MW01699350

Autodesk AutoCAD
Fundamentals

Elise Moss

ISBN:
978-1-58503-554-0 (Text only)
978-1-58503-592-2 (Text bundled with 13-month license AutoCAD® 2011)

autodesk®
authorized publisher

SDC
PUBLICATIONS

Schroff Development Corporation

www.SDCpublications.com

Schroff Development Corporation
P.O. Box 1334
Mission, KS 66222
(913) 262-2664
www.SDCpublications.com

Publisher: Stephen Schroff

Trademarks

The following are registered trademarks of Autodesk, Inc.: AutoCAD, AutoCAD Mechanical Desktop, Inventor, Autodesk, AutoLISP, AutoCAD Design Center, Autodesk Device Interface, and HEIDI
Microsoft, Windows, Word, and Excel are either registered trademarks or trademarks of Microsoft Corporation.
All other trademarks are trademarks of their respective holders.

Copyright © 2010 by Elise Moss

All rights reserved. No part of this book may be reproduced, stored in a retrieval system, or transcribed in any form or by any means – electronic, mechanical, photocopying, recording, or otherwise – without the prior written permission of Schroff Development Corporation.

Moss, Elise
Autodesk AutoCAD 2011: Fundamentals
Elise Moss
ISBN: 978-1-58503-554-0 (Text Only)
ISBN 978-1-58503-594-6 (Text bundled with AutoCAD 2011)

The author and publisher of this book have used their best efforts in preparing this book. These efforts include the development, research, and testing of material presented. The author and publisher shall not be held liable in any event for incidental or consequential damages with, or arising out of, the furnishing, performance, or use of the material herein.

Examination Copies:

Books received as examination copies are for review purposes only and may not be made available for student use. Resale of examination copies is prohibited.

Electronic Files:

Any electronic files associated with this book are licensed to the original user only. These files may not be transferred to any other party.

Printed and bound in the United States of America.

Preface

This book began as a series of class notes and power points during my tenure at Silicon Valley College. The material was expanded and grew for my classes at DeAnza Community College. When Schroff Development Corporation approached me to write this textbook, I was initially reluctant. After all, there are a plethora of textbooks on the market for AutoCAD and I didn't feel that I had anything additional I could add.

I was convinced to go forward with this text because the class notes I prepared for my classes would often go through double and even triple printings at the DeAnza College Bookstore. This meant that people who were not even enrolled in my class were coming into the bookstore to purchase my notes. Obviously, my material was filling in gaps.

The major gap was applying the knowledge of AutoCAD to mechanical drafting. Knowing how to draw a line in AutoCAD is not the same as understanding which line type is required when creating technical drawings. This text provides the necessary information on how to use AutoCAD as a tool to work as a mechanical drafter or designer.

This text should be used to in combination with a basic AutoCAD reference manual or with an instructor who can provide guidance on basic AutoCAD.

Files used in this text can be downloaded from
www.schroff.com/resources.

Acknowledgements

The effort and support of the editorial and production staff of Schroff Development Corporation is gratefully acknowledged. I especially thank Stephen Schroff for his helpful suggestions regarding the format of this text.

Feel free to email me if you have any questions, comments, or problems with any of the exercises in this text. I get email from all over the world and usually respond within twenty-four hours. My email address is elise_moss@mossdesigns.com.

Finally, truly infinite thanks to Ari for his encouragement and his faith.

Elise Moss
Los Gatos, CA

Classroom Setup

Each student should be equipped with an AutoCAD workstation using either Windows XP Professional , Windows Vista or Windows 7. AutoCAD 2011 is certified by Autodesk to work in Windows 7. The student exercises should be copied to each student workstation in a directory called c:\class. A backup of each exercise should be kept in a safe place either on each computer or on a network server to refresh the drawing files after each class. Auto Tracking should be turned off before the class starts and not turned on until it is covered in class.

In order to demonstrate commands and exercise solutions, the instructor workstation should be equipped with an overhead projector, large screen television/monitor or a VGA splitter that feeds multiple VGA monitors on each student desk.

If students are working off a network and are not assigned a specific workstation, they should be aware that any modifications they make to their toolbars or display will change when they move to a different workstation. For this reason, the use of profiles and workspaces is covered early in the text. I recommend to my students to use a flash or "jump" drive to save their work. This protects them from other students messing with their work, either on purpose or by accident, as well as any hardware or server failures. The exercises demonstrate how to plot to dwf files because each classroom may have a different printer type available and there is no way to cover all the different printer type setups. However, students can certainly submit any assignment to the instructor using dwf files, thus cutting down on paper and toner usage. 2011 includes a PDF driver so students can also print to PDF if they desire. Many students ask me if there is anyway to avoid the STUDENT VERSION watermark when they plot as they want to use their classwork to show a prospective employer. To those students, I recommend a screen capture software, such as SnagIt or HyperSnap. Simply do a Plot Preview and then screen capture the previewed plot minus the water mark and print that.

Autodesk offers free software with 13 month licenses to all students in an accredited course. I urge students to take advantage of this opportunity. For more information, visit www.student.autodesk.com or ask your instructor.

NOTES:

Table of Contents

NOTES:

Lesson 1.0 – The AutoCAD Environment

Estimated Class Time: 1.5 Hours

Objectives

This section introduces the interface available within AutoCAD starting with the Pointing Device. The AutoCAD window includes the Pull-Down (POP) menus, Toolbars, the Drawing Window, Command Prompt, Work Spaces and Status Bar. In addition, you will learn special Keyboard options and Shortcut (Cursor) menus, how to use the Dialog Boxes, and how to access AutoCAD's on-line Help.

- **Work Space**
  Customize which menus and toolbars are available; modify the appearance of the work environment
- **Pointing Device**
  Use the mouse for selecting options in the AutoCAD window.
- **Shortcut Menus**
  Right-click your pointing device to display context sensitive Shortcut (Cursor) menus.
- **AutoCAD Window**
  The AutoCAD window consists of the following areas:
- **Title Bar**
  Minimize and maximize the AutoCAD window from the title bar.
- **Pull-Down Menu**
  Select commands from the Pull-Down (POP) menu headings.
- **Toolbars**
  Use AutoCAD toolbars as another method for selecting commands.
- **Drawing Window**
  Create your drawing and drawing layouts in this area.
- **Command Prompt**
  The Command Prompt will prompt you for the next step.
- **Status Bar**
  This area contains handy toggle switches and displays the x,y,z coordinates.
- **Dialog Boxes**
  Create your drawing and drawing layouts in this area.
- **Keyboard Options**
  Use the keyboard to type command options, text, or press Escape to cancel commands.
- **Help Menu**
  Use the AutoCAD Help menu to learn more about the program.

Work Space

Overview

The Workspace tool allows you to customize the appearance of your work environment.

By default, AutoCAD comes with four defined workspaces:

3D Modeling, 2D Design, Sheet Layout and Publishing, and AutoCAD Classic.

This text will be working in the AutoCAD Classic environment.

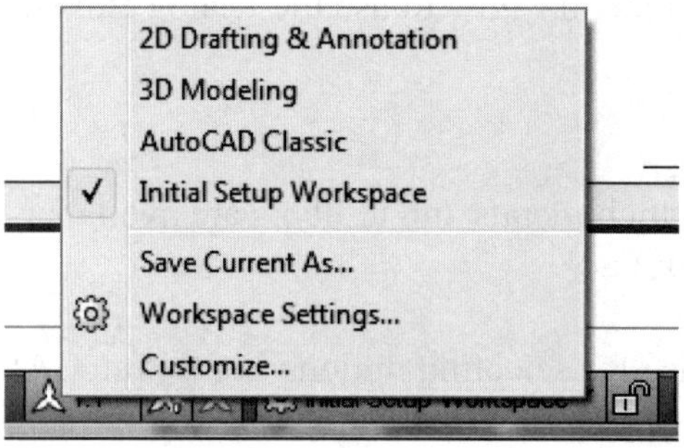

The Workspace control has moved to the Status Bar on the lower right of the graphics window.

If you want to save your current work environment (system settings, active toolbars, and menus) simply select 'Save Current As' to apply the active settings to a new or existing workspace.

Command Exercise

Exercise 1-1 – User Interface

Drawing Name: **(none, start from scratch)**
Estimated Time to Completion: 5 Minutes

Scope

Set the workspace to the AutoCAD Classic environment
Close the Tool Palettes.

1. *Locate the AutoCAD Classic workspace on the toolbar.*
2. *Set the AutoCAD Classic workspace as Current.*

Solution

1. 

Locate the Workspace toolbar located on the lower right Status Bar.

Select the down arrow.

2. 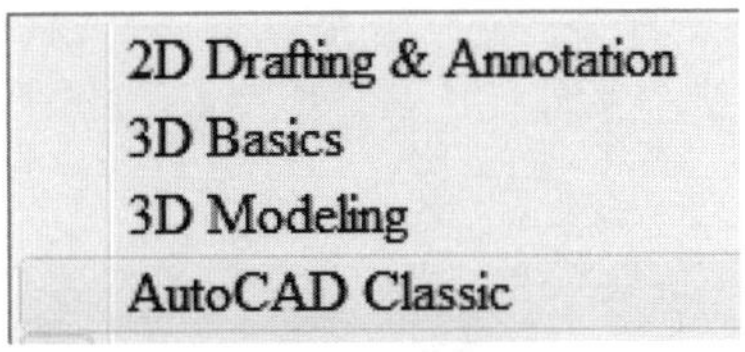

Enable **AutoCAD Classic**.

The user interface is modified.

3. 

Close the Tool Palette by pressing the X in the upper left corner.

4. 

Locate the **Workspace** toolbar. The default location is the upper left above the display window.

5. 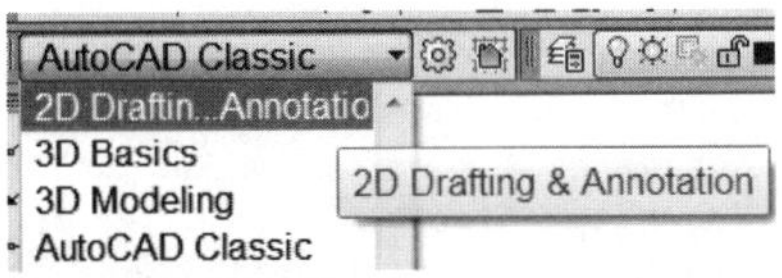

By pressing down on the drop-down list, you can see all the different work space settings.

Select the **2D Drafting & Annotation** workspace.

6. 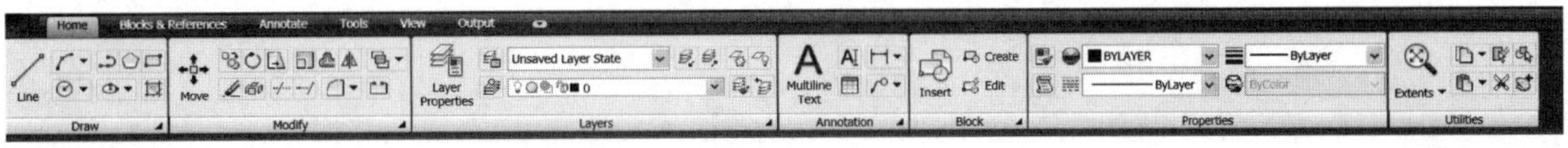

All the toolbars disappear and are replaced by a ribbon panel.

7. 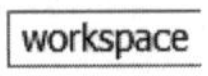

Type **workspace** at the Command Prompt.

8. 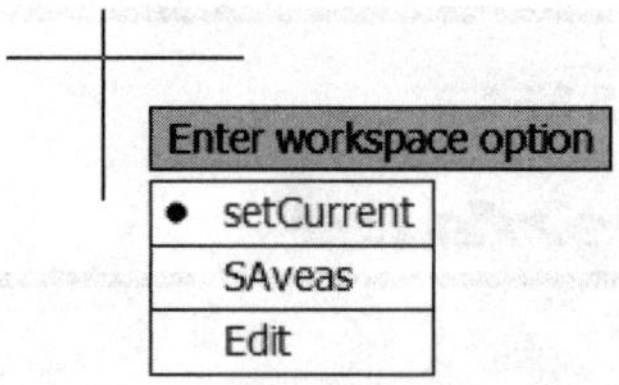

Right click and select the **setCurrent** option.

9. 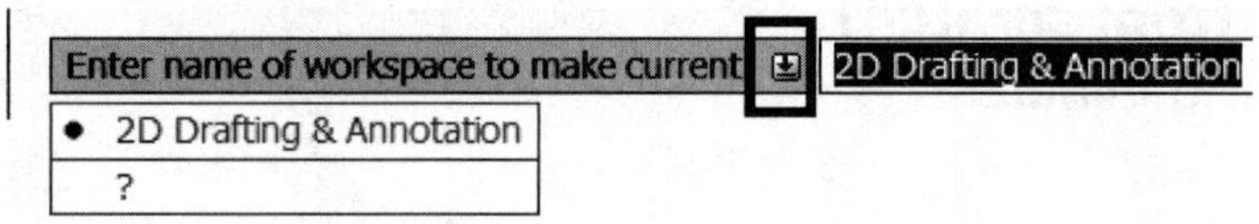

Press the down arrow on your keyboard.

10. 

Then select the **?**.
Or type it in the edit field

11. 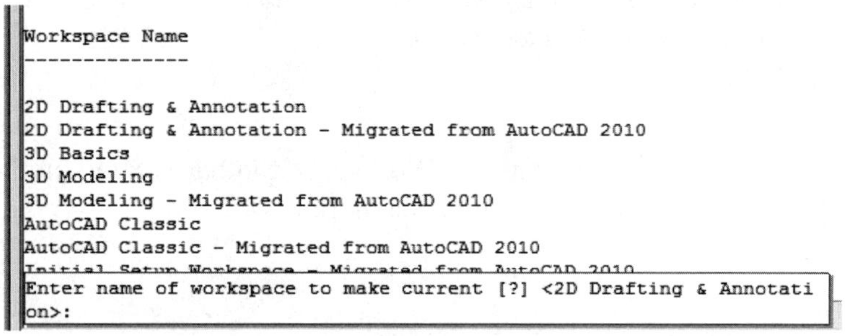

The workspaces are listed.

Type **AutoCAD Classic**.

12. 

Press Enter.

13. The interface returns to AutoCAD Classic.

> ***Tip:*** *When you make any changes, they will automatically be saved to the active workspace.*

Pointing Device

Overview

Use the pointing device to select objects and options. This tutorial reviews the functions of a two or three-button mouse, though there are other pointing devices available. The pointing device is configured in the *Systems Tab* in the *Options* dialog box. The default setting is automatically set to the "current system pointing" device, this will typically be a two button mouse, the three button mouse, or the Microsoft IntelliMouse®. The left button (LMB) is typically the Pick button and the right button (RMB) is the <ENTER> button. Pressing the <ENTER> button, when the cursor is in the Drawing Window, activates a Shortcut Menu with the option to repeat the last command. This feature can be disabled in the *User Preferences* Tab of the *Options* dialog box, by removing the checkmark from "Shortcut menus in drawing area". If this option is selected, pressing the right button on the mouse (RMB) will either execute a command, proceed with the command (by accepting the default option), or if the Command Prompt is blank, repeat the last command. Using shift + the <ENTER> button, activates the Object Snap shortcut menu. These shortcut menus will be covered later in this Tutorial in the topics that follow.

Two Button Mouse:

Button	**Action**
Left (LMB)	Use to pick or select objects or options
Right (RMB)	Use to <ENTER> to complete the command, repeat the last command, or access a context sensitive cursor menu
Shift + Right (RMB)	Brings up the Object Snap cursor menu

Three Button Mouse:

Button	**Action**
Left (LMB)	Use to pick or select objects or options
Right (RMB)	Use to <ENTER> to complete the command, repeat the last command, or access a context sensitive cursor menu
Middle Button	Brings up the Object Snap cursor menu

Microsoft IntelliMouse:

Button	**Action**
Left (LMB)	Use to pick or select objects or options
Right (RMB)	Use to <ENTER> to complete the command, repeat the last command, or access a context sensitive cursor menu
Shift + Right (RMB)	Brings up the Object Snap cursor menu
Middle Button (press + drag)	Use to pan the drawing
Middle Button (roll)	Use to zoom the drawing.

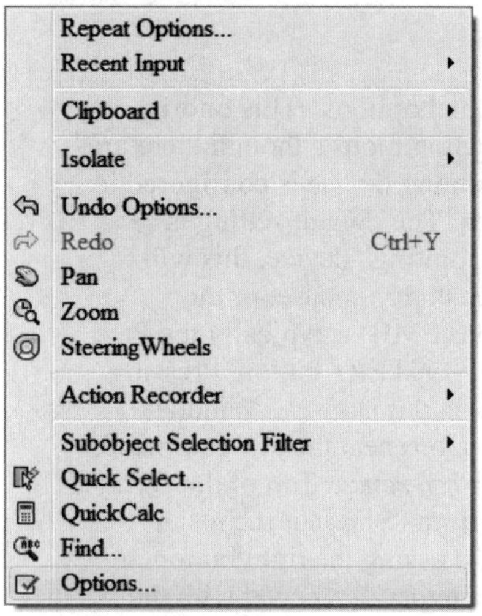

Figure 1 – The RMB Shortcut Menu

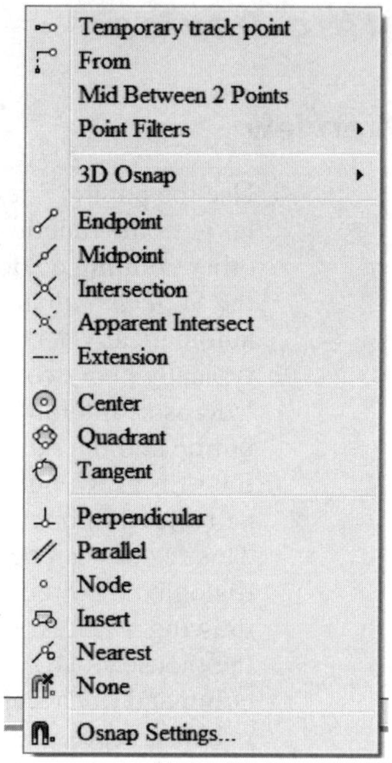

Figure 2 – The Shift Key + RMB Shortcut Menu

General Procedures

1. Pick a command from the toolbar using the left button on the mouse.
2. Follow the Command Prompt prompts.
3. Press <ENTER> to complete the command or continue to the next step. Press <ENTER> again to repeat the command, or select a choice from the Shortcut menu.

- Picking in a blank area of the drawing window will create a selection window. Press escape to cancel this selection window, or simply make the other corner.
- Making a selection window from right to left will select all objects the window crosses. Making a selection window from left to right will only select the objects completely within the selection window.
- Picking objects in the drawing window when the Command Prompt is blank will highlight the objects and display the *grips*. Press Escape (**Esc** on the keyboard) two times to cancel the grips and the selection.
- The left and right button functions can be reversed from the Windows Settings menu (from the Start bar). Select "Control Panel" then select "Mouse".

Command Exercise

Exercise 1-2 – Pointing Device

Drawing Name: **(none, start from scratch)**
Estimated Time to Completion: 5 Minutes

Scope

Practice the Left and Right button mouse functions:

1. *Draw line segments.*
2. *Press the right button on the mouse to repeat the line command.*
3. *Practice selecting a single object.*
4. *Practice making a selection window.*
5. *Activate the object snap shortcut (cursor) menu.*
6. *Activate the toolbar short cut menu.*
7. *Activate the Command Prompt short cut menu.*

Solution

1. Locate the line command from the Draw Toolbar and draw some line segments. Press the right button on the mouse. This will bring up a context sensitive cursor menu. Select 'Enter' to complete the line command, so that the Command Prompt is blank.

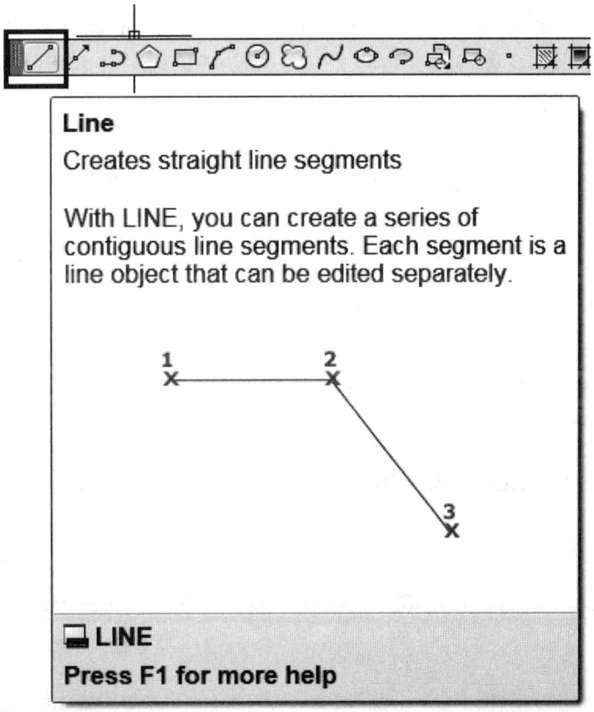

> ***Tip:*** *To turn off the rollover help tips, type ROLLOVERTIPS on the Command Prompt and enter 0.*

2. Press the right button on the mouse again. This will bring up a context sensitive cursor menu. Select 'Repeat Line' to repeat the line command. Complete the line command, so that the Command Prompt is blank.

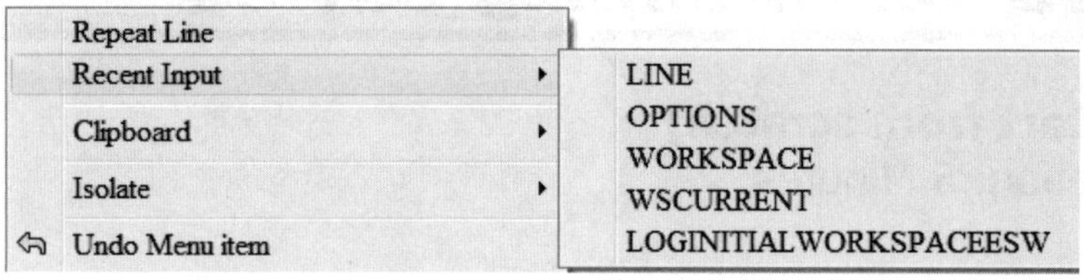

Note that if you expand Recent Input, you can select any of your most recent commands.

3. Pick one of the line segments. Notice that it is highlighted and notice the grips (these are the blue boxes on the line). Press <ESC> once to cancel and clear the grips.

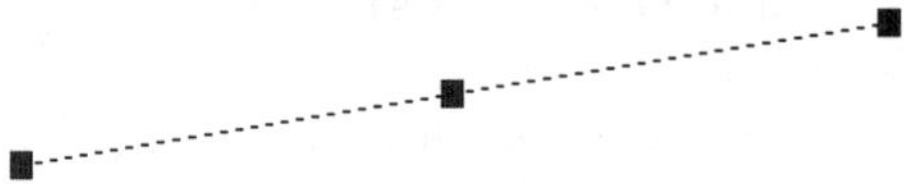

4. Pick in the blank area of the drawing. Notice this will create a rectangular selection window. You will be prompted to select the other corner. Make the selection window from Left to Right and notice that only the objects completely within the window will be selected. Press <ESC> to cancel the selection. Now make the window from right to left and notice that the lines that are crossed by the selection box are now highlighted. Press <ESC> again to exit.

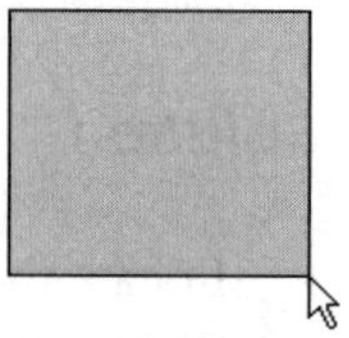

5. Activate the object snap shortcut (cursor) menu using the mouse button according to the pointing device you are using. Press <ESC> to cancel this menu.

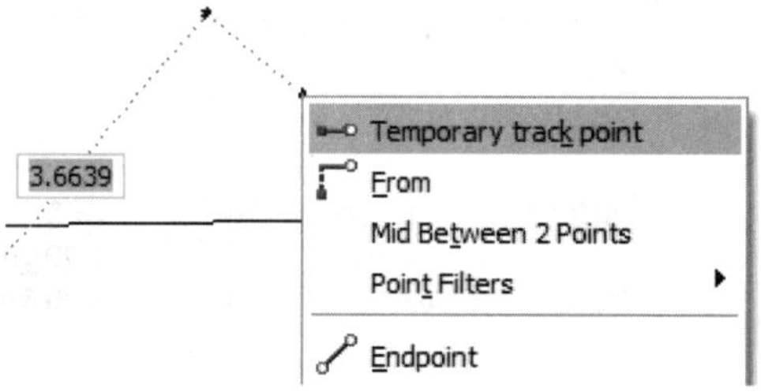

6. Press the RMB with the cursor over a toolbar icon. This will bring up the toolbar menu. Press <ESC> to cancel.

7. Press the RMB in the Command Prompt area to view the menu shown below. Press <ESC> to cancel.

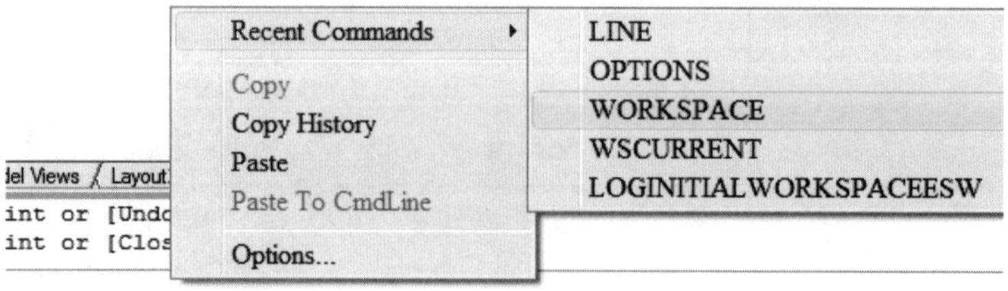

> ***Tip:*** *The short cut menus are context sensitive and are determined by the location of the cursor when the right button on the mouse is selected.*

Extra: *If you have the Microsoft Intellimouse, roll the middle button to zoom the drawing in and out in the drawing. Press the middle button and drag to pan.*

AutoCAD Window

Overview

The AutoCAD window consists of a Title Bar, Pull-Down Menus, Toolbars, a Drawing Window, the Ribbon, the Command Prompt, and the Status Bar.

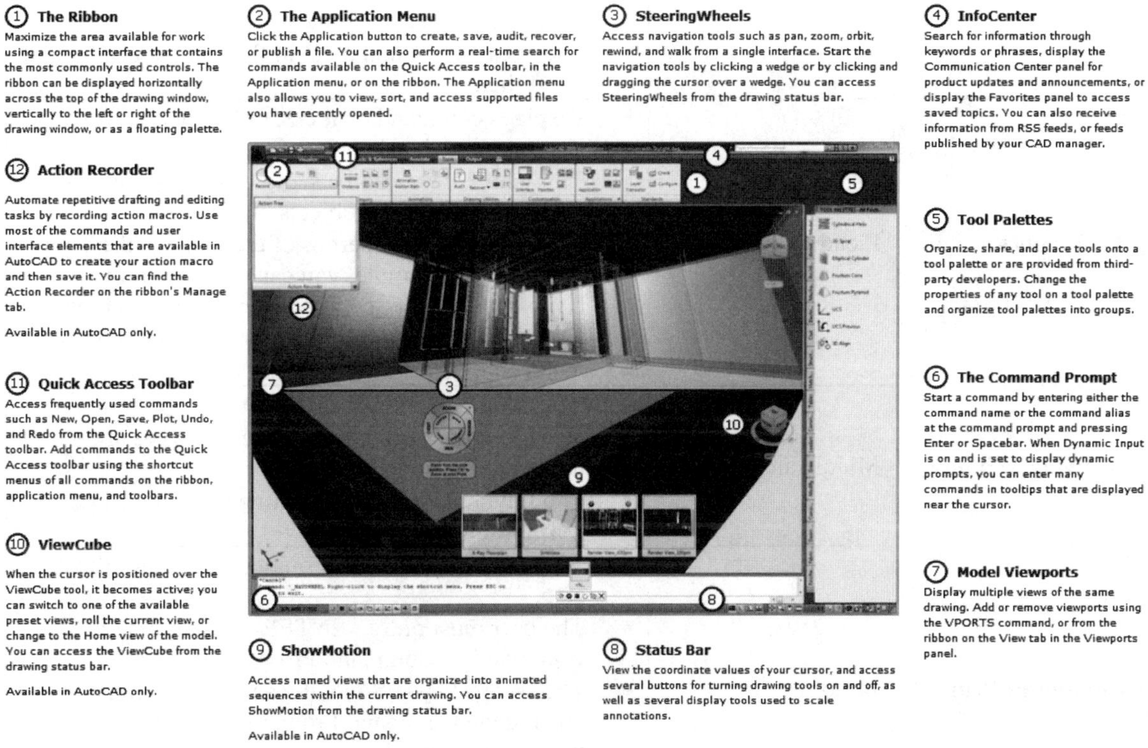

Figure 3 – The AutoCAD Window

AutoCAD Window Detail	Location	Function Overview
Title Bar	Top	• Lists the name of the current drawing. • Contains buttons to minimize, maximize or exit AutoCAD • Contains buttons to minimize, maximize or close the current drawing.
Pull-Down Menu	Beneath the Title Bar	• Lists AutoCAD commands by category • Also referred to as "POP" • Words followed by a black arrow ‣ will display an additional list of related options. • Words followed by an *ellipsis* (…) will open a *dialog box.*
Toolbars	Docked at sides or floating in the drawing window	• Displays commands as icons (buttons) in related toolbar categories • The toolbar pictured in the top row is the *Standard Toolbar.* • The toolbar beneath it is the *Object Properties Toolbar.* • Accessing a command from a toolbar is usually a faster, more direct approach. • The toolbars contain most of the commands, but not all of them.
Tool Palettes	Floating or Docked	• Displays commands, blocks, or hatches as icons (buttons) in related categories • The Tool Palette can be set to be transparent, so you can see drawing objects underneath. • You can set the properties of the tools on the Tool Palette. For example, you can set a line tool to always place on a specific layer and/or line type. • You can create a Tool Palette for all your blocks • You can hide or display Tool Palettes easily.
Drawing Window	Middle area	• Area where the drawing is created. • The Model tab is for creating the drawing or 3-dimensional model. • The Layout tabs are for creating the finished layout for plotting or printing.
Command Prompt	Bottom	• Area where AutoCAD prompts the user for the next step. • The user must press <ENTER> after typing the Command or Command Prompt options • The escape key (ESC) will cancel any command leaving the Command Prompt blank and ready for the next command. • Ctl+9 displays or hides the Command Prompt window
Status Bar	Beneath the Command Prompt	• Displays the coordinates of the cursor location. • Displays the ON/OFF status of special toggle switches). • Single-click to toggle these options ON or OFF.
Dynamic Input	At the end of the cursor	• When DYN is enabled, you can close the Command Prompt window and enter prompts at a smaller window located at the end of the cursor

Title Bar

Locator

Overview

The Title Bar will display the name of the drawing. Buttons are displayed in the upper right-hand corner to minimize, maximize, re-size, or close the AutoCAD window or an individual drawing file. Remember that when any program is minimized, it will remain listed in the Start Bar.

General Procedures

1. To maximize the AutoCAD Window, select the following icon:

2. To maximize the Drawing Window, select the following icon:

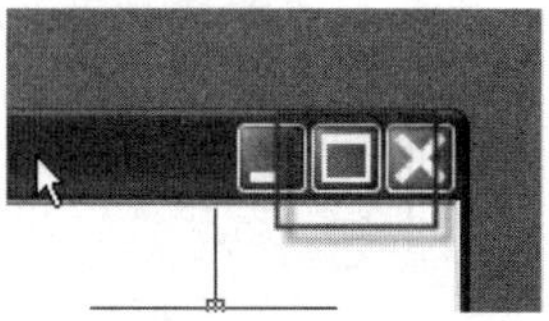

3. To minimize the AutoCAD or Drawing Windows, select the the minimize button:

4. To bring the AutoCAD Window to the foreground, select AutoCAD from the Start bar.

Tips & Tricks

- Keep the AutoCAD and Drawing windows maximized for optimum drawing space.
- Use the Alt+Tab keys to alternate between programs, or select the program from the Start bar.
- Practice Minimizing and Maximizing the AutoCAD and Drawing Windows.

Toolbars

Locator

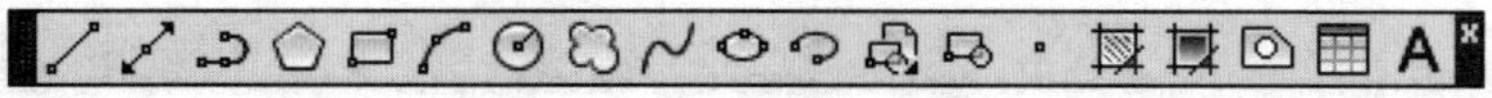

Toolbar Menu	
Pull Down Menu	**View / Toolbars….**
Command	**Toolbar**
Alias	**to**
RMB Shortcut Menu	**Right click on any visible toolbar.**
Dialog Box	**Toolbars**

Overview

Selecting a Toolbar button or *icon* is generally a faster and more efficient way to initiate a command. Toolbars can be floating or docked. A floating toolbar can be resized, and the title will be displayed at the top. You can more quickly and easily turn them on and off by simply right-clicking on any toolbar to get a shortcut menu. Some toolbar buttons have "fly-out" options. These are the ones with black arrows in the lower right corner of the button.

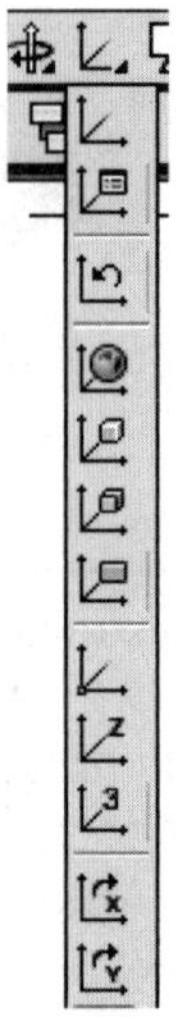

Figure 4 – Toolbar with Fly-Out

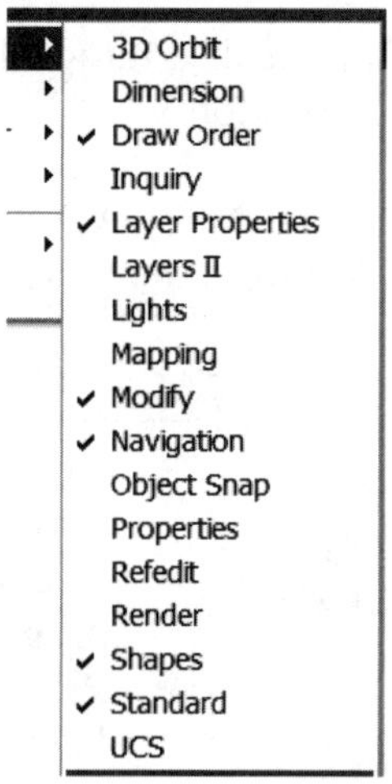

Figure 5 – Toolbar Shortcut Menu

The default toolbars are Standard, Layer Properties, Draw, and Modify.

General Procedures

To open or close a toolbar using the short-cut menu:

1. Right-Click over any toolbar to access the shortcut menu.
2. Select the desired toolbar from the list.

To open or close a toolbar using the Toolbar dialog box:

1. Select 'Toolbars…' from the View pull-down menu
2. Place a checkmark before the desired toolbar, then Close the dialog box.

To dock or undock a toolbar:

1. To dock a toolbar, place your pointer on the background or toolbar title bar, then press the left button on the mouse and drag the toolbar to the side, top, or bottom of the drawing window.
2. When the outline of the toolbar appears in the docking area, release the pointing device.
3. To move a docked toolbar into the drawing window, place your pointer on the toolbar (but not on an icon), then press the pick button (LMB) and drag the toolbar into the drawing area.

To re-size a floating toolbar:

1. Place your pointer on the edge of the toolbar. When the pointer image changes to a double black arrow, press the pick button and drag the mouse to re-size the toolbar.

To select a fly-out option from the toolbar:

1. Move the pointer over the fly-out button. Press and hold the pick button (LMB) to display the fly-out options, then move the pointer to select the desired button.
2. The newly selected fly-out button will remain on top. Simply select this button the next time around, or select a new fly-out option if desired.

Tips & Tricks

- Selecting a Toolbar button or icon is generally a faster and more efficient way to initiate a command.
- When pointing to a toolbar button, a label will appear with the command name, and a Tool Tip will appear at the bottom of the screen.
- The Standard Toolbar is normally docked at the top, and the Object Properties toolbar is beneath it.

Drawing Window

Locator

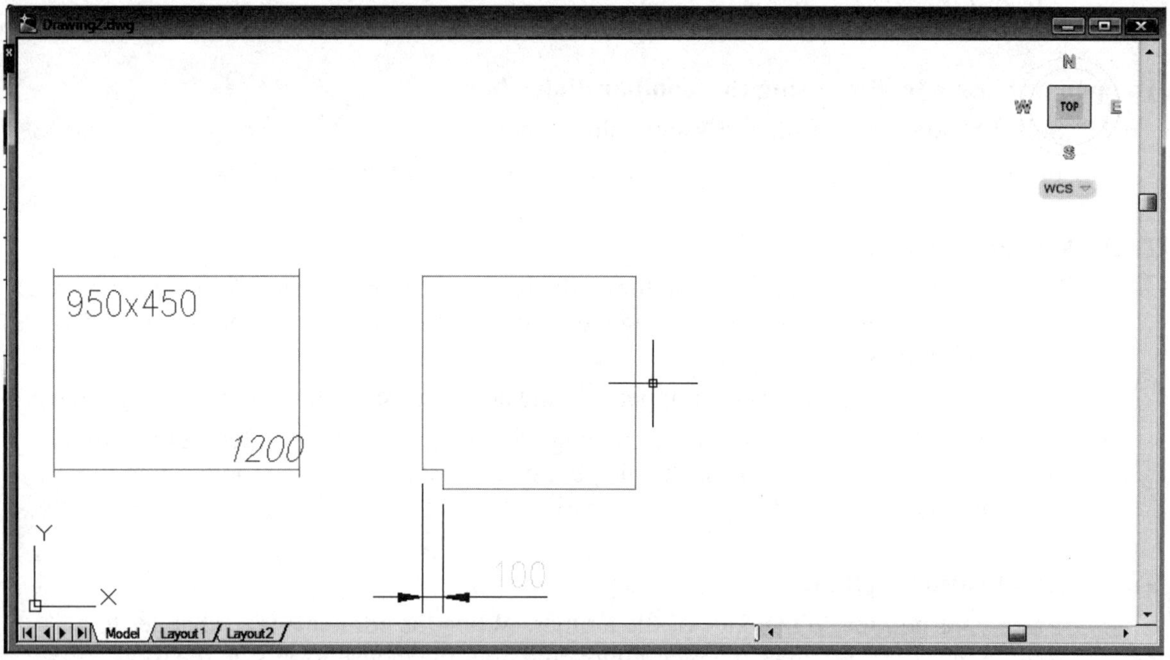

Figure 6 – AutoCAD Drawing Window

Overview

When working in the Drawing Window, be sure that the Model Tab is selected. Later this text will cover how to create a drawing Layout. The cursor must be in the Drawing window in order to pick points for drawing objects, or select objects to modify. Right-click in the drawing window to execute a command, proceed with the next step of the command, or if the Command Prompt is blank, repeat the last command. Picking (LMB) in a blank area of the drawing window will initiate a selection window or box. You must pick the opposite corner whether you want to select an object or not, or press Escape to cancel the selection window. Multiple drawings may be opened in one AutoCAD session. Minimize a drawing window, or use the options from the **Window** Pull-Down menu to select the current drawing. Close the drawings that are not being used.

General Procedures

To minimize, maximize / re-size, or close a drawing window:

1. Select this button to minimize the drawing window.

2. Select this button to maximize a drawing window.

3. Select this button to re-size a drawing window.

4. Select this button to close a drawing.

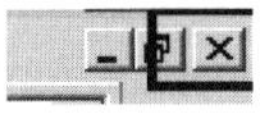

Tips & Tricks

- The Model Tab should be selected when creating a drawing.
- The cursor must be in the Drawing window in order to pick points for drawing objects, or select objects to modify.
- Right-click in the drawing window to execute a command, proceed with the next step of the command, or if the Command Prompt is blank, repeat the last command.
- Picking (LMB) in a blank area of the drawing window will initiate a selection window or box. You must pick the opposite corner whether you want to select an object or not, or press Escape to cancel the selection window.
- Close drawings that are not being used.

Command Prompt

Locator

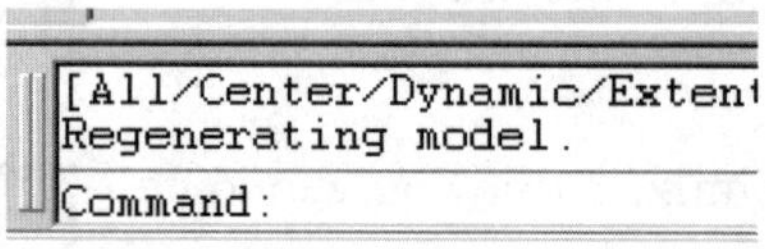

Figure 7 – AutoCAD Command Prompt Area

Overview

The Command Prompt at the bottom of the AutoCAD window will prompt the user for the next step. It is important to read the Command Prompt. A blank Command Prompt means that AutoCAD is waiting for the user to begin a command. Remember to press <ENTER>, after typing a command, a command alias, a Command Prompt option, or after selecting objects. Generally it is best to view three lines of text at the Command Prompt. The scroll bar to the right of the Command Prompt window can be used to view previous Command Prompts. The **F2** function key will display the entire Text Window. The up and down arrows on the keyboard will carry the last option typed to the bottom Command Prompt. A Command Prompt option that is in parenthesis or < > is known as the *default.* It is unnecessary to type the default option over again, simply press <ENTER> to accept the default. Pressing the <ENTER> button on the mouse (RMB) when the cursor is in the Command Prompt area will bring up a Shortcut Menu.

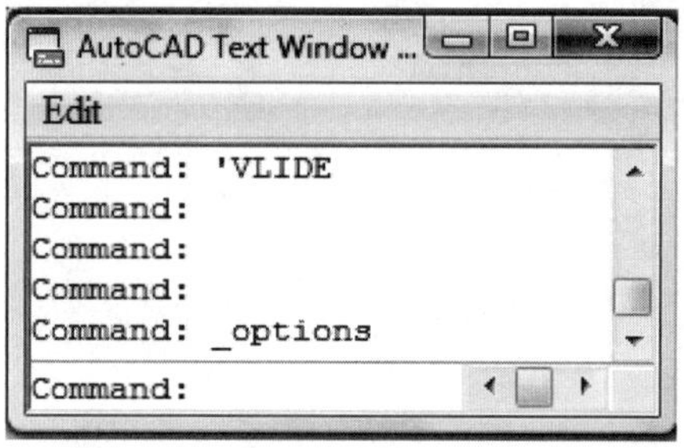

Figure 8 – The AutoCAD Text Window

The F2 function key will open the AutoCAD Text Window, which will display all previous Command Prompts. These lines can be viewed and copied, but they cannot be changed. Press the x in the upper right hand corner to close the AutoCAD Text Window.

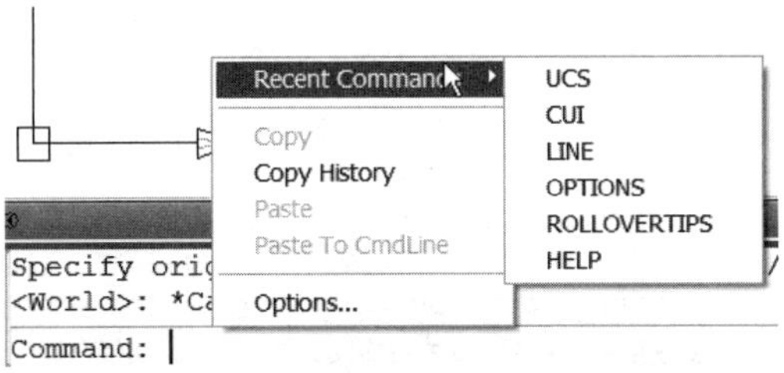

Figure 9 – Command Prompt Shortcut Menu

Right-click (RMB) in the Command Prompt area to bring up the Command Prompt shortcut menu. This can be used to copy highlighted text, or access the Options dialog box.

Command Prompt Cursor Menu Option (RMB)	Overview
Recent Commands	Lists recently used commands
Paste to CmdLine	Pastes highlighted words from the text window to the Command Prompt.
Copy	Copies highlighted words from the text window to a clipboard.
Copy History	Copies everything from the text window to the Clipboard.
Paste	Pastes copied text to the Command Prompt.
Options...	Opens the Options dialog box to set user preferences.

General Procedures

How to follow the Command Prompt prompts:

1. Type the command, the command alias or the Command Prompt option and Press <ENTER>.
2. Follow the Command Prompt prompts:
    - When prompted to select objects, pick the objects then press <ENTER> to continue.
    - When presented with Command Prompt options, type the capitalized letter of the option and press <ENTER> to continue.
    - When presented with a default choice in parenthesis or < > press <ENTER> to accept the default, or type the preferred option and press <ENTER>.

Tips & Tricks

- It is important to remember to read the Command Prompt, as this is your line of communication with AutoCAD.
- Use the keyboard <ENTER> button or the right button (RMB) on the mouse.
- When using the RMB, be sure that the cursor is in the drawing window.
- To disable the command options cursor menu, select Options, the User Preferences tab, "Right Click Customization" and "Repeat Last Command". Apply & Close.

Status Bar

Locator

Figure 10 – ApplicationStatus Bar

Overview

The Application Status Bar is at the bottom of the AutoCAD window. Select (LMB) the buttons to turn the options ON or OFF, or use the corresponding function keys. Right-click (RMB) to access the Settings dialog box for the corresponding Status Bar options or other option that apply.

Status Bar Option	Overview	Function Key
INFER CONSTRAINTS	Applies constraints to 2D sketch geometry	
SNAP	Snap ON will restrict the cursor to select points at designated X and Y increments. Snap spacing may or may not be equal to the Grid spacing. However, if the Grid spacing is set to 0, it will be equal the Snap spacing.	**F9**
GRID	This switch turns the Grid ON and OFF. The Grid is a visual tool, and does not restrict cursor selection. Grid spacing may or may not be equal to the Snap spacing. However, if the Grid spacing is set to 0, it will be equal to the Snap spacing.	**F7**
ORTHO	Use Ortho (for orthogonal) ON when dragging the mouse to: Draw straight lines Move, Copy, or Mirror objects along a linear plane Rotate objects in 90-degree increments. ORTHO is either ON or OFF and does not have a Settings option.	**F8**
POLAR TRACKING	Turns Polar Snap ON/OFF. When Polar Snap is ON, the angular direction and the distance from the last point selected will be tracked and displayed according to the Polar Tracking settings.	**F10**
OSNAP	When Object Snap (OSNAP) is ON, the cursor will always gravitate to specified points on objects in the drawing. Unlike SNAP, which follows a grid pattern, OSNAP refers to objects in the drawing and will display object snap markers.	**F3**
3D OSNAP	Snaps to grips on 3D solids	
OTRACK	Object Snap Tracking (OTRACK), when ON, will combine with OSNAP (which must also be ON) to allow the cursor to track along alignment paths based on other object snap points in the drawing. To use object snap tracking, you must turn on one or more object snaps.	**F11**
DUCS	Dynamic UCS – this controls the appearance of the UCS icon when modeling in 3D	

Status Bar Option	Overview	Function Key
DYN	Dynamic Input controls the appearance of the cursor. When enabled, cursor will display the dimensions related to the drawing object. To turn off the input display, disable the toggle. 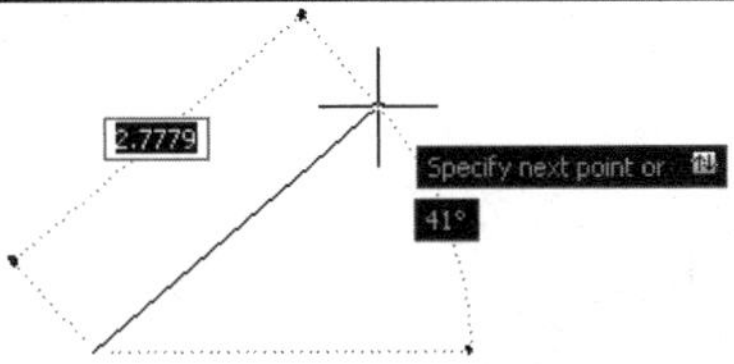	
LWT	Line weights can be specified according to the LWT settings and applied to the lines being drawn when LWT is on. When LWT is off, objects will be drawn using the line weights as designated by the layer (ByLayer). Visibility of lineweight is controlled from the lineweight settings dialog box (choose it from the Format POP, or type *lineweight*). Select "Display Lineweight".	
TRANSPARENCY	Changes the selected object to be transparent	
QUICK PROPERTIES	Controls the display of Quick Properties and allows the user to set which properties are displayed	**CTL + SHIFT+P**
Selection Cycling	When enabled, displays a list of objects which are overlapping each other to allow easy selection.	

General Procedures

1. Select the Status Bar option to turn it ON or OFF.
2. Right-click the Status Bar option to access the corresponding Settings dialog box.

Tips & Tricks

- Select either the Status Bar button, or select the corresponding function key from the keyboard.
- A Status Bar option can be turned ON or OFF while using a draw or modify command. Therefore, beginning the Line command, and deciding to turn ORTHO on or off while in the middle of the command is acceptable.

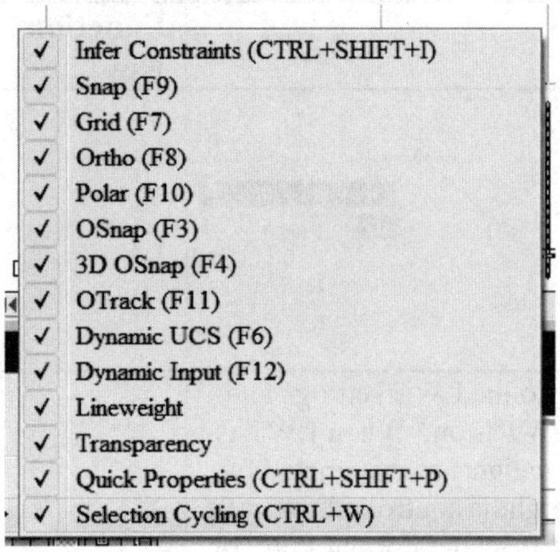

Left click on the down arrow and a list of available buttons appears. A check mark next to the name indicates that the button is active and visible. To hide a button, simply left click on the name.

Note that the Status buttons have their own submenu.

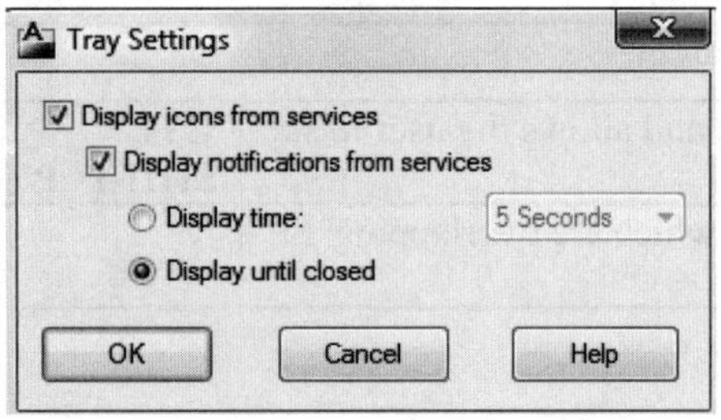

If you select the Tray Settings… option, you can control the balloon notifications. Balloons will display when you plot, when updates are available, etc. To turn off the balloon notifications, you can simply disable the boxes and press ‘OK’.

Dialog Boxes

Locator

Toolbar Menu	**Certain command buttons will activate a dialog box.**
Pull Down Menu	**Commands or Options followed by and ellipsis (…) will open a dialog box.**
Command	**Certain typed commands will activate a dialog box.**
Alias	**Certain commands aliases will activate a dialog box.**
RMB Shortcut Menu	**Select within the white text or list areas or dialog box.**
Dialog Box	**The name or title will be listed at the top the dialog box.**

Overview

Certain commands and options will launch dialog boxes. Commands from the Pull-Down or Shortcut menus followed by an ellipsis (…) will open a Dialog Box. When opened, it is not possible to type at the Command Prompt, or use any of the commands other than those listed in the Dialog Box. Use the text boxes to type information, select the appropriate tabs, buttons, or check boxes, and select OK to exit. It is also possible to press the Escape key, select the Cancel button, or the X in the upper right-hand corner of the Dialog Box to exit.

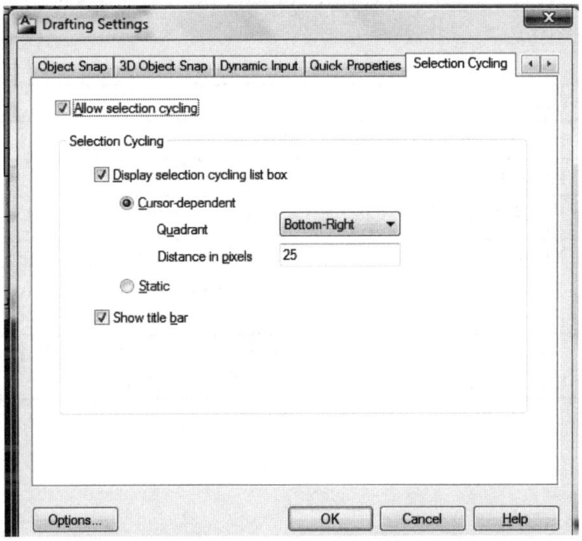

Figure 11 – Drafting Settings Dialog Box

General Procedures

1. When a dialog box is opened, select or type the desired options.
2. Press 'OK' to exit the dialog box.

Tips & Tricks

- To move the Dialog Box select the Title bar, press and drag.
- To type over text in the Text Areas, drag the cursor over selected text, or double click to select the entire text; then type over it.
- Select the Help button in the Dialog Box for more information.
- Choices that are not available will be gray.

Keyboard Options

Locator

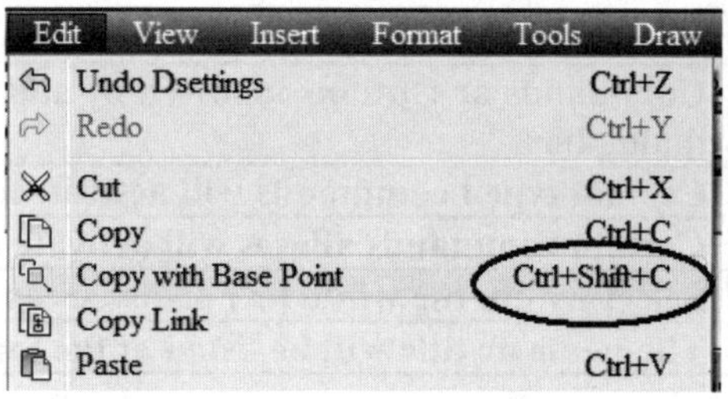

Overview

Commands, command aliases, or *system variables* can be typed at the keyboard. It is important to remember to press <ENTER> to execute the command, and follow the Command Prompt prompts. When choosing a Command Prompt option, type the capitalized letter(s) of the desired option. Pressing <ENTER> or the spacebar will execute the command. When typing Text, however, the <ENTER> key is the same as a carriage return on a typewriter, and the spacebar will type a space. Function Keys are used to toggle some options ON or OFF.

Keyboard Option	Overview
ESC	Escape. Cancels all commands
Enter	Executes a command.
Spacebar	Works like the <ENTER> key except when typing text.
Arrows	Moves the cursor position. In the case of the Command Prompt, the up and down arrows will bring the previously typed information to the last Command Prompt.
Ctrl	Use the Control key + single keys to begin selected commands as indicated in the Pull-Down menus. (i.e. Ctrl+S, will Save)

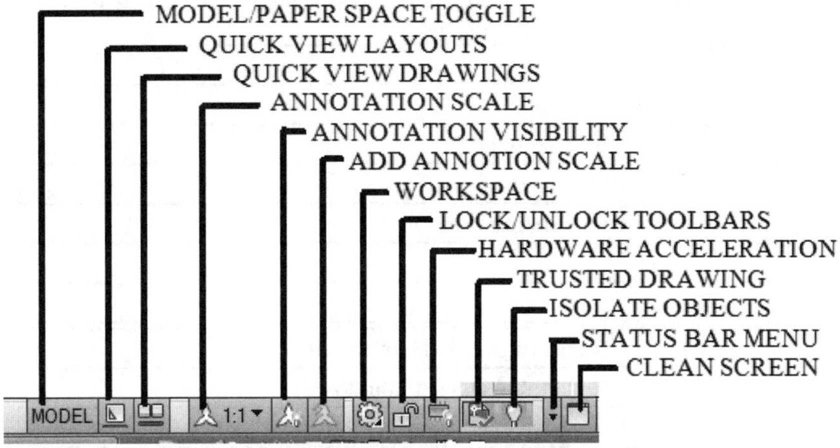

Figure 12 – Right Side Status Bar

AutoCAD 2011 has extended the use of the Status Bar to provide more icons to help the user navigate as they go.

Command Alias	**Command Aliases are shortcut keys that can by typed to access a command, when the Command Prompt is blank. Some of the command aliases include:**
A	Arc
B	Block Definition dialog box
C	Circle
CO	Copy
D	Dimension Style Manager dialog box
E	Erase
ED	Edit Text
F	Fillet
H	Boundary Hatch dialog box
I	Insert Block dialog box
L	Line
LA	Layers Properties Manager dialog box
M	Move
O	Offset
P	Real-Time Pan
PE	Edit Polyline
PL	Draw Polyline
PU	Purge
R	Redraw
Re	Regenerate Drawing

Function Keys	Function Keys, located at the top or side of the keyboard, activate the following options:
S	Stretch
T	Multiline Text
U	Undo (last command)
V	View dialog box
W	Write Block dialog box
X	Explode
Z	Zoom
F1	Activates the AutoCAD Help Menu
F2	Opens the AutoCAD Text Window
F3	Turns OSNAP (object snap) ON or OFF
F4	Turns the Tablet ON or OFF (if one has been calibrated)
F5	Toggles through the three Isoplanes: Top, Right, and Left.
F6	Toggles through the three coordinate options: ON, OFF or display Polor Coordinates.
F7	Turns the GRID ON or OFF
F8	Turns ORTHO ON or OFF
F9	Turns SNAP ON or OFF
F10	Turns POLAR Tracking ON or OFF
F11	Turns OTRACK (object snap tracking) ON or OFF

General Procedures

1. Type the command, command alias, or system variable at the Command Prompt.
2. Press <ENTER> to execute the command, or follow the Command Prompt prompts.

Tips & Tricks

- Remember to press the <ENTER> key after typing a command, a command alias, or a system variable.
- Commands, aliases, or system variables are not case sensitive.
- A *default* is the most common or last option selected and will be shown in parentheses. Press <ENTER> to accept the default. It is not necessary to type the default over again.
- When in doubt about a command location, type it (and remember to press <ENTER>). This will usually begin the desired command.
- System variable settings will be covered in this tutorial at the appropriate topic.

Help Menu

Command Locator

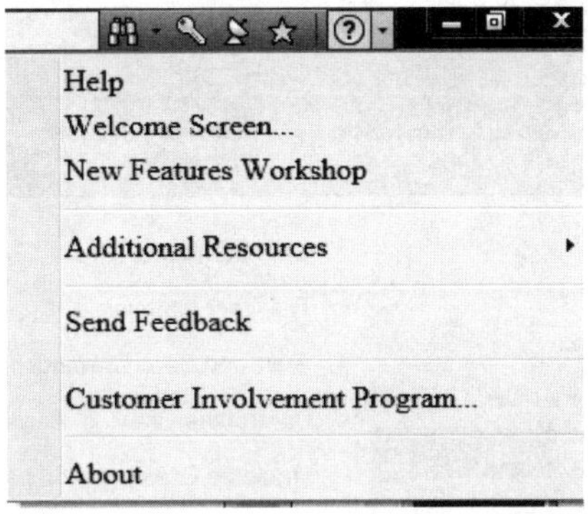

Pull Down Menu	**Help / AutoCAD Help Topics**
Command	**Help**
Alias	**F1**
RMB Shortcut Menu	
Dialog Box	**Help Topics: AutoCAD Help**

Command Overview

AutoCAD Help can be invoked at any time. If the Command Prompt is blank, the Help menu will open at one of the tabs, depending on which tab was selected the last time Help was used. If help is invoked while in the middle of a command, the Help menu will open to the page covering that command. There are three tabs to the Help menu: Contents, Index, and Find. This Help menu follows a format typical among Windows programs.

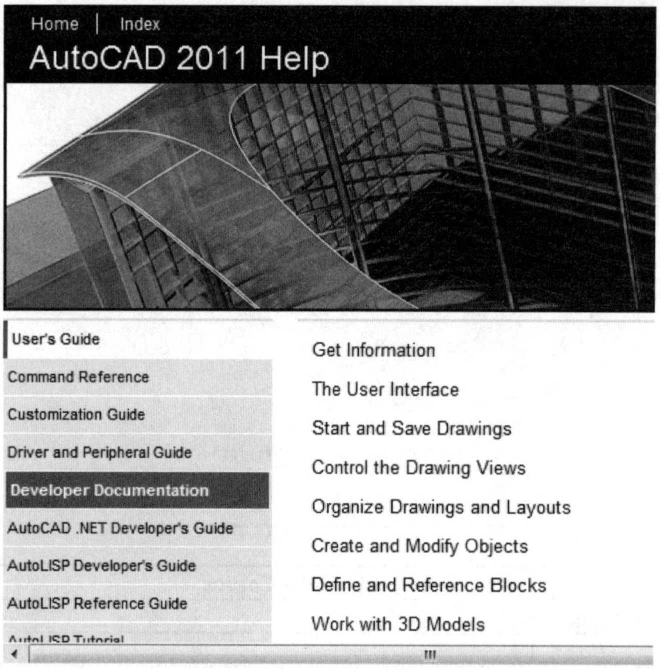

Figure 13 – AutoCAD Help Dialog Box

General Procedures

To access help when in the middle of a command:

1. Select the question mark in the toolbar.

To use the Help Contents tab:

1. Select Help Topics / Contents Tab.
2. Open a topic by double clicking on it, or single-click and select Open.

To use the Help menu Index tab:

1. Select Help Topics / Index Tab.
2. Begin to type the word.
3. Double-click the index entry, or single-click and select Display

To use the Help menu Find tab:

1. Select Help Topics / Find Tab.
2. If the setup Wizard appears, select Next.
3. Begin to type the word.
4. Double-click the index entry, or single-click and select Display

Command Exercise

Exercise 1-3 – Dynamic Input

Drawing Name: **(none, start from scratch)**
Estimated Time to Completion: 5 Minutes

Scope

Control the appearance of Dynamic Input

Solution

1.

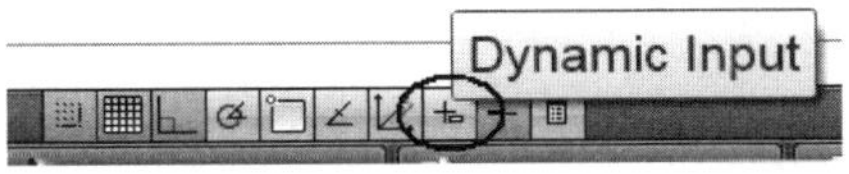

Verify that ORTHO and DYN are both enabled. Start the Line command. Move the cursor around the drawing window. Note how the coordinates in the input bar change depending on the cursor location.

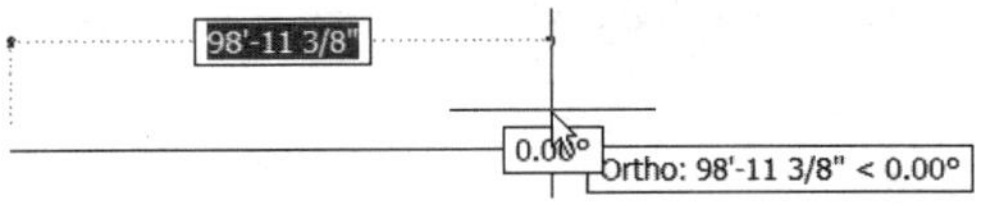

2.

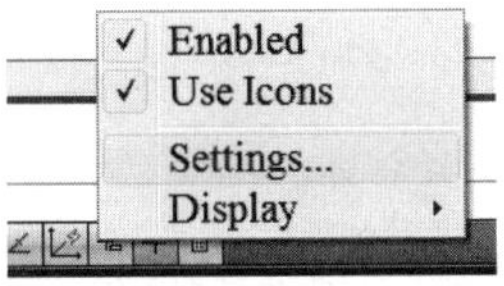

Place your cursor over the DYN toggle button. Right click and select **Settings**.

3.

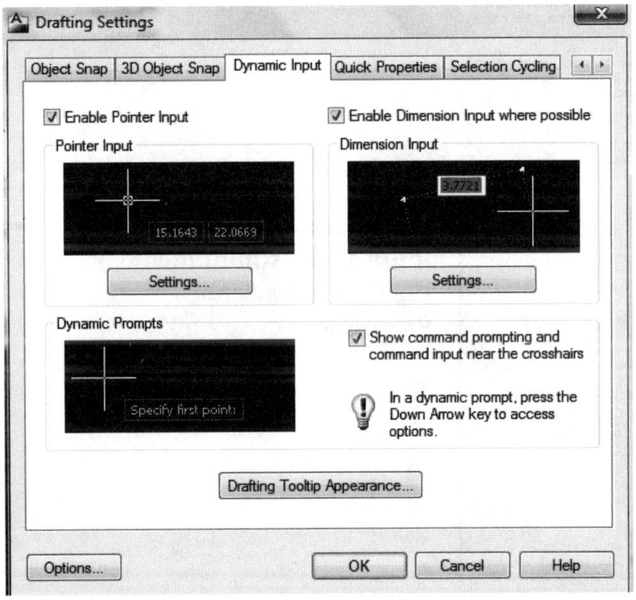

Select the **Settings** button under Pointer Input.

4.

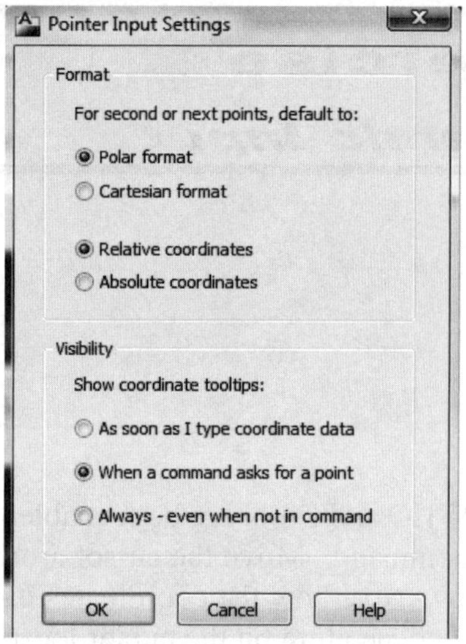

Press **OK**.

5.

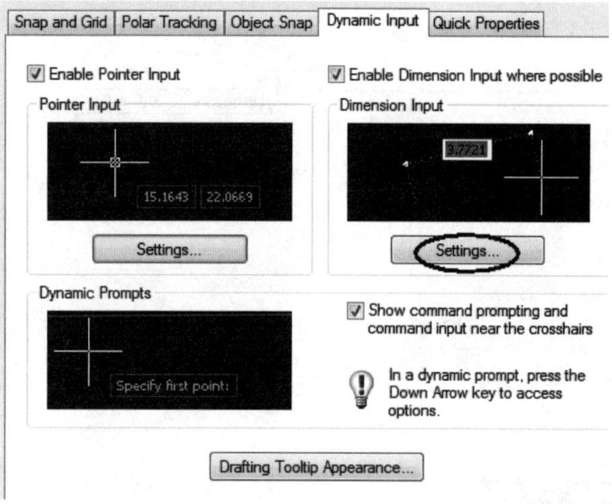

Select the **Settings** button under Dimension Input.

6.

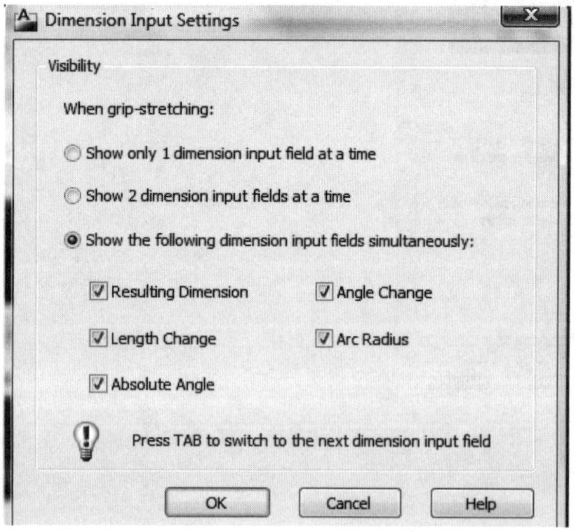

Enable **Show the following dimension input fields simultaneously**.
Enable all the options.
Press **OK**.

7. 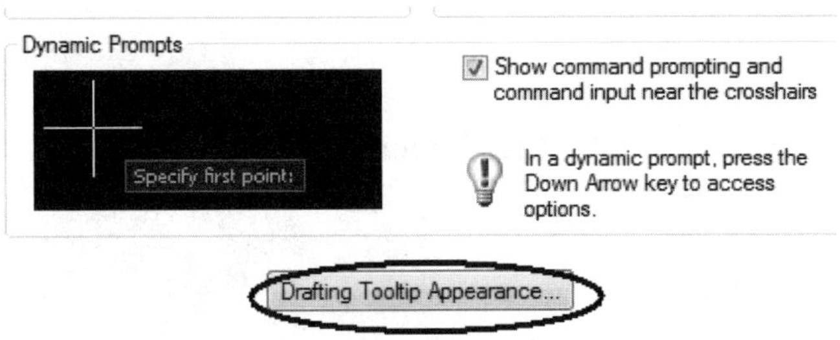

Select **Drafting Tooltip Appearance** under Dynamic Prompts.

8. 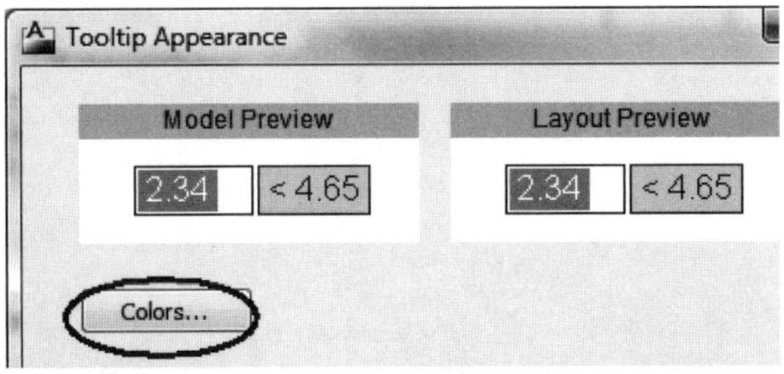

Select the **Colors** button.

9. 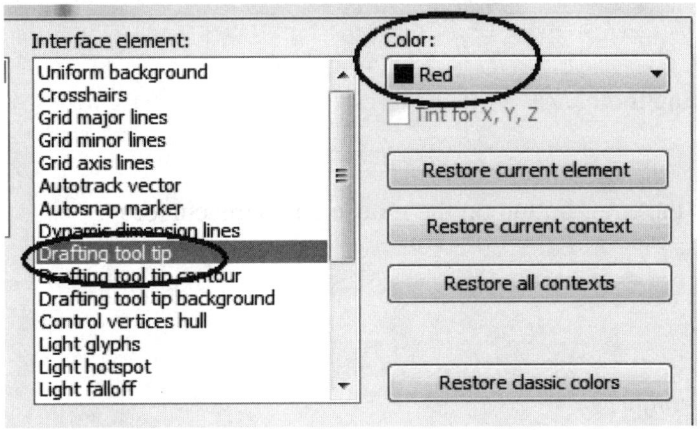

Highlight the **Drafting tool tip** in the Interface element box.
Set the color to **RED**.
Press **Apply**.

10. 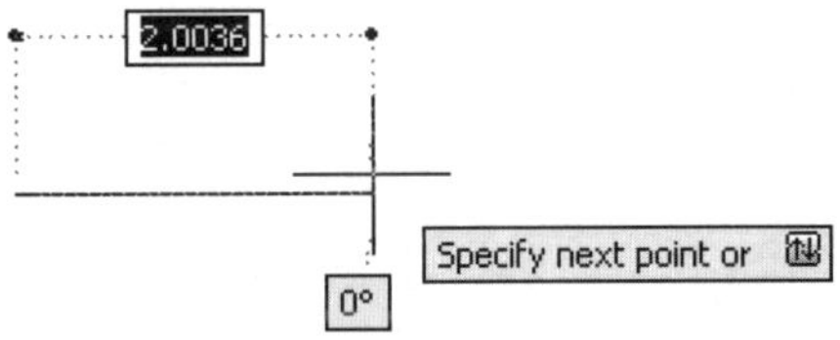

Press **OK** twice to close the dialog.

Note how the display has changed.

11. 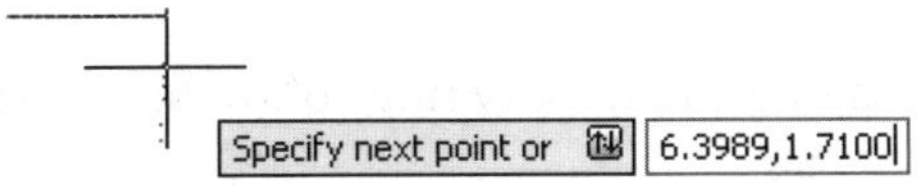

Pick a point to start the line.

Press the up and down arrows on your keyboard. Note that AutoCAD is keeping track of the coordinates selected.

12. 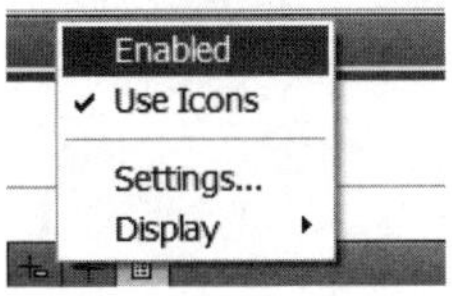

Toggle DYN off.

Note that the cursor dynamic input is now turned off.

Review Questions

1. Which is the Pick button and which is the <ENTER> button on the mouse?

2. Name the areas of the AutoCAD Screen:

3. How do you move a floating toolbar?

4. How do you dock a floating toolbar?

5. How do you make a docked toolbar floating again?

6. How do you re-size a floating toolbar?

7. What happens if you press the enter button on the mouse when the cursor is:

In the drawing window?

Over a toolbar?

Over the Command Prompt?

8. What does the Escape key do?

9. How can a dialog box be closed?

10. At a blank command prompt, what commands are initiated by typing following letters?

E	**C**	**M**
A	**L**	**P**
R	**Z**	**U**

11. Where is the Standard toolbar?

12. Where is the Object Properties toolbar?

Review Answers

1. Which is the Pick button and which is the <ENTER> button on the mouse?

   Left Button (LMB) : Pick

   Right Button (RMB): <ENTER>

2. Name the areas of the AutoCAD Screen:

   Title Bar, Pull-Down Menus, Toolbars, Drawing Window, Command Prompt, Status Bar

3. How do you move a floating toolbar?

   Pick in the frame or title bar of the toolbar (anywhere but the icon), drag to a new location and release the pick button.

4. How do you dock a floating toolbar?

   Drag the toolbar to any of the four sides of the drawing window until the rectangle shape appears, then release the pick button.

5. How do you make a docked toolbar floating again?

   Pick anywhere on the toolbar except an icon. Press and drag it into the drawing window.

6. How do you re-size a floating toolbar?

   Move the cursor to any of the four sides of the toolbar until a double arrow symbol appears. Press and drag to re-size the toolbar.

7. What happens if you press the enter button on the mouse when the cursor is:

   In the drawing window?

   A Shortcut Menu appears related to the last or current command.

   Over a toolbar?

   The toolbar Shortcut Menu appears.

   Over the Command Prompt?

   The Command Prompt Shortcut Menu appears.

8. What does the Escape key do?

   Cancels a command.

9. How can a dialog box be closed?

   Select OK, Close, the X in the upper right hand corner, or the Escape key

10. At a blank command prompt, what commands are initiated by typing following letters?

E *Erase*	**C** *Circle*	**M** *Move*
A *Arc*	**L** *Line*	**P** *Pan*
R *Redraw*	**Z** *Zoom*	**U** *Undo*

11. Where is the Standard Toolbar?

    The docked toolbar at the top.

12. Where is the Object Properties Toolbar?

    The docked toolbar at the top, beneath the Standard Toolbar.

NOTES:

Lesson 2.0 – View Commands

Estimated Class Time – 1 Hour

Objectives

This Lesson will cover the different ways to view drawings. Learn to Pan and Zoom in *real time*, and use the other Zoom options. Views can be Named and Saved, then Restored. The drawing window can be divided into Multiple Viewports.

- **Pan Realtime**
  Pan the drawing with the motion of the cursor in *real time*.
- **Zoom Realtime**
  Zoom the drawing with the up and down motion of the cursor in *real time*.
- **Zoom Window**
  Make a zoom window around an area to view close up.
- **Zoom Previous**
- **Zoom Options**
  Additional zoom options are located in the fly-out on the Standard Toolbar.
- **Regen**
  Regenerate the drawing to smooth out circles and arcs.
- **Named Views**
  Name and Save drawing Views and make them current when needed.
- **Multiple Viewports**
  Display different views of the drawing in multiple viewports.

Pan Realtime

Command Locator

Toolbar Menu	**Navigation / Pan Realtime**
Command	**Pan**
Alias	**P**
RMB Shortcut Menu	**Drawing Window**

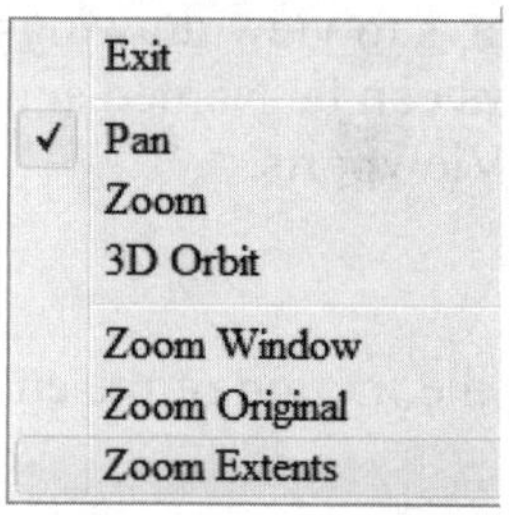

Figure 1 – Pan Realtime Shortcut Menu

Real Time Pan / Zoom Short-Cut Menu Options:	Overview
Exit	Exits the Realtime Pan or Zoom commands
Pan	Invokes the Realtime Pan command.
Zoom	Invokes the Realtime Zoom command.
3D Orbit	Rotates the drawing three-dimensionally
Zoom Window	Zooms to a window made by pressing the pick button and dragging it around the area to view.
Zoom Original	Displays the drawing in the original zoom setting.
Zoom Extents	Zooms to the extents of the drawing objects.

Command Overview

With the Pan Realtime command, pick a point in the drawing window. Press the LMB and drag the drawing view in real time. Right click (RMB) to access the shortcut menu and select Exit, or one of the other options. The Escape key will also exit the Pan Realtime command.

General Procedures

1. Invoke the Pan Realtime command.
2. Pick a point in the drawing window (LMB), press and drag to pan the view.
3. Right-click (RMB) to access the shortcut menu and pick Exit.

Tips & Tricks

- The shortcut menus for Pan Realtime and Zoom Realtime are identical.
- When dragging the cursor in Pan Realtime, the mouse can be picked up and relocated in the drawing window, if the cursor reaches the edge of the drawing window.

Zoom Realtime

Command Locator

Toolbar Menu	**Navigation / Zoom**
Command	**Zoom**
Alias	**Z**
RMB Shortcut Menu	**Drawing Window**

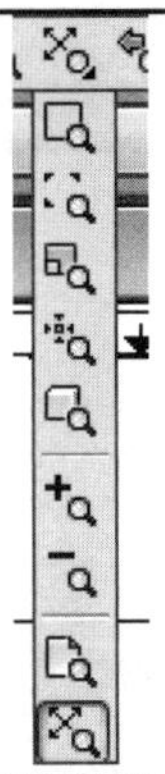

Command Overview

With the Zoom command, pick a point in the drawing window. Drag the mouse up or down to zoom in or out. Right click (RMB) to access the shortcut menu and select Exit, or one of the other options. The Escape Key will also exit the Zoom command.

General Procedures

1. Invoke the Zoom command.
2. Pick a point in the drawing window (LMB), press and drag up to zoom in and down to zoom out.
3. Right-click (RMB) to access the shortcut menu and select Exit or one of the other options.

Tips & Tricks

- Remember to drag up to zoom in and down to zoom out.
- When dragging the cursor in Zoom, the mouse can be picked up and relocated in the drawing window, if the cursor reaches the top or bottom of the drawing window.

Zoom Window

Command Locator

Toolbar Menu	**Navigation / Zoom Flyout**
Command	**Zoom, Window**
Alias	**Z**

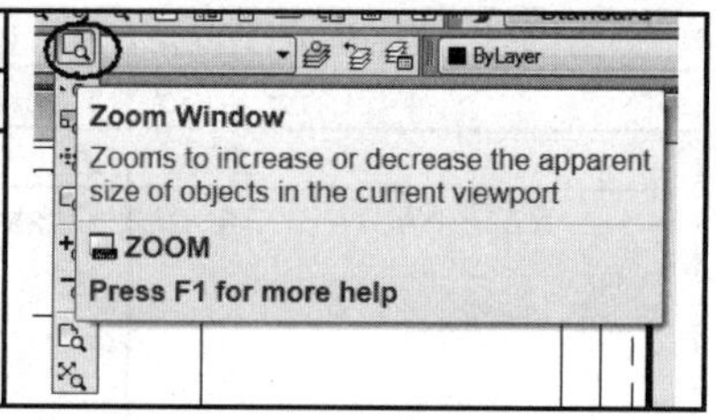

Command Overview

Use the Zoom window command to view a selected area of the drawing.

General Procedures

1. Invoke the Zoom Window command.
2. Pick the first corner of the view window, then drag the mouse and pick the opposite corner.

Tips & Tricks

- When the Zoom Window command is invoked, the opposite corner of the window must be made or Escape to cancel the Zoom command.
- When invoking the Zoom command, the Window option is a default. Just begin the first corner of the zoom window.
- Zoom commands can be used while in the middle of other commands.

Zoom Previous

Command Locator

Toolbar Menu	**Navigation / Zoom Previous**
Command	**Zoom / P**
Alias	**Z / P**

Command Overview

The Zoom Previous command displays the previous view.

General Procedures

1. Invoke the Zoom Previous command using the button in the Standard toolbar. If typing the alias Z, press <ENTER>, then type P (and <ENTER> for the Previous option).

Tips & Tricks

- Zoom previous can be accessed from the Zoom command by typing 'P' and pressing <ENTER>.
- Zoom Previous can go back until no previous views are found.

Zoom Options

Command Locator

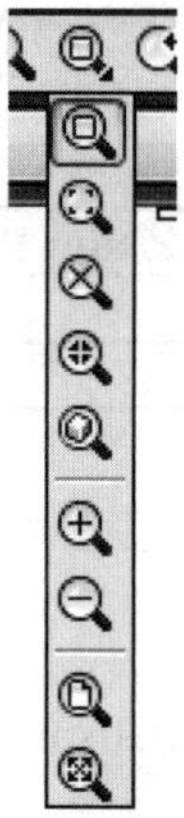

Toolbar Menu	**Navigation / Zoom Fly-out**
Command	**Zoom (type capitalized letter of the desired option)**
Alias	**Z (type capitalized letter of the desired option)**

Command Overview

Other zoom options are available within the Zoom command. These can be accessed from the fly-out button on the Standard Toolbar under the Zoom Window command. These options are also available by typing the capitalized letter of the desired option after invoking the Zoom command.

Zoom Option	Button	Overview
Zoom		Zoom Realtime – zoom in and out
Zoom Previous		Zoom back through previous views
Zoom Window		Zooms to a selected window.
Zoom Dynamic		Displays the zoom window. LMB to scale or pan the view window. RMB to display the Shortcut menu.
Zoom Scale		Zoom to a specific scale relevant to the last zoom or to actual scale in paper space (x/xp).
Zoom Center		Makes a selected point in the drawing the Center of the drawing.
Zoom Object		Select an entity in your drawing and the view will adjust to center on the select object.
Zoom In		This will zoom at a scale of .5x.
Zoom Out		This will zoom at a scale of 2x.
Zoom All		This will zoom to view all of the geometry in the drawing as well as the area designated by the Drawing Limits.
Zoom Extents		This will zoom to view only the geometry in the drawing.

General Procedures

1. Invoke the Zoom command option from the fly-out in the Standard Toolbar.
2. If typing the alias Z, press <ENTER>, then type the capitalized letter of the desired option and press <ENTER>.

Tips & Tricks

- The most important Zoom options are Window, All and Extents.
- Zoom All or Extents occasionally to be sure bits of the drawing have not gotten thrown out into space.
- If the desired fly-out option is the visible button on the Standard Toolbar, simply select it. It is not necessary to display the fly-out list to select that option.

Command Exercise

Exercise 2-1 – Real Time Zoom

Drawing Name: **pan1.dwg**
Estimated Time to Completion: 10 Minutes

Scope

Zoom and Pan the drawing in real time. Use the RMB to switch between some basic zoom modes.

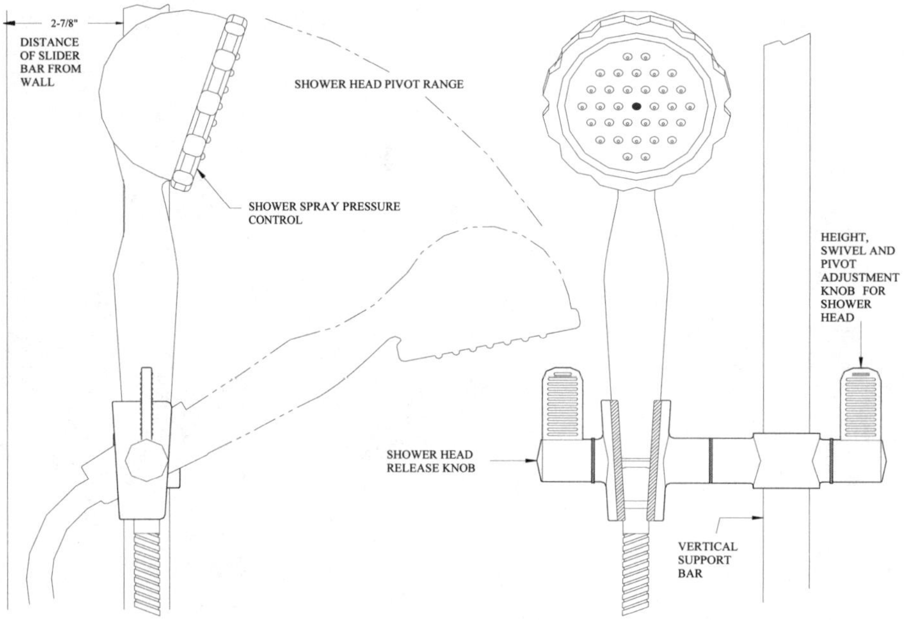

Figure 2 – Zoom and Pan Exercise

Solution

1. Invoke the Zoom command (z or zoom).

2. *Press ESC or ENTER to exit, or right-click to display shortcut menu.*
   Pick a point in the middle of the drawing window. Hold the LMB down and drag the mouse up and down. Notice how you zoom in as you move the mouse up and zoom out as you move the mouse down.

3. *Press ESC or ENTER to exit, or right-click to display shortcut menu:*
   Hold the mouse down and drag the mouse to the top of the screen. Let go of the LMB and move the mouse to the center of the screen. Hold the LMB down and drag the mouse to the top of the screen. This allows you to continue to zoom in. Repeat the process but zoom out by dragging the mouse down instead of up.

4. *Press ESC or ENTER to exit, or right-click to display shortcut menu:*
Press the <ENTER> or <ESC> key to end the command.

5. Invoke the Pan command (p or pan).

6. *Press ESC or ENTER to exit, or right-click to display shortcut menu:*
Select a location in the middle of the screen and hold your LMB down and drag your mouse up, down, right and left. Notice how the drawing pans as you move your mouse. Let go of the LMB reposition the mouse and repeat the steps above to continue panning in one direction.

7. *Press ESC or ENTER to exit, or right-click to display shortcut menu:*
Press the RMB and select zoom from the view shortcut menu. Zoom in or out by holding the LMB down and dragging the mouse up and down.

8. *Press ESC or ENTER to exit, or right-click to display shortcut menu:*

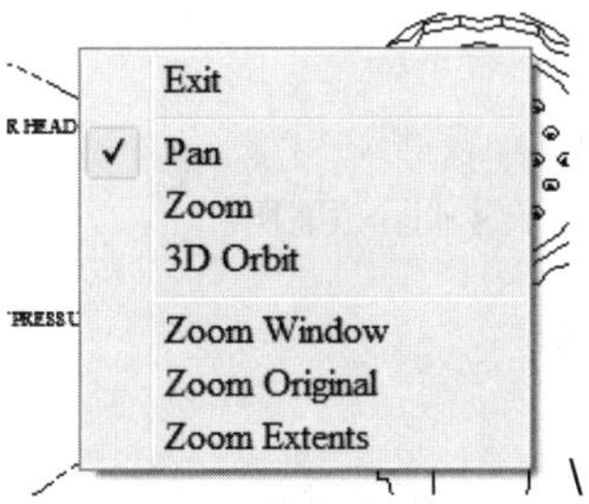

Press the RMB and switch back to Pan. Pan through the drawing.

9. *Press ESC or ENTER to exit, or right-click to display shortcut menu:*
Press the RMB and switch to Zoom Window in the shortcut menu. You will create a window with your mouse that will represent the area to zoom in on. Position your mouse to create a rectangular window. Hold your LMB down and drag the mouse diagonally to create a window. Release the left mouse button to finish the command and zoom in on the drawing. Notice that this method is a *drag and release* and works slightly differently then the regular Zoom Window command.

10. *Press ESC or ENTER to exit, or right-click to display shortcut menu:*
Press the RMB and select Zoom Extents. Notice how AutoCAD zooms to the extents of the drawing. Press the RMB and select the Zoom Original option in the shortcut menu. Notice how the drawing zooms to the original settings that existed when the ZOOM / PAN command was first invoked.

> ***Tip:*** *The Microsoft IntelliMouse offers many user friendly viewing options that are automatically invoked by using the Wheel on the IntelliMouse. AutoDesk recommends using the Microsoft IntelliMouse with AutoCAD.*

Regen

Command Locator

Pull Down Menu	**View / Regen**
Command	**Regen**
Alias	**Re**

Command Overview

The REGEN command is used to smooth out circles or arcs in the drawing. Regen All is used when there are multiple viewports in the drawing. Whereas Redraw refreshes the drawing window, Regen recalculates the mathematics of the drawing and though it may take longer, is a more thorough command.

General Procedures

1. Select Regen from the View pull-down or type Re and press <ENTER>.

- Sometimes REGEN will happen automatically, as with certain zoom commands.
- Regen can be used frequently. It recalculates the mathematics of the drawing and displays the objects with greater accuracy.

Command Exercise

Exercise 2-2 – Zoom and Regen

Drawing Name: **zoom1.dwg**
Estimated Time to Completion: 10 Minutes

Scope

Zoom this drawing out several times then use the Zoom Window option and pick just inside the corners of the red rectangle. Regen to see the arcs and circles smooth out.

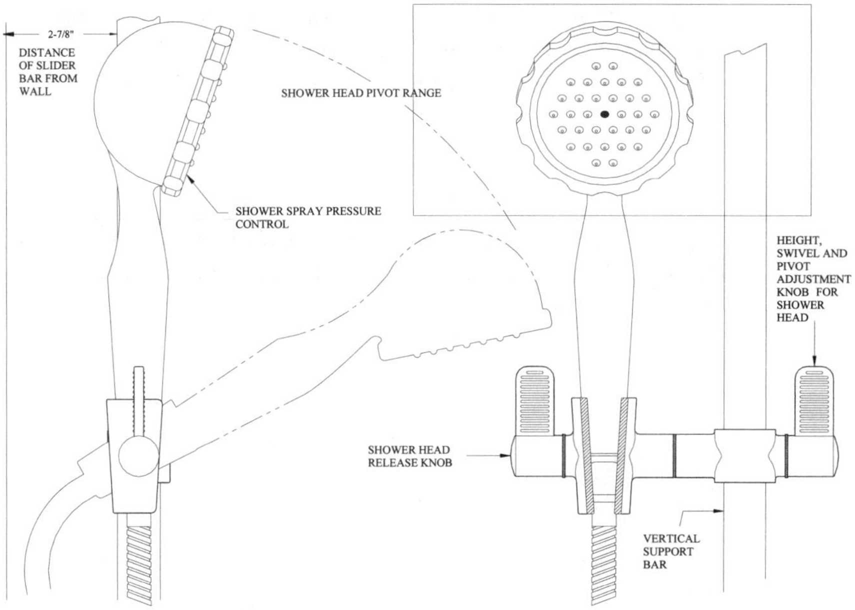

Figure 3 – Zoom and Regen Exercise

Solution

1. Invoke the Zoom command (z or zoom and <ENTER> once).

2. *Press ESC or ENTER to exit, or right-click to display shortcut menu.*
   Press the LMB in the middle of the drawing and drag down to zoom out of the drawing.

3. *Press ESC or ENTER to exit, or right-click to display shortcut menu.*
   Press <ENTER> to end the command.

4. Invoke the Regen command by selecting Regen from the View pull-down (re or regen).

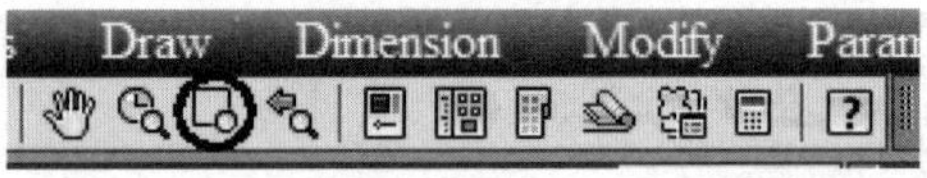

5. Invoke the Zoom Window command (z or zoom and <ENTER> once).

6. *[All/Center/Dynamic/Extents/Previous/Scale/Window/Object] <real time>:*
Create a window with your mouse that will represent the area to zoom in on. Position your mouse inside a corner of the red box and click the LMB. Move the mouse diagonally to another corner of the box and click the LMB again. Notice how the Arcs and Circles are represented by small straight segments.

7. Invoke the Regen command by selecting Regen from the View pull-down (re or regen).

Extra: *From the <VIEW<ZOOM pull-down experiment with all the different zoom options available. Scale, Dynamic, Center, In, Out, Previous and All. Which method of viewing your drawing is the easiest?*

Tip: *You can invoke the Zoom Window function directly by typing Z <ENTER> and specifying the opposite corners of the Zoom Window (the Window option is the default).*

Named Views

Command Locator

Toolbar Menu	**Views/ Named Views**
Pull Down Menu	**View / Named View**
Command	**View**
Alias	**V**
Dialog Box	**View**

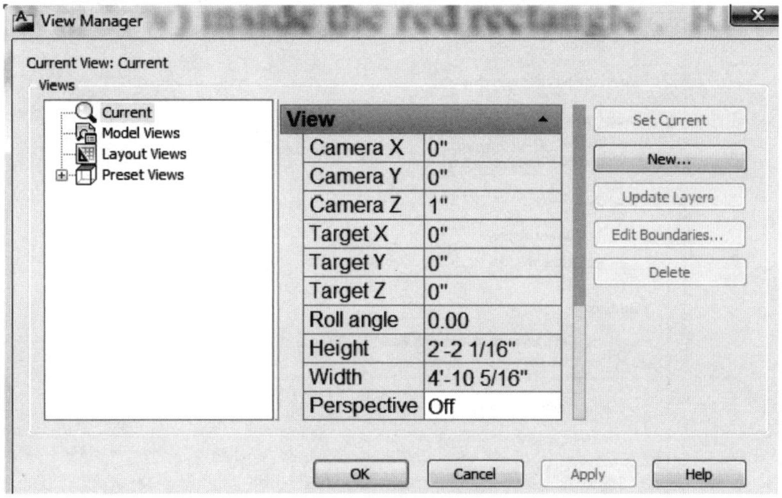

Figure 4 – View Dialog Box

Command Overview

Views can be saved and restored with the Named View command. This will save the time it takes to zoom out and in, to a frequently selected view. This tutorial will focus on the Named Views area of the View dialog box. New views can be Named as the Current display or defined by a new view (Define Window). Named Views from the list can be selected and set as the Current view.

General Procedures

1. Begin the Named Views command. Highlight 'Current' and select 'New'.
2. In the New View window, type the view name. Select 'Current display' or 'Define Window'. If Define Window is selected, select the cursor arrow and make a window around the desired view in the drawing. If this view is okay, select OK, otherwise try again.
3. Named Views can now be selected from the list and "Set Current"
4. To Delete or Rename a Named View, select it, then right click (RMB) and select the desired option.

- Named Views are saved with the drawing file.
- Certain characters are not allowed for the View name.
- Remember to select Current display or Define window for the New Named View.
- You can save layer settings with Named Views to create different views for your layouts.
- The name can be up to 255 characters long and contain letters, digits, and the special characters dollar sign ($), hyphen (–), and underscore (_).
- Named Views can be placed on sheets.

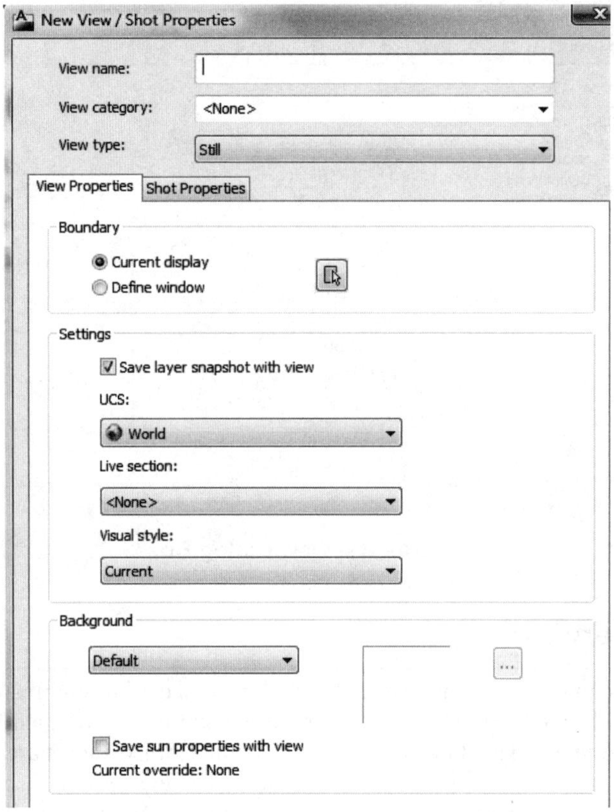

Figure 5 – New Named View

View Name	Name of your saved view
View Category	The category is used in the Sheet Set Manager to organize your views. You can add a category or select one from the list. This entry is optional.
View Type	Options are Still, Cinematic and Recorded Walk
Boundary	Sets the limits of the view
Save layer snapshot View	Saves the current layer settings
UCS Name	Allows you to set the view to a specific UCS
Live section	Displays the live section applied when the view is restored. This option is only available when in the Model space
Visual Style	Allows you to specify a visual style to be assigned to a view
Background	Allows you to set a different background color than the current setting. This can only be done for model space views in shaded mode.

Command Exercise

Exercise 2-3 – Saving Named Views

Drawing Name: **nview1.dwg**
Estimated Time to Completion: 5 Minutes

Scope

Zoom the specified area. With the Named Views command, name the view BALLAST and save it. Zoom All, then restore the named view.

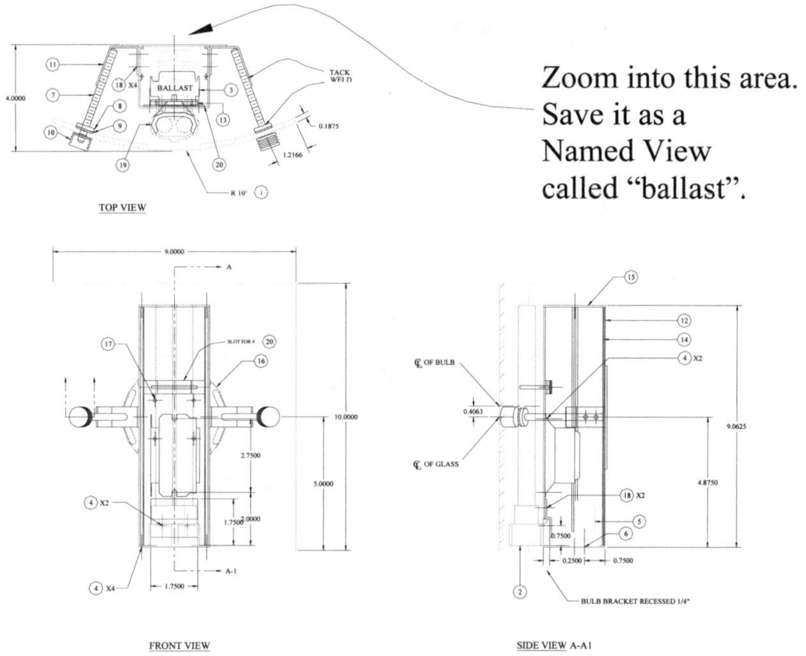

Figure 6 – Named View Exercise

Solution

1. Invoke the Zoom Window command (z or zoom).

2. *[All/Center/Dynamic/Extents/Previous/Scale/Window/Object] <real time>:*
   Create a window around the desired area of the screen (upper left corner).

3. Regenerate the drawing by selecting Regen from the View pull-down or by typing 'RE' or 'REGEN' and pressing <ENTER>. Notice how the arcs and circles smooth out.

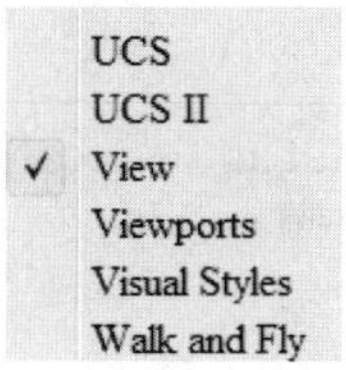

If the View toolbar is not visible, right click on any toolbar and enable **View**.

4. Invoke the Named Views command (view).

5. Press the **New** button.

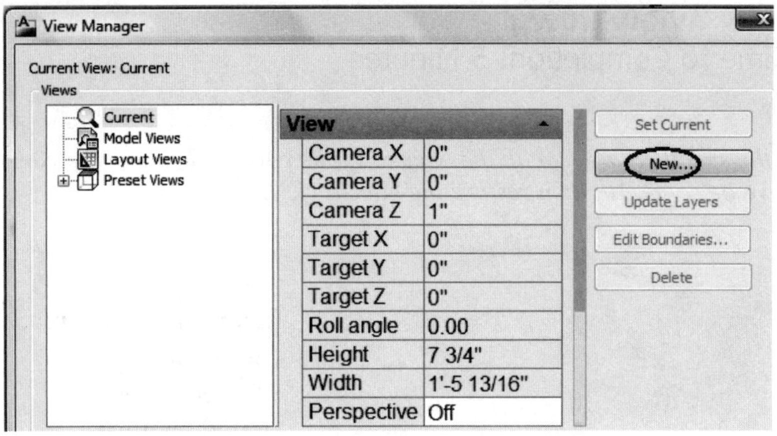

Figure 7 – View Dialog Box

6. In the New View dialog box, fill out the information as shown in the next figure and press **Apply**.

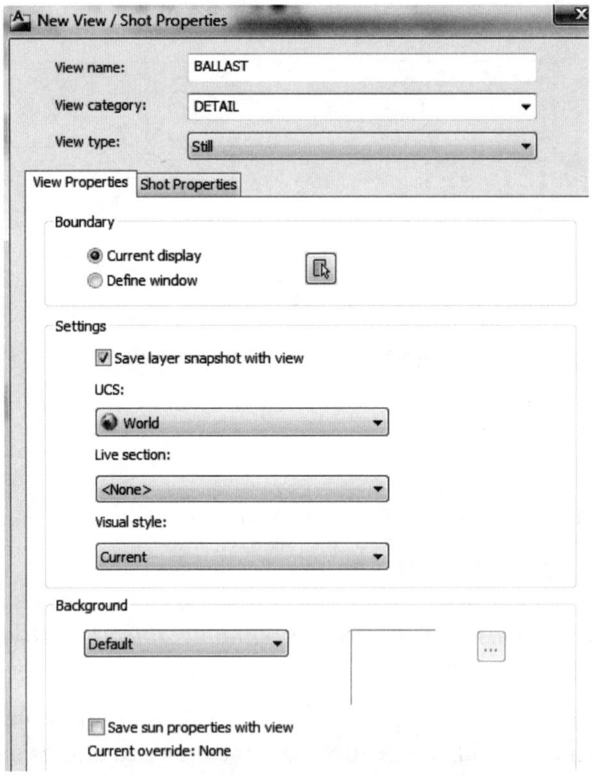

Figure 8 – New View Dialog Box

7. Close the View dialog box by pressing **OK**. You have just saved a view that can be recalled at any time. We will zoom out and then restore the view you have just created called **BALLAST**.

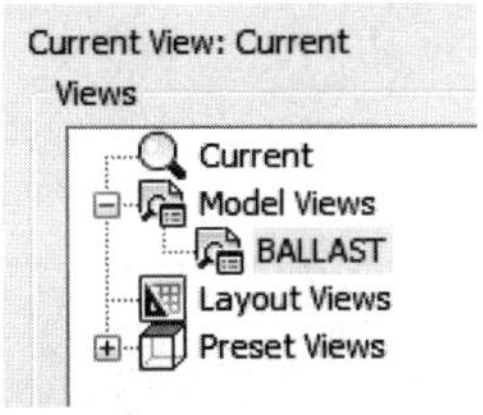

The view you created is listed in the View Manager.

Press **OK** to close the View Manager dialog.

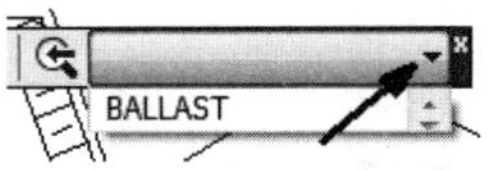

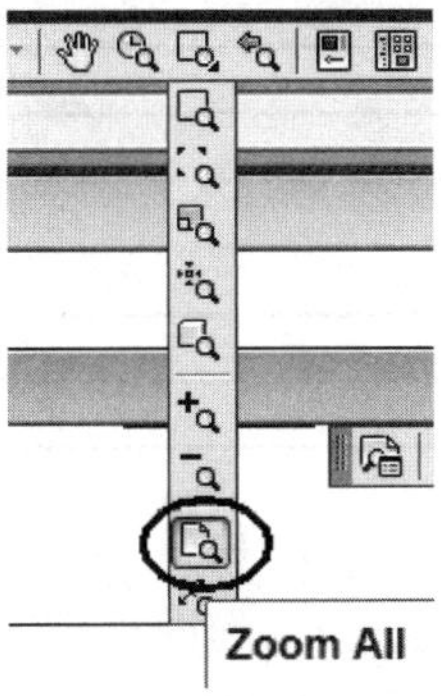

8. Invoke the Zoom All command (z or zoom, option a). Notice that the entire drawing is now visible in the drawing window.

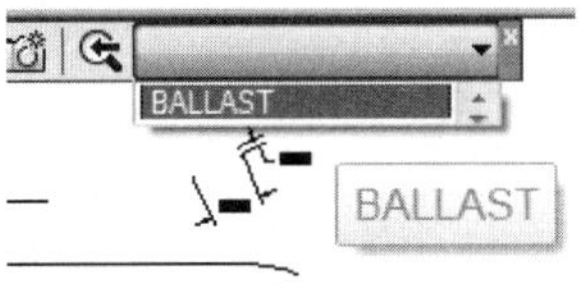

9. Press the down arrow on the View toolbar and select **BALLAST**.

10. Notice how the drawing window now displays the BALLAST view you created at the beginning of the exercise.

Extra: *Practice saving other views in the drawing.*

Multiple Viewports

Command Locator

Toolbar Menu	**Viewports/New Viewports**
Pull Down Menu	**View / Viewports / (select option)**
Command	**Viewports**
Alias	**Vports**
RMB Shortcut Menu	**List box**
Dialog Box	**Viewports**

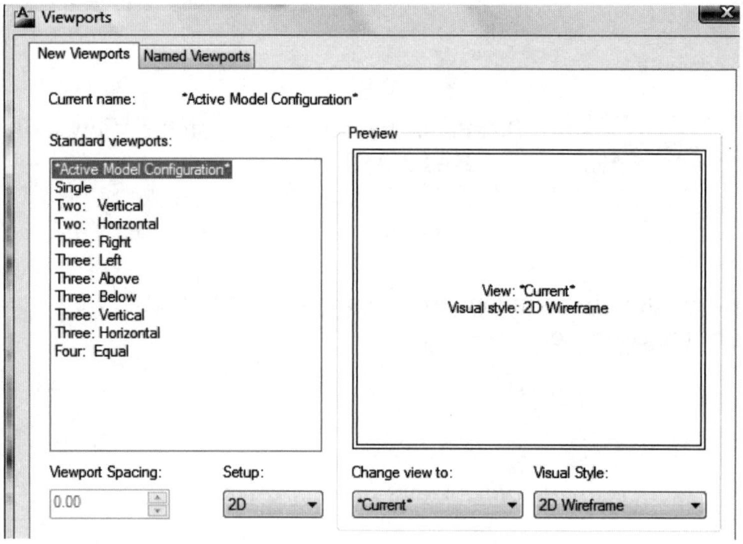

Figure 9 – Viewports Dialog Box

Command Overview

The Model view of the drawing can be divided into Multiple Viewports. Each viewport can display a different part of the drawing, however, only one viewport may be active. Tiled viewports configurations, including the views within each viewport can be named and selected to be current later in the drawing.

General Procedures

To create one, two, three, etc. viewports:

1. Select the desired number of viewports from the Pull-Down (POP) menu, View / (select 1, 2, 3, or 4 viewports).
2. Follow the command line prompts. For three viewports, "Right" is the default location for the largest viewport.

To create viewports using the Viewports dialog box:

1. Type vports, or select the POP option View / Viewports / New Viewports…
2. Select the viewport configuration from the list.

To use Multiple Viewports:

1. Select a viewport to make it active.
2. Use any of the Zoom commands. To draw between viewports, click on one viewport and pick a point, then click on the other viewport to continue drawing the object.

To Save a Viewport Configuration:

1. From the Viewport dialog box, select the New Viewports tab.
2. Type in the New name for the current viewport configuration.
3. This name will appear in the list, and later can be selected and made current.

Tips & Tricks

- An active viewport is the one with the bolder border around it. The cursor crosshairs will also be visible in the active viewport.
- Named Viewport configurations are saved with the drawing file.

Command Exercise

Exercise 2-4 – Multiple Viewports

Drawing Name: **vport1.dwg**
Estimated Time to Completion: 10 Minutes

Scope

Create four tiled viewports. Restore a named view in each viewport. Save the viewport configuration as V1. Join two adjacent views and save this as V2. Change to a single viewport. Restore the Saved viewport configurations.

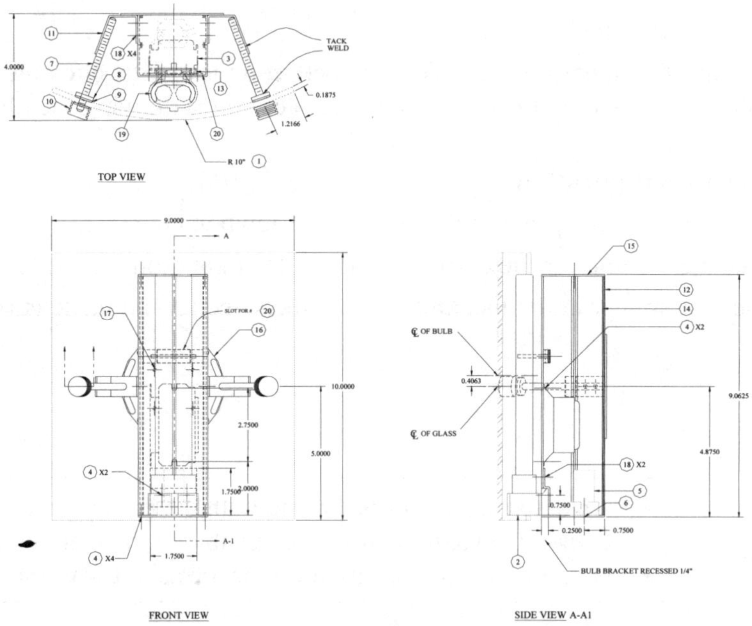

Figure 10 – Multiple Viewports Exercise

Solution

1. Start the exercise by creating four tiled viewports. Select **VIEW→VIEWPORTS→4 VIEWPORTS** from the pull-down menus.

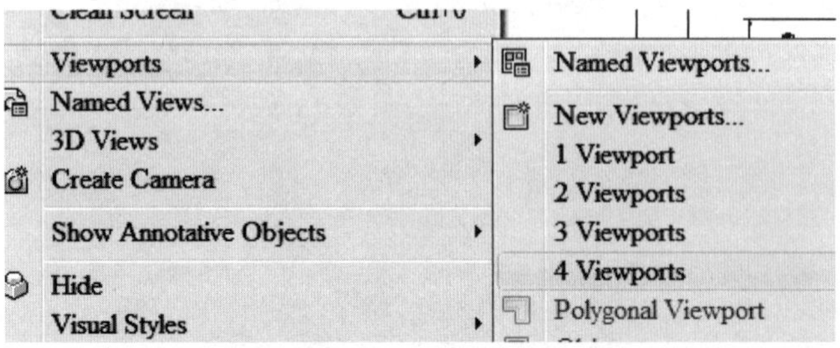

2. Notice how the drawing window is divided into 4 viewports. The same view is displayed in all four viewports. We will now restore different Named Views in each viewport.

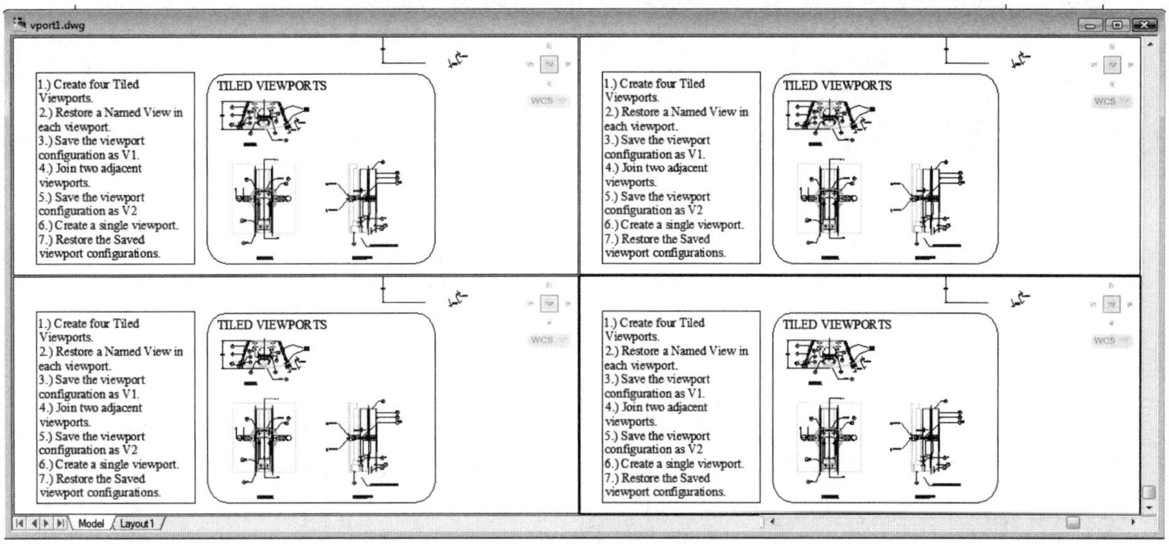

Figure 11 – Four Viewports

3. Move your pointer to the upper left corner viewport and activate the viewport by clicking inside it with your LMB.

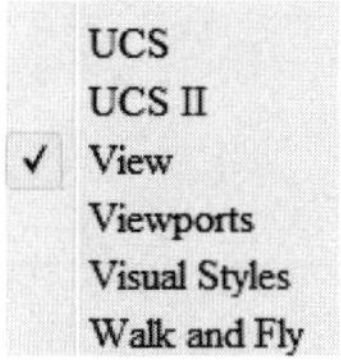

If the View toolbar is not visible, right click on any toolbar and enable **View**.

4. Invoke the Named Views command (view).

5. In the View dialog box, double-click on ‘TOP’ to set it current for the viewport. Press ‘OK’.

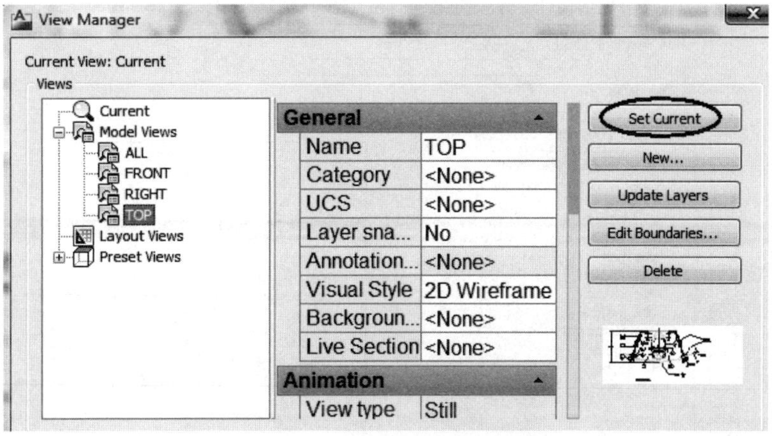

Figure 12 – View Dialog Box

6. Repeat the process for the other viewports by selecting other named views for each. When finished, your drawing may look similar to the next figure.

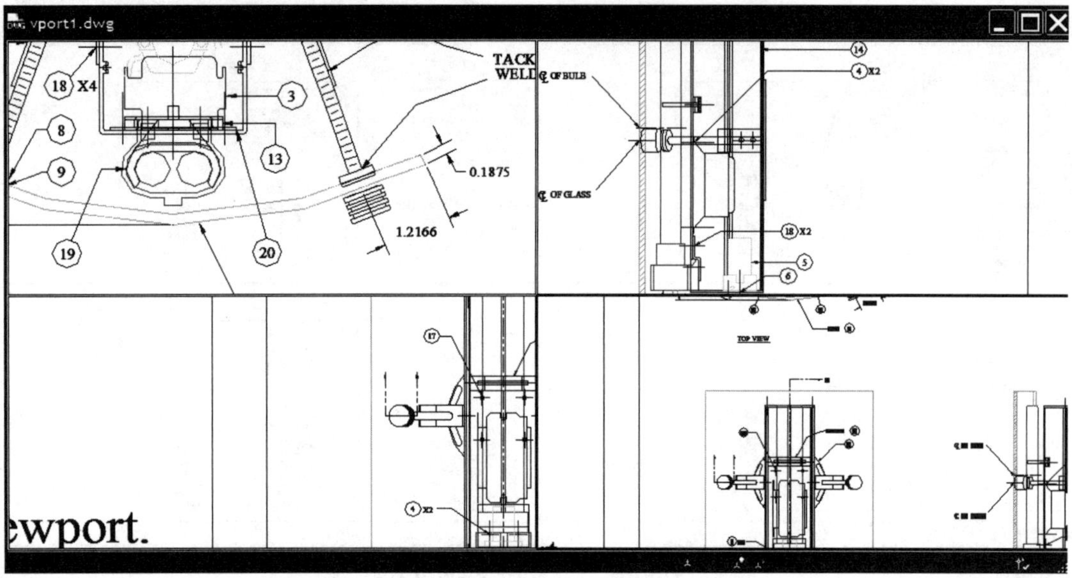

Figure 13 – Four Viewports after Changing the Views

7. Once you have created the layout above, save the configuration. Select **VIEW→ VIEWPORTS→NEW VIEWPORTS**… from the pull-down menu.

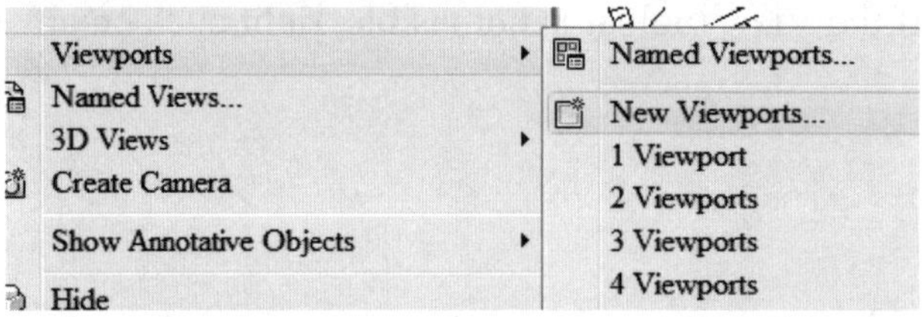

8. In the Viewports dialog box enter the information displayed in the following figure. Enter **V1** for the new name. Press **OK** to save. You have just saved a viewport configuration that can be restored at any time.

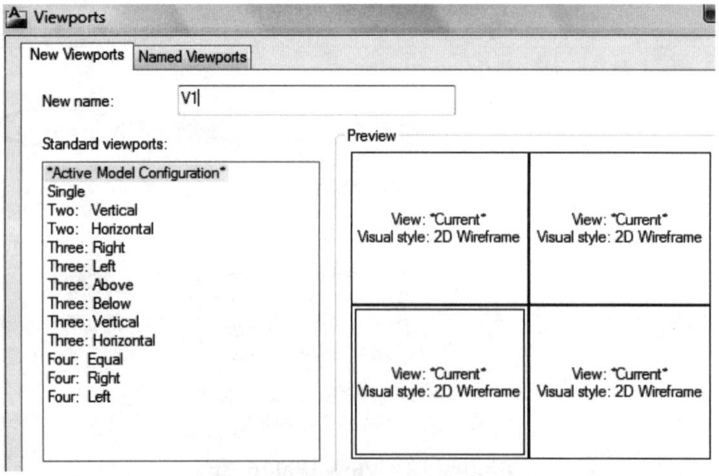

Figure 14 – Viewports Dialog Box

9. Select **VIEW→VIEWPORTS→NEW VIEWPORTS**… from the pull-down menu.

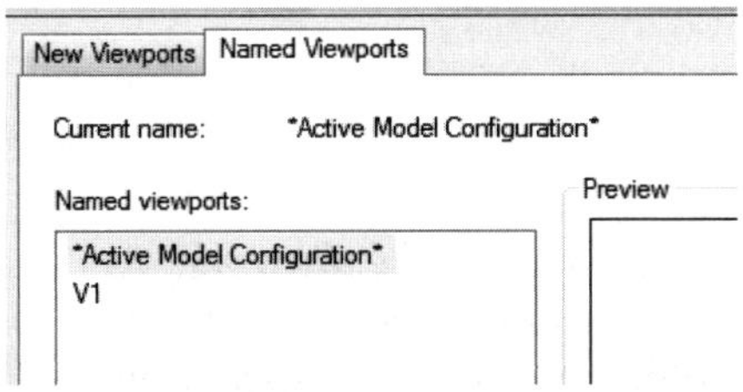

In the Named Viewports tab, the V1 configuration is listed.

10. Close the dialog box.

***Tip:** Use your RMB to activate a pop up dialog box that will allow you to delete or rename your viewport configurations (Named Viewports) in the Viewports dialog box.*

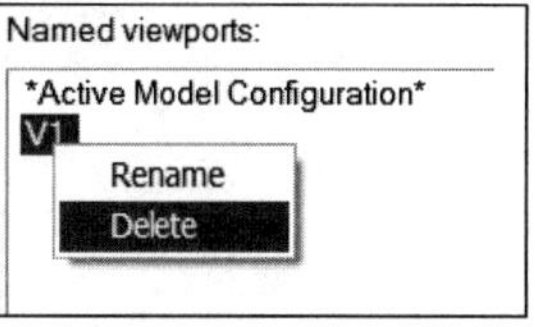

Lesson Exercise

Exercise 2-5

Viewing Drawings

Drawing Name: **Lesson 2 MCAD.dwg**
Estimated Time to Completion: 15 Minutes

Scope

Use the commands you have learned in the past Lesson to view the drawing. Determine which viewing commands are easier for you to use. Locate information on the drawing and fill out the table below. Follow the instructions on the drawing for creating a named view and tiled viewport layout.

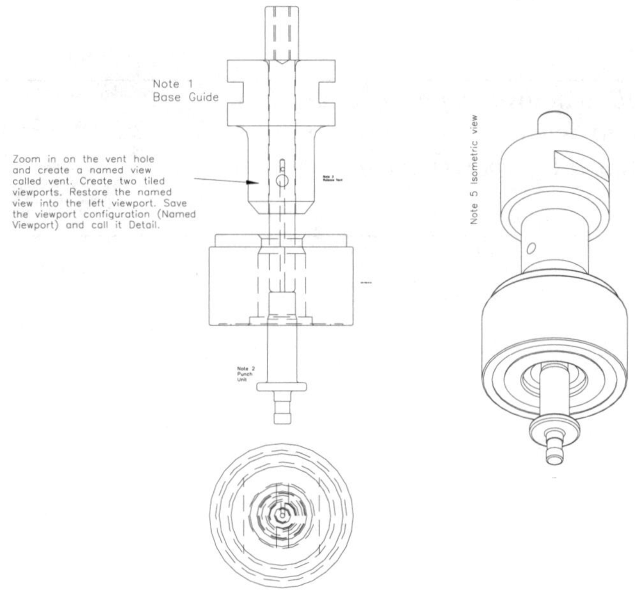

Figure 15 – Viewing Drawings

Hints

1. Choose a zoom command you feel comfortable with. The author likes the Zoom Window and Zoom Previous commands.
2. Note 6 is under the Isometric drawing. Note 7 is under the number 6 in Note 6.
3. Use the named views command and named viewports command to complete the second part of the exercise.

Lesson Exercise

Exercise 2-6

View Commands

Drawing Name: **Lesson 2 aec.dwg**
Estimated Time to Completion: **15 Minutes**

Scope

Using the commands learned in this Lesson, zoom and pan around the drawing. Examine the named views in the drawing and create named views of the kitchen, bath and small bedroom. View the drawing with multiple viewports.

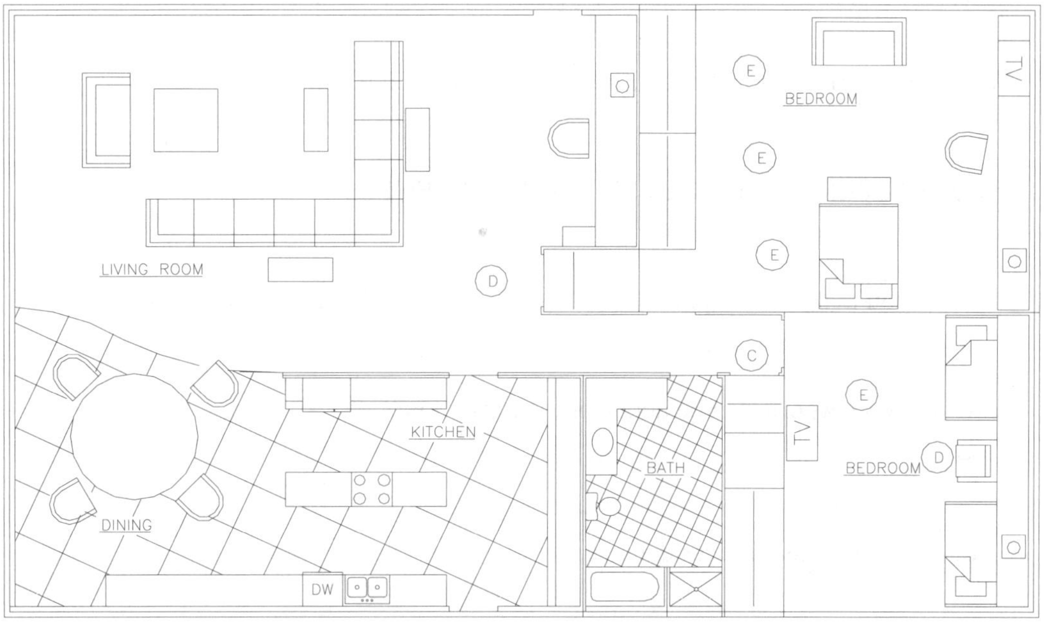

Figure 16 – View Commands Lesson Exercise

Hints

1. Use the different zoom options to become familiar with all of them.
2. Zoom in on the kitchen and create a named view of it. Do the same for the bathroom and small bedroom.
3. Use the Viewports command to bring up multiple viewports and show a different room in each viewport.

Review Questions

1. Identify the following icons by writing the command and the toolbars where they can be found:

		Command	Toolbars
a.			
b.			
c.			
d.			
e.			
f.			
g.			

2. What is the difference between Zoom Extents and Zoom All?

3. What is the difference between REDRAW and REGEN?

4. How do you make a viewport active? How can you tell that a viewport is active?

5. How many viewports can be active at the same time?

- ❑ 1
- ❑ 2
- ❑ 3
- ❑ As many as the user decides.

6. Can you create a new Viewport configuration (Named Viewport) if you activate the Viewport dialog box by selecting <VIEW<VIEWPORTS<NAMED VIEWPORTS… and Not <VIEW<VIEWPORTS<NEW VIEWPORTS…?

7. When restoring Viewport configurations (Named Viewports) does AutoCAD regenerate the drawing? Try It.

Review Answers

1. Identify the following icons by writing the command and the toolbars where they can be found:

a. *Named View / Standard*
b. *Pan Real-time / Standard*
c. *Zoom / Standard*
d. *Zoom Window / Standard & Zoom Toolbar*
e. *Zoom Previous / Standard*
f. *Zoom All / Standard & Zoom Toolbar*
g. *Zoom Extents / Standard & Zoom Toolbar*

2. What is the difference between Zoom Extents and Zoom All?

Zoom Extents will zoom only all of the geometry in the drawing. Zoom All will zoom everything - the drawing geometry and the drawing limits (grid area).

3. What is the difference between REDRAW and REGEN?

REDRAW refreshes the drawing screen, whereas REGEN recalculates the mathematics of the drawing database.

4. How do you make a viewport active? How can you tell that a viewport is active?

a. To make a viewport active, place the cursor in the viewport and select the left button on the mouse (LMB).

b. An active viewport will have a slightly bolder border around it, and will show the cursor crosshairs in it.

5. How many viewports can be active at the same time?

■ 1
❑ 2
❑ 3
❑ As many as the user decides.

Only one viewport can be active in AutoCAD at one time.

6. Can you create a new Viewport configuration (Named Viewport) if you activate the Viewport dialog box by selecting <VIEW<VIEWPORTS<NAMED VIEWPORTS… and Not <VIEW<VIEWPORTS<NEW VIEWPORTS…?

Yes, The viewport dialog box has two tabs: Named Viewports and New Viewports. Users can switch to either tab no matter how the dialog box was activated.

7. When restoring Viewport configurations (Named Viewports) does AutoCAD regenerate the drawing?

Try it.

NOTES:

Lesson 3.0 – Drawing Lines

Estimated Class Time: 2 Hours

Objectives

This section introduces AutoCAD commands, for creating a simple drawing. Starting with a New drawing, the user will learn to draw lines using different methods.

- **Start From Scratch**
  Use the New command to begin a new drawing from "scratch".
- **Line**
  Draw line segments.
  Using Direct Distance Method
  Using Polar Tracking
  Using Cartesian Coordinates
  Absolute Coordinates
  Relative Coordinates
  Polar Coordinates
  Drag Method
- **Coordinate Entry**
- **Erase**
  Deleting AutoCAD entities

Start from Scratch

Command Locator

Toolbar Menu	**Standard/New**
Pull Down Menu	**File / New**
Command	**New**
Alias	**Ctrl+N**

For the exercises in this section, we will be using the *acad.dwt* template. This template setting was made when AutoCAD was installed. If you want to set a different default template to be used, go to the **Options** dialog and select the default template you wish to use.

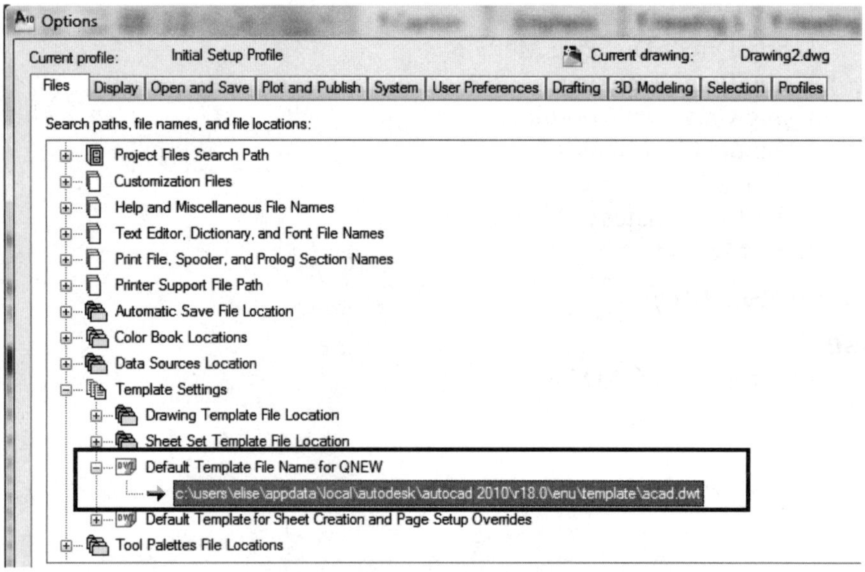

Figure 1 – The Options Dialog

Command Overview

To Create a New drawing, choose New. Every time the New drawing command is invoked, a new drawing is created with the title Drawing1, Drawing2, Drawing3, etc.

General Procedures

1. Select the New button from the Standard Toolbar

> - Make it a habit to select the New file icon from the Standard Toolbar. This is a quicker way to access the command, then from the Pull-Down menu.
> - Close drawings that are not being used.

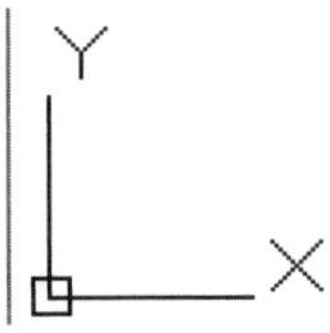

The graphics window uses a Cartesian coordinate system. The lower left corner of the screen shows a UCS (user coordinate system) icon. The icon shows x for horizontal and y for vertical. The z-axis is pointed toward the user. The UCS is located at the 0,0 or origin point.

At the lower left corner of your screen, you will see some numbers. These numbers reflect the coordinate point (x, y) of your mouse. Move your mouse around and note how the coordinate values change.

Tip: *Use F6 to toggle your coordinates ON and off.*

Your graphics window in AutoCAD emulates a piece of paper. LIMITS controls the size of your piece of paper. When you start a new file, you can specify the size of paper you want to draw on using Wizards or Templates. AutoCAD really doesn't care where you draw in your graphics window. You can draw outside the limits with impunity.

AutoCAD allows you to draw geometry using four methods:

- Absolute Coordinates
- Relative Coordinates
- Polar Coordinates
- Direct Entry

Absolute Coordinates use absolute values relative to the origin.

Relative Coordinates use coordinates relative to the last point selected.

Polar Coordinates use a distance and angle relative to the last point selected.

Direct Entry allows the user to set ORTHO on (this is like using a ruler to draw a straight line), move the mouse in the desired direction, and then enter in the desired distance.

Line

Command Locator

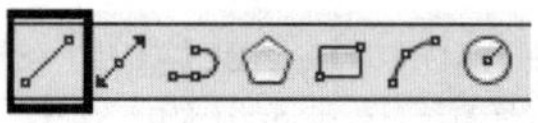

Toolbar Menu	**Draw/Line**
Pull Down Menu	**Draw/Line**
Command	**Line**
Alias	**L**

Command Overview

A line is defined by two endpoints. A line has 0 width and 0 thickness. When drawing a line, specify the first point, then specify the next point. Press the enter button on the mouse (with the cursor in the drawing window) to access the Line Shortcut menu. Type C to close two or more line segments.

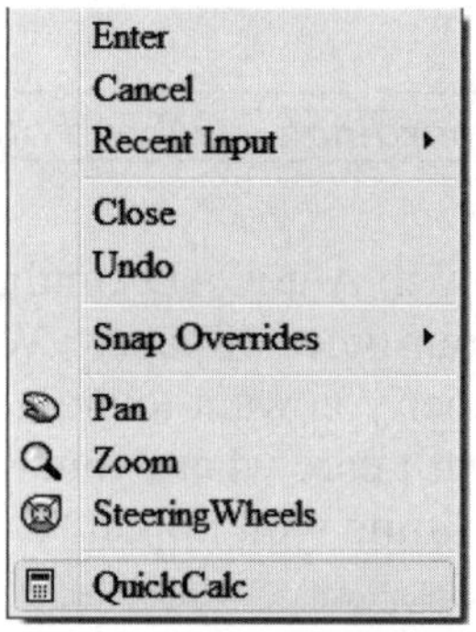

Figure 2 – Line Shortcut Menu

Line Short-Cut Menu Option:	Overview
Enter	Select to exit the Line command.
Cancel	Cancels the command.
Recent Input	Lists the most recently entered point coordinates
Close	Closes the line to form a closed polygon.
Undo	Undoes the last segment of the line.
Snap Overrides	Allows the user to select a snap
Pan	Begins Real-Time Pan
Zoom	Begins Real-Time Zoom
Steering Wheels	Launches the Steering Wheel control
QuickCalc	Launches a calculator

General Procedures

1. Begin the line command by selecting the line icon in the Draw Toolbar or typing L at the blank command prompt.
2. Select the first point, select the next point, and continue selecting the endpoints of each successive line segment.
3. Press the <ENTER> button on the mouse (with the cursor in the drawing window), then select <ENTER> to end the Line command.
4. Press <ENTER> to Repeat the Line command.

- Move the mouse after selecting each endpoint of the line. This will make it easier to see the last line segment created.
- Double click on ORTHO in the Status Bar (or press F8) to alternate between drawing straight or angled line segments.
- Typing U for Undo in the middle of the line command will undo the last line segment. Typing U after completing line segments (at the blank command prompt) will Undo the entire line command.

Command Exercise

Exercise 3-1 – Line using Direct Distance Method

Drawing Name: **Begin a new drawing**
Estimated Time to Completion: 10 Minutes

Scope

Start a New drawing using the acad.dwt template. Enable DYN. With ORTHO on, draw the object below. Drag the line in the desired direction and type the distance. Do not add the dimensions.

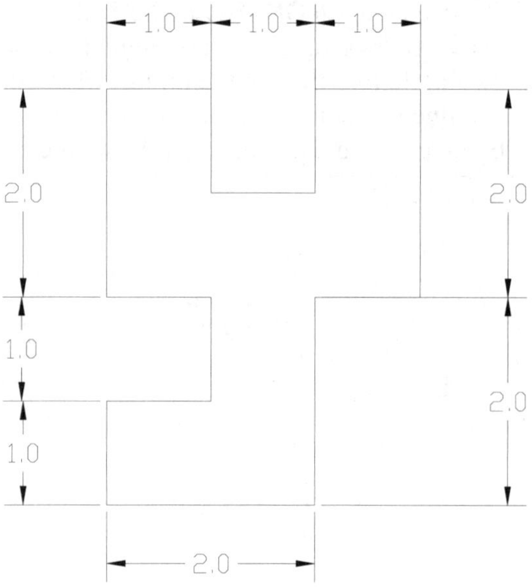

Figure 3 – Line Exercise

Solution

1. 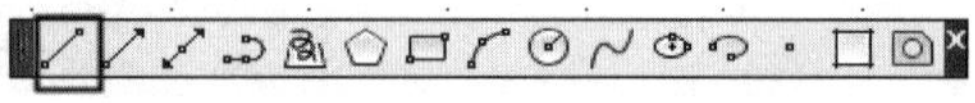 Turn **ORTHO** on by pressing <F8> until the command line says '<Ortho on>'.

2. 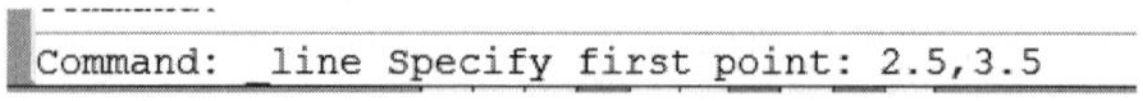

Invoke the **Line** command (l or line).

3. *Specify next point or [Undo]:*
Type **2.5** for the X-coordinate. Type **3.5** for the Y-coordinate. Press <**ENTER**>.

4. 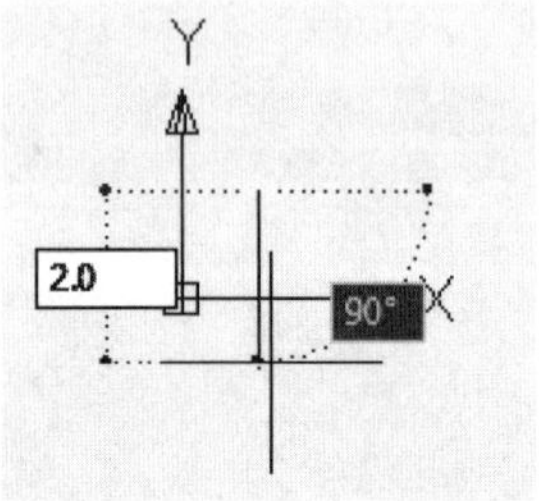

Specify next point or [Undo]:
Drag the cursor downward and type **2.00** and press <ENTER>.

5. 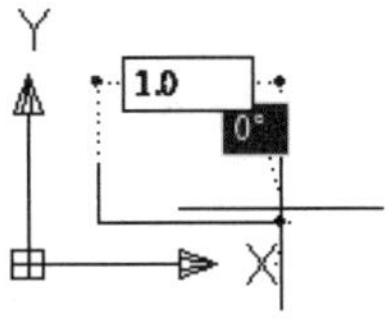

Specify next point or [Undo]:
Drag the cursor to the right and type **1.00** and press <ENTER>.

6. 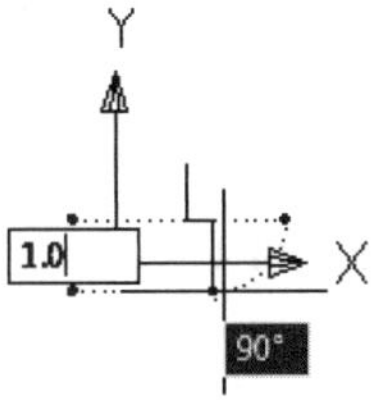

Specify next point or [Close/Undo]:
Drag the cursor downward and type **1.00** and press <ENTER>.

7. 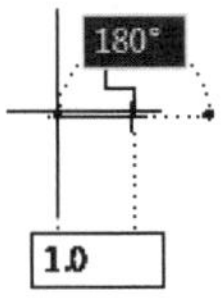

Specify next point or [Close/Undo]:
Drag the cursor to the right and type **1.00** and press <ENTER>.

8. 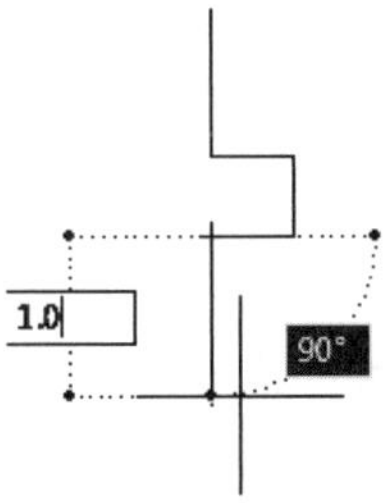

Specify next point or [Close/Undo]:
Drag the cursor downward and type **1.00** and press <ENTER>.

9. 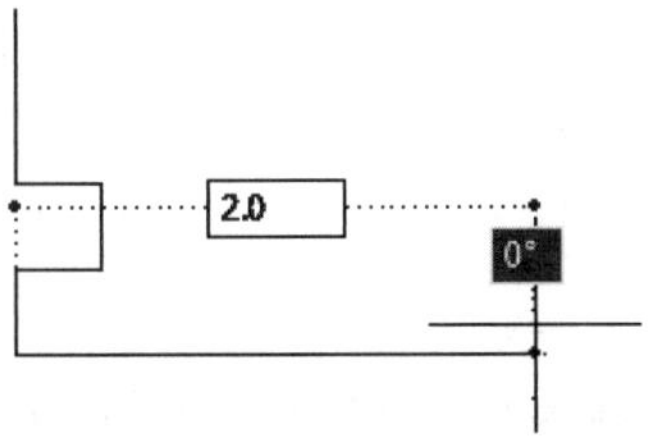

Specify next point or [Close/Undo]:
Drag the cursor to the right and type **2.00** and press <ENTER>.

10. 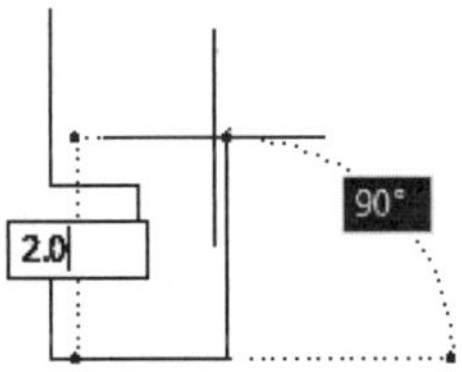

Specify next point or [Close/Undo]:
Drag the cursor up and type **2.00** and press <ENTER>.

11. 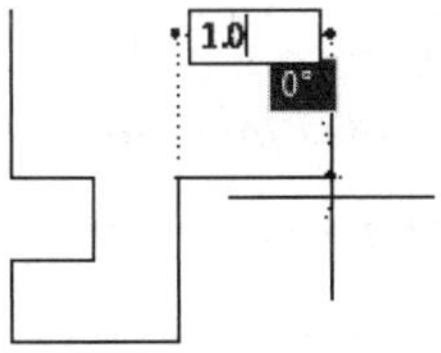

Specify next point or [Close/Undo]:
Drag the cursor to the right and type **1.00** and press <ENTER>.

12. 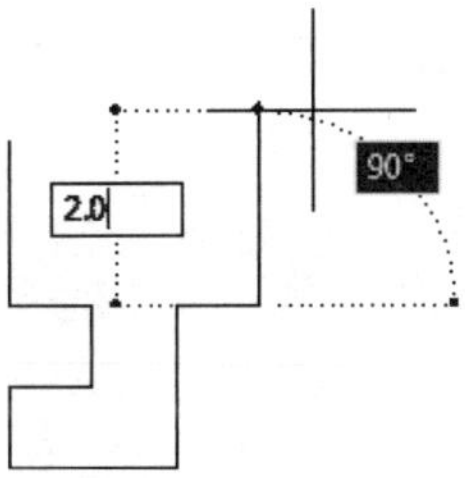

Specify next point or [Close/ Undo]:
Drag the cursor upward and type **2.00** and press <ENTER>.

13.

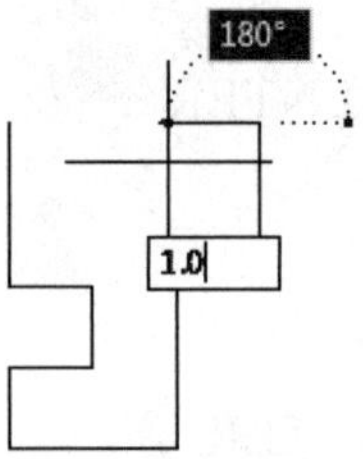

Specify next point or [Close/Undo]:
Drag the cursor to the right and type **1.00** and press <ENTER>.

14.

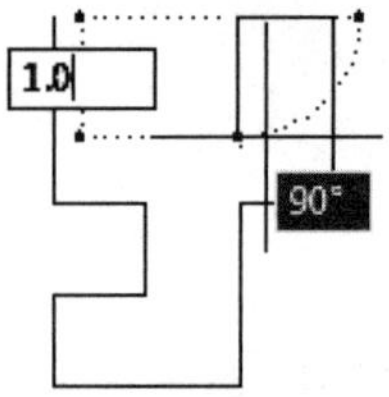

Specify next point or [Close/Undo]:
Drag the cursor downward and type **1.00** and press <ENTER>.

15.

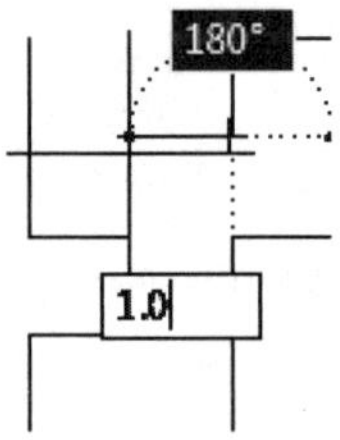

Specify next point or [Close/Undo]:
Drag the cursor to the left and type **1.00** and press <ENTER>.

16.

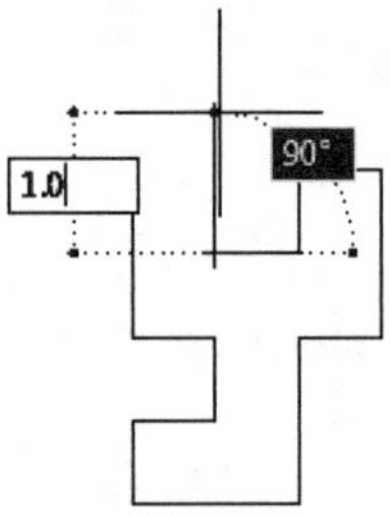

Specify next point or [Close/Undo]:
Drag the cursor upward and type **1.00** and press <ENTER>.

17.

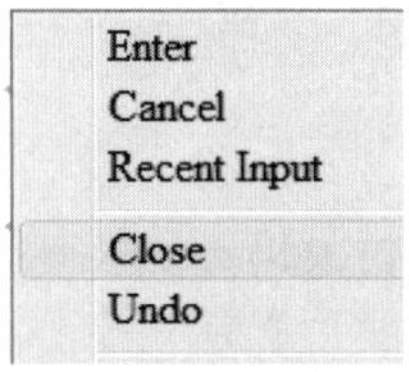

Specify next point or [Close/Undo]:
Right-click in the drawing area and select 'Close' or type 'C' and press <ENTER>.

> ***Tip:** If the lines look crooked, then ORTHO is not on. You must begin again. Try to draw all of the line segments without starting and stopping the line command.*
>
> *The **Close** option only works if you draw in one continuous line. Otherwise, you can simply draw a closing line from endpoint to endpoint.*

Command Exercise

Exercise 3-2 – Line Using Polar Tracking

Drawing Name: **Line2.dwg**
Estimated Time to Completion: 10 Minutes

Scope

Open 'line2.dwg' and draw the object shown in the example using the line command with POLAR enabled. Polar settings have already been made to create the necessary angles. When you have completed the third segment, type C to close the object. Press <ENTER> to repeat the line command, press <ENTER> again, and see that the line picks up from the last point selected.

Figure 4 – Line Exercise

Solution

1. 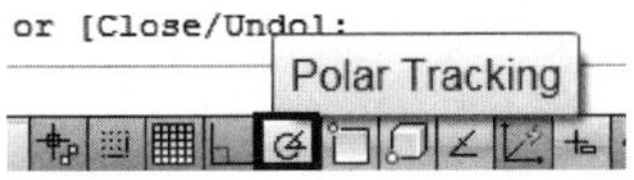

Turn **POLAR** on.

2. 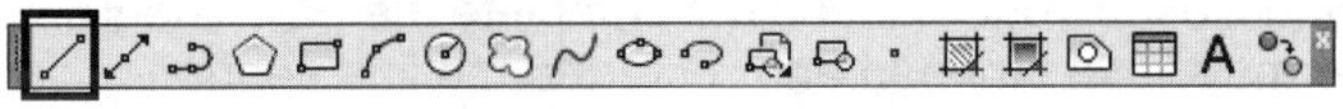
Invoke the **Line** command (l or line).

3. *Specify first point:*
Pick a start point of the line with your left mouse button near the #1 on the drawing.

4. 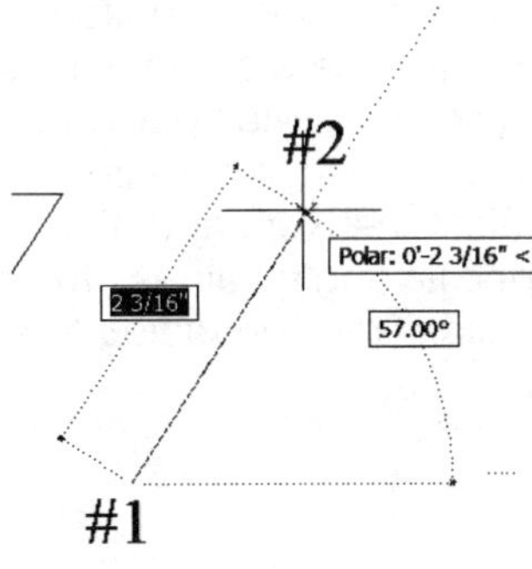

Specify next point or [Undo]:
Pick a second point near the #2 on the drawing.

As you draw your line up to the #2, look for the Tooltip indicating the 57-degree angle.

5. 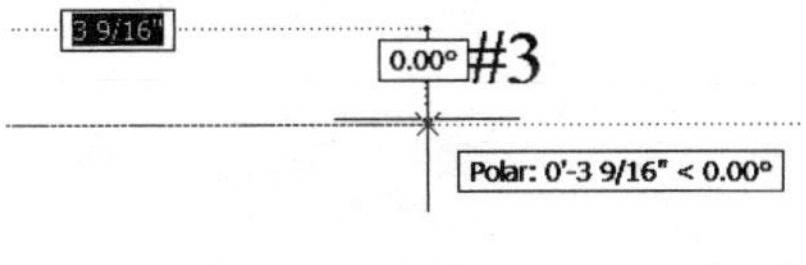

Specify next point or [Undo]:
Move your mouse near #3 and click to complete the second line segment.

As you draw your line up to the #2, look for the Tooltip indicating the 0-degree angle.

6.

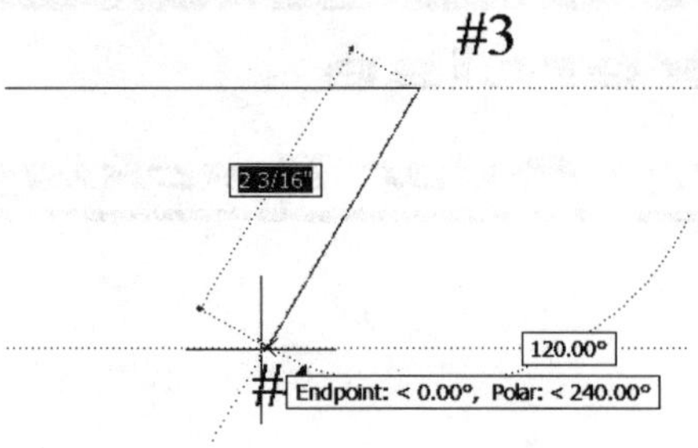

Specify next point or [Close/Undo]:
Use Object Tracking to line up your end point and set the Polar Angle to 240-degrees.

7.

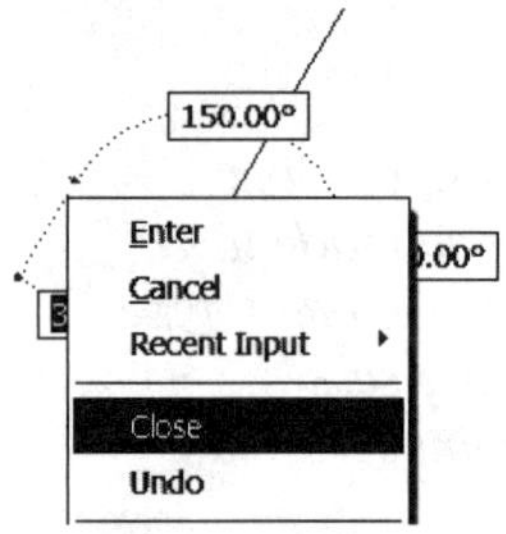

Specify next point or [Close/Undo]:
Right-click in the drawing area and select **Close** or type 'C' or 'CLOSE' and press <ENTER> at the command line to create the final line segment.

8. *Specify next point or [Close/Undo]:*
Right-click in the drawing area and select **Close** or type 'C' or 'CLOSE' and press <ENTER> at the command line to create the final line segment.

9. Right-click in the drawing area and select **Repeat Line** or press <ENTER> to repeat the line command.

10. *Specify first point:*
Press <ENTER> to start the line at the last point selected.

11. *Specify next point or [Undo]:*
Press <Esc> to clear the command line.

- When you closed your object did it complete the parallelogram? If not, you may have stopped and restarted the line sequence, in which case the close option will refer to the new start point.
- Move your mouse, as you work to see what line segments you have just completed.
- Click on ORTHO in the Status bar, or press the <F8> function key; whichever is more convenient at the time; to create straight lines.
- Make a habit of using the <ENTER> key to complete your AutoCAD commands, and to repeat the last command used. Alternately, you may click the right mouse button and select the Repeat option.
- In order for Polar Tracking to click to specific angle values, you have to have them set. Use Settings in the Polar Tracking dialog to add angles you want to use in your drafting.

Command Exercise

Exercise 3-3 – Line Using Cartesian Coordinates

Drawing Name: **Begin a new drawing**
Estimated Time to Completion: 10 Minutes

Scope

Start a New Drawing using the acad.dwt template and draw the object shown in the example using the line command with Cartesian Coordinates. When you have completed the third segment, type C to close the object. Press <ENTER> to repeat the line command, press <ENTER> again, and see that the line picks up from the last point selected. Turn DYN off and ORTHO on for this exercise.

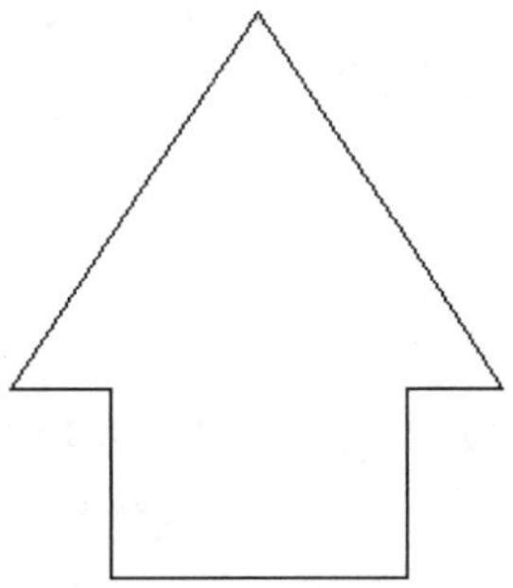

Figure 5 – Line Exercise

Solution

1. Invoke the **Line** command (l or line). 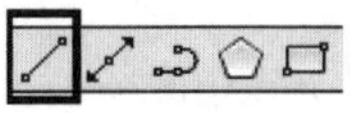
2. *Specify first point:* Type **0,0** at the command line.
3. *Specify next point or [Undo]:* Type **3,0**.
4. *Specify next point or [Undo]:* **3,2**
5. *Specify next point or [Close/Undo]:* **4,2**
6. *Specify next point or [Close/Undo]:* **1.5,6**
7. *Specify next point or [Close/Undo]:* **-1,2**
8. *Specify next point or [Close/Undo]:* **0,2**
9. *Specify next point or [Close/Undo]:*
   Right-click in the drawing area and select 'Close' or type 'C' or 'CLOSE' and press <ENTER> at the command line to create the final line segment.

> ***Tip:*** *If your drawing did not turn out properly, make sure you had DYN OFF. To check your data entry, press F2 and the text window will open and you can review your entries.*

Coordinate Entry

Command Overview

Once the Units have been established, coordinates can be typed to specify points or distances. Always draw full scale. There are four ways to specify coordinates: absolute, relative, polar, and direct distance.

Coordinate Entry Method	*Overview*	*Examples*
Absolute Coordinates	The x and y coordinates are determined by an absolute Origin point of 0,0.	X,Y 1,5
Relative Coordinates	The x and y coordinates reference the last point selected in the drawing.	@x,y @3,5
Polar Coordinates	The distance and angle specified references the last point selected in the drawing	@distance<angle @5<45
Direct Distance	Select the first point, then drag the cursor in the desired direction and type the distance.	Type the distance 4

General Procedures

Using Absolute Coordinates:

1. When prompted to specify a point, type the Absolute coordinates for x and y (x,y)
2. Type the Absolute Coordinate for each successive point (x,y).

Typical Example: Inserting a Title Block or an Externally Referenced Drawing at a specific location.

Using Relative Coordinates:

1. When prompted to specify a point, select a point in the drawing.
2. Type the Relative Coordinate for each successive point (@x,y).

Typical Example: Drawing a Rectangle.

Using Polar Coordinates:

1. When prompted to specify a point, select a point in the drawing.
2. Type the Polar Coordinate for each successive point (@distance < angle).

Typical Example: Drawing lines or moving objects at a specified distance and angle other then orthogonal angles.

Using Direct Distance:

1. When prompted to specify a point, select a point in the drawing.
2. Turn ORTHO on and drag the cursor in the desired direction.
3. Type the distance and press <ENTER>.

Typical Example: Drawing lines or using the Move, Copy or Stretch commands.

- Always use object snap for selecting specific points in the drawing.
- Remember to separate the x and y coordinates by a comma.
  Example: 1,5 means the absolute coordinate where x=1 and y=5.
- It is not necessary to type the z coordinate when z = 0.
- Angles are typically measured counter-clockwise. Angle 0 is typically East.
- Precede Relative and Polar coordinate information with an @ sign (over the number 2 on the keyboard).
- ORTHO should be on when using the direct distance method.
- When drawing lines, or moving objects at specific angles(other than with ORTHO on), type the polar coordinate (example: @10<45) or use Polar Tracking Settings.
- Typing the minimum number of keystrokes is important for drawing efficiently. AutoCAD will fill in leading and trailing zeros and the appropriate Unit endings.
- AutoCAD will convert decimal equivalents to feet and inches.
- AutoCAD will assume inches, unless the foot mark ' is typed.
- The Coordinates Display can be turned on or off from the Status Bar by double clicking on it (LMB). If in the middle of a Draw or Modify command, a third option will display the distance and <angle.
- The DYN toggle can be used to display and enter coordinates.

Command Exercise

Exercise 3-4 – Absolute Coordinates

Drawing Name: **entry1.dwg**
Estimated Time to Completion: 5 Minutes

Scope

Start the line command. Draw the objects using the absolute coordinates in the order indicated. Connect the points using only the keyboard. Turn DYN off and ORTHO on.

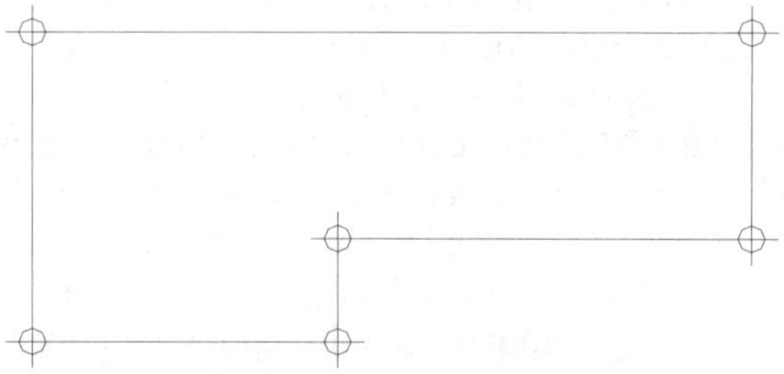

Figure 6 – Absolute Coordinates Exercise

Solution

1. Invoke the **Line** command (l or line).

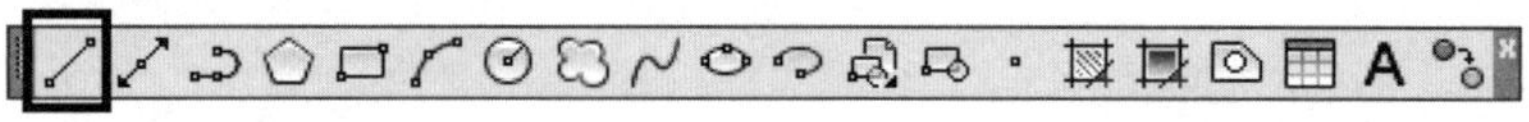

2. *Specify first point:*
   Type **1,1** at the command line and press <ENTER>. Notice where the first point of the line is created.
3. *Specify next point or [Undo]:*
   Type **4,1** at the command line and press <ENTER>.
4. *Specify next point or [Undo]:*
   Type **4,2** at the command line and press <ENTER>.
5. *Specify next point or [Close/Undo]:*
   Type **8,2** and press <ENTER>.
6. *Specify next point or [Close/Undo]:*
   Type **8,4** and press <ENTER>.
7. *Specify next point or [Close/Undo]:*
   Type **1,4** and press <ENTER>.
8. *Specify next point or [Close/Undo]:*
   Type **1,1** and press <ENTER>.
9. *Specify next point or [Close/Undo]:*
   Press the <ENTER> key to end the command.

> ***Tip:*** *You can also use the close option to complete the exercise rather than typing in the final '1,1'.*

Command Exercise

Exercise 3-5 – Relative Coordinates

Drawing Name: **entry2.dwg**
Estimated Time to Completion: 5 Minutes

Scope

Start the line command. Draw the objects using the relative coordinates in the order indicated. Connect the points using only the keyboard.

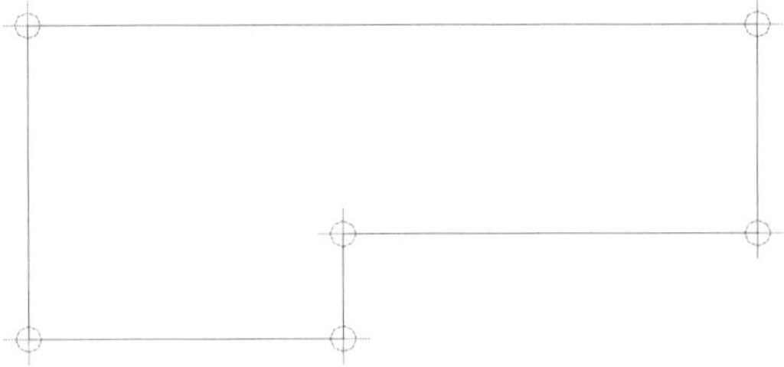

Figure 7 – Relative Coordinates Exercise

Solution

1. Invoke the **Line** command (l or line).

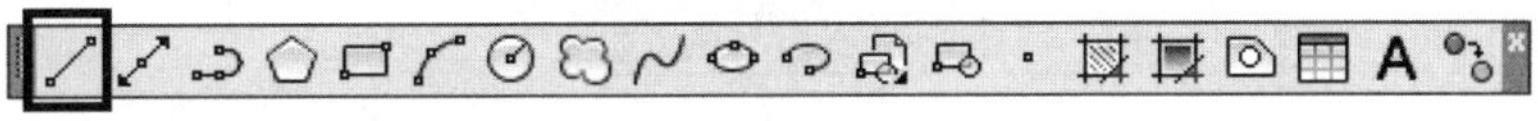

2. *Specify first point:*
   Type **1,1** at the command line and press <ENTER>.
   Notice where the first point of the line is created.
3. *Specify next point or [Undo]:*
   Type **@3,0** at the command line and press <ENTER>.
4. *Specify next point or [Undo]:*
   Type **@0,1** at the command line and press <ENTER>.
5. *Specify next point or [Close/Undo]:*
   Type **@4,0** and press <ENTER>.
6. *Specify next point or [Close/Undo]:*
   Type **@0,2** and press <ENTER>.
7. *Specify next point or [Close/Undo]:*
   Type **@-7,0** and press <ENTER>.
8. *Specify next point or [Close/Undo]:*
   Type **@0,-3** and press <ENTER>.
9. *Specify next point or [Close/Undo]:*
   Press the <ENTER> key to end the command.

Extra: *What would you type in to create the shape in a clockwise fashion instead of counter clockwise direction? Try It.*

Command Exercise

Exercise 3-6 – Polar Coordinates

Drawing Name: **entry3.dwg**
Estimated Time to Completion: 5 Minutes

Scope

Start the line command. Draw the objects using the polar coordinates in the order indicated. Connect the points using only the keyboard.

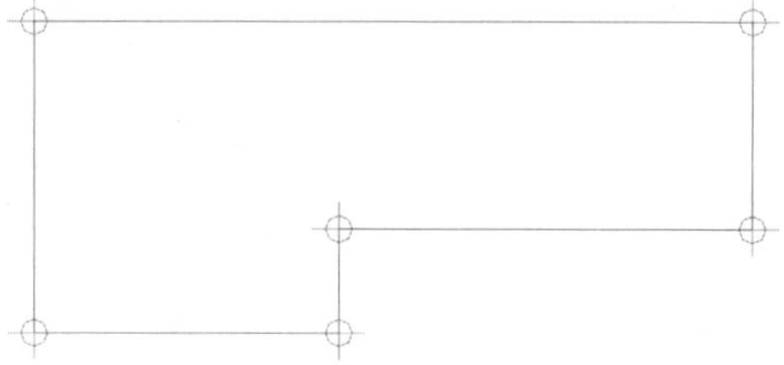

Figure 8 – Polar Coordinates Exercise

Solution

1. Invoke the **Line** command (l or line).

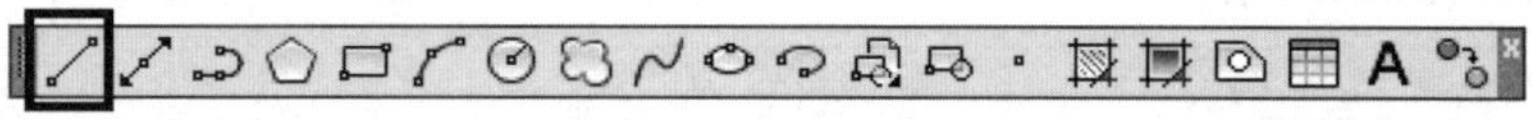

2. *Specify first point:*
   Type **1,1** at the command line and press <ENTER>.
   Notice where the first point of the line is created.
3. *Specify next point or [Undo]:*
   Type **@3<0** at the command line and press <ENTER>.
4. *Specify next point or [Undo]:*
   Type **@1<90** and press <ENTER>.
5. *Specify next point or [Close/Undo]:*
   Type **@4<0** and press <ENTER>.
6. *Specify next point or [Close/Undo]:*
   Type **@2<90** and press <ENTER>.
7. *Specify next point or [Close/Undo]:*
   Type **@7<180** and press <ENTER>.
8. *Specify next point or [Close/Undo]:*
   Type **@3<270** and press <ENTER>.
9. *Specify next point or [Close/Undo]:*
   Press the <ENTER> key to end the command.

Extra: *What would happen if you typed @-3<180 in step 3 in the exercise? Try it.*

Command Exercise

Exercise 3-7 – Drag Method

Drawing Name: **entry4.dwg**
Estimated Time to Completion: 5 Minutes

Scope

Start the line command. Draw the objects using the direct distance method to draw the object.

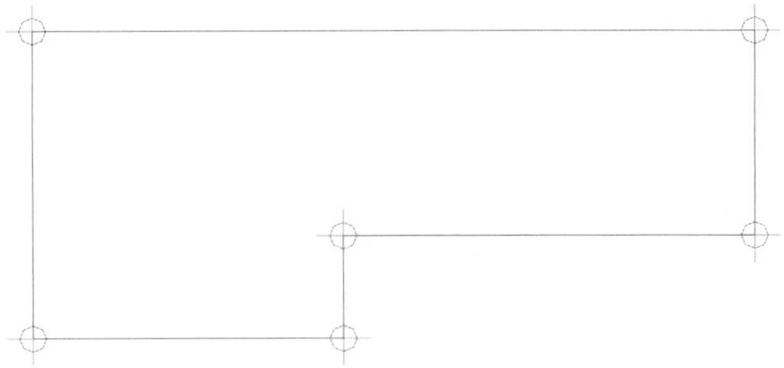

Figure 9 – Drag Method Exercise

Solution

1. Invoke the Line command (l or line).

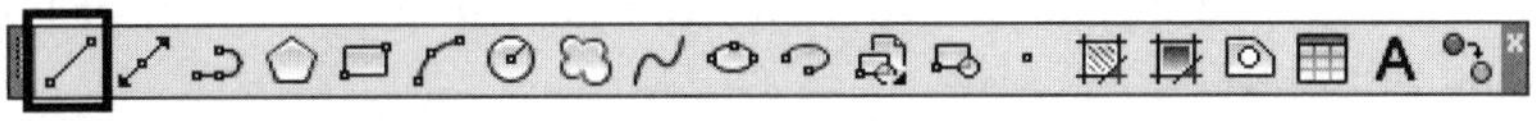

2. *Specify first point:*
   Type **1,1** and press <ENTER>. Notice where the first point of the line is created.
3. *Specify next point or [Undo]:*
   Toggle **ORTHO** on at the Status Bar.
4. *Specify next point or [Undo]:*
   Drag the mouse to the right, type **3** and press <ENTER>.
5. *Specify next point or [Undo]:*
   Drag the mouse upward, type **1** and press <ENTER>.
6. *Specify next point or [Close/Undo]:*
   Drag the mouse to the right, type **4** and press <ENTER>.
7. *Specify next point or [Close/Undo]:*
   Drag the mouse upward, type **2** and press <ENTER>.
8. *Specify next point or [Close/Undo]:*
   Drag the mouse to the left, type **7** and press <ENTER>.
9. *Specify next point or [Close/Undo]:*
   Drag the mouse downward, type **3** and press <ENTER>.
10. *Specify next point or [Close/Undo]:*
    Press the <ENTER> key to end the command.

Erase

Command Locator

Toolbar Menu	**Modify/Erase**
Pull Down Menu	**Modify/Erase**
Command	**Erase**
Alias	**E**

Command Overview

Erase deletes selected objects. Press <ENTER> after selecting the objects to erase to execute the command. Type OOPS to bring back the last set of erased objects, even if other objects were drawn since the last erase.

General Procedures

1. Begin the erase command by selecting the Erase icon from the Modify Toolbar or typing E at the blank command prompt.
2. Place the cursor over the objects to erase and pick (LMB).

Tips & Tricks

- If the cursor is not over an object, a selection window will appear. Make the other corner of the selection window.
- A Selection Window made from Left to Right will select only the objects completely in the window.
- A Selection Window made from Right to Left will select all objects the window crosses.
- Typing All (and pressing <ENTER>) will select all objects in the drawing to erase. Press <ENTER> to execute the command.

Command Exercise

Exercise 3-8 – Erase

Drawing Name: **erase1.dwg**
Estimated Time to Completion: 5 Minutes

Scope

Erase the objects in the drawing. Draw some more lines. Type OOPS to bring back the last set of erased objects.

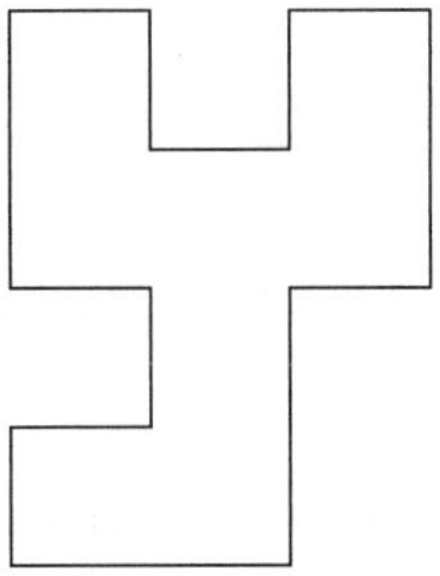

Figure 10 – Erase Exercise

Solution

1. Invoke the **Erase** command (e or erase).

2. *Select objects:*
   Select the objects by typing **ALL** and pressing <ENTER>, picking each line individually, or using the Window method. When all the objects are highlighted, press <ENTER> to execute the Erase command.
3. Invoke the **Line** command (l or line).

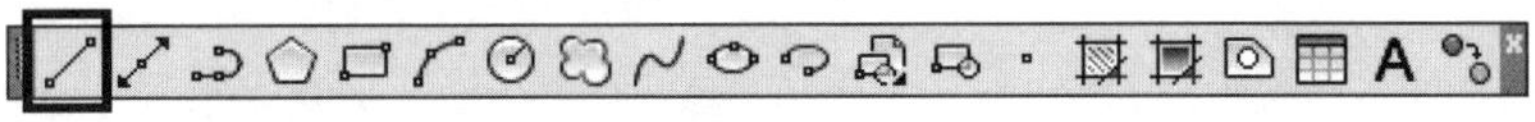

4. *Specify first point:*
   Use your LMB to pick the start point of a line segment. Select any location on the drawing.
5. *Specify next point or [Undo]:*
   Continue to use the LMB to create lines on the drawing.
6. *Specify next point or [Close/Undo]:*
   Press the <ENTER> key to end the line command.
7. Type **OOPS** at the command line and press the <ENTER> key.

> ***Tip:*** *Select all the objects to erase, then press <ENTER> to execute the command. To remove an object from the selection set, hold down the shift key and select the object again. See that it is removed from the selection set. Then press <ENTER>.*

Review Questions

1. At the select object prompt, what letter must you type to select using a window?
   - ❑ W
   - ❑ SO
   - ❑ SP
   - ❑ S

2. Write down the letter to type for each of the following Object Selection options:

   Previous ____________________

   Last ____________________

   Fence ____________________

   All ____________________

   Crossing Window ____________________

   Crossing Polygon ____________________

   Window Polygon ____________________

3. When selecting objects by picking in a blank area in the drawing window, what is the difference between the following:

   Making a select box from right to left. ________

   Making a select box from left to right. ________

4. When using the POLAR method of coordinate entry, which tray button should be enabled?

5. When entering direct coordinates, which tray button should be disabled?

Review Answers

1. At the select object prompt, what letter must you type to select using a window?
    - ❑ W *(W for window)*

2. Write down the letter to type for each of the following Object Selection options:
    P,L,F,A or enter, CW, CP, CW.

3. When selecting objects by picking in a blank area in the drawing window, what is the difference between the following:
    WINDOW, CROSSING

4. When using the POLAR method of coordinate entry, which tray button should be enabled?
    POLAR

5. When entering direct coordinates, which tray button should be disabled?
    DYN

NOTES:

Lesson 4.0 – Toolbars and Profiles

Estimated Class Time: 2 Hours

Objectives

Customizing AutoCAD is a topic that can be quite extensive. This chapter will introduce a few simple ways to customize AutoCAD. This includes how to Create **Custom Toolbars** and **Profiles**. Access to Profiles, which contain the personalized settings for the drawing environment, such as the drawing Display Color, and the location of toolbars, is done through the Options dialog.

- **Options Dialog - Profiles**
- **Creating Custom Toolbars**

Options Dialog – Profiles

Command Locator

Pull Down Menu	**Tools / Options**
Command	**Options**
RMB Shortcut Menu	**Right Click on Command Line / Options**
Dialog Box	**Options**

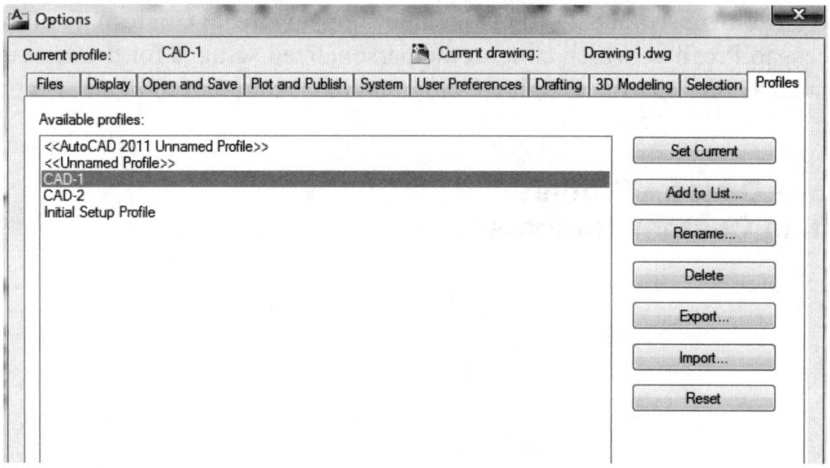

Figure 1 – Options Dialog Box, Profiles Tab

Command Overview

The Profiles Tab of the Options dialog box allows you to copy your Preferences settings, including toolbar arrangement, to a personalize profile (.ARG file). This can be exported to the network or a floppy disk. When you use AutoCAD on another computer workstation, simply import your own .arg profile file.

Available Profiles – List all available profiles for the system.

Set Current – Makes the selected profile the current profile.

Add to List – Displays the Add Profile dialog box to save the selected profile under a different name.

Rename – Selecting this button will open the Change Profile dialog box allowing you to rename and change the description of the selected profile.

Delete – Deletes the selected profile (unless it is the current profile).

Export – Exports a selected profile as an .ARG file

Import – – Imports a selected profile that was created by using the Export option.

Reset – Resets the values in the selected profile to the system default settings.

Command Exercise

Exercise 4-1 – Options – Profiles

Drawing Name: **pref4.dwg**
Estimated Time to Completion: 10 Minutes

Scope

Using the Profile tab in Options, copy the current profile as CAD–1 and CAD–2, then make CAD–1 the current profile. In the Display tab, deselect Scroll Bars, change the background color, and Apply. Open and rearrange some toolbars. Next use the Options / Profile command to make each profile current and view the changes made to the AutoCAD window.

Solution

1.

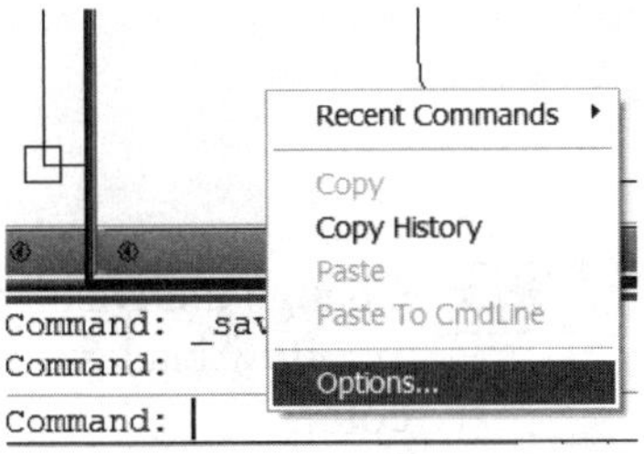

Invoke the Options command by right-clicking in the command line area of the screen and selecting **Options…**

2.

Select the *Profiles* tab and copy the current profile by using the **Add to List…** button.

3.

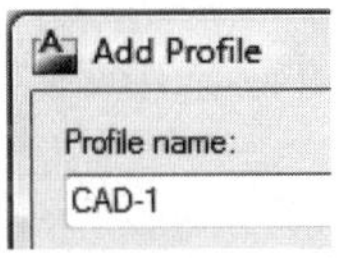

Name one profile *CAD–1* and press **Apply & Close**.

4.

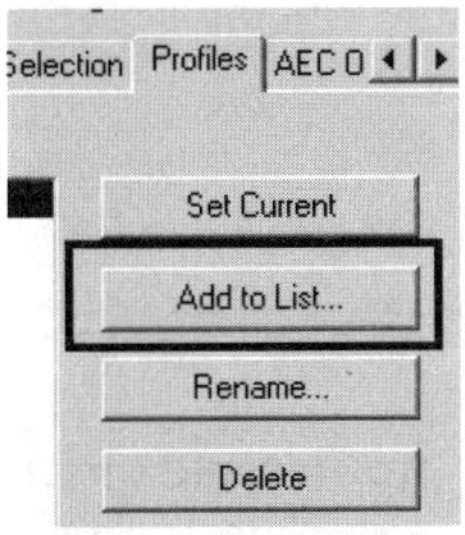

Highlight the *CAD-1* Profile and select **Add to List** to create another profile.

5.

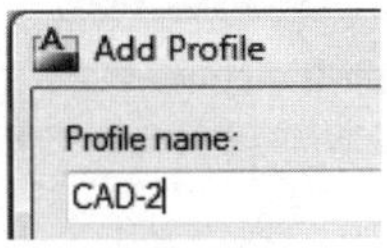

Name this profile *CAD-2* and press **Apply & Close**.

6. 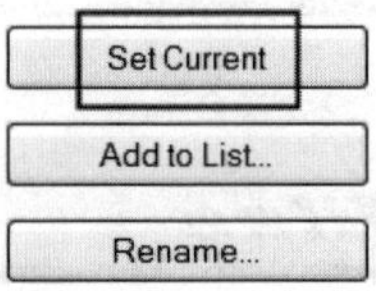

Highlight the *CAD-1* profile and select **Set Current**.

7. 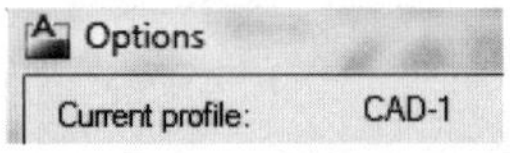

You will see the *CAD-1* Profile listed as the current profile.

8. 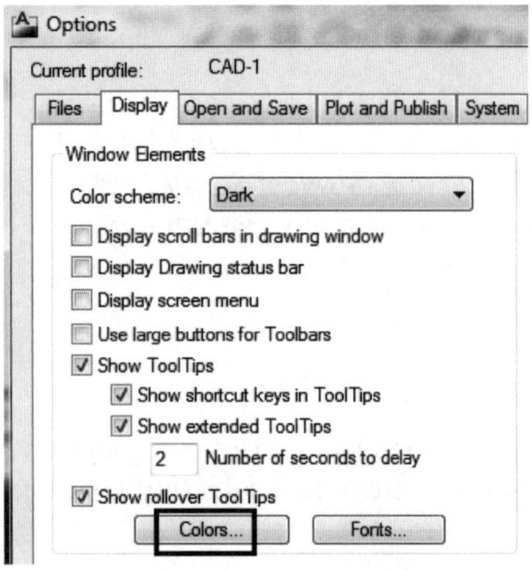

In the Display tab of the dialog box, enable **Display Scroll Bars**.

Select the **Colors** button.

9. 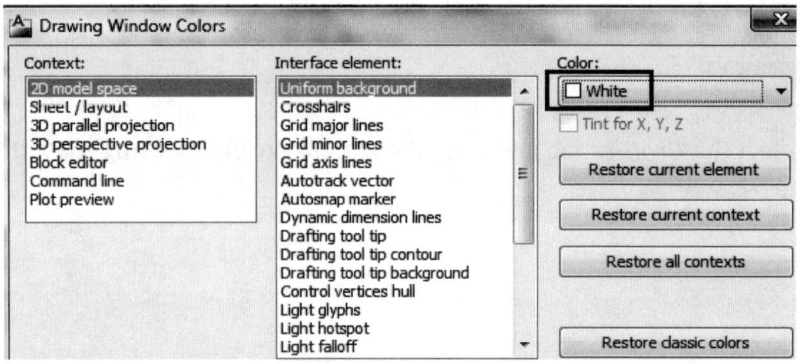

Change the Display Window background color.
Press **Apply & Close**.

10. Press **OK** to apply the changes and exit the dialog box.

11. Re–arrange the toolbars.

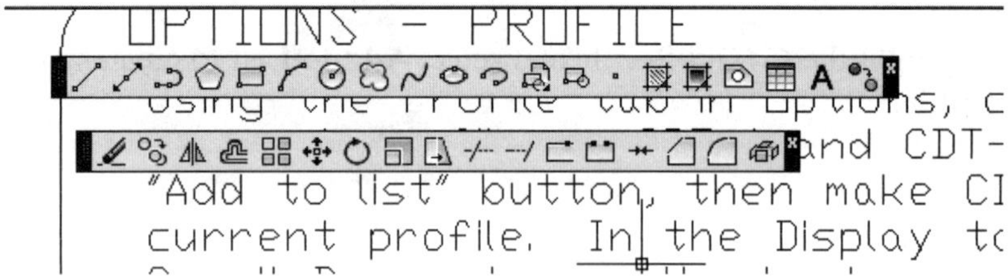

12. Return to the Options dialog box, Profiles tab. Switch between user profiles and observe the changes.

Creating Custom Toolbars

Command Locator

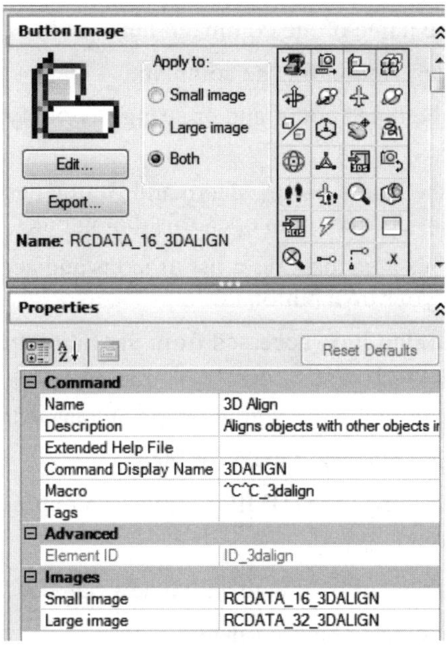

Figure 2 – Button Properties Dialog Box

Command Overview

Using the Toolbar dialog box and options, you can create custom toolbars, modify existing toolbars, and add buttons with macros to execute special functions. This can be very useful, and also fun to do.

Options

Toolbars dialog box:

Toolbars – Lists the toolbars from a selected Menu Group.

Menu Group – Lists the menus that have been loaded into the AutoCAD program.

Large Buttons – Select this to make the icons larger.

Show Tool Tips – When pointing to an icon, a label with the command will be displayed.

New – Created a new Toolbar.

Delete – Deletes a selected Toolbar (be careful!).

Customize – Accesses the Customize Toolbars dialog box.

Properties – Displays the properties of the toolbar, such as the alias name.

Customize Toolbars dialog box (accessed from the Customize Button):

Categories – Lists the categories for the AutoCAD commands and icons.

Description – Displays the definition of selected icons.

Close – Closes the Customize Toolbar dialog box. Note: This must be closed to successfully perform the next options available in the Button Properties dialog box.

Button Properties dialog box (accessed by right–clicking over any icon when the Toolbar dialog box is opened):

Name – Write the name of the command here.

Help – Write a description for the command.

Macro – Write the typed command or string several typed command options together.

Apply – Apply the Name, Help, Macro and Button design to a selected button (the one you right–clicked on to open this dialog box).

Button Icon – This area displays a list of icons and access to the Edit button to change or create your own button design.

Button Editor dialog box (accessed from the Edit button in the Button Properties dialog box):

Grid – Displays a grid on the button image area as a drawing aid.

Clear – Clears the image and makes it blank.

Open – Opens an image file (BMP) to save as a button design.

Undo – Reverses the last step.

Save As – Saves the button image with a new name.

Save – Saves the current button image.

Close – Closes the dialog box

Drawing tools – At the top of the dialog box; shows a pencil, line, circle, and eraser.

Colors – Are displayed on the right side of the dialog box.

Bitmap image – This is the picture you create using the drawing tools and colors.

Tips & Tricks

- Check in the Categories to see if the command you want does not already exist.
- Check the Bonus or Express tools to see if the command you want, or a comparable command does not already exist there.
- When creating a button image, perform a **SaveAs** and save the image to a special folder for button icons. That way if you ever lose the button icons, you can re-attach them to your custom tools without having to recreate them.
- Use a graphics program, like PaintShop Pro or Microsoft Paint, to create your tool button icons.
- If you create a tool that uses a LISP routine, be sure to add the lisp routine to the Startup Suite to ensure that the lisp routine is loaded every time you create or open a drawing.

Command Exercise

Exercise 4-2 – Creating Custom Toolbars

Drawing Name: **new drawing**
Estimated Time to Completion: 15 Minutes

Scope

Using the Toolbar dialog box, create a New toolbar named Custom. Drag and drop some commands onto the custom toolbar. Test the tools on the custom toolbar.

Solution

1. Type **CUI** at the command line.

2. 

Select the **Customize** tab.

Set the *Main CUI File (acad.cuix)* in the drop-down list.

3. 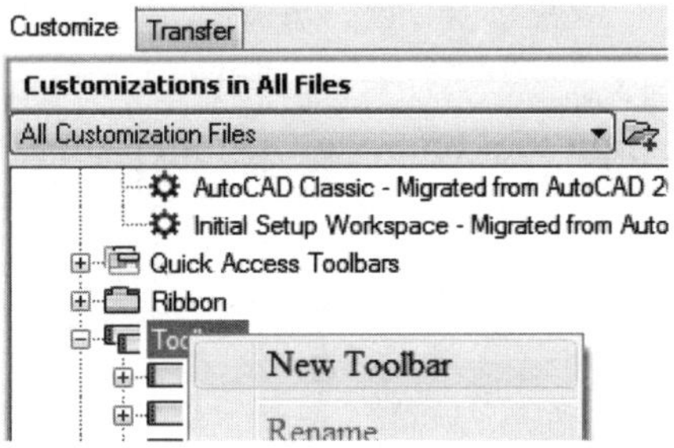

Highlight the *Toolbar* category.
Right click and select **New→Toolbar**.

4. 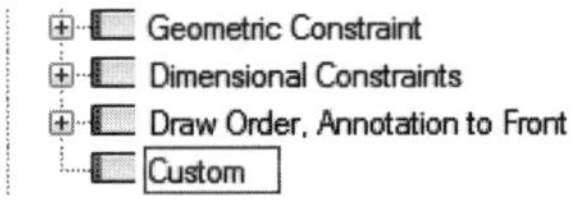

The new toolbar will appear at the bottom of the toolbar list. Rename the toolbar *Custom.*

To rename, you can right click and select **Rename**.

5. 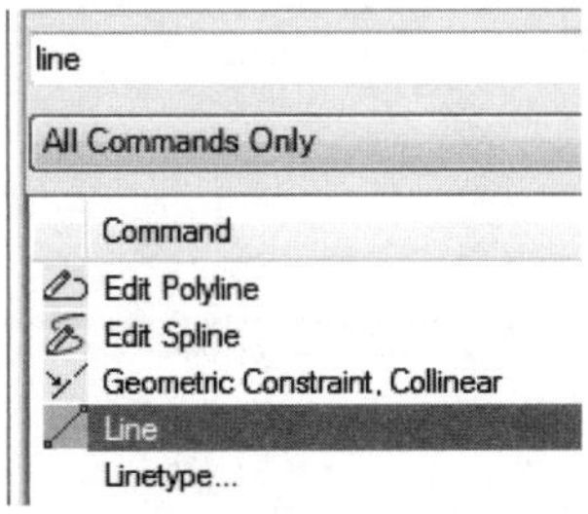

In the lower left panel, you see a Command List. You can scroll through the list to see all the commands or type the command in the search field.

Locate the Line command.

6. 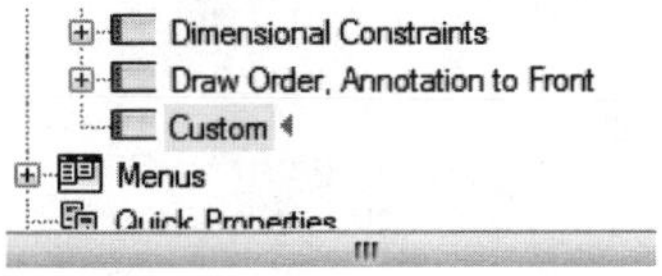

Drag and drop the Line command from the lower left pane to the upper left pane.

7. 

To place into the Custom toolbar, you should see an arrow symbol and then release the mouse button to place the Line tool onto the toolbar.

8. 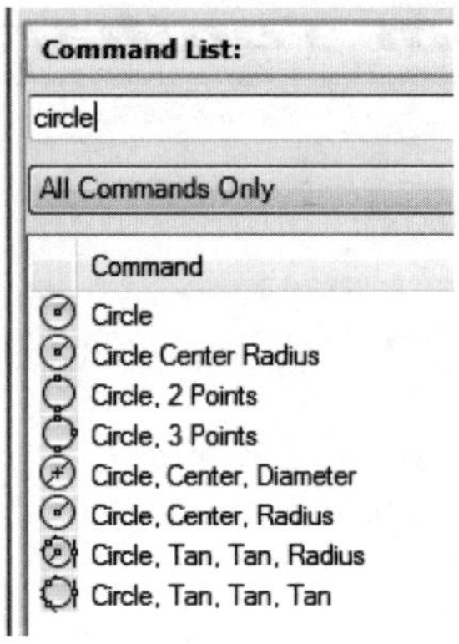

Locate the **Circle, Center, Diameter** tool in the Command List.

9. 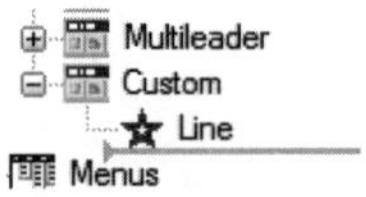

Drag and drop the **Circle, Center, Diameter** tool onto the Custom toolbar.

10. 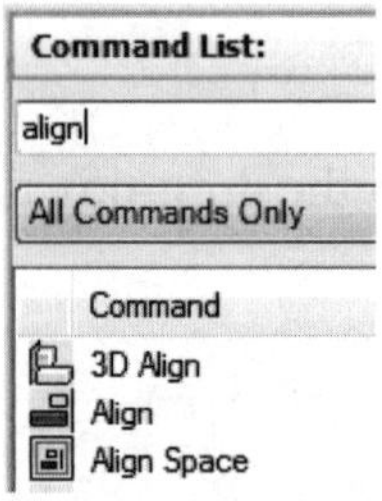

Locate the **Align** tool in the Command List.

11. 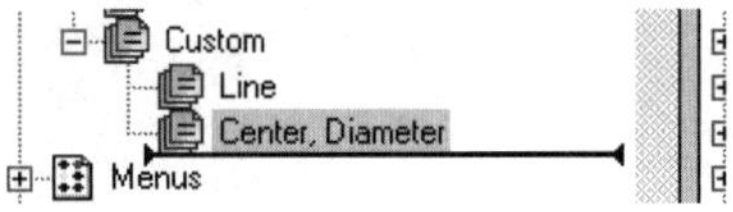

Drag and drop the **Align** tool onto the Custom toolbar.

12. 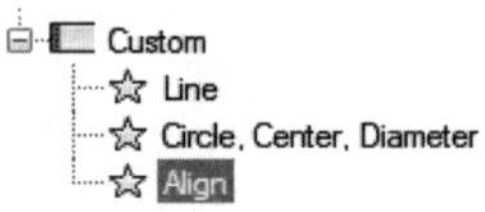

Press **Apply** and **OK**.

13. 
Your Custom toolbar is visible.

14. Test the tools to see how they work.

Command Exercise

Exercise 4-3 – Creating a Custom Command Tool

Drawing Name: **new drawing**
Estimated Time to Completion: 15 Minutes

Scope

Create a custom command. Assign the custom command to a tool icon. Download the 'thaw.bmp' file from the publisher's website to use as the tool icon's image. Add the custom tool to a toolbar.

Solution

1. Type **CUI** at the command line.

2. 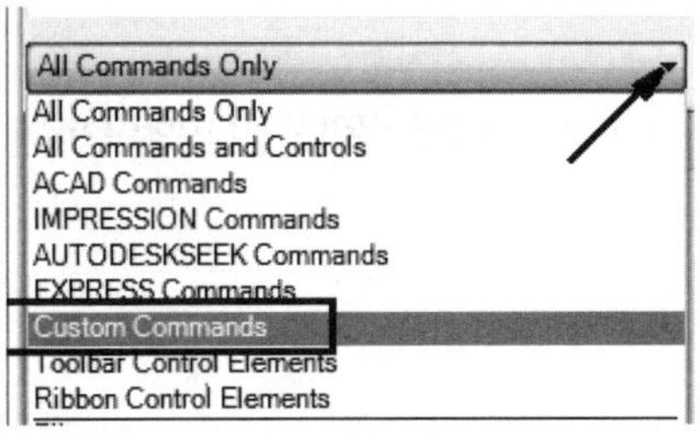

In the Commands window (lower left), select **Custom Commands** from the Categories list.

3. 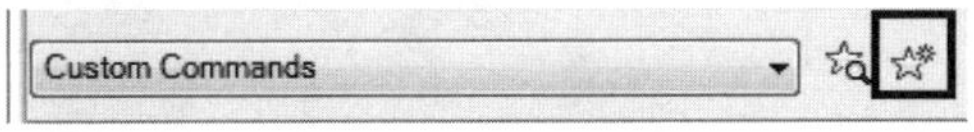

Press the **New** button.

4. 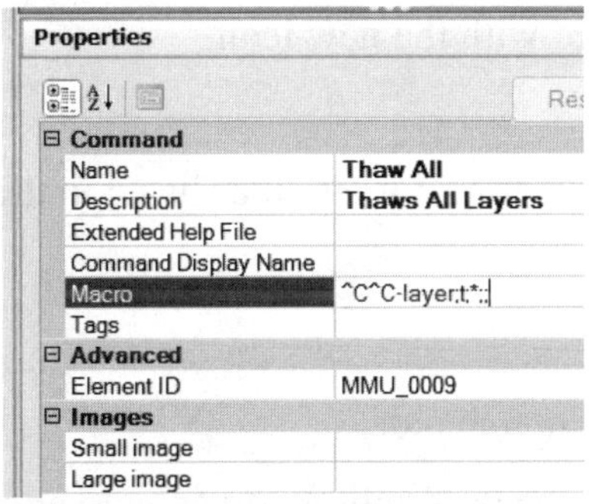

In the Properties window (lower right):

In the Name field type, '**Thaw All**'.
In the Description field, type '**Thaws all layers**'.
Click in the Macro field after the '^C^C'.
Type '**–layer;t;*;;**'

5. 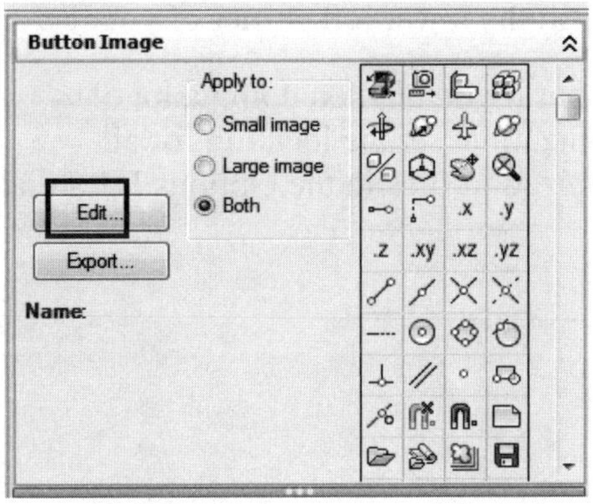

In the Button Image window (top right):

Select any icon on the right and press **Edit**.

6. 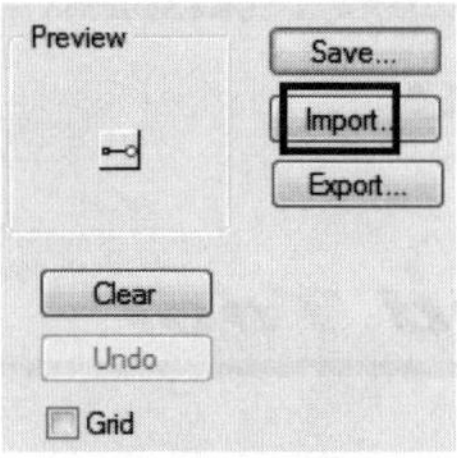

Press the **Import** button.

7. 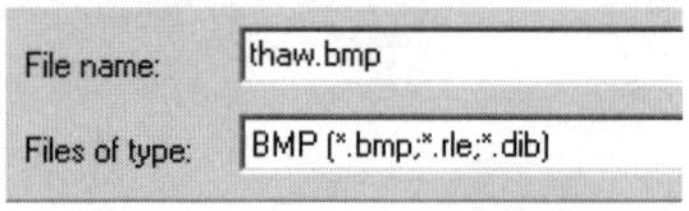

Download and locate the *thaw.bmp* file.

This image was created using Paintshop Pro. If you plan on creating a lot of custom commands, you might want to use a graphics program to create your icons. You can also download many free icon images from the Internet.

8. 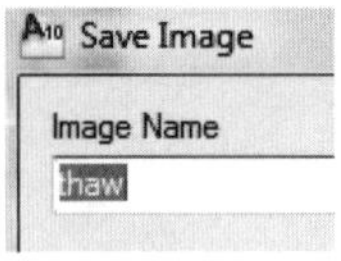

Press **Save**.

Accept the default image name.

Press OK.

Press **Close**.

9. 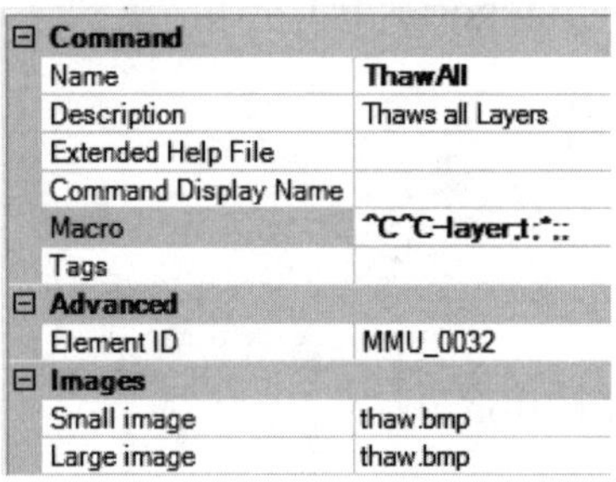

Note the image is automatically assigned in the dialog.

10. 

Note that the custom command has updated with the new icon.

11. 

Drag and drop the custom command onto your custom toolbar listed in the upper left window.

Press **Apply** and **OK**.

12. 

The custom toolbar updates with the new command.

Note that when you mouse over the icon, the description you entered appears. The description you entered appears in the lower left corner of your screen.

13. 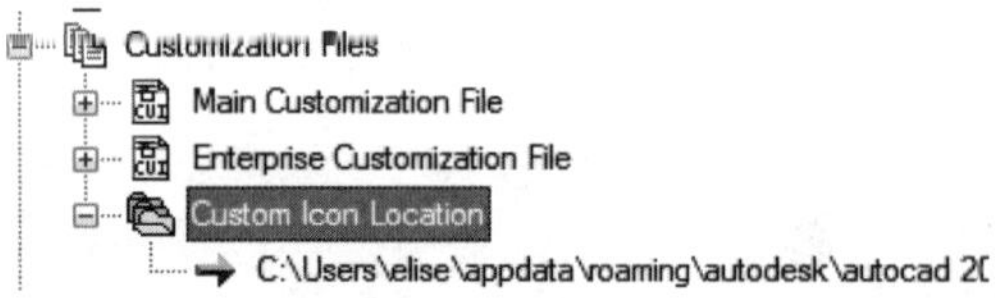

Note that if you plan on doing a lot of customization, set the location for all customization files in the Options/Files dialog.

Using AutoLISP

AutoLISP is a programming language used with AutoCAD. Using AutoLISP, users can create scripts and automate functions to save time and be more productive in their work. LISP routines are used to replace repetitive tasks. If you find yourself performing the same task over and over using the same commands, then you have a candidate for a LISP routine. Even if you are not interested in writing LISP routines yourself, you can download millions of free routines from websites such as www.augi.com, www.cadalyst.com, and www.cadville.com for your use. Once you start using LISP routines, you may find they are somewhat addictive as they make your work less tedious and more enjoyable.

LISP programs define a custom command. This command is usually the same as the name of the file; i.e. *a2t.lsp* will be run by typing **a2t** on the command line. If you are unsure of what command is required to run a LISP routine, open the file using Notepad and search for the term *defun c:*. This command stands for "define function" and indicates the name for the custom command. Whatever characters follow the **c:** are used to run the program.

Once you have begun to rely on a few custom routines, you may decide to add some tool icons to your custom toolbar so that you can access your routines faster. This is simpler than having to type in the LISP command on the command line.

The next exercise guides you through how to add a LISP routine to the Startup Suite, create a command tool, and add the tool to the custom toolbar. A LISP routine is provided for your use from the publisher's website, but any LISP routine will work.

In order to run a LISP routine, it must be loaded into AutoCAD first. To load any LISP routine, you can type **APPLOAD** on the command line. By adding a LISP routine to the Startup Suite, it is automatically loaded every time you open or create a new drawing. Once the LISP routine is loaded, it can be initiated by typing the custom command on the command line. By creating a custom tool for a LISP routine, you eliminate the need to type the command.

Command Exercise

Exercise 4-4 –Creating Tools for LISP Routines

Drawing Name: **new drawing**
Estimated Time to Completion: 20 Minutes

Scope

Add a LISP routine to the Startup Suite. Create a custom command button for a LISP routine. Add the button to a toolbar.

Solution

1. 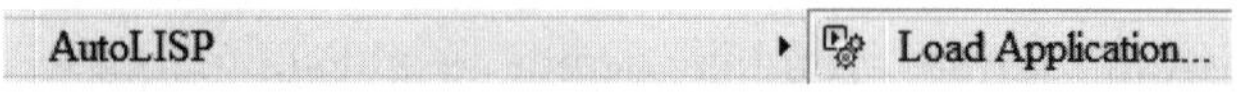

Go to **Tools→AutoLISP→Load Application**.

2. 

In the lower right corner, select the **Contents** button under Startup Suite.

3. 

Select the **Add** button located on the lower left of the dialog.

4. 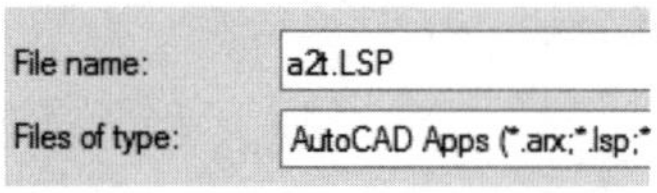

Locate the *a2t.LSP* downloaded from the publisher's website.

Press **Add**.

5. 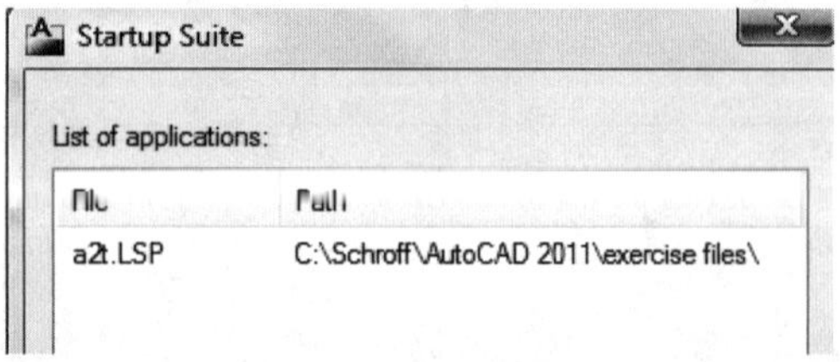

The file will be listed now.

Press **Close**.

6. 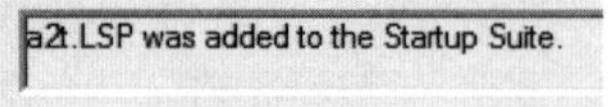

A message should appear in the lower left indicating that the LISP file has been added to the Startup Suite.

You should also see the routine listed under Loaded Applications.

Press **Close**.

7. Type **CUI** at the command line.

8. 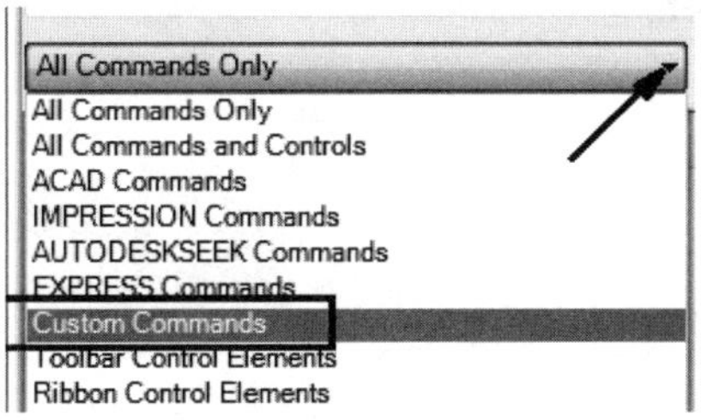

In the Commands window (lower left), select **Custom Commands** from the Categories list.

9. 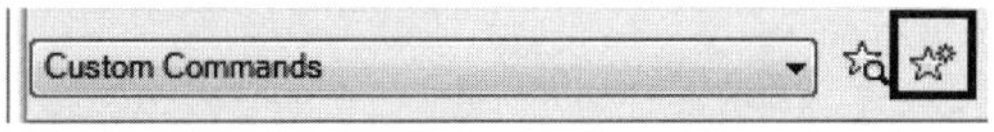

Press the **New** button.

10. 

In the Properties window (lower right):

In the Name field type **A2T**.

In the Description field, type **Converts All Attributes to Text**.

Click in the Macro field after the '^C^C'.

Type **a2t**.

11. 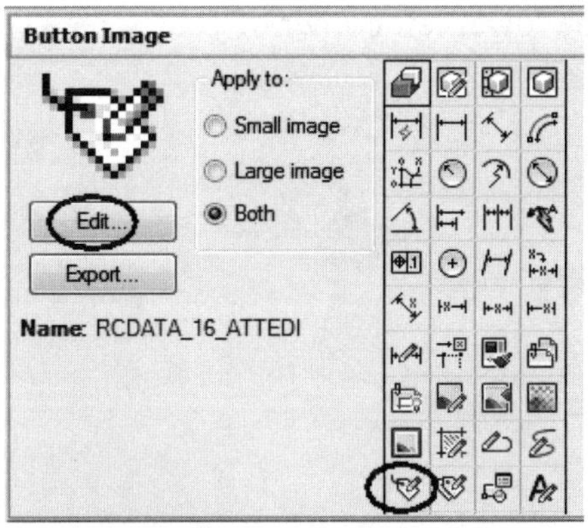

In the Button Image window (top right):

Select the Edit Attribute icon on the icon palette and press **Edit**.

12. 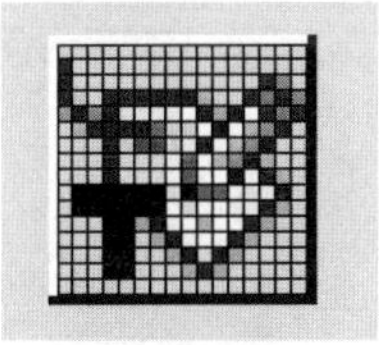

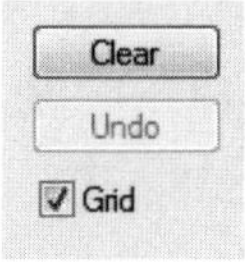

Add a **T** to the image.

Enable Grid to make it easier to place.

Press **Save**.

13. 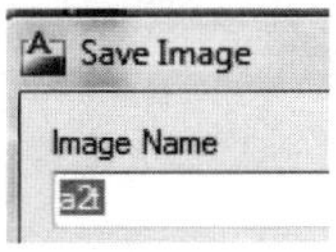

The custom icon will automatically be saved to the location specified in Options for custom icons.

Enter 'a2t' for the file name.

Press **OK**.

14. 

Press **Close**.

15. 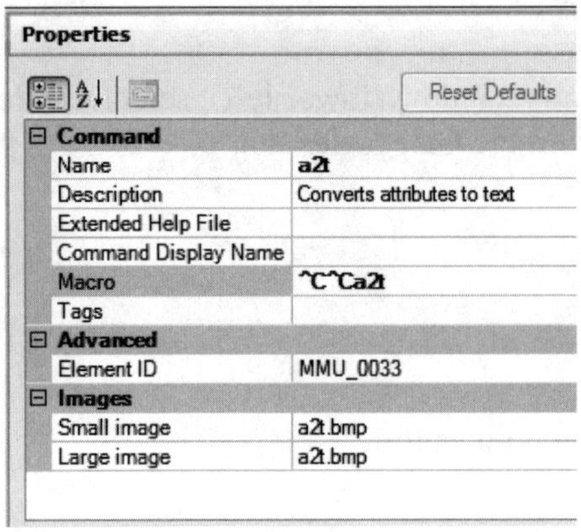

The properties will automatically update with the new bitmap icon.

16. 

Note that the custom command has updated with the new icon.

17. 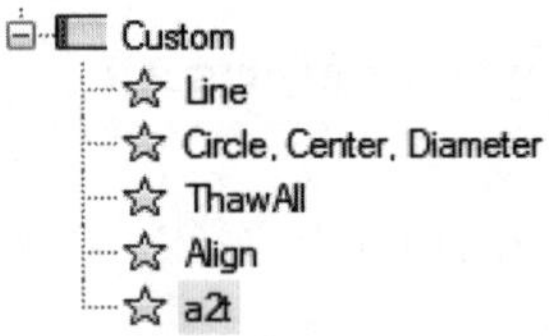

Drag and drop the custom command onto your custom toolbar listed in the upper left window.

Press **Apply** and **OK**.

18. 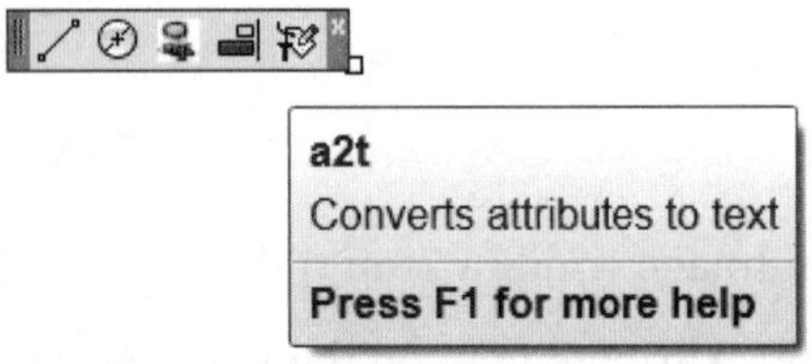

The custom toolbar updates with the new command.

Note that when you mouse over the icon, the name you entered appears. The description you entered appears in the lower left corner of your screen.

Lesson 5.0 – Draw Commands

Estimated Class Time: 4 Hours

Objectives

This section introduces AutoCAD commands, for creating a simple drawing. The user will learn to use the commands on the Draw toolbar.

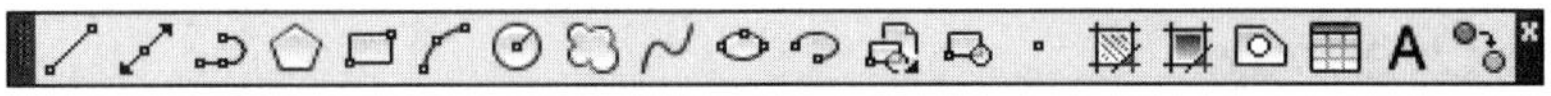

- **Polyline**
  Draw polylines.
- **Polygon**
  Draw multi-sided polylines.
- **Rectangle**
  Draw rectangular polylines.
- **Arc**
  Draw arcs several different ways.
- **Circle**
  Draw circles using six different methods.
- **Donut**
  Draw a donut – a circle with a thick outline.
- **Spline**
  Draw splines by using Points to control the spline shape.
- **Ellipse**
  Draw ellipses using two different methods.
- **Ellipse Arc**
  Draw an elliptical arc.
- **AddSelected**
  Adds selected elements using source properties.

Polyline

Command Locator

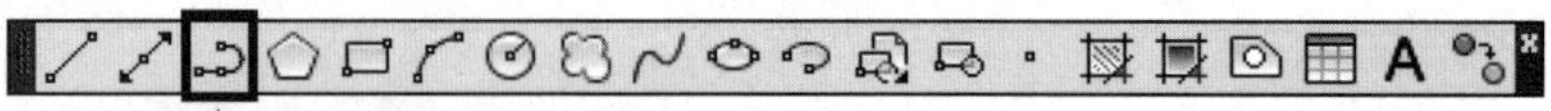

Toolbar Menu	**Draw / Polyline**
Pull Down Menu	**Draw / Polyline**
Command	**Pline**
Alias	**PL**
RMB Shortcut Menu	**Drawing Window**

Command Overview

Polylines are essential to drawing in AutoCAD. Polylines are line and arc segments with common endpoints that are joined to make one object. A rectangle is an example of a polyline. Polylines can be more efficient because selecting one polyline segment will automatically select the entire polyline, and offsetting a Polyline will Offset all of the segments equally. Sometimes it is necessary to  Explode a Polyline, then use the  Edit Polyline command to *join* all the line and arc segments. When drawing a Polyline, the user will be presented with many command line options, however, for all practical purposes, drawing a Polyline is much like drawing line segments.

Primarily, GIS drafters and architects use polylines. Mechanical drafters use polylines to create drawing borders, arrows and cutting plane lines. Cutting plane lines are used for section views.

A polyline is similar to a line but it can have thickness. Additionally, you can "join" or connect more than one line to create a single object. Polylines can have varying thickness or widths.

You can draw your object using lines and arcs and convert it to polyline using the polyline edit command. You can convert polylines and polyarcs back to lines and arcs using the EXPLODE command.

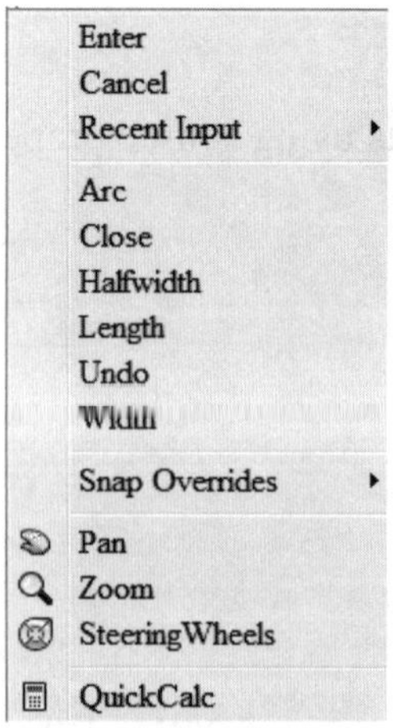

Figure 1 – Polyline Shortcut Menu Options

Polyline Option	Overview
Specify next point	This is the default option. Simply pick the next polyline point, much like drawing line segments.
Arc	This option, used within the Polyline command will invoke the polyline Arc option, creating a Polyarc. There are a few ways to draw a polyline arc, one way is to simply drag the cursor in the desired direction (ORTHO on or off) and type the distance. Then type L to return to the Polyline Line segment option.
Close	This option closes a polyline so that the first and last points are connected.
Halfwidth	This option will make the polyline width half the designated distance.
Length	The length option will extend the polyline being drawn, a designated length.
Undo	The Undo option will undo the last polyline segment.
Width	Type W for width, then specify a start width and an ending width.

General Procedures

1. Invoke the Pline command.
2. Specify a start point.
3. Type W for width (and <ENTER>)
4. Specify a starting width (and <ENTER>) and an ending width (and <ENTER>). The default ending width is usually equal to the starting width, unless drawing an object such as an arrowhead.
5. Specify the next point, using the methods learned in drawing line segments.
6. Optional: Type U (and <ENTER>) to Undo the last polyline segment without exiting the polyline command.
7. Optional: Type A (and <ENTER>) to go invoke the Arc option without exiting the polyline command. Type L (and <ENTER>) to return to the Line mode.
8. Optional: Type C (and <ENTER>) to Close the polyline.

- It is more typical, and usually more practical, to draw regular line and arc segments then use the Edit Polyline command to join them (see next section).
- When drawing a Polyline, the most common options used are Width and "Specify next point".
- The default polyline width is 0. When the width is changed, it will remain the latest width setting until changed again.
- Polyline starting and ending widths can be specified by picking points in the drawing window.
- Draw polylines in continuous segments. If the polylines are drawn as separate segments, the intersections will appear jagged. If the polyline is not closed, there will be a jagged edge at that opened intersection.
- Do not cross polyline segments. Example: 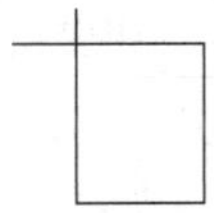

Sometimes it is easier for the beginner drafter to create the geometry using standard lines and arcs and then convert the geometry into polylines and polyarcs. To change a regular line to a polyline, use the PEDIT command. PEDIT can also be used to modify the width to an existing polylines and append geometry.

The Polyline Edit command can be initiated as follows:

Pull Down Menu	**Modify/ Object/Polyline**
Command	**Pedit**
Double Click	**Double left mouse click on polyline**
Alias	**PE**

The PEDIT command has several options:

```
Enter an option [Close/Join/Width/Edit vertex/Fit/Spline/Decurve/Ltype gen/Reverse/Undo]:
```

Close	Creates the closing segment of the polyline, connecting the last segment with the first. AutoCAD considers the polyline open unless you close it using the Close option.
Join	Adds lines, arcs, or polylines to the end of an open polyline and removes the curve fitting from a curve-fit polyline. For objects to join the polyline, their endpoints must touch unless you use the Multiple option at the first PEDIT prompt. In this case, you can join polylines that do not touch if the fuzz distance is set to a value large enough to include the endpoints.
Width	Specifies a new uniform width for the entire polyline.
Edit Vertex	Marks the first vertex of the polyline by drawing an X on the screen. If you have specified a tangent direction for this vertex, an arrow is also drawn in that direction.
Fit	Creates a smooth curve consisting of pairs of arcs joining each pair of vertices. The curve passes through all vertices of the polyline and uses any tangent direction you specify.
Spline	Uses the vertices of the selected polyline as the control points, or frame, of a curve. The curve passes through the first and last control points unless the original polyline was closed. The curve is pulled toward the other points but does not necessarily pass through them. The more control points you specify in a particular part of the frame, the more pull they exert on the curve. The technical term for this type of curve is *B-spline.* AutoCAD can generate quadratic and cubic spline-fit polylines.
Decurve	Removes extra vertices inserted by a fit or spline curve and straightens all segments of the polyline. Retains tangent information assigned to the polyline vertices for use in subsequent fit curve requests. If you edit a spline-fit polyline with commands such as BREAK or TRIM, you cannot use the Decurve option.
Ltype gen	Generates the linetype in a continuous pattern through the vertices of the polyline. When turned off, this option generates the linetype starting and ending with a dash at each vertex. Ltype Gen does not apply to polylines with tapered segments.
Reverse	Reverses the direction of the polyline
Undo	Reverses operations as far back as the beginning of the PEDIT session.

> ***Tip:*** *The PLINEGEN system variable controls the linetype pattern display around and the smoothness of the vertices of a 2D polyline. Setting PLINEGEN to 1 generates new polylines in a continuous pattern around the vertices of the completed polyline. Setting PLINEGEN to 0 starts and ends the polyline with a dash at each vertex. PLINEGEN does not apply to polylines with tapered segments.*
>
> *PLINETYPE controls both the creation of new polylines with the PLINE command and the conversion of existing polylines in drawings from previous releases.*
>
> *0 Polylines in older drawings are not converted when opened; PLINE creates old-format polylines*
> *1 Polylines in older drawings are not converted when opened; PLINE creates optimized polylines*
> *2 Polylines in older drawings are converted when opened; PLINE creates optimized polylines*
>
> *The CONVERT command can be used to optimize polylines created in AutoCAD R13 or earlier.*

Command Exercise

Exercise 5-1 – Polyline

Drawing Name: **pline1.dwg**
Estimated Time to Completion: 10 Minutes

Scope

Using the Polyline command with the Width, Arc and Line options, draw the object as indicated with a polyline width of '0.3'. Ortho should be on.

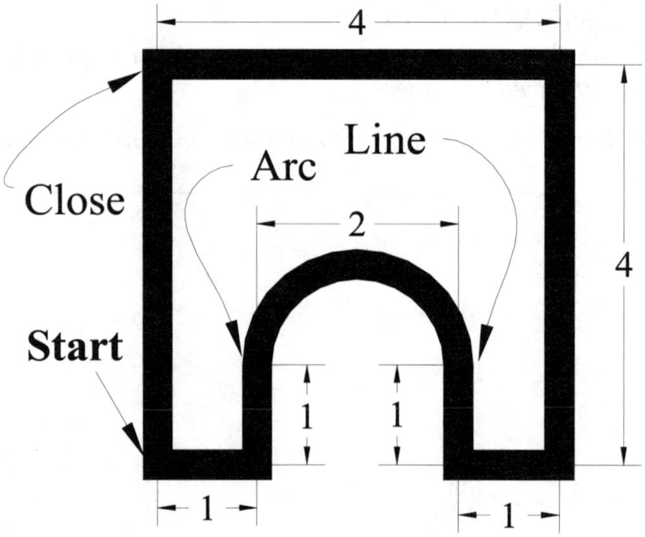

Figure 2 – Polyline Exercise

Solution

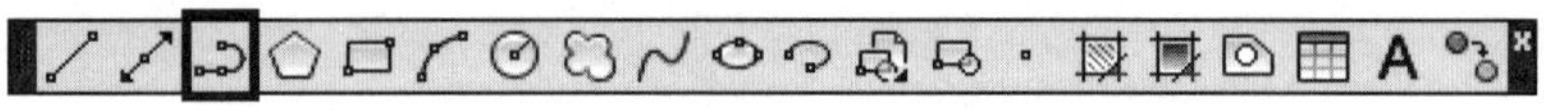

1. Invoke the Polyline command (pl or pline).
2. *Specify start point:*
   Pick the start point with the LMB.
3. *Specify next point or [Arc /Halfwidth/Length/Undo/Width]:*

   `Specify next point or [Arc/Halfwidth/Length/Undo/Width]:`

   Right-click in the drawing window and select 'Width' or type 'W' for width and press <ENTER>.
4. *Specify starting width <0.0000>:*
   Type '0.3' and press <ENTER>.
5. *Specify ending width <0.3000>:*
   Press <ENTER>.
6. *Specify next point or [Arc/Close/Halfwidth/Length/Undo/Width]:*
   Make sure ORTHO is ON. Drag the mouse to the right. Type '1' and press <ENTER>.

7. *Specify next point or [Arc/Close/Halfwidth/Length/Undo/Width]:*
   Drag the mouse upward. Type '1' and press <ENTER>.
8. *Specify next point or [Arc/Close/Halfwidth/Length/Undo/Width]:*
   Right-click in the drawing window and select 'Arc' or type 'A' for arc and press <ENTER>.
9. *Specify endpoint of arc or [Angle/CEnter/CLose/Direction/Halfwidth/Line/Radius/Second pt/ Undo/Width]:*
   Drag the mouse to the right. Type '2' and press <ENTER>.
10. *Specify endpoint of arc or [Angle/CEnter/CLose/Direction/Halfwidth/Line/Radius/Second pt/ Undo/Width]:*
    Type 'L' for line and press <ENTER>.
11. *Specify next point or [Arc/Close/Halfwidth/Length/Undo/Width]:*
    Drag the mouse downward. Type '1' and press <ENTER>.
12. *Specify next point or [Arc/Close/Halfwidth/Length/Undo/Width]:*
    Drag the mouse to the right. Type '1' and press <ENTER>.
13. *Specify next point or [Arc/Close/Halfwidth/Length/Undo/Width]:*
    Drag the mouse upward. Type '4' and press <ENTER>.
14. *Specify next point or [Arc/Close/Halfwidth/Length/Undo/Width]:*
    Drag the mouse to the left. Type '4' and press <ENTER>.
15. *Specify next point or [Arc/Close/Halfwidth/Length/Undo/Width]:*
    Right-click in the drawing window and select 'Close' or type 'C' for close to complete the exercise.

***Extra:** Explode the polyline. What happens? Undo the explode command. Move the objects by selecting the arc only. Notice that the entire polyline is selected.*

***Tip:** Do not start and stop the polyline segments. Use the polyline UNDO option if an incorrect endpoint is selected.*

Command Exercise

Exercise 5-2 – Polyline

Drawing Name: **new drawing**
Estimated Time to Completion: 10 Minutes

Scope

Using the Polyline command with the Width and Line options, draw an arrow. ORTHO should be enabled.

Solution

1.  Invoke the Polyline command (pl or pline).

2. When prompted for the start point, enter **2,2**.

```
Command: _pline
Specify start point: 2,2
```

3. Right click and select **W** for width.

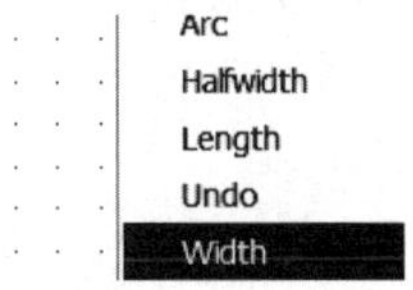

4. Set the starting width to **0**.
Set the ending width to **0.8**.

```
Specify starting width <0'-0">: 0
Specify ending width <0'-0">: 0.8
```

5. Specify the next point as **.75**.

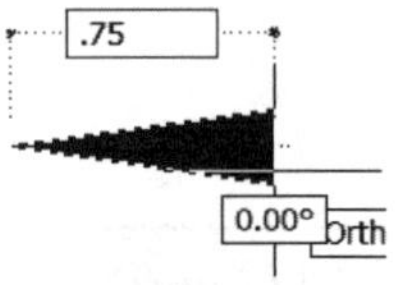

6. Right click and select **W** for width.

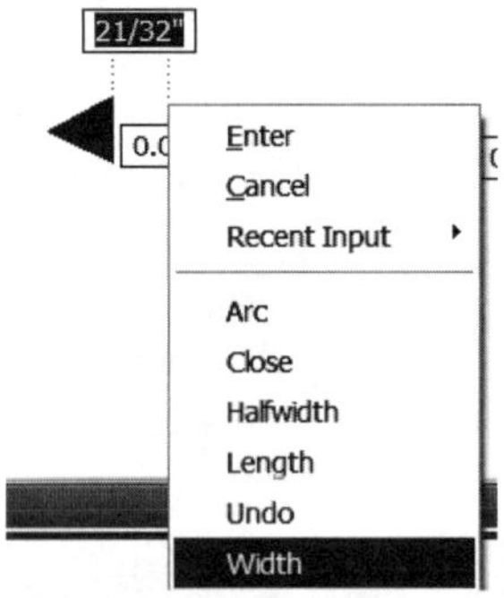

7. Set the starting width to **0.4**.
Set the ending width to **0.4**.

```
Specify starting width <0'-0 13/16">: .4
Specify ending width <0'-0 13/32">: .4
```

8. Set the distance to **5**.

Press <**ENTER**> to exit the command.

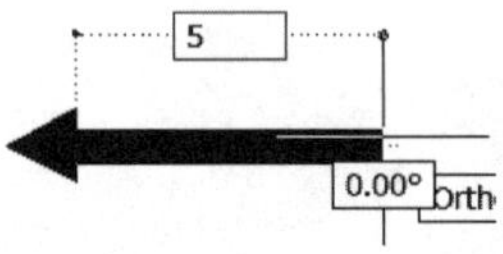

Polygon

Command Locator

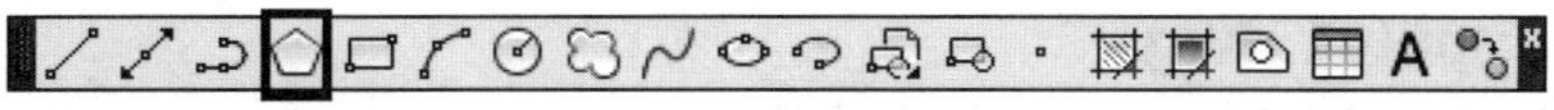

Toolbar Menu	**Draw / Polygon**
Pull Down Menu	**Draw / Polygon**
Command	**Polygon**
Alias	**Pol**

Command Overview

Polygons are polylines with equal line segments. First determine the number of sides for the polygon then select a center point. A polygon may be either Inscribed (I) within or Circumscribed (C) around an imaginary circle. Typing the radius of this circle will determine the size of the polygon. A Polygon may also be constructed using the Edge option, and specifying the length of the Polygon Edge.

General Procedures

1. Begin the Polygon command. Type the number of sides, and press <ENTER>.
2. Specify the center of the Polygon.
3. Determine whether it is Inscribed (I) or Circumscribed (C) about the radius of the circle.
4. Specify the radius.

- After specifying the number of sides to the polygon, type E (for Edge mode) to specify the length and direction of the polygon edge.
- There is no polygon Center. Use the Tracking Object Snap or draw a construction line.

Command Exercise

Exercise 5-3 – Polygon

Drawing Name: **poly1.dwg**
Estimated Time to Completion: 5 Minutes

Scope

Practice the options for drawing a polygon:

1.) Draw a 6-sided polygon making the overall radius 2, using the Inscribed option.

2.) Draw a 6 sided polygon making the overall radius 2, using the Circumscribed option.

3.) Draw a 6 sided polygon using the Edge option, with a length of 1. Notice that the angle of the polygon is determined by the cursor direction as it is dragged from the first pick point.

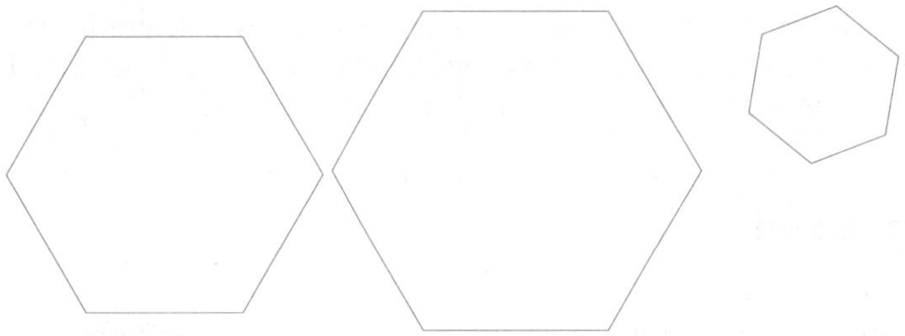

Solution

1. Invoke the Polygon command (polygon).

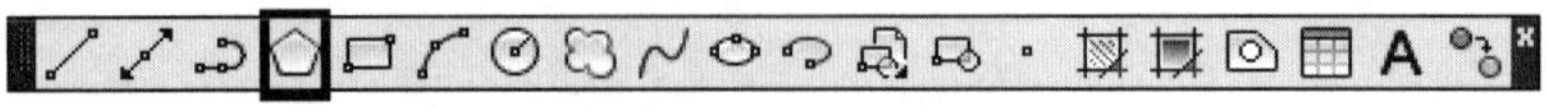

2. *Enter number of sides <4>:*
Type '6' at the command line for the number of sides and press <ENTER>.
3. *Specify center of polygon or [Edge]:*
Pick a point on your drawing with the LMB.
4. *Enter an option [Inscribed in circle/Circumscribed about circle] <I>:*
If the default value is <I> for inscribed. Press <ENTER> to accept this value, right-click in the drawing window and select 'Inscribed in circle' or type 'I' and press <ENTER>.
5. *Specify radius of circle:*
Type '2' and press <ENTER> for the radius in which the polygon is inscribed.
6. Repeat the Polygon command with the RMB.

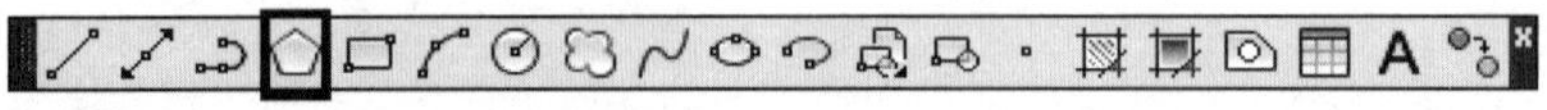

7. *Enter number of sides <6>:*
Press <ENTER> to accept the default.
8. *Specify center of polygon or [Edge]:*
Pick a point with your LMB.

9. *Enter an option [Inscribed in circle/Circumscribed about circle] <I>:*
Right-click in the drawing window and select 'Circumscribed about circle' or type 'C' at the command line and press <ENTER>.

10. *Specify radius of circle:*
Type '2' and press <ENTER> for the radius of the circle about which the polygon is circumscribed.

11. Repeat the Polygon command with the RMB.

12. *Enter number of sides <6>:*
Press <ENTER> to accept the default.

13. *Specify center of polygon or [Edge]:*
Right-click in the drawing window and select 'Edge' or type 'E' and press <ENTER> for the edge option.

14. *Specify first endpoint of edge:*
Pick the first point with the LMB.

15. *Specify first endpoint of edge:*
To specify second endpoint of the edge, drag the mouse away from the first point and type '1' at the command line and press <ENTER>. Notice what happens as the cursor is dragged if ORTHO is ON or OFF.

Tip: *Can the Center Object Snap be used to select the center of the polygon? Try it. How would you draw a line from the center point of one polygon to the next?*

Rectangle

Command Locator

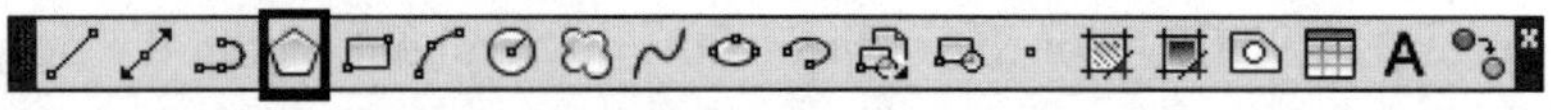

Toolbar Menu	**Draw / Rectangle**
Pull Down Menu	**Draw / Rectangle**
Command	**Rectangle**
Alias	**Rectang**
RMB Shortcut Menu	**Drawing Window (before select the first corner point)**

Command Overview

Rectangles are polylines. All of the line segments are connected. Draw rectangles by designating the opposite corners.

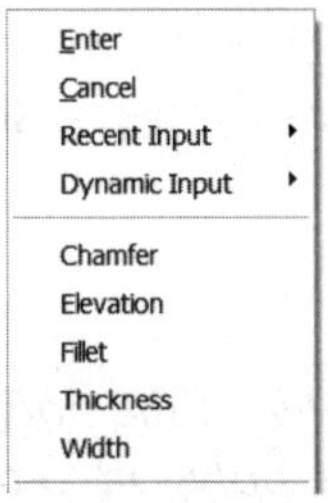

RMB Shortcut Menu for the Rectangle Command Before Selecting a Point

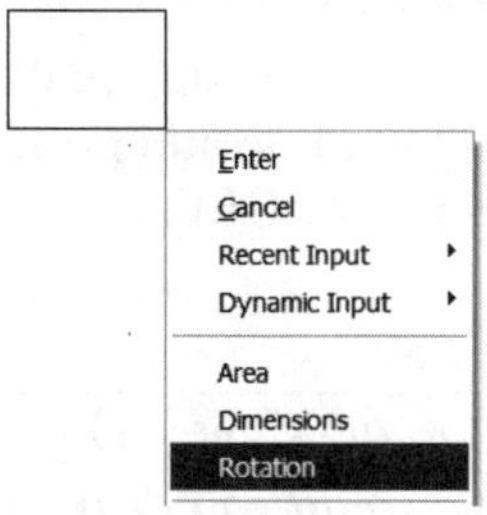

RMB Shortcut Menu for the Rectangle Command After Selecting a Point

General Procedures

To draw a rectangle by picking opposite corners:

1. Begin the rectangle command, and pick the first corner.
2. Drag the mouse and pick the opposite corner.

To draw a rectangle using coordinates:

1. Begin the rectangle command, and pick the first corner.
2. Type '@5,3' to create a 5 x 3 rectangle. The @ means "relative to the last point picked", the first number is the distance in the x direction, the second number is the distance in the y direction. The rectangle will be drawn 5 units to the right, and up 3 units. If a negative coordinate is type, i.e. @-5,-3 the rectangle will be drawn to the left and down from the point picked.

- Use the Rectangle command rather than drawing four separate line segments. This is quicker to make, and a more efficient object, since it is a polyline.
- Beginners should ignore the other Rectangle options, which appear at the command line, until they have had more experience using AutoCAD. The Chamfer and Fillet options will automatically add those features to the corners of the rectangle. Width will change the width of the rectangle's lines. Thickness and Elevation are for 3D drawing. Area allows the user to set the area of the rectangle. The user is still prompted for the length of one side of the rectangle and AutoCAD performs the calculation to determine the length of the other side based on the area provided. Rotation allows you to create a rectangle at an angle.

Command Exercise

Exercise 5-4 – Rectangle

Drawing Name: **rect1.dwg**
Estimated Time to Completion: 5 Minutes

Scope

Draw rectangles as they are in the example. Turn Snap on to make the small rectangles. Turn Snap off to make the large rectangle.

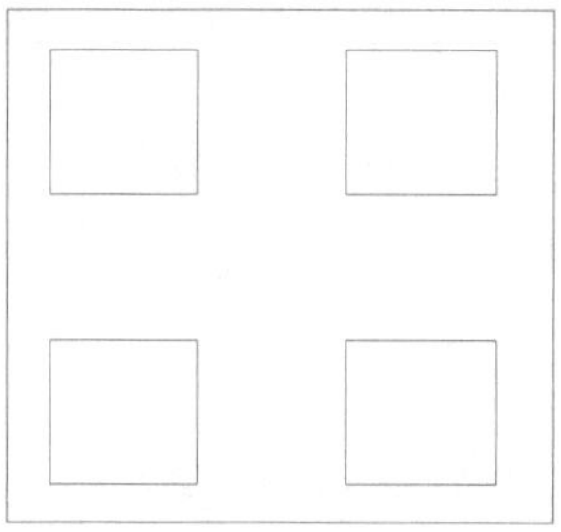

Solution

1. Start by creating the small rectangles. Turn <Snap on> by pressing the <F9> key, or use your LMB to toggle SNAP on at the Status Bar.
2. Invoke the **Rectangle** command (rectang).

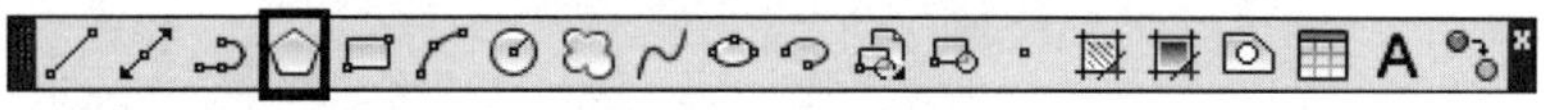

3. *Specify first corner point or [Chamfer/Elevation/Fillet/Thickness/Width]:*
   Position your pointer to the desired location and pick the first point with your LMB.
4. *Specify other corner point:*
   Move your pointer diagonally to the second desired location and pick the point with your LMB.
5. Repeat the Rectangle command by pressing the RMB or the <ENTER> key. Select the fist corner of for the rectangle and then the second corner. Repeat the command to finish the small rectangles.
6. Turn Snap off by pressing the <F9> key or using the LMB to toggle snap off at the Status Bar.
7. Repeat the Rectangle command by right-clicking in the drawing area and selecting 'Repeat'.
8. *Specify first corner point or [Chamfer/Elevation/Fillet/Thickness/Width]:*
   Pick the first corner of the large rectangle with your LMB.
9. *Specify other corner point:*
   Pick a second diagonal corner to complete the large rectangle.

> ***Tip:*** *You can toggle the SNAP on and off in the middle of the rectangle command. Try it.*

Arc

Command Locator

Toolbar Menu	**Draw / Arc**
Pull Down Menu	**Draw / Arc / (select option)**
Command	**Arc**
Alias	**A**
RMB Shortcut Menu	**Drawing Window**
Dialog Box	

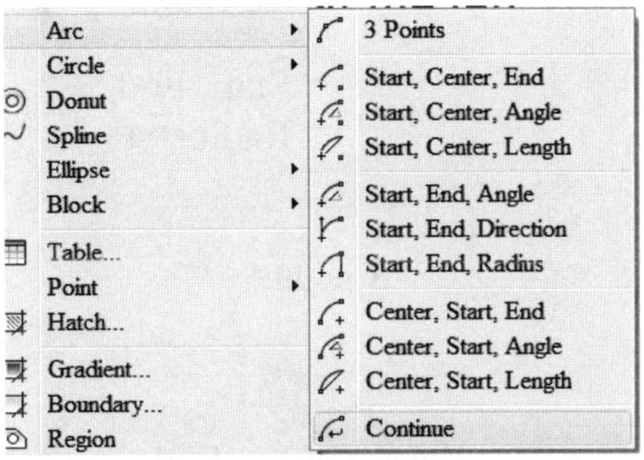

Arc options from the Draw (Arc) Pull-Down Menu

Command Overview

There are many arc options. We will look at the following Arc options: '3 points', 'Start, Center, End', and 'Start, End, Radius'. These Arc options will work in most instances.

Invoke the Arc command from the toolbar or by typing A at the command line. This will draw a '3-point' Arc through three consecutive points. Other Arc options can be selected from the Pull-Down menu. Arcs are constructed in a counter-clockwise direction, except when drawing a 3-point Arc.

General Procedures

1. Begin the Arc command, from the toolbar to draw a 3-point arc, or select one of the Arc options from the Pull-Down Menu.
2. Follow the Command Line prompts.
3. Press the RMB, with the cursor in the Drawing Window to repeat the Arc command.

- Arcs are constructed in a counter-clockwise direction, except when drawing a 3-point Arc.
- Press the right button on the mouse to repeat the Arc command.
- When the cursor is in the Drawing Window, the Shortcut Menu (RMB) will provide an option to repeat the same Arc command.
- When the cursor is over the Command Line, the shortcut Menu (RMB) will provide and option to repeat the Arc command, but it will be the generic 3-point Arc.

Command Exercise

Exercise 5-5 – Arc

Drawing Name: **arc1.dwg**
Estimated Time to Completion: 10 Minutes

Scope

Draw the object on the left using the appropriate Arc and Object Snap options. Use running object snaps (Endpoint and Midpoint).

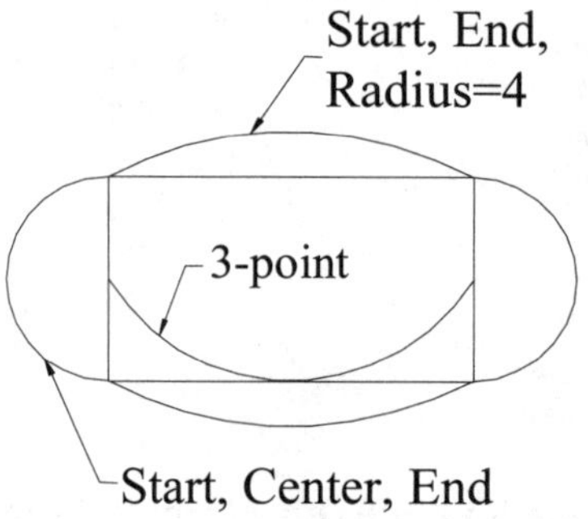

Arc Exercise

Solution

1. Start by toggling OSNAP on. Press the **OSNAP** button on the Status Bar.

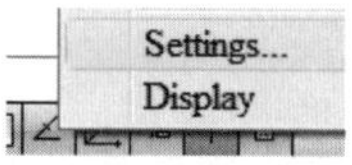

2. Right click on the Object Snap Tracking button on the Status Bar. Select **Settings**.
3. Enable Midpoint and Endpoint running object snaps as shown below.

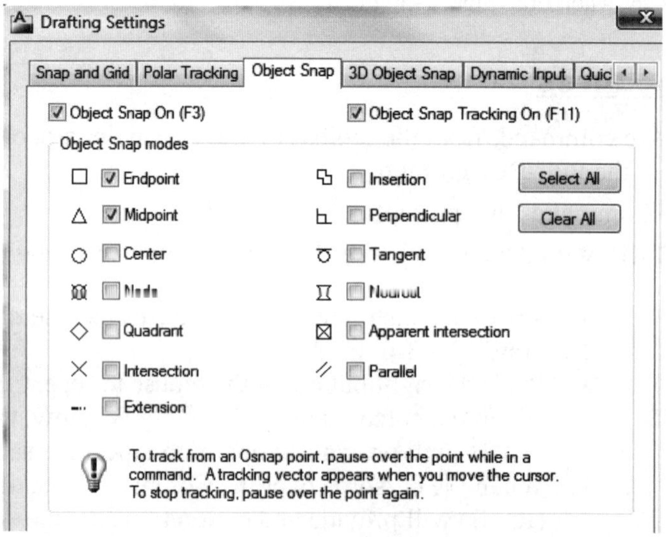

4. Invoke the Start, Center, End ARC command from the pull-down menu (<DRAW<ARC<START,CENTER,END…).

5. *Specify start point of arc or [CEnter]:*
Move near the upper left corner of the box until the desired Object Snap Marker appears. Select the point with the LMB.

6. *Specify second point of arc or [CEnter/ENd]: _c Specify center point of arc:*
Move the pointer near the middle of the left side of the box until the Midpoint Object Snap appears. Select the point with the LMB.

7. *Specify end point of arc or [Angle/chord Length]:*
Move near the bottom left corner of the box. Use your LMB when the Endpoint Object Snap appears.

8. Repeat the Start,Center,End Arc command with the RMB.

9. *Specify start point of arc or [CEnter]:*
Repeat the exact procedure for the right side of the box but start the arc at the lower right corner.

10. Invoke the Start, End, Radius Arc command from the pull-down menu (<DRAW<ARC<START,END,RADIUS).

11. *Specify start point of arc or [CEnter]:*
Select a point near the upper right corner of the box. Remember to use the LMB when the desired Endpoint Object Snap Marker appears.

12. *Specify second point of arc or [CEnter/ENd]:*
Select the end point of the arc at the upper left corner of the box.

13. *Specify center point of arc or [Angle/Direction/Radius]: _r Specify radius of arc:*
Type '4' for the radius of the Arc.

14. Repeat the Start, End, Radius Arc command with the RMB. Repeat the process above. Start your Start, End, Radius Arc at the lower left corner of the box.

15. Invoke the Three Point Arc command by selecting it from the tool bar or by typing 'A' or 'ARC' at the command line and pressing <ENTER>.

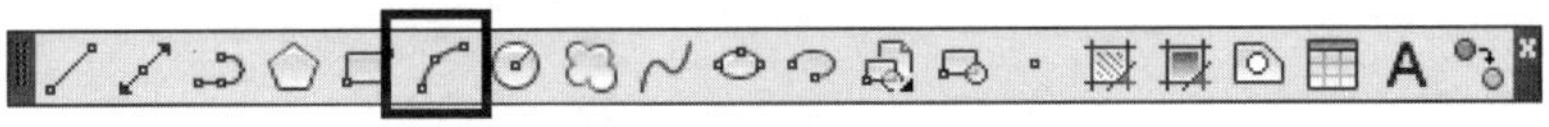

16. *Specify start point of arc or [CEnter]:*
Pick the midpoint of the right side of the box.

17. *Specify second point of arc or [CEnter/ENd]:*
Pick the midpoint of the bottom of the box.

18. *Specify end point of arc:*
Pick the midpoint of the left side of the box. This will complete the arc.

> ***Tip:*** *Notice how the first two sets of arcs were created in a counter-clockwise fashion. What happens if they were created in a clockwise fashion? Try it.*

Circle

Command Locator

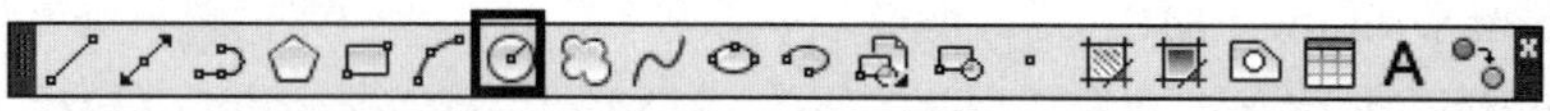

Toolbar Menu	**Draw / Circle**
Pull Down Menu	**Draw / Circle (select option)**
Command	**Circle**
Alias	**C**
RMB Shortcut Menu	**Drawing Window**

Command Overview

There are several ways to draw a Circle. The most common way is to pick the center point then designate a radius. Right click to view the shortcut menu for options. If a center point is selected first, the shortcut menu option for circle is Diameter. If no center point is selected, the shortcut menu will display other options.

Circle Options	Overview
Radius / Diameter	If a center point is selected, type or pick the Radius. Right-click to select the Diameter option or type D and <Enter>.
3P	Draws a circle by selecting 3 Points on the circumference.
2P	Draws a circle by selecting 2 Points on the diameter.
TTR	Draws a circle by selecting two Tangents and typing a radius
Tangent, Tangent, Tangent	(Accessed from the Draw Pull-Down menu only) Draws a circle by selecting three Tangents.

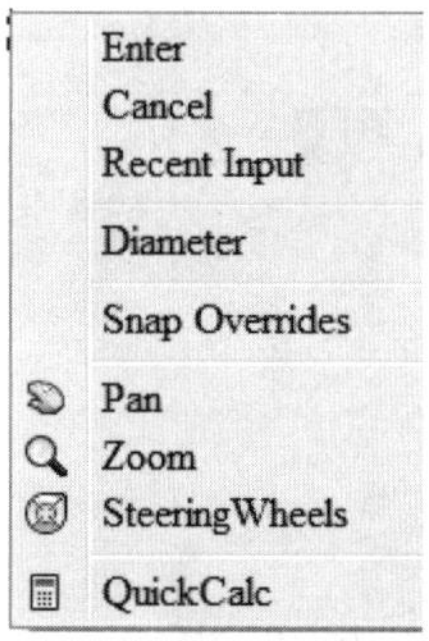

**Circle Shortcut Menu
(center point selected)**

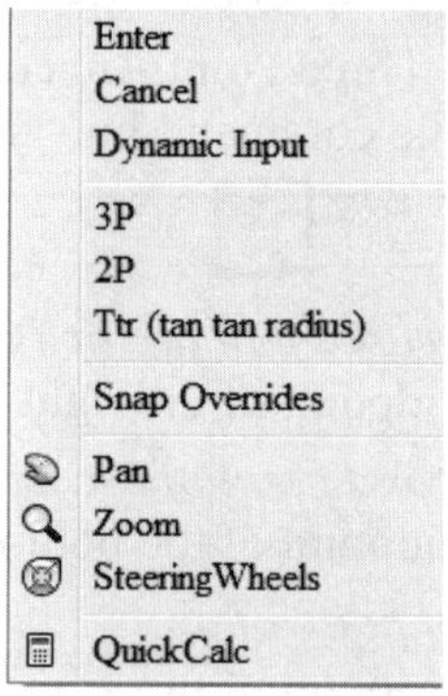

**Circle Shortcut Menu
(no center point selected)**

General Procedures

1. Begin the Circle command, and pick the center point.
2. Type the radius, or press <ENTER> and select the Diameter option. Then type the diameter.

Tips & Tricks

- To make a circle the same size as the previous circle, press <ENTER> to accept the *default* (the radius or diameter that appears in brackets).
- The Tangent, Tangent, Tangent option can only be accessed from the Draw Pull-Down menu.
- When selecting a circle, for example to Erase, pick the circumference.

Donut

Command Locator

Toolbar Menu	**– Must be Added using Customize**
Pull Down Menu	**Draw / Donut**
Command	**Donut**
Alias	**DO**

Command Overview

A Donut has an inner diameter and an outer diameter. When prompted for inner and outer diameters, type it, or press <ENTER> to accept the default.

General Procedures

1. Begin the Donut Command by typing DO (and <ENTER>) or selecting it from the Draw Pull-Down Menu.
2. Type the inside diameter or press <ENTER> to accept the *default.*
3. Type the outside diameter or accept the *default.*
4. Specify the center of the donut by picking in the drawing window. <ENTER> to exit.

Tips & Tricks

- For a solid filled Donut, make the inner diameter zero (0).
- The diameters can also be determined by picking two points in the AutoCAD Window.

Command Exercise

Exercise 5-6 – Circle and Donut

Drawing Name: **circle1.dwg**
Estimated Time to Completion: 10 Minutes

Scope

Draw the large circle using the Tan, Tan, Tan option. With Snap On, draw the inner ring using the Center, Diameter (3) option. With Snap On, draw four circles the same size using the Center, Radius (0.25) option. Place a donut with an inside diameter of 0 and an outside diameter of 0.5 as designated.

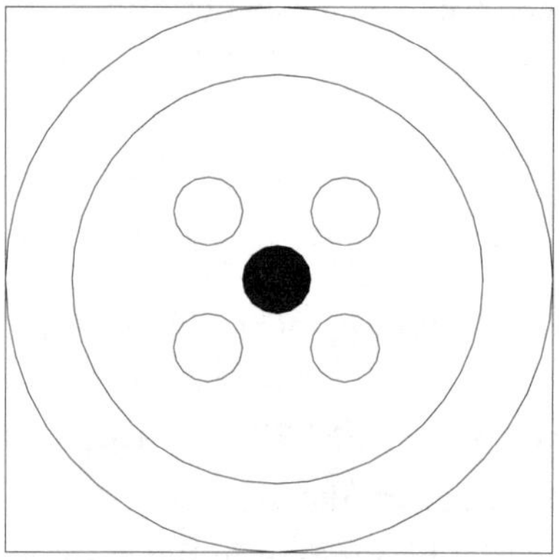

Circle Exercise

Solution

1. Invoke the circle command by using the **DRAW→CIRCLE→TAN, TAN, TAN** command from the pull-down menus.
2. *Specify first point on circle: _tan to*
   Select the top line segment of the box with the LMB. You will notice a symbol appearing when your pointer is on the line segment.
3. *Specify second point on circle: _tan to*
   Select the left or right side of the box with the LMB. (Notice the symbol that appears)
4. *Specify third point on circle: _tan to*
   Select the bottom of the box with the LMB. (Notice the symbol that appears). The Circle is automatically drawn.
5. Turn Snap on with the <F9> key or use your mouse to toggle snap on at the Status Bar.
6. Invoke the circle command by using the **DRAW→CIRCLE→CENTER, DIAMETER** command from the pull-down menu.
7. *Specify center point for circle or [3P/2P/Ttr (tan tan radius)]:*
   Pick in the center of the box.
8. *Specify diameter of circle:*
   Type ‘3’ at the command line and press <ENTER>.

9. Invoke the circle command from the toolbar or by typing **C** or **CIRCLE** at the command line and pressing <ENTER>.

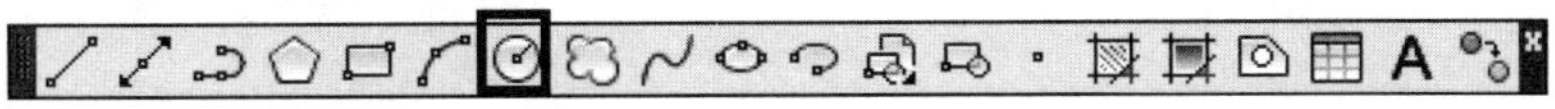

10. *Specify center point for circle or [3P/2P/Ttr (tan tan radius)]:*
Use your LMB to pick the desired center point of the first small circle.

11. *Specify radius of circle or [Diameter] <1.5000>:*
Type **0.25** at the command line and press <ENTER>.

12. Repeat the Circle command by pressing <ENTER> or the RMB.

13. *Specify center point for circle or [3P/2P/Ttr (tan tan radius)]:*
Select the desired center point for the second small circle.

14. *Specify radius of circle or [Diameter] <0.2500>:*
Press <ENTER> to accept the radius setting of 0.25.

15. Repeat the command to complete the remaining circles.

16. Invoke the Donut command by selecting Donut from the Draw pull-down menu (donut).

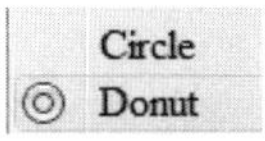

17. *Specify inside diameter of donut <0.5000>:*
Type **0** and press <ENTER>.

18. *Specify outside diameter of donut <1.0000>:*
Type **0.5** and press <ENTER>.

19. *Specify center of donut or <exit>:*
Use your LMB to pick the center point for the donut.

20. *Specify center of donut or <exit>:*
Press <ENTER> to end the command.

> ***Tip:*** *AutoCAD remembers the radius of the last circle that was created. If you start the Circle command by typing 'C' or 'Circle' you can enter a radius by default. If you would like to enter a diameter, type 'D' and press <ENTER> after you have selected the center point of the circle and then enter the diameter of the circle.*

Spline

Command Locator

Toolbar Menu	**Draw/ Spline**
Pull Down Menu	**Draw / Spline**
Command	**Spline**
Alias	**spl**

Command Overview

You can make a spline from a polyline using the Pedit command. An easy way to create a spline is to define the points where the arcs (both concave and convex) are to be placed and use those points to control your spline's shape.

General Procedures

1. Begin the Spline command.
2. Pick a point.
3. Pick a second point.
4. You can right click at this point to see the spline options.
5. Continue picking points until you are done. Press <ENTER> or 'Close' to exit the command.

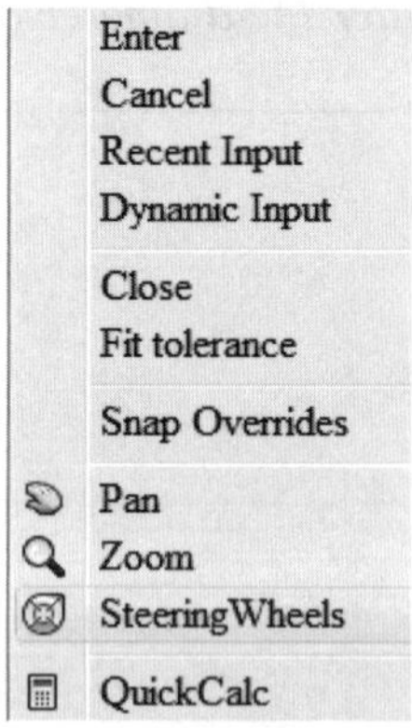

Spline Shortcut Menu Options

You can use the Fit tolerance option to define a spline using points. If you set the fit tolerance to 0, then the spline will pass through the selected points. If you set the fit tolerance to a number greater than 0, it will create a spline using the tolerance to get as close to the points as the tolerance allows. Dynamic Input only appears in the shortcut menu if the DYN button is enabled.

Command Exercise

Exercise 5-7 – Spline

Drawing Name: **spline1.dwg**
Estimated Time to Completion: 5 Minutes

Scope

Use the points to assist you in creating your spline.

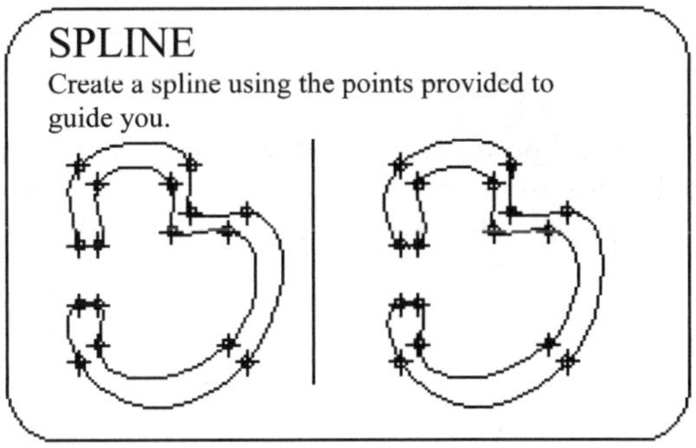

Spline Exercise

Solution

1. Invoke the **Spline** command.

2. Select a point.
3. Follow the points along to create your spline object.
4. At the last point, right click and select **Close** and then <ENTER>.

Ellipse

Command Locator

Toolbar Menu	**Draw/ Ellipse**
Pull Down Menu	**Draw / Ellipse**
Command	**Ellipse**
Alias	**el**

Command Overview

The Ellipse command prompts for a center point, an axis end point, and then a radius distance to the perpendicular axis. Users can also determine the size of the ellipse based on rotation. Ellipse Arc allows the user to create a partial ellipse.

General Procedures

1. Begin the Ellipse command.
2. Pick a center point.
3. Pick a second point to indicate one axis end of the ellipse.
4. Move the mouse in a perpendicular direction from the second point to set the second axis. Enter a radius distance or select a point.

Command Exercise

Exercise 5-8 – Ellipse & Ellipse Arc

Drawing Name: **ellipse1.dwg**
Estimated Time to Completion: 5 Minutes

Scope

Use the points to assist you in creating your ellipse.

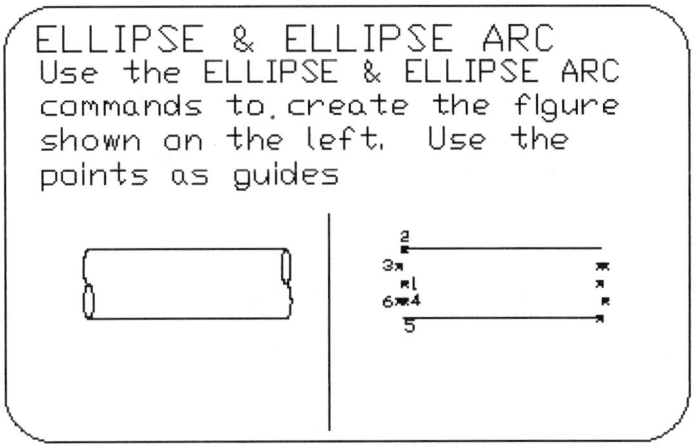

Ellipse Exercise

Solution

1. 

   Invoke the **Ellipse** command.

2. 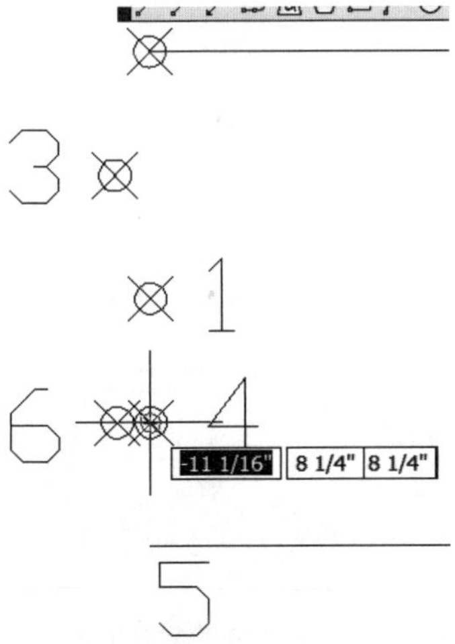

   Select Point 4.

   The NODE OSNAP should be enabled to assist you in selecting the points.

3. 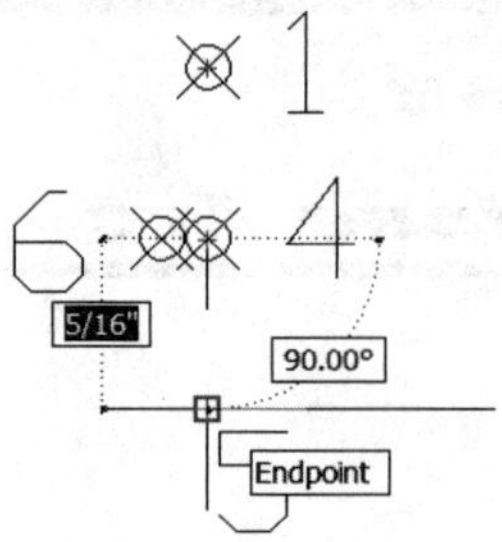

Select the endpoint located at Point 5.

4. 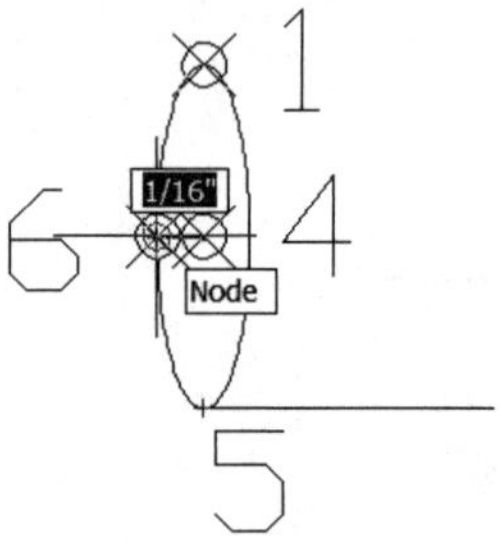

Select Point 6 when prompted for the distance to other axis.

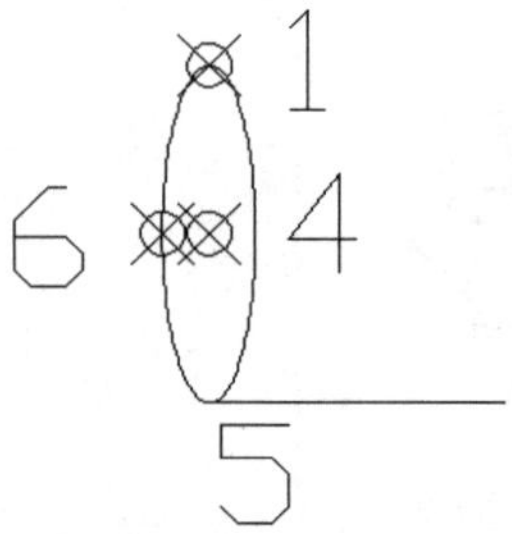

The ellipse is placed.

5. 

Select the Ellipse Arc tool.

6. 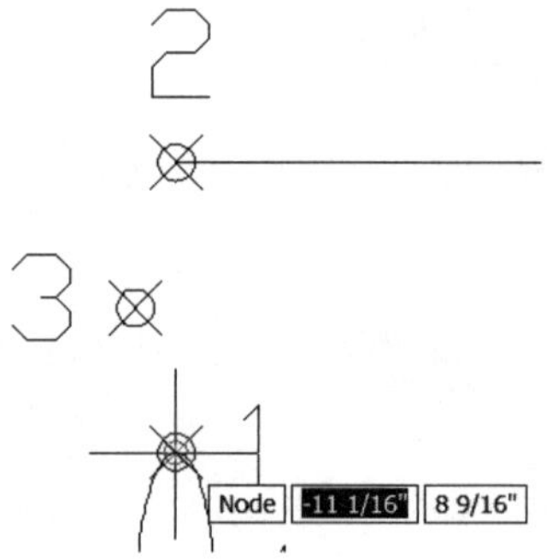

Select Point 1.

7. 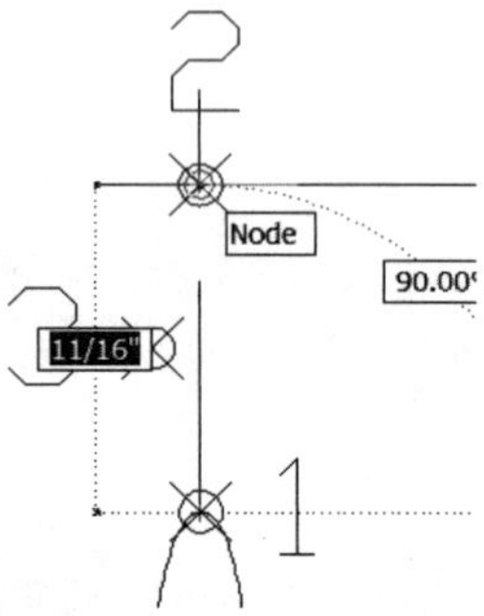

Select Point 2.

8.

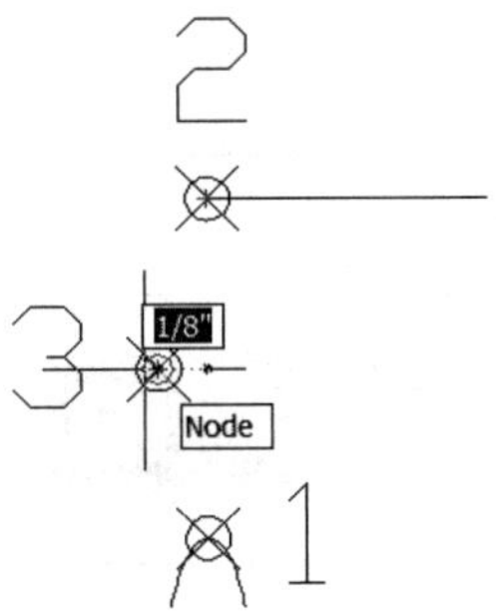

Select Point 3.

9.

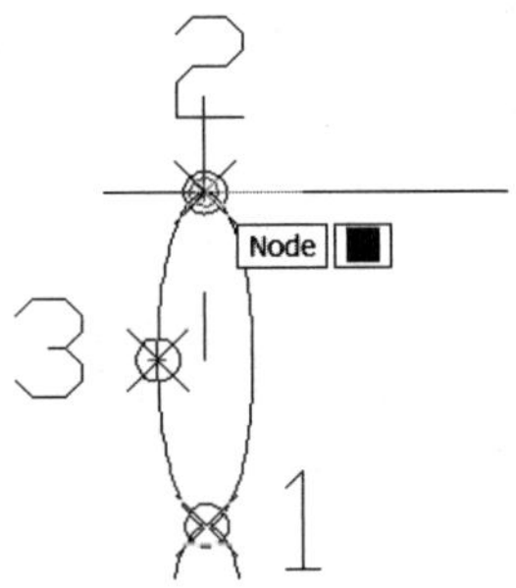

Select Point 2 as the start point for the angle.

10.

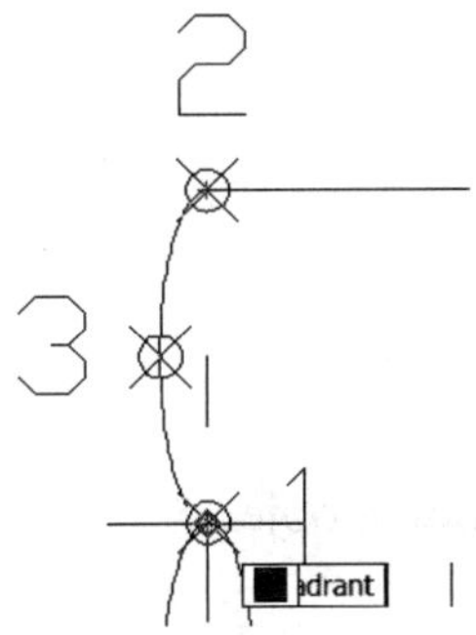

Select Point 1 as the end point for the angle.

11.

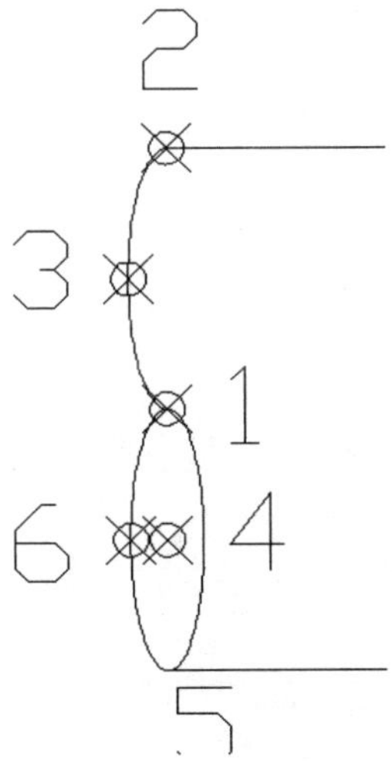

One end of your wire is completed.

Repeat the steps for the other side.

AddSelected

Command Locator

Toolbar Menu	**Draw/ AddSelected**
Shortcut Menu	**Select an object, right click and select Add Selected**
Command	**addselected**

Command Overview

With the ADDSELECTED command, you can create a new object using a source object. The new object will have the same layer, color, and line type as the source object, however the user can define new location points, and new sizes.

General Procedures

1. Select an object.
2. The command which is used to create the selected object is initiated.
3. Create a new object.
4. The new object has the same layer, color, linetype, etc. as the source object.

Command Exercise

Exercise 5-9 – AddSelected

Drawing Name: **addselected.dwg**
Estimated Time to Completion: 5 Minutes

Scope

Use AddSelected to add lines and a circle.
Note that the new entities have the same properties as the source entities: layer, color, etc.

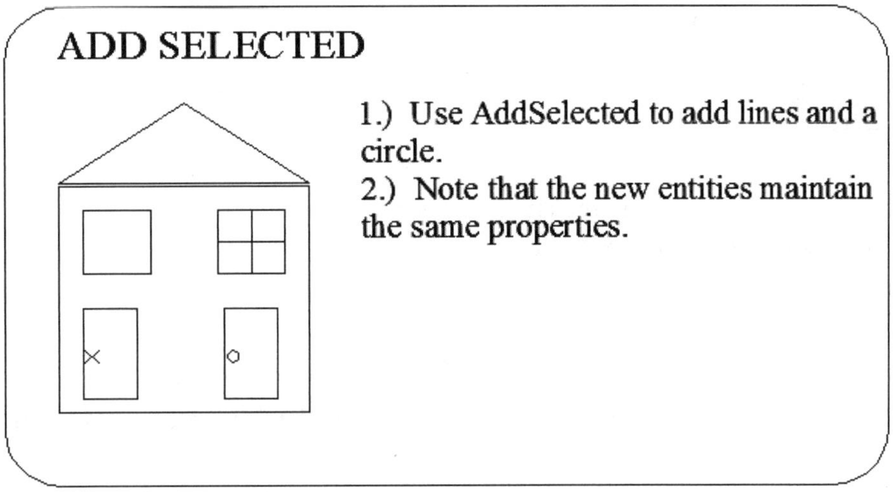

AddSelected Exercise

Solution

1.  Note that the current layer is 0.

2. 

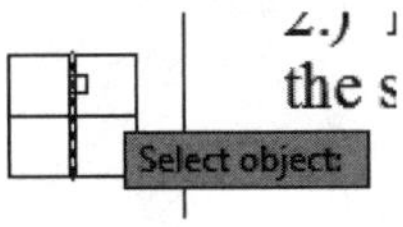

Select the **AddSelected** tool.
Then, select the vertical blue line.

3. 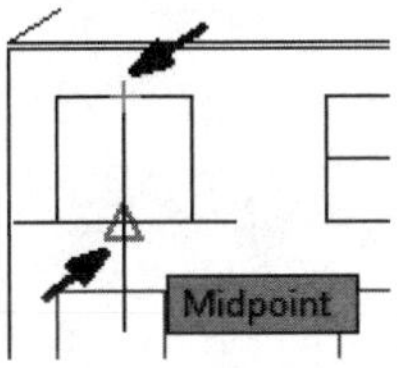

Select the top and bottom midpoints to place the new line.

4.

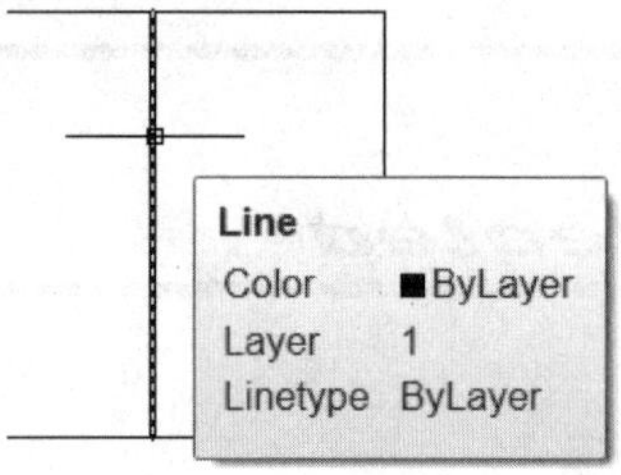

Note that the new line is placed on the same layer and is the same color as the line selected.

Verify that the current layer is still layer 0.

5.

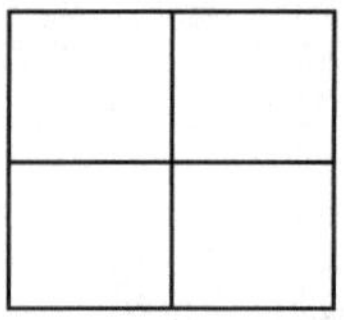

Repeat to place the horizontal line.

6.

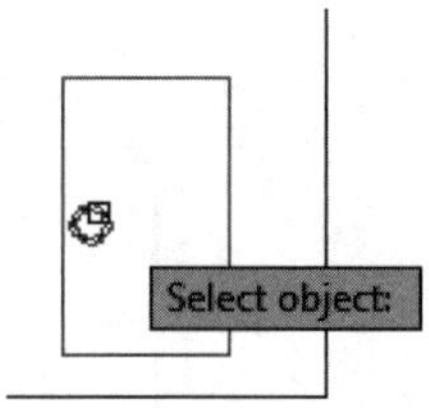

Select the **AddSelected** tool.
Then, select the orange circle.

7.

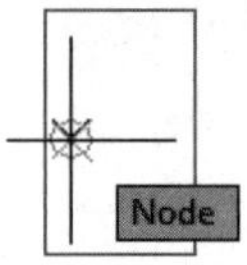

Select the point in the left-side door to place the circle.
Specify a radius of 1/8″.

Note: You can change the radius of the circle.

8.

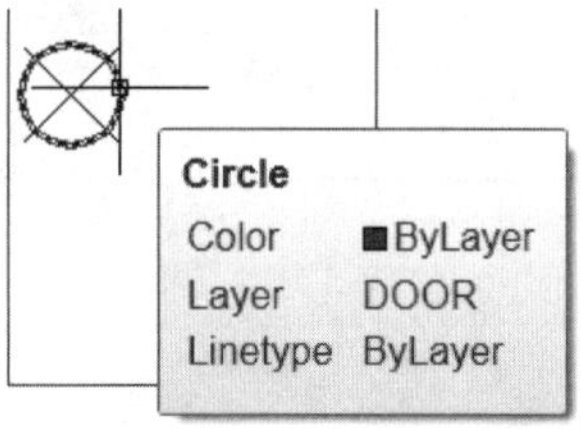

Note that the new circle has the same properties as the selected circle.

Verify that the current layer is still layer 0.

Section Exercise

Exercise 5-10 – Standard Bracket

Drawing Name: **create a new drawing**
Estimated Time to Completion: **15 Minutes**

Scope

Use the commands you have learned in the past section to create the three view orthographic drawing of the bracket in the figure below. Do not worry about a title block, drawing dimensions or hidden lines. Try to place the polygon and circle in the middle of the upper and lower plates. Remember to use the most efficient commands. (i.e. Running Object Snap).

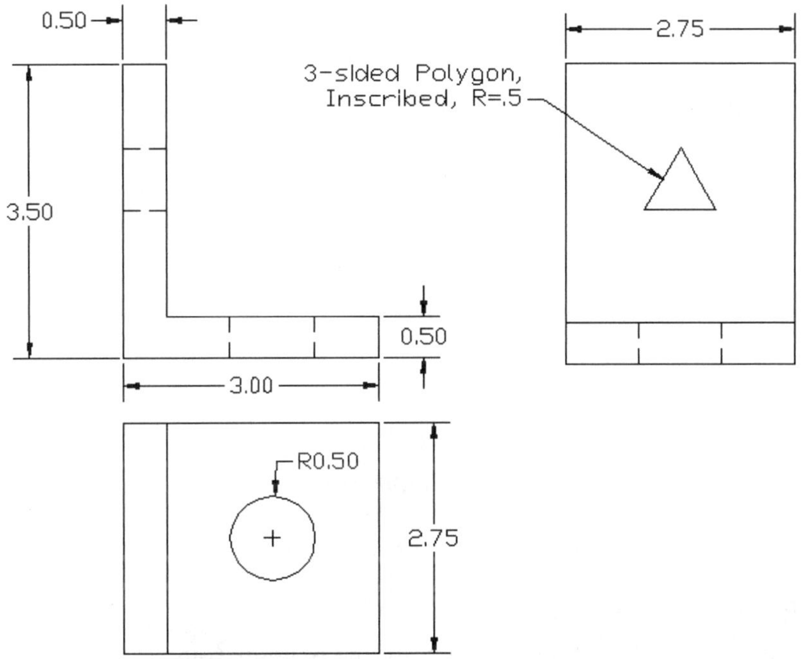

Standard Bracket

Hints

1. Start by setting the Endpoint, Midpoint, Intersection and Quadrant Running Object Snaps. Turn OTRACK on.
2. Try to use the Line and Rectangle commands to create the overall geometry. Try the Polygon command to create the Triangle, and the circle command to make the hole.
3. Use the ORTHO mode to create vertical and horizontal lines.

Section Exercise

Exercise 5-11 – Simple House

Drawing Name: **create a new drawing**
Estimated Time to Completion: **15 Minutes**

Scope

Using the commands learned in this section, draw this simplified house.

Simple House

Hints

1. Use Rectangles for the basic shapes.
2. Use lines with midpoint object snaps for the window frames.
3. Draw extra shapes with the polygon command and then erase them.

Review Questions

1. Identify the following icons by writing the name of the command and the toolbar where it can be found. *Extra: Write the command line shortcut, or alias.*

Command

a)  ______________________

b)  ______________________

c)  ______________________

d)  ______________________

e)  ______________________

2. Name the six options for creating a circle.

3. Name three options for creating an arc.

4. You construct a circle using the 2P option. What does this option prompt you for?

5. True or False: Using AddSelected automatically changes the active layer.

6. Identify the properties which are copied when using **AddSelected**.

    a) Color
    b) Layer
    c) Linetype
    d) Location

Review Answers

1. Identify the following icons by writing the name of the command.
   a. *Line / Draw / L*
   b. *Rectangle / Draw / REC*
   c. *Circle / Draw / C*
   d. *Arc / Draw / A*
   e. *Polygon / Draw / POL*

2. Name the six methods for creating a circle.
   Center, Radius
   Center, Diameter
   2P
   3P
   Tan, Tan, Tan
   Tan, Tan, Radius

3. Name three methods for creating an arc.

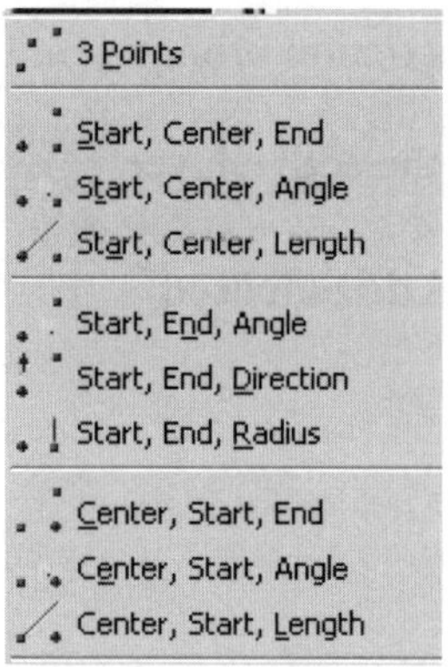

4. You construct a circle using the 2P option. What does this option prompt you for?
   The two end points of the diameter

5. *False*

6. *a, b, c*

Lesson 6.0 – Modify Commands

Estimated Class Time: 2 Hours

Objectives

This section introduces AutoCAD commands for modifying objects in a simple drawing. This lesson reviews the following commands on the Modify toolbar:

- **Copy**
  Copy selected objects to a new location.
- **Mirror**
  Mirror selected objects about a mirror line.
- **Offset**
  Offset selected objects a set distance.
- **Array**
  Rectangular and Polar Arrays.
- **Move**
  Move selected objects to a new location.
- **Rotate**
  Rotate selected objects to a new angle.
- **Scale**
  Scale objects to make them larger or smaller.
- **Stretch**
  Use stretch to lengthen and widen geometry.
- **Trim**
  Trim objects to a cutting edge.
- **Extend**
  Extend objects to a selected boundary.
- **Fillet**
  Use fillets.
- **Undo and Redo**
  Undo previous commands and redo the "undo".

Copy

Command Locator

Toolbar Menu	**Modify**
Pull Down Menu	**Modify→Copy**
Command	**Copy**
Alias	**CO or CP**
RMB Shortcut Menu	**Drawing Window**

Command Overview

To Copy an object, pick the base point, drag the mouse and pick the location for the copied object. In AutoCAD 2006, copy is automatically set to make multiple copies. You will continue to place copies until you press <ESC> or <ENTER>.

General Procedures

To Create a single copy:

1. Invoke the Copy Command.
2. Select the objects to Copy, and press <ENTER>.
3. Pick a point on or near the object as the base point.
4. Drag the mouse and pick the location for the copied object.
5. Press <ESC> to exit the command or right click and select <ENTER>.

Tips & Tricks

- Use Object Snaps for picking the base point and the new location.
- If using direct distance to relocate the object, be sure ORTHO is ON.
- Remember to use the LMB to pick the base point and the new location of the object.
- Be sure SNAP (in the Status Bar) is off, when selecting objects.
- The Copy command is automatically in MUTLIPLE mode if you are using AutoCAD 2005 or above. If you are using a lower revision of AutoCAD, you need to use the M option to create multiple copies in a single command.

Command Exercise

Exercise 6-1 – Copy

Drawing Name: **copy1.dwg**
Estimated Time to Completion: 5 Minutes

Scope

Copy the objects in the rectangle on the left into the rectangle on the right

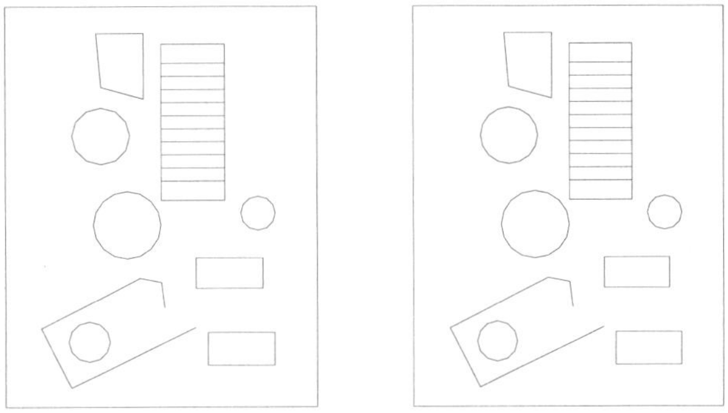

Copy Exercise

Solution

1. Invoke the Copy command (co or copy).

2. *Select objects:*
   Select all of the objects using a window inside the red box.
3. *Specify base point or displacement:*
   You may want to turn OSNAP off. Use your LMB to select in the middle of the red box with the objects somewhere. This is the point from which the objects will be copied.
4. *Specify second point of displacement or <use first point as displacement>:*
   Move your mouse to position the rectangles in the red box on the right and press the LMB to specify the second point of displacement.
5. Press **<ESC>** to exit the command.

> ***Tip:*** *You may also leave OSNAP on, and snap to a corner of the left red box for the base point and the same corner of the right red box for the second point of displacement.*

Command Exercise

Exercise 6-2 – Copy Multiple

Drawing Name: **copy2.dwg**
Estimated Time to Completion: 5 Minutes

Scope

Decorate the tree on the right by making multiple copies of the star as indicated in the drawing on the left.

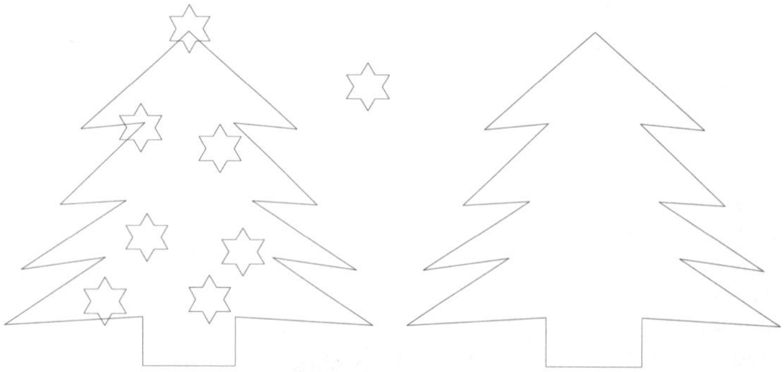

Copy Multiple Exercise

Solution

1. Invoke the Copy command (cp or copy).

2. *Select objects:*
Select the star between the trees with the LMB. Close the selection set with the <ENTER> key or RMB.
3. *Specify base point:*
You may want to turn OSNAP off. Use your LMB to select in the middle of the selected star. This is the point from which the stars will be copied multiple times.
4. *Specify second point of displacement or <use first point as displacement>:*
Move your mouse to position the star on the tree on the right and press the LMB to specify the second point of displacement. Move your mouse to another location and press the LMB to copy another star. Repeat the process to decorate the tree. Right click and select <ENTER> to exit the command.

Extra: *What happens when you use the Undo command after making multiple copies? Try making multiple copies of multiple objects.*

Mirror

Command Locator

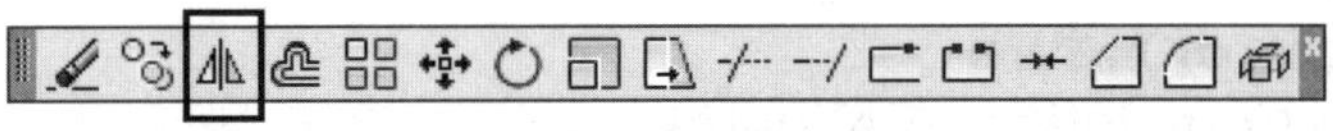

Toolbar Menu	**Modify / Mirror**
Pull Down Menu	**Modify / Mirror**
Command	**Mirror**
Alias	**MI**
RMB Shortcut Menu	**Drawing Window**

Command Overview

Mirror selected objects around a mirror line with ORTHO on or off. Use the MIRRTEXT system variable to control whether text will mirror or not.

General Procedures

To use the Mirror command:

1. Invoke the Mirror Command.
2. Select the objects to mirror, and press <ENTER>.
3. Pick the first point of the mirror line. Drag the mouse and pick the second line.
4. At the prompt Delete source objects? [Yes/No] <N>, press <ENTER> to accept the default or type Y to delete the source objects.

To use the Mirror command without mirroring text:

1. Type MIRRTEXT, and press <ENTER>.
2. Type 0 to turn MIRRTEXT off.
3. Proceed with the Mirror command.

Command Exercise

Exercise 6-3 – Mirror

Drawing Name: **mirror1.dwg**
Estimated Time to Completion: 5 Minutes

Scope

Mirror the lines below using the endpoints of the upper and lower lines for the Mirror Line.

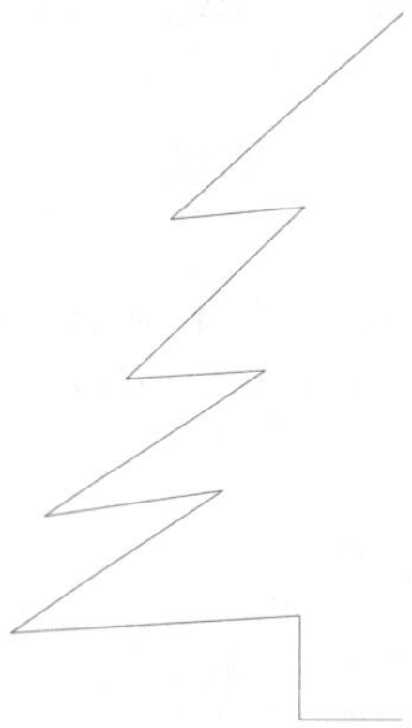

Mirror Exercise

Solution

1. Invoke the Mirror command (mirror).

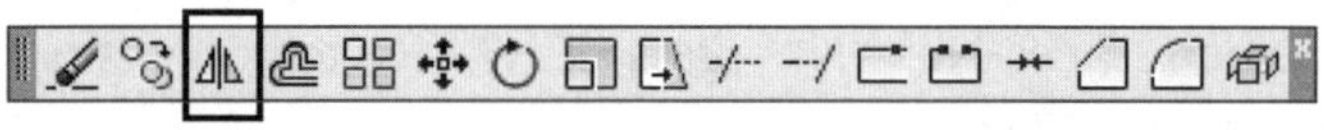

2. *Select objects:*
   Select the left side of the tree and press <ENTER> to end the selection.
3. *Specify first point of mirror line:*
   Make sure OSNAP is on. Pick the endpoint of the line that will represent the top of the tree with the LMB.
4. *Specify second point of mirror line:*
   Use the LMB and object snap to select the end point that represents the bottom of the tree.
5. *Erase source objects? [Yes/No] <N>:*
   Right-click in the drawing area and select 'No' or just press <ENTER> to accept the default (N).

Extra: *Mirror the word MIRROR. Type 'MIRRTEXT' at the command line and press <ENTER>. Type 0 <ENTER>. Mirror the word MIRROR again. What is the difference? Try It.*

Command Exercise

Exercise 6-4 – Mirror

Drawing Name: **mirror2.dwg**
Estimated Time to Completion: 5 Minutes

Scope

Turn the mirror text system variable MIRRTEXT off, and mirror the objects using the endpoints of the upper and lower lines for the mirror line.

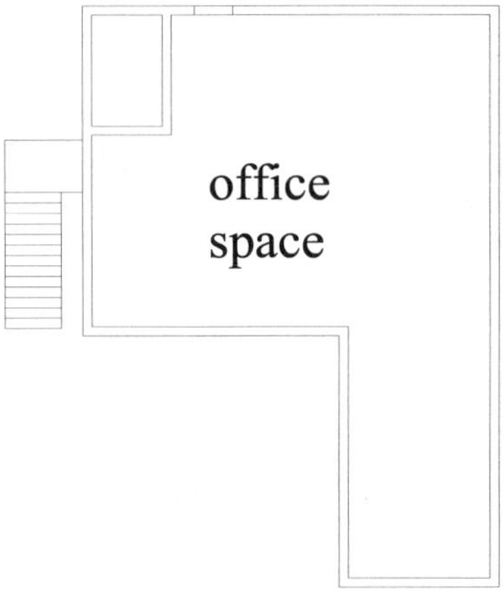

Mirror Exercise

Solution

1. Start the exercise by making sure the Endpoint running object snap is activated.
2. Type 'MIRRTEXT' at the command line and press <ENTER>.
3. *Enter new value for MIRRTEXT <1>:*
   Type '0' and press <ENTER>.
4. Invoke the Mirror command (mirror).

5. *Select objects:*
   Select the objects that make up the office space. Include the text.
6. *Select objects:*
   Close the selection set by pressing <ENTER>.
7. *Specify first point of mirror line:*
   Select the upper right hand corner of the office space. Remember to use the object snap.
8. *Specify second point of mirror line:*
   Toggle ORTHO on. Move the mouse near the bottom right corner of the office space and click the LMB.
9. *Erase source objects? [Yes/No] <N>:*
   Right-click in the drawing area and select 'No' or just press <ENTER> to accept the default option of 'No'.

Offset

Command Locator

Toolbar Menu	**Modify / Offset**
Pull Down Menu	**Modify / Offset**
Command	**Offset**
Alias	**O**
RMB Shortcut Menu	**Drawing Window**

Command Overview

To Offset a single object, first set the offset distance by picking two points in the Drawing Window, or typing the offset distance. Select the object to offset and the side to offset.

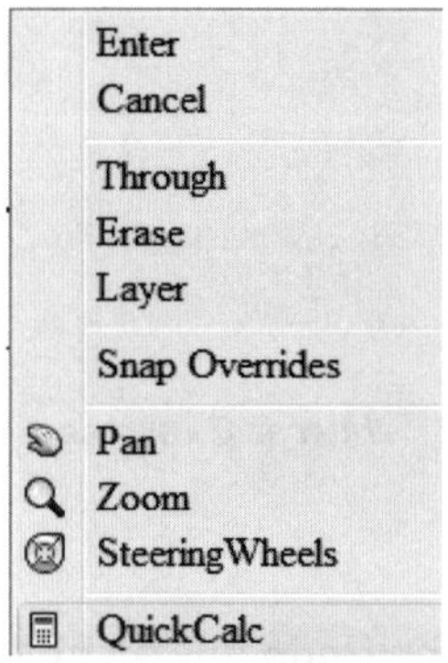

Offset Shortcut Menu

Offset Option	Overview
Through	Use this option to use a second object or point to set the distance for the offset.
Erase	Use this option to delete the source object after it is offset.
Layer	Use this option to set what layer the offset/new object will be assigned. You can set the new object to the current layer or the layer used by the source object.

General Procedures

1. Invoke the Offset Command.
2. Type the Offset distance.
3. Select the object to Offset, then pick the side to offset the object.

Tips & Tricks

- Offset lines, circles, arcs and polylines.

Command Exercise

Exercise 6-5 – Offset

Drawing Name: **offset1.dwg**
Estimated Time to Completion: 5 Minutes

Scope

Offset the objects with an offset distance of 0.25.

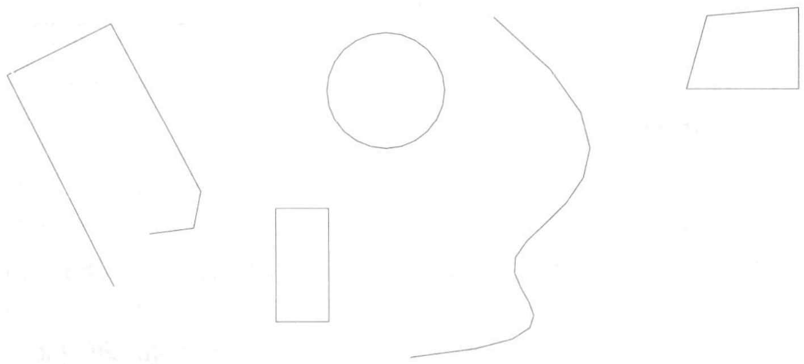

Offset Exercise

Solution

1. Start the Offset Command (o or offset).

2. *Specify offset distance or [Through] <Through>:*
   Type '0.25' at the command line and press <ENTER>.
3. *Select object to offset or <exit>:*
   Select the desired object with the LMB.
4. *Specify point on side to offset:*
   Select the side of the object to create the offset on.
5. *Select object to offset or <exit>:*
   Repeat the process offsetting all the objects on the screen.

Array

Command Locator

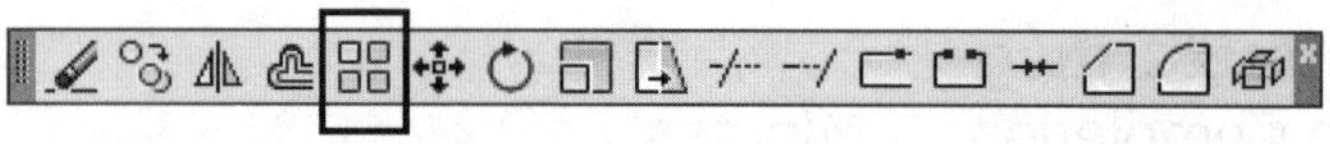

Toolbar Menu	**Modify / Array**
Pull Down Menu	**Modify / Array**
Command	**Array**
Alias	**AR**
RMB Shortcut Menu	**Drawing Window**

Command Overview

Rectangular Array copies objects in rows and columns. The rectangular array can also be set to copy a linear pattern at an angle.

Polar Array copies objects in a circular pattern. Specify which method of array is preferred and follow the Command line prompts.

A rectangular Array copies the objects into rows and columns with designated distances between the objects. Columns are copied in the positive X direction, and Rows are copied in the positive Y direction. A negative distance will copy the objects in the negative X and Y directions, respectively.

A polar array copies objects around a center point. Specify the total number of objects, the angle to fill (360 degrees or less) and whether the objects should be rotated.

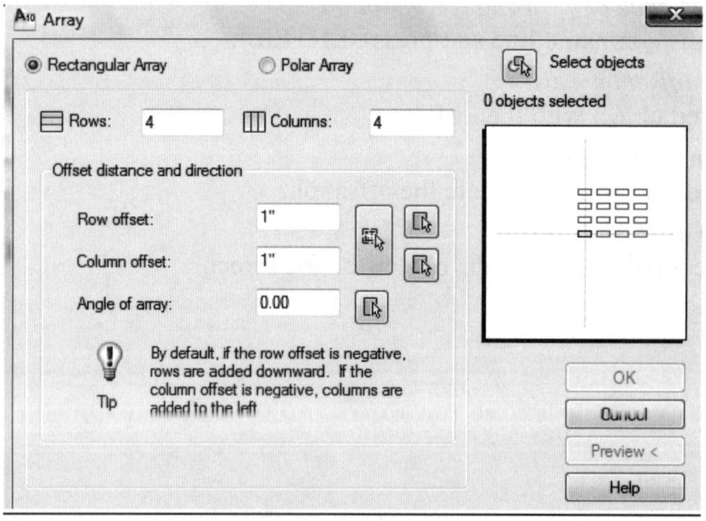

Rectangular Array Dialog

General Procedures

To create a Rectangular Array:

1. Invoke the Array command.
2. Select the objects to Array and press <ENTER>.
3. Enable the Rectangular Array.
4. Enter the number of rows, then enter the number of columns.
5. Type the distance between the rows and the columns.
6. Use the Preview button to check your array settings.

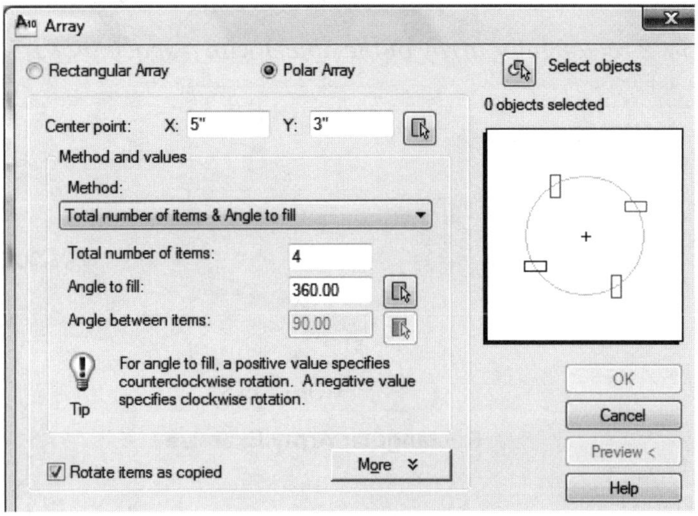

Polar Array Dialog

To create a Polar Array:

1. Invoke the Array command.
2. Select the objects to Array and press <ENTER>.
3. Enable the Polar Array radio button.
4. Specify the center point of the array.
5. Enter the total number of items for the array.
6. Specify the angle to fill. Press <ENTER> for 360, or type the angle.
7. Press <ENTER> to accept the default to rotate the arrayed objects.

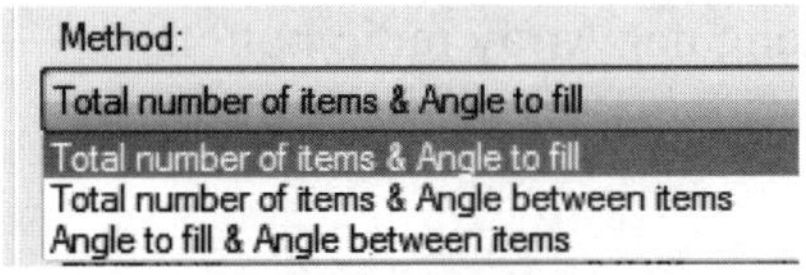

Polar Array Options

The Polar Array has three options for creating the array:

- Total number of items & Angle to fill
- Total number of items & Angle between items
- Angle to fill & Angle between items

Tips & Tricks

- For Rectangular Array, a negative distance between columns will array the objects in the negative x (-x) direction (right to left). A negative distance between rows, will arrays objects in the negative y (-y) direction (below one another).
- For Polar Array, a negative angle arrays objects in a counter-clockwise direction.
- For Rectangular Array, one row or one column will array objects in one direction only.
- The MINSERT command (typed) will insert blocks in rows and columns. Individual blocks cannot be deleted or Exploded.
- For Rectangular Array, you can set an angle to array from.

Command Exercise

Exercise 6-6 – Rectangular Array

Drawing Name: **arrayr1.dwg**
Estimated Time to Completion: 5 Minutes

Scope

Create a 3 x 2 rectangular array of the object with a spacing of 1.5.

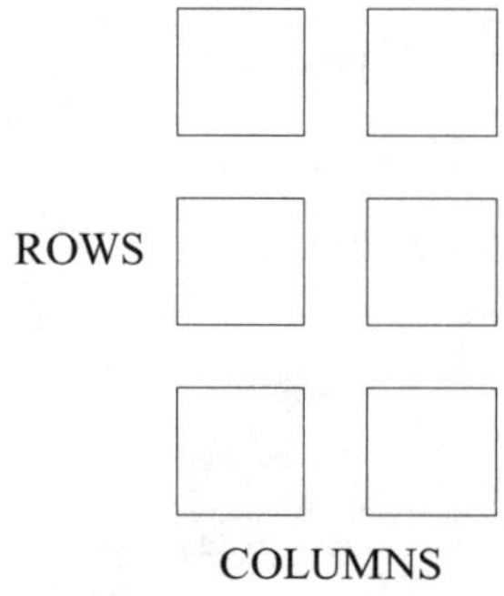

Rectangular Array Exercise

Solution

1. 

Invoke the Array command (array).

2. 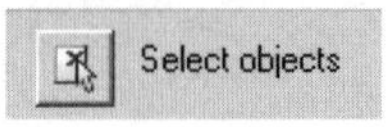

Pick the *Select objects button:*
Select the rectangle on the right.

3. 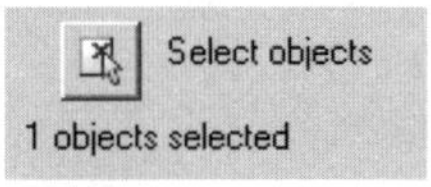

Select objects:
Press <ENTER> when it has been selected.
The dialog will show *1 object selected.*

4. 

Enable the Rectangular Array radio button.

5. 

In the Rows field: Type '3'

6. 

In the Columns field: Type '2'

7. 

In the Row offset: Type '1.5'

8. 

In the Column offset: Type '1.5'

9. 

Press the 'Preview' button.

10.
```
Pick or press Esc to return to dialog or <Right-click to accept array>:
```

If the array looks correct, RMB. Otherwise, LMB and check your settings.

Command Exercise

Exercise 6-7 – Rectangular Array at an Angle

Drawing Name: **arrayr2.dwg**
Estimated Time to Completion: 5 Minutes

Scope

Create a 3 x 2 rectangular array of the object with a spacing of 1.5 at a 30-degree angle.

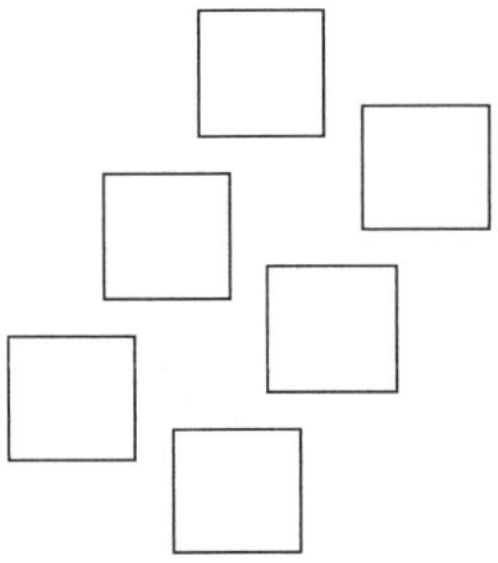

Rectangular Array Exercise

Solution

1. 

Invoke the Array command (array).

2. 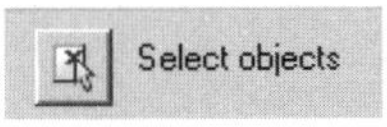

Pick the *Select objects button:*
Select the rectangle on the right.

3. 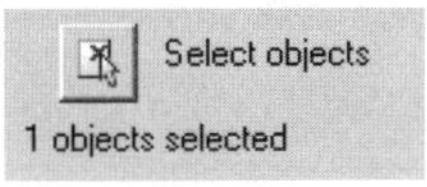

Select objects:
Press <ENTER> when it has been selected.
The dialog will show *1 objects selected.*

4. 

Enable the Rectangular Array radio button.

5. 

In the Rows field: Type '3'

6. 

In the Columns field: Type '2'

7. 

In the Row offset: Type '1.5'

8. 

In the Column offset: Type '1.5'

9. 

Set the Angle of array to '-30'.

10. 

Press the 'Preview' button.

11.

```
Pick or press Esc to return to dialog or <Right-click to accept array>:
```

If the array looks correct, press RMB; otherwise, select LMB and check your settings.

Command Exercise

Exercise 6-8 – Polar Array

Drawing Name: **arrayp1.dwg**
Estimated Time to Completion: 5 Minutes

Scope

Array the hex object using the polar array option as indicated in the drawing. The number of items is 8 (total).

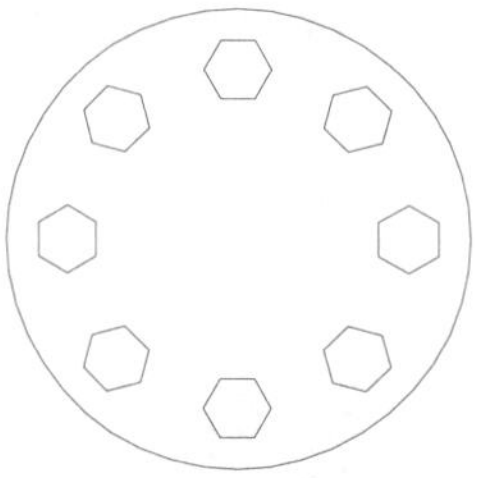

Polar Array Exercise

Solution

1.

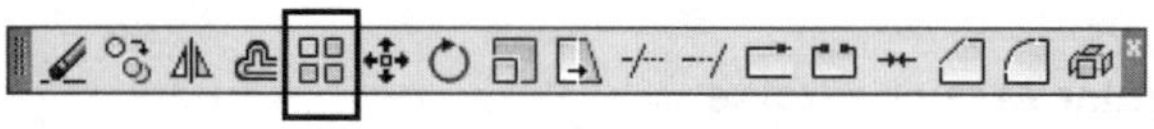

Invoke the Array command (array).

2.

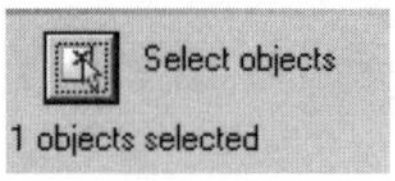

Press the *Select objects* button
Select the polygon on the right. The dialog will show *1 objects selected.*

3.

Enable the Polar Array option.

4.

Select the 'Pick Center Point' button.

5.

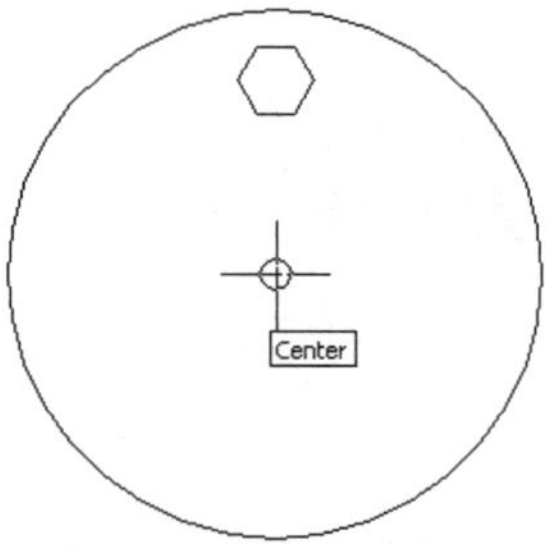

Pick the center of the circle as the base point.

6.

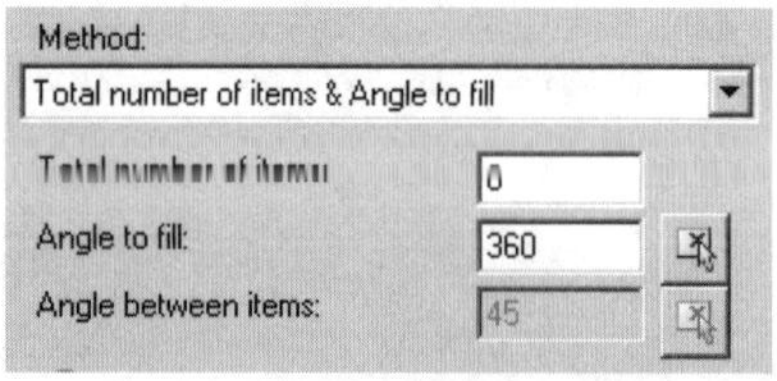

Set the Method to: *Total number of items & Angle to fill.*
In the number of items in the array field: Type '8'.
In the Angle to fill field: Accept the default of '360'.

7.

Place a check in the 'Rotate items as copied' box.
Press the 'Preview' button.

8.

```
Pick or press Esc to return to dialog or <Right-click to accept array>:
```

If the array looks correct, press 'Accept'; otherwise, select 'Modify" and check your settings.

Extra: *Undo the polar array and repeat the exercise. Do not rotate the objects as they are copied.*

Move

Command Locator

Toolbar Menu	**Modify**
Pull Down Menu	**Modify / Move**
Command	**Move**
Alias	**M**

Command Overview

To Move an object, pick the base point, drag the object and pick or use any of the methods previously discussed to input coordinates.

General Procedures

1. Invoke the Move Command.
2. Select the objects to Move, and press <ENTER>.
3. Pick a point on or near the object for the base point.
4. Drag the mouse and pick the new location or use absolute, relative coordinates, polar coordinates, or the direct distance method to relocate the object.

Tips & Tricks

- Use Object Snaps for picking the base point and the new location.
- If using the direct distance to relocate the object, be sure ORTHO is ON.
- Remember to use the pick button (LMB) to select the base point and the new location of the object.
- Be sure SNAP (in the Status Bar) is off, when selecting objects.
- Use ORTHO TRACKING to help align objects being moved.

Command Exercise

Exercise 6-9 – Move

Drawing Name: **move1.dwg**
Estimated Time to Completion: 5 Minutes

Scope

Turn Snap off and Move the blue objects into the red rectangle.

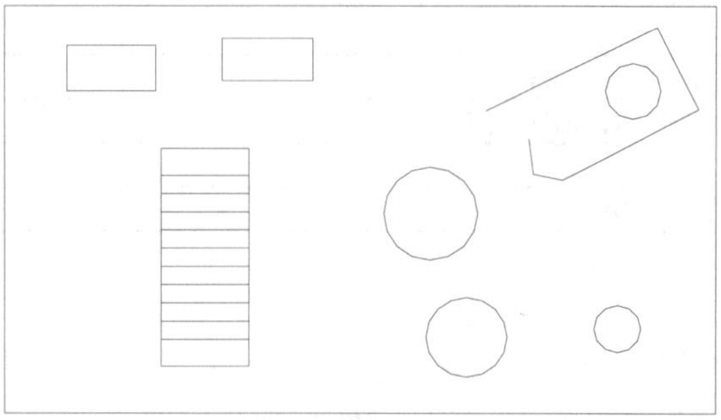

Move Exercise

Solution

1. Invoke the Move command (m or move).

2. *Select objects:*
   Start by selecting a rectangle with the LMB. Close the selection set with the <ENTER> key or RMB.
3. *Specify base point or displacement:*
   You may want to turn OSNAP off. Use your LMB to select in the middle of the rectangle. This is the point from which the rectangle will be moved.
4. *Specify second point of displacement or <use first point as displacement>:*
   Move your mouse to position the rectangle in the in the red box and press the LMB to specify the second point of displacement.
5. Repeat the Move command with the RMB (m, move or <ENTER>).

6. *Select objects:*
   Select another object.
7. *Specify base point or displacement:*
   Pick near the middle of the object. This will be the point from which it is moved.
8. *Specify second point of displacement or <use first point as displacement>:*
   Select a point inside the red box for the second point.
9. Repeat the Move command with the RMB (m, move or <ENTER>) and move the rest of the objects into the red box, one at a time or in groups.

> ***Extra:*** *Undo the command and repeat the exercise using different methods of selecting objects.*

Rotate

Command Locator

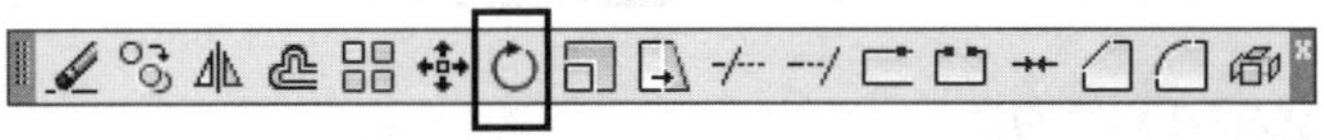

Toolbar Menu	**Modify / Rotate**
Pull Down Menu	**Modify / Rotate**
Command	**Rotate**
Alias	**RO**
RMB Shortcut Menu	**Drawing Window**

Command Overview

Rotate selected objects in a counter clockwise direction with a positive rotation angle. Rotate in a clockwise direction with a negative angle. The Reference option permits the user to reference the angle of an existing line in the drawing and type a new angle.

General Procedures

To use the Rotate command:

1. Invoke the Rotate Command.
2. Select the objects to rotate, and press <ENTER>.
3. Pick a base point on or near the object.
4. Type the rotation angle or drag the mouse and pick the rotation angle.

To use the Rotate command with the Reference option:

1. Invoke the Rotate Command.
2. Select the objects to rotate, and press <ENTER>.
3. Pick a base point on or near the object. Type R for reference, or press the RMB and select Reference from the shortcut menu.
4. Using Object Snap, select the endpoints of the line to reference. This will determine the precise reference angle.
5. Type the new rotation angle.

Tips & Tricks

- Turn ORTHO on to rotate in 90 degree increments, relative to the current rotation angle.
- When rotating the object with ORTHO on, keep the cursor close to the base point to make it easier to rotate the object.
- Toggle through the Coordinates display by selecting F6 or double clicking the coordinates in the Status Bar to view the distance and angle option.
- When using the Reference option to straighten objects, it is more accurate to reference the angle of a line in the drawing using the object snap, than to try to find the angle of the line and rotate it in the negative direction.
- Objects will be rotated around the rotation base point.
- The Rotate Command now has a COPY option, so that you can create a copy in addition to rotating selected objects.

Command Exercise

Exercise 6-10 – Rotate

Drawing Name: **rotate1.dwg**
Estimated Time to Completion: 5 Minutes

Scope

Rotate the objects as indicated in the drawing.

Rotate Exercise

Solution

1. Invoke the Rotate command (rotate).

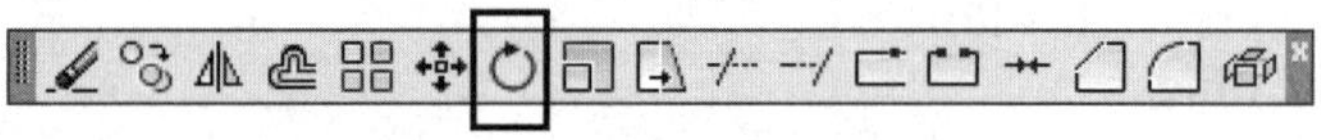

2. *Select objects:*
   Select the box and text on the left.
3. *Select objects:*
   Press <ENTER> to close the selection set.
4. *Specify base point:*
   Pick a point inside the rectangle. This is the point about which the objects will be rotated.
5. *Specify rotation angle or [Reference]:*
   Type '45' and press <ENTER>.
6. Repeat the Rotate command with the RMB (rotate or <ENTER>).

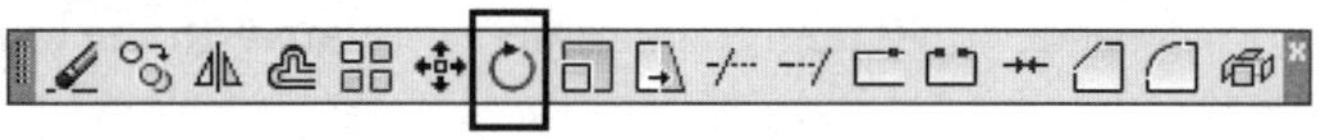

7. *Select objects:*
   Select the box and text on the right.
8. *Select objects:*
   Press <ENTER> to close the selection set.
9. *Specify base point:*
   Toggle ORTHO on. Pick a point inside the box on the right with the LMB.
10. *Specify rotation angle or [Reference]:*
    Drag the mouse upward and click to rotate the objects 90 degrees counter clockwise.

Command Exercise

Exercise 6-11 – Rotate

Drawing Name: **rotate2.dwg**
Estimated Time to Completion: 5 Minutes

Scope

Straighten the object using the reference option with rotate.

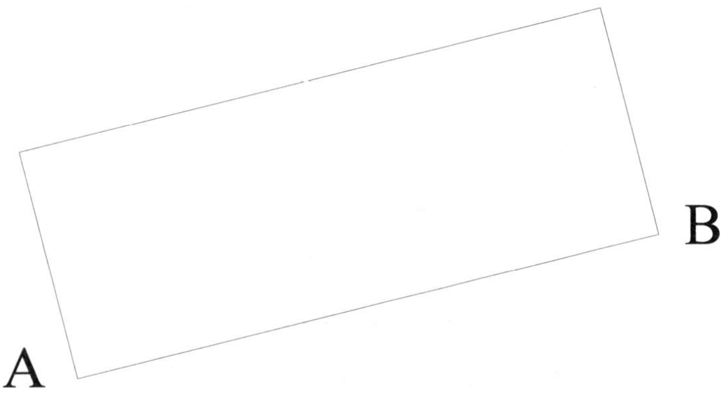

Rotate Exercise

Solution

1. Invoke the Rotate command (rotate).

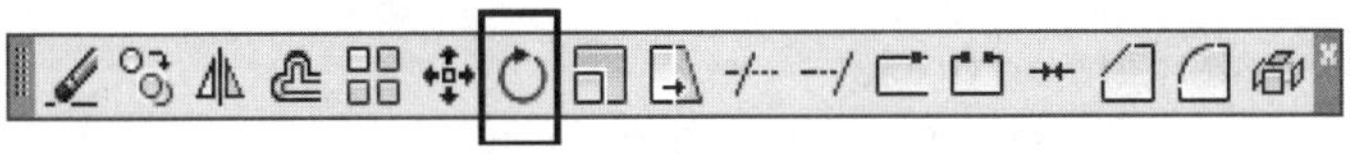

2. *Select objects:*
   Select the rectangle with the LMB.
3. *Select objects:*
   Close the selection set by pressing <ENTER>
4. *Specify base point:*
   Pick the lower left corner of the rectangle (A). Remember to use Object Snaps.
5. *Specify rotation angle or [Reference]:*
   Right-click in the drawing area and select 'Reference' or type 'R' for Reference and press <ENTER>.
6. *Specify the reference angle <0>:*
   Pick the same point on the rectangle (A).
7. *Specify second point:*
   Pick the lower right corner of the rectangle (B).
8. *Specify the new angle or [Points] <0>:*
   Type '0' at the command line and press <ENTER>.
   (The Points option allows you to select two points to specify the new angle.)

Command Exercise

Exercise 6-12 – Rotate and Copy

Drawing Name: **rotate3.dwg**
Estimated Time to Completion: 5 Minutes

Scope

Use Rotate to Copy and Rotate an object.

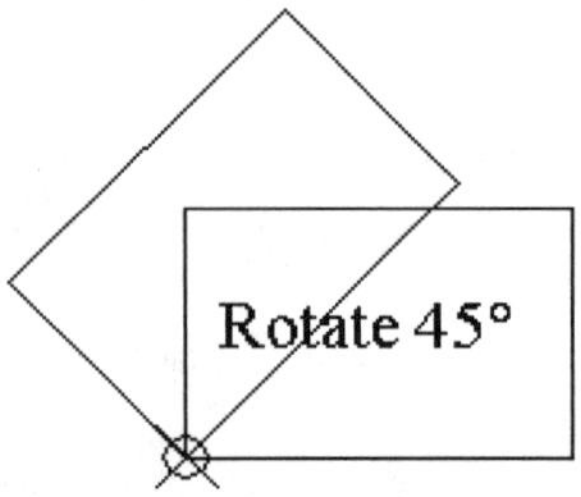

Rotate and Copy Exercise

Solution

1. Invoke the Rotate command (rotate).

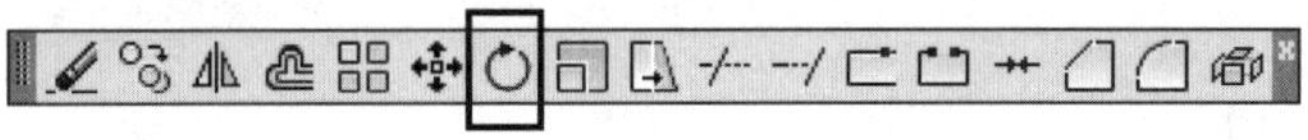

2.

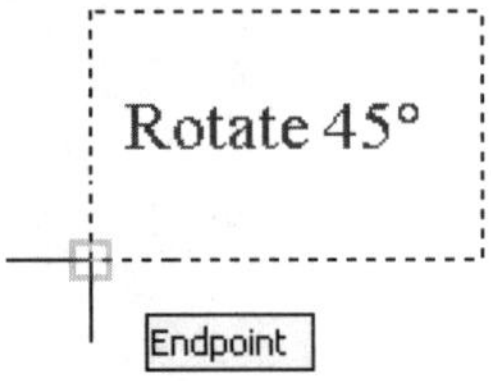

Select the rectangle on the left.
Select the lower left corner as the base point.

3.

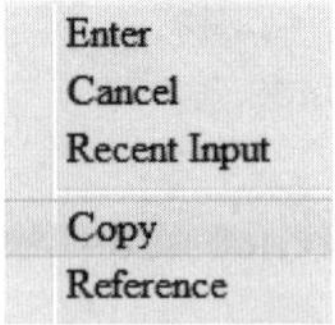

RMB and select **Copy**.

4.

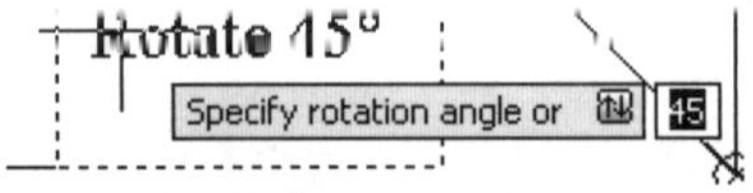

Type '**45**' as the rotation angle.

Scale

Command Locator

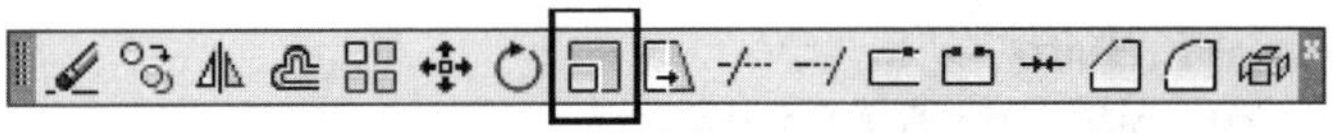

Toolbar Menu	**Modify / Scale**
Pull Down Menu	**Modify / Scale**
Command	**Scale**
Alias	**SC**
RMB Shortcut Menu	**Drawing Window**

Command Overview

Scale objects *up* or *down* from a selected base point. Use the Reference option to reference a known length, then type the new length to scale the object proportionately.

General Procedures

To use the Scale command:

1. Invoke the Scale Command.
2. Select the objects to Scale, and press <ENTER>.
3. Pick a base point on or near the object.
4. Type the Scale Factor and press <ENTER>.

To use the Scale command with the Reference option:

1. Invoke the Scale Command.
2. Select the objects to Scale, and press <ENTER>.
3. Pick a base point on or near the object. Type R for reference (and press <ENTER>), or press the RMB and select Reference from the shortcut menu.
4. Use Object Snaps, to specify the reference length, or type the reference length, if known.
5. Type the new length.

Command Exercise

Exercise 6-13 – Scale

Drawing Name: **scale1.dwg**
Estimated Time to Completion: 5 Minutes

Scope

Scale the images as indicated in the drawing.

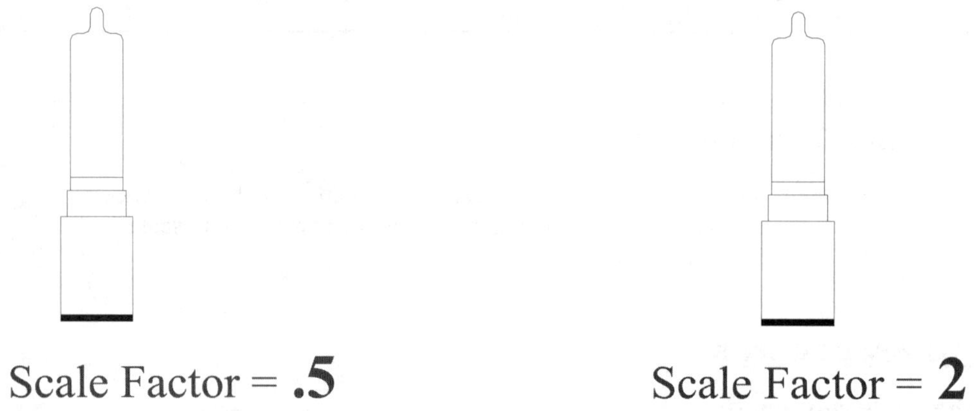

Scale Exercise

Solution

1. Invoke the Scale command (scale).

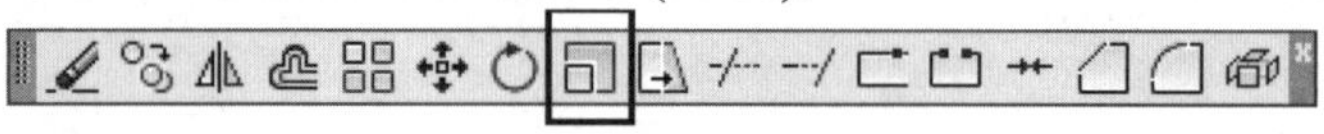

2. *Select objects:*
   Select the objects that make up the part on the left.
3. *Select objects:*
   Press <ENTER> to close the selection set.
4. *Specify base point:*
   Select a point near the base of the part.
5. *Specify scale factor or [Reference]:*
   Type '0.5' and press <ENTER>.
6. Repeat the Scale command with the RMB (scale or <ENTER>).

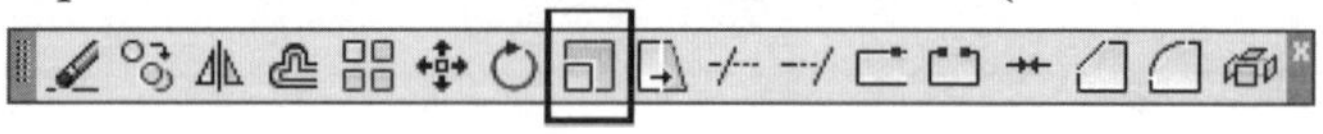

7. *Select objects:*
   Select the objects that make up the part on the right.
8. *Select objects:*
   Press <ENTER> to close the selection set.
9. *Specify base point:*
   Select a point near the base of the part.
10. *Specify scale factor or [Reference]:*
    Type '2' and <ENTER>.

Command Exercise

Exercise 6-14 – Scale

Drawing Name: **scale2.dwg**
Estimated Time to Completion: 5 Minutes

Scope

Using the Reference option, scale the image so that the overall height is 4.

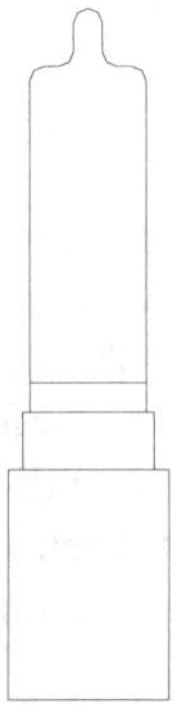

Scale Exercise

Solution

1. Invoke the Scale command (scale).

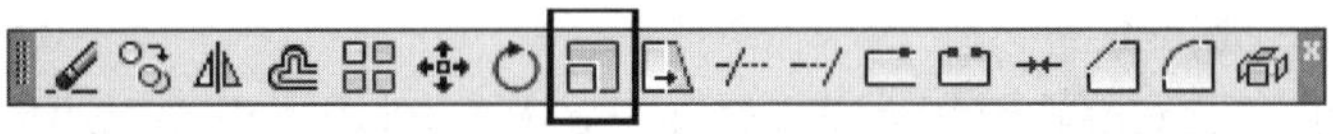

2. *Select objects:*
   Select the objects that make up the part.
3. *Select objects:*
   Press <ENTER> to close the selection set.
4. *Specify base point:*
   Select the Midpoint of the base with the LMB. Remember to use the Object Snap.
5. *Specify scale factor or [Reference]:*
   Right-click in the drawing window and select 'Reference' or type 'R' for Reference and press <ENTER>.
6. *Specify reference length <1>:*
   Pick the Midpoint or Quadrant of the top with the LMB.
7. *Specify second point:*
   Pick the Midpoint or Perpendicular to the bottom with the LMB. Remember to use the running object snap.
8. *Specify new length:*
   Type '4' and press <ENTER>.

Stretch

Command Locator

Toolbar Menu	**Modify / Stretch**
Pull Down Menu	**Modify→Stretch**
Command	**Stretch**
Alias	**s**

Command Overview

Learning how to use the Stretch command is tricky at first. Always use a Crossing Window or Crossing Polygon to select the objects to stretch. The endpoints or vertices, of the objects selected will be stretched, or *moved*, to a new location, while the objects outside of the selection window will remain anchored. Once the objects are selected, press <ENTER> and pick a base point, then with ORTHO on, drag the object in the desired direction and type a distance.

General Procedures

1. Begin the Stretch command.
2. Select objects using the automatic Crossing Window option (right to left). Frame the object so that the endpoints to be moved are completely within the selection box.
3. Pick a base point on or near the object.
4. Select the second point of displacement drag the object in the desired direction (with ORTHO on) and type the distance.

Tips & Tricks

- Circles can not be stretched with this command, but can be stretched using grips (grips will be covered at the end of this chapter).
- Objects that are completely within the selection window will be moved.
- If a crossing window is not used, only the objects completely within the window will be moved, and not stretched.
- Blocks can not be stretched.
- When selecting the Second point of displacement, use the direct distance method with ORTHO on. Drag the cursor in the desired direction and type the distance.
- When selecting points (base point or second point of displacement), picking points with or without Object Snap, Relative Coordinates, or Polar Coordinates are all acceptable methods. However, the direct distance with ORTHO on works best.

Command Exercise

Exercise 6-15 – Stretch

Drawing Name: **stretch1.dwg**
Estimated Time to Completion: 5 Minutes

Scope

Use the crossing window option to select objects to stretch.

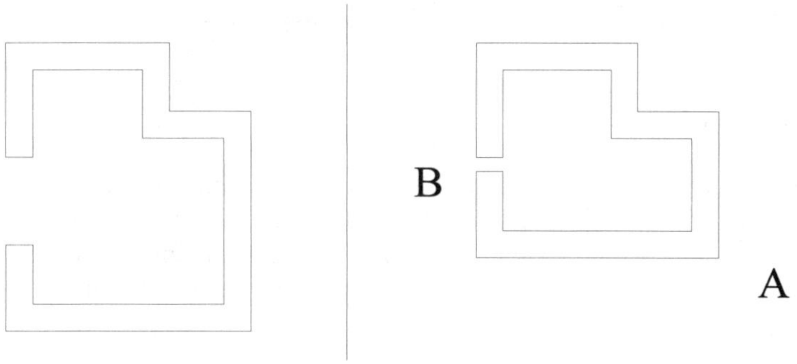

Stretch Exercise

Solution

1. Invoke the Stretch command (stretch).

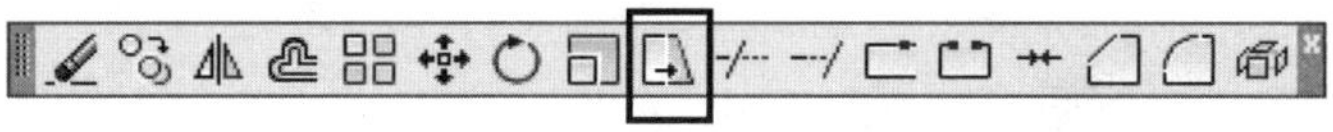

2. *Select objects:*
   Use a crossing window to select the lower half of the object.
3. *Select objects:*
   Press <ENTER> to continue.
4. *Specify base point or displacement:*
   Turn ORTHO on and pick a point from which the part will be stretched with the LMB. ***(Hint:** Using the midpoint of the bottom horizontal line works well.)*
5. *Specify second point of displacement:*
   Drag the mouse downward. Type '1' at the command line and press <ENTER>.

> ***Tip:** Notice that the line segments that are fully contained in the crossing selection window are moved the lines that are crossed are stretched.*

Trim

Command Locator

Toolbar Menu	**Modify / Trim**
Pull Down Menu	**Modify / Trim**
Command	**Trim**
Alias	**TR**
RMB Shortcut Menu	**Drawing Window**

Command Overview

Trim objects to a cutting edge. The cutting edge may or may not cross the object to trim. If the objects do not cross or intersect, the Edge mode must be set to "Extend". The Project option is for 3D. Undo is an option that can be used within the Trim command, without completely exiting the command.

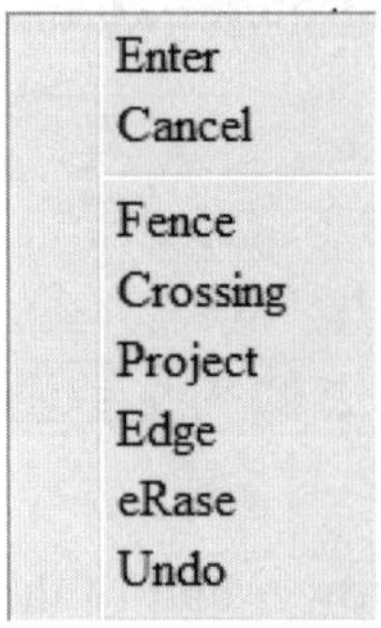

Trim Shortcut Menu

Trim Option	Overview
Fence	When this option is selected, the user draws an imaginary fence line that is used as the cutting edge.
Crossing	The crossing option is used to designate the objects which are to be retained following the Trim operation.
Project	The Project option is used when you are working in 3D space and you wish to trim using objects which may be at a different elevation or work plane.
Edge	The Edge object is also used when working in 3D space to designate either a projected edge or an edge which is actually intersecting the object to be trimmed.
Erase	Deletes selected objects – temporarily suspends the trim command to allow the user to erase unwanted objects and then returns to the Trim command.

General Procedures

Regular Trim (No Extend):

1. Invoke the Trim command.
2. Select the cutting edges, and press <ENTER>.
3. Select the objects to trim.

Trim using the Extend option:

1. Invoke the Trim command.
2. Select the cutting edges, and press <ENTER>.
3. Type E (for Edge) and press <ENTER>.
4. Type E (for Extend) and press <ENTER>.
5. Select the objects to trim.

Tips & Tricks

- Selecting Multiple lines to trim is acceptable, such as lines that trim to each other.
- An object must be crossed by the cutting edge to be trimmed (unless the Edge mode Extend option is selected and the object would cross the cutting edge if extended).
- A circle must be crossed twice by the cutting edge in order to be trimmed.
- The object will be trimmed on the side of the cutting edge where it is selected.

Command Exercise

Exercise 6-16 – Trim

Drawing Name: **trim1.dwg**
Estimated Time to Completion: 5 Minutes

Scope

Trim the lines outside the red box select the line individually. Repeat the exercise but select the lines to trim using the Fence (F) option.

Trim Exercise

Solution

1. Invoke the Trim command (trim).
2. *Select objects:*
   Use the LMB to select the red box as the cutting edges.
3. *Select objects:*
   Press <ENTER> to finish selecting cutting edges.
4. *Select object to trim or [Project/Edge/Undo]:*
   Use the left mouse button to select the portion of the top black line that extends outside the left side of the red box.
5. *Select object to trim or [Project/Edge/Undo]:*
   Repeat the process for all the lines along the left side of the red box. Press <ENTER> when finished.
6. Repeat the Trim command with the RMB (trim or <ENTER>).

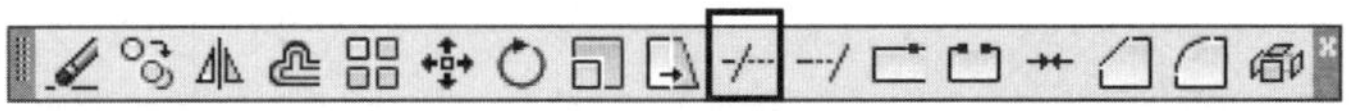

7. *Select objects:*
   Use the LMB to select the red box as the cutting edges.
8. *Select objects:*
   Press <ENTER> to finish selecting cutting edges.
9. *Select object to trim or [Project/Edge/Undo]:*
   Type 'F' at the command line for Fence and press <ENTER>.
10. *First fence point:*
    Create a fence line that cuts all the line segments that extend outside the red box on the right.
11. *Specify endpoint of line or [Undo]:*
    Finish creating the fence and press <ENTER> to trim the selected line segments.
12. *Select object to trim or [Project/Edge/Undo]:*
    Press <ENTER> to finish the exercise.

Extra: *Undo all the trimming and try removing the lines inside the red box. Undo again. Can a cutting edge be trimmed? Try it. Select all lines as the cutting edge, then trim the red rectangle and the lines.*

Extend

Command Locator

Toolbar Menu	**Modify / Extend**
Pull Down Menu	**Modify / Extend**
Command	**Extend**
Alias	**EX**
RMB Shortcut Menu	**Drawing Window**

Command Overview

Extend objects to a boundary, by selecting the object towards the end to be extended. The boundary may or may not reach the object being extended. If the objects do not reach the boundary, the Edge mode must be set to "Extend". Typically this option is set to "No Extend". The Project option is for 3D. Undo can be used as an option within the Extend command without completely exiting the command.

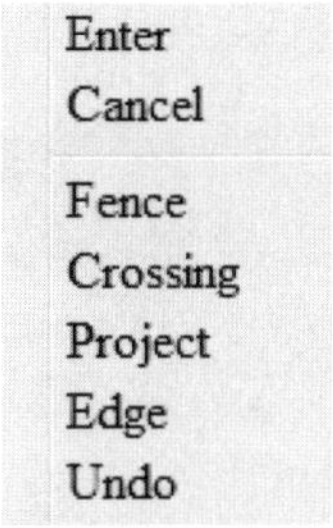

Extend Shortcut Menu

Extend Option	Overview
Fence	When this option is selected, the user draws an imaginary fence line that is used as the cutting edge.
Crossing	The crossing option is used to designate the objects which are to be retained following the Trim operation.
Project	The Project option is used when you are working in 3D space and you wish to trim using objects which may be at a different elevation or work plane.
Edge	The Edge object is also used when working in 3D space to designate either a projected edge or an edge which is actually intersecting the object to be trimmed.

General Procedures

Regular Extend (No Extend):

1. Invoke the Extend command.
2. Select the boundary edges, and press <ENTER>.
3. Select the objects to extend towards the boundary edge.

Trim using the Extend option:

1. Invoke the Extend command.
2. Select the boundary edges, and press <ENTER>.
3. Type E (for Edge) and press <ENTER>.
4. Type E (for the Extend option) and press <ENTER>.
5. Select the objects to extend towards the boundary edge.

Tips & Tricks

- The Undo option will undo one step at a time, without exiting the Extend command.
- An object must be able to meet the boundary edge to be trimmed (unless the Edge mode Extend option is selected and the object would meet the boundary edge if extended).
- Select the object to Extend anywhere on the half that is closest to the boundary.

Command Exercise

Exercise 6-17 – Extend

Drawing Name: **extend1.dwg**
Estimated Time to Completion: 5 Minutes

Scope

Extend the horizontal line to the sides of the red rectangle.

Extend Exercise

Solution

1. Invoke the Extend command (extend).

2. *Select objects:*
   Pick the red rectangle with the LMB as the boundary edge.
3. *Select objects:*
   Close the selection of boundary edges by pressing <ENTER>.
4. *Select object to extend or [Project/Edge/Undo]:*
   Pick on the left side of the top dark line. Notice that the line extends from the side of the line you have selected.
5. *Select object to extend or [Project/Edge/Undo]:*
   Pick the other side of the same line.
6. *Select object to extend or [Project/Edge/Undo]:*
   Repeat the process with the rest of the lines to finish the exercise.

Extra: *Create a line segment that is outside the red box. Start the Extend command and use the red box as the boundary edge. Extend the line to the outside of the rectangle and then extend the line through the rectangle to the opposite side.*

Tip: *You can extend Arcs to a boundary. Try It.*

Fillet

Command Locator

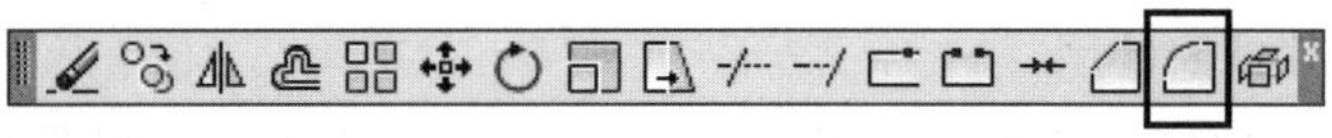

Toolbar Menu	**Modify / Fillet**
Pull Down Menu	**Modify / Fillet**
Command	**Fillet**
Alias	**F**
RMB Shortcut Menu	**Drawing Window**

Command Overview

Radius corners with the FILLET command. Clean up corners with the Fillet radius set to 0.

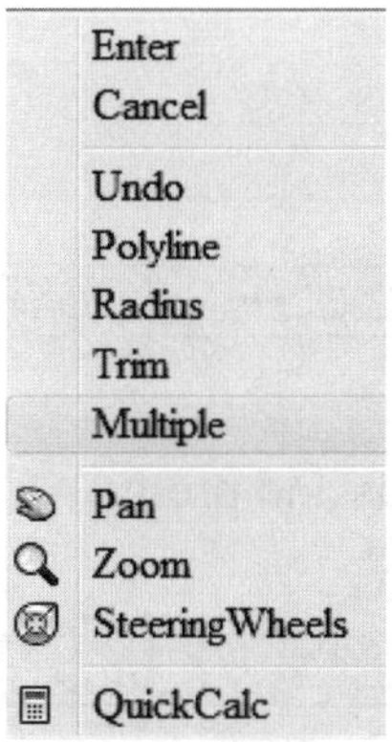

Fillet Shortcut Menu Options

Fillet Option	Overview
Select first object	This is the default selection. Select the first object towards the corner to fillet.
Select second object	Select the second object towards the corner to fillet. This object must be adjacent or parallel to the first line selected.
Polyline	Type P to fillet all of the corners of a polyline at once.
Radius	Type R to change the Radius of the fillet. This setting remains until it is changed again. The default radius setting when starting a new drawing is .50.
Trim	Type T to invoke the Trim or No Trim options. No trim (N) will leave the original lines when making a fillet.
Multiple	Type U to create more than one fillet. Works similar to the Multiple option of the Copy command.

General Procedures

1. Begin the Fillet command.
2. To change the current radius, type R (and <ENTER>). Type the desired radius (and <ENTER>). Press <ENTER> to repeat to the Fillet command.
3. Select the first object, then select the second object.

Tips Tricks

- It is not necessary to set the radius to fillet parallel lines.
- Fillet will now work if the lines or arcs are separate polylines, or at the arc intersections of polylines.
- Set a Radius value of 0 to create a 90-degree angle and trim corners.

Command Exercise

Exercise 6-18 – Fillet

Drawing Name: **fillet1.dwg**
Estimated Time to Completion: 5 Minutes

Scope

Use the fillet command with a fillet radius of 0, to clean up the corners of the lines as indicated. Remember to change the fillet radius first.

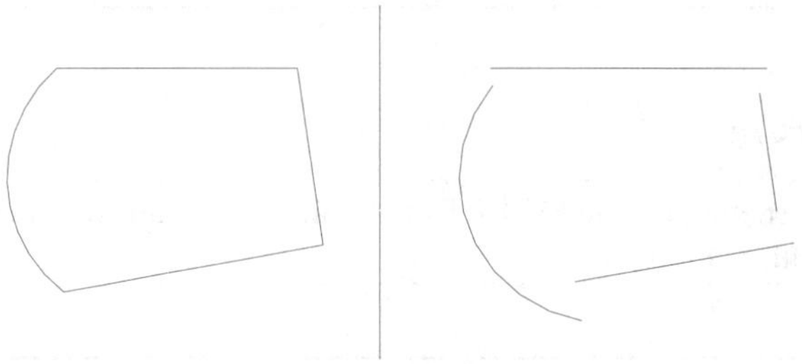

Fillet Exercise

Solution

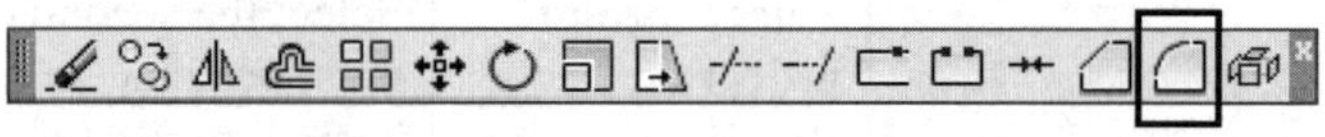

1. Invoke the Fillet command (f or fillet).
2. *Select first object or [Polyline/Radius/Trim]:*
   Right-click in the drawing window and select 'Radius' or type 'R' for Radius and press <ENTER>.

3. *Specify fillet radius <0.5000>:*
   Type '0' and press <ENTER>.
4. *Select first object or [Polyline/Radius/Trim]:*
   Use the LMB to select the arc.
5. *Select second object:*
   Use the LMB to select the top line segment.

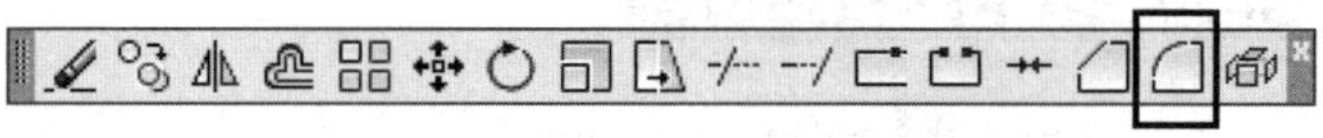

6. Repeat the Fillet command with the RMB (f, fillet or <ENTER>).
7. *Select first object or [Polyline/Radius/Trim]:*
   Select the top line with the LMB.
8. *Select second object:*
   Pick the line on the right side with the LMB.
9. Continue the process of repeating the fillet command, selecting two adjacent segments to cleanup the corners of the object.

Tips & Tricks

- Notice you can not select all of the segments in one step. You must repeat the fillet command for each corner, unless the object is a polyline and the Fillet command is used with the Polyline option. Try it on a rectangle.
- It is not necessary to set the radius to fillet parallel lines.

Undo and Redo

Command Locator

Toolbar Menu	**Standard / Undo and Standard / Redo**
Pull Down Menu	**Edit / Undo and Edit / Redo**
Command	**Undo or Redo**
Alias	**U (no alias for redo)**
RMB Shortcut Menu	**Drawing Window (for Undo options)**

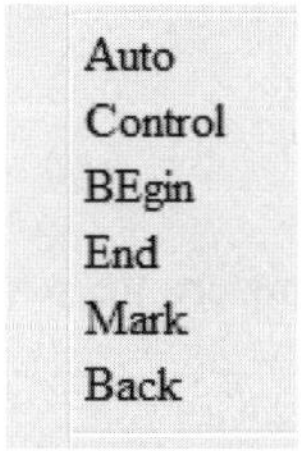

Undo Shortcut Menu

Command Overview

Type U for undo or select the button in the Standard Toolbar. This will reverse previous commands. Undo can be taken all the way back to the beginning of the drawing. Redo must immediately follow the Undo command and will reverse the last Undo commands in order

General Procedures

1. Select the Undo button or type U at the command line, and press <ENTER>.
2. Press the <ENTER> key to repeat the undo command until satisfied.

Tips & Tricks

- Be careful not to press the <ENTER> key too many times.
- Use U rather than typing the entire UNDO command.
- The Undo shortcut menu appears only when the entire word 'UNDO' is typed.
- Use the **Mark** option for Undo to mark a point before you start an edit sequence. You can then undo back to the point you have bookmarked.

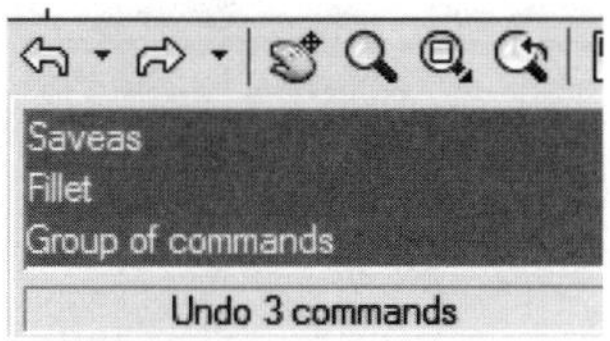

The UNDO and REDO tools have a drop-down list to help decide how far back or forward you want to undo/redo.

You can not skip commands on this list or select individual commands using the CTL key. You can only select commands in the order they were given.

Command Exercise

Exercise 6-19 – Undo and Redo

Drawing Name: **undo1.dwg**
Estimated Time to Completion: 5 Minutes

Scope:

Draw several lines, circles and rectangles. Undo your drawing several steps back. Next try to Redo several steps. Notice that both Undo and Redo keep track of the commands issued.

Solution:

1. Invoke the Line command (l or line) and create several lines on the drawing.

2. Invoke the Circle command (c or circle) and create several circles on the drawing.

3. Invoke the Rectangle command (rectang) and create several rectangles on the drawing.

4. Invoke the Erase command (e or erase) and erase one or two of the objects you have just created.

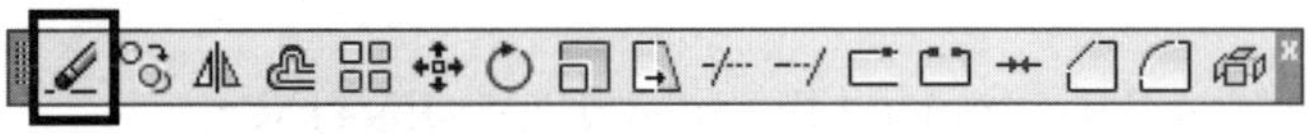

5. Invoke the Undo command by using the standard Windows icon at the top of the screen or typing 'U' at the command line.

6. Repeat the command until about half of your objects are gone.

7. Invoke the REDO command by using the standard Windows icon at the top of the screen.

Section Exercise

Exercise 6-20 – Modify Commands

Drawing Name: **Lesson 6 aec.dwg**
Estimated Time to Completion: **15 Minutes**

Scope

Using the modify commands, furnish the apartment as shown.

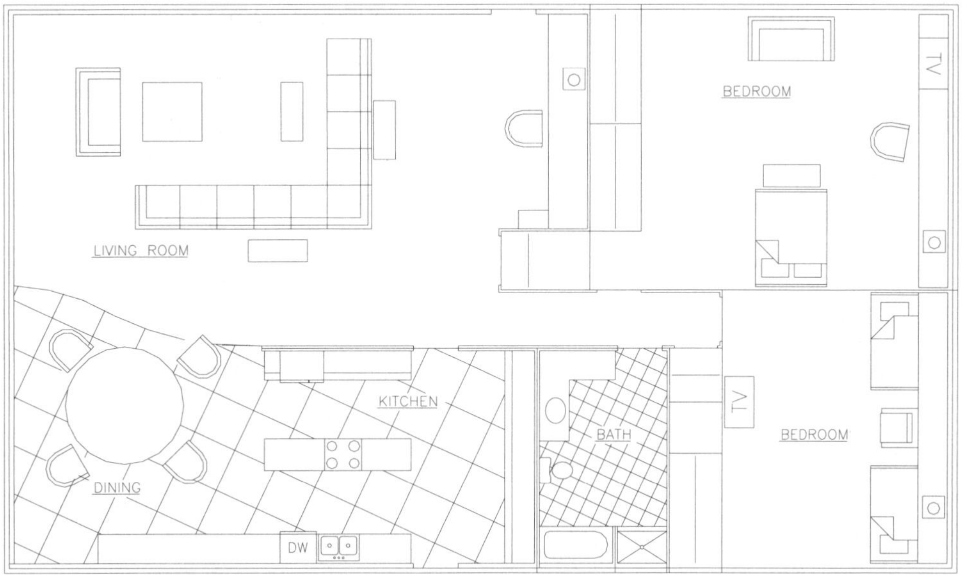

Modify Commands Exercise

Hints

1. Copy the chairs and sofa sections.
2. Use the mirror command to create the second single bed.
3. Move most of the pieces into place.

Review Questions

1. You construct a circle. You now want to copy the circle. What option can you use at the Select objects prompt to select the last object you created.

2. You wish to mirror some text. What value should MIRRTEXT be set to ensure that the text mirrors properly?

3. You need to duplicate an object in a rectangular pattern. What command allows you to do this?

4. You enter the TRIM command. When prompted to select the cutting edges, you press the <ENTER> key. What is the result?

5. You wish to offset an object and delete the source object. What is the best way to do this?

6. Identify the following icons that are all located in the Modify Toolbar:

   a.  ____________________

   b.  ____________________

   c.  ____________________

   d.  ____________________

   e.  ____________________

   f.  ____________________

   g.  ____________________

   h.  ____________________

   i.  ____________________

7. Typing the letter R at the command line invokes which command?
   - ❑ Scale
   - ❑ Rotate
   - ❑ Redraw
   - ❑ Regen

8. What does the R option stand for in the Scale command?

9. What does the U option stand for in the trim and extend commands?

10. Explain the similarities between the Copy and Move commands.

11. Can you trim a line that is acting as a cutting edge? Try It.

Review Answers

1. *Type L at the command line to select the last object created.*

2. *Set **MIRRTEXT** to 1.*

3. *ARRAY*

4. *All objects in the drawing may now be used as a cutting edge.*

5. *Use the **ERASE** option for OFFSET.*

6. *a. erase*
   b. copy
   c. mirror
   d. offset
   e. move
   f. scale
   g. rotate
   h. trim
   i. Extend

7. *Redraw*

8. *Reference*

9. *Undo*

10. *The steps to move an object are similar to copying an object. The major difference is that the copy command leaves the original object in place.*

11. *Yes. Cutting edges can be trimmed as long as they cross another object.*

NOTES:

Lesson 7.0 – Selecting Objects

Estimated Class Time: 1 hour

Objectives

This section introduces different methods of selecting objects and what to do with the objects once they are selected.

- **Selecting Objects**
- **Quick Select**
- **Quick Properties**

Selecting Objects

Command Overview

Knowing how to select objects is an important aspect to being able to manipulate objects inside of AutoCAD. Typically one begins with a specific Modify command, then selects the objects to modify. When an object is selected, it will be highlighted. Continue to select (or de-select) objects at the "Select objects" prompt, then press <ENTER> to continue. Objects can be selected individually, with the selection window, or by invoking one of the options at the *Select object* prompt.

Select Object Option	Key	Overview
Pick		Place the cursor over the object and pick it using the LMB
Window (Left to Right)		Making a selection window from left to right will create a window in which only the objects that are completely within the window will be selected. Place the cursor in the blank area of the drawing to the left of the objects to select and pick (LMB). Drag the mouse to the right to display the selection window, and pick the opposite corner.
Window (Right to Left)		Making a selection window from right to left will create a crossing window. All objects that are crossed by this window will be selected. Place the cursor in the blank area of the drawing to the right of the objects to select and pick (LMB). Drag the mouse to the left to display the selection window, the pick the opposite corner.
Deselecting objects		To deselect an previously selected object, press the shift key and select it again using any of the selection methods.
Last	L	At the Select objects prompt, type L to select the last object drawn.
All	ALL	At the Select objects prompt, type ALL to select all objects in the drawing.
Fence	F	At the Select objects prompt, type F to initiate the Fence option. All objects crossed by the fence line will be selected.
Window Polygon	WP	At the Select objects prompt, type WP to initiate a Window Polygon. Create the polygon by picking points around the objects to select. This will be easier if ORTHO is off. Only objects completely within the Window Polygon will be selected.
Crossing Polygon	CP	At the Select objects prompt, type CP to initiate a Crossing Polygon. Create the polygon by picking points that cross the objects to select. This will be easier if ORTHO is off. All objects crossed by the Polygon will be selected.
Previous	P	At the Select objects prompt, type P to select the Previous objects selected.

General Procedures

1. Select a Modify Command.
2. At the Select object prompt, initiate a Selection option (remember to press <ENTER>).
3. When all of the desired objects have been selected, press <ENTER> to continue with the Modify Command.

Tips & Tricks

- After objects have been selected, press <ENTER> to continue, even if All objects have been selected.
- If the selection window is accidentally initiated, try to utilize the crossing window to select the object. If there is no way to properly cross the object with a window to select it (right to left), make a window that selects nothing and try to select the object again, without exiting the modify command.
- It is very difficult to select objects if SNAP is ON.
- Objects may also be selected first, then a Modify command can be selected. When objects are selected first, they will be highlighted and will display small boxes at various points of the object. These boxes are called Grips and will be covered in greater detail in the section on Advanced Commands.
- At the Select objects prompt, type S to view the list of command line options. Type the capitalized letter(s) of the Select Object option, and press <ENTER>. It is not necessary to view this list in order to invoke the select object option.

Command Exercise

Exercise 7-1 – Selecting Objects

Drawing Name: **select1.dwg**
Estimated Time to Completion: 5 Minutes

Scope

Using the erase command, practice selecting the blue and red objects in the drawing. Optional: use the select objects as indicated. Use the fence (F) option to select the red lines on the left. Use the Window Polygon (WP) to select the blue objects on the right.

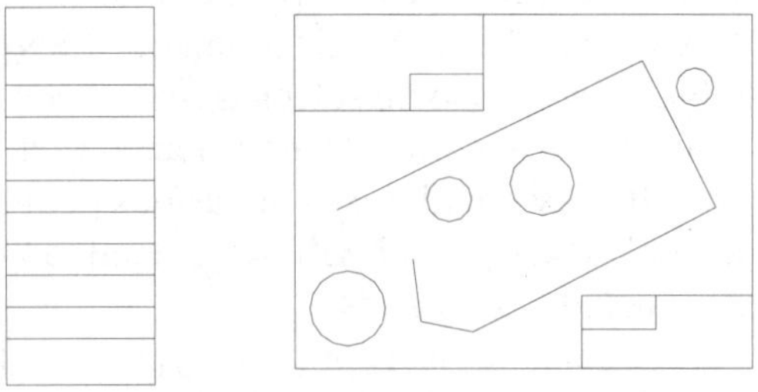

Selecting Objects Exercise

Solution

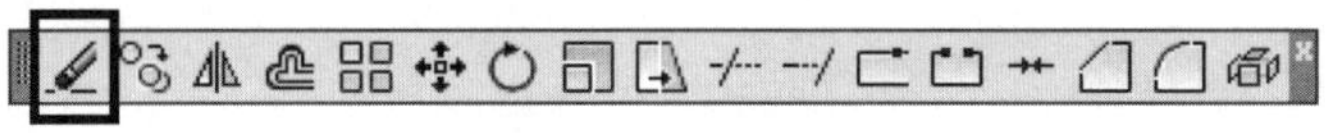

1. Invoke the Erase command (e or erase).
2. *Select objects:*
   Activate the Fence option by typing ‘F’ and pressing <ENTER>.
3. *First fence point:*
   Pick just above the top redline with the LMB. You may want to toggle OSNAP off.
4. *Specify endpoint of line or [Undo]:*
   Pick just below the bottom red line with the LMB. Press <ENTER> to close the selection set.
5. *Select objects:*
   Press <ENTER> again to erase the selected lines.
6. Repeat the Erase command with the RMB (e, erase or <ENTER>).
7. *Select objects:*
   Activate the Window Polygon option by typing ‘WP’ and pressing <ENTER> (make sure ORTHO is off).
8. *First polygon point:*
   Create a polygon around the blue objects similar to that shown in the figure to the right. Select the objects with a window polygon.

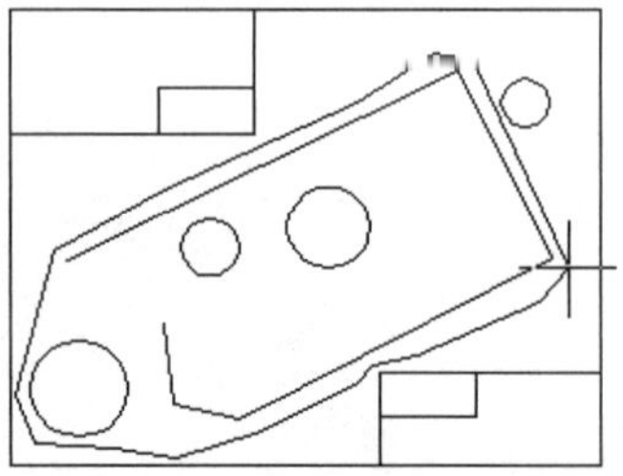

9. *Specify endpoint of line or [Undo]:*
   Press the <ENTER> key to close the selection set.
10. *Select objects:*
    Press the <ENTER> key again to complete the exercise by erasing the selection set.

Extra: *Use the Undo Command to bring the erased objects back. Experiment with different methods of selecting objects. Can you use the Fence selection method followed by the Crossing Polygon method to create a single selection set? Try it. Use the <Shift> key to remove an object from your selection set..*

Tip: *Dashed lines displayed on the screen when using selection methods indicates that objects that are touched or crossed are selected. Solid lines indicate that only objects fully contained will be selected.*

Command Exercise

Exercise 7-2 – Selecting Objects using Properties

Drawing Name: **select2.dwg**
Estimated Time to Completion: 5 Minutes

Scope

Use the Properties dialog to filter out selected objects.

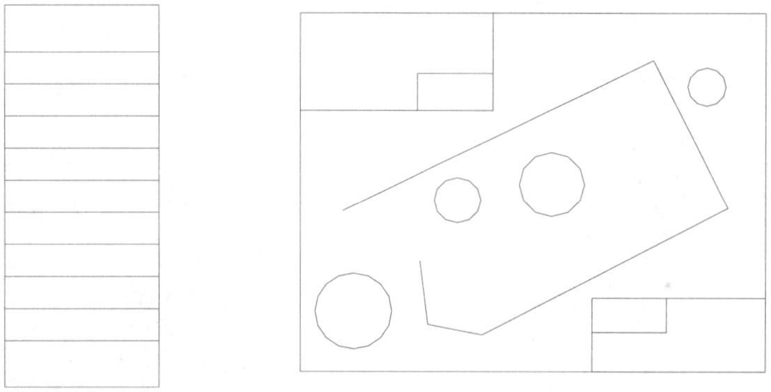

Selecting Objects Exercise

Solution

1. Window around all the objects so that they are highlighted.

2. 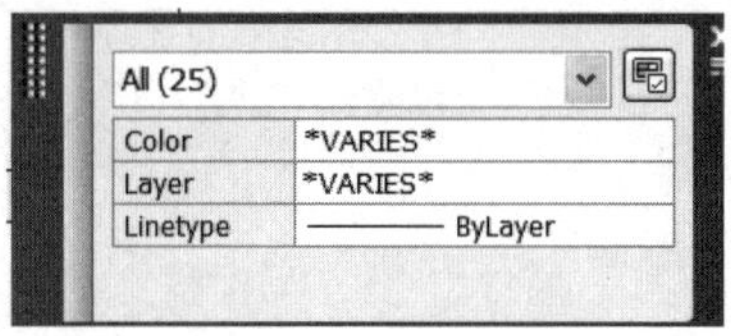

The Quick Properties dialog will appear automatically.

3. 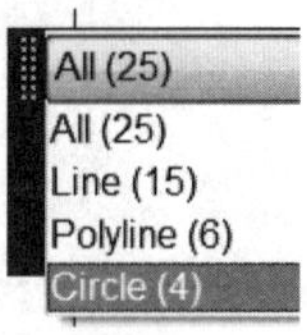

From the drop-down list, select **Circle**.

4. 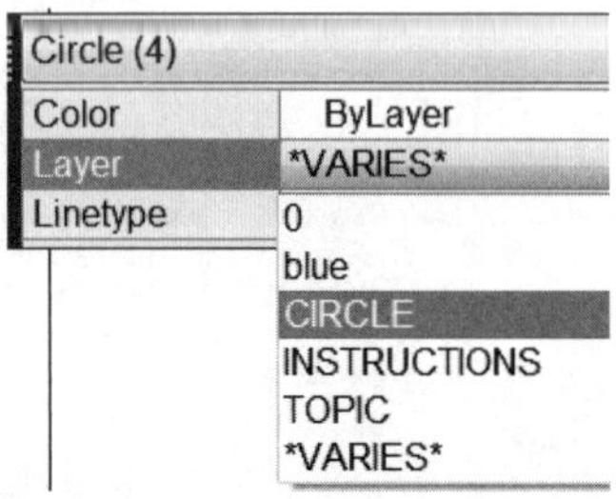

Select the **Circle** layer from the drop-down list for layers.

5. The circles will be moved to the circle layer.

Quick Select

Command Locator

Pull Down Menu	**Tools/Quick Select…**
Command	**qselect**
RMB Shortcut Menu	**Quick Select…**
Dialog Box	**Quick Select**

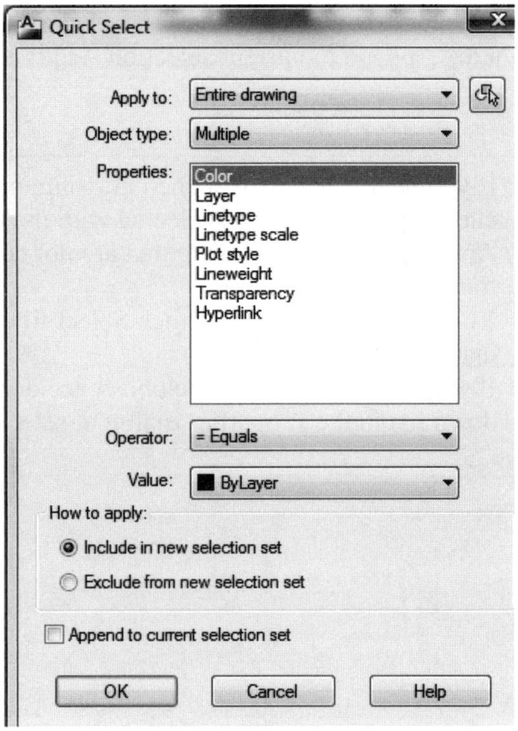

Quick Select Dialog Box

Command Overview

The Quick Select command allows you to specify filtering criteria and then decide how you want AutoCAD to create the selection set from that criterion. You are given the option to restrict the filter selection to currently selected entities or allow it to apply to the entire drawing. The Quick Select dialog box then presents you with the option to choose the object type. These options are "Multiple", or choose the drop down list which will display every type of entity currently in the drawing. After selecting the object type, you can further filter the selection set by choosing one of the entities properties and then selecting an operator and value for that property. You are then given the option of how to apply this filter to the current selection set. You can choose to Include or Exclude the filter entities from the current selection set. Lastly you can decide whether or not to append to the current selection set.

General Procedures

Using Quick Select to create a filtered selection set

1. Invoke the Quick Select command.
2. In the Quick Select dialog box, select the entity type in the Object Type drop down list.
3. In the Properties list, if applicable select a specific property for the objects being selected and set the operator and value fields accordingly.
4. Select whether to "Include objects in new selection set", or "Exclude objects from new selection set".
5. Select whether or not to "Append to current selection set."
6. Press 'OK'.

Tips & Tricks

- If you have a partially opened drawing, only objects that are currently loaded can be selected with the Quick Select command. Any objects in the drawing that are not currently loaded cannot be found by the command.
- You can also access the Quick Select filter using the Properties dialog.
- If you select more than one object accidentally, you can use the drop-down list in the Properties dialog to select the desired object.

Command Exercise

Exercise 7-3 –
Quick Select

Drawing Name: **qselect1.dwg**
Estimated Time to Completion: 10 Minutes

Scope

Using Quick Select, select all lines in the drawings and place on the lines layer. Next select all polylines in the drawing and place on the polyline layer. Repeat the process for all Mtext, Text, and blocks.

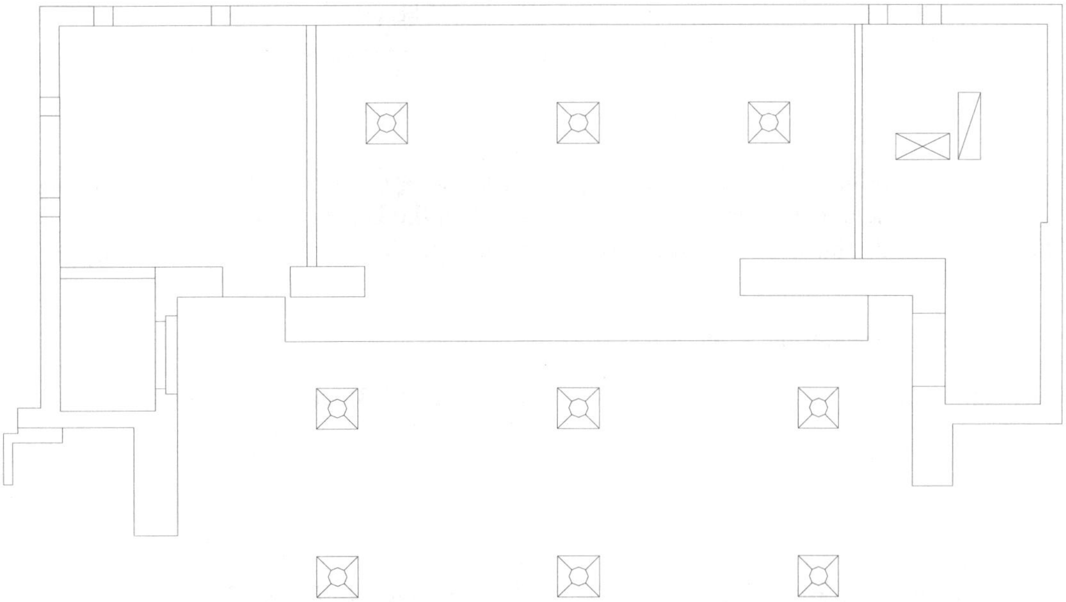

Quick Select Exercise

Solution

1. From the Tools menu, select **Quick Select**.

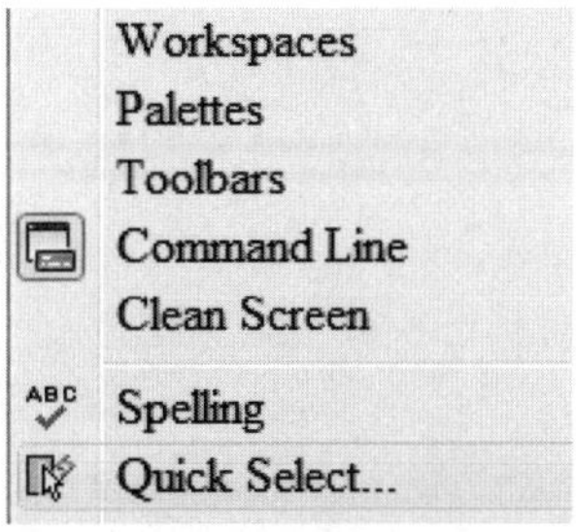

2. Select 'Line' in the Object Type drop down list.

3. In the properties section, select 'Color', 'Equal =' as Operator, and 'Bylayer' as value.

4. In the 'How to apply' section, choose 'Include in new selection set.'

5. Uncheck the 'Append to selection set' if it is currently checked and select OK.

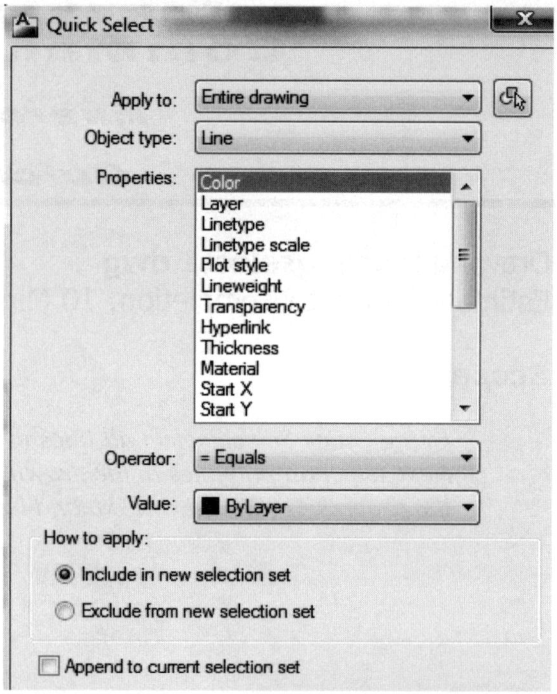

6. With all the lines selected in the drawing, use the Layer drop down list on the object properties tool bar and select the Lines layer. This will place the selected entities on the Lines layer.

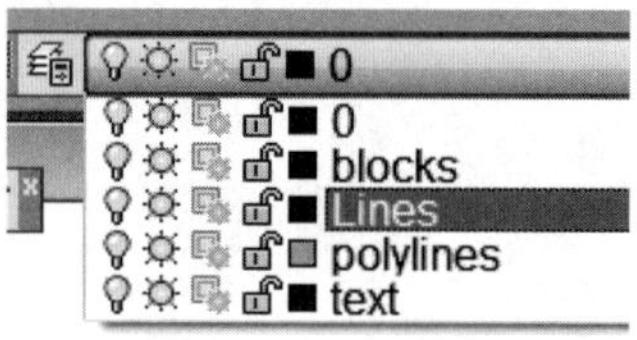

7. Press <ESC> to clear the selection set.

8. Repeat the above process for Polylines, Text, Mtext, and Blocks.

Extra: *You select several objects, including lines, circles, and rectangles. How can you filter the selection so that you change the layer of only the rectangles?*

Quick Properties

Command Locator

Status Toolbar	**Quick Properties toggle**
Command	**quickproperties**
RMB Shortcut Menu	**Quick Properties…**
Shortcut Key	**Ctl+Shift+P**
Dialog Box	**Quick Properties**

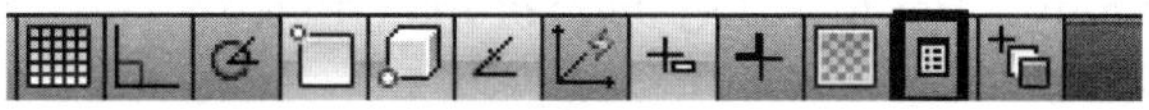

To enable Quick Properties, use the Quick Properties toggle located on the Status Bar.

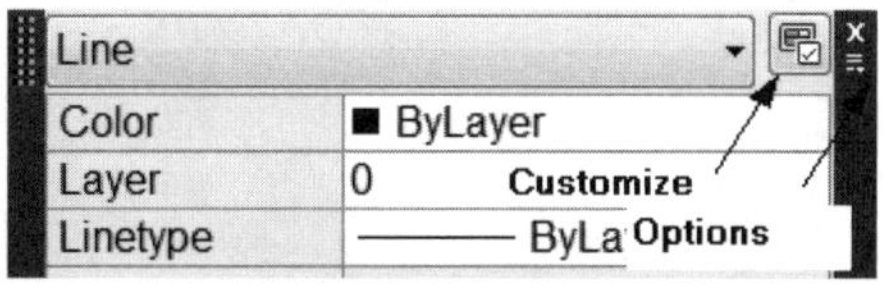

If no selection is made, the Quick Properties dialog is empty. You can customize what Properties are displayed/included in the dialog. The Options buttons allows you to control where the dialog will appear when any object is selected.

Command Exercise

Exercise 7-4 – Customize Quick Properties

Drawing Name: **qprops1.dwg**
Estimated Time to Completion: 5 Minutes

Scope

Learn how to set which fields will appear in the Quick Properties dialog.

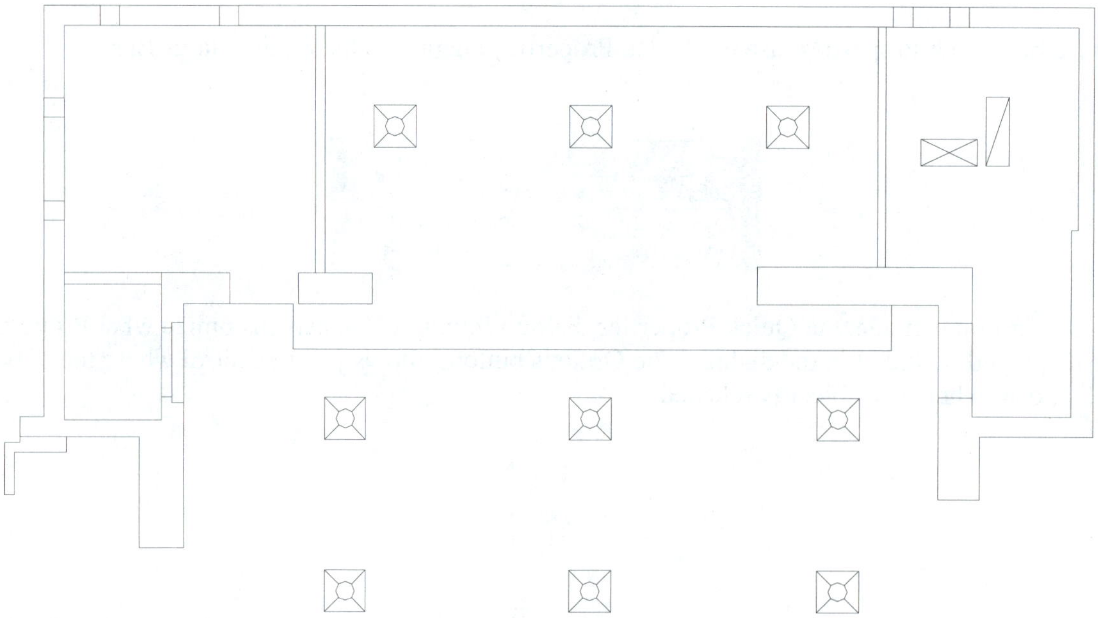

Quick Properties Exercise

Solution

1. 

Toggle **Quick Properties** ON using the Status Bar button.

2. 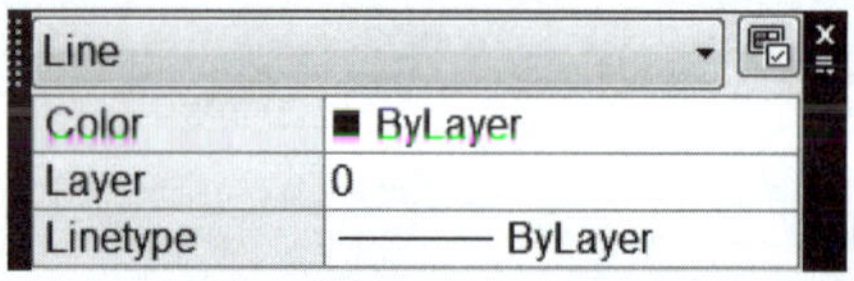

Select a line in the drawing.

The Quick Properties dialog will display information about the line.

Note which properties are listed: Color, Layer, Linetype, etc.

3. 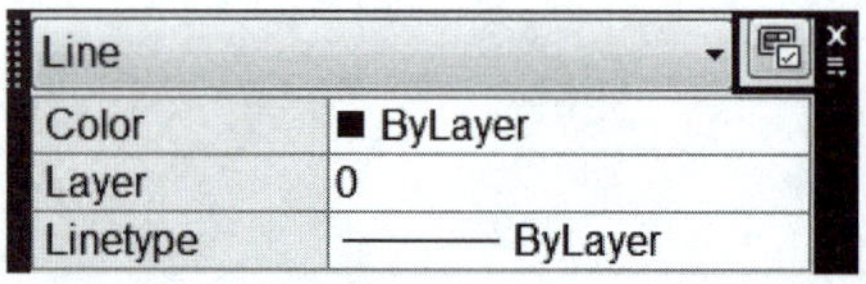

Select the **Customize** button.

4.

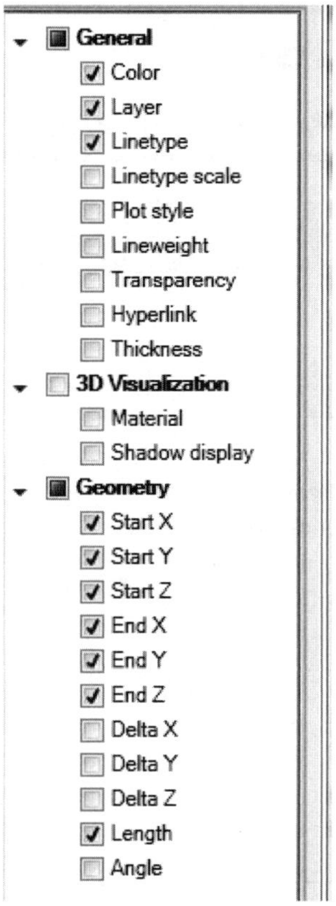

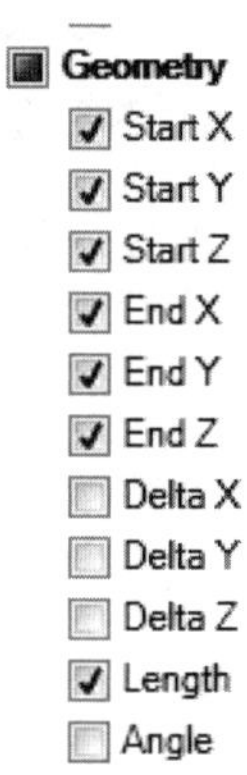

In the right hand pane, you see a list of properties that can be displayed in the Quick Properties dialog. A checkmark indicates it will be displayed.

Place a check mark in front of the Start X, Start Y, Start Z, and End X, End Y, End Z and Length.

These display the start and end coordinates of the selected line.

Press **Apply** and **OK** to close the dialog.

5.

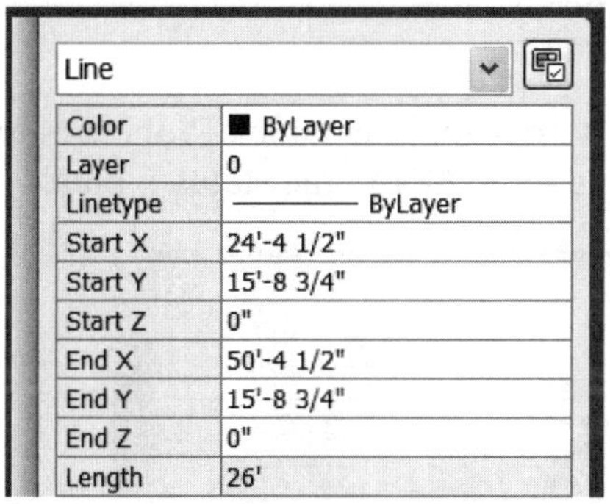

Select a line again.

Quick Properties displays the selected properties.

Close the file without saving.

Command Exercise

Exercise 7-5 – Use Quick Properties

Drawing Name: **qprops2.dwg**
Estimated Time to Completion: 5 Minutes

Scope

Learn how to use Quick Properties to modify objects easily…

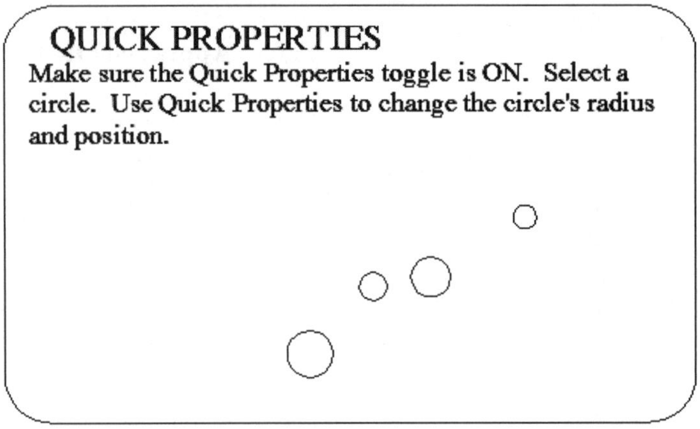

Quick Properties Exercise

Solution

1.  Verify that the Quick Properties toggle is set to ON in the status toolbar.

2. Select a circle.

   The Quick Properties dialog should pop up immediately.

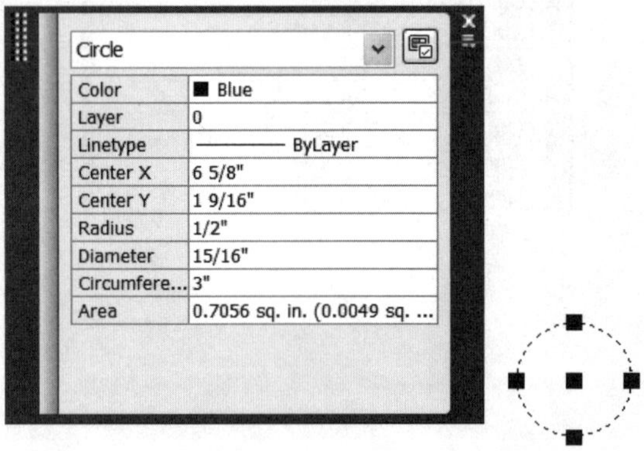

3. 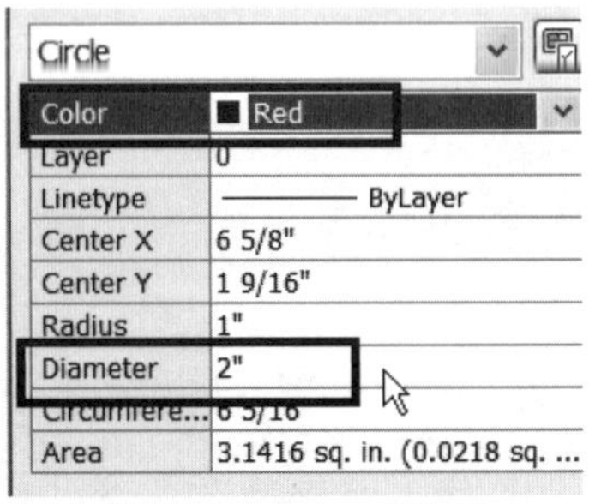

   Change the Color to **Red**.

   Change the Diameter to **2″**.

   Try this with the other circles.

4. Close without saving.

Selection Cycling

Command Locator

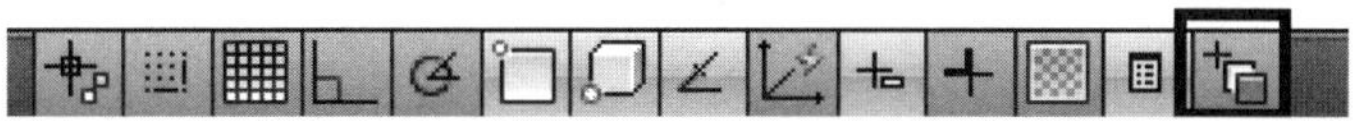

Selection cycling is used when creating or modifying a 3D model. Some edges or faces are often hidden. Rather than rotate the model, the user can use selection cyling to pick the desired entity.

To use selection cycling, toggle the Selection Cycling button on the Status Bar.

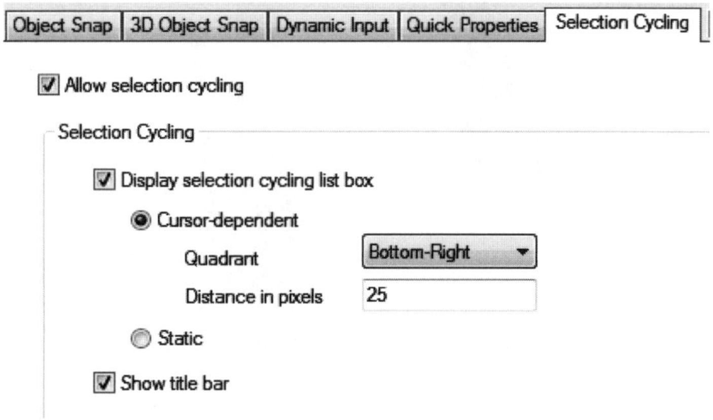

As you position your cursor, a dialog will appear to aid you in your selection.

	Vertex filtering is on	Shift + F2
	Edge filtering is on	Shift + F3
	Face filtering is on	Shift + F4
	History subobject filtering is on	Shift + F5
	Subobject filtering is off	Shift + F1

Command Exercise

Exercise 7-6 – Selection Cycling

Drawing Name: **selcycling1.dwg**
Estimated Time to Completion: 5 Minutes

Scope

Learn how to use Selection Cycling with 3D objects

Selection Cycling Exercise

Solution

1. 
Verify that the Selection Cycling toggle is set to ON in the status toolbar.

2. 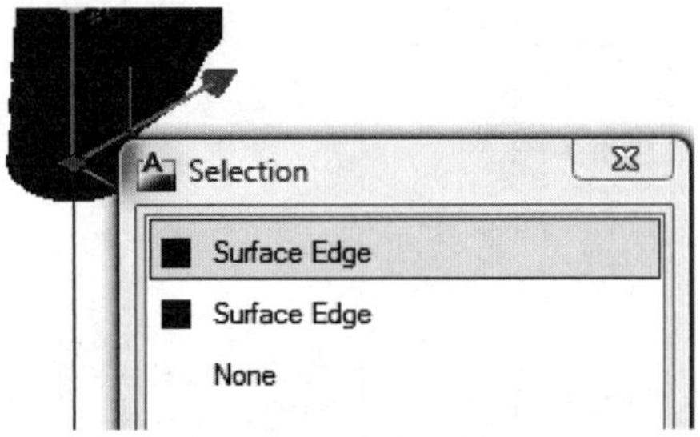

Hold down the Control key.

Left pick anywhere on the model.

A dialog list will appear with available selections.

Close the dialog.

3.
```
Enter variable name or [?] <SUBOBJSELECTIONMODE>: SubObjSelectionMode
Enter new value for SUBOBJSELECTIONMODE <1>: 2
```

Press **Shift + F3** to enable edge filtering.
The command line will show that the selection mode has been modified.

4. 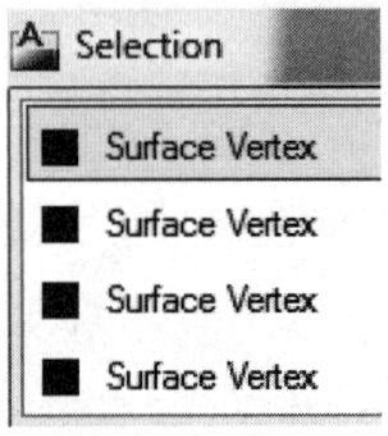

Hold down the Control key.

Left pick anywhere on the model.

A dialog list will appear with available selections.

Close the dialog.

Review Questions

1. Name three methods of selecting an object.

2. Quick Select is used to filter through a drawing or selection to quickly select objects. Which object in the list below can be selected using the Quick Select dialog?
    a. Lines
    b. Circles
    c. Dimensions
    d. Polygons
    e. All of the above

3. To customize the properties in the Quick Properties dialog:
    a. Go to Options and select the Properties
    b. Go to Settings and select the Quick Properties tab
    c. Right click on the Quick Properties dialog and select Customize
    d. All of the above

4. True or False:
   You can determine where the Quick Properties will appear when an object is selected.

5. Use this menu to locate the Quick Select tool.
    a. Tools
    b. View
    c. Design
    d. Draw

6. To deselect an object:
    a. Press Esc
    b. Press the Shift and pick the object again
    c. Press Enter
    d. A and B

Review Answers

1. Name three methods of selecting an object.

   Pick, Window, Crossing

2. Quick Select is used to filter through a drawing or selection to quickly select objects. Which object in the list below can be selected using the Quick Select dialog?

   e

3. To customize the properties in the Quick Properties dialog:

   c

4. True or False:
   You can determine where the Quick Properties will appear when an object is selected.

   True

5. Use this menu to locate the Quick Select tool.

   a

6. To deselect an object:

   d

Section 8.0 – Object Properties

Estimated Class Time – 3 Hours

Objectives

This section will focus on the Object Properties Toolbar. Object properties include Color, Layer, Linetype, Linetype Scale, Lineweight, and Thickness. The Match Properties and Properties commands can be used to change specific features as well as the properties of a selected object. Layers will help keep the drawing information organized. Use the drop down Layer Control list to make a layer current or change a layer state. Use the Layer Properties Manager dialog box to create new Layers. These settings can be saved to a drawing that can be used as a prototype or template for other drawings.

- **Layer Manager**
  Control the Layer states from this drop down list.
- **Make an Object's Layer Current**
  Select an object in the drawing and make the layer it is on the current layer.
- **Color Control**
  Control the Color of the objects being drawn.
- **Linetype Control**
  Control the Linetype of the objects being drawn.
- **Lineweight Control**
  Control the Lineweight of the objects being drawn.
- **Layer Properties Manager**
  Use the Layer Properties Manager dialog box to create a system of layers for the current drawing.
- **Match Properties Command**
  Match the properties of a selected object to other objects.
- **Properties Command**
  Change the object properties as well as specific features of a selected object.

When you start AutoCAD, the only line type available is CONTINUOUS. This is the linetype used primarily for object lines. In order to keep file sizes small, the user must load any other desired linetype before he can draw using that line style.

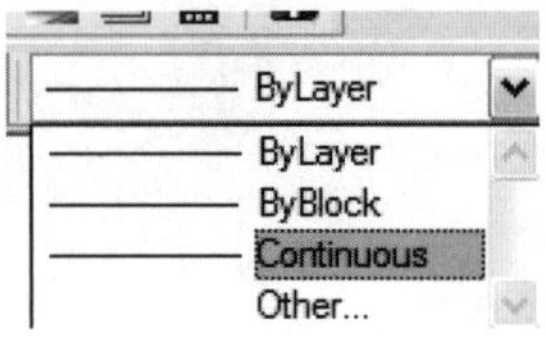

> ***Tip:*** *Once you load a linetype it remains in the drawing's database even if you don't have any geometry with that linetype. To keep your file size small, you should routinely run the PURGE command to eliminate unused linetypes and layers.*

The architectural industry has set up layer standards defining colors and linetypes to be used when creating drawings. The mechanical engineering industry has not developed a standard to be used for layers. Each company usually creates their own standards to be used for all technical documents. This ensures that the drawings have a uniform appearance.

> ***Tip:*** *One method to ensure that all drafters comply with a company's standards is to use a template set up with layers and linetypes. Use of templates is discussed later in this text.*
>
> *AutoCAD 2004 and above come with a CAD Standards tool to help you ensure that drawings meet company standards.*

Layers are used to organize your drawing. Industry standard is to place object lines, hidden, dimensions, etc. each on a separate layer. Many drafters organize their drawings by placing object types on separate layers. For example, fasteners, doors, walls, gears might each be placed on a separate layer. Layer names should be short but easy to understand.

You can use the Layer Control and Linetype control to set up your layers to use the different linetypes and colors.

Layer Manager

Command Locator

Toolbar Menu	**Properties / Layer Manager**
Pull Down Menu	**Format/Layer Manager**
Command	**Layer**
Alias	**la**
Dialog Box	**Layer Manager**

Command Overview

Layers may be conveniently selected from the Layer Control drop down list. Layers may be made current, or the *layer state* may be changed. The options include: On or Off, Freeze or Thaw, Lock or Unlock, and making a layer plottable or not. A layer may be made current by selecting it from the list. When the command line is blank, the properties of a selected object will be identified in the Object Properties Toolbar, and can be placed on a different Layer by selecting a different Layer from the drop down list. This feature applies to the Color, Linetype, and Lineweight Controls as well.

Layer State	Overview
Make a Layer Current	Select the name of the layer in the drop down list to make it current. Objects drawn on the current layer will have the properties assigned to that layer.
Turn a Layer On or Off	Select the light bulb to turn that layer on (yellow). Select it again to turn it off (gray). A layer is not visible when it is turned off, however it may be current. A layer that is off and current at the same time would be odd, because the new objects drawn would be invisible until the layer is turned on again.
Freeze or Thaw in All Viewports	Select the sun to freeze that layer (snowflake). Select the snowflake to thaw that layer (sun). A layer is not visible when it is frozen. It is also completely ignored in a regeneration, which will make the regeneration time faster. A layer that is made current cannot be frozen.
Lock or Unlock a layer	Objects on a Locked layer can not be changed. When a layer is locked current, objects may be drawn on that layer, but can not be changed.
Make a layer plottable or non-plottable	Whether a layer is plotted or not can be controlled by selecting this feature. This way the layer may be visible, but will not plot.

General Procedures

To make a Layer current:

1. Select the down arrow in the Layer list.
2. Select the layer (name) to make it current.

To change a Layer state:

1. Select the down arrow in the Layer list.
2. Select the desired option: On/Off, Freeze/Thaw, Lock/Unlock, Plot/no plot.

To move objects from one Layer to another:

1. With the Command Line blank (press Escape), select the objects to change.
2. Select the down arrow in the Layer list. And select the desired layer.
3. Press Escape two times to deselect the object and cancel the *grips*.

Tips & Tricks

- If there are no objects on a layer, the layer key will appear grayed out.
- The Layer Control list will appear gray when in the middle of a command. Press Escape to cancel the command and the Layers Control list will be accessible.
- Use the Freeze option instead of Off. A frozen layer is completely ignored in a drawing regeneration and will therefore make a faster regeneration.

Command Exercise

Exercise 8-1 – Layer Control

Drawing Name: **layerc1.dwg**
Estimated Time to Completion: 15 Minutes

Scope

Using Layer Control drop down list, draw the objects on the appropriate layer. Make the layer current before you draw. Practice the Freeze and Thaw options.

Solution

1. 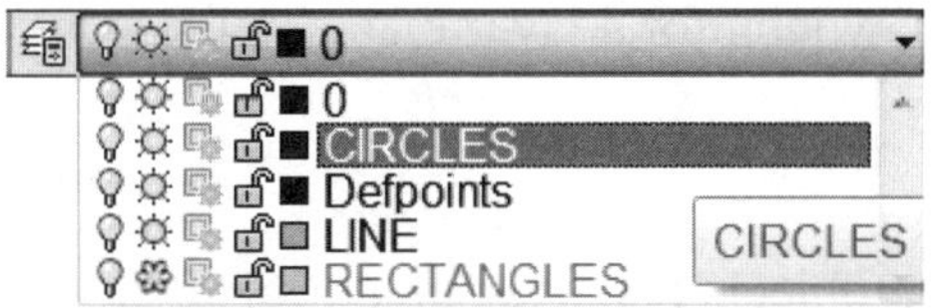

Start the exercise by selecting the **CIRCLES** layer in the Layer Control drop down list.

2. 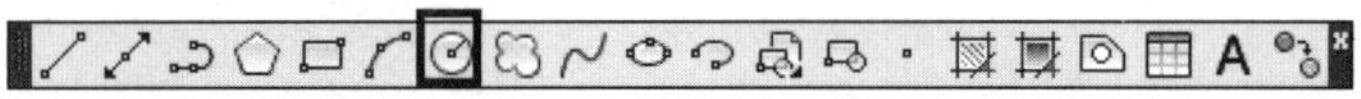

Invoke the **Circle** command (c or circle).

3. *Specify center point for circle or [3P/2P/Ttr (tan tan radius)]:*
Pick a point on the screen with the LMB.

4. *Specify radius of circle or [Diameter]:*
Use the LMB to determine the radius. Notice that the Circle is purple. This is a visual indicator that the Circle is located on the CIRCLES layer.

5. 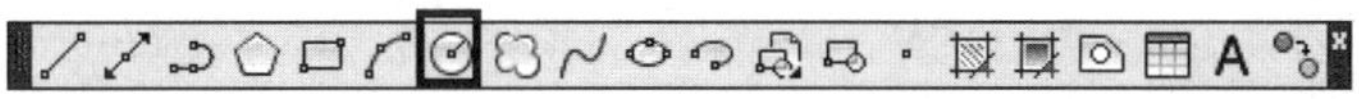

Repeat the circle command and create more circles on the Circles layer.

6. 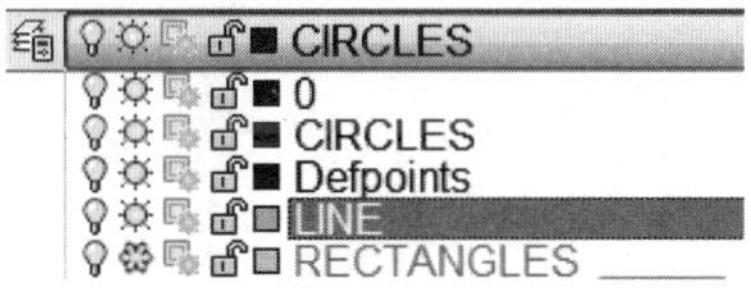

Use the Layer Control drop down list to select the LINE layer as the current layer.

7. 
Invoke the **Line** command (l or line).

8. *Specify first point:*
Use the LMB to pick the first point.

9. *Specify next point or [Undo]:*
Use the LMB to pick the second point. Notice that the line is green.

10. Create more line segments on the LINE layer and press <ENTER> to end the command.

11. 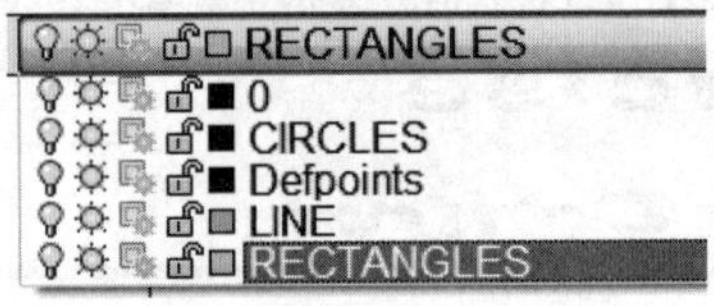

Use the Layer control drop down list to select the **RECTANGLES** layer.

12. 

Invoke the **Rectangle** command (rectang).

13. *Specify first corner point or [Chamfer/Elevation/Fillet/Thickness/Width]:*
Use the LMB to select the first corner of the rectangle.

14. *Specify other corner point:*
Use the LMB to specify the second point of the rectangle.

15. Repeat the command to create multiple rectangles on the RECTANGLES layer.

16. 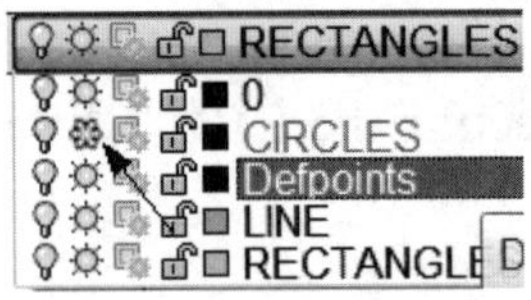

Freeze a layer by selecting the Layer Control drop down list and selecting the Freeze / Thaw icon for a layer that is not current.

17. Repeat the process by thawing a layer. Notice that objects that exist on a Frozen layer are not visible.

Extra: *Try freezing the current layer. What happens? Try turning a layer ON and OFF. Try drawing on a layer that is OFF.*

Tip: *You can draw on a layer that is turned OFF. But you cannot draw on a layer that is frozen. AutoCAD will not REGEN objects on a frozen layer. Locking a layer is a good way filter the selection of objects. Entities on a locked layer cannot be edited.*

Make an Object's Layer Current

Command Locator

Toolbar Menu	**Layer**
Command	**LAYMCUR**

Command Overview

Make a layer current by selecting an object in the drawing on that layer.

General Procedures

1. Select the Make Object's Layer Current button from the Properties toolbar.
2. Select the desired object.

Tips & Tricks

> ➢ An object's layer can be identified first by selecting it with the Command Line blank.

Color Control

Command Locator

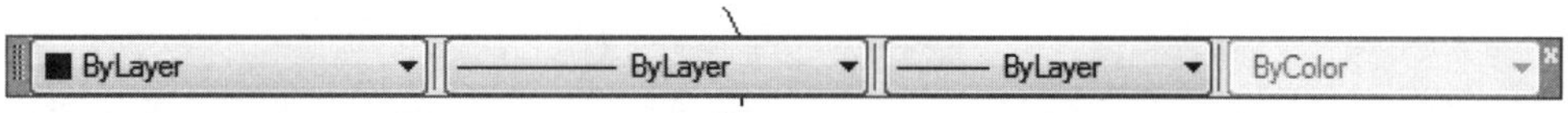

Toolbar Menu	**Properties / Color Control**
Pull Down Menu	**Format / Color**
Command	**Color**
Alias	**COL**
Dialog Box	**Select Color**

Command Overview

This option controls the color of the objects currently being drawn. Typically, the colors of objects in the drawing should be determined *by the layer*, and it is not advisable to mix colors in the same layer. This is because the user will usually want to know at a glance that all objects that are Blue, for instance, are on a particular layer. Be sure that "ByLayer" appears in the Color Control box. When an object is selected with the Command Line blank, selecting a color from the drop down list will automatically apply the color to the selected object.

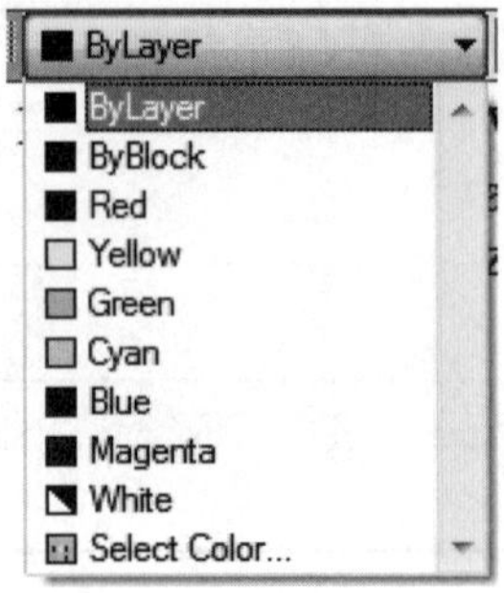

Color Control Drop-down List

General Procedures

1. Select the down arrow in the Color Control list.
2. Select "ByLayer".

- When drawing, make sure that the word "BYLAYER" appears in the Color Control window. This is a suggestion, but not the rule.
- The Color Control list will appear gray when in the middle of a command. Press Escape to cancel the command and the Color Control list will be accessible.
- Selecting "Other…" from the Color Control drop down list will display the Select Color dialog box and full Color Spectrum.

Linetype Control

Command Locator

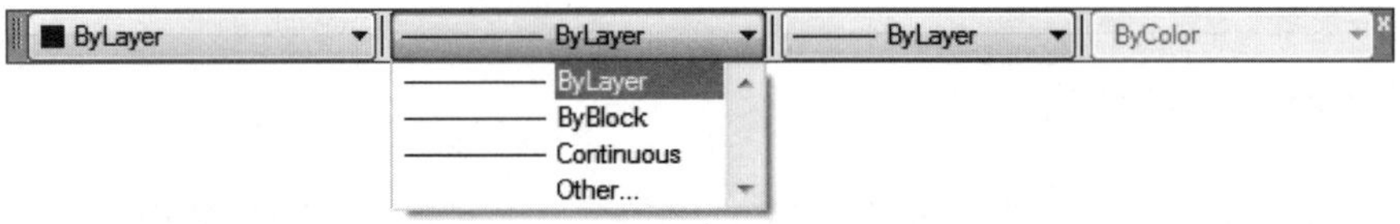

Toolbar Menu	**Properties / Linetype Control**
Pull Down Menu	**Format / Linetype**
Command	**Linetype**
Alias	**LTYPE**
Dialog Box	**Linetype Manager**

Command Overview

This option controls the Linetype of the objects currently being drawn. It is typical that a variety of linetypes may be present on the same layer, such as Continuous, Center and Hidden. However, it is best to leave the Linetype Control setting to ByLayer. Selecting "Other…" from the drop down list will display the Linetype Manager dialog box. The user can Load additional linetypes into the drawing using either this dialog box or the Layer Properties Manager dialog box which will be covered further on in this chapter.

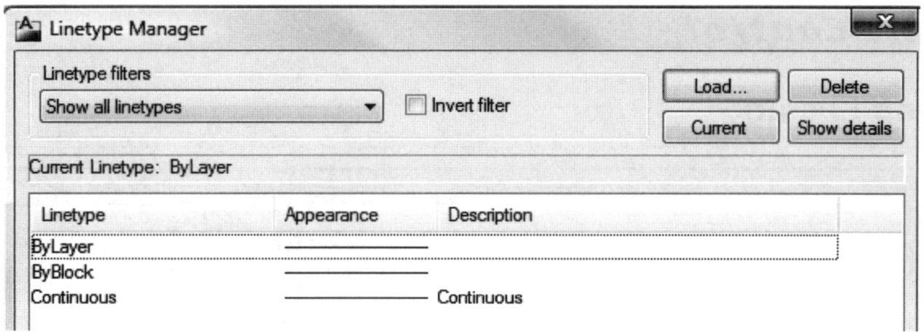

Linetype Manager Dialog Box

General Procedures

To load a linetype into the drawing:

1. Select the down arrow in the Linetype Control list.
2. Select "Other…"
3. From the Linetype Manager dialog box, select Load, then scroll through the list to find and select the linetypes to load into the drawing. Hold down the Control key to select alternate linetypes, hold down the Shift key to select several linetypes. Then select OK (two times) to exit.

- Be sure that the word "ByLayer" appears in the Linetype Control window. If making another linetype current for a specific reason, remember to change it back to ByLayer.
- Linetypes can be assigned to a Layer. This will be covered further on in this chapter.
- The system variable, LTSCALE, will globally control the scale of the linetypes in the drawing.
- Linetypes beginning with ACAD_ISO are for Metric drawings.

Lineweight Control

Command Locator

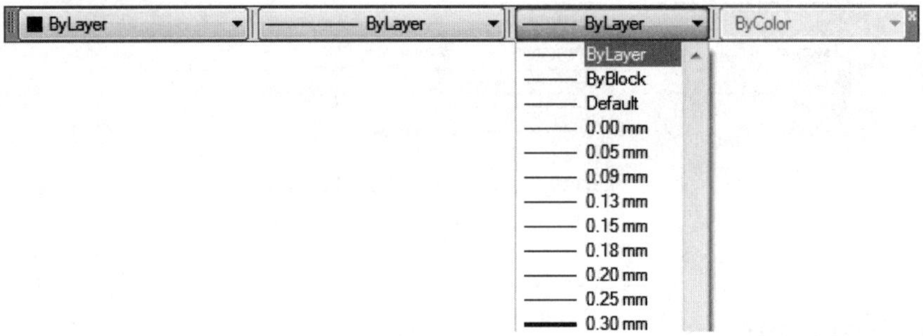

Toolbar Menu	**Properties / Lineweight Control**
Pull Down Menu	**Format / Lineweight**
Command	**Lineweight**
Alias	**LWEIGHT**
Dialog Box	**Lineweight Settings**

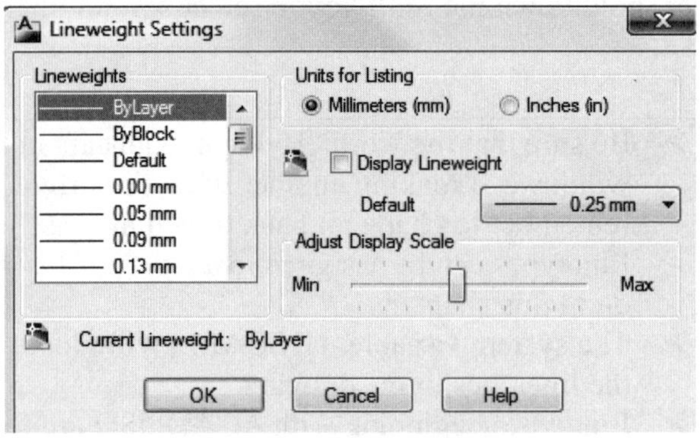

Lineweight Settings Dialog Box

Command Overview

The Lineweight of the objects in the drawing can be controlled individually or by the Layer when set to ByLayer. This chapter will cover how to determine linetypes by the Layer in the section that covers the Layer Properties Manager dialog box.

General Procedures

To make a lineweight the current setting:

1. Select the down arrow in the Linetype Control list.
2. Select the desired linewidth.

To change the lineweight of an existing object:

1. With the Command Line blank, select the objects in the drawing to change.
2. Select the down arrow in the Linetype Control list.
3. Select the desired linewidth. Once the lineweights of the objects have changed, press Escape two times to cancel the selection.

Tips Tricks

- Be sure that the word "ByLayer" appears in the Lineweight Control window. If selecting another lineweight current for a specific reason, remember to change it back to ByLayer.
- Lineweights can be assigned to a Layer. This will be covered further on in this chapter.
- Lineweights will not be visible unless "Display Lineweight" is selected in the Lineweight Settings dialog box.

Layer Properties Manager

Command Locator

Toolbar Menu	**Properties / Layers**
Pull Down Menu	**Format / Layer...**
Command	**Layer**
Alias	**LA**
RMB Shortcut Menu	**In the list area of the Layer Properties Manager dialog box**
Dialog Box	**Layer Properties Manager**

Command Overview

Use the Layer Properties Manager dialog box to create drawing Layers with specified Names, Colors, Linetypes, Lineweights, and Plot Styles (plot colors) and Plot variables (plottable or not). The layer lists may be sorted in ascending or descending order by double-clicking the heading, such as Name. Layer 0 is a default standard layer and can not be renamed or deleted. This makes it a good "working layer". Other layers may only be deleted if there is no geometry on those layers and they are not "current". Layers may be made current, frozen, thawed, locked, unlocked, turned on or off from this dialog box. Once objects are created, they may be moved to other layers using the Match Properties, or the Properties commands (see next section), or by selecting the object with the Command line blank and selecting the layer to move it to from the drop down list (shown in the previous section). Create a system of layers to save as a prototype or template drawing.

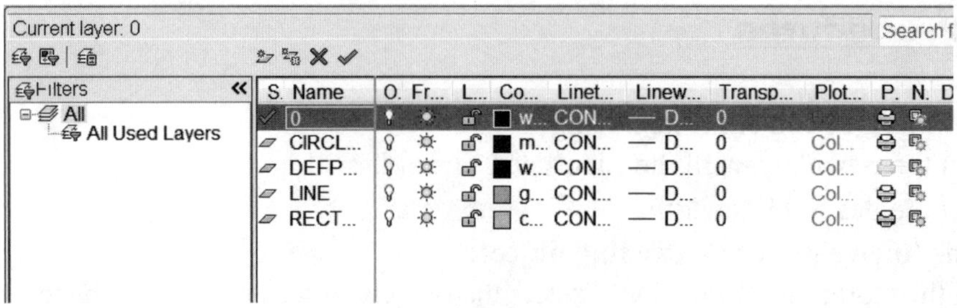

Layer Properties Manager

Feature	Overview
Named Layer Filters	This section controls what layer names are visible. For all practical purposes, the words "Show all layers" should be visible in the text window and the Invert Filter and Apply to Object Properties toolbar options should not be checked.
New	Select this button to create a New layer. The default name will be Layer1, Layer2, Layer3, etc. Type in a different layer name, or select the layer name twice to rename it.
Delete	This option allows selected layers to be deleted, only if the layer contains no geometry, or is not current.
Current	Select this option to make a highlighted layer current. A layer that is current can not be frozen. You can also use the "Make Object's Layer Current" icon found in the Object Properties Toolbar to make a layer current. Select the object whose layer will become current.
Show details	This option will expand the layer dialog box to display additional details. For all practical purposes, it is not necessary to display the additional layer details.

Layer List Heading	Icon	Overview
Name		Lists the layer name. Select two times to rename a layer. Spaces and certain characters are not allowed. To select a layer in the dialog box, pick it (LMB), to deselect it, pick it again, select another layer or pick in the blank area of the dialog box. To select all layers, right-click (RMB) in the blank area and choose "Select All".
On / Off		Turns selected layers on or off. A layer that is turned OFF may still be current, but will not be visible. This is an odd state, because objects drawn on that layer will not be seen until the layer is turned back on.
Freeze / Thaw in all VP		Freezes or thaws selected layers in all view ports. A frozen layer is not visible and cannot be made current.
Lock / Unlock		Locks or unlocks selected layers. It is possible to lock a current layer and draw on a locked layer, but not modify the objects on that layer until it is unlocked.
Color		Pick the color for the corresponding layer(s) to access the Select Color dialog box. Pick a color from the Standard Colors or the Full Color Palette to apply to a selected layer.
Linetype		Pick the linetype for the corresponding layer(s) to access the Select Linetype dialog box. Pick a linetype from "Loaded linetypes" list to apply to a selected layer. Select the Load button to access and select from the "Available linetypes" list.
Lineweight		Pick the lineweight for the corresponding layer(s) to access the Lineweight dialog box. Pick a lineweight from the list to apply to a selected layer.
Transparency		Sets the level of transparency for the layer; is level is set to 0, then layer is not transparent. Transparency can be set from 0 – 90, where 90 is fully transparent.
Plot		Makes a layer plottable or not

General Procedures

1. Invoke the Layer command.
2. In the Layer Properties Manager dialog box, select New. Name the layer.
3. Select the corresponding color, to access the Select Color dialog box, pick a color, then select OK.
4. Select the corresponding linetype, to access the Select Linetype dialog box, and pick a linetype from the list. If the desired linetype is not in the list, select "Load…" and pick a linetype from the list. Select OK or Cancel to exit the Linetype dialog boxes.
5. Select OK to close the Layer Properties Manager dialog box.

Tips & Tricks

- Use the Freeze option instead of Off. Layers that are frozen are completely ignored in a regeneration, and hence will speed regeneration time.
- Deleting a selected Layer or linetype is similar to the PURGE command.
- A layer can be renamed any time. This will help to organize the information in the drawing.
- Layer 0 cannot be renamed or deleted.
- The Color, Linetype and Lineweight Control options in the Properties Toolbar should be set to Bylayer. In this way these options will be determined by the layer.
- The system variable LTSCALE controls the global scale of the linetypes in the drawing. The effects of LTSCALE apply to linetypes that contain spaces and dashes (i.e. the hidden or the center linetypes).
- Refer to Scale Factor Chart to help determine an appropriate LTSCALE.
- You can create more than one layer at a time by typing a comma at the end of your layer name.
- Transparency controls how bright objects appear.
- To rename a layer: double click on the name with the LMB to activate a cursor that will allow you to type a new name.
- Double clicking on a layer will also set it to be the current layer.

Command Exercise

Exercise 8-2 – Drawing on Layers

Drawing Name: **layers1.dwg**
Estimated Time to Completion: 15 Minutes

Scope

In the layers dialog box, create the designated layers and draw the object using the appropriate layers. Do not simply copy the objects from the left side to the right side! Learn to create layers.

Layers Exercise

Solution

1. 

Invoke the **Layers** command (layer) to open the Layer Properties Manager dialog box.

2. 

In the Layer Properties Manager dialog box press the **New** button with the LMB. This will create a new layer called 'Layer1' in rename mode.

3. 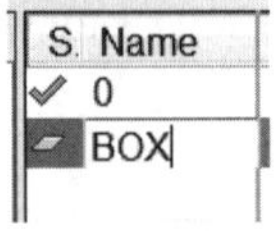

In the dialog box, rename LAYER1 to **BOX**.

4. 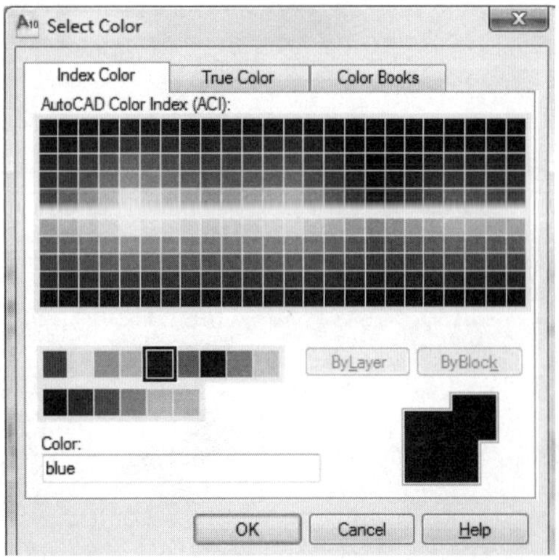

Use the LMB to select the color box to change the color associated with the BOX layer. Use the LMB to select BLUE from the Standard Colors section in the Select Color dialog box.

5. 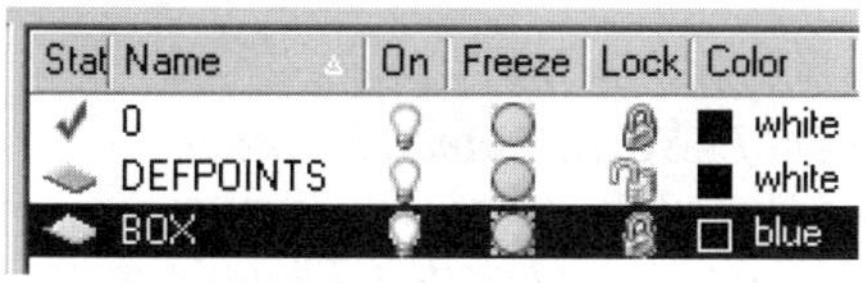

Press '**OK**' to complete the change.

6. 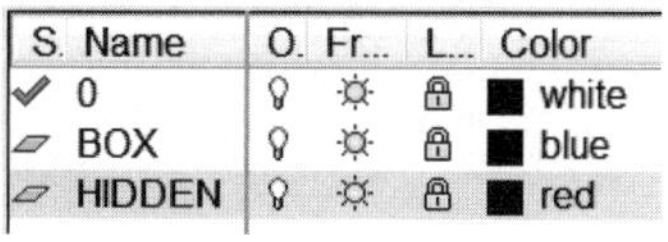

Create a third layer by pressing the **New** button in the Layer Properties Manager dialog box. Rename the new layer to **HIDDEN**. Set the color to **RED**.

7. 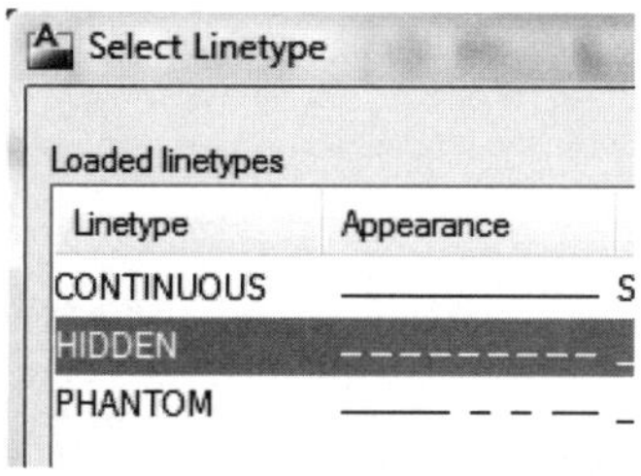

Use the LMB and press on the Word CONTINUOUS under Linetype for the HIDDEN layer. This will activate the Select Linetype dialog box.

Use the LMB to select the **HIDDEN** Linetype

8. 

LMB on the **0** under the Transparency column. Enter the value 50 in the dialog and press **OK** to continue.

9. 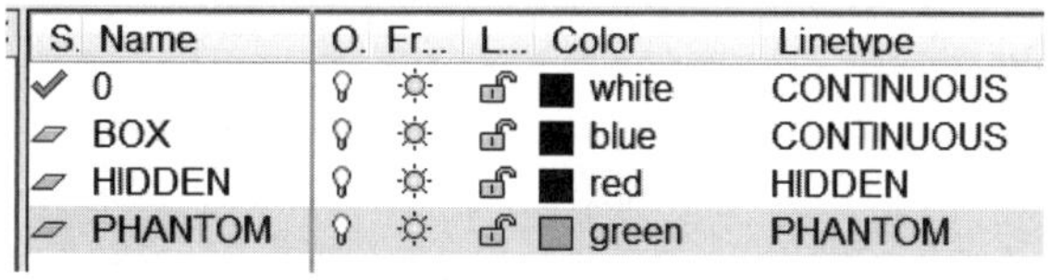

Create a layer called SUPPORT. Press the **New** button in the Layer Properties Manager dialog box and rename the new layer to **SUPPORT**. Change the color to green, and set the linetype to **PHANTOM**.

10. 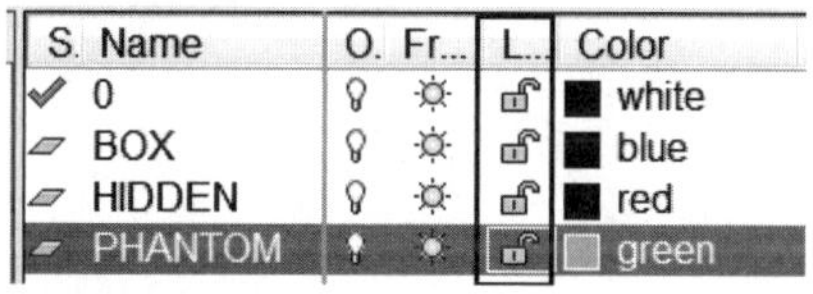

Make sure that your layers are UNLOCKED or you will not be able to edit any objects you place on that layer.

11. 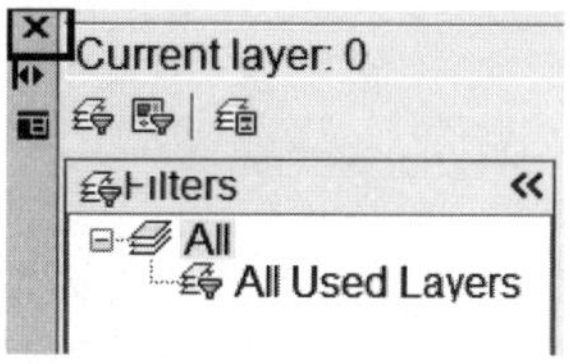

When you have finished creating the three layers, close the dialog box by pressing the 'x' button in the upper left corner.

12. 

Start by setting the BOX layer current before you create the blue box. Select the BOX layer from the Layer Dropdown list in the Object Properties toolbar.

13. 
Invoke the **rectangle** command (rectang).

14. Use your mouse and LMB to create the rectangle.

15. Repeat the same steps to finish the drawing. Remember to set the correct layer current before drawing the object. Use Object Snaps, Copy and Mirror as needed.

EXTRA: *Type LTSCALE at the command line and change the linetype scale to 0.75. View the changes to your drawing. Repeat LTSCALE, and change it to 0.25. View the drawing, then set it back to 0.5. From the Layer Properties dialog box change the colors associated with the layers you created. Change the linetype of the layers. View your drawing.*

Command Exercise

Exercise 8-3 – Creating Layers

Drawing Name: **new drawing**
Estimated Time to Completion: 20 Minutes

Scope

Practice creating layers, loading linetypes and assigning linetypes and colors to the layers.

Solution

1.  Select the **Layer Properties Manager** button.

2.  Select the **New Layer** tool.

3. 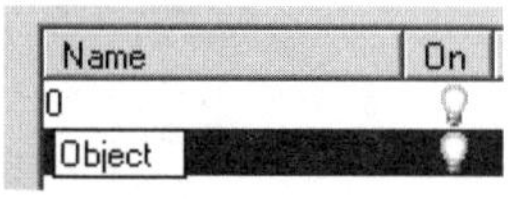

In the edit field, type **Object**.

4. 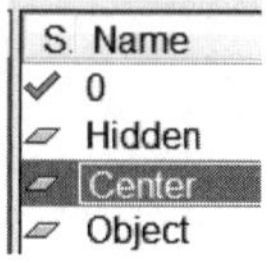

Create three layers in all:
   - Object
   - Hidden
   - Center

> ***Tip:*** *If you type a comma after you enter the layer name, AutoCAD will automatically drop a line so you can add the next layer.*

5. 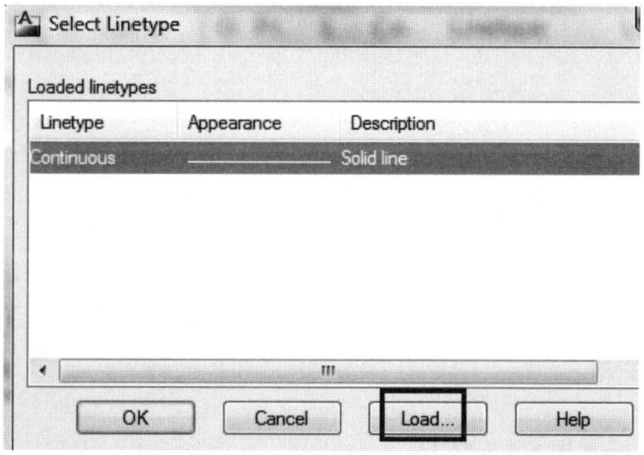

Highlight the **Hidden** layer. Pick the word **Continuous**.

   Press the **LOAD** button.

6. 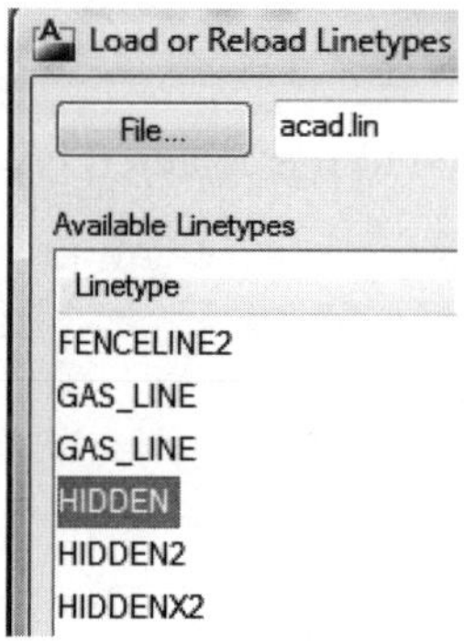

Select the **Hidden** linetype.

   Press **OK**.

   This loads the selected linetype into the active drawing.

   *You can select more than one linetype to load by holding down the **Control** key.*

7. 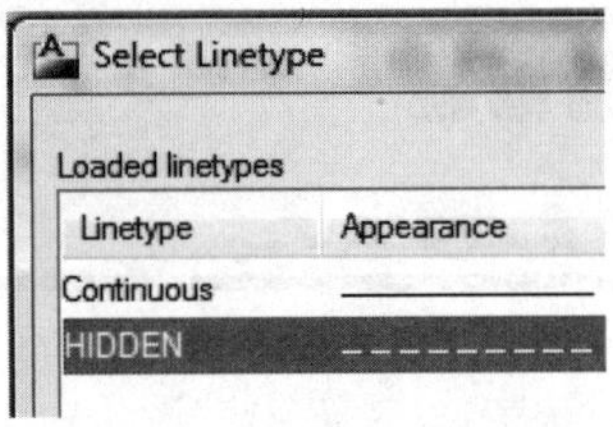

Highlight HIDDEN.

Press **OK**.

This assigns the HIDDEN linetype to the selected layer.

8. 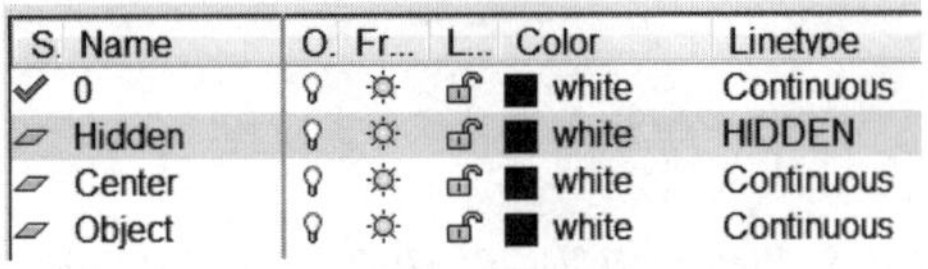

Note that the layer HIDDEN now has been assigned the HIDDEN linetype.

9. 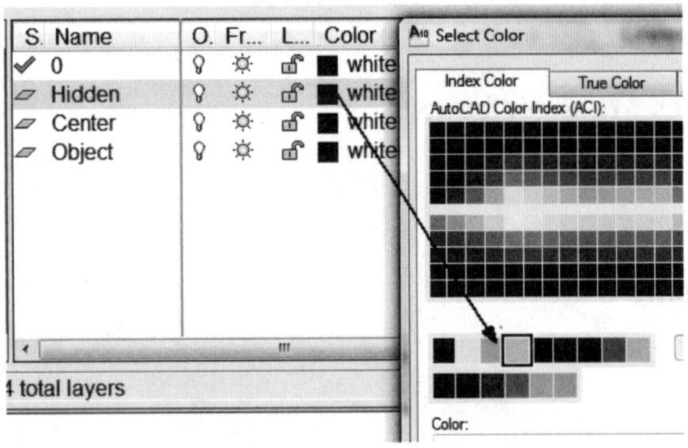

Highlight the HIDDEN layer.

Pick the Color button.

Select the **Cyan** color.

Press **OK**.

10. 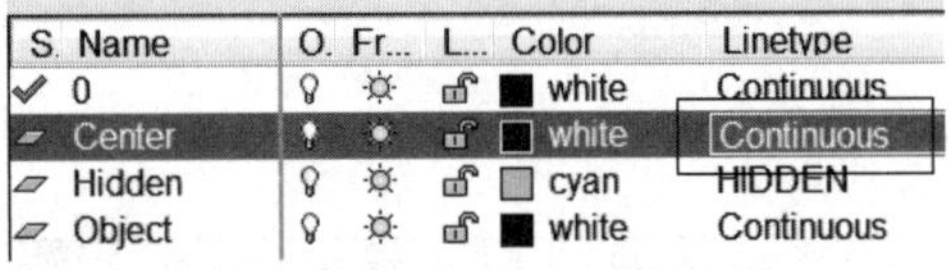

Highlight the **Center** layer.

Pick the word **Continuous**.

11. 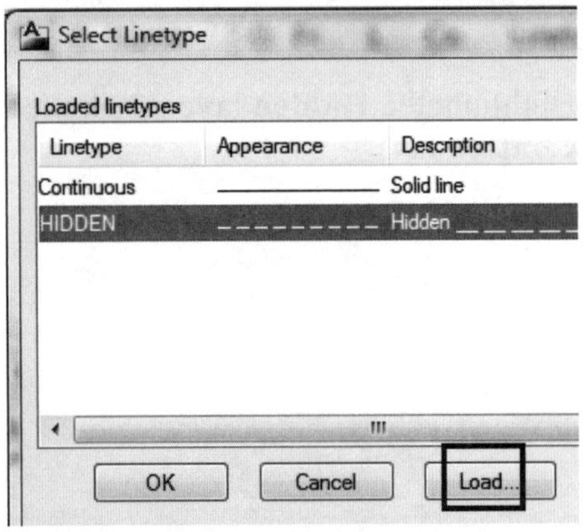

Press the **LOAD** button.

12. 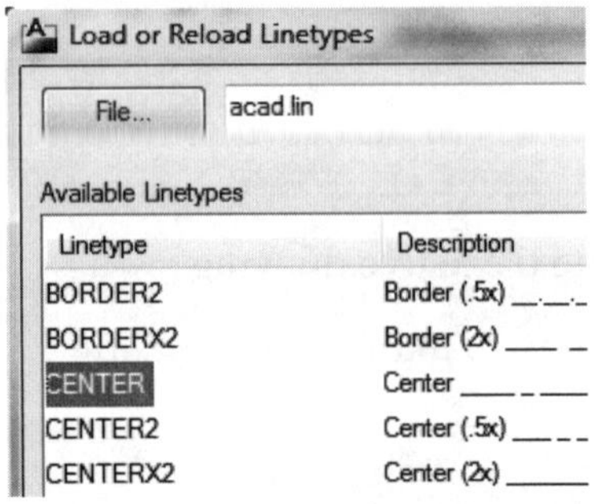

Select the **CENTER** linetype.

Press **OK**.

This assigns the CENTER linetype to the selected layer.

13. 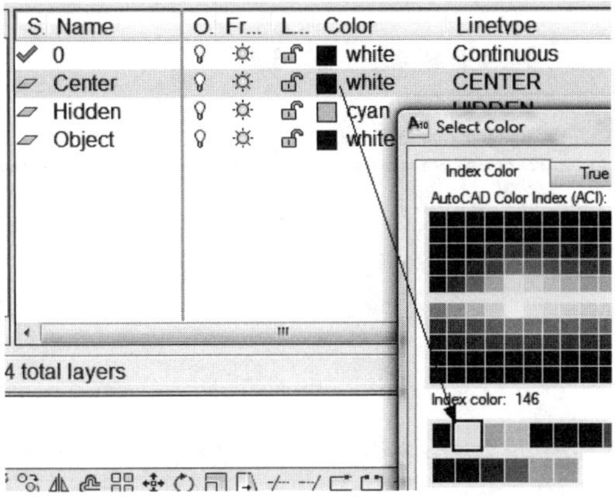

Pick the Color button.

Select the **yellow** color.

Press **OK**.

14. 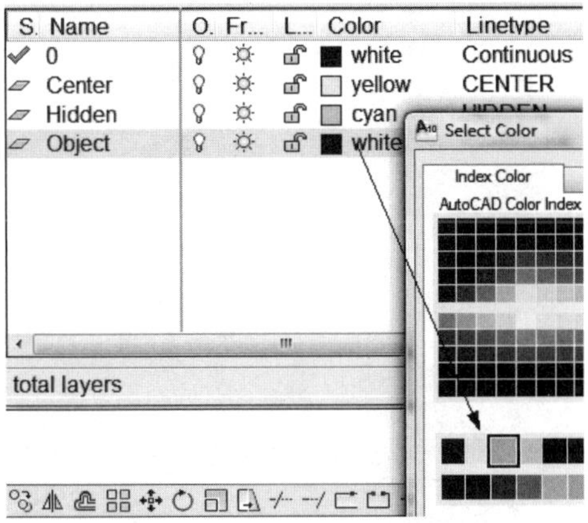

Set the Object layer to the **green** color.

15. 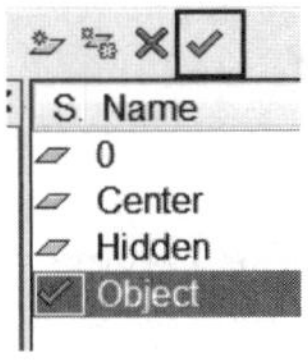

Highlight **Object** and select the green check mark. This sets the Object Layer current.

We want the Object layer to be the Current layer – the layer where any entities we create are placed.

16. 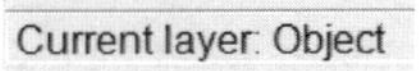

The Current Layer is noted at the top bar of the Layer dialog.

17. 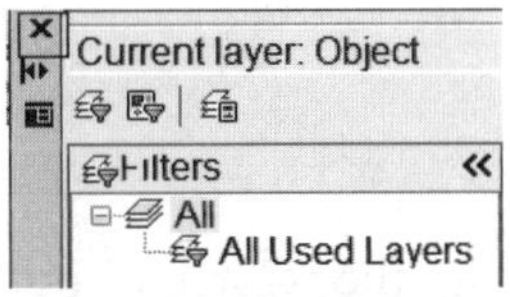

Close the Layer Manager dialog by pressing the X in the dialog corner.

18. 

The current layer is shown in the layer drop-down list.

19. 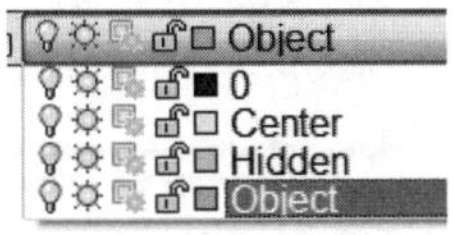

Your layers are listed in the layer drop-down.

You can set a layer current by selecting it from the drop-down list.

You can also quickly assign an object to a layer by selecting it and then selecting the layer from the drop-down list.

Command Exercise

Exercise 8-4 – Rename Layers

Drawing Name: **layers2.dwg**
Estimated Time to Completion: 5 Minutes

Scope

In the Layer Properties dialog box, Rename layer #1 to WINDOW. Make the House Layer current. Select all, then Freeze all.

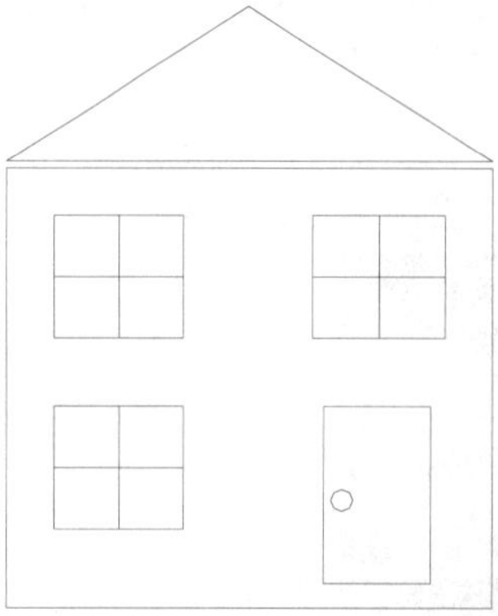

Layers Exercise

Solution

1. 

Invoke the Layers command (layer) to open the Layer Properties Manager dialog box.

2. 

In the Layer Properties Manager, double click on the name of Layer '1' to rename it to **WINDOW**.

3. 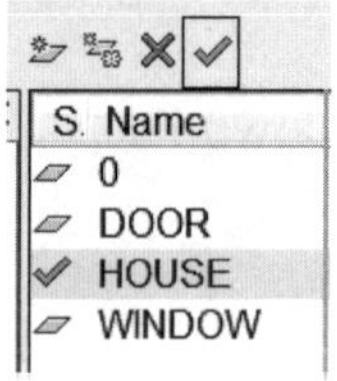

Select the HOUSE layer and set it current by pressing the 'Current' button.

4. 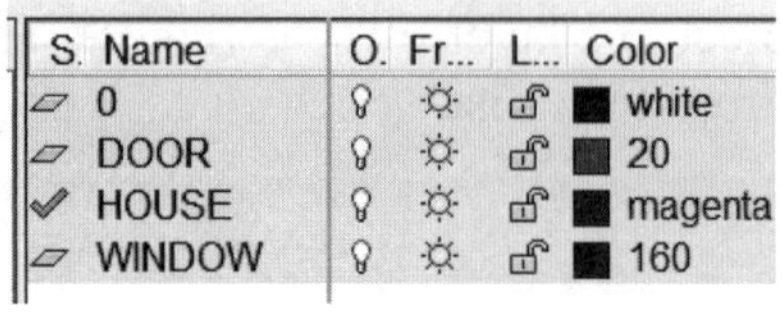

Hold down the <SHIFT> key to select all the layers so they are highlighted.

5. 

LMB click the sun in the Freeze column on the first row.

6. 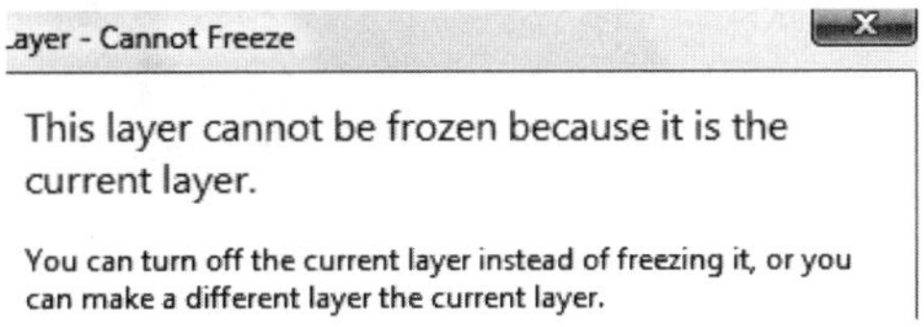

A warning message will appear.

Press **Close**.

7. 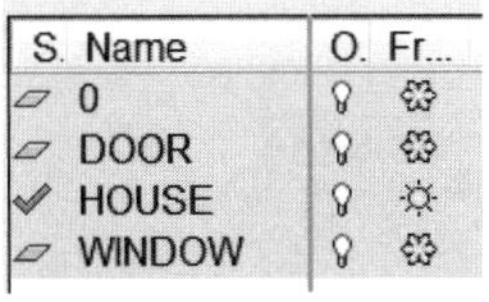

All the layers will be frozen except for the current layer – House.

8. 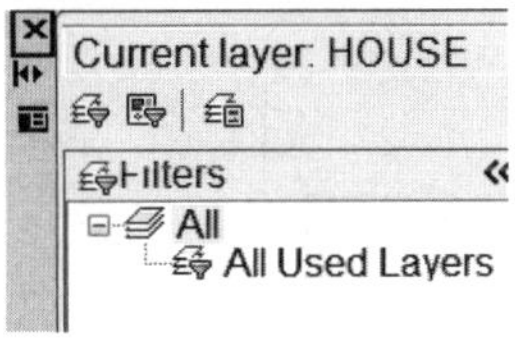

Close the dialog by pressing the X in the corner.

Extra: *Try Freezing and Thawing different layers. Try turning different layers ON or OFF.*

> ***Tip:*** *Remember visually turning layers OFF is similar to Freezing but time can be saved during regeneration if a layer is Frozen.*

When you first start out as a drafter, chances are you won't be creating drawings from scratch. Instead, you will be given legacy drawings to work on. (A legacy drawing is an older drawing that needs to be updated to comply with engineering changes or standards.) Your first step upon opening up a legacy drawing should be to identify how the drawing is organized; i.e. which objects are on which layers. Once you have determined how the drawing is organized, you may opt to move objects onto different layers to make it easier to work on the drawing or in order to comply with your company's CAD standards.

Command Exercise

Exercise 8-5 – Identifying Layers

Drawing Name: **Site Plan.dwg**
Estimated Time to Completion: 10 Minutes

Scope

Use the Layer Translator to identify the layers in a drawing.

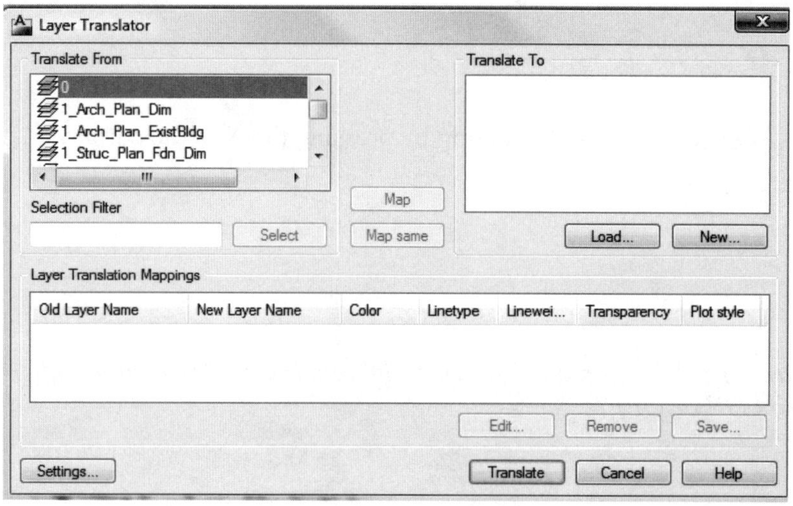

Layer Translator Dialog

Solution

1. 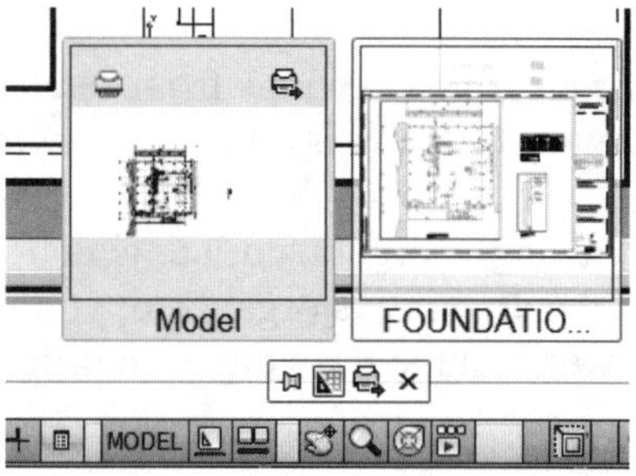

Select the **Model** icon on the Status Bar.

2. 

Go to **Tools→CAD Standards→Layer Translator**.

3. 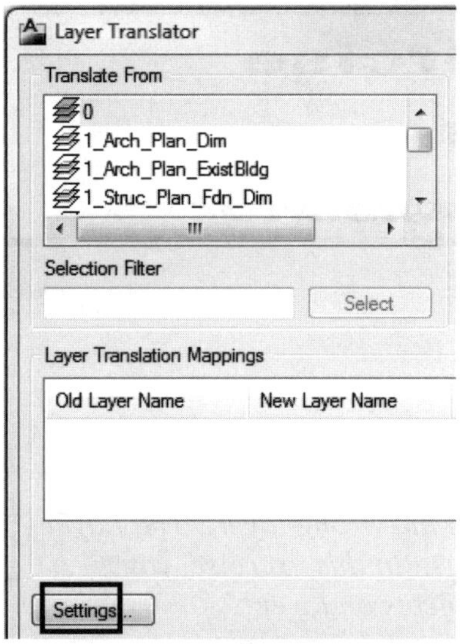

Select **Settings**.

4. 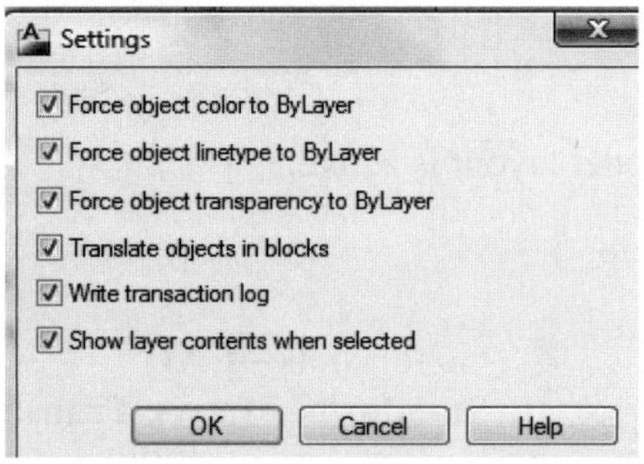

Enable **Show layer contents when selected**.

Press **OK**.

5. 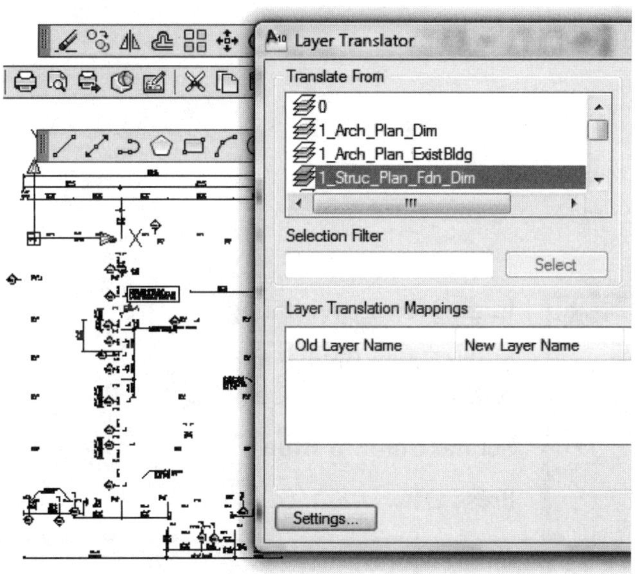

Move the Layer Translator dialog to the side so you can see the drawing.

Select each layer in the Translate From list. Note which objects are visible when which layers are highlighted.

Note that several layers don't have anything on them.

6. Close the Layer Translator.

7. Close the file without saving.

Command Exercise

Exercise 8-6 – Using the Layer Translator

Drawing Name: **Elevation.dwg**
Estimated Time to Completion: 15 Minutes

Scope

Often you will work on a file with objects residing on the wrong layer. The Layer Translator makes it easy for you to organize drawings. In this exercise, you learn how to use the Layer Translator to organize objects on layers.

Solution

1.  Select the **Model** icon. Verify that the model layout is active.

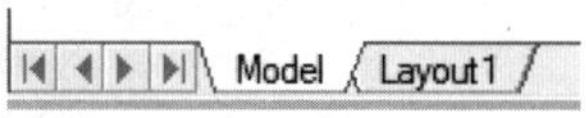

2. 

Go to **Tools→CAD Standards→Layer Translator**.

3. 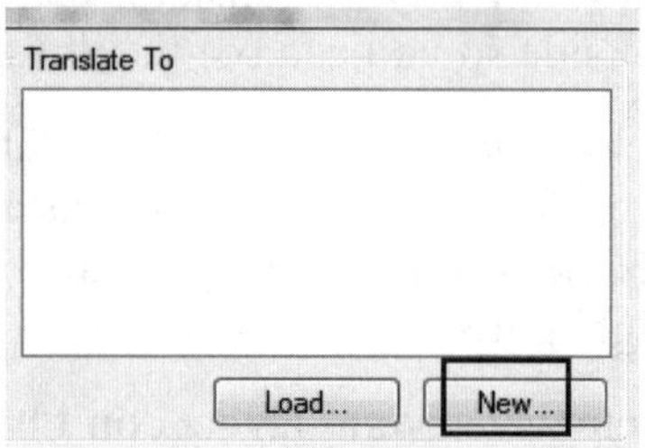

Select the **New** button.

4. 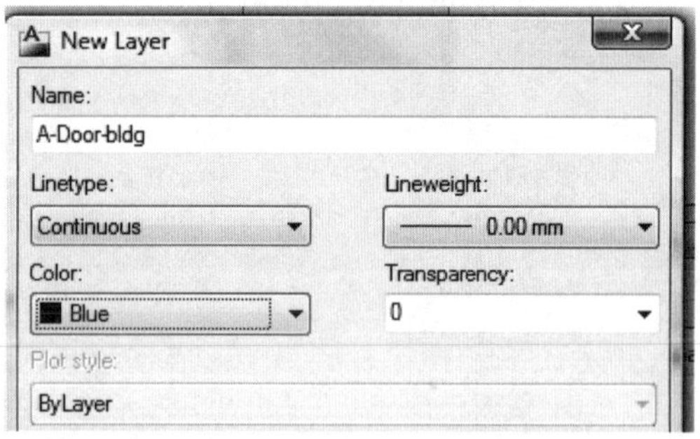

In the New Layer dialog:

In the Name field, enter **A-Door-bldg**.

Set the Color to **Blue**.

Press **OK**.

5. 

Select the New button.

6. 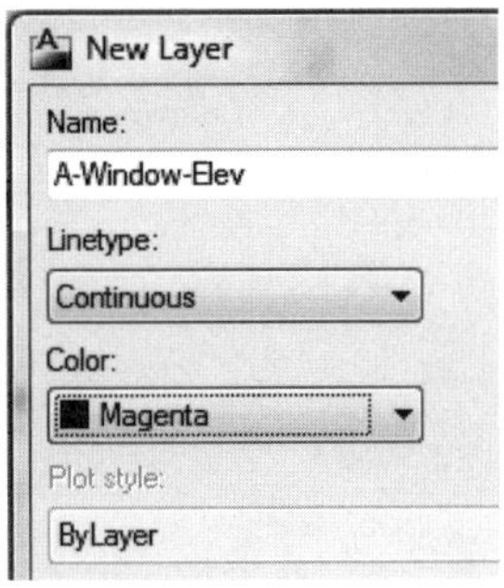

In the New Layer dialog:

In the Name field, enter **A-Window-Elev**.

Set the Color to **Magenta**.

Press **OK**.

7. 

Select the **New** button.

8. 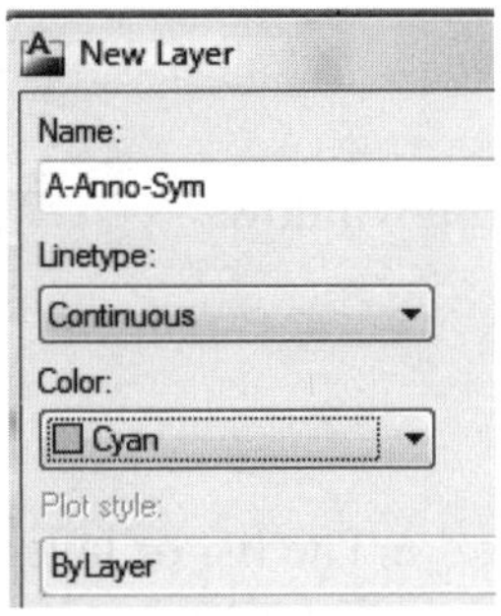

In the New Layer dialog:

In the Name field, enter **A-Anno-Sym**.

Set the Color to **Cyan**.

Press **OK**.

9. 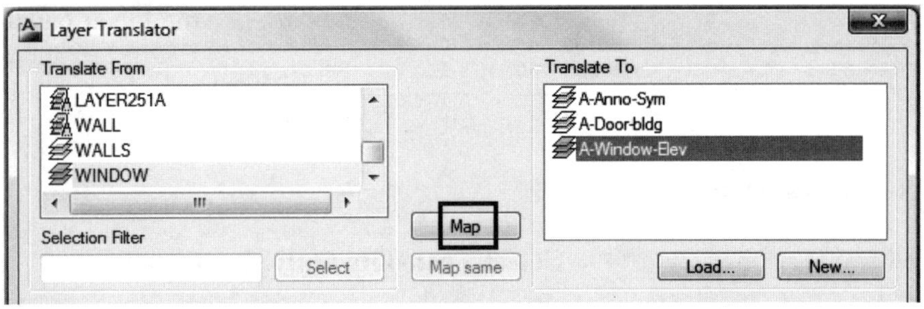

Highlight **WINDOWS** in the Translate From window.
Highlight **A-Window-Elev** in the Translate To window.
Select **Map**.

10. 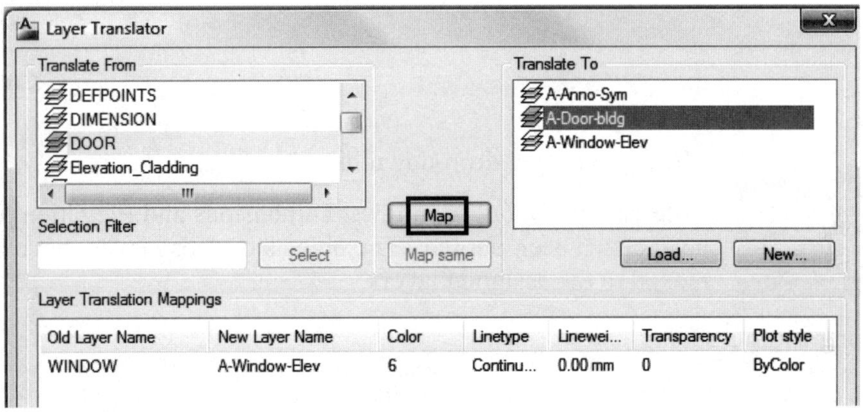

Highlight **DOOR** in the Translate From window.
Highlight **A-Door-bldg** in the Translate To window.
Select **Map**.

11.

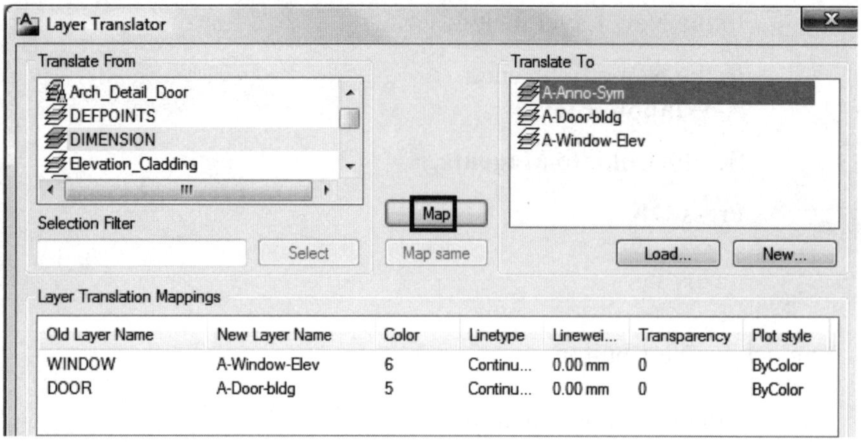

Hold down the Control key.
Highlight **DIMENSIONS** and **Elevation_Dim** in the Translate From window.
Highlight **A-ANNO-SYM** in the Translate To window.
Select **Map**.

You can map more than one layer at a time.

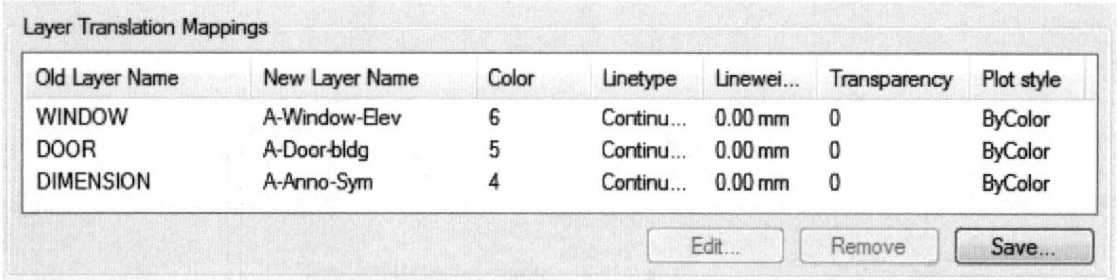

The list of layers to translate are listed in the lower panel

12. 

Select **Translate**.

13.

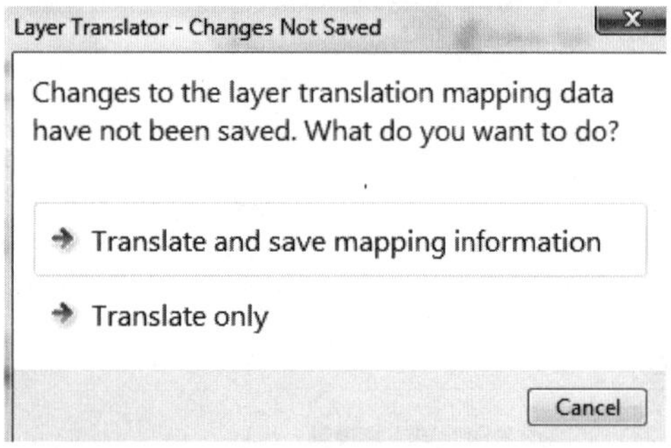

Select **Translate Only**.

You may wish to Save your mapping settings if you plan to translate more than one drawing from the same source.

14.

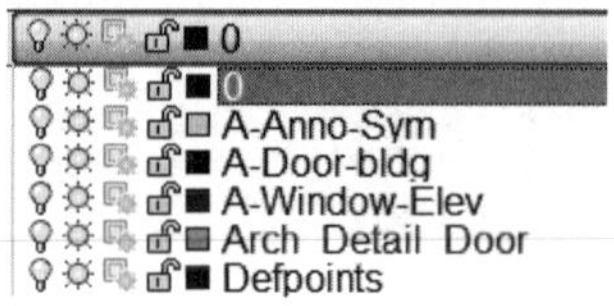

Check your layer drop-down list.

Note that the Doors, Windows, Dimensions and Elevation_Dim layers have been purged. The objects on those layers have been moved to the assigned layers.

15. Close the drawing without saving.

Match Properties Command

Command Locator

Toolbar Menu	**Standard**
Pull Down Menu	**Modify / Match Properties**
Command	**Matchprop**
Alias	**MA**
RMB Shortcut Menu	**Drawing Window**
Dialog Box	**Property Settings**

Command Overview

Object Properties of a selected object can be matched to other objects in the drawing. Select the Source object first, then select the destination object(s). The Matching Properties command will apply the Color, Layer, Linetype, Linetype Scale, Lineweight, Thickness (for 3D), and Dimension, Text, and Hatch styles. Type S to invoke the Settings option or press the RMB to access the shortcut menu and select Settings. Remove the checkmark from any items not to match.

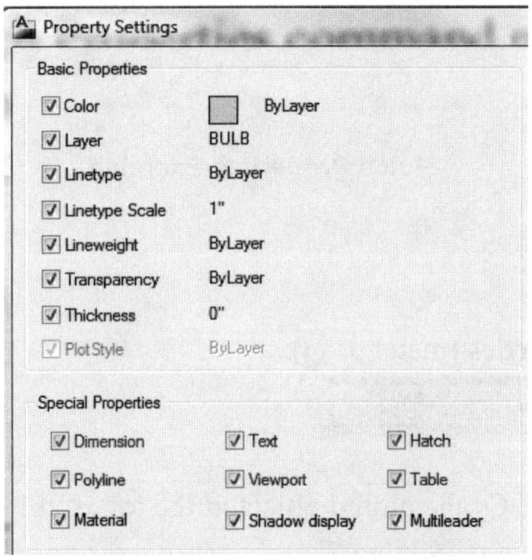

Property Settings Dialog Box

General Procedures

1. Select the Match Properties command from the Standard Toolbar.
2. Select the Source object.
3. Select the destination objects.
4. Press <ENTER> to Exit the command.

Tips & Tricks

- This option is similar to the Microsoft Word *Property Painter.*

Command Exercise

Exercise 8-7 – Match Properties

Drawing Name: **match1.dwg**
Estimated Time to Completion: 5 Minutes

Scope

Using the Match Properties command, match the properties of the colored objects to the similar objects on layer 0 (Black or White). Zoom Window for a close-up view of the drawing.

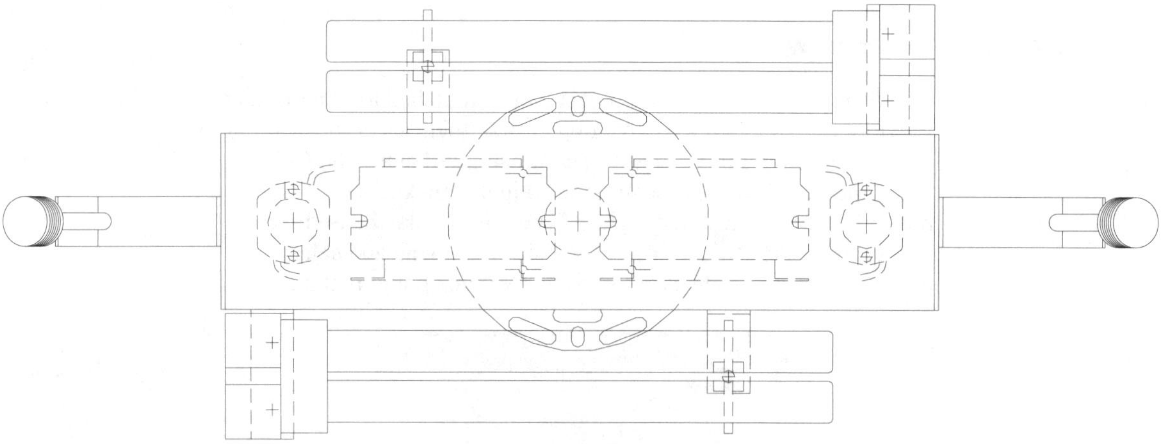

Match Properties Exercise

Solution

1. Invoke the **Match Properties** (matchprop).

2. *Select source object:*
   Use the LMB to select the Cyan colored object at the top of the assembly.
3. *Select destination object(s) or [Settings]:*
   Pick the corresponding part at the bottom of the assembly.
4. *Select destination object(s) or [Settings]:*
   Press the <ENTER> key to end the command.
5. Repeat the process by repeating the Match Properties command. Select the source object first and then apply the properties of the source object to the desired part in the assembly.

> ***Tip:*** *The properties of the dark blue object can be applied to multiple objects.*

Properties Command

Command Locator

Toolbar Menu	**Properties**
Pull Down Menu	**Modify / Properties**
Command	**Properties**
Dialog Box	**Properties**

Command Overview

The Properties of selected objects can be changed using the Properties command. The list in the Properties dialog box will correspond to the objects that are selected. Objects may be selected before or after the Properties command is invoked. The most common features to change are Layer and Linetype. When one item is selected, the Properties dialog box will display options relevant to the features of that object, such as the radius or diameter of a circle, or the contents of selected Text. The Properties dialog box can be moved to select items in the drawing that may appear behind it. Press Escape to deselect objects, and pick new objects to modify.

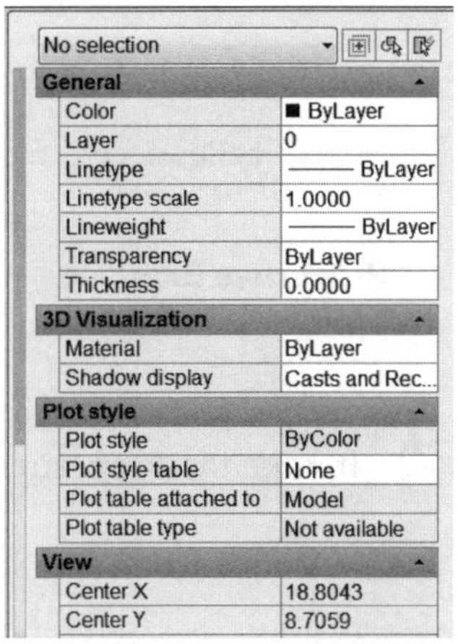

Properties Dialog Box

General Procedures

1. Invoke the Properties command, then select the object(s) to change.
2. Select the option to change from the list, and select or type the new option.
3. Press Escape to deselect the objects.
4. Select the X in the upper right-hand corner to close the dialog box.

Tips & Tricks

- The linetype scale will be multiplied by the global LTSCALE for the objects selected. This change will only affect linetypes other than Continuous.
- The beginners' rule is that the colors of objects should be set to BYLAYER.
- Only layers that are already created will be available in the Select Layer list.
- Only linetypes that have already been loaded will be available in the Select Linetype list.

Command Exercise

Exercise 8-8 – Properties

Drawing Name: **change1.dwg**
Estimated Time to Completion: 10 Minutes

Scope

Using the Properties command, place the shaft on the SHAFT layer, the bellows on the BELLOWS Layer, and the CV joints on the CV Layer.

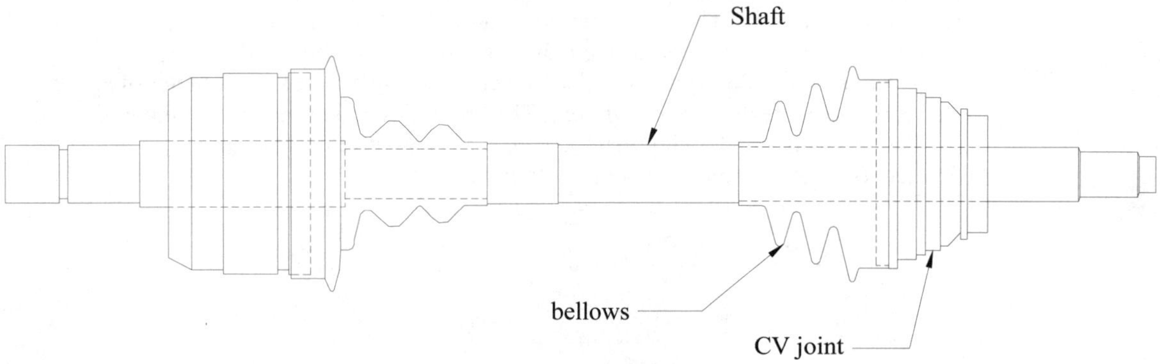

Properties Exercise

Solution

1.  Invoke the Properties command (properties).

2. 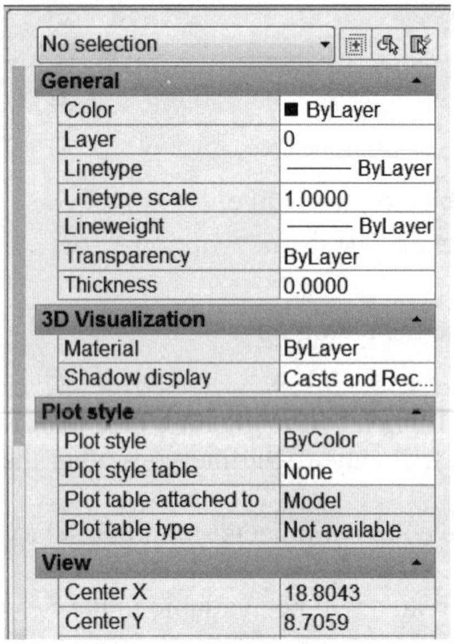

Your Screen will look similar to the following figure.

3. 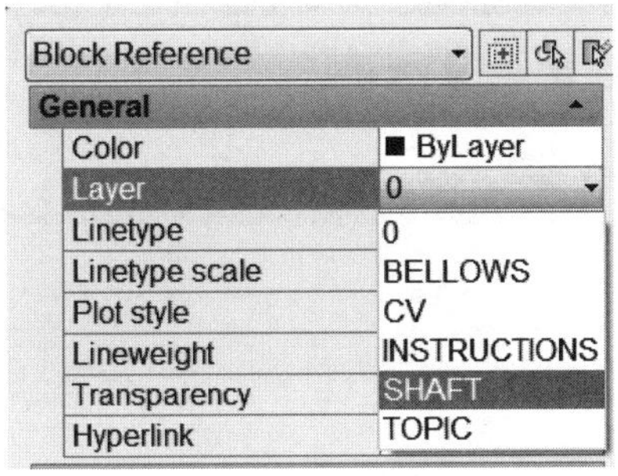

Use the LMB to select the Shaft. Notice that it is highlighted when selected and the information in the Properties Dialog box changes. Change the layer the shaft is on to the SHAFT layer. Pick 0 next to the word Layer in the Properties dialog box.

4. In the drop down list that appears select the SHAFT Layer. Notice that the Shaft changes color. Press the <ESC> key to clear the selection.

5. 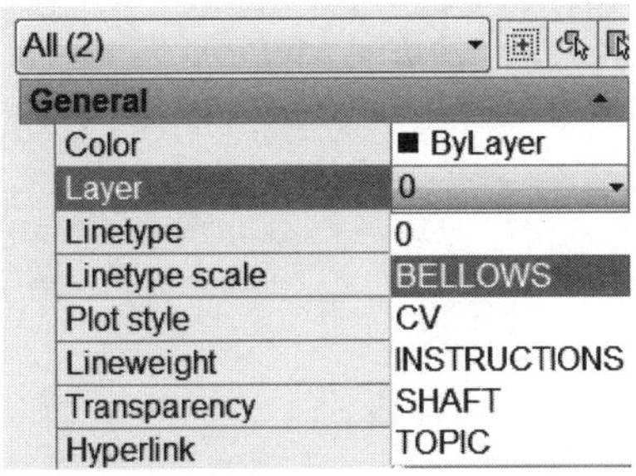

Select the two Bellows with the LMB. Notice how the information in the Properties Dialog box changes. Activate the Drop down list next to the word Layer and select BELLOWS. Note that the Properties dialog displays that two items have been selected.

6. 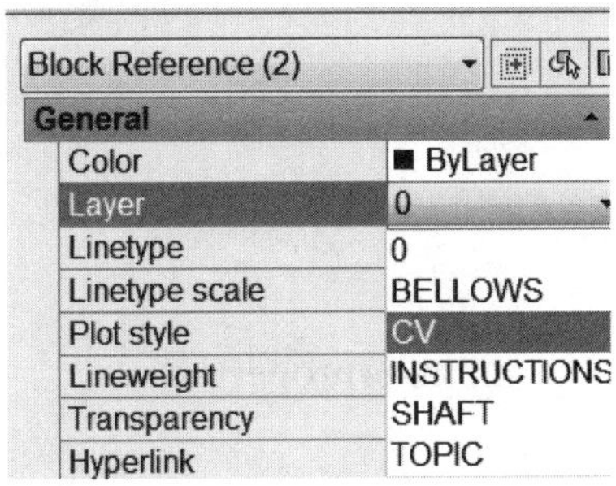

Press <ESC>. Select the two CV joints and change the layer in the Properties dialog box to CV.

Press <ESC>.

Extra: *Try undocking the Properties dialog box from the side of the screen and float it in the drawing area. If it is already floating, try to dock it.*

Command Exercise

Exercise 8-9 – Change Properties

Drawing Name: **change2.dwg**
Estimated Time to Completion: 10 Minutes

Scope

Using the Properties command, change the radius of the circle to 2, the layer to "Circle" and the center point to the midpoint of the line. Perform all these changes in the Properties dialog box. Using the Properties dialog, switch between the circle and the line selection. Change the layer for the line.

Properties Exercise

Solution

1.  Invoke the Properties command (properties).

2. Select the circle and the line using window or crossing.

3. 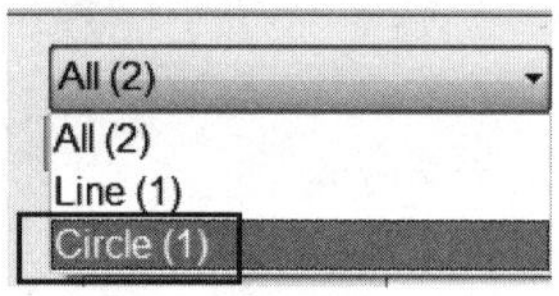

Two items are listed in the Properties dialog.
Select the drop-down arrow.
Select the Circle in the list.

4. 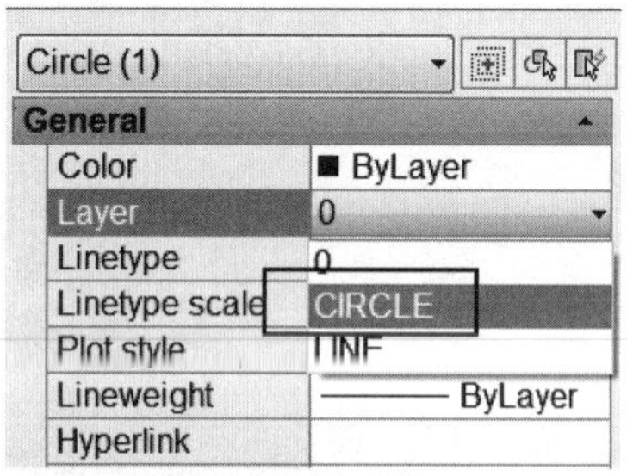

Change the layer to the CIRCLE layer in the properties dialog box.

5. 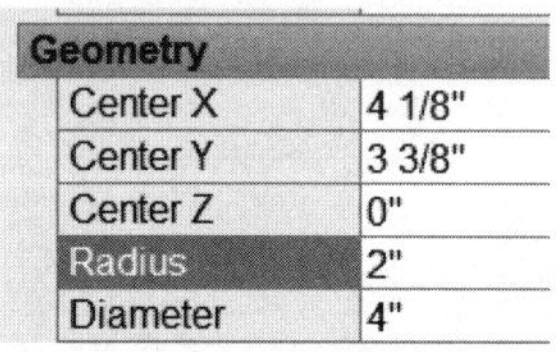

Select the Radius property and change it to 2.0

6. 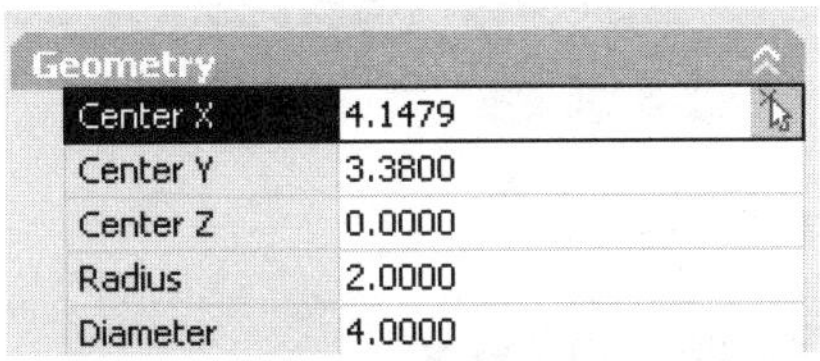

Under the Geometry properties of the circle select the Center X property.

7. 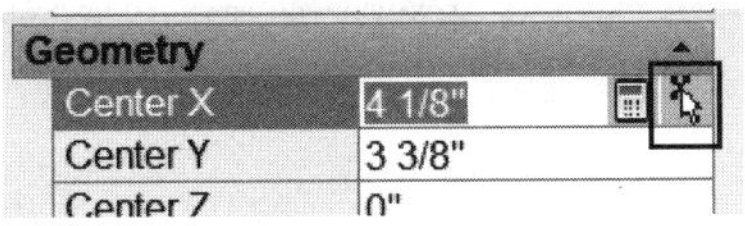

Pick the pointer icon that appears next to the Center X property in the dialog box.

8. 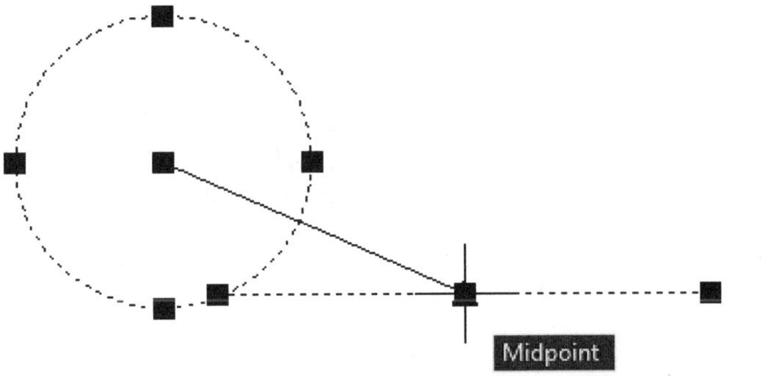

Pick a point in the drawing. Use your OSNAP to select the midpoint of the line. Notice how the circle has been changed.

9. 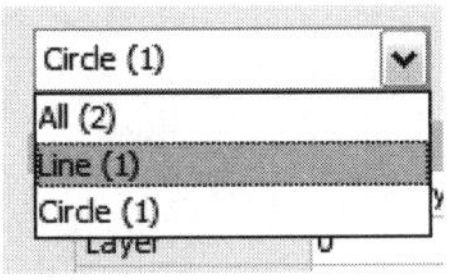

Select the Line from the drop-down list on the Properties dialog.

10. 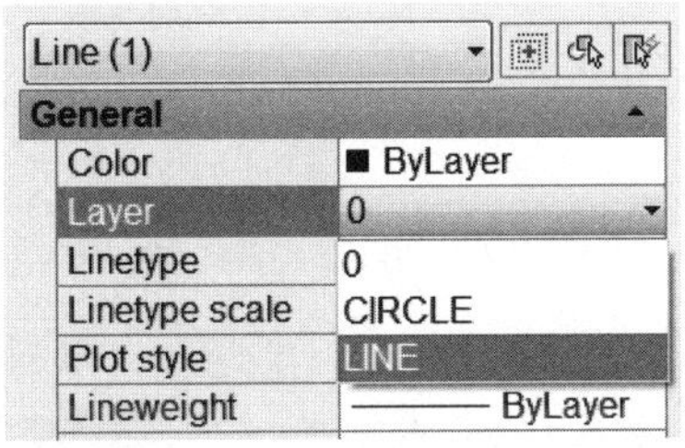

Assign the Line to the LINE layer.

11. 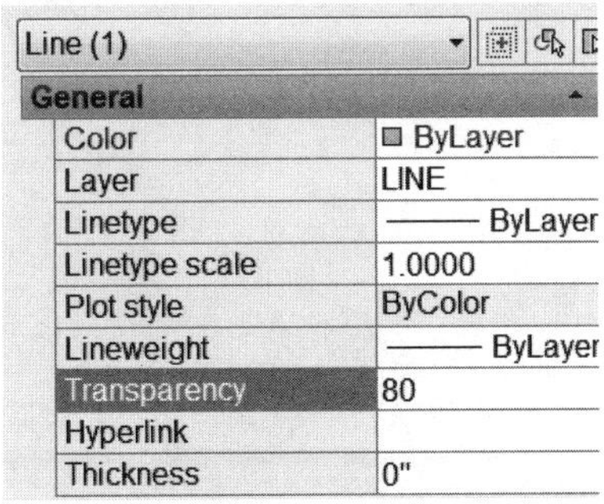

Set the Transparency of the line to 80.

Extra: *Try changing the Area and Circumference of the circle.*

Section Exercise

Exercise 8-10 – Organize Your Drawing

Drawing Name: **Lesson 8 MCAD.dwg**
Estimated Time to Completion: 15 Minutes

Scope

Use the commands you have learned in the past section to organize the drawing into different layers. Create a Layer for each part in the assembly. Use the Properties tools to place the corresponding part on the correct layer.

Layer Name:	*Color:*
NUT	*GREEN*
UPPERBODY	*RED*
LOWERBODY	*YELLOW*
POST	*91*
PLATE	*65*
SHOULDERSCREW	*CYAN*
BILL_OF_MATERIAL	*YELLOW*
TEXT	*250*

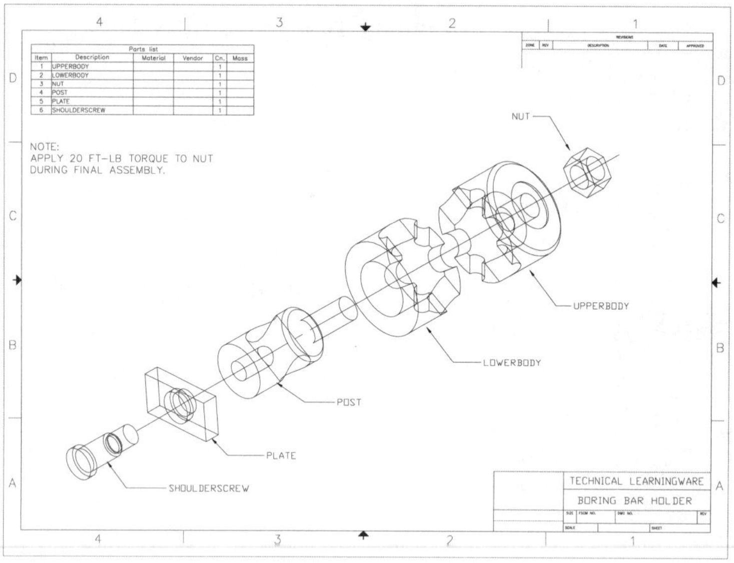

Object Properties MCAD Section Exercise

Hints

1. Start by creating the 8 new layers using the Layers Command. Notice that a layer for the title block already exists.
2. Use the Properties Command and different selection methods to make sure each part is on the correct layer.

Review Questions

1. Identify the following icons and briefly describe each function:

a.  ______________________________

b.  ______________________________

c.  ______________________________

2. What are the two options (what the image represents and its opposite) for the individual icons in the layers control dialog box?

a. 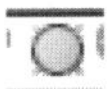 ______________________________

b.  ______________________________

c.  ______________________________

3. What is the difference between FREEZE and OFF when controlling layers?

4. You can turn the current layer OFF. Can you FREEZE the current layer? Can you draw on a layer that is OFF? Try It.

5. What command will remove used layers thus decreasing the file size of your drawing?

- ❑ CLEAN
- ❑ DRAIN
- ❑ PURGE
- ❑ FLUSH

6. What does it mean to choose the color BYLAYER?

- ❑ Objects choose their own color randomly
- ❑ Objects default to the 0 layer and are black or white depending on the drawing window back ground color.
- ❑ Objects take on the color of the current layer they are assigned to.
- ❑ Objects take on an assigned color no matter what layer they are on.

7. What does the LTSCALE command do?

8. How can you control the Match Properties command so only specific features are matched like Line Type? Try It.

9. Transparency

- ❑ Makes objects invisible
- ❑ Can be controlled using Layers
- ❑ Can be set in the Properties Dialog
- ❑ Can be used in overlays

Review Answers

1. Identify the following icons and briefly describe each function:
   a. *Layers Command, opens the Layers dialog box*
   b. *Match Properties, matches the properties of one or more objects to the first selected*
   c. *Make Object's Layer Current, makes the layer of the selected object current*

2. What are the two options (what the image represents and its opposite) for the individual icons in the layers control dialog box?
   a. *Freeze & Thaw*
   b. *On & Off*
   c. *Lock & Unlock*

3. What is the difference between FREEZE and OFF when controlling layers?

   The layers are not visible. Frozen layer is ignored in a regeneration (Saving time when you regen), a layer that is simply turned Off will still be processed in a regeneration (saving no time in a regen). Therefore, use FREEZE instead of OFFF.

4. You can turn the current layer OFF. Can you FREEZE the current layer? Can you draw on a layer that is OFF? Try It.

   You can not FREEZE the current layer. You can turn OFF the current layer. You can draw on a layer that is turned OFF. It is not recommended to draw on layers that are turned off, though, because you cannot see what you are drawing.

5. What command will remove used layers thus decreasing the file size of your drawing?

   - *PURGE*

   The Purge command will delete unused layers and other objects such as linetypes, blocks, etc. You may also delete unused layers and linetypes in the Layers dialog box.

6. What does it mean to choose colors BYLAYER?

   - *Objects take on the color of the current layer they are assigned to.*

   Objects will take on the color of the current layer, when the color control is set to ByLayer. In the Object Properties dialog box, selecting BYLAYER will assign color to the selected object according the layer it is on.

7. What does the LTSCALE command do?

   LTSCALE is a system variable that controls the linetype scale.

8. How can you control the Match Properties command so only specific features are matched like Line Type? Try It.

   Right click and select Settings to enable/disable Match Property Options.

9. Transparency

   ✓ *Can be controlled using Layers*

   ✓ *Can be set in the Properties Dialog*

   ✓ *Can be used in overlays*

Lesson 9.0 – Drafting Settings and Object Snaps

Estimated Class Time – 2 Hours

Objectives

Students will practice setting different drafting and object snap settings and using the active settings to control how geometry is drawn.

- **Drafting Settings**
- **Object Snaps**
- **Creating Orthographic Views**

Drafting Settings

Command Locator

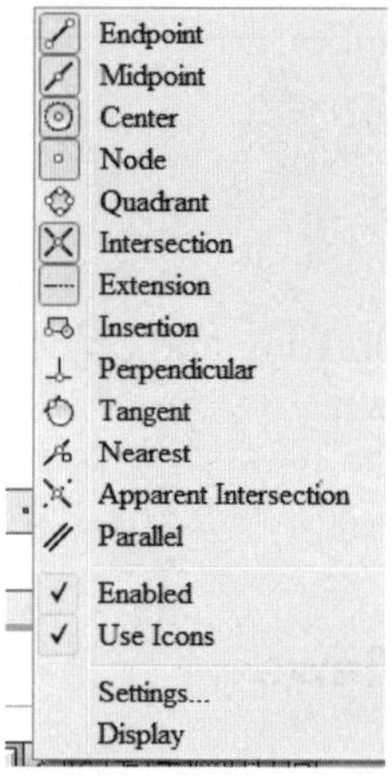

Pull Down Menu	**Tools→Drafting Settings…**
Command	**dsettings**
Alias	**ds**
RMB Shortcut Menu	**Over SNAP, GRID, POLAR, OSNAP or OTRACK in the Status Bar**
Dialog Box	**Drafting Settings**

Command Overview

The Drafting Settings dialog box contains five tabs:

- Snap and Grid
- Polar Tracking
- Object Snap
- Dynamic Input
- Quick Properties

Select the Status Bar option using the LMB to turn these functions ON or OFF. Use the RMB to access the Drafting Settings dialog box. In 2011, you can quickly enable and disable object snaps by mousing over the OSNAP button and selecting/deselecting the preferred OSNAPs.

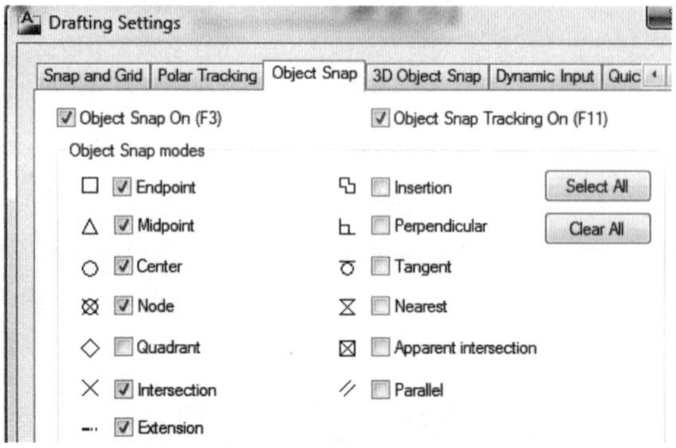

Drafting Settings Dialog Box, Object SnapTab

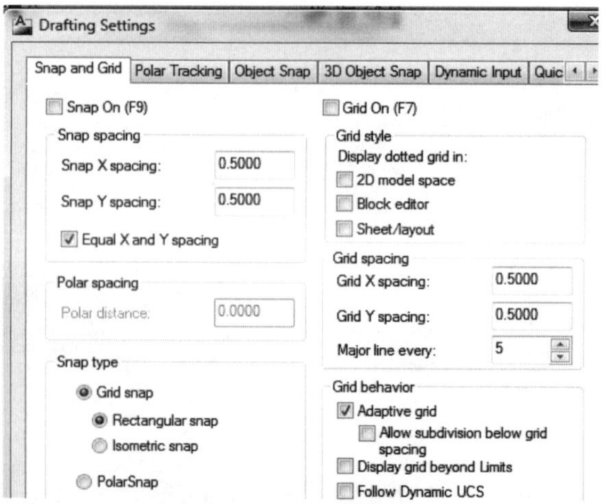

Drafting Settings Dialog Box, Snap and Grid Tab

Command Exercise

Exercise 9-1 – Drafting Settings

Drawing Name: **drsettings1.dwg**
Estimated Time to Completion: 5 Minutes

Scope

In the Drafting Settings dialog box, Set the Grid spacing to 0,0. Set the Snap Spacing to .5,.5. Turn the Snap and Grid ON. Select OK. Notice how the snap and grid spacing change.

Solution

1. Activate the Drafting Settings dialog box by right-clicking on 'Snap' or 'Grid' on the status bar and selecting 'Settings…' or by typing 'DSETTINGS' at the command line and pressing <ENTER>.

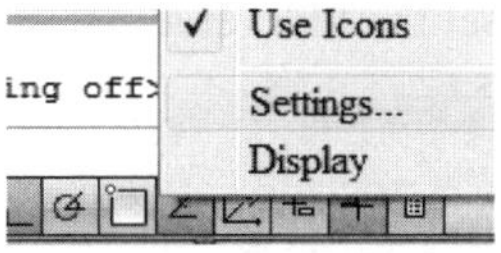

2. Fill out the settings in the dialog box as shown in the following figure.

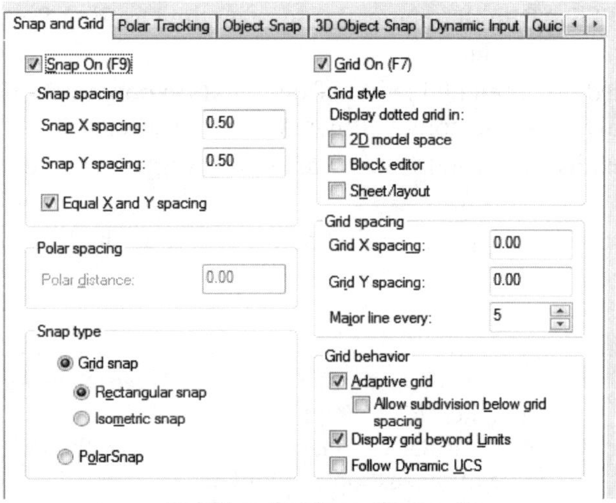

Drafting Settings Dialog Box

3. Press 'OK' to continue.
4. Notice how the Grip spacing defaults to the Snap spacing.

Extra: *What happens if you set the snap spacing to 1,1 and Grid spacing to .3,.3? Try It.*

Tip: *Use the Isometric Snap option in the dialog box above to create an isometric drawing. Turn Ortho ON and use the F5 function key or Ctrl+E to toggle through the isoplanes.*

Drafting Settings: Polar Tracking Tab

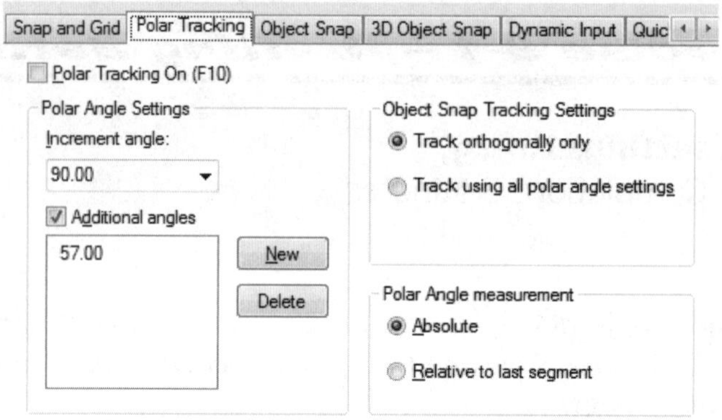

Drafting Settings Dialog Box, Polar Tracking Tab

Polar Snap works independently from SNAP. With Polar Snap turned ON incremental angles will be displayed as the line being dragged approaches that angle. Set the "Incremental angle" from the drop down list, or add "New" angles.

General Procedures

1. Right-click on POLAR in the Status Bar to open the Drafting Settings dialog box and select the Polar Tracking tab.
2. Select the desired "Incremental angle" from the drop down list. Check "Track orthogonally only" and "Absolute" Polar Angle measurement.
3. "Track orthogonally only" and "Absolute" Polar Angle measurement should also be selected.
4. Using the Line command, pick the first point, then drag the line to see the Polar Angle display.

Tips & Tricks

- With the desired polar angle displayed, type the length of the line and press the <ENTER> key.
- Select "Relative to last segment" to see the Polar Angle in relation to the angle of the last object drawn.

Drafting Settings: Object Snap Tab

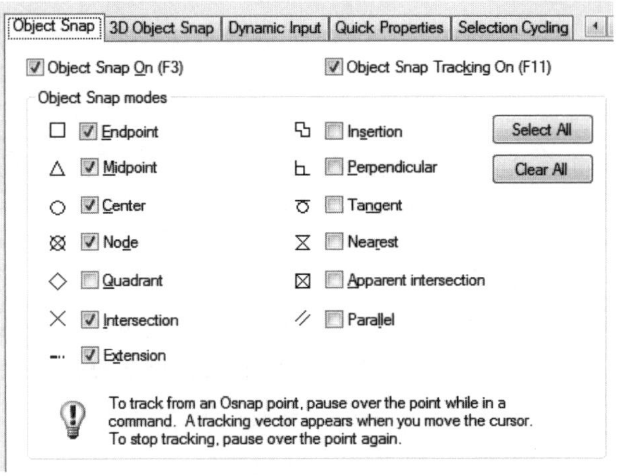

Drafting Settings Dialog Box, Object Snap Tab

When an Object Snap mode is selected, and a draw or modify command has been invoked, the OSNAP will be displayed as the cursor moves over a line or object. The cursor will want to "snap" to that point. If the cursor is held over that snap point, a label will display the snap mode. Once the cursor is moved away from that point, the Object Snap will no longer be displayed or selected. Toggle the OSNAP settings on and off from the Status Bar.

General Procedures

1. Right-click on OSNAP to open the Drafting Settings dialog box and select the Object Snap tab.
2. Select the desired Object Snap modes (i.e. Endpoint, Midpoint, and Intersection).
3. Select OK to exit the dialog box and draw using Object Snap.

Tips & Tricks

- OSNAP settings when selected will remain constant, or "running," if OSNAP is on. Object Snap options can be selected individually using the Object Snap toolbar (see next section), whether OSNAP is on or off.
- Object Snap will want to gravitate to the nearest OSNAP setting. When two options are selected that might make one option impossible to select (such as Center and Quadrant of a circle or arc), use the Tab key to toggle through the options. When the desired Object Snap is displayed, use the pick button to select it.
- Do not check all the Object Snap modes in the dialog box. This will make selecting objects tedious and no longer a handy tool.
- When no Object Snap modes are selected ("Clear All"), selecting OSNAP from the Status Bar will automatically open the Drafting Settings dialog box at the Object Snap tab. Once object snap modes are selected, OSNAP is an ON/OFF switch.
- Select Options from the dialog box to change the AutoSnap marker color and AutoSnap marker size.
- Type OS to open the Drafting Settings dialog box at the Object Snap tab.

Object Snap

Command Locator

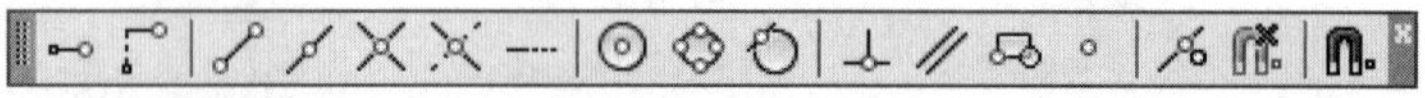

Toolbar Menu	**Object Snap Fly-Out or Object Snap**
Alias	**End, mid, int, per, etc. (the first three letters of the option), then press <ENTER>**
RMB Shortcut Menu	**2-Button Mouse: Shift + <ENTER> with the cursor in drawing window** **3-Button Mouse: Middle button with the cursor in drawing window**

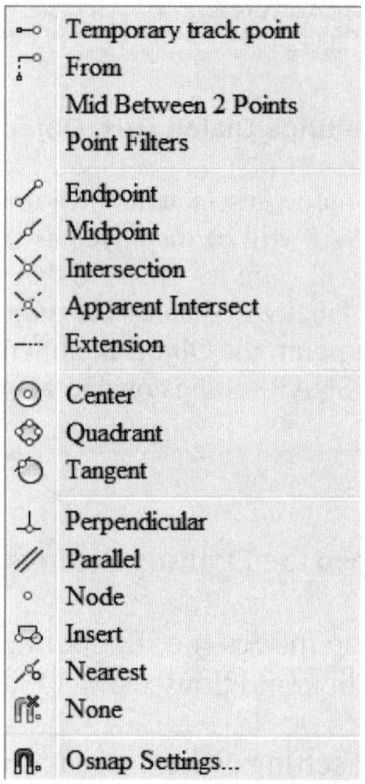

Object Snap Shortcut Menu

Command Overview

Object Snaps are used in combination with other commands. Use an object snap option when prompted to select a point and a specific object snap is desired. Unlike the OSNAP settings, which keep the OSNAP option "running", these object snaps are used for single selections.

Object Snap Option	Button	Overview
Endpoint	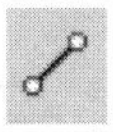	selects the endpoint of a line or arc.
Midpoint	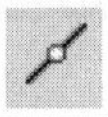	selects the midpoint of a line or arc.
Intersection	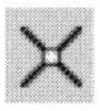	selects the intersection or projected intersection of two lines.
Apparent Intersect	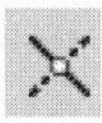	selects the virtual intersection of an existing line and the extension of another line.
Extension	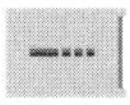	selects a point extending from a line's endpoint.
Center	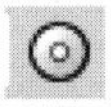	selects the center of a circle or arc.
Quadrant		selects one of the four quadrants of a circle or arc.
Tangent		makes the object drawn, tangent to the object selected.
Perpendicular		makes the object drawn perpendicular to the object selected.
Parallel	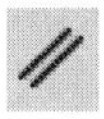	draws an object parallel to the selected object.
Node	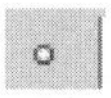	selects a point – you must have placed a point using the POINT command.
Insert		selects the point on the object where it was inserted –works for blocks, xrefs, and text.
Nearest	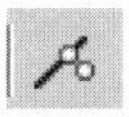	selects a point on the object selected at the location where it was picked.
None		turns off all active object snap settings during the active command.
OSNAP Settings		opens the Drafting Settings dialog box.

General Procedures

1. Begin a Draw (or Modify) command.
2. When prompted for a selection point, choose an Object Snap option.
3. Place the cursor over the object, when the marker appears at the desired location, use the LMB to select.

Tips & Tricks

- Remember to select the Object Snap each time before picking a point.
- When specifying the center of a circle, be sure to pick the circumference.
- The "Apparent Intersection" Object Snap is for 3D modeling.
- Selecting two object snaps in a row, such as Endpoint and Midpoint, will cancel both Object Snap selections (it doesn't understand the "endpoint of the midpoint").
- If the wrong Object Snap option is mistakenly selected, pick in a blank area of the Drawing Window, then select the proper Object Snap option again.
- Single object snaps can be used in combination with the running OSNAP settings.

Command Exercise

Exercise 9-2 – Object Snap

Drawing Name: **osnap1.dwg**
Estimated Time to Completion: 5 Minutes

Scope

Practice using single object snaps. Draw the objects shown using the object snaps as indicated.

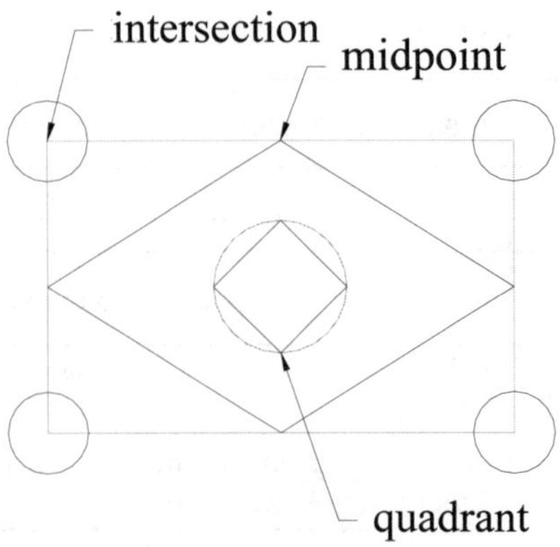

Object Snap Exercise

Solution

1. Make sure Running Object Snap is turned off. Use your LMB to toggle OSNAP off at the status bar.
2. Create the four circles first. Invoke the Circle command (c or circle).

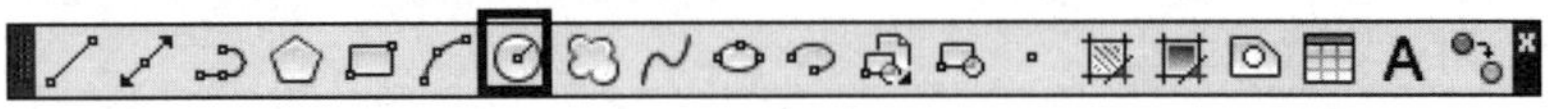

3. *Specify center point for circle or [3P/2P/Ttr (tan tan radius)]:*
   Before you pick the first center point of the circle hold your <Shift> key down and press the RMB to bring up the Object Snap shortcut menu. Select intersection.
4. *Specify center point for circle or [3P/2P/Ttr (tan tan radius)]: _int of*
   Move your pointer near the desired intersection until the Intersection Object Snap Marker appears. Pick the point with your LMB. Notice how the center of the circle is exactly at the intersection of the 2 lines.
5. *Specify radius of circle or [Diameter]:*
   Use your mouse to estimate the radius of the circle.
6. Repeat the process to complete the remaining circles.
7. Invoke the Line command (l or line).

8. *Specify first point:*
Before you pick the start point of the line hold your <Shift> key down and press the RMB. This will bring up the Object Snap shortcut menu. Select Midpoint.

9. *Specify first point: _mid of*
Move your pointer near one of the sides of the box until the Midpoint Object Snap Marker appears. Select the point with the LMB.

10. *Specify next point or [Undo]:*
Hold your <Shift> key down and press the RMB to activate the Object Snap shortcut menu. Select Midpoint.

11. *Specify next point or [Undo]: _mid of*
Move your pointer to the desired side of the box to compete the first line segment.

12. *Specify next point or [Close/Undo]:*
Repeat the process using the midpoint object snap to finish the four line segments in the Box.

13. We will finish the exercise by creating the 4 line segments in the center circle. Invoke the Line command (l or line).

14. *Specify first point:*
Hold the <Shift> key down and press the RMB to active the Object Snap shortcut menu. Select the Quadrant object snap.

15. *Specify first point: _qua of*
Move the pointer near the top of the center circle and press the LMB once the Quadrant Object Snap Marker appears.

16. *Specify next point or [Undo]:* Repeat the process of using the <Shift> RMB to activate the shortcut menu. Remember to select the Quadrant Object Snap before selecting a point with the LMB.

> ***Tip:*** *The Object Snap symbols help to indicate were the selection point will be placed. The Object Snap tool bar can also be used to select the desired Object Snap. Move your pointer near the circumference of a circle when using the Center Object Snap.*

Command Exercise

Exercise 9-3 – Object Snap

Drawing Name: **osnap2.dwg**
Estimated Time to Completion: 5 Minutes

Scope

Using the single object snap option. Draw the object on the left using the object snaps as indicated each time you select a point.

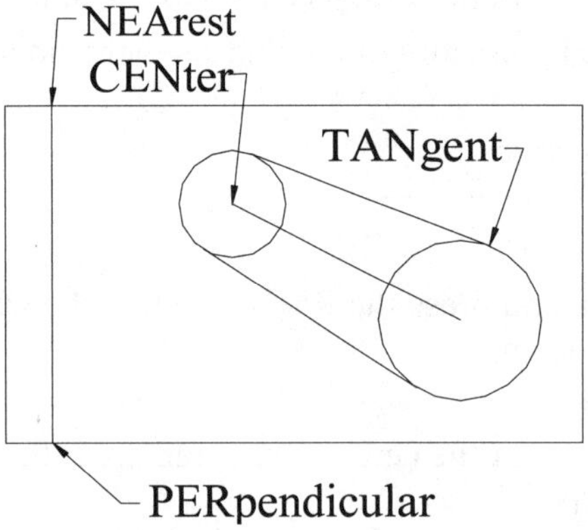

Object Snap Exercise

Solution

1. Start by creating the vertical line using the Perpendicular and Nearest Object Snaps. Invoke the Line command (l or line).

2. *Specify first point:*
Hold the <Shift> key down and press the RMB to activate the Object Snap shortcut menu. Select the Nearest Object Snap
3. *Specify first point: _per to*
Move the pointer to the top of the box and press the LMB when the Nearest Object Snap Marker appears.
4. *Specify next point or [Undo]:*
Hold the <Shift> key down and press the RMB to activate the Object Snap shortcut menu. Select the Perpendicular Object Snap.
5. *Specify next point or [Undo]: _nea*
Move the pointer to the bottom of the box and select the desired point that will create the vertical line segment. Notice that the line is perpendicular to the bottom line segment and positioned at the second point you have selected.

6. Create the two lines that are tangent to the circles. Start by invoking the Line command (l or line).

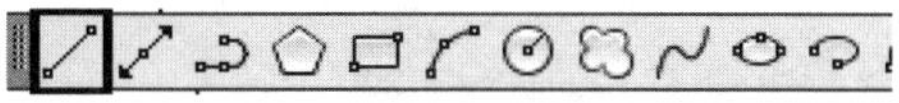

7. *Specify first point:*
Hold your <Shift> key down and press the RMB to activate the Object Snap shortcut menu. Select Tangent.

8. *Specify first point: _tan to*
Move the pointer to the general area for the start point of the line and press LMB when the Tangent Object Snap Marker appears.

9. *Specify next point or [Undo]:*
Hold your <Shift> key down and press the RMB to activate the Object Snap shortcut menu.

10. *Specify first point: _tan to*
Move the pointer to the general area for the end point of the line and press LMB when the Tangent Object Snap Marker appears. Repeat the process for the second line that is tangent to the 2 circles.

11. Finish the exercise by creating a line from the center point of the first circle to the center point of the second circle. Invoke the Line command (l or line).

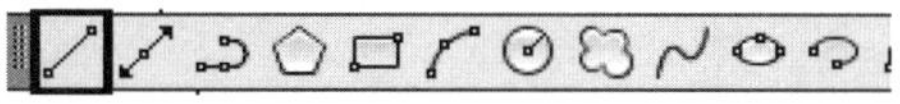

12. *Specify first point:*
Hold your <Shift> key down and press the RMB to activate the Object Snap shortcut menu. Select Center.

13. *Specify first point: _cen to*
Move the pointer to the center of the circle for the start point of the line and press LMB when the Center Object Snap Marker appears.

14. *Specify next point or [Undo]:*
Hold your <Shift> key down and press the RMB to activate the Object Snap shortcut menu. Select Center.

15. *Specify next point or [Undo]: _cen of*
Move the pointer to the center of the second circle for the end of the line. Press the LMB when the Center Object Snap Marker appears.

> ***Tip:*** *AutoCAD will not display lines when using Perpendicular or Tangent Object snap until an end point is selected. This occurs because the first point is dependant on the second point selected when using the Tangent and Perpendicular Object Snap.*

Command Exercise

Exercise 9-4 – Object Snap

Drawing Name: **osnap3.dwg**
Estimated Time to Completion: 5 Minutes

Scope

Draw the object on the left using Running Object Snaps. Double click on OSNAP, or select <TOOLS<DRAFTING SETTINGS. Activate the Endpoint, Midpoint and Quadrant running object snaps. Note that this exercise is similar to the previous single object snap exercise, except that Object Snap options will remain ON.

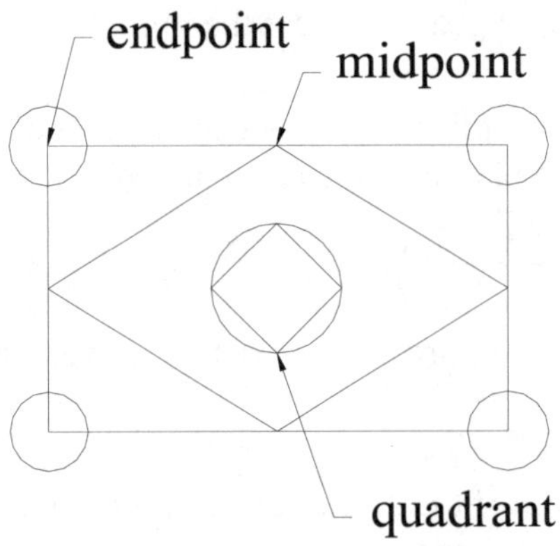

Running Object Snap Exercise

Solution

1. Start by making sure the Running Object Snaps are set. Use your LMB to toggle OSNAP on at the status bar.
2. Set the correct running object snaps by right-clicking on 'OSNAP' on the status bar and selecting 'Settings…'

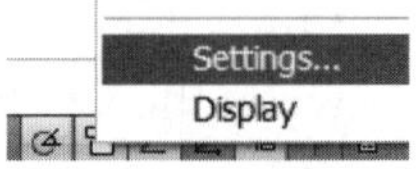

3. In the Drafting Tools dialog box, select the Object Snap tab and select the options shown in the next figure.

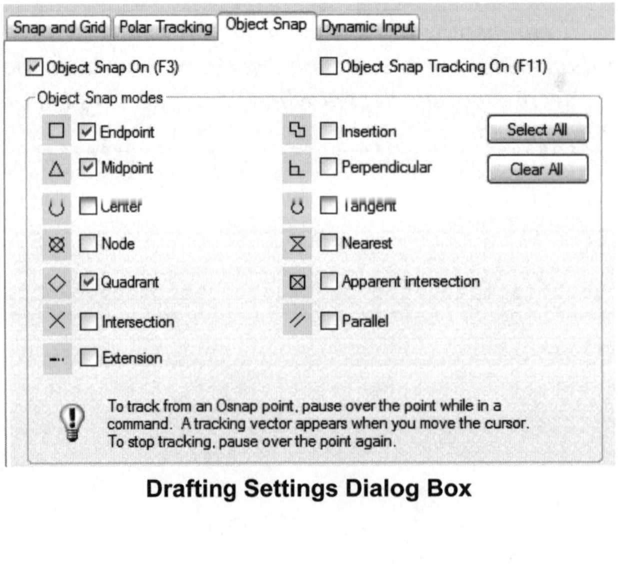

Drafting Settings Dialog Box

4. Press ‘OK’ to continue.
5. Invoke the circle command (c or circle).

6. *Specify center point for circle or [3P/2P/Ttr (tan tan radius)]:*
   Move your pointer to near one of the desired corners until the End Object Snap Marker appears. Pick the point with the LMB.
7. *Specify radius of circle or [Diameter]:*
   Use your mouse and LMB to finish the first circle.
8. Repeat the circle command by pressing <ENTER> or right-clicking in the drawing window and selecting 'Repeat'.

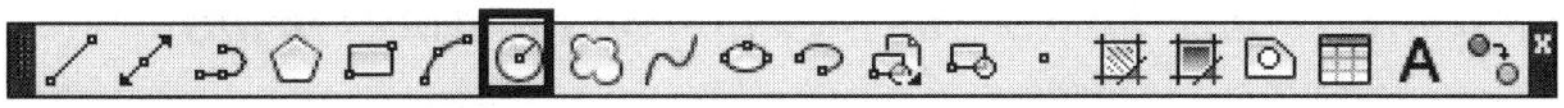

9. *Specify center point for circle or [3P/2P/Ttr (tan tan radius)]:*
   Move your pointer to the next corner until the desired End Object Snap Marker appears. Pick with your LMB.
10. *Specify radius of circle or [Diameter] <x.xx>:*
    Press <ENTER> to finish the second circle with the same radius. Repeat the process to complete the remaining circles.
11. Invoke the line command (l or line).

12. *Specify first point:*
    Move your pointer to one of the sides of the box. You will see the Midpoint Object Snap Marker appear. Pick with your left mouse button. This creates the start point of the line.
13. *Specify next point or [Undo]:*
    Move your pointer to another side to compete the first line segment. Remember to use your LMB when the desired object snap marker appears. Let the cursor *snap* into the Object Snap marker. Repeat the command to complete the four line segments.
14. Invoke the Line command (l or line) to finish the exercise by creating the diamond in the center circle.

15. *Specify first point:*
    Move your pointer near the top quadrant of the center circle. Press the LMB to select the start point of the line segment.
16. *Specify next point or [Undo]:*
    Repeat the process by moving the pointer near the desired quadrant and pressing the LMB when the Quadrant Object Snap appears.

- Before you start drafting set running object snaps. Most commonly used object snaps are Endpoint, Midpoint, Intersection and Center. Use your <Tab> key to cycle through the different object snaps that overlap each other (i.e., Quadrant and Center or multiple object snap options that are close together.
- Remember to use the regular Intersection object snap to find the Intersection or Extended Intersection of two objects. Apparent Intersection is for 3D. Choosing an object snap option from the toolbar, shortcut menu, or by typing the alias, will override Running Object Snap.

Command Exercise

Exercise 9-5 – Object Snap

Drawing Name: **osnap4.dwg**
Estimated Time to Completion: 5 Minutes

Scope

Draw a circle with the Center at the projected intersection of the two lines as indicated in the figure below. Notice how the intersection option works in this exercise.

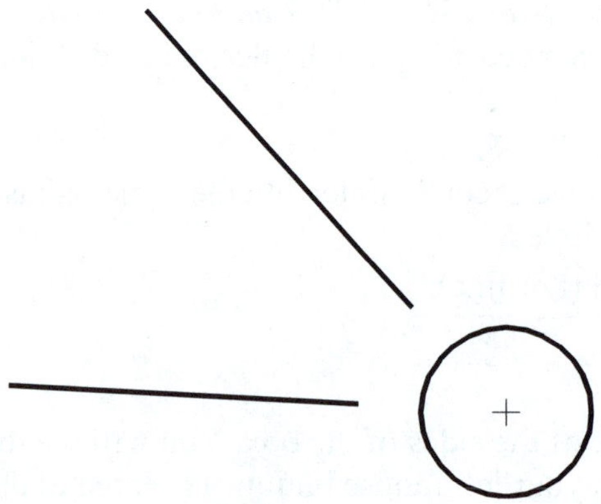

Object Snap Exercise

Solution

1. Invoke the circle command (c or circle).

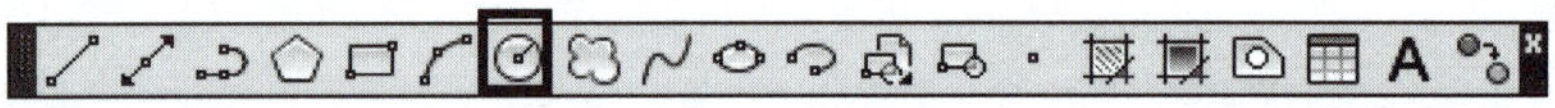

2. *Specify center point for circle or [3P/2P/Ttr (tan tan radius)]:*
Hold the <Shift> key down and press the RMB to activate the Object Snap shortcut menu. Select Intersection.
3. *Specify center point for circle or [3P/2P/Ttr (tan tan radius)]: _int of*
Move the pointer to the lower end of the top line and press the LMB. Notice the Object Snap tool tip will say "Extended Intersection".
4. *Specify center point for circle or [3P/2P/Ttr (tan tan radius)]: _int of and*
Move the pointer near the end of the second line. Notice where the Intersection Object Snap appears. Press the LMB to select the center of the circle.
5. *Specify radius of circle or [Diameter]:*
Use the mouse to determine the radius of the circle and complete the exercise.

Command Exercise

Exercise 9-6 – Object Tracking

Drawing Name: **new drawing**
Estimated Time to Completion: 20 Minutes

Scope

Enable Object Snaps and Object Tracking in order to draw the figure. Enable ORTHO ON.

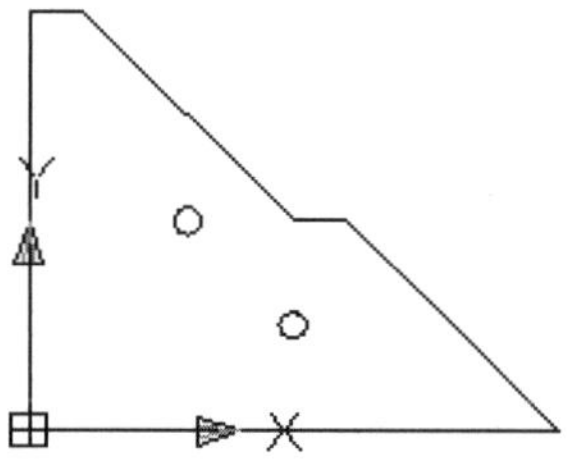

Object Tracking

Solution

1. 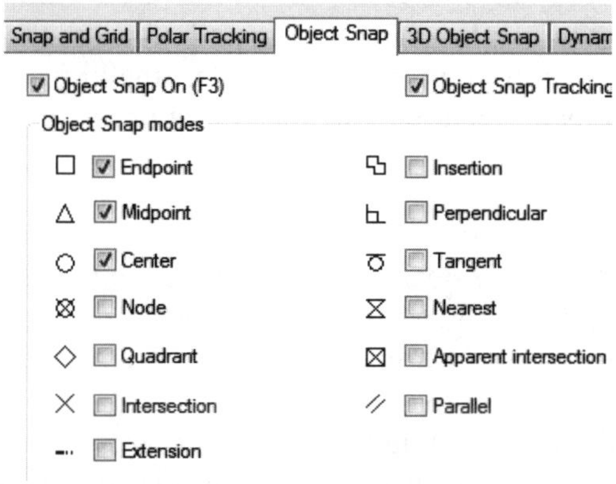

Verify that the Endpoint, Midpoint, and Center are enabled in the Object Snap settings.

2. 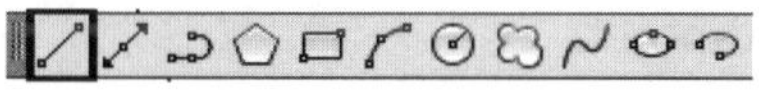

Start the **Line** command.

3. 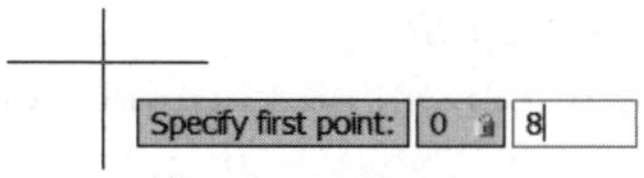

Specify the first point as **0,8**.

4. 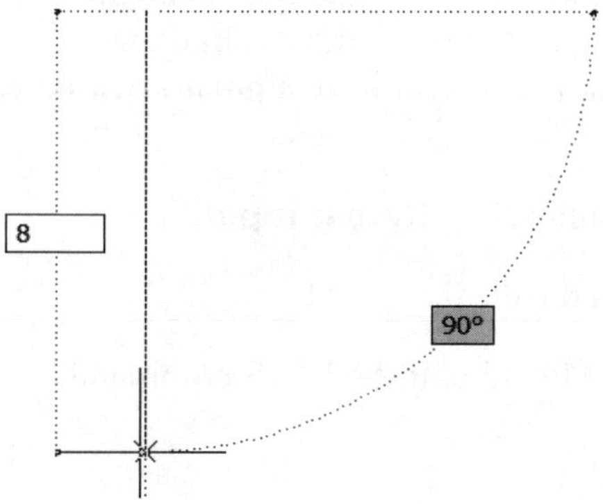

Move the cursor down and enter **8**.

5.

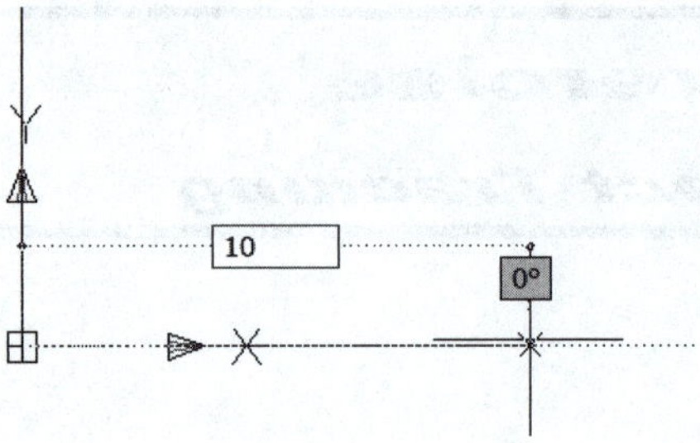

Specify next point or [Undo]:
Move the cursor towards the right until a temporary polar tracking path of 0 degrees displays as shown in the next figure. Type **10** and press <ENTER> while this path is showing.

Disable the ORTHO toggle.

6.

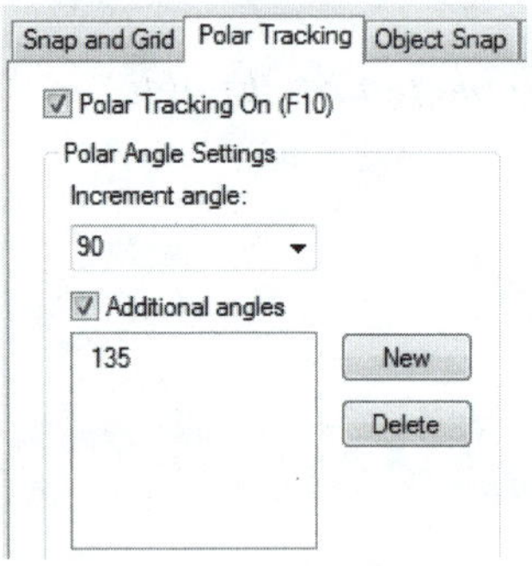

Set Polar Tracking to 135.

Enable **POLAR** ON.

7.

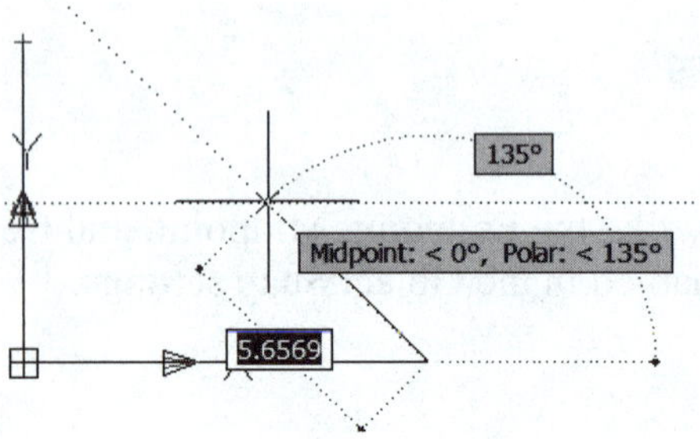

Specify next point or [Close/Undo]:
Move the cursor near the midpoint of the vertical line until it is acquired (a + sign shows up at the midpoint and a tooltip also appears). Then move the cursor to the right to display the tracking path through the midpoint until you also have a polar tracking path of 135 degrees. Then click to select that point.

8.

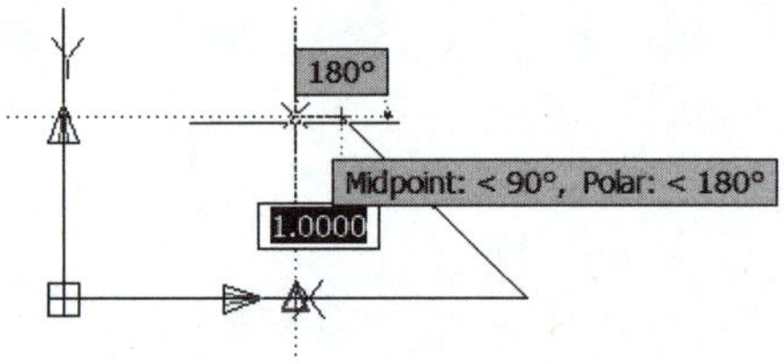

Specify next point or [Close/Undo]:
Move the cursor near the midpoint of the horizontal line until it is acquired (a + sign shows up at the midpoint and a tooltip also appears). Then move the cursor upward to display the tracking path through the midpoint until you also have a polar tracking path of 180 degrees as shown in the next figure. Then click to select that point.

9.

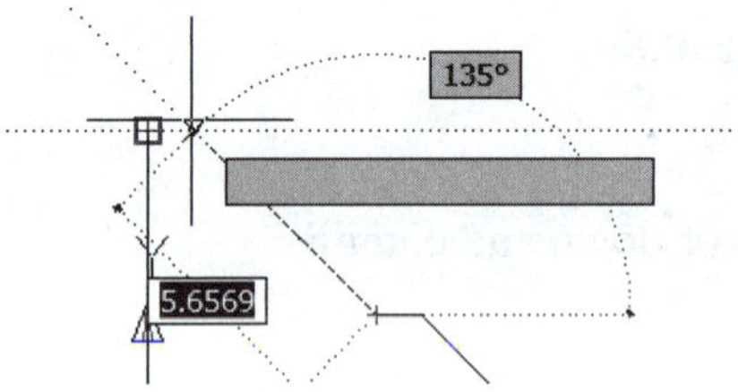

Specify next point or [Close/Undo]:
Move the cursor near the upper endpoint of the vertical line until it is acquired (a + sign shows up at the endpoint and a tooltip also appears). Then move the cursor to the right to display the tracking path through the endpoint until you also have a polar tracking path of 135 degrees. Then click to select that point.

10.

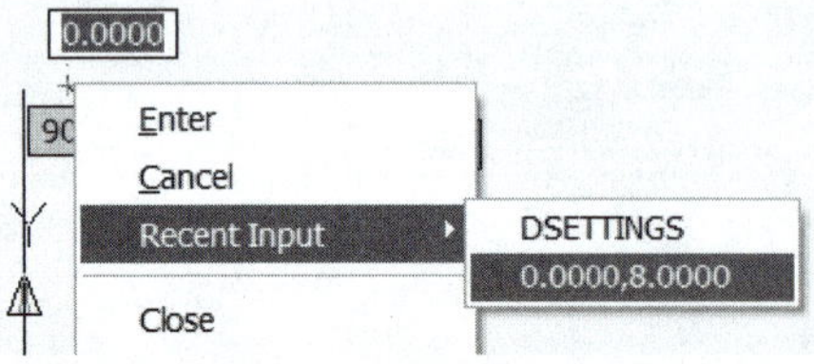

Right click and select **Recent Input**.

Select **0,8** as the closing point.

Press <ENTER> to exit the LINE command.

11. 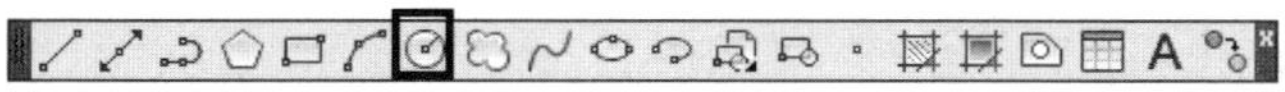

Invoke the **Circle** command (c or circle).

12. 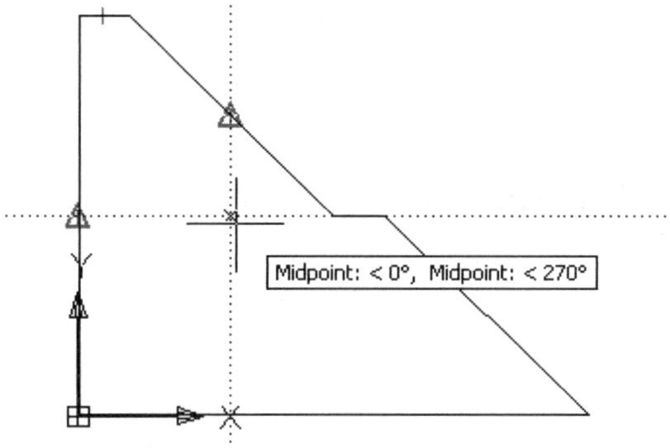

Specify center point for circle or [3P/2P/Ttr (tan tan radius)]:
Move the cursor near midpoint of the vertical line until it is acquired (a + sign shows up at the midpoint and a tooltip also appears). Then move the cursor near midpoint of the upper inclined line until it is acquired. Finally, move downward until tracking paths display through both of the midpoints as shown in the next figure. Then click to select that point.

13. 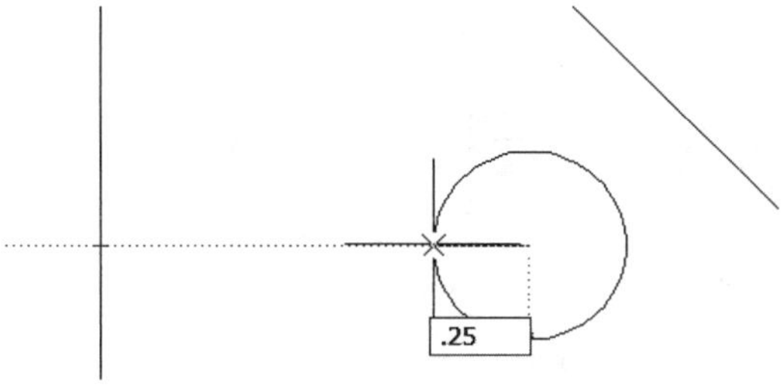

Specify radius of circle or [Diameter] <x.xx>:
Type **0.25** and press <ENTER>.

14. 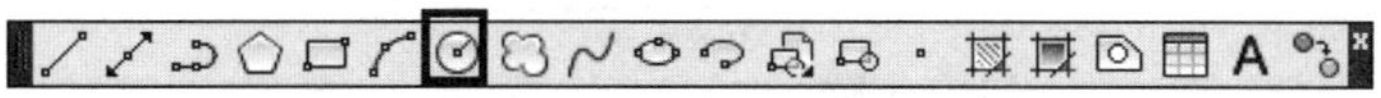

Repeat the Circle command (right-click and select 'Repeat', or type c or circle).

15. *Specify center point for circle or [3P/2P/Ttr (tan tan radius)]:*
Move the cursor near endpoint of the upper horizontal line until it is acquired (a + sign shows up at the midpoint and a tooltip also appears).

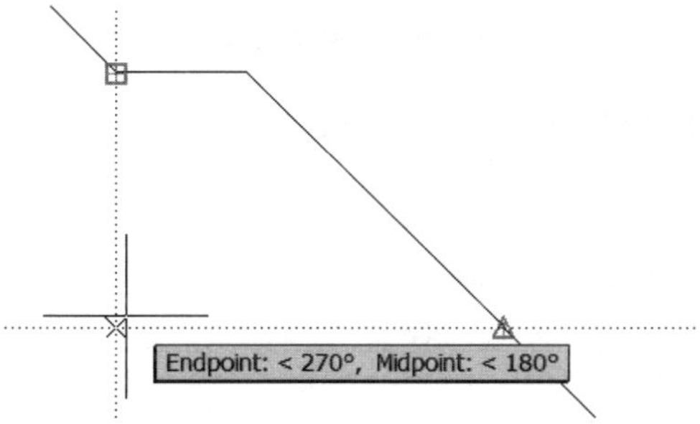

Then move the cursor near midpoint of the lower angled line until it is acquired. Finally, move to the left until tracking paths display through both of the midpoints as shown in the next figure. Then click to select that point.

16. 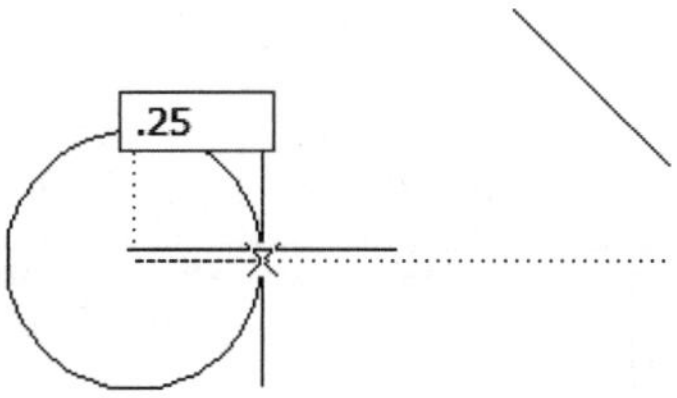

Specify radius of circle or [Diameter] <x.xx>:
Type '0.25' and press <ENTER>.

> ***Tip:*** *Draw a line with a random angle, then draw another line that is parallel to it. Use the Parallel Object Snap option.*

Creating Orthographic Views

You can use the drafting settings to create the views required for a 2D drawing layout.

FIRST-ANGLE PROJECTION

The U.S. and Canada uses Third-Angle Projection.

The rest of the world uses first-angle projection.

All countries start with a FRONT VIEW.

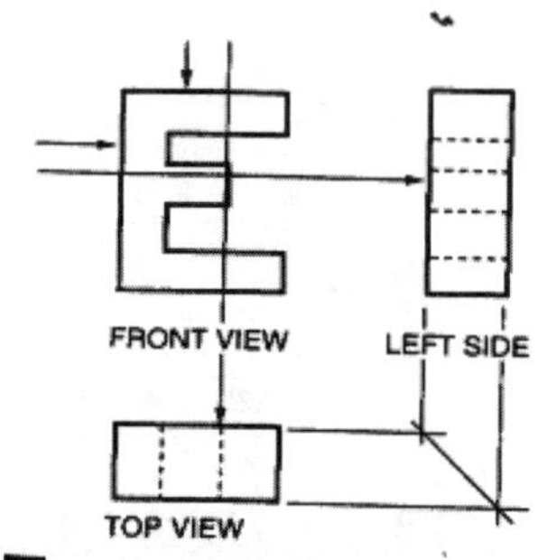

First-angle projection

THIRD- ANGLE PROJECTION

THIS IS THE LAYOUT USED IN THE UNITED STATES & CANADA.

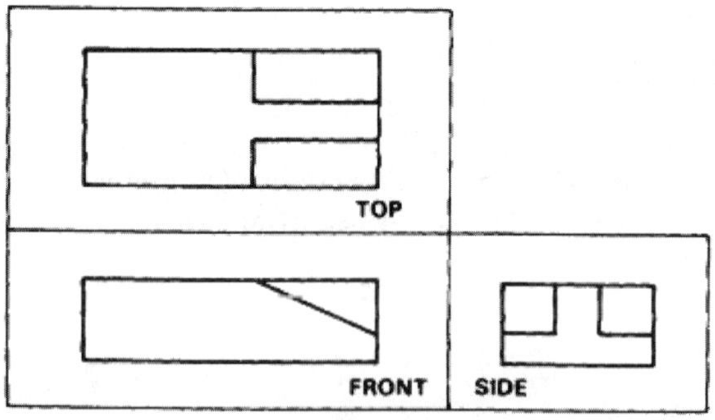

ORTHO LAYOUT WORKSHEET

SELECT THE CORRECT LAYOUT FOR THE THREE ISOMETRIC OBJECTS

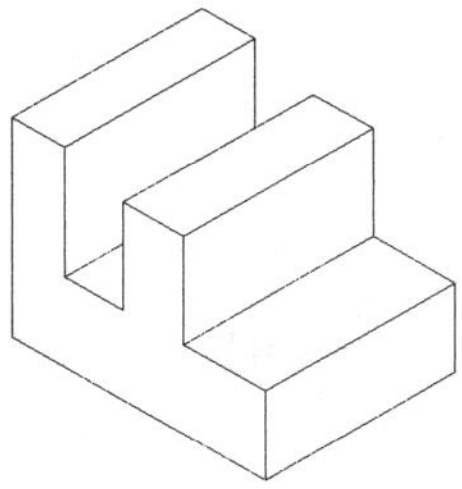

PROBLEM 1:

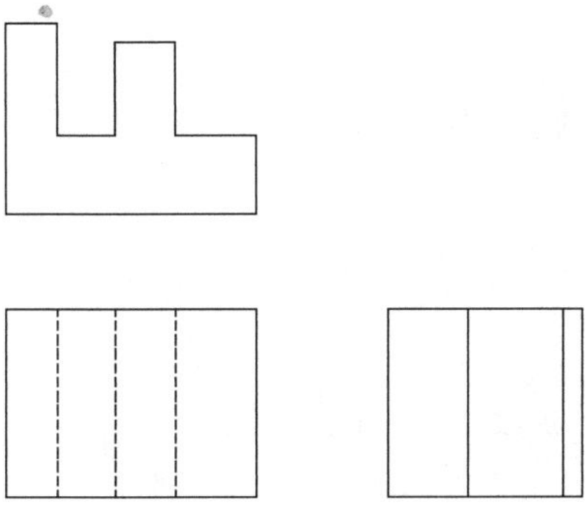

LAYOUT 1-A

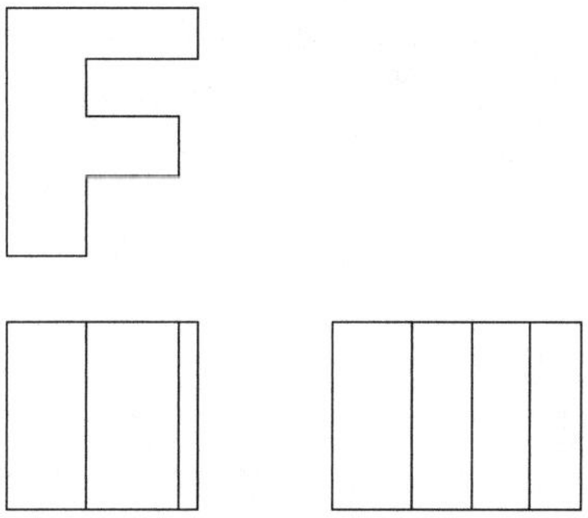

LAYOUT 1-B

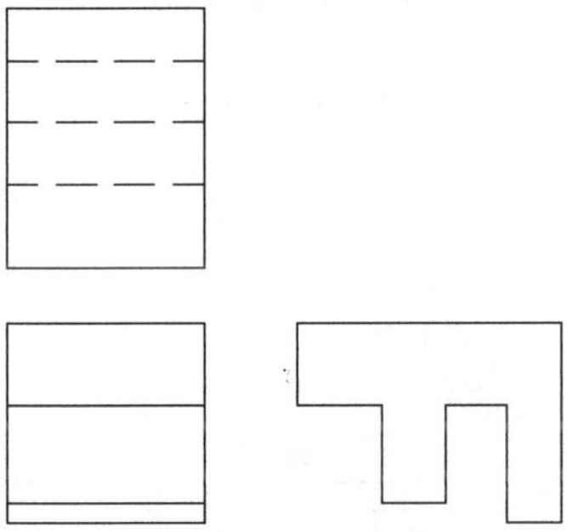

LAYOUT 1-C

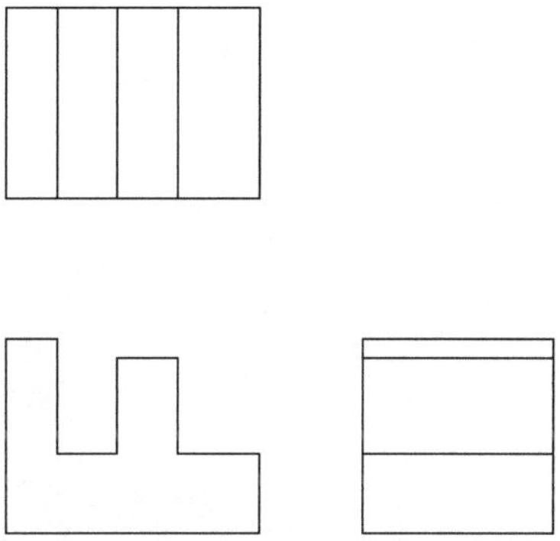

LAYOUT 1-D

SELECT THE CORRECT LAYOUT

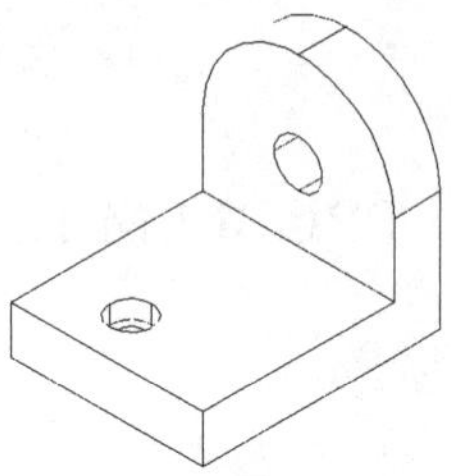

PROBLEM 2:

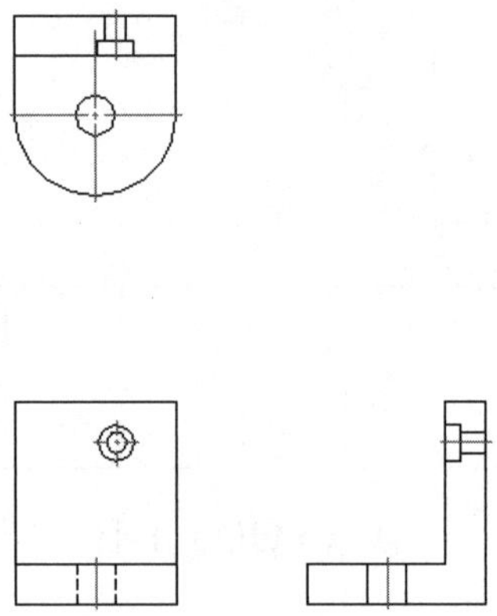

LAYOUT 2-A

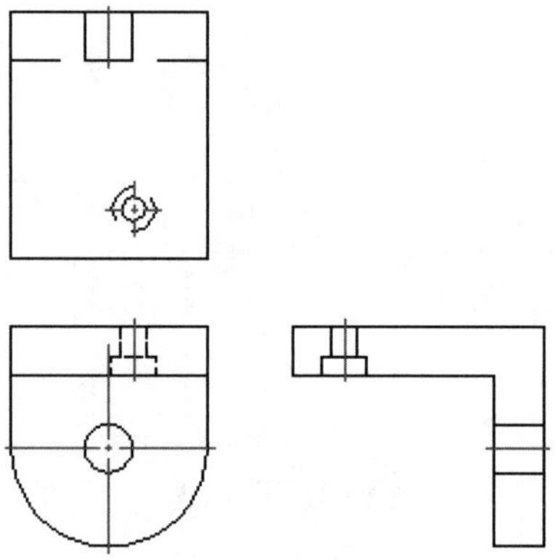

LAYOUT 2-B

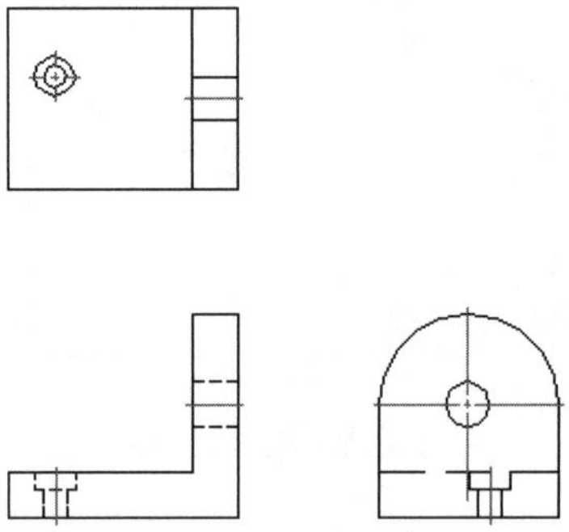

LAYOUT 2-C

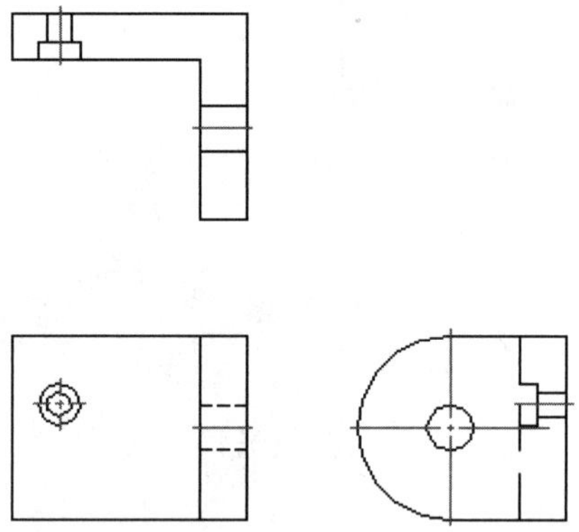

LAYOUT 2-D

SELECT THE CORRECT LAYOUT

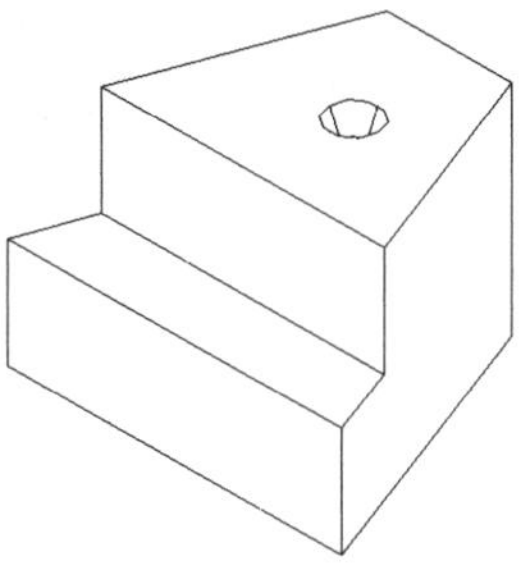

PROBLEM 3:

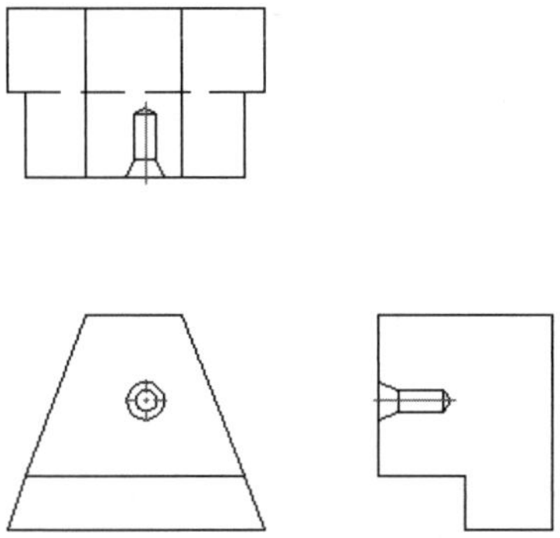

LAYOUT 3-A

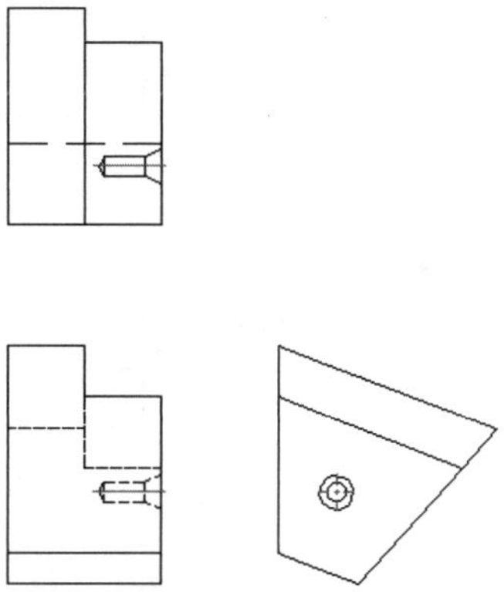

LAYOUT 3-B

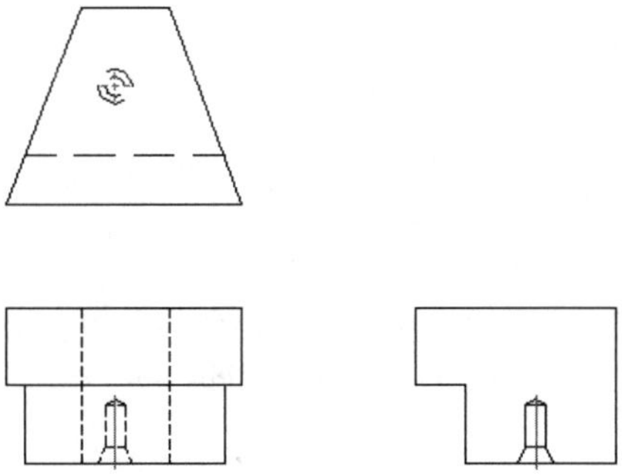

LAYOUT 3-C

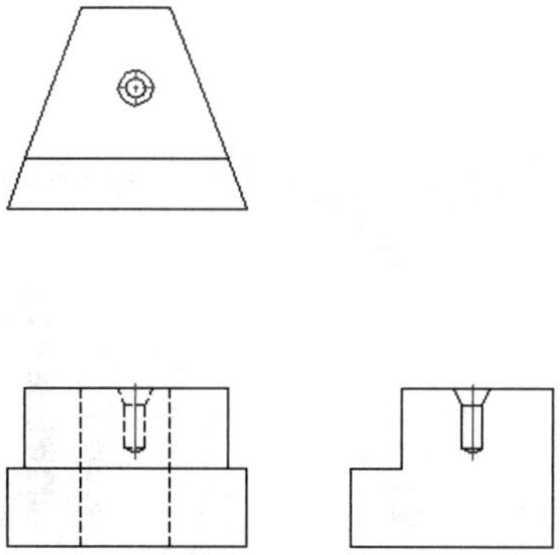

LAYOUT 3-D

Command Exercise

Exercise 9-7 – Using Object Tracking to Create a Layout

Drawing Name: **new drawing**
Estimated Time to Completion: 20 Minutes

Scope

The goal of this exercise is to create an orthographic layout without using any construction lines. Use OTRACK, OSNAP, and OFFSET. If you have to draw and erase any lines, you have not done the exercise properly.

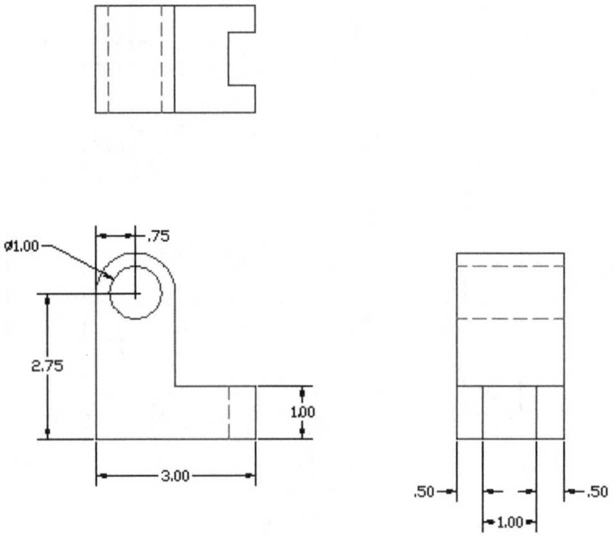

Orthographic Layout

Solution

1. 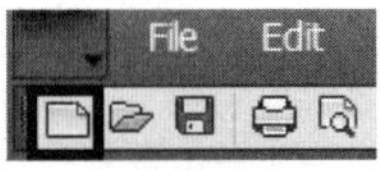

Select **QNEW**.

2. 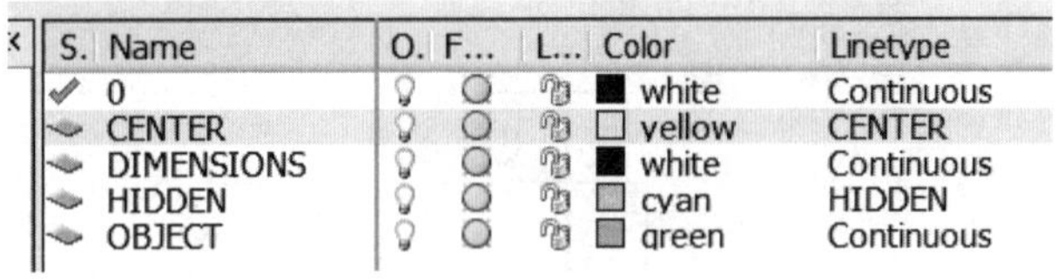

S.	Name	O.	F...	L...	Color	Linetype
✓	0				white	Continuous
	CENTER				yellow	CENTER
	DIMENSIONS				white	Continuous
	HIDDEN				cyan	HIDDEN
	OBJECT				green	Continuous

Set up layers for object, hidden, center, and dimensions.

3. 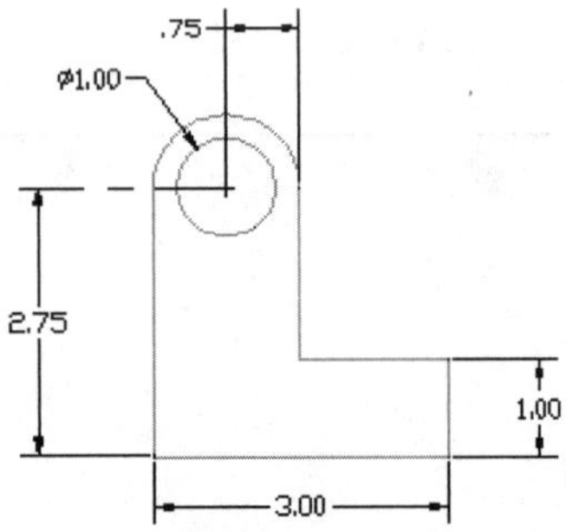

Draw the front view of this object.

Add dimensions.

4. 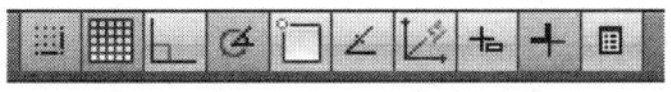 Enable OSNAP, ORTHO, and OTRACK.

5. 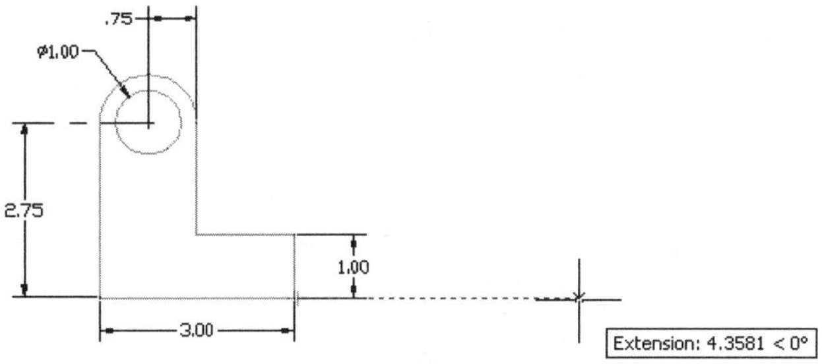

Use ORTHO TRACKing to line up the end point of the right side view.

6. 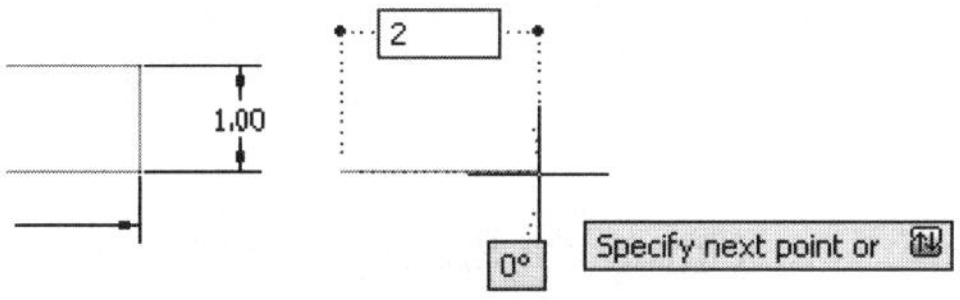

Create the first line approximately 2 units to the right of the first view.

Move to the right and enter a distance of 2 units.

7. 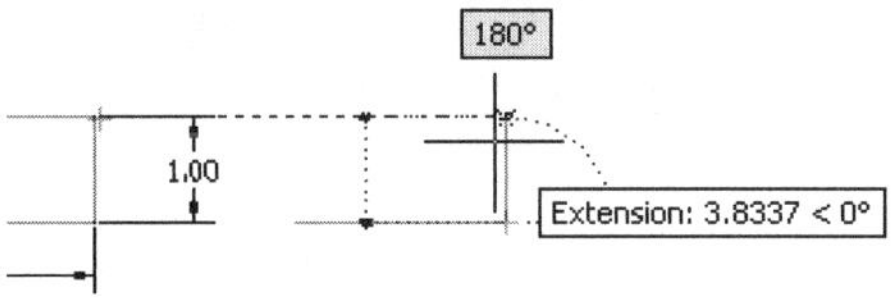

Move up in the vertical direction and align with the horizontal line on the first view.

8. 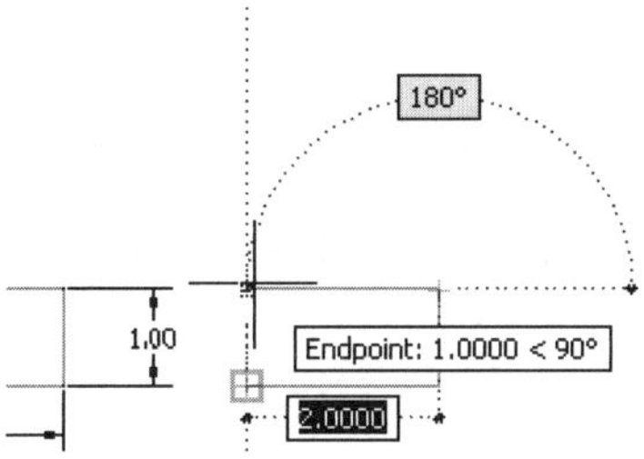

Use ORTHO TRACKING to locate the end point of the top horizontal line.

Right click and select **CLOSE**.

9. 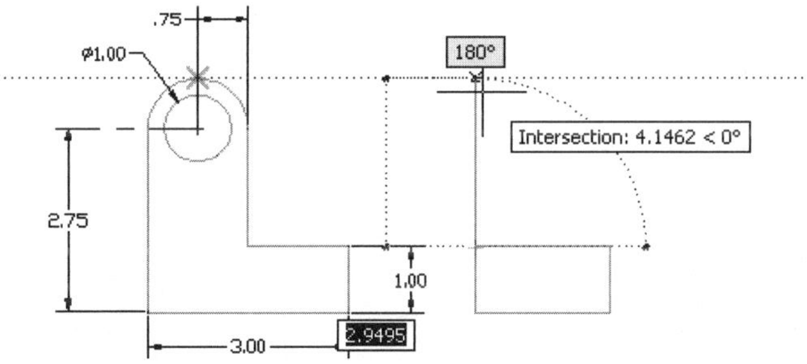

Locate the top of the right side view.

10. 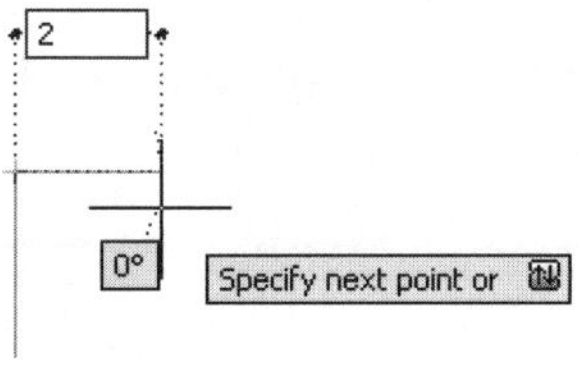

Draw a 2 unit horizontal line.

11. 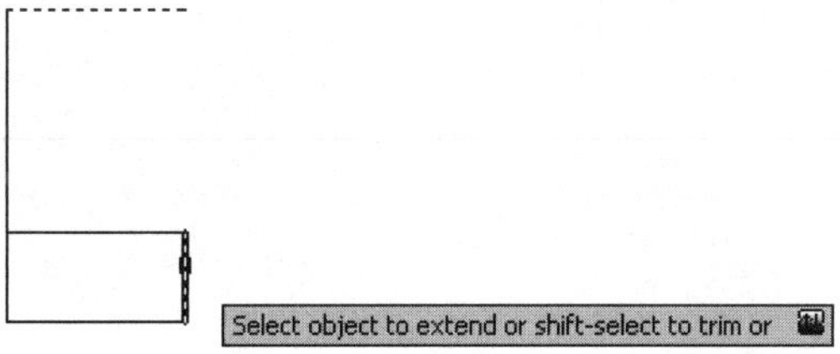

Use EXTEND to lengthen the vertical line to meet the top horizontal line.

12.

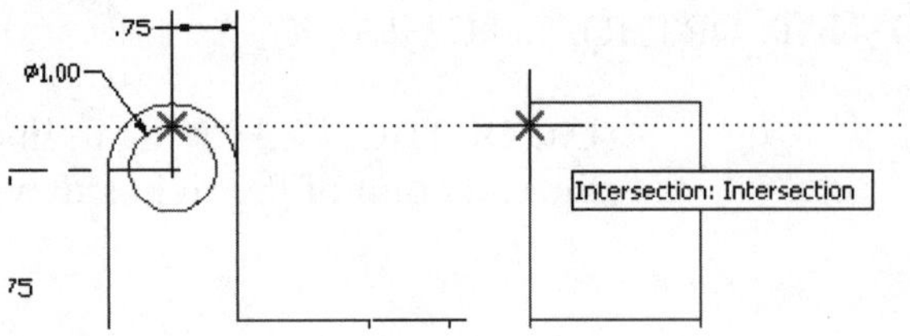

Switch to the **hidden** layer.
Locate the hidden line for the hole using OTRACK.

13.

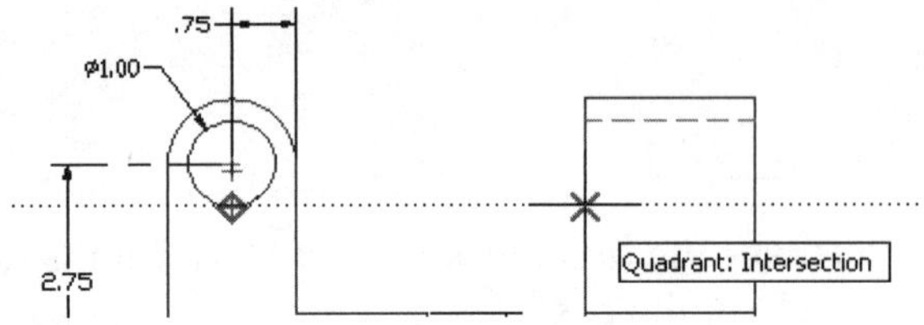

Create the bottom hidden line for the hole using OTRACK.

Be aware that if you don't have the OSNAP settings set correctly, you may accidentally line up with the wrong elements.

14.

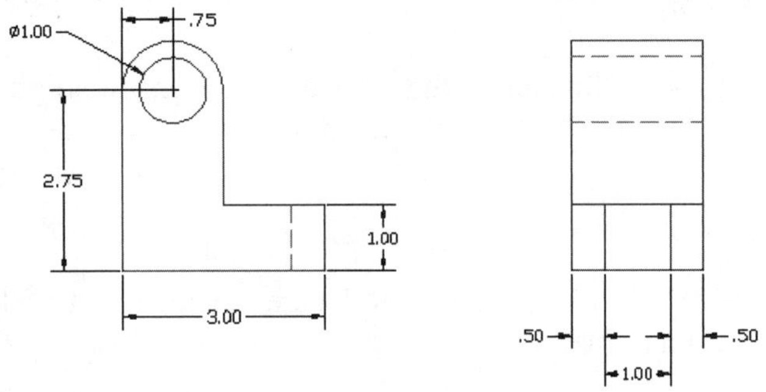

Complete the right side view as shown.

15.

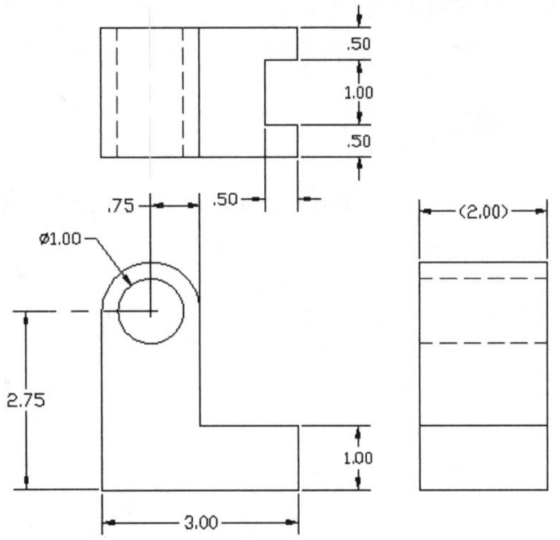

Create the top view using OSNAPs, OTRACKS, and OFFSET.

16.

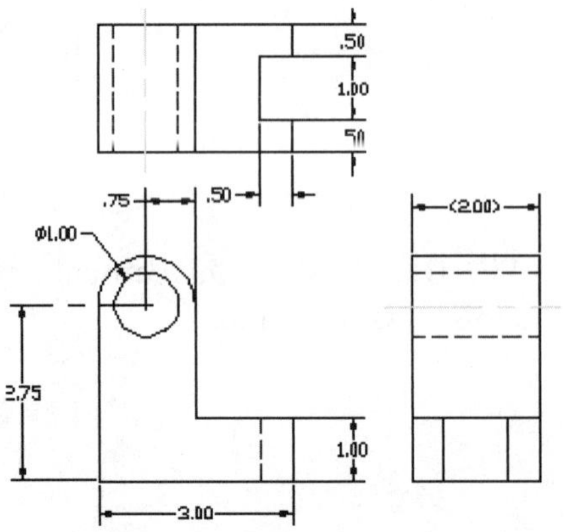

Complete the drawing by placing the missing lines in the right side view.

Review Questions

1. Identify the following object snap options:

a.  __________________

b.  __________________

c. 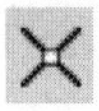 __________________

d.  __________________

e.  __________________

f.  __________________

g.  __________________

h.  __________________

i.  __________________

2. How can you access an object snap option for a single selection (not OSNAP)?

3. What control in the Status Bar turns the Object Snap Settings ON or OFF

4. What does the DSETTINGS command do?

- ❑ Invokes the Object Snap Pop up Menu
- ❑ Allows you to adjust the running object snap settings
- ❑ Toggles the OSNAP command on and off.
- ❑ Nothing

5. How would you select the exact center of a circle? How would you select the exact center of a 6 or 4 or 3 sided polygon? Try it.

Review Answers

1. Identify the following object snap options:
   - *a.* *Endpoint*
   - *b.* *Perpendicular*
   - *c.* *Intersection*
   - *d.* *Center*
   - *e.* *Nearest*
   - *f.* *Midpoint*
   - *g.* *Tangent*
   - *h.* *Quadrant*
   - *i.* *Object Snap Settings*

2. How can you access an object snap option for a single selection (not OSNAP)?

   Press the <Shift> key and RMB to access the Object Snap Pop up dialog box.

3. What control in the Status Bar turns the Object Snap Settings ON or OFF

   OSNAP

4. What does the DSETTINGS command do?

   - ■ *Invokes the Object Snap Pop up Menu*
   - ❑ Allows you to adjust the running object snap settings *(You can toggle OSNAP on and off)*
   - ❑ Toggles the OSNAP command on and off.
   - ❑ Nothing

5. How would you select the exact center of a circle? How would you select the exact center of a 6, 4 or 3 sided polygon? Try it.

   Use your line command coupled with object snaps to create intersection points at the center of the polygon. Use the Intersection object snap to select the center and erase your construction lines.

Lesson 10.0 – Dimensions

Estimated Class Time – 2 Hours

Objectives

Dimensioning a drawing is easy. If placed correctly, the dimensions will be as accurate as the drawing. Students will learn how to create Dimension Styles to suit the drawing specifications. Dimensions can be created in English/Standard or Metric units, or both. Edit selected dimensions or make changes to the Dimension Style for a global update.

- **Dimensions**
  Place dimensions using different dimension tools.
- **Ordinate Dimensions**
- **Dimension Space**
- **Dimension Break**
- **Dimension Style**
  Control the appearance of dimensions, including text color and size, arrowheads, and spacing.
- **Edit Dimension Location**
  Use grips to edit the placement of dimensions.
- **Edit Dimension Text**
- **Edit Dimension Properties**
  Edit dimensions globally by modifying the dimension styles or individually with the Properties command.

Dimensions

If you are a mechanical drafter, you will be expected to use ANSI standards when applying dimensions. If you are an architectural drafter, you will be expected to apply AIA standards.

Architects will often create many different styles to manage the requirements of different counties and cities. Most mechanical drafters will create one style for standard (inch) dimensioning and one style for metric. Dimensioning styles for mechanical drawings are dictated by the American Society of Mechanical Engineers (ASME). A copy of the standards can be purchased through the ASME website at www.asme.org. The current dimensioning standards are ASME Y14.5M-1994. Most mechanical design jobs require drafters to be familiar with ANSI dimensioning standards.

Some simple rules to keep in mind when applying ANSI standards:

1. Center the dimension. You can use GRIPS or DIMTEDIT to shift the dimension text position to set it centered.
2. Always place your dimensions between views.
3. Always place overall dimensions (length, height, and width).
4. Place the shortest dimensions closest to the object.
5. Never place dimensions on top or inside of the object.
6. Leaders are placed at a 30, 45, or 60 degree angle.
7. When dimensioning holes, use a diameter dimension NOT a radius.
8. Never dimension to hidden or center lines.
9. Do not double dimension (that is apply a dimension that is already shown in a different view or the same view.)
10. When using inches, suppress leading zeros.

Command Overview

Learn how to Dimension a drawing using the dimension variables. Dimensions will be as accurate as the drawing, provided the objects were chosen correctly. To open the Dimension Toolbar, place the cursor over any icon and press the right button on the mouse, then place a checkmark before "Dimension". This section will cover individual dimension commands, how to select the object to dimension and pick the dimension location. The easiest way to adjust the dimension locations after they have been placed is to use the Grips. Some Dimension commands, such as Ordinate Dimensions and Tolerance, will not be covered in this Tutorial. Dimension Style and Edit Dimension commands and options will be covered in the next section.

Dimension Command	Button	Overview
Linear Dimension	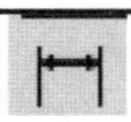	This option is for horizontal or vertical dimensions. Use object snap to select the first and second extension line origin or press return to select the object. Drag the cursor and pick to place the dimension.
Aligned Dimension		This option will align a dimension with an angled line. Use object snap to select the first and second extension line origin or press return to select the object. Drag the cursor and pick to place the dimension.
Arc Length		Dimension the length of an arc.
Ordinate Dimension		Places ordinate dimensions. Right click to select the Origin option to set the origin for the Ordinate Dimension
Radius		Select a circle or arc for the Radius Dimension. Drag the cursor and pick to place the dimension.
Jogged		Places a jogged leader on a circle or arc.
Diameter Dimension		Select a circle or arc for the diameter dimension. Drag the cursor and pick to place the dimension.
Angular Dimension	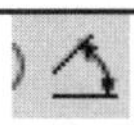	This option will place an angular dimension between selected lines. Select two angular lines and pick the dimension location.
Quick Dimension		Quick Dimension (QDIM) allows the user to select an object that contains multiple lines and place multiple dimensions with the Continuous, Staggered, Baseline, Ordinate, Radius, Diameter, datum, Point, and Edit options.
Baseline Dimension	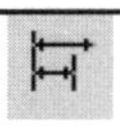	This option builds a baseline dimension from the first extension line of a linear, aligned or angular dimension. Begin with the linear, aligned or angular dimension first, using object snaps to select the origin points. Next invoke Baseline Dimension and select the next extension line origin. Continue then press <ENTER> to exit the command.
Continued Dimension	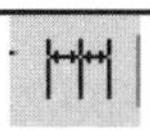	This option creates continuous dimensions from the second extension line of a linear, aligned or angular dimension. Begin with the linear, aligned or angular dimension first, using object snaps to select the origin points. Next invoke the Continued Dimension and select the next extension line origin. Continue then press <ENTER> to exit the command.
Dimension Space		Dimension Space allows you to quickly adjust the spacing between linear dimensions so that they do not overlap.
Dimension Break	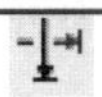	This creates a gap in the extension line of a dimension. Select the dimension, then select the object (a line or point) where you wish to place the gap.
Tolerance		Places a GD&T symbol
Center Mark		Select a circle or arc to place a center mark in the drawing. Center mark styles can be modified in the Dimension Style dialog box.
Inspection		Select existing dimensions to be used for inspection purposes.

Dimension Command	Button	Overview
Jogged Linear		Add a jog to an existing dimension so that it can be foreshortened as needed.
Dimension Edit		Shifts dimension text
Dimension Text Edit		Edit the value of dimension text
Dimension Update		Update the dimension style applied to a dimension
Dimension Style drop-down	Standard	Use this drop-down box to select a dimension style on the fly.
Dimension Style		Launches the Dimension Style Manager dialog.

General Procedures

For Linear or Aligned dimensions:

1. Select the desired dimension command.
2. Use the appropriate Object Snaps to select the dimension line origin points. Drag the cursor and pick the dimension location. *Note: To dimension a single line segment, press <ENTER>, then select the line.*

For Radius, Diameter, or Center Mark dimensions:

1. Select the desired dimension command.
2. Pick the Circle, Arc, or Line to dimension. Drag the cursor and pick the dimension location. *Note: Center Mark will simply be placed at the center.*

For Baseline or Continued Dimensions:

1. Begin by placing a Linear, Aligned or Angular Dimension, using Object Snaps to select the origin points.
2. Invoke the Baseline or Continued Dimension. Using Object Snaps, pick the next dimension line origins. When finished, press <ENTER> to Exit the command.

For Quick Dimensions (QDIM):

1. Invoke the Quick Dimension command.
2. Window the objects to be dimensioned, or pick them individually, and press <ENTER>.
3. Specify the dimension line position by dragging in the desired direction. The default dimension option will appear in parenthesis.
4. Pick to place the dimension, or type the capitalized letter of the desired option and <ENTER>. The pick (LMB) to place the dimension.

Tips & Tricks

- Use Object Snaps or set the OSNAP settings when selecting dimension line origin points.
- Do not explode dimensions. Associativity to the object will be lost and the dimension will be broken into as many as 10 separate objects.
- Adjust dimension locations after they are placed using grips.
- Begin the Baseline and Continued dimensions by placing a Linear, Aligned or Angular dimension first.
- Leader text will have "no wrap" unless a width is specified

Command Exercise

Exercise 10-1 – Dimensions

Drawing Name: **dim1.dwg**
Estimated Time to Completion: 5 Minutes

Scope

Dimension the object as indicated using Linear and Aligned Dimensions

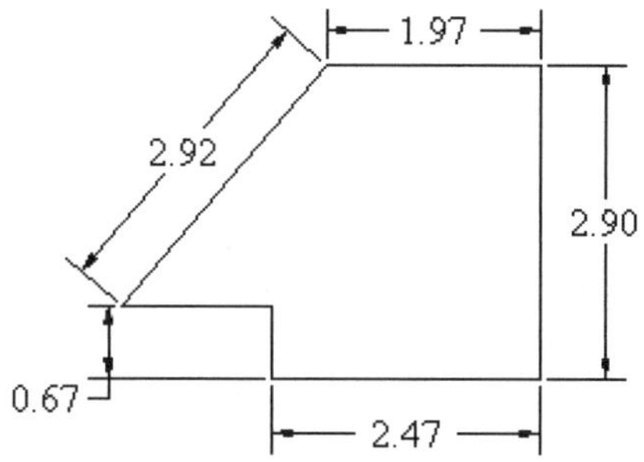

Dimensions Exercise

Solution

If you are still in the AutoCAD Classic workspace, we will now move over to the 2D Drafting and Annotation workspace.

*Go to the **Workspace** tool on the lower right of the screen or the Workspace toolbar.*

*Set **2D Drafting and Annotation** workspace current.*

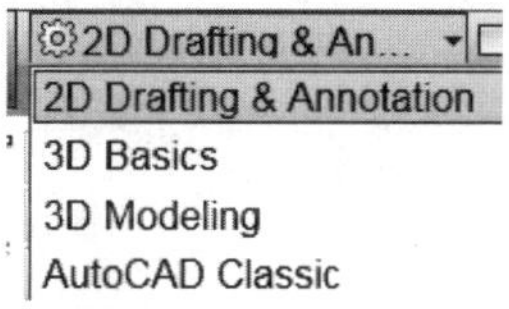

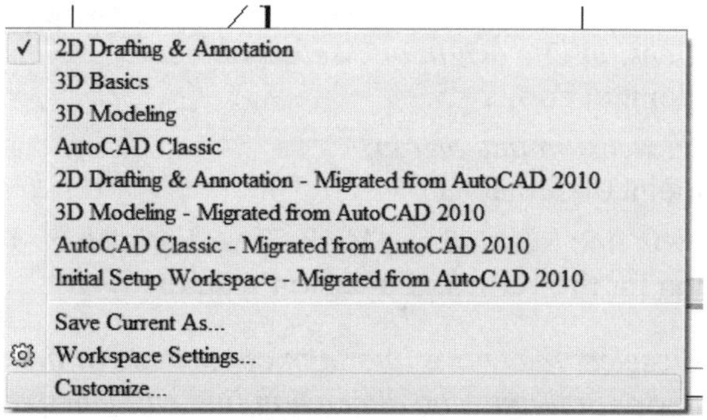

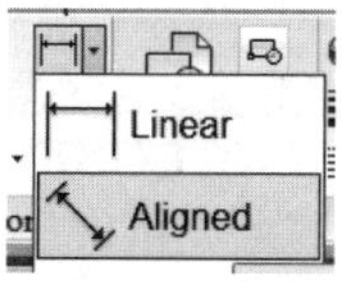

1. Invoke the Aligned Dimension command (dimaligned). On the Ribbon panel, locate the Aligned tool in the Annotations drop-down.
2. *Specify first extension line origin or <select object>:*
   Press <ENTER> to select the object.
3. *Select object to dimension:*
   Select the angled line between 1 and 2.
4. *Specify dimension line location or [Mtext/Text/Angle]:*
   Select a location for the dimension with the LMB.

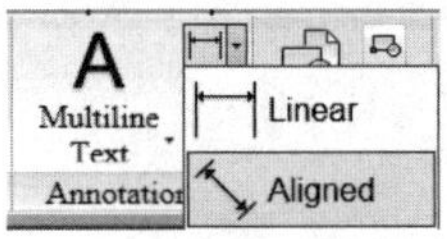

5. Invoke the Linear Dimension command (dimlinear). Select the Linear Dimension command from the Annotation Ribbon tab.
6. *Specify first extension line origin or <select object>:*
   Press <ENTER> to select the object.
7. *Select object to dimension:*
   Select the line between 2 and 3.
8. *Specify dimension line location or [Mtext/Text/Angle/Horizontal/Vertical/Rotated]:*
   Select a location for the horizontal dimension with the LMB.

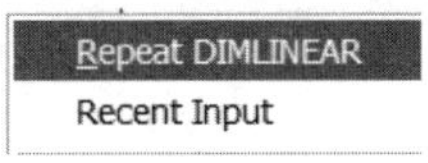

9. Repeat the Linear Dimension command with the RMB (dimlinear or <ENTER>).
10. *Specify first extension line origin or <select object>:*
    Press <ENTER> to select the object.
11. *Select object to dimension:*
    Select the angled line between 3 and 4.
12. *Specify dimension line location or [Mtext/Text/Angle/Horizontal/Vertical/Rotated]:*
    Select a location for the vertical dimension with the LMB.

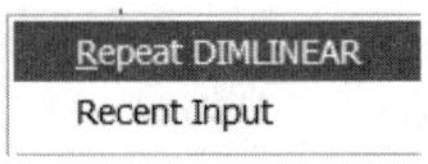

13. Repeat the Linear Dimension command with the RMB (dimlinear or <ENTER>).
14. *Specify first extension line origin or <select object>:*
    Press <ENTER> to select the object.
15. *Select object to dimension:*
    Select the angled line between 4 and 5.
16. *Specify dimension line location or [Mtext/Text/Angle/Horizontal/Vertical/Rotated]:*
    Select a location for the horizontal dimension with the LMB.

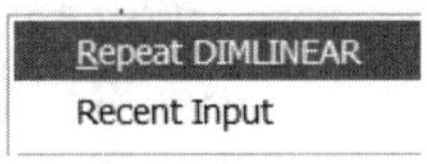

17. Repeat the Linear Dimension command with the RMB (dimlinear or <ENTER>).
18. *Specify first extension line origin or <select object>:*
    Select the endpoint of corner #5.
19. *Specify second extension line origin:*
    Select the endpoint of corner #1.
20. *Specify dimension line location or [Mtext/Text/Angle/Horizontal/Vertical/Rotated]:*
    Select a location for the vertical dimension with the LMB.

> ***Note:*** *If you select the entire line segment instead of the corners of the object for the first and second origin points, the dimension line will run over the object and not gap will be visible between the object and the dimension line.*

21. To close the file, go to **File→Close** or type **CLOSE**.

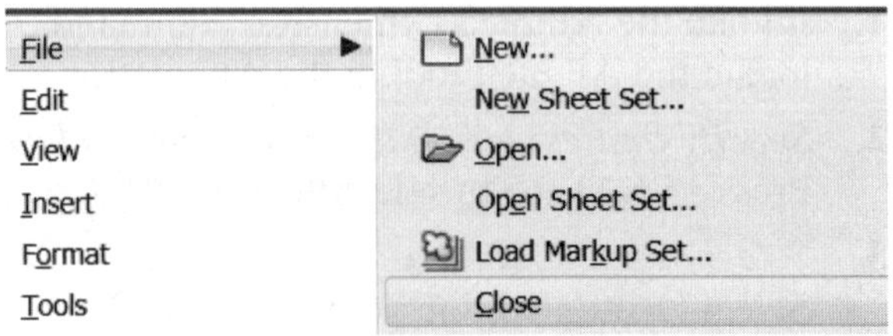

Command Exercise

Exercise 10-2 – Accessing the Dimension Toolbar

Drawing Name: **new drawing**
Estimated Time to Completion: 5 Minutes

Scope

Activate the AutoCAD Classic Workspace.
Activate the Dimension Toolbar.

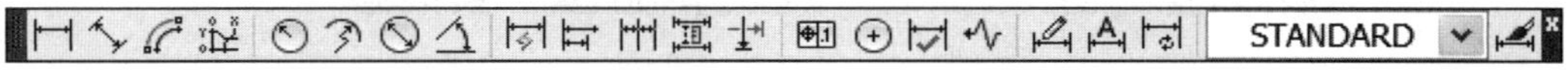

Solution

1. Type **Workspace** at the command line.

2. 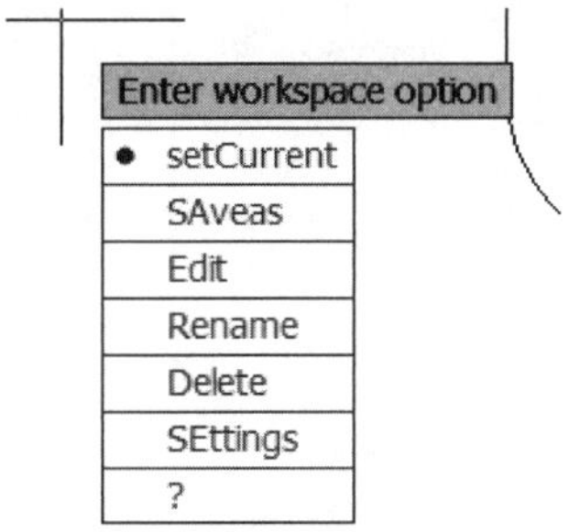

Press <**ENTER**> to accept the setCurrent option as the default.

3. 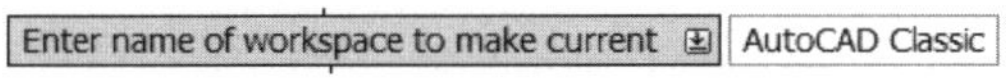

Type **AutoCAD Classic** to return to the AutoCAD Classic workspace.

   Press <**ENTER**>.

4. 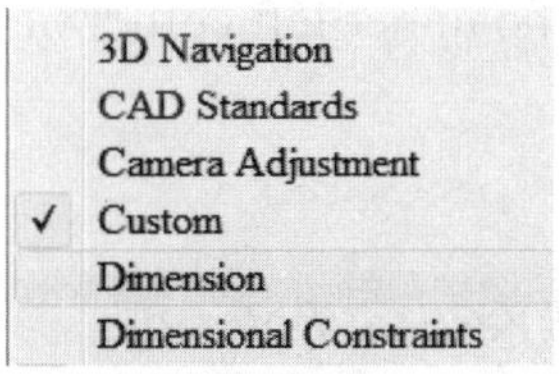

Right click on the gray area at the top of the screen.

   Select **AutoCAD→Dimension** to activate the Dimension toolbar.

5. 

Close the drawing without saving.

Command Exercise

Exercise 10-3 – Dimensions

Drawing Name: **dim2.dwg**
Estimated Time to Completion: 5 Minutes

Scope

OSNAP should be enabled with ENDPOINT.
Dimension the object as indicated using Continuous and Baseline Dimensions

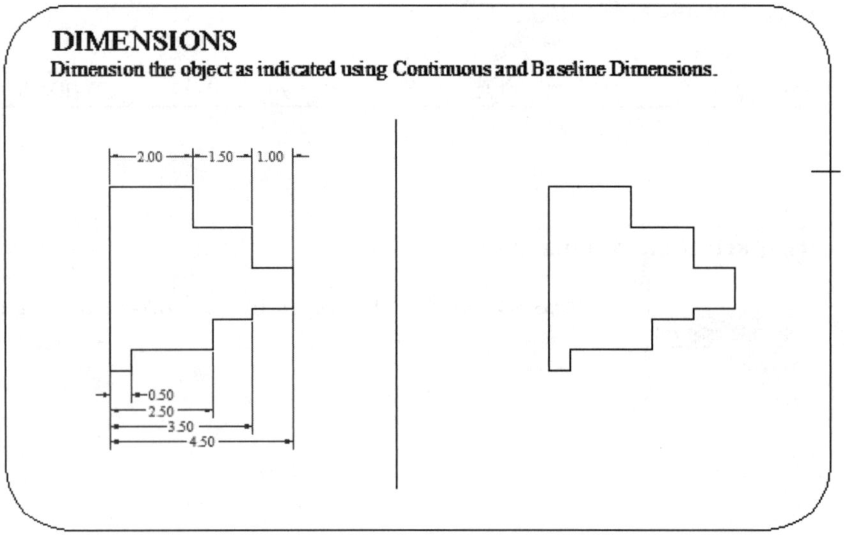

Dimensions Exercise

Solution

1. Select the **Linear Dimension** command from the Dimension toolbar. 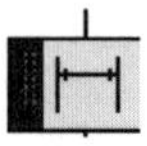
2. *Specify first extension line origin or <select object>:*
   Make sure the Intersection Running Object Snap is active. Pick the upper left corner of the object with the LMB.
3. *Specify second extension line origin:*
   Pick corner A with the LMB.
4. *Specify dimension line location or [Mtext/Text/Angle/Horizontal/Vertical/Rotated]:*
   Select a location for the dimension with the LMB.
5. Invoke the Continue Dimension command (dimcontinue). 
6. *Specify a second extension line origin or [Undo/Select] <Select>:*
   Select corner B.
7. *Specify a second extension line origin or [Undo/Select] <Select>:*
   Select corner C.
8. *Specify a second extension line origin or [Undo/Select] <Select>:*
   Right click and select <ENTER> to end the command.

9. Invoke the Linear Dimension command (dimlinear).

10. *Specify first extension line origin or <select object>:*
Select the lower left corner of the object with the LMB.

11. *Specify second extension line origin:*
Select corner 1.

12. *Specify dimension line location or [Mtext/Text/Angle/Horizontal/Vertical/Rotated]:*
Select a location for the dimension with the LMB.

13. Invoke the Baseline Dimension command (dimbaseline).

14. *Specify a second extension line origin or [Undo/Select] <Select>:*
Select corner 2.

15. *Specify a second extension line origin or [Undo/Select] <Select>:*
Select corner 3.

16. *Specify a second extension line origin or [Undo/Select] <Select>:*
Press <ENTER>.

17. *Select base dimension:*
Right click and select <ENTER> to end the command.

Note: *You will get the best results if you start with a linear, angular, or aligned dimension and immediately follow with the Baseline or Continued Dimension command*

Command Exercise

Exercise 10-4 – Dimensions

Drawing Name: **dim3.dwg**
Estimated Time to Completion: 5 Minutes

Scope

Dimension the object as indicated using Angular, Radius, Diameter Dimensions, and Center Mark.

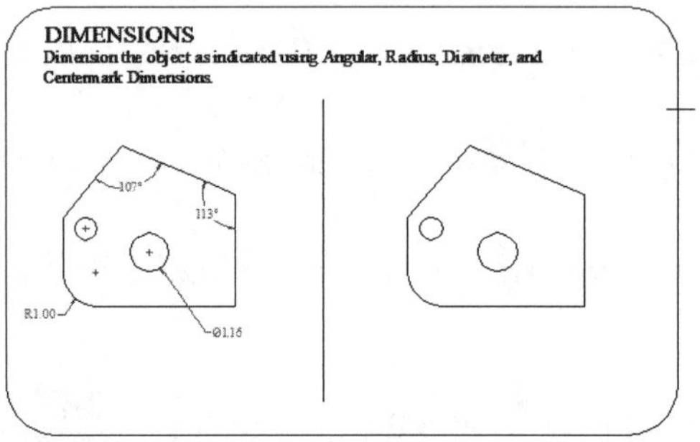

Dimension Exercise

Solution

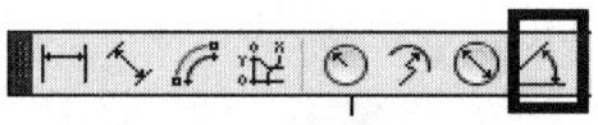

1. Invoke the Angular Dimension command (dimangular).
2. *Select arc, circle, line, or <specify vertex>:*
   Pick the line segment marked #1.
3. *Select second line:*
   Pick the line segment marked #2.
4. *Specify dimension arc line location or [Mtext/Text/Angle]:*
   Select a location for the dimension.

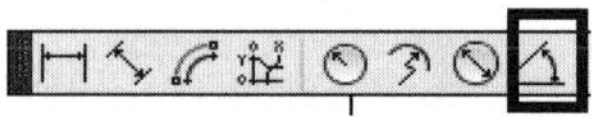

5. Repeat the Angular Dimension command with the RMB (dimangular or <ENTER>).
6. *Select arc, circle, line, or <specify vertex>:*
   Pick the line segment marked #3.
7. *Select second line:*
   Pick the line segment marked #4.
8. *Specify dimension arc line location or [Mtext/Text/Angle]:*
   Select a location for the dimension.

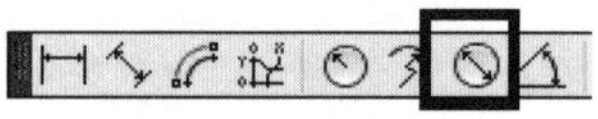

9. Invoke the Diameter Dimension command (dimdiameter).
10. *Select arc or circle:*
    Select the large circle.
11. *Specify dimension line location or [Mtext/Text/Angle]:*
    Select a location for the dimension.

12. Invoke the Radius Dimension command (dimradius).
13. *Select arc or circle:*
    Select the arc marked #5.
14. *Specify dimension line location or [Mtext/Text/Angle]:*
    Select a location for the dimension.

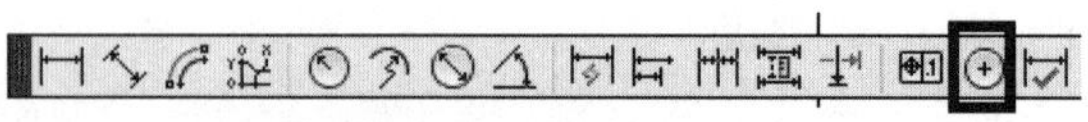

15. Invoke the Center Mark command (dimcenter).
16. *Select arc or circle:*
    Select the small circle.

Command Exercise

Exercise 10-5 – Quick Dimension

Drawing Name: **qdim.dwg**
Estimated Time to Completion: 10 Minutes

Scope

Use the Quick Dimension command to create continuous, staggered, baseline and ordinate dimensions of the same geometry under the appropriate headings. Select the geometry of the continuous set and remove one of the dimension points.

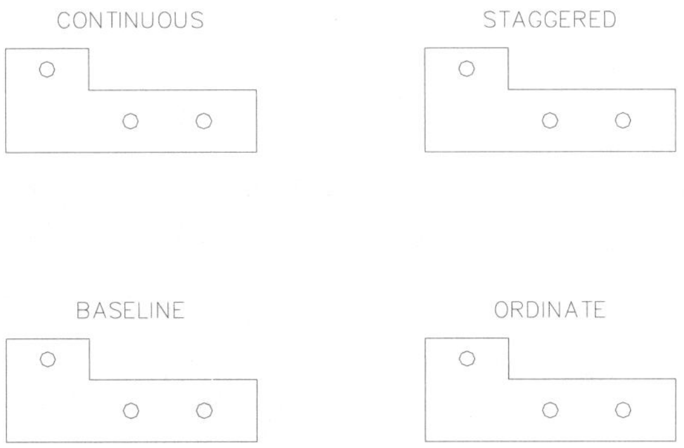

Quick Dimension – Before

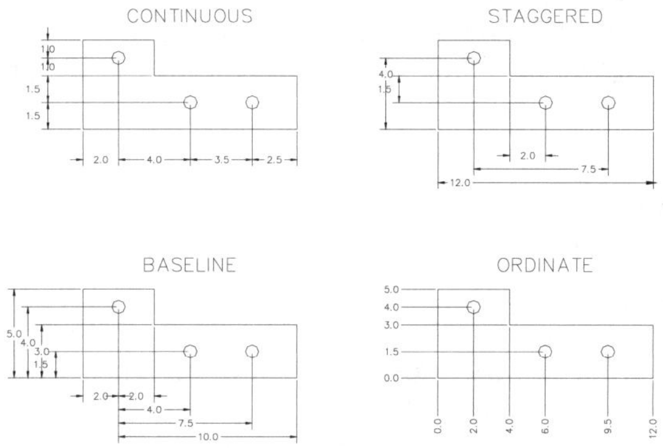

Quick Dimension – After

Solution

Continuous

1. Invoke the **Quick Dimension** command (qdim).

2. *Select geometry to dimension:*
   Select all of the geometry underneath the word 'CONTINUOUS'.
3. *Select geometry to dimension:*
   Press <ENTER> when all of the geometry is selected.
4. *[Continuous/Staggered/Baseline/Ordinate/Radius/Diameter/datumPoint/Edit] <Continuous>:*
   Select a placement point below the geometry to create the horizontal dimensions.
5. Repeat the **Quick Dimension** command with the RMB (press <ENTER> or qdim).

6. *Select geometry to dimension:*
   Select the same set of geometry (type 'P' and press <ENTER>).
7. *Select geometry to dimension:*
   Press <ENTER> when all of the geometry is selected.
8. *[Continuous/Staggered/Baseline/Ordinate/Radius/Diameter/datumPoint/Edit] <Continuous>:*
   Select a placement point to the left of the geometry to create the vertical dimensions.

Staggered

9. Repeat the **Quick Dimension** command with the RMB (press <ENTER> or qdim).
10. *Select geometry to dimension:*
    Select all of the geometry underneath the word 'STAGGERED'.
11. *Select geometry to dimension:*
    Press <ENTER> when all of the geometry is selected.
12. *[Continuous/Staggered/Baseline/Ordinate/Radius/Diameter/datumPoint/Edit] <Continuous>:*
    Right-click in the drawing area and select 'Staggered' or type 'S' and press <ENTER> to select staggered dimensions.
13. *[Continuous/Staggered/Baseline/Ordinate/Radius/Diameter/datumPoint/Edit] <Staggered>:*
    Select a placement point below the geometry to create the horizontal dimensions.
14. Repeat the **Quick Dimension** command with the RMB (press <ENTER> or qdim).

15. *Select geometry to dimension:*
    Select the same set of geometry (type 'P' and press <ENTER>).
16. *Select geometry to dimension:*
    Press <ENTER> when all of the geometry is selected.
17. *[Continuous/Staggered/Baseline/Ordinate/Radius/Diameter/datumPoint/Edit] <Staggered>:*
    Select a placement point to the left of the geometry to create the vertical dimensions.

Baseline

18. Repeat the **Quick Dimension** command with the RMB (press <ENTER> or qdim).
19. *Select geometry to dimension:*
    Select all of the geometry underneath the word 'BASELINE'.
20. *Select geometry to dimension:*
    Press <ENTER> when all of the geometry is selected.
21. *[Continuous/Staggered/Baseline/Ordinate/Radius/Diameter/datumPoint/Edit] <Staggered>:*
    Right-click in the drawing area and select 'Baseline' or type 'B' and press <ENTER> to select baseline dimensions.
22. *[Continuous/Staggered/Baseline/Ordinate/Radius/Diameter/datumPoint/Edit] <Baseline>:*
    Select a placement point below the geometry to create the horizontal dimensions.
23. Repeat the **Quick Dimension** command with the RMB (press <ENTER> or qdim).

24. *Select geometry to dimension:*
    Select the same set of geometry (type 'P' and press <ENTER>).
25. *Select geometry to dimension:*
    Press <ENTER> when all of the geometry is selected.
26. *[Continuous/Staggered/Baseline/Ordinate/Radius/Diameter/datumPoint/Edit] <Baseline>:*
    Select a placement point to the left of the geometry to create the vertical dimensions.

Ordinate

27. Repeat the **Quick Dimension** command with the RMB (press <ENTER> or qdim).
28. *Select geometry to dimension:*
    Select all of the geometry underneath the word 'ORDINATE'.
29. *Select geometry to dimension:*
    Press <ENTER> when all of the geometry is selected.

30. *[Continuous/Staggered/Baseline/Ordinate/Radius/Diameter/datumPoint/Edit] <Baseline>:* Right-click in the drawing area and select 'Ordinate' or type 'O' and press <ENTER> to select ordinate dimensions.
31. *[Continuous/Staggered/Baseline/Ordinate/Radius/Diameter/datumPoint/Edit] <Ordinate>:* Right-click in the drawing area and select 'datumPoint' or type 'P' and press <ENTER> to select a new datum point.
32. *Select new datum point:* Using an object snap, select the lower left corner of the geometry.
33. *[Continuous/Staggered/Baseline/Ordinate/Radius/Diameter/datumPoint/Edit] <Ordinate>:* Select a placement point below the geometry to create the horizontal dimensions.
34. Repeat the **Quick Dimension** command with the RMB (press <ENTER> or qdim).

35. *Select geometry to dimension:* Select the same set of geometry (type 'P' and press <ENTER>).
36. *Select geometry to dimension:* Press <ENTER> when all of the geometry is selected.
37. *[Continuous/Staggered/Baseline/Ordinate/Radius/Diameter/datumPoint/Edit] <Ordinate>:* Select a placement point to the left of the geometry to create the vertical dimensions.

Remove a Dimension Point

38. Invoke the **Erase** command (e or erase).

39. *Select objects:* Select the horizontal continuous dimensions.
40. *Select objects:* Once the dimensions have been selected, press <ENTER> to erase them.
41. Invoke the **Quick Dimension** command (qdim).

42. *Select geometry to dimension:* Select all of the geometry underneath the word 'CONTINUOUS'.
43. *Select geometry to dimension:* Press <ENTER> when all of the geometry is selected.
44. *[Continuous/Staggered/Baseline/Ordinate/Radius/Diameter/datumPoint/Edit] <Ordinate>:* Right-click in the drawing area and select 'Edit' or type 'E' and press <ENTER> to edit the dimension points.
45. *Indicate dimension point to remove, or [Add/eXit] <eXit>:* Select the two points indicated in the next figure. Remove the Indicated Points.

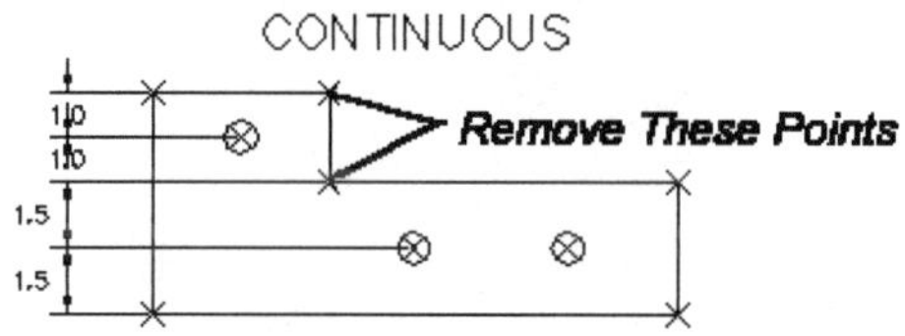

46. *Indicate dimension point to remove, or [Add/eXit] <eXit>:* Press <ENTER> to exit edit mode.
47. *[Continuous/Staggered/Baseline/Ordinate/Radius/Diameter/datumPoint/Edit] <Ordinate>:* Right-click in the drawing area and select 'Continuous' or type 'C' and press <ENTER> to change back to continuous dimensions.
48. *[Continuous/Staggered/Baseline/Ordinate/Radius/Diameter/datumPoint/Edit] <Continuous>:* Select a placement point below the geometry to create the horizontal dimensions.

Ordinate Dimension

Command Locator

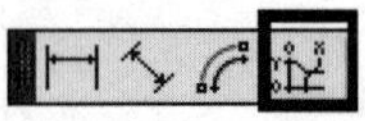

Toolbar Menu	**Dimension**
Pull Down Menu	**Dimension / Ordinate**
Command	**Dimord**
Alias	**D**

Command Overview

This dimension tool places ordinate dimensions in both the horizontal and vertical directions. You can add and delete points as well as set the origin.

Command Exercise

Exercise 10-6 – Ordinate Dimension

Drawing Name: **dimord.dwg**
Estimated Time to Completion: 10 Minutes

Scope

Use the Ordinate Dimension tool to place vertical and horizontal dimensions. Set the Origin for the Ordinate Dimension by setting the UCS.

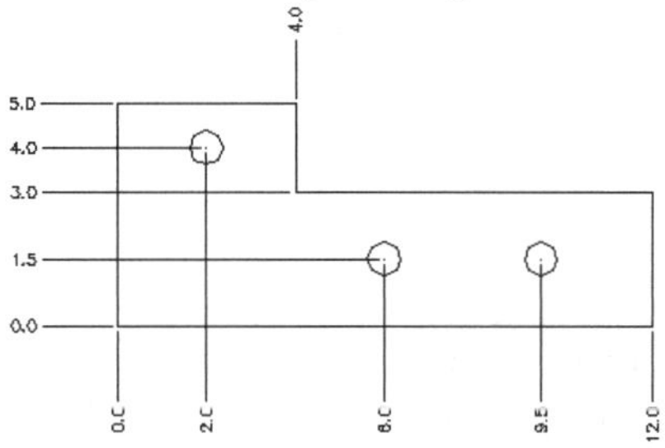

Ordinate Dimensions

Solution

1.

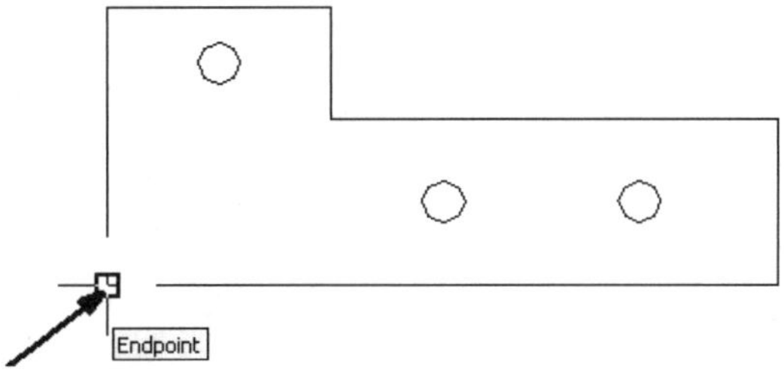

Type **UCS** on the command line.

Select the lower left corner of the object to set the origin for the ordinate dimensions.

Press <ENTER> when prompted to specify the X-axis.

2.

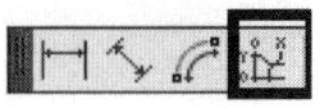

Select the Ordinate Dimension tool.

3.

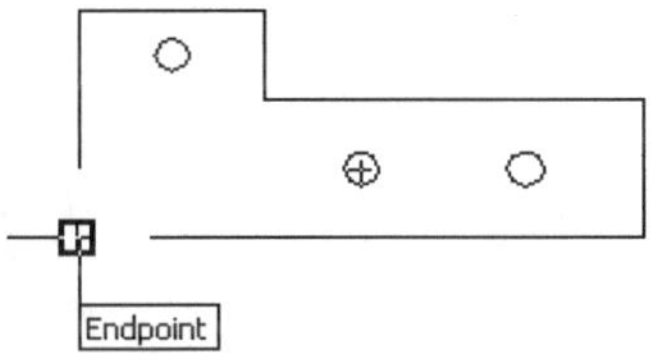

The prompt will ask you to select a feature.

Select the same point as the origin.

4.

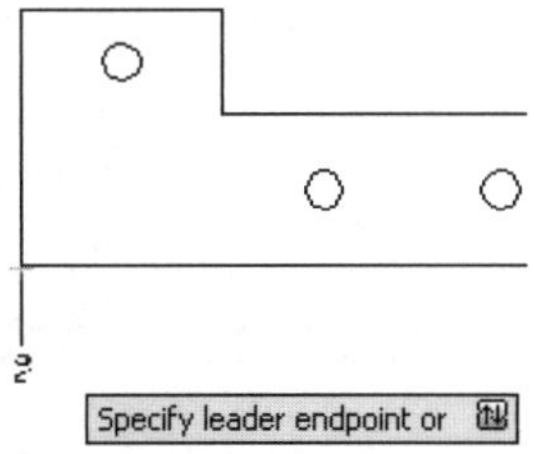

Bring the mouse down vertically to place the dimension.

5.

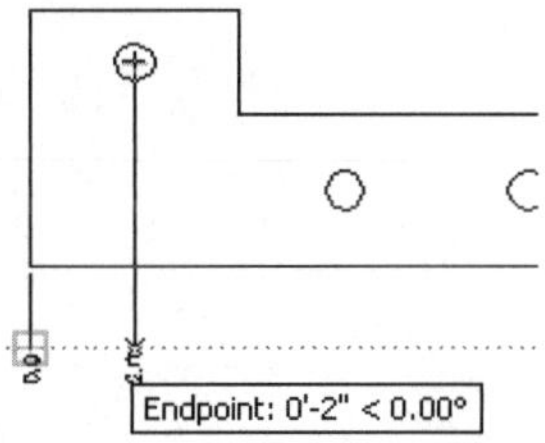

Use Object Tracking to line up the next ordinate dimension.

Place the remaining dimensions.

Dimension Space

Command Locator

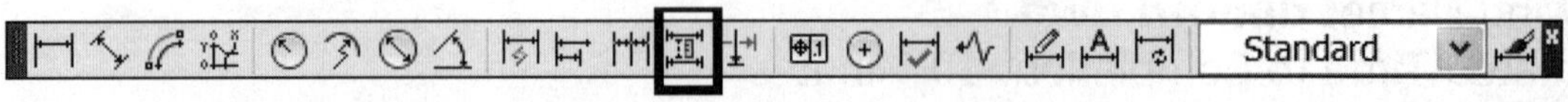

Toolbar Menu	**Dimension Space**
Pull Down Menu	**Dimension / Dimension Space**
Command	**DIMSPACE**

Command Overview

This dimension tool aligns and/or spaces linear and angular dimensions. It uses the spacing value set in the DIMDLI system variable. You can also set the spacing value within the command.

Command Exercise

Exercise 10-7 – Dimension Space

Drawing Name: **dimspace.dwg**
Estimated Time to Completion: 5 Minutes

Scope

Use the DIMSPACE tool to adjust the spacing of the overlapping linear dimensions.

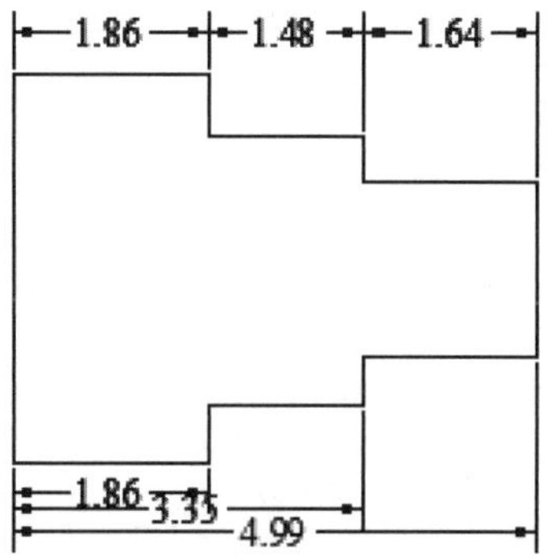

DIMSPACE

Solution

1.

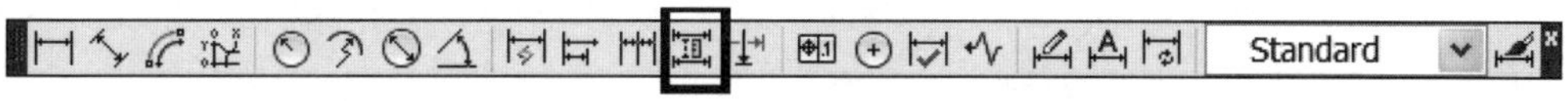

Select the DIMSPACE tool from the DIMENSION toolbar.

2. Select the 1.86 dimension. It will highlight when you mouse over it to indicate it will be selected.

3. Select the **3.35** dimension.
Select the **4.99** dimension.

4. 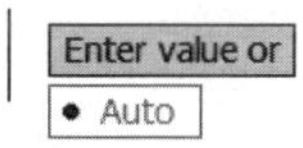

You will be prompted to enter a spacing value or select Auto. Auto is the default and uses the value stored in the DIMDLI system variable.

5. 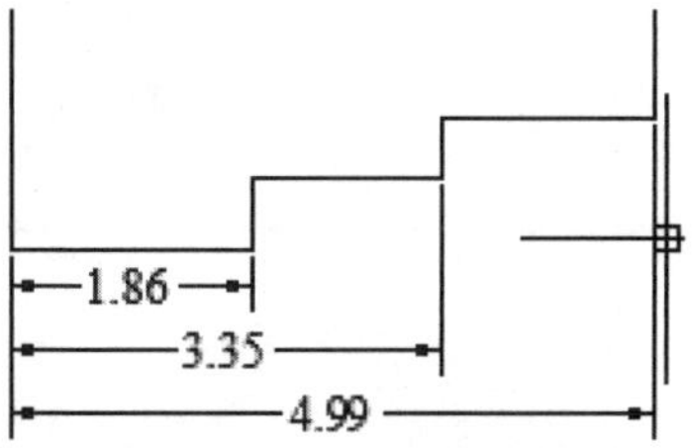

Press **Enter** to accept the default value.

The dimensions will adjust to the correct spacing.

Dimension Break

Command Locator

Toolbar Menu	**Dimension Break**
Pull Down Menu	**Dimension / Dimension Break**
Command	**DIMBREAK**
RMB Shortcut Menu	**Auto/Restore/Manual**

Command Overview

This dimension tool places or removes gaps in the extension lines of dimensions. This is used to create a cleaner drawing. The AUTO option requires the user to select an object such as a line to be used as the midpoint for the gap. The RESTORE option removes any breaks placed in the dimensions. The MANUAL option requires the user to select two points to define the gap. If the AUTO option is used, the gap will adjust if the selected object or the dimension is modified.

Command Exercise

Exercise 10-8 – Dimension Break

Drawing Name: **dimbreak.dwg**
Estimated Time to Completion: 15 Minutes

Scope

Use the DIMBREAK tool to place gaps in the extension lines using the AUTO and MANUAL methods. Use the RESTORE option to eliminate the breaks.

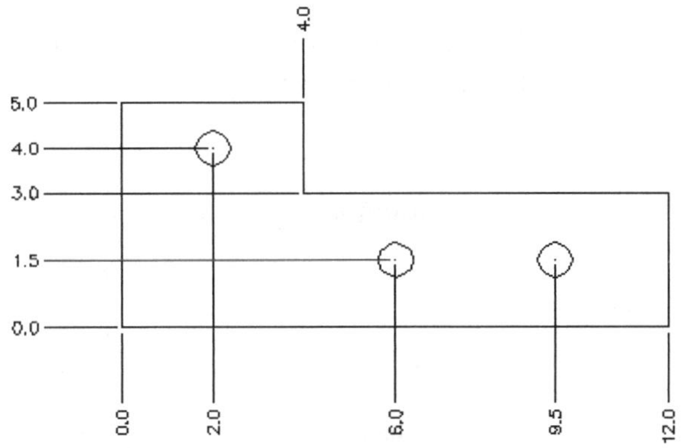

DIMBREAK

Solution

1. 

   Select the **DIMBREAK** tool from the Dimension toolbar.

2. 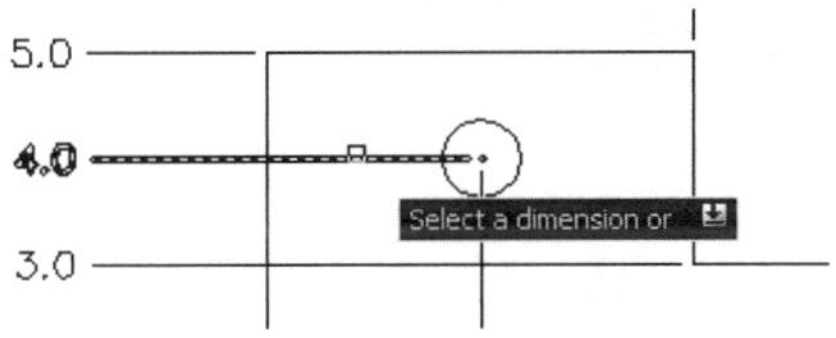

   Select the 4.0 vertical dimension.

3. 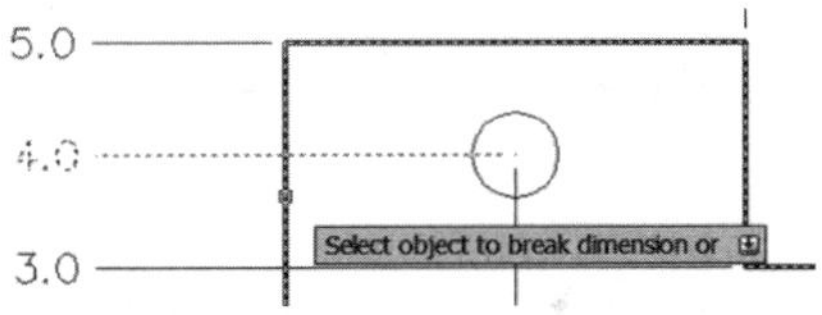

   Select the polygon object.

4. 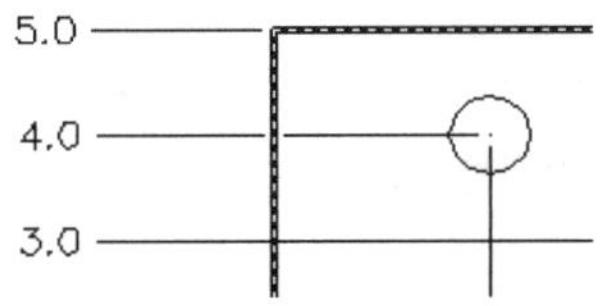

   A gap is placed in the dimension.

   Press ENTER to exit the command.

5. 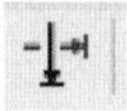 Select the **DIMBREAK** tool again.

6. 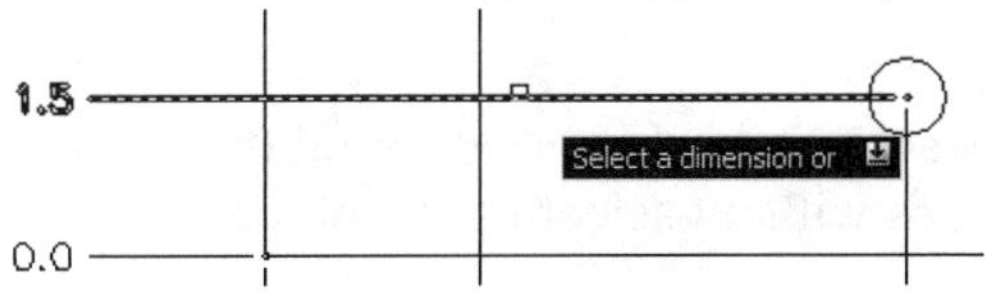

   Select the 1.5 vertical dimension.

7. 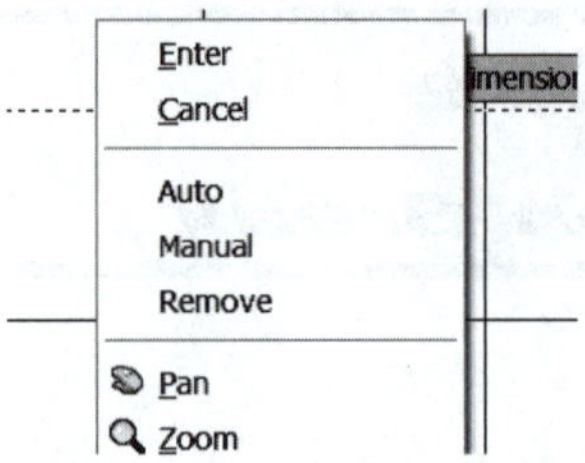

RMB and select **Manual**.

8. 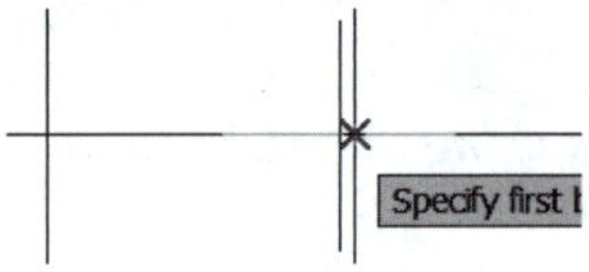

Select the horizontal dimension line between the circle and the 1.5 dimension as your first point.

9. 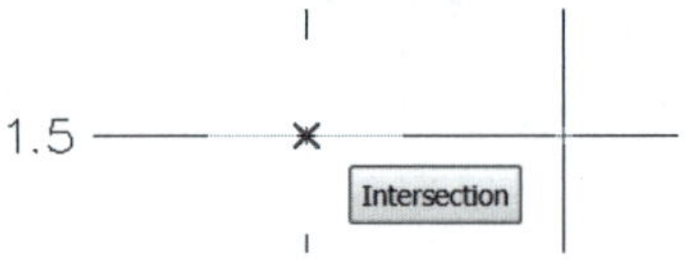

Select the intersection between the object and the extension line as the second point.

10. 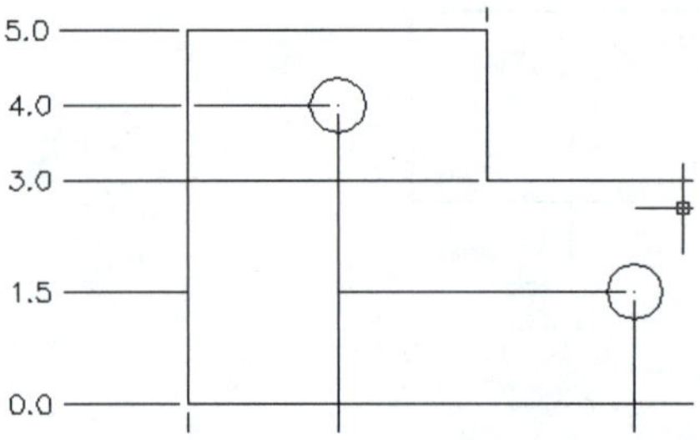

Note the gap created.

11. 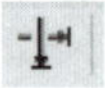 Select the **DIMBREAK** tool again.

12. 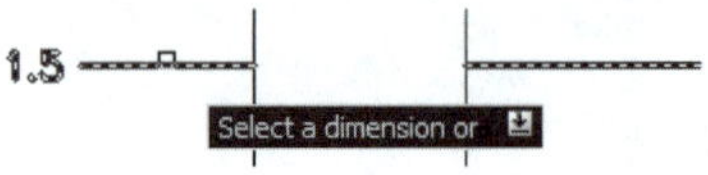

Select the 1.5 vertical dimension you just modified.

13. 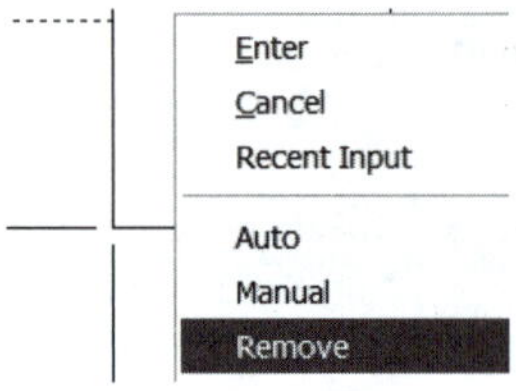

RMB and select **Remove**.

14. 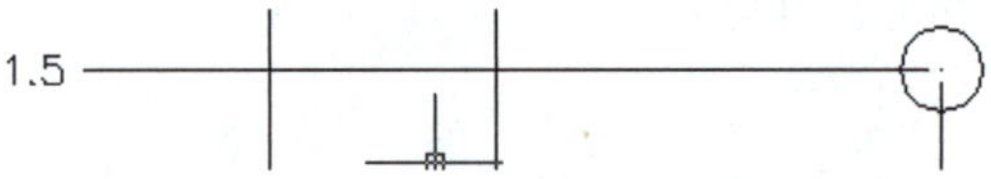

The gap is removed.

15. 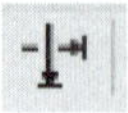 Select the **DIMBREAK** tool again.

RMB and select **Multiple**.

16. 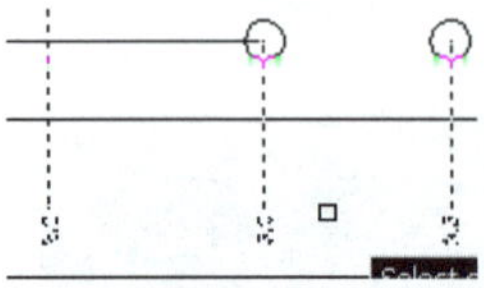
Select the three middle horizontal dimensions .

Press **ENTER**.

17. 

RMB and select **ENTER**.

18. 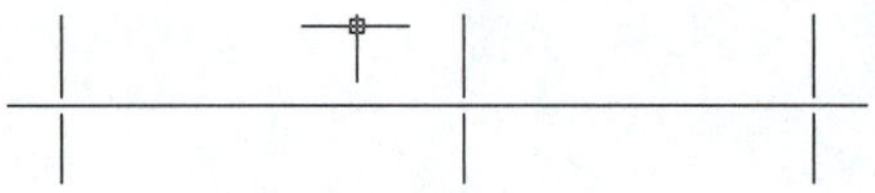
A gap is automatically placed for all three dimensions without selecting the object.

Dimension Style

Command Locator

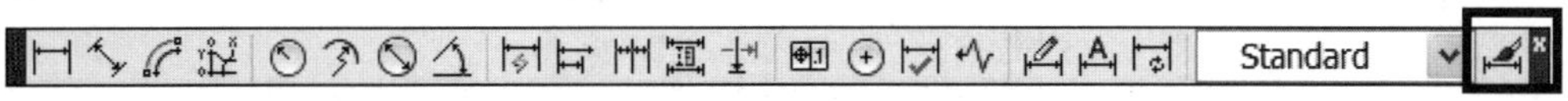

Toolbar Menu	**Dimension**
Pull Down Menu	**Dimension / Style…**
Command	**Dimstyle**
Alias	**D**
Dialog Box	**Dimension Style Manager**

Command Overview

The Standard Dimension Style is sufficient for most beginners. However, it may be necessary to make minor changes to the Standard Dimension Style or create additional Dimension Styles. The Dimension Style Manager dialog box lists and previews selected dimension styles. Select Modify to access the Modify Dimension Style options. Changes made to the Dimension Styles will globally affect the dimensions in the drawing that reference the style being modified, unless the change was made to an individual dimension. Only common modifications to dimension styles will be discussed in this tutorial.

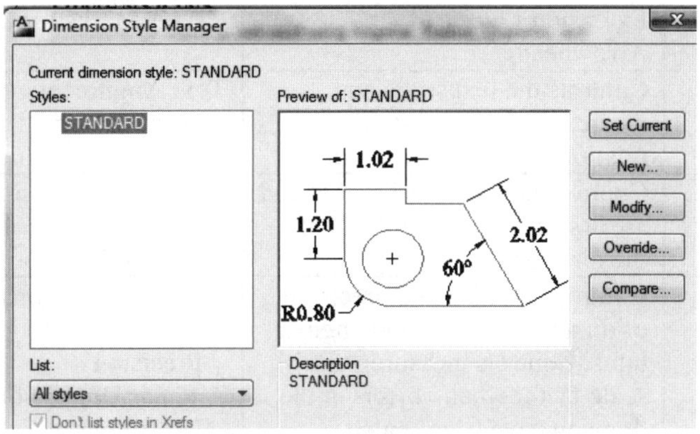

Dimension Style Manager Dialog Box

Dimension Style Manager	Overview
Current Dimstyle	Displays the name of the current dimension style
Styles:	Lists the dimension styles in the drawing.
List	Controls the display of either all dimension style names in the drawing or only the dimension styles in use.
Preview of : Standard	Shows a Preview image of the current [Standard] dimension style.
Set Current	Makes a selected dimension style current.
New…	Invokes the New Dimension Style dialog box where a new style name can be typed, starting with or based on a selected dimension style, for all or selected dimensions (linear, angular, radial…etc.).
Modify…	Invokes the Modify Dimension Style dialog box. Changes made to the current dimension style will be applied to dimensions placed in the drawing using that style (see next section).
Override…	Works similar to the Modify option however changes will be applied to dimensions placed after the Override modifications have been made.
Compare…	Compares selected dimension styles and displays the differences.

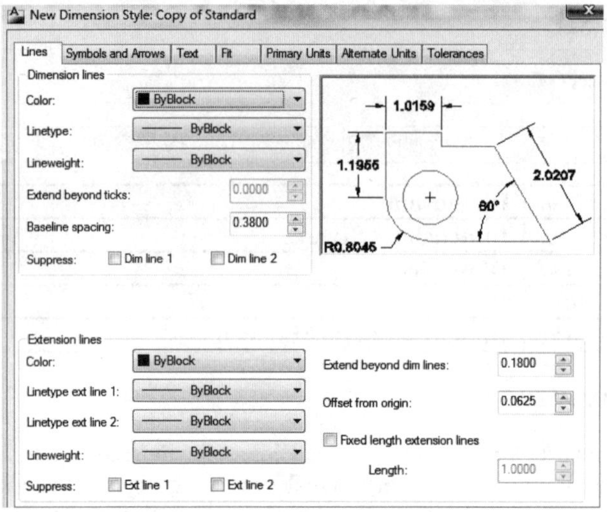

Modify Dimension Style Dialog Box

Modify Dimension Style dialog box tab	Overview	Typical Options to Change
Lines and Arrows	Controls the features of the Extension Lines and Arrowheads.	Arrowhead style Center Marks for Circles
Text	Controls the text style, and where the text is located in relation to the dimension lines.	Text Alignment: Horizontal or Aligned with dimension line
Fit	Controls how dimension text and arrows fit within or outside of the dimension lines.	Scale for Dimension Features: Use Overall Scale (type a scale factor) Scale dimensions to layout (paperspace)
Primary Units	Controls the type and precision of dimension linear and angular units. Controls measurement scale factor when objects in the drawing have been scaled.	Linear Dimensions: Unit Format Precision Angular Dimensions: Units Format Precision Measurent Scale: Scale Factor
Alternate Units	Controls the display of Alternate Units, the Unit format, and the Multiplier for alternate units.	Display Alternate Units Precision
Tolerances	Controls Tolerance Format.	Tolerance Format Method Precision Values

General Procedures

To Create a New Dimension Style:

1. Invoke the Dimension Style command.
2. Select a dimension style to start with from the drop down list. Select the New button, then type the New Style Name, or accept the default name.
3. Select Continue to access the Modify Dimension Style dialog box.

To Modify a Dimension Style:

1. Invoke the Dimension Style command.
2. Select the dimension style, then select the Modify button.
3. Select the appropriate tab in the Modify Dimension Style dialog box. Select OK and Close to Continue.

To Delete a Dimension Style:

1. Invoke the Dimension Style command.
2. Select the dimension style from the list, then right-click (RMB) to access the shortcut menu.
3. Select delete. The dimension style will not be deleted if it is current, or if there are any dimensions in the drawing using that dimension style.

Tips & Tricks

- The Purge command can also be used to delete unreferenced Dimension Styles. Select File / Drawing Utilities / Purge (select option or All).
- The Standard Dimension Style will be adequate for most beginners.
- When creating a new dimension style, base the new style on Standard, and apply changes to it, leaving Standard alone, unless only minor changes are needed.
- Make global modifications to dimensions in the drawing by changing the Dimension Style. Existing dimensions should automatically update. If for some reason they do not update, select the dimension Update command from the Dimension toolbar or from the Dimension pull-down menu.

Command Exercise

Exercise 10-9 – Dimension Styles

Drawing Name: **dimsty1.dwg**
Estimated Time to Completion: 30 Minutes

Scope

Dimension the object on the left using the standard dimension style. Create a new Dimension Style called TEST based on the Standard dimension style with overall scale (Geometry) of 2 (remember to set current). Dimension the object on the right.

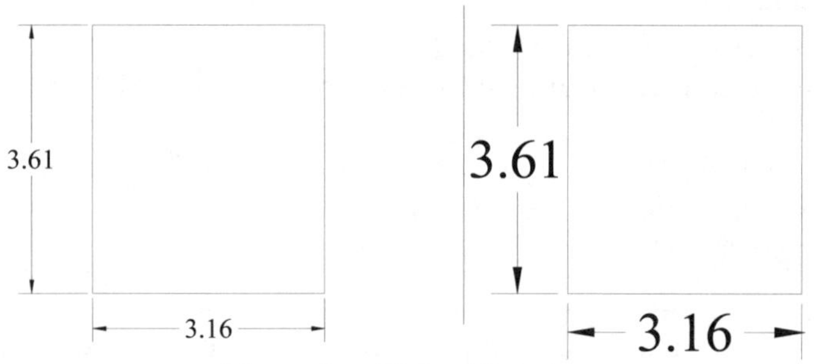

Dimension Styles Exercise

Solution

1. 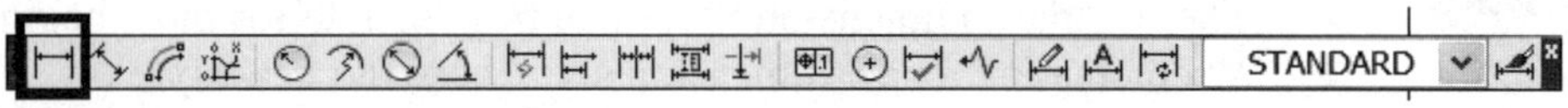

Invoke the **Linear Dimension** command (dimlinear).

2. *Specify first extension line origin or <select object>:*
Press <ENTER> to select an object.

3. *Select object to dimension:*
Select the left side of the left box.

4. *Specify dimension line location or [Mtext/Text/Angle/Horizontal/Vertical/Rotated:*
Select a location for the vertical dimension.

5. 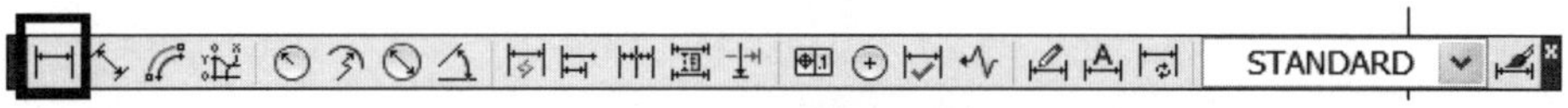

Repeat the Linear Dimension command with the RMB (dimlinear or <ENTER>).

6. *Specify first extension line origin or <select object>:*
Press <ENTER> to select an object.

7. *Select object to dimension:*
Select the bottom of the left box.

8. *Specify dimension line location or [Mtext/Text/Angle/Horizontal/Vertical/Rotated:*
Select a location for the horizontal dimension.

9. 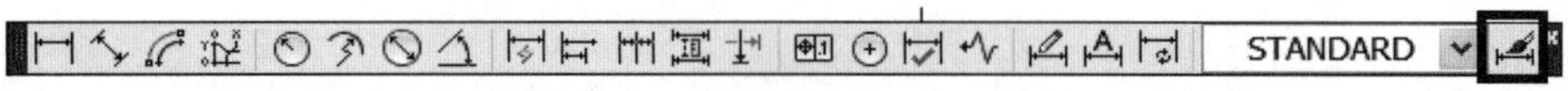

Invoke the Dimension Style command (dimstyle).

10.

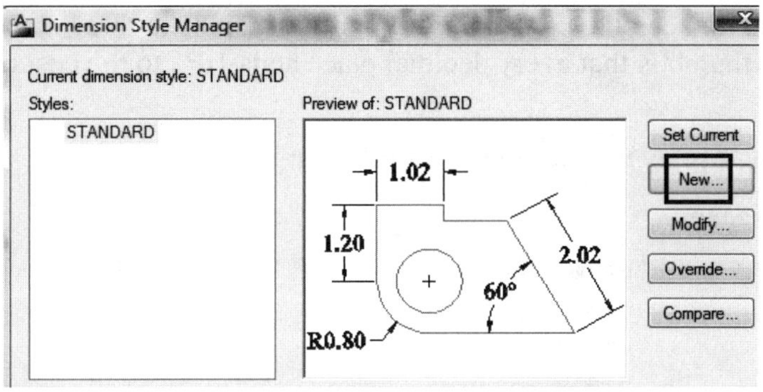

In the Dimension Style Manager dialog box, press **New...** to create a new dimension style.

11.

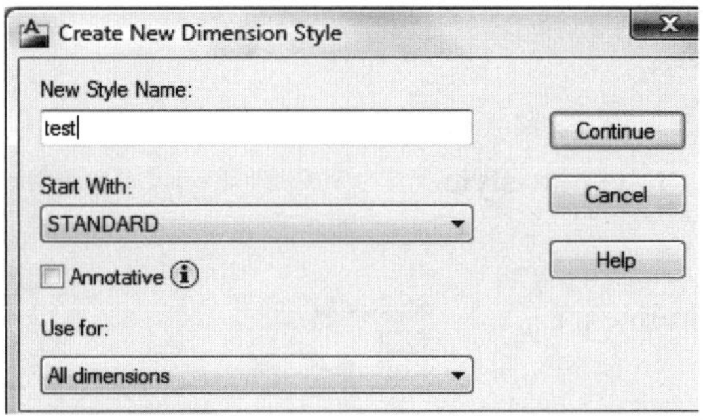

In the Create New Dimension Style dialog box, enter the new name for the new dimension style based on the standard dimension style and press **Continue**.

12.

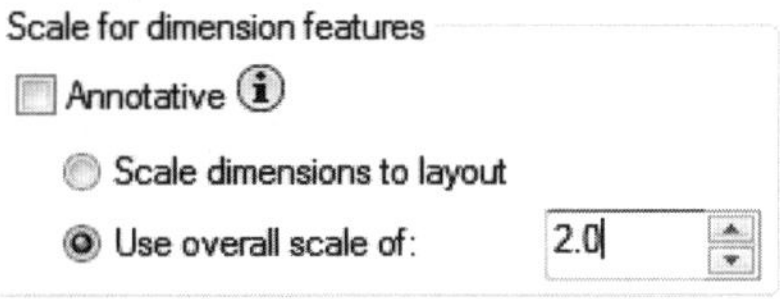

In the Fit tab of the dialog box, change the overall scale to **2**.

13.

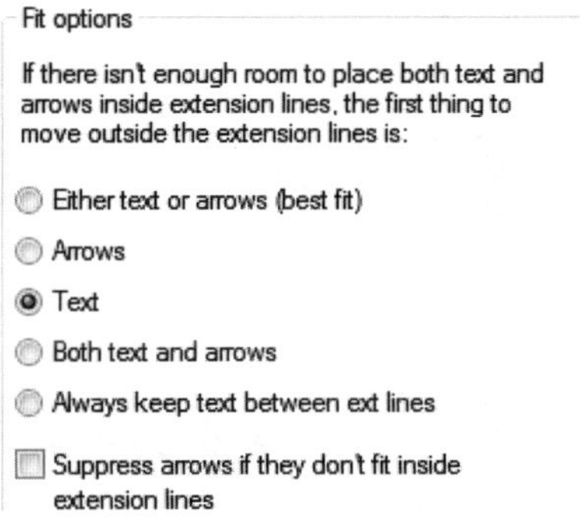

Under Fit options:
Enable **Text**.

Notice how the radial dimension changes in preview window.

14.

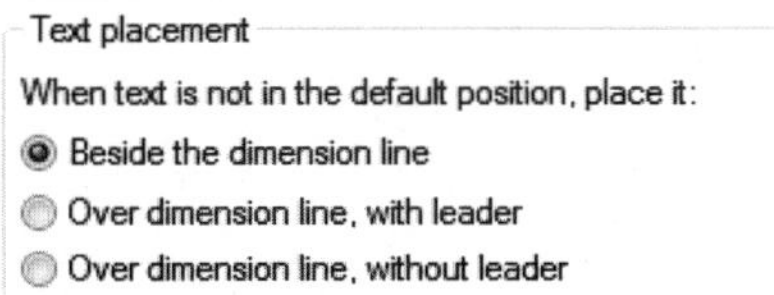

Under Text placement:

Enable **Beside the dimension line**.

15.

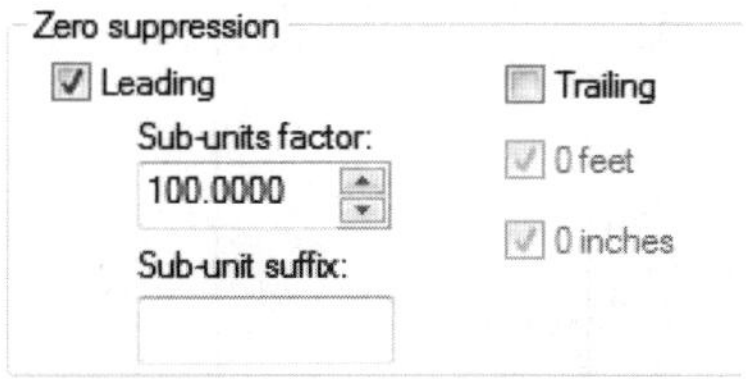

Select the Primary Units tab.

Enable **Leading** under Zero suppression.

16.

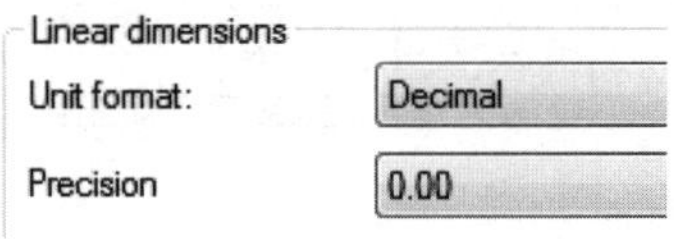

Under Linear Dimensions:

Set the Precision to **0.00**.

17. In mechanical design, you want to keep the precision for your dimensions to three decimal places or less. A good rule of thumb is that every decimal place adds 10% to the cost of fabrication.

Note how the Preview window display updates to reflect the changes.

18. Select the Symbols and Arrows tab.

Under Arrowheads:

Set the Arrow size to **0.200**.

Press the **OK** button to continue.

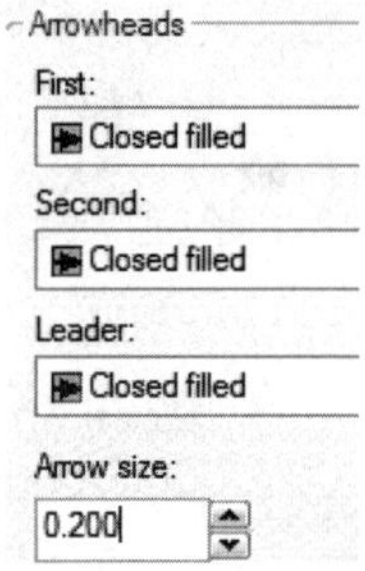

19. Note that the current dimension style is set to the new style.

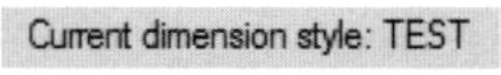

20. Press **Close** to continue.

21. Invoke the Linear Dimension command (dimlinear).

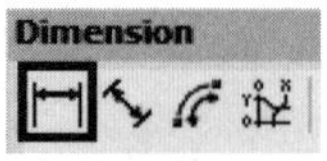

22. *Specify first extension line origin or <select object>:*
Press <ENTER> to select an object.

23. *Select object to dimension:*
Select the left side of the box on the right.

24. *Specify dimension line location or [Mtext/Text/Angle/Horizontal/Vertical/Rotated:*
Select a location for the vertical dimension.

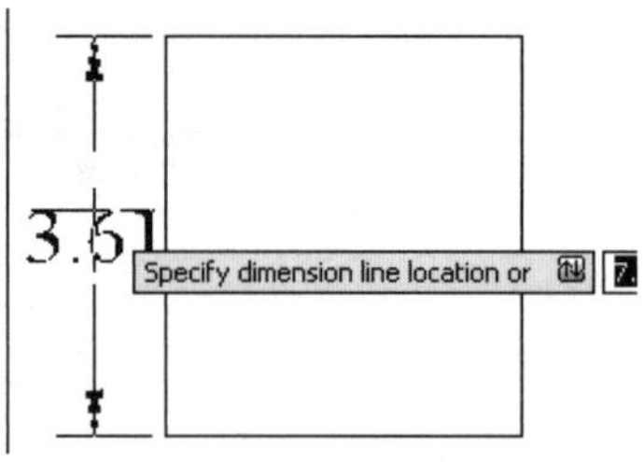

25. Repeat the Linear Dimension command with the RMB (dimlinear or <ENTER>).

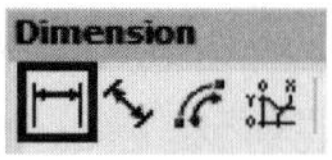

26. *Specify first extension line origin or <select object>:*
Press <ENTER> to select an object.

27. *Select object to dimension:*
Select the bottom of the box on the right.

28. *Specify dimension line location or [Mtext/Text/Angle/Horizontal/Vertical/Rotated:*
Select a location for the horizontal dimension.

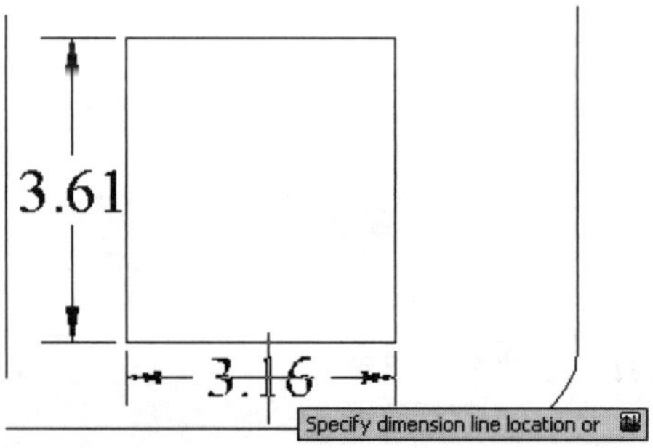

Edit Dimension Location

Command Locator

Command	**(Command line must be blank)**

Command Overview

The placement of the dimension lines and text can be adjusted using Grips. With the command line blank, select the dimension. Select the grip at the either arrow point, or on the dimension text, drag the cursor then pick the new location. The location of the dimension text can be moved closer to one extension line or the other using the same method. This is also a good way to move the extension line origin points, should they be incorrectly selected.

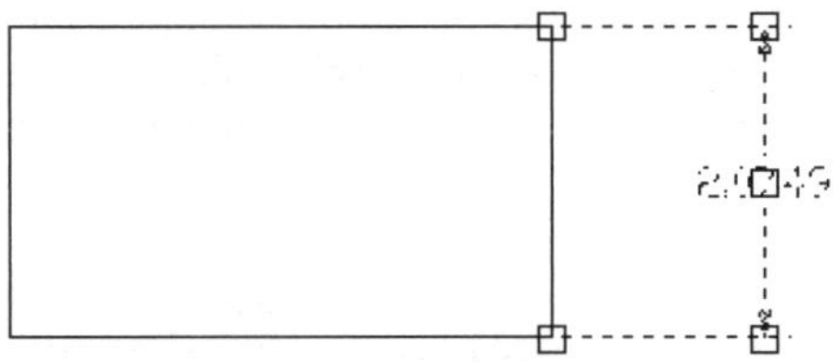

Grips on a Dimension Line

General Procedures

To move the dimension line:

1. With the Command line blank, select the dimension.
2. Select either the text, or arrowhead grip. The default grip mode will be Stretch.
3. Stretch the dimension line and pick the new location. Press Escape two times to cancel the grip selection.

To move the dimension text:

1. With the Command line blank, select the dimension.
2. Select the dimension text. The default grip mode will be Stretch.
3. Drag the dimension text toward one extension line or the other, or to a new location. Press Escape two times to cancel the grip selection.

To move a dimension origin point:

1. Zoom into the area where the dimension origin point should meet the object (intersection, endpoint…etc.). With the Command line blank, select the dimension.
2. Select the dimension origin point. The default grip mode will be Stretch.
3. Use Object Snap to drag the origin point to the correct location on the object. Press Escape two times to cancel the grip selection. ***Note:*** *Sometimes both the object and the dimension may be selected and the origin point dragged to the grip of the object being dimensioned.*

Tips & Tricks

- Remember to press the Escape key two times to cancel the grip selection. Pressing <ENTER> will repeat the last command (which may have been the Erase command!).

Edit Dimension Text

Command Locator

Toolbar Menu	**Text/ Edit Text**
Pull Down Menu	**Modify / Text...**
Command	**Ddedit**
RMB Shortcut Menu	**Text area of the Multiline Text Editor**
Dialog Box	**Multiline Text Editor**

Command Overview

AutoCAD dimensions are *associated* with the object being dimensioned, therefore, if the dimension text appears to be incorrect, it is either because the dimension line origin points were incorrectly selected, or the drawing is incorrect. Check first to see that the origin points are at the correct location (see previous section). If this seems to be correct, then go back and correct the drawing. The Edit Text command (DDEDIT) should be used to add annotation to the dimension text and not to delete or overwrite existing dimension text. In the Multiline Text Editor, the dimension text will be represented as the *greater than* and *less than* symbols < >. Place the cursor before or after these symbols to type additional text. Do not overwrite or delete the < > symbols representing the dimension text. Deleting or typing over these symbols will break *associativity* between the dimension and the objects being dimensioned. It is better to make corrections to the geometry in the drawing.

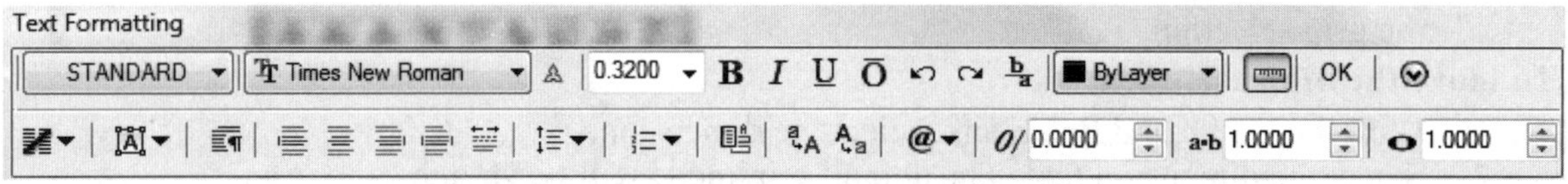

Multiline Text Editor Dialog Box

General Procedures

1. Invoke the Edit Text command.
2. Select the dimension to edit.
3. Place the cursor before or after the < > symbols and type additional annotation. Select OK to exit.

- Never delete these < > symbols, or type in between these symbols.
- By maintaining *associativity* between the dimension and the object being dimensioned, changes made to the object will automatically update the dimension text.
- If you ever accidentally delete or modify a dimension, you can select the dimension and type <> and the true dimension will automatically be recovered.

Edit Dimension Properties

Command Locator

Toolbar Menu	**Standard** *(Select dimension first)*
Command	*(Select dimension first)* **Properties**
Dialog Box	**Properties**

Command Overview

When changing dimensions properties, decide first whether this change should apply globally to the dimension style, or to a single dimension.

For instance, if the precision of the primary units of a dimension style are set to four decimal places, and the user wants the precision of radial dimensions to always be two decimal places, then a subset style for Radius dimensions needs to be created from the original dimension style. Use the Dimension Style Manager dialog box, to make the desired changes, and all of the radial dimensions in the drawing will be automatically updated to reflect the change.

If you want to change only a selected dimension in the drawing, use the Properties command. Changes made to individual dimensions will usually not update globally if a change is later made to that Dimension Style.

The Styles toolbar

The Styles toolbar allows you to select the current dimension style, the current text style and the current table style. Simply select the style you want to make active from the drop-down list.

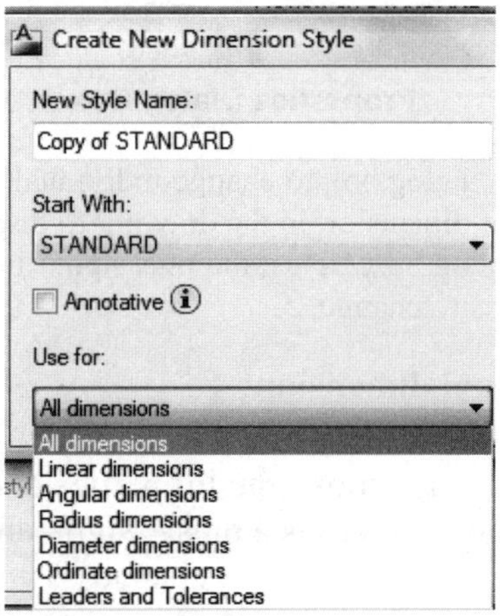

Dimension Style Manager Dialog Box

Use the **Dimension Style Manager** dialog box to make global changes to dimensions in the drawing. This will automatically apply modifications made to the dimension style. When creating a subset from a dimension style with changes to specific dimensions, select New, then choose the type of dimension from the list alongside "Use for". Then select Continue to make the desired changes.

General Procedures

To change the Dimension Style Properties:

1. Invoke the Dimension Style command.
2. In the Dimension Style Manager box, select the dimension style to change then select the Modify button.
3. Select the options to change from the corresponding tab in the Modify Dimension Style dialog box. Then select OK to exit.

To make a change to a specific feature of an existing the Dimension Style Properties:

1. Invoke the Dimension Style command.
2. In the Dimension Style Manager box, select the dimension style to change then select the New button.
3. From the New Dimension Style dialog box select the dimension type (Angular, Radius, etc. from the "Use for" list. Select Continue.
4. Select the options to change from the corresponding tab in the Modify Dimension Style dialog box. Then select OK to exit.

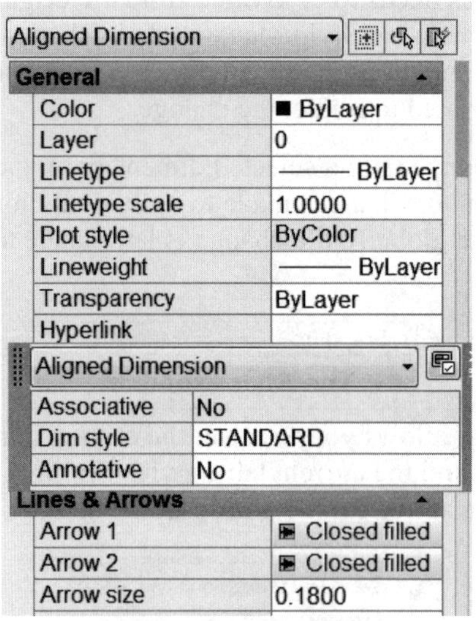

Properties Dialog Box

Use the **Properties** dialog box to change individual dimensions in the drawing. Select the dimension in the drawing to display the dimension properties in the dialog box. Select the plus sign + before the property to access the options to change.

To make a change to an individual dimension:

1. Invoke Properties command.
2. Select the dimension to change (move the Properties dialog box if necessary)
3. Select the option to change. If there is a plus + sign before the option to change, select the plus sign first, then select the option to change. Type or select the new option.
4. Select OK to exit.

- When editing dimensions, determine whether you want to apply the change globally by making the change to the Dimension Style, or individually by using the Properties command.
- Changes made to individual dimensions will usually not update if a change is later made to that Dimension Style.

Command Exercise

Exercise 10-10 – Edit Dimension

Drawing Name: **dimedit1.dwg**
Estimated Time to Completion: 5 Minutes

Scope

Use the Properties command to modify the dimensions as indicated.

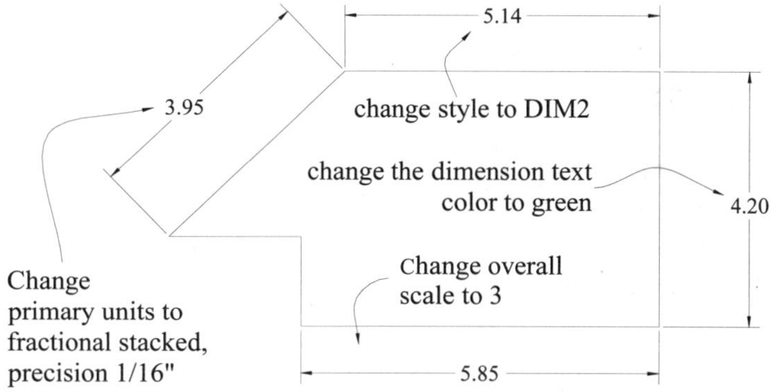

Edit Dimension Exercise

Solution

1.  Invoke the **Properties** command (properties).

2. 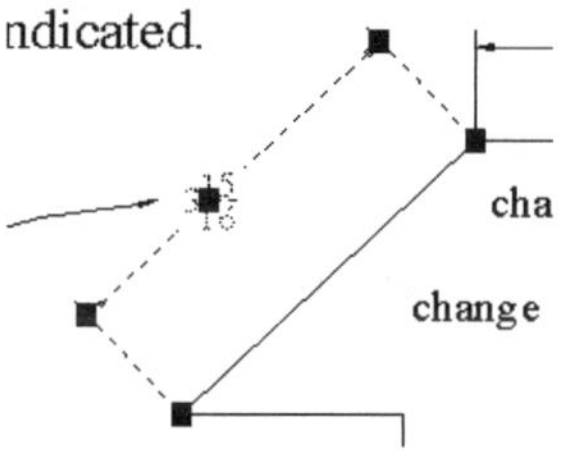

Select the aligned dimension that will be changed to fractional stacked.

3. 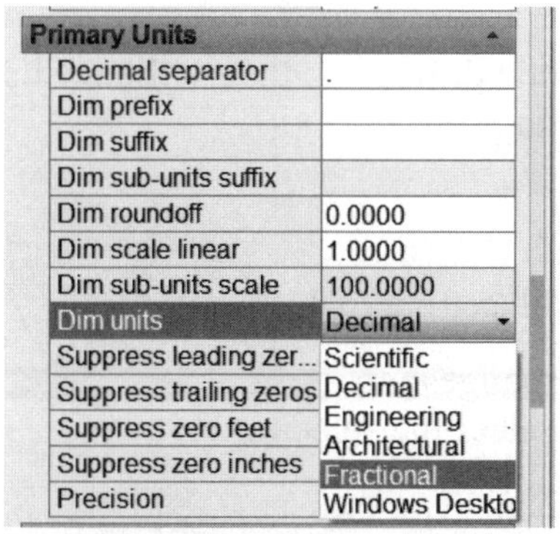

In the Properties dialog box, change the 'Dim units' to **Fractional**.

4. 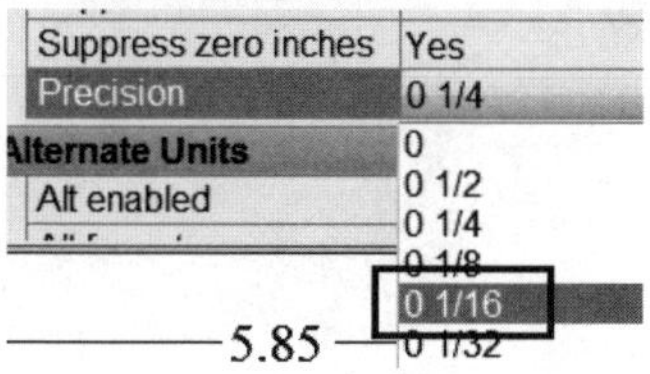

Change the 'Precision' to **'0 1/16'**.

5. 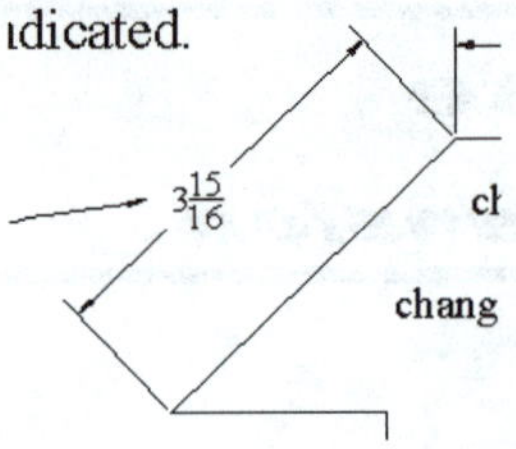

Click a point in the drawing window with the LMB. Notice how the Dimension changes. Press the <Esc> key once to clear the selection.

6. 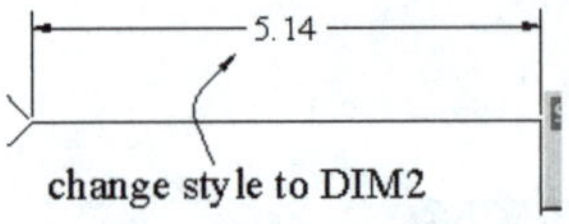

Pick the top horizontal dimension that will have its style changed to DIM2.

7. 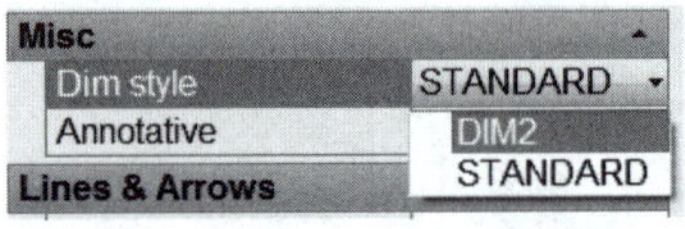

Using the Quick Properties dialog (the abbreviated Properties dialog):

Change the 'Dim style' to **DIM2**.

8. 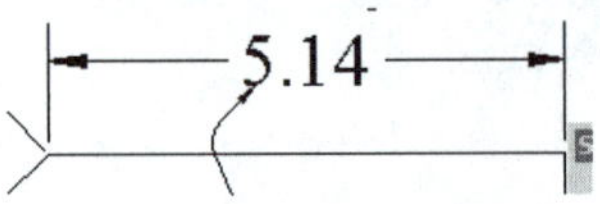

Notice how the Dimension changes. Press the <Esc> key once to clear the selection.

9. 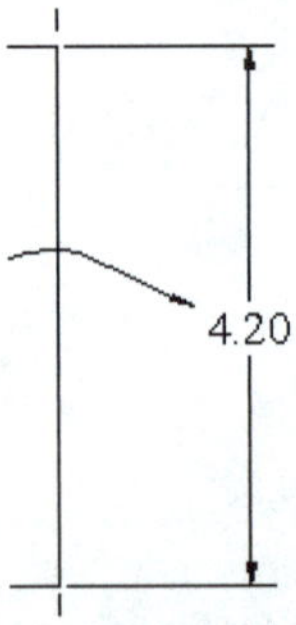

Pick the vertical dimension that will have its text color changed to green.

10. 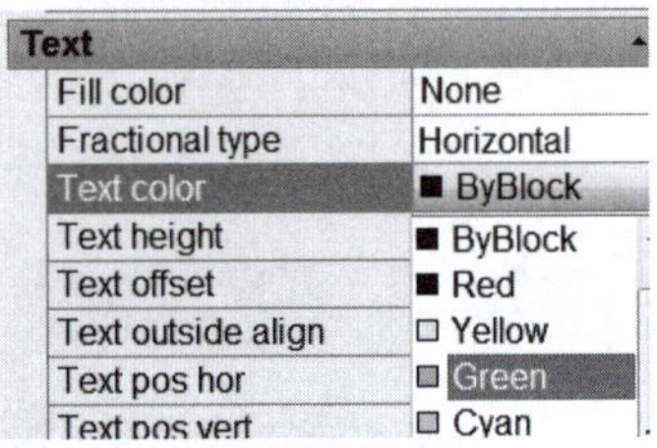

Change the 'Text color' to **Green**.

Notice how the Dimension changes.
Press the <Esc> key once to clear the selection.

11. 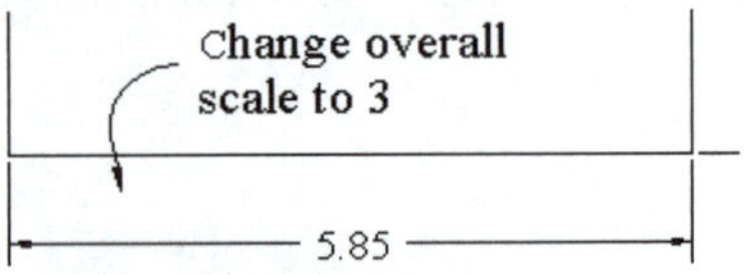

Pick the lower horizontal dimension that will have its overall scale changed to 3.

12. 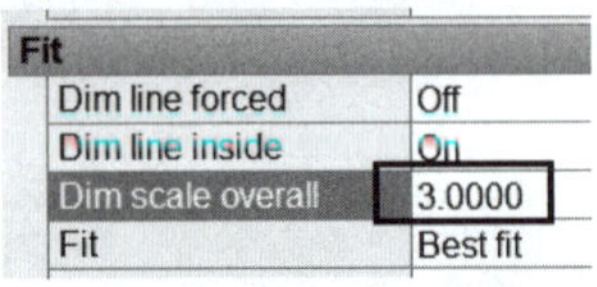

Change the 'Dim scale overall' setting to **3**.

Notice how the Dimension changes.
Press the <Esc> key once to clear the selection.

Close the Properties dialog box.

Command Exercise

Exercise 10-11 – Edit Dimension

Drawing Name: **dimedit2.dwg**
Estimated Time to Completion: 10 Minutes

Scope

Use the Properties command to edit the top dimension. Use the Edit Text command to make changes to the bottom dimension.

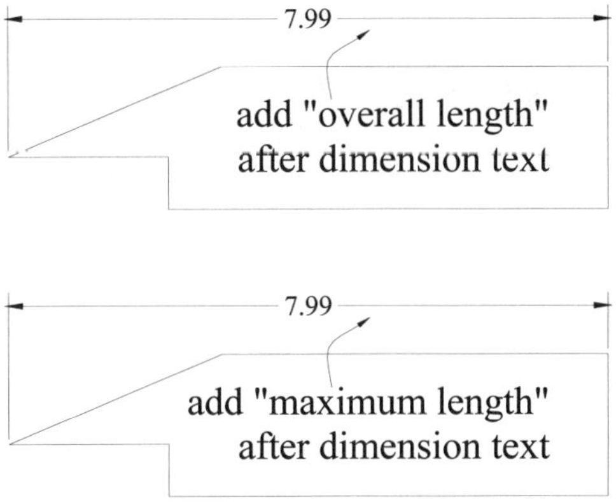

Edit Dimension Exercise

Solution

1.  Invoke the **Properties** command (properties).

2. 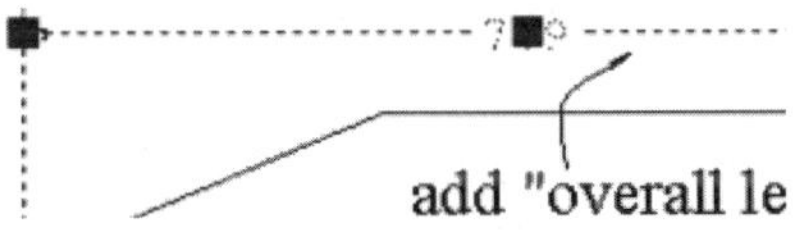

Pick the top dimension with the LMB.

3. 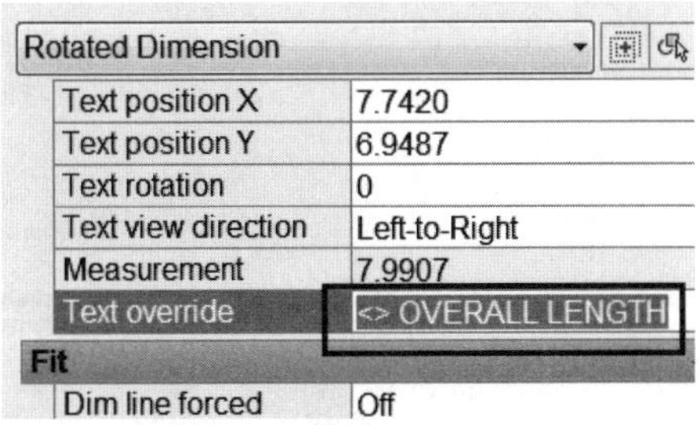

In the Properties dialog box, change the Text override to <> **OVERALL LENGTH**.

4. 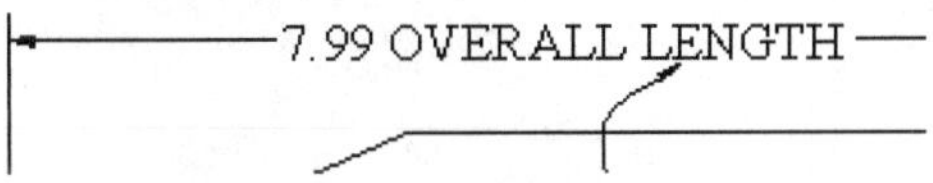

Close the dialog box and press <ESC> once to clear the selection.

5.  Invoke the Edit Text command (**ddedit**).

6. 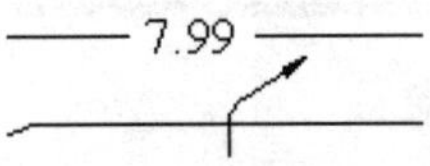

Select an annotation object or [Undo]:
Pick the lower dimension with the LMB.

7. 

Type in the desired text in the Multiline Text Editor and press ‘OK’.

8. *Select an annotation object or [Undo]:*
Press <ENTER> to end the command.

> ***Tip:*** *Typing <> indicates the original dimension value.*

Command Exercise

Exercise 10-12 – Editing Dimensions

Drawing Name: **dimedit3.dwg**
Estimated Time to Completion: 10 Minutes

Scope

Use the Align Text Option in the Dimensions Menu.
Use Grips to adjust the dimensions as indicated.

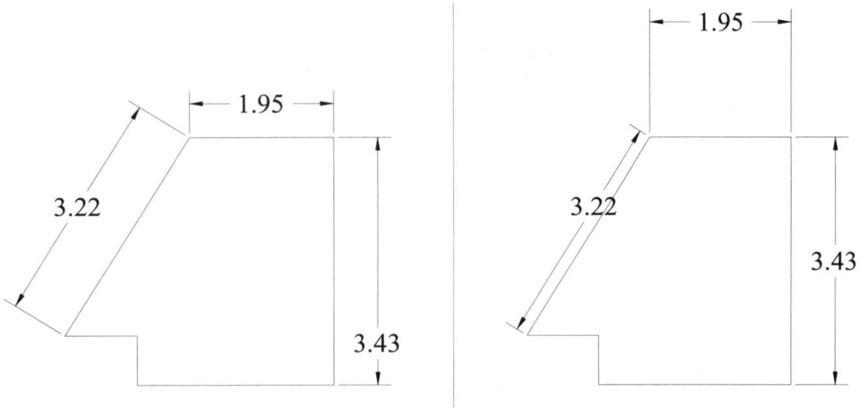

Edit Dimension Exercise

Solution

1. 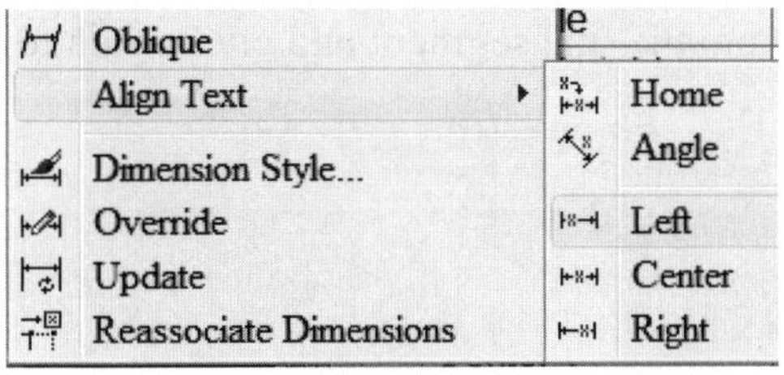

Go to the Dimensions Menu.
Select **Align Text→Left**.

2. 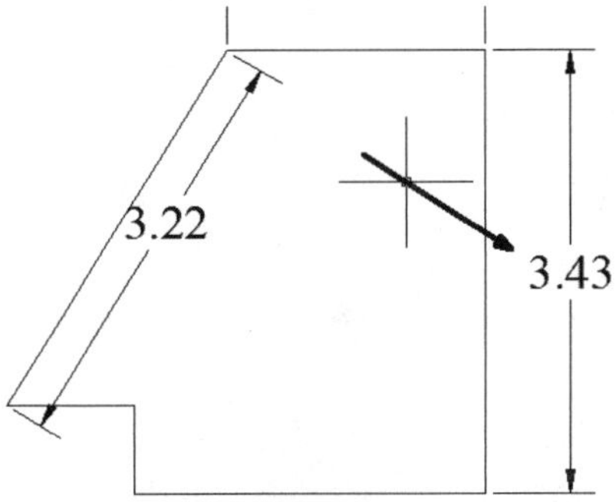

Pick the 3.43 vertical dimension on the right side figure.

The dimension will automatically pop in place.

3. 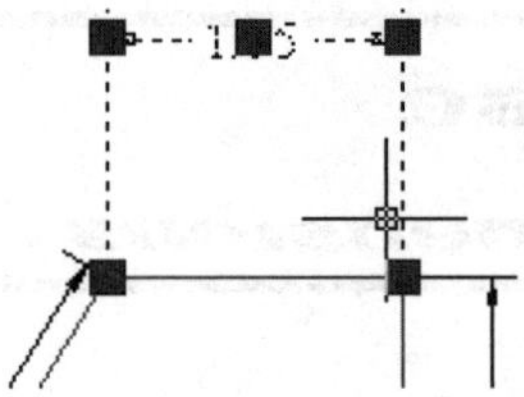
Pick the horizontal dimension at the top of the object on the right.

4. Select one of the grips along the dimension line.

5. 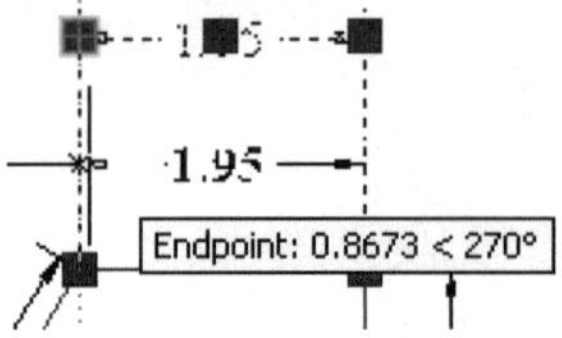

Specify stretch point or [Base point/Copy/Undo/eXit]:
Move the dimension down closer to the top line segment and click again.

6. Press <ESC> once to clear the selection.

7. 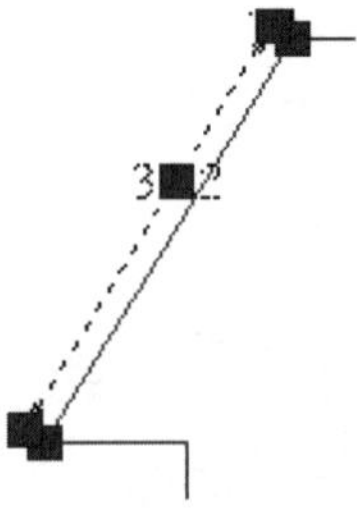
Pick the Aligned dimension.

8. 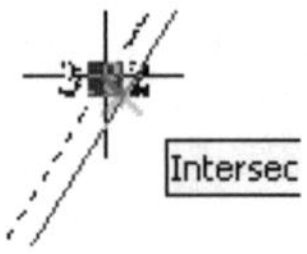

Select the grip over the text.

9. 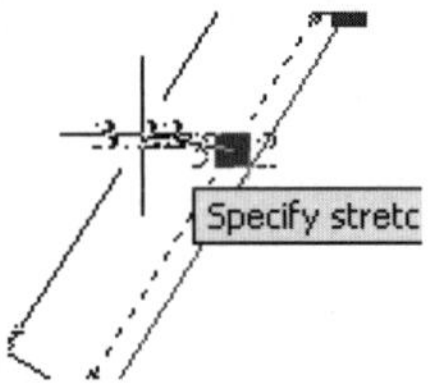

Specify stretch point or [Base point/Copy/Undo/eXit]:
Move the dimension away from the line segment and click again to place.

Press <ESC> to deselect.

Command Exercise

Exercise 10-13 – Editing Dimensions

Drawing Name: **dimedit4.dwg**
Estimated Time to Completion: 10 Minutes

Scope

Use the Stretch command to modify the part. Notice that the dimensions will change automatically.

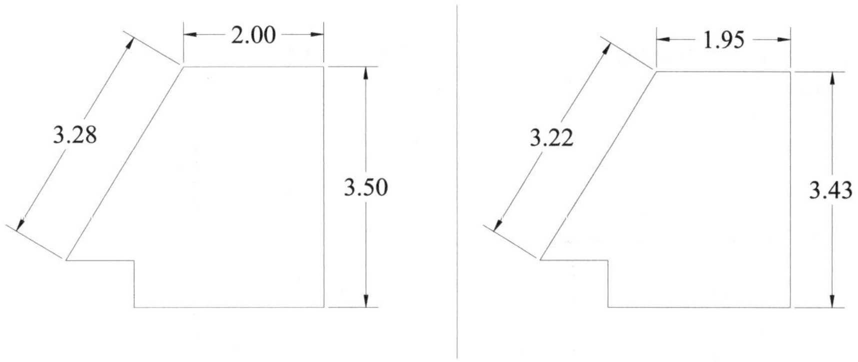

Edit Dimension Exercise

Solution

1. Invoke the Stretch command (stretch). 
2. *Select objects:*
   Using a crossing window, select the bottom portion of the part, include crossing over the dimensions.
3. *Select objects:*
   Press <ENTER>
4. *Specify base point or displacement:*
   Pick a base point near the center of the object.
5. *Specify second point of displacement:*
   Type '@0,-0.07' and press <ENTER>. Notice how the part changes as well as the dimensions.
6. Repeat the Stretch command with the RMB (stretch or <ENTER>). 
7. *Select objects:*
   Using a crossing window, select the right side, include crossing over the horizontal dimension.
8. *Select objects:*
   Press <ENTER>
9. *Specify base point or displacement:*
   Pick a base point near the center of the object.
10. *Specify second point of displacement:*
    Type @0.05<0 and press <ENTER>.

***Tip:** Turn ORTHO off and use direct distance instead of polar coordinates.*

Section Exercise

Exercise 10-14 – Dimensioning a Drawing

Drawing Name: **new drawing**
Estimated Time to Completion: 30 Minutes

Scope

Create a drawing from scratch using standard orthographic views and dimension.

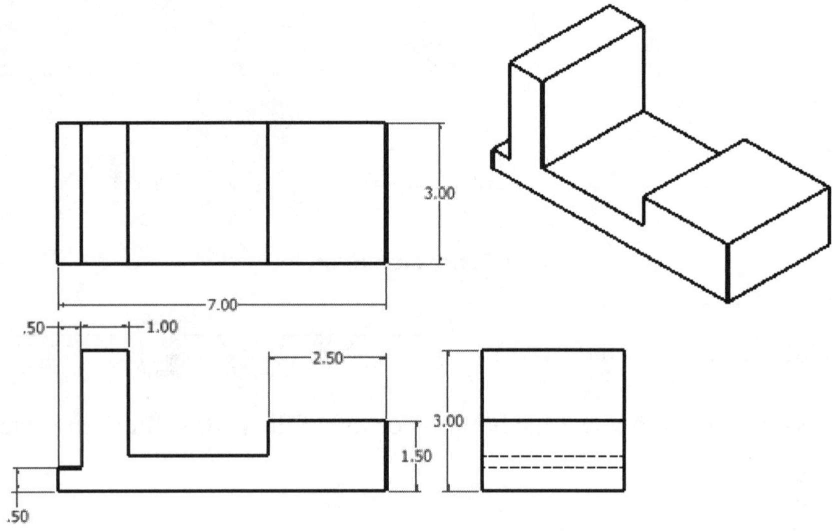

Dimension Exercise

Solution

1. Set Drawing Precision to 2.
2. Create three layers:

Object	Green
Hidden	Cyan
Dimension	Red

3. Draw a front, top, and right side view as shown.

Section Exercise

Exercise 10-15 –

Dimensioning a Drawing

Drawing Name: **new drawing**
Estimated Time to Completion: 30 Minutes

Scope

Create a drawing from scratch using standard orthographic views and dimension.

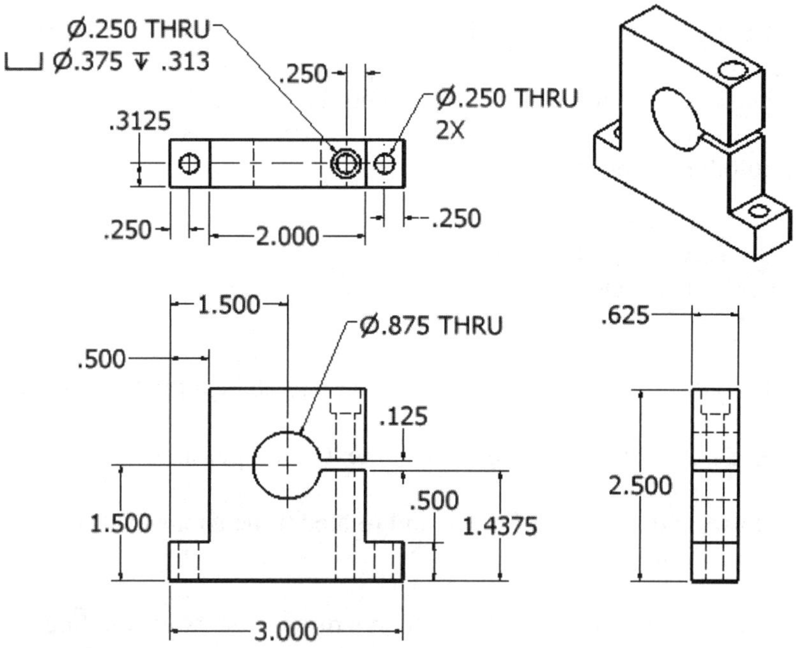

Dimension Exercise

Solution

1. Set Drawing Precision to 3.
2. Draw a front, top, and right side view as shown.
3. Create three layers:

Object	Green
Hidden	Cyan
Dimension	Red

Review Questions

1. Which dimensioning units are most often used for Mechanical technical drawings?

   - ❑ A. Decimal
   - ❑ B. Engineering
   - ❑ C. Architectural
   - ❑ D. Scientific

2. The _______ dialog box is used to control dimension styles and variables.

   - ❑ A. DIMENSION
   - ❑ B. DIMSTYLE
   - ❑ C. Dimension Style Manager
   - ❑ D.STYLE

3. **T F** The DIMASO system variable governs the creation of associative dimensioning.

4. **T F** The size of dimension arrows can not be modified.

5. The default dimension style is called:

   - ❑ A. DEFAULT
   - ❑ B. STANDARD
   - ❑ C. OVERRIDE
   - ❑ D.STYLE1

6. **T F** The DIMSTYLE command allows you to change the text style of the dimension.

7. **T F** Adding text to existing dimension text is not possible.

8. **T F** Horizontal, vertical, aligned, and rotated dimensions cannot be associative dimensions.

9. **T F** You can trim and extend associative dimension extension lines.

10. **T F** Dimension Styles can not be named.

Review Answers

1. Which dimensioning units are most often used for Mechanical technical drawings?

   A. Decimal

2. The _______ dialog box is used to control dimension styles and variables.

   C. Dimension Style Manager

3. **T F** The DIMASO system variable governs the creation of associative dimensioning.

   True

4. **T F** The size of dimension arrows can not be modified.

   False

5. The default dimension style is called:

   B. STANDARD

6. **T F** The DIMSTYLE command allows you to change the text style of the dimension.

   True

7. **T F** Adding text to existing dimension text is not possible.

   False

8. **T F** Horizontal, vertical, aligned, and rotated dimensions cannot be associative dimensions.

   False

9. **T F** You can trim and extend associative dimension extension lines.

   False

10. **T F** Dimension Styles can not be named.

    False

NOTES:

Lesson 11.0 – Text Tools

Estimated Class Time – 2 hours

Objectives

This section will cover how to use Text. Learn to type Text in either single or multiple lines, edit Text and check for spelling errors. Create Text Styles choosing from a variety of fonts.

- **Single Line Text**
  Type a single line of text for simple notes.
- **Multiline Text**
  Use the Multiline Text editor to create paragraphs of text or sentences that can be stretched into wider or narrower paragraphs using Grips.
- **Text Style**
  Create several Text Styles for specific text requirements.
- **Edit Text**
  Use the Edit Text command to change the content of Single Line or Multiline text. Use the Properties command to change other features of the text in the drawing.
- **Find and Replace**
  Use the Find and Replace to search and change text in the drawing.
- **Spell Check**
  Use the Spell command to check for spelling errors.
- **Fields**
  Fields are tied to drawing properties and can be used as a more dynamic and powerful version of attributes
- **Tables**
  Tables may be used for tabulated drawings, parts lists, and material lists. Fields, attributes and texts can all be inserted into a table.

Single Line Text

Command Locator

Draw Menu

Text Toolbar Menu	
Pull Down Menu	**Draw / Text / Single Line Text**
Command	**Dtext**
Alias	**DT**
RMB Shortcut Menu	**Drawing Window**

Command Overview

Text can be typed a single line at a time with the DTEXT command. Text can be moved, copied, rotated, scaled or changed after it has been placed in the drawing. When typing text, the spacebar will create a space, and the <ENTER> key will act as a carriage return and bring the cursor to the next line. The <ENTER> button on the mouse (RMB) will not work with text. Use the <ENTER> key on the keyboard. The easiest way to use the Single Line Text command is to pick a start point and follow the prompts for the Text height, and Text rotation angle, then begin typing. It is important to press <ENTER> twice to end the DTEXT command. This is because the first time <ENTER> is pressed, the cursor will move to the next line, but the text will not be placed until <ENTER> is pressed again. Single Line Text is best when used for simple notes that contain only a few words or a short sentence.

DTEXT Option	Overview
Start point	Pick a start point for the text in the Drawing Window.
Specify height	Type in a height, or press <ENTER> to accept the default text height.
Specify rotation angle	Type in a rotation angle or press <ENTER> to accept the default rotation angle.

Two less common options within the DTEXT command are Justify and Style. Type J (and <ENTER>) to access the Justification options. The more common Justification options are: Align, Fit, Center, Middle, and Right. The other options TL, TC, TR, for Top Left, Top Center, Top Right, etc., are more options than any beginner needs to know! Justifications will not display until the DTEXT command is completely executed. The default start point is Left Justification, and need not be typed. The Text Style option will be covered in the next section.

Justification	Overview
Align	Aligns the text between two points, scaling the text height proportionately.
Fit	Fits the text between two points, maintaining the text height.
Center	Centers the text at the (bottom center).
Middle	Centers the text right in the middle of the text.
Right	Justifies the text to the right.

General Procedures

Typing Single Line Text:

1. Begin the Single Line Text command by typing DT (and <ENTER>).
2. Pick a start point in the Drawing Window.
3. Type the text height, or press <ENTER> to accept the default Text height.
4. Press <ENTER> to accept the default rotation angle (0) or type a new angle.
5. Type the first line of text. Press <ENTER>. Type the second line of text. Press <ENTER> twice to complete the dtext command.

Tips & Tricks

- Single Line Text (DTEXT) is referred as dynamic or *displayed* text, because it is displayed on the screen as it is being typed.
- When the Dtext (Single Line Text) command is repeated, the last line of text will be highlighted to show the height and rotation. Pressing enter will automatically place the text cursor under the last line of text. The cursor can be moved at any time to locate new start points.
- Remember to press <ENTER> at the Keyboard.
- You will not be prompted for a text height if one is specified in the current text style.

Command Exercise

Exercise 11-1 – Single LineText

Drawing Name: **text1.dwg**
Estimated Time to Completion: 5 Minutes

Scope

Create the two lines of text as indicated in the drawing using the Single Line text command.

Figure 1 – Text Exercise

Solution

1. 

Invoke the Single Line Text command, from the Draw pull-down, select Text> Single Line Text (or type *dt, dtext* or *text*).

2. *Specify start point of text or [Justify/Style]:*
Use the LMB to pick the start point of the text. Remember that the text will be created from this pick point.

3. 

Specify height <0.2000>:
Type **0.4** and press <ENTER>.

4. 

Specify rotation angle of text <0>:
Type **0** and press <ENTER> or simply press <ENTER> to accept the default value.

5. 

Type the first line of text **HAVE A GOOD** and press <ENTER> once.

6. 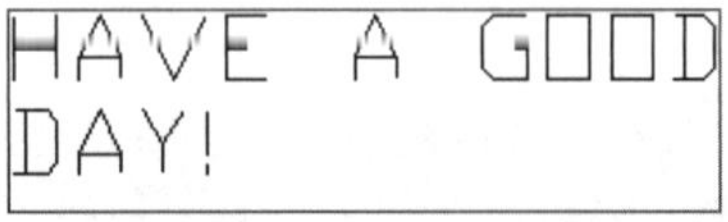

Type the second line of text **DAY!** and press <ENTER>.

7. Press <ESC > to exit the command.

Command Exercise

Exercise 11-2 – Single Line Text Options

Drawing Name: **text2.dwg**
Estimated Time to Completion: 5 Minutes

Scope

Recreate the single line text. Use the different methods of justifying the text. Note that the text justifications will not be displayed until the Enter key is pressed twice to complete the DTEXT command

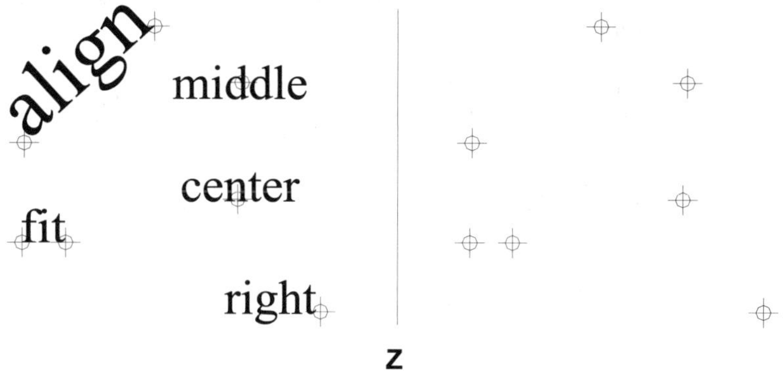

Figure 2 – Text Exercise

Solution

1. 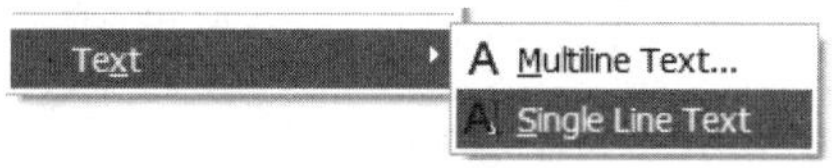

Invoke the Single Line Text command, from the Draw pull-down, select Text>Single Line Text (or type *dt, dtext* or *text*).

2. 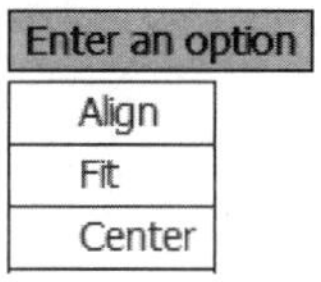

When prompted for a starting point, type **J** for justify.

   A short cut menu will appear.

   Select **Align**.

3. 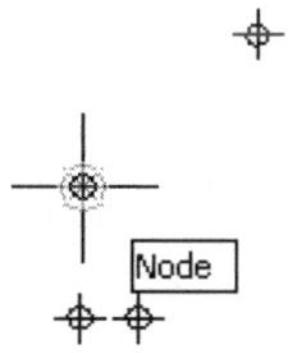

Specify first endpoint of text baseline:
Make sure the Node running object snap is activated. Pick the first point with the LMB.

4. 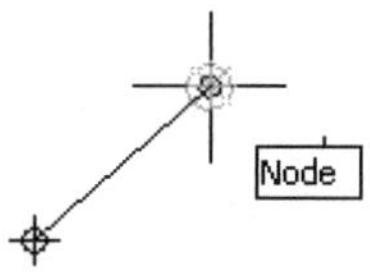

Specify second endpoint of text baseline:
Select the second align point with the LMB.

5. 

Type **align** and press <ENTER>.

   Press <ESC> to exit the command.

6. 

Repeat the Single Line Text command with the RMB (dt, dtext, text or <ENTER>).

7. 

Type **J** for Justify and press <ENTER>.

8. 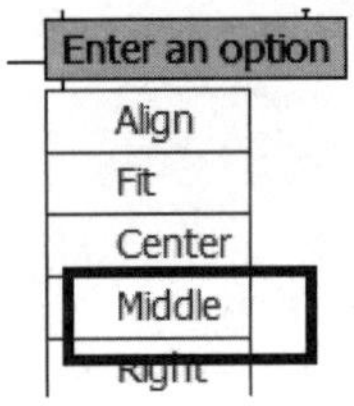

Select **Middle** and press <ENTER>.

9. 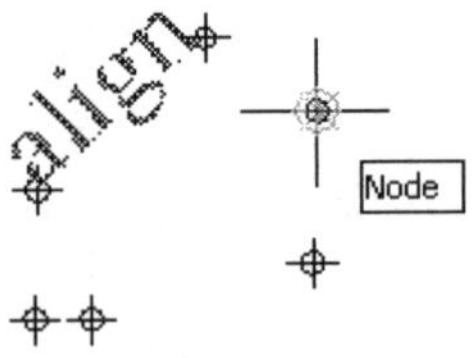

With the Node OSNAP enabled, pick the node to be used for the middle text.

Specify height <0.5000>:
Press <ENTER>.

Specify rotation angle of text <0>:
Press <ENTER>.

10. 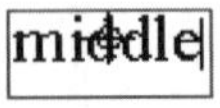

Enter text:
Type **middle** and press <ENTER>.

Press <ESC> to exit the command.

11. 

Repeat the Single Line Text command with the RMB (dt, dtext, text or <ENTER>).

12. 

Type **J** for Justify and press <ENTER>.

13. 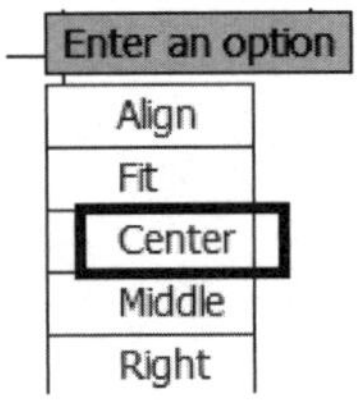

Select **Center** or type 'C' for Center and press <ENTER>.

14. 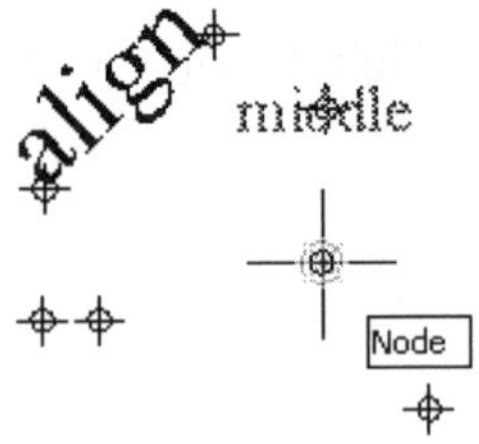

Specify center point of text:
Pick the center point with the LMB.

Specify height <0.5000>:
Press <ENTER>.

Specify rotation angle of text <0>:
Press <ENTER>.

15. 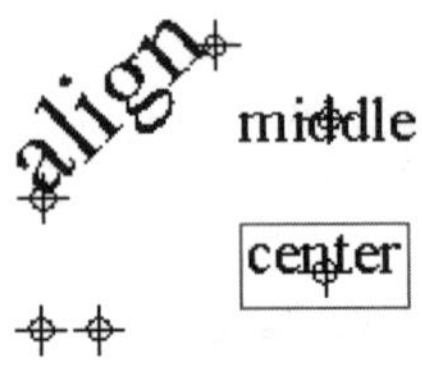

Enter text:
Type **center** and press <ENTER>.

Press <ESC> to exit the command.

16. 

Repeat the Single Line Text command with the RMB (dt, dtext, text or <ENTER>).

17. 

Type **J** for Justify and press <ENTER>.

18. 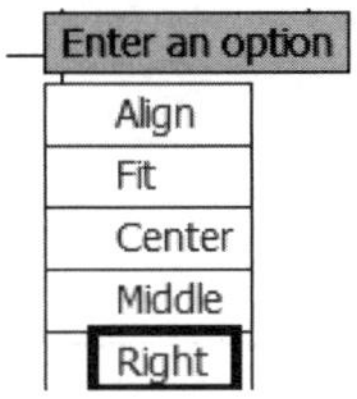

Select **Right** or type **R** for Right and press <ENTER>.

19. 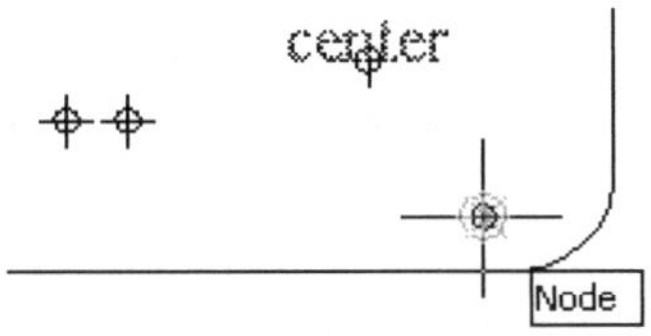

Specify right end point of text:
Pick the right end point with the LMB.

Specify height <0.5000>:
Press <ENTER>.

Specify rotation angle of text <0>:
Press <ENTER>.

20. 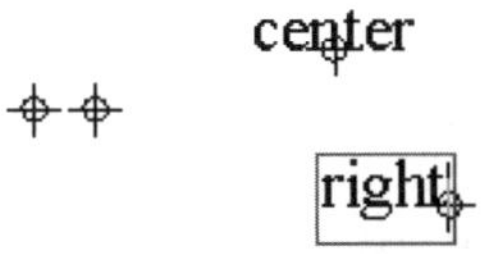

Enter text:
Type **right** and press <ENTER>.

Press <ESC> to exit the command.

21. 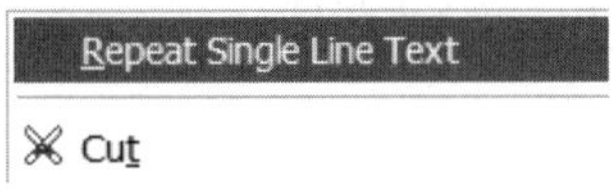

Repeat the Single Line Text command with the RMB (dt, dtext, text or <ENTER>).

22. 

Type **J** for Justify and press <ENTER>.

23. 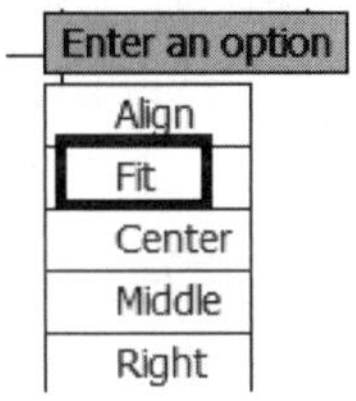

Select **Fit** or type **F** for Fit and press <ENTER>.

24. 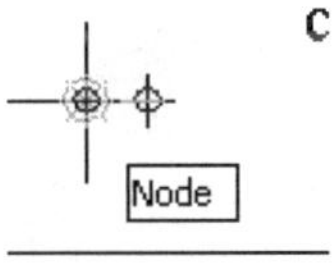

Specify first endpoint of text baseline:
Pick the first point with the LMB.

25. 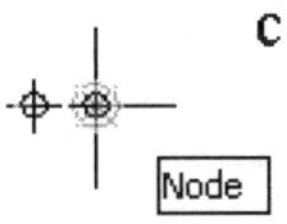

Specify second endpoint of text baseline:
Pick the second point with the LMB.

Specify height <0.5000>:
Press <ENTER>.

26. 

Enter text:
Type **fit** and press <ENTER>.

Press <ESC> to exit the command.

Tip: *Remember to press <ESC> to exit the TEXT command.*

Multiline Text

Command Locator

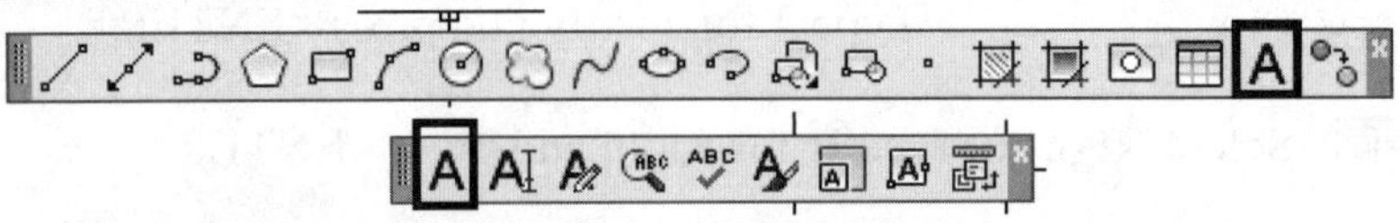

Toolbar Menu	**Draw, Text**
Pull Down Menu	**Draw→Text→Multiline Text**
Command	**Mtext**
Alias	**T**
RMB Shortcut Menu	**Multiline Text Editor**
Dialog Box	**Multiline Text Editor**

Command Overview

Create paragraphs of text with the Multiline Text command. Define the area where the Multiline text should appear in the drawing, by picking the opposite corners of the *text box* in the drawing window. Type the text in the Multiline Text Editor dialog box. Multiline Text can be moved, rotated, scaled, copied or changed after it has been placed in the drawing. Use the grips to adjust the paragraph width. When typing in the text editor, the spacebar will create a space, and the <ENTER> key will act as a carriage return and bring the cursor to the next line. The cursor may be place between letters by picking once (LMB). A double click will select an entire word and a triple click will select the entire sentence. The <ENTER> button on the mouse (RMB) when placed within the Multiline Text Editor dialog box will invoke a shortcut menu with options to Cut, Copy, and Paste selected text. To resize the Multiline Text Editor, select a corner of the window with the LMB and drag. The Editor contains four tabs: Character, Properties, Line Spacing, and Find/Replace. Begin the Multiline text command, specify the first corner, then the opposite corner of the window. Type text in the Multiline Text Editor, use the available options, then select OK to place the text in the drawing. The Edit Text command will open the same Text Editor dialog box with the selected text for editing.

Multiline Text Editor Dialog Box

Multiline Text Editor Option	**Overview**
Font	Change the font of selected words with this option. This option should be used when changing only a few selected words. If a global font change is preferred, use the Text Style command.
Font height	Change the height of selected words.
Bold	Make selected text Bold, when applicable to the font.
Italics	Make selected text *Italic,* when applicable to the font.
Underline	Underlines selected text.

Multiline Text Editor Option	Overview
Undo	This option will undo the last step in the dialog box.
Redo	This option will undo the last undo.
Stack	This option will stack selected words or text when separated by a forward slash.
Color	This option will make selected text a different color. Select a color from the list. Color changes to selected text will override color changes applied to the layer or the object.

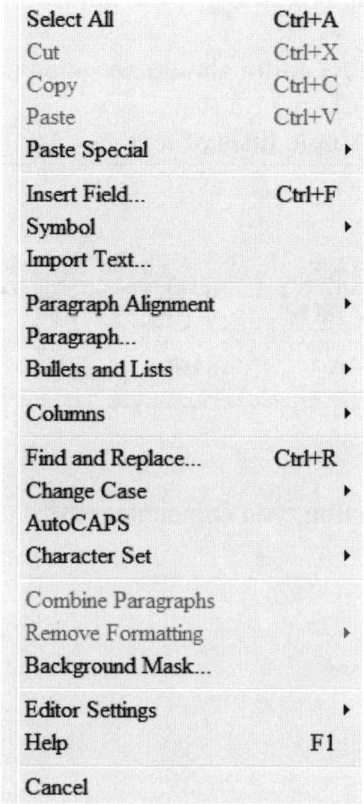

MTEXT Options Shortcut Menu

If you RMB click in the MTEXT window, you have several more options available to you, including placing Indents and Tabs, insert symbols, insert fields, and modify the text.

General Procedures

1. Invoke the Multiline Text command by typing T or selecting the icon from the draw toolbar.
2. Specify Text area by picking the first corner, then the opposite corner in the drawing Window.
3. Type the Multiline Text Editor dialog box.
4. Select OK to exit.

- In the Multiline Text editor, single click (LMB) to insert words or letters. Double click to highlight the entire word. Triple click to select the entire sentence.
- Pressing the <ENTER> button on the mouse (RMB), with the cursor in the text box, will bring up the cursor menu with the Windows Edit options.
- Type text using the space bar (and not <ENTER>) to allow sentences to wrap.
- After exiting the multiline text dialog box, use grips to adjust the width of the Multiline Text.
- Documents to be imported into the text editor should be saved in Text (.txt) or Rich Text Format (.rtf).
- Exploding Multiline text will make single lines of text.

MTEXT Dialog

If you select the Options button at the far right of the MTEXT dialog, you can control the appearance of the MTEXT dialog box.

Command Exercise

Exercise 11-3 – Multiline Text

Drawing Name: **mtext1.dwg**
Estimated Time to Completion: 5 Minutes

Scope

Use the Multiline text command to create the text as indicated.

Figure 3 – Multiline Text Exercise

Solution

1.  Invoke the Multiline Text command (mt or mtext).

2. *Specify first corner:*
Use the Node Object Snap to select the upper left point.

> ***Tip:*** *The text is wrapped automatically to fit into the specified window. Use the grips to adjust the paragraph width.*

3. 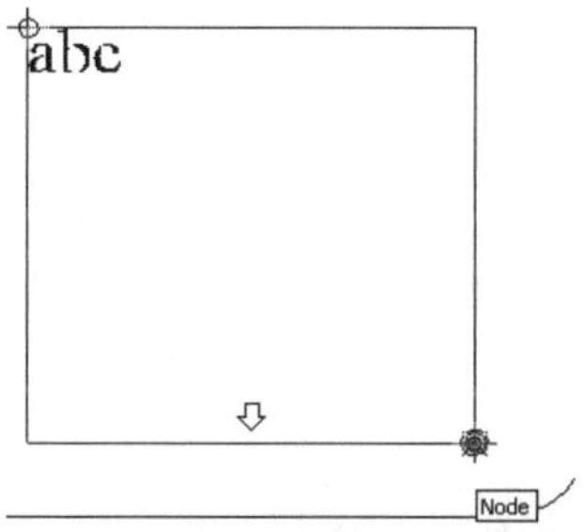

Specify opposite corner or [Height/Justify/Line spacing/ Rotation/Style/Width]:
Use the Node Object Snap to select the lower right point.

4. 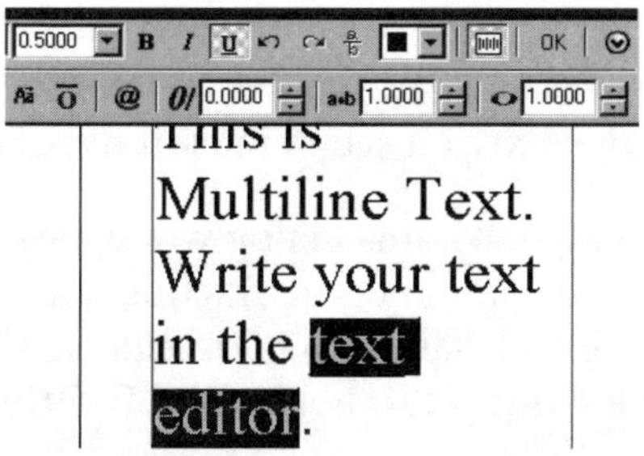

Type the text as shown on the left side of the screen.
Use your mouse and click and drag with the LMB to highlight the last two words **text editor**.

5.  Press the U (Underline) button to underline the text.

6. 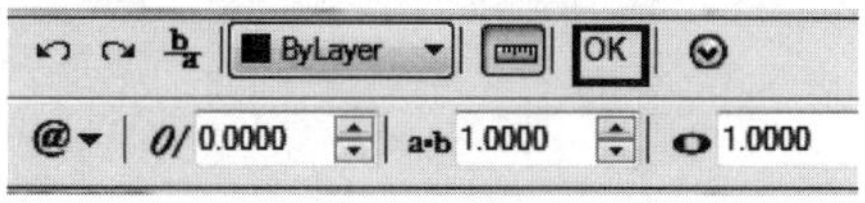

Press **OK** to close the dialog.

Command Exercise

Exercise 11-4 – Formatting Multiline Text

Drawing Name: **mtext2.dwg**
Estimated Time to Completion: 5 Minutes

Scope

Use the Multiline text command type and format the text as indicated.

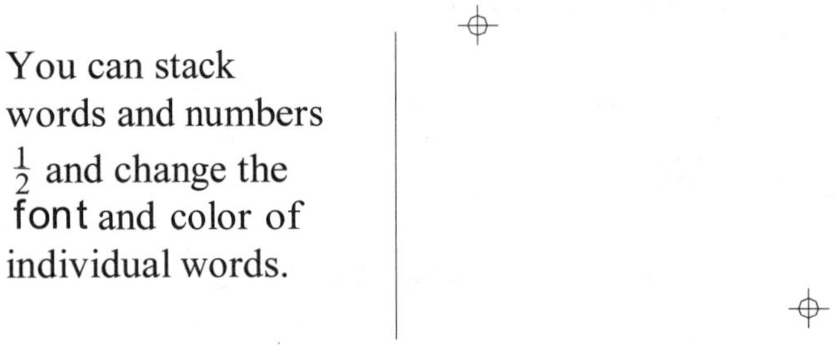

Figure 4 – Multiline Text Exercise

Solution

1. 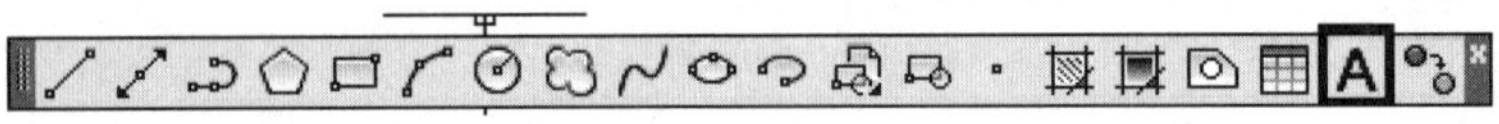

   Invoke the Multiline Text command (mt or mtext).

2. *Specify first corner:*
   Use the Node Object Snap to select the upper left point.

3. 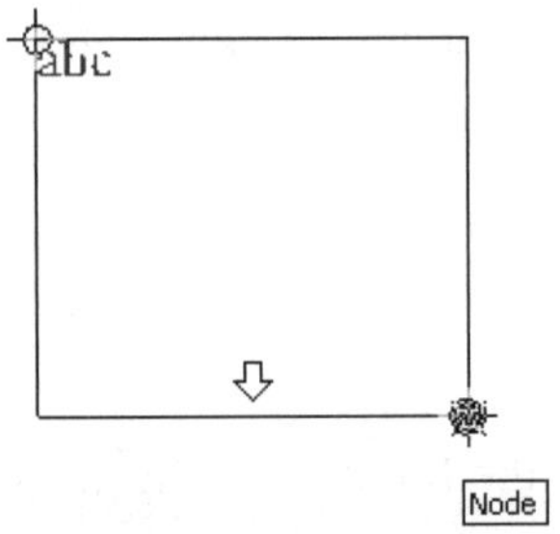

   Specify opposite corner or [Height/Justify/Line spacing/Rotation/Style/Width]:
   Use the LMB and Node Object Snap to pick the second corner.

4. 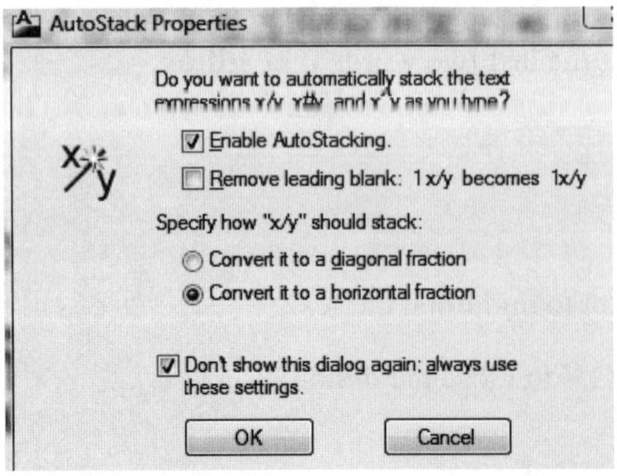

   Type in the text you see in the left hand pane.

   When you type ½, this dialog will appear. You have the option of the fraction appearing with a diagonal slash or a horizontal slash. Select the **Convert to horizontal fraction** option.

   Press **OK**.

5.

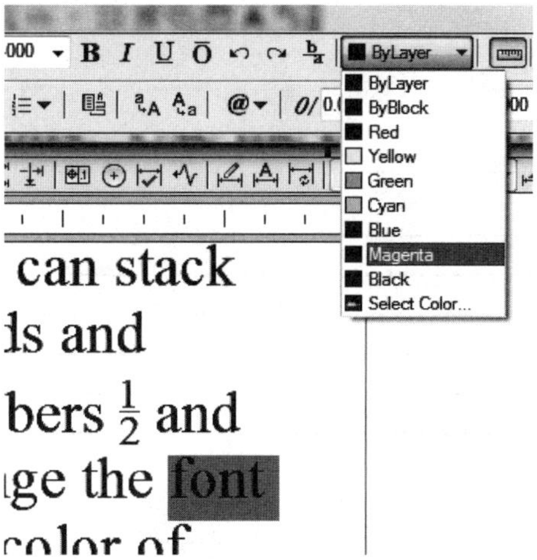

Highlight the word **color**. Select the desired color for the selected text from the drop-down list.

6.

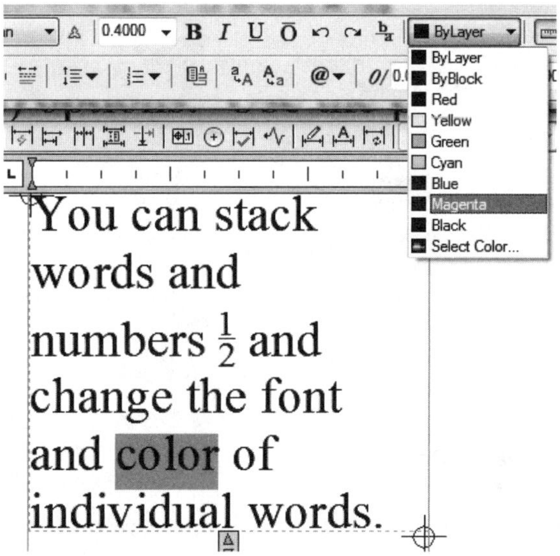

Repeat the process to change the color of the word **font**.

7.

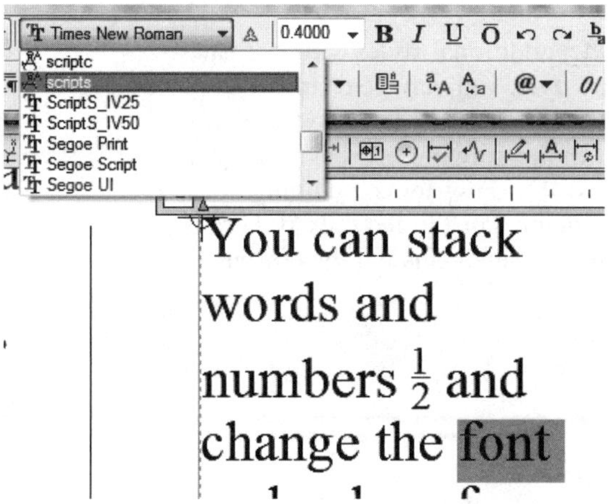

While the word **font** is still highlighted adjust the font style for the selected text by using the drop-down list box. Set it to the **scripts** font.

Press the **OK** button to close the dialog.

Text Style

Command Locator

Toolbar Menu	**Styles, Text**
Pull Down Menu	**Format / Text Style…**
Command	**Style**
Alias	**ST**
Dialog Box	**Text Style**

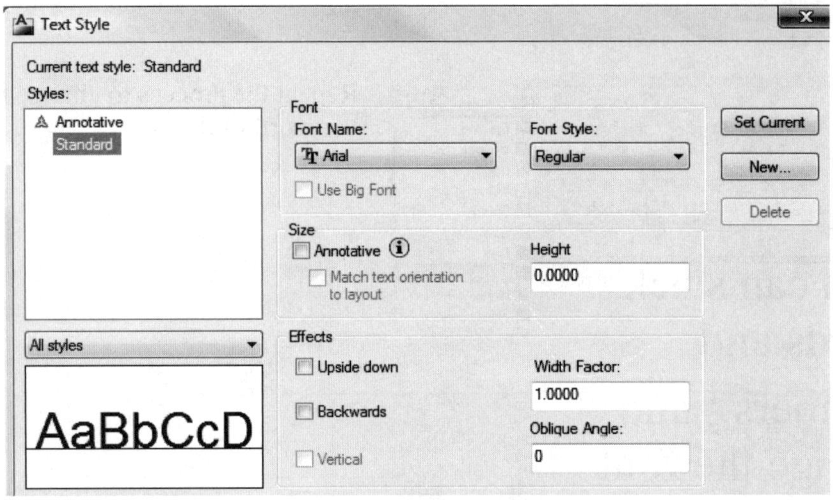

Text Style Dialog Box

Command Overview

In addition to the Standard Text Style, additional styles can be created. Text will be typed in the current text style, and may be changed from one style to another. Applying a different font to a Text Style will globally change the font of any text in the drawing that has been typed in that style. AutoCAD supports most Windows fonts including TrueType fonts. Text Styles may be deleted or Purged only if there is no text in the drawing referencing that style, or it is not the current style.

Text Style Option	Overview
Style Name	The current style will be at the top of the list of Text Style in the drawing. The default style is Standard with the txt.shx font.
New	Select this button to make a new Text Style. The default name will be style1, however it may be renamed.
Rename…	Select this button to rename a selected Text Style.
Delete	Select this option to delete a selected Text Style. There can not be text in the drawing using that Style.
Font	Select a Font from the Font Name list. The default font for the Standard style is txt.shx. AutoCAD supports most Windows fonts including TrueType fonts.
Font Style	Font style options will be displayed according to the Font selected. Some fonts do not have Font style options.
Font Size	When the Text Style height is 0.0, the user will always be prompted for a text height when using the DTEXT command. Text style height can be pre-set, however, it is always possible to change the height of text in the drawing. When Annotative is enabled, the text will automatically be scaled depending on the annotative scale. Instead of creating text styles for different text heights, you can use annotative scale to control the size of the text.
Effects	These are hardly used options that include Upside down, Backwards, and Vertical. A Width factor of 1.0 is a normal width. Greater than 1 is a wider letter, and less than 1 is a narrower letter. Oblique Angle creates a slant letter.
Set Current	Select this button to apply changes to the Text Style before exiting the dialog box.

General Procedures

Making changes to the Standard Text Style:

1. Invoke the Text Style command.
2. Select a different Font from the drop down list.
3. Select Apply, then Close the dialog box.

Creating a New Text Style:

1. Invoke the Text Style command.
2. Select "New" and type a name for that style (or accept the default name).
3. Select a Font from the drop down list. Optional: Type the Height for the new text style.
4. Select Apply, then Close the dialog box.

Tips & Tricks

- Use this dialog box to make a Text Style current.
- Changes applied to a Text Style will globally affect any text in the drawing referencing that style.
- Avoid having an excessive number of Text Styles. Some common text styles might be made for notes, dimensions, and the Title Block.
- Refer to the following Text Height Chart for large format drawings. For instance, if the drawing area is 12 x 9, a text height of .2 might be good. However if the drawing area is 120 x 90, a text height of 2 would be more appropriate (.2 x 10).

Text Height Chart			
This chart is for drawings using Architectural or Fractional Units. The text sizes are based on what would typically be the plotted scale			
Drawing Scale	**Scale Factor**	**Plotted Scale**	**Text Size In Drawing**
1/16 in.= 1 ft.	192	1/16 in	12 in.
		3/32 in.	18 in.
		1/8 in.	24 in.
		3/16 in.	36 in.
		1/4 in.	48 in.
1/8 in.= 1 ft.	96	1/16 in.	6 in.
		3/32 in.	9 in.
		1/8 in.	12 in.
		3/16 in.	18 in.
		1/4 in.	24 in.
3/16 in.= 1 ft.	64	1/16 in.	4 in.
		3/32 in.	6 in.
		1/8 in.	8 in.
		3/16 in.	12 in.
		1/4 in.	16 in.
¼ in.= 1 ft.	48	1/16 in.	3 in.
		3/32 in.	4.5 in.
		1/8 in.	6 in.
		3/16 in.	9 in.
		1/4 in.	12 in.
3/8 in.= 1 ft.	32	1/16 in.	2 in.
		3/32 in.	3 in.
		1/8 in.	4 in.
		3/16 in.	6 in.
		1/4 in.	8 in.
½ in.= 1 ft.	24	1/16 in.	1.5 in.
		3/32 in.	2.25 in.
		1/8 in.	3 in.
		3/16 in.	4.5 in.
		1/4 in.	6 in.
3/4 in.= 1 ft.	16	1/16 in.	1 in.
		3/32 in.	1.5 in.
		1/8 in.	2 in.
		3/16 in.	3 in.
		1/4 in.	4 in.
1 in.= 1 ft.	12	1/16 in.	0.75 in.
		3/32 in.	1.125 in.
		1/8 in.	1.5 in.
		3/16 in.	2.25 in.
		1/4 in.	3 in.

Drawing Scale	Scale Factor	Plotted Scale	Text Size In Drawing
1.5 in.= 1 ft.	8	1/16 in.	0.5 in.
		3/32 in.	0.75 in.
		1/8 in.	1 in.
		3/16 in.	1.5 in.
		1/4 in.	2 in.
1 in.= 20 ft.	240	1/16 in.	15 in.
		3/32 in.	22.5 in.
		1/8 in.	30 in.
		3/16 in.	45 in.
		1/4 in.	60 in.
1 in.= 30 ft.	240	1/16 in.	22.5 in.
		3/32 in.	33.75 in.
		1/8 in.	45 in.
		3/16 in.	67.5 in.
		1/4 in.	90 in.
1 in.= 40 ft.	480	1/16 in.	30 in.
		3/32 in.	45 in.
		1/8 in.	60 in.
		3/16 in.	90 in.
		1/4 in.	120 in.
1 in.= 50 ft.	600	1/16 in.	37.5 in.
		3/32 in.	56.25 in.
		1/8 in.	75 in.
		3/16 in.	112.5 in.
		1/4 in.	150 in.
1 in.= 60 ft.	720	1/16 in.	45 in.
		3/32 in.	67.5 in.
		1/8 in.	90 in.
		3/16 in.	135 in.
		1/4 in.	180 in.

Command Exercise

Exercise 11-5 – Creating Text Styles

Drawing Name: **style1.dwg**
Estimated Time to Completion: 10 Minutes

Scope

Create a text style called TEXT1 and apply a text height of 0.4 and the font called Arial to that style. Type the text as indicated in the new style.

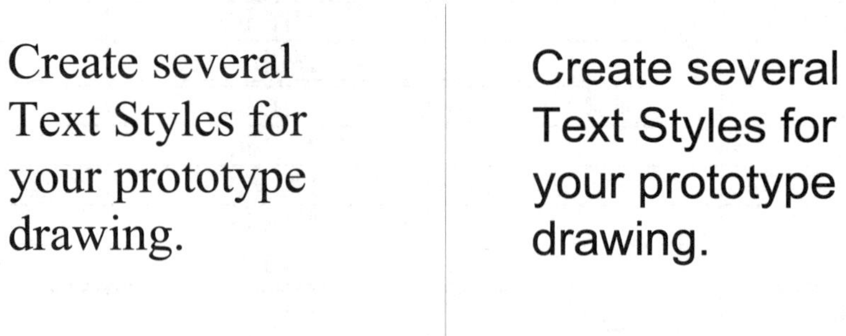

Figure 5 – Text Styles Exercise

Solution

1. 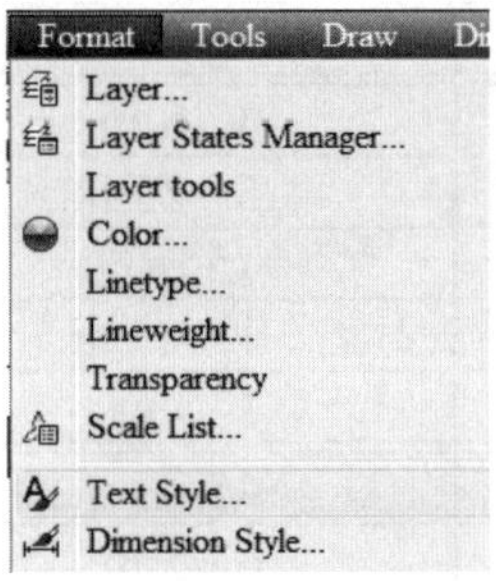

Invoke the Text Style command, from the Format pull-down, select **Text Style…**

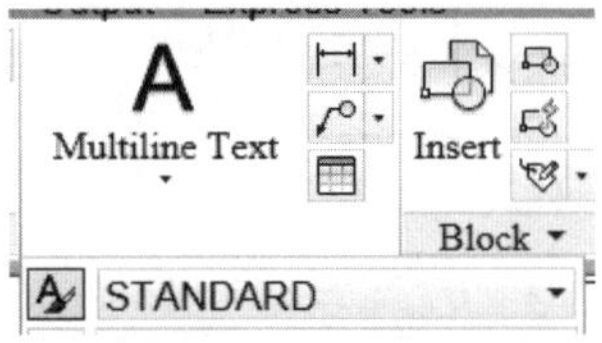

You can also set the **2D Drafting and Annotation** workspace current.

Then select **Text Style** from the ribbon under Annotation.

2. 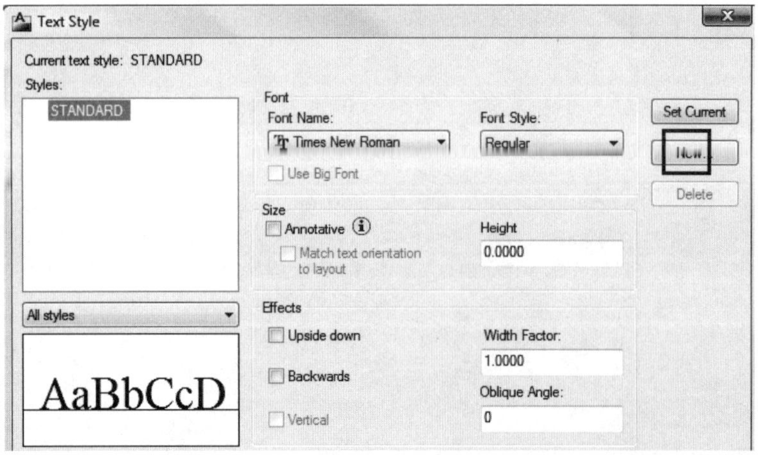

Press the **New** button in the Text Styles dialog box.

3. 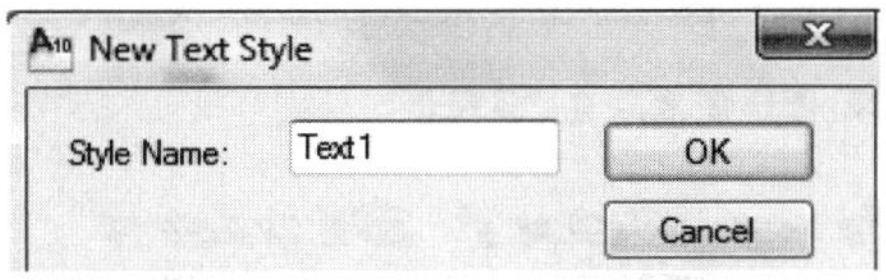

In the New Text Style dialog box, enter **TEXT1** for the name of the new text style and press **OK**.

4. 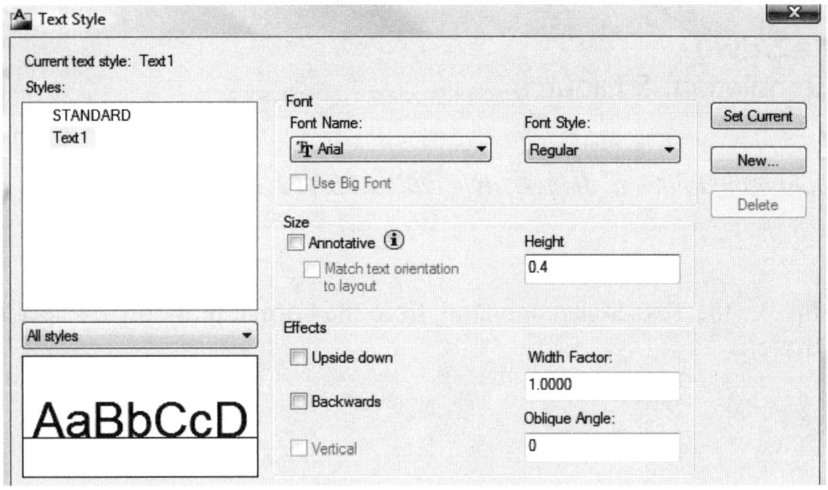

Fill in the remaining information in the Text Style dialog box as shown.

Set the Font Name to **Arial**.
Set the Font Style to **Regular**.
Set the Height to **0.4**.

5. Press the **Apply** button first and then the **Close** button to apply the changes to TEXT1 and then close the dialog box.

6. 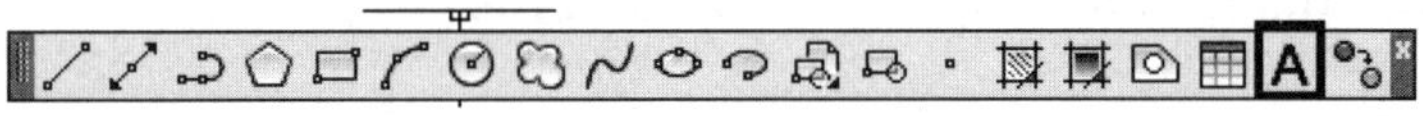

Invoke the Multiline Text command (mt or mtext).

7. *Specify first corner:*
Notice that the current style is TEXT1. Pick the upper left corner of the multiline text window with the LMB.

8. 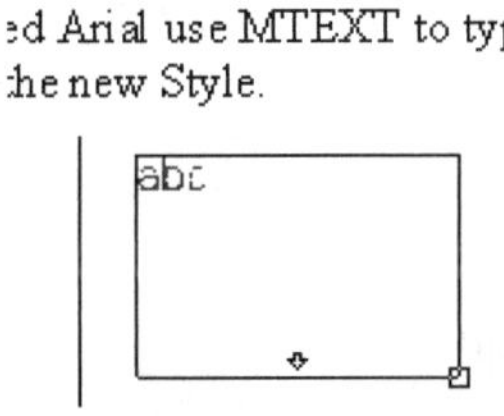

Specify opposite corner or [Height/Justify/Line spacing/ Rotation /Style/Width]:
Pick the lower right corner of the multiline text window.

9. 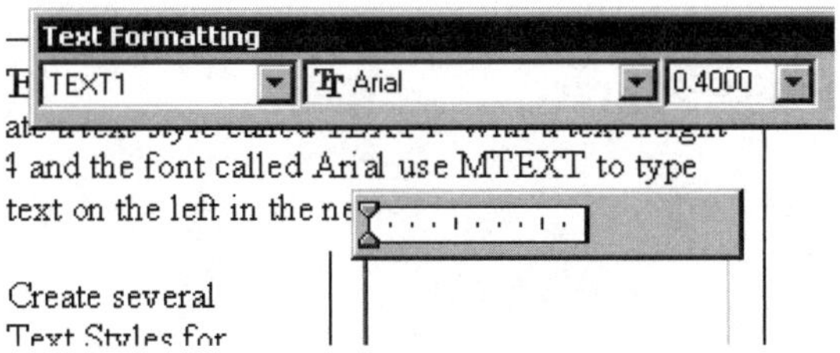

Type the desired text into the Multiline Text Editor and press 'OK'. Note that the text style you just created is the current text style.

- You can use PURGE to eliminate any unused text styles from your drawing.
- You can import text styles from one drawing to another using the Design Center.
- You can store text styles in your template for easier access.

Command Exercise

Exercise 11-6 – Purging Text Styles

Drawing Name: **style2.dwg**
Estimated Time to Completion: 5 Minutes

Scope

Use the Purge command to delete the text style called TEXT2, or delete it from the dialog box.

Solution

1.

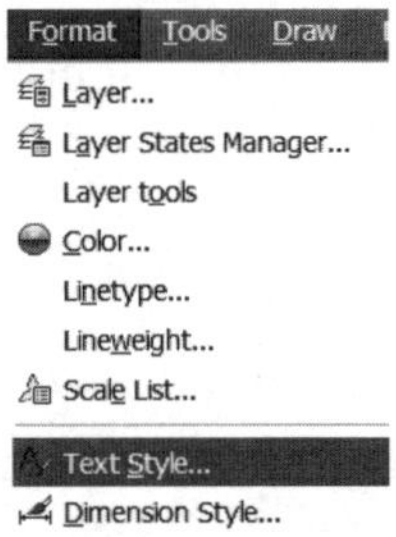

Invoke the Text Style command, from the Format pull-down, select **Text Style…**

2.

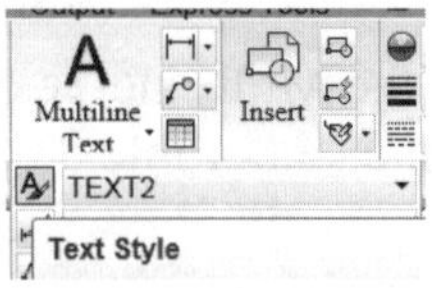

From the Annotation ribbon, select **Text Style.**

3.

Highlight the **Standard** text style and press the **Set Current** button to make it current.

Press **Close** to close the Text Style dialog box.

4.

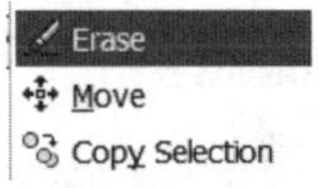

Select the text.
RMB and select **Erase**.

5.

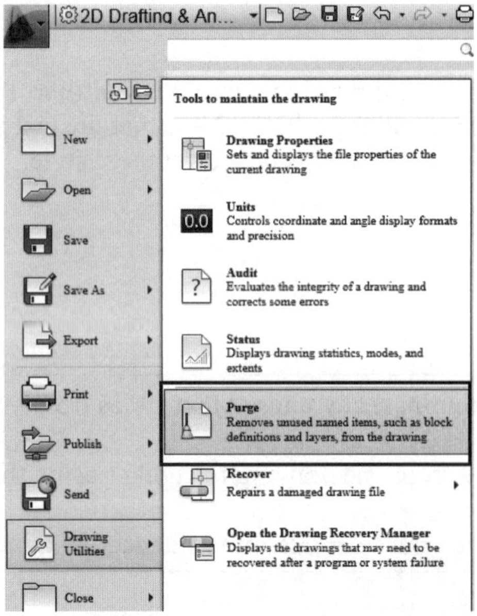

Invoke the Purge command.

From the File ribbon panel, select **Drawing Utilities→Purge**.

6. 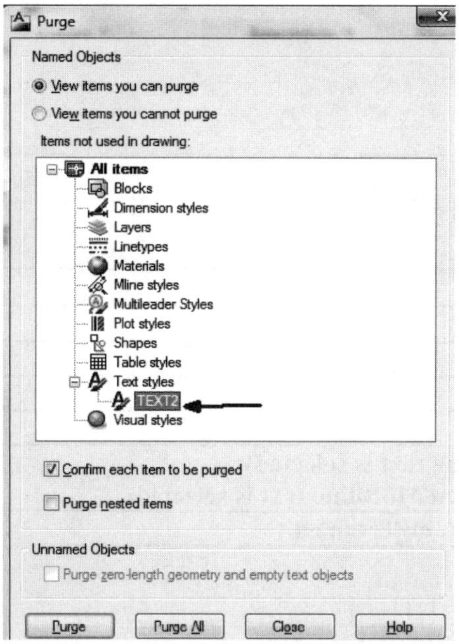

Expand the Text Styles category. Highlight **TEXT2**.

7. 

Select the **Purge** button.

8. 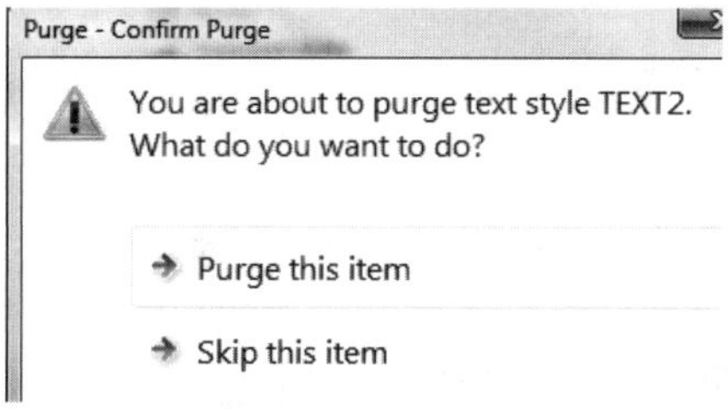

A dialog will pop up to verify that you want to purge the text style.

Select **Purge this item**.

Press the **Close** button.

9. 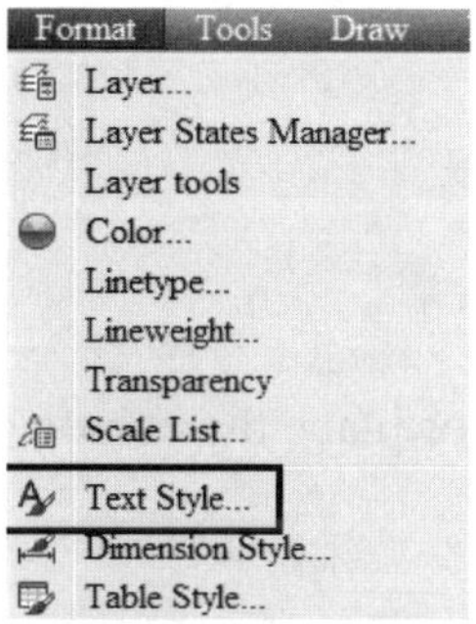

Invoke the Text Style command, from the Format pull-down, select **Text Style…**

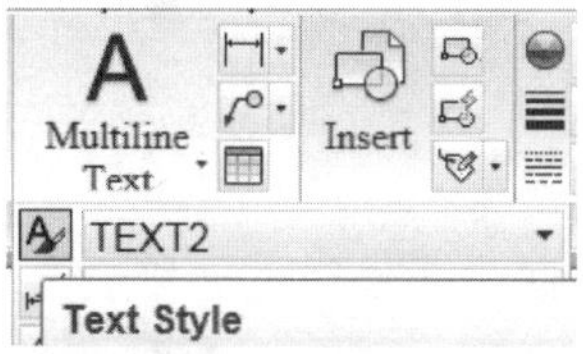

From the Annotation ribbon, select **Text Style**.

10. 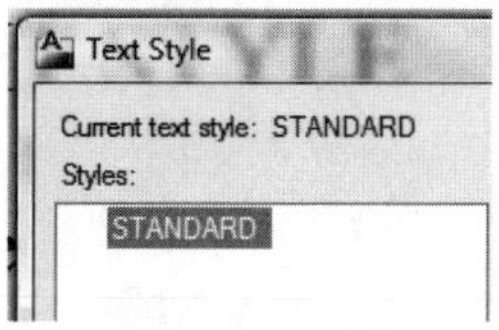

The TEXT2 text style is no longer available.

> ***Tip:*** *If any text exists in the drawing with the TEXT2 style the purge command will not be able to remove the text style because it is still being used.*

The Styles toolbar can be used to quickly switch from one text style to another.

Edit Text

Command Locator

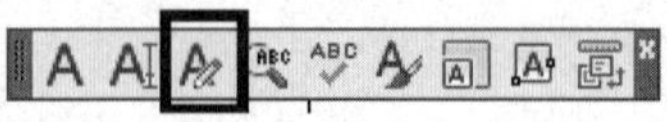

Toolbar Menu	**Text→Edit Text**
Pull Down Menu	**Modify→Text...**
Command	**Ddedit**
Alias	**ED**
RMB Shortcut Menu	**Text Window**
Dialog Box	**Edit Text (when Single Line text is selected)** **Multiline Text Editor (when Multiline text is selected)**
	Double left click on the text object to edit

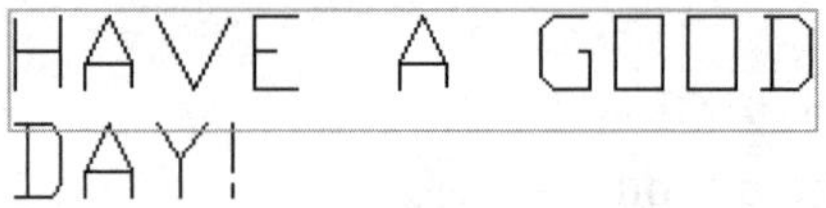

Edit Text Dialog Box

Command Overview

Use the Edit Text command to change the contents of Text in the drawing. For Single Line text, this will display the single line Text Editor. Text may also be edited using the Properties command. This contains additional options to change the text properties.

General Procedures

1. Invoke the Edit Text command (ED). Select the text to edit.
2. Make corrections to the text by typing over the highlighted text, or place the cursor between letters or words and type.
3. Select OK to exit.

Command Exercise

Exercise 11-7 – Edit Text

Drawing Name: **etext1.dwg**
Estimated Time to Completion: 5 Minutes

Scope

Edit the Single Line and Multiline Text using the Edit Text (DDEDIT) command. Edit the text on the right to be like the text on the left.

HAVE A GOOD DAY!	This is Single Line Text
The Text command issues the Multiline Text option.	This is Multiline Text.

Figure 6 – Edit Text Exercise

Solution

1. *Select an annotation object or [Undo]:*
   Double left click to edit the "This is Single Line Text". In the Edit Text dialog box, type over the existing text.

2. 

   Alternate method:
   Double click on the single line text to bring up the edit box.

3. Type **HAVE A GOOD DAY!** and press <ENTER>.

4. 

   Double LMB click on the multiline text to activate the edit box.

5. 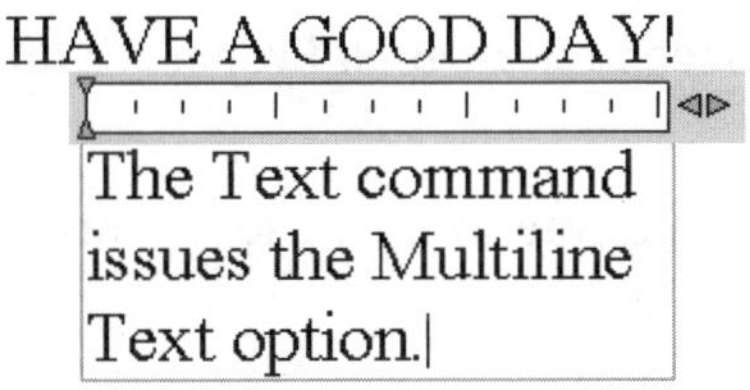

   Modify the text and press **OK**.

Tips & Tricks

- Place the cursor in the text area and press the RMB to Copy, Cut, Paste, or Delete selected text.
- The Edit Text command works with dimension text, Multiline Text, and Single Line Text.
- To exit the Edit Text mode, simply left click outside the text edit box.

Command Exercise

Exercise 11-8 – Edit Text Properties

Drawing Name: **etext2.dwg**
Estimated Time to Completion: 10 Minutes

Scope

Edit the Single Line and Multiline text using the new Quick Properties tool.

HAVE A GOOD DAY!
Multiline text can be adjusted with grips. Let the text wrap naturally, using the space bar instead of the Enter key.

This is Single Line Text

This is Multiline Text. Highlight the text you wish to modify in the Text Editor dialog box.

Figure 7 – Edit Text Exercise

Solution

1. 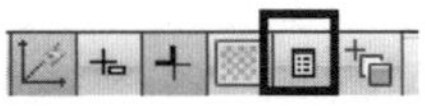
Verify that the Quick Properties button is enabled on the Status Bar.

2. Use the LMB to select the single line of text located on the right side of the drawing.

3. 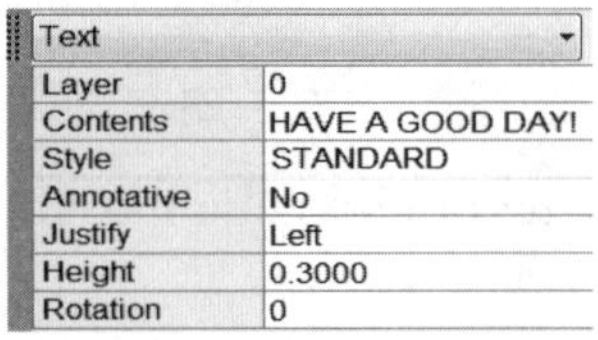

In the Quick Properties dialog box, highlight the existing text and change it to **HAVE A GOOD DAY!**

4. 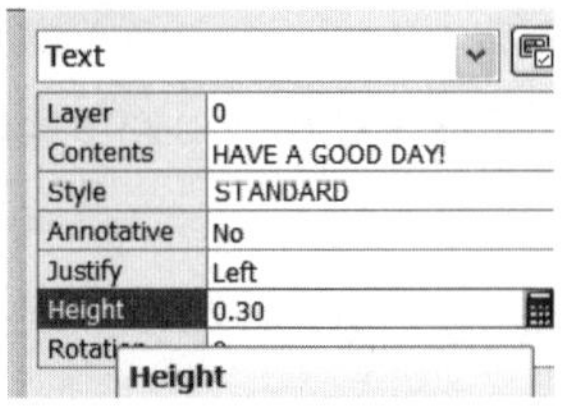

Adjust the Height to **0.3**.

Press the <ESC> button to release the selection. Notice how the text changes.

5. Use the LMB to pick the Multiline Text. Notice the changes in the Quick Properties dialog box.

6. 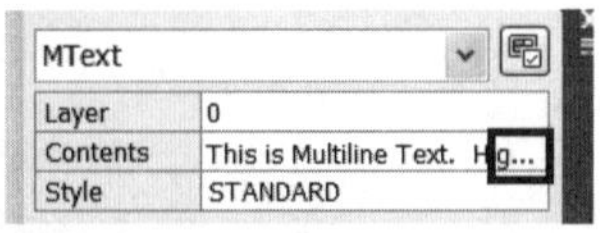

Pick the '…' Button next to the Contents of the text. This will activate the Multiline Text Editor.

7. 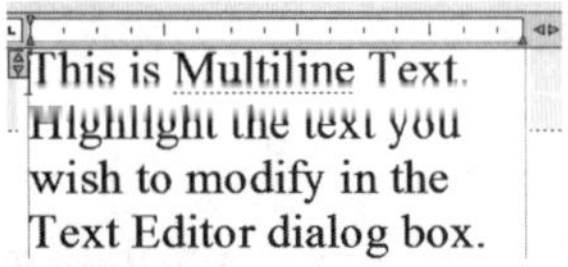

Highlight the existing text, type in the new text and press **OK**.

8. 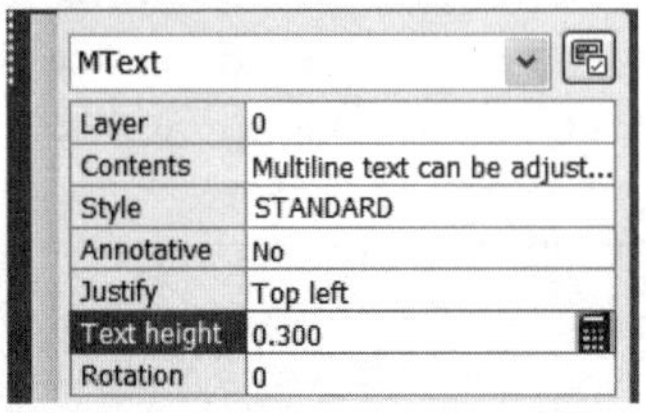

Back in the Quick Properties dialog box, change the height to **0.3000**.

Press the <ESC> button to release the selection. Notice how the text changes.

Close the Properties dialog box.

Command Exercise

Exercise 11-9 – Edit Text with Grips

Drawing Name: **etext3.dwg**
Estimated Time to Completion: 5 Minutes

Scope

Using grips, move and stretch the multiline text paragraph into the box.

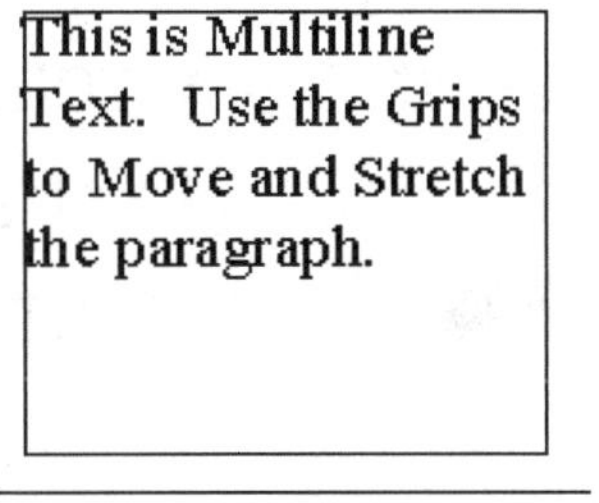

Figure 8 – Edit Text Exercise

Solution

1. 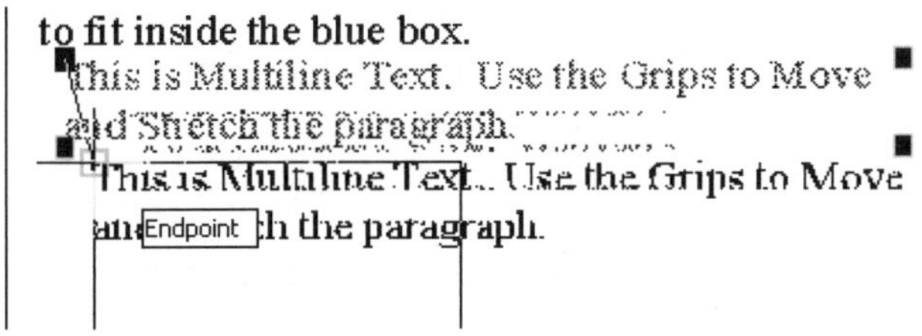

Make sure the command line is clear. Select the black multiline text and the box with the LMB.

Notice how the grip points appear.

2. *Specify stretch point or [Base point/Copy/Undo/eXit]:*
Click the upper left grip point on the text, it will turn red. Move to the upper left grip point of the box and click again. The text will move down to the box.

3. 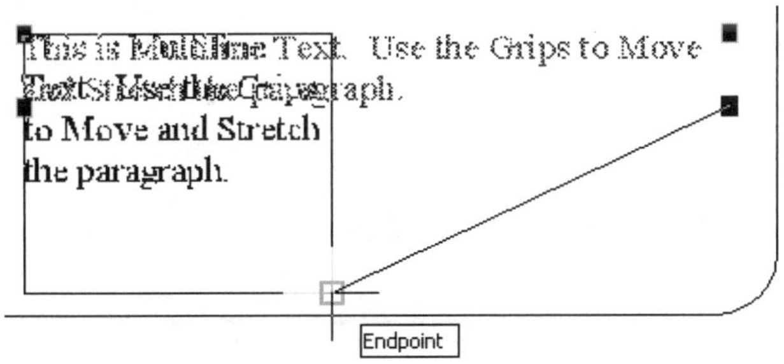

Specify stretch point or [Base point/Copy/Undo/eXit]:
Click the lower right grip point on the text. Move to the lower right grip point of the box and click again. The text will stretch itself to fit inside the box.

Command Exercise

Exercise 11-10 – Edit Text Properties

Drawing Name: **etext4.dwg**
Estimated Time to Completion: 5 Minutes

Scope

Change the Style of the text to TEXT2 using the Quick Properties dialog.

Figure 9 – Edit Text Exercise

Solution

1. 

Select the text with the LMB to activate the grips. The Quick Properties dialog will appear.

2. 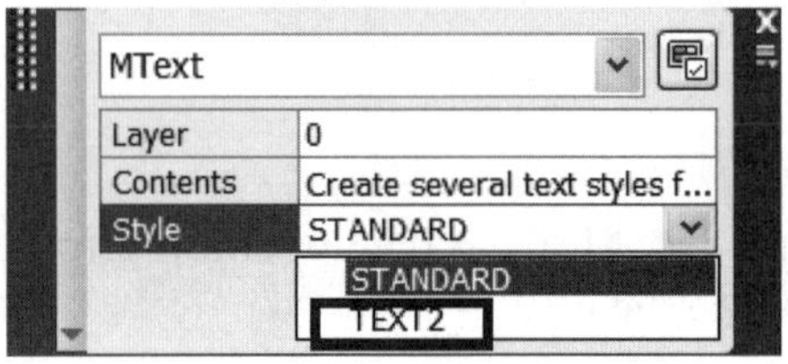

In the Properties dialog box change the Style to **TEXT2**.

3. Press <**ESC**> to release the selection.

Find and Replace

Command Locator

Pull Down Menu	**Edit→Find**
Command	**Find**
RMB Shortcut Menu	**Text Windows in the dialog box**
Dialog Box	**Find and Replace**
Annotate Ribbon	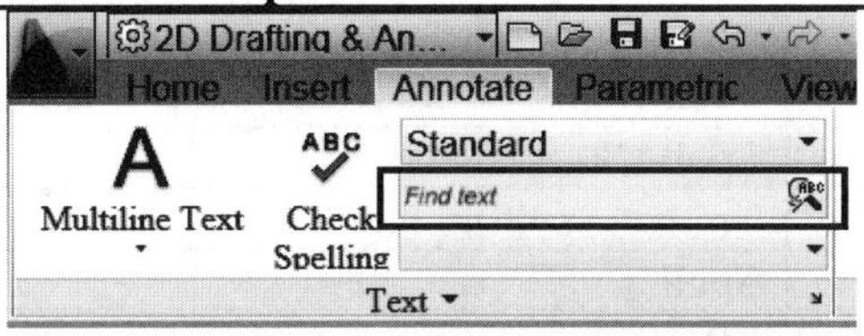

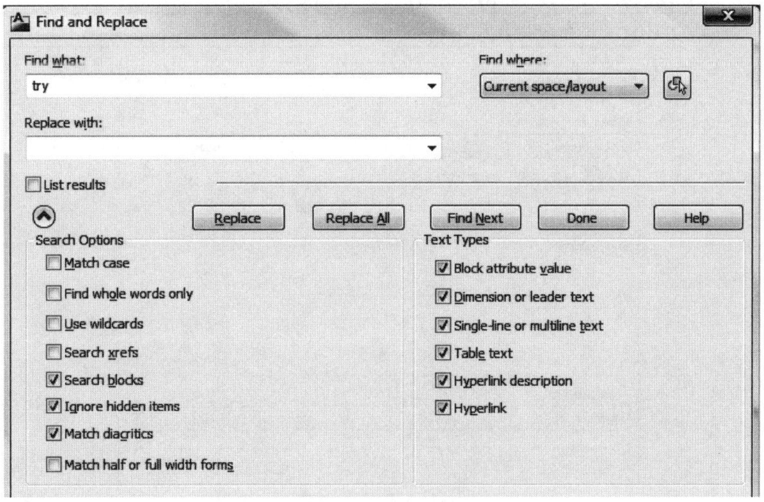

Find and Replace Dialog Box

Command Overview

The Find and Replace command provides text search with the options to perform a global search or to search selected text. Type in the Text string to find, and type the replacement text.

General Procedures

1. Invoke the Find and Replace command.
2. Type the text string to Find, and type the replacement text.
3. Select the Find button, then select "Replace All".

Tips Tricks

- Using this command with selected text is the same as using options in the Find/Replace tab of the Multiline Text dialog box.
- Use the Window option located in the upper right corner to limit the find and replace operation to a specific section of a drawing.

Spell Check

Command Locator

Annotate Ribbon	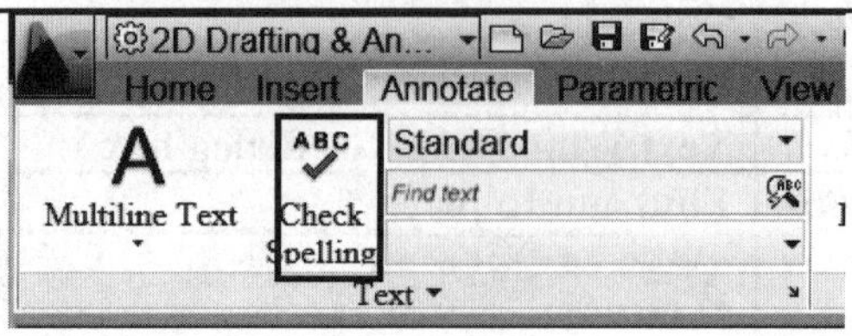
Text Toolbar	**Spell Check**
Pull Down Menu	**Tools→Spelling**
Command	**Spell**
Alias	**SP**
RMB Shortcut Menu	**Text Window of the dialog box**
Dialog Box	**Check Spelling**

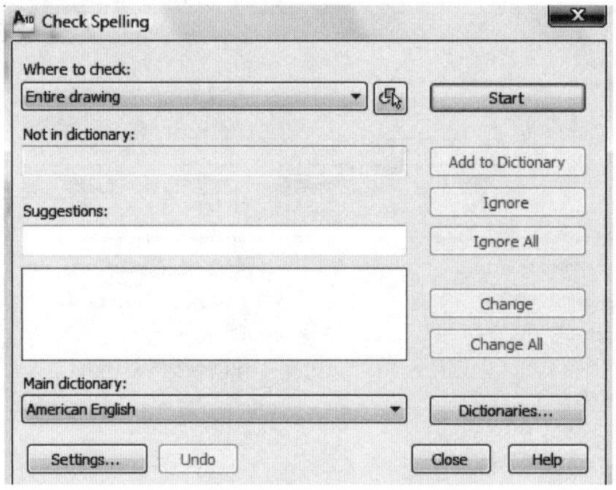

Check Spelling Dialog Box

Command Overview

Check for spelling errors. Select one line of text or all the text in the drawing. Add words to build a custom dictionary.

Spell Check Option	Overview
Current word	The misspelled word will appear in this area.
Suggestions	Spell check will provide a list of suggested words.
Ignore / Ignore All	Ignore will keep the misspelled word or words as they are.
Change / Change All	This option will substitute the misspelled word or words for a suggested word.
Add	Build a custom dictionary with the Add option.
Lookup	This option will look up more words based on the highlighted suggestion.
Change Dictionary	There are several language dictionaries available with Spell Check, including the custom dictionary.
Context	The sentence context of the misspelled word will appear in this area.

General Procedures

1. Invoke the Spell command. Select the text to check.
2. Select a suggestion from the list if the current word is incorrect.
3. Select Change, then select OK.

Tips & Tricks

- Building a custom dictionary is useful when abbreviations are used frequently in the drawing.

Command Exercise

Exercise 11-11 – Spell Check

Drawing Name: **spell1.dwg**
Estimated Time to Completion: 5 Minutes

Scope

Correct the spelling in the text provided.

Solution

1. 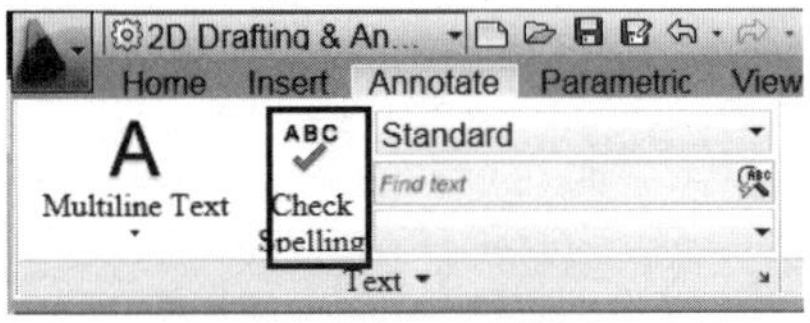

Invoke the Spell Checker; from the Tools pull-down, select **Spelling**.

From the Annotate ribbon, select Check Spelling.

2. 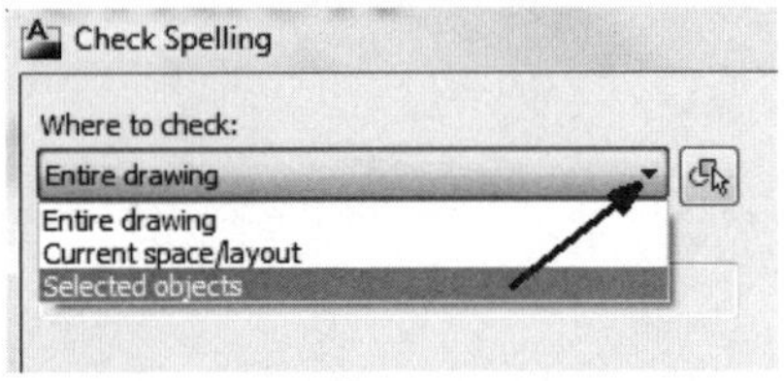

In the Where to check: drop-down, select **Selected objects**.

3.  Press the Select tool to activate the selection mode.

4. *Select objects:*
Use the LMB to pick the text to check and press <ENTER> or type **ALL** to check the spelling for the entire drawing.

5. 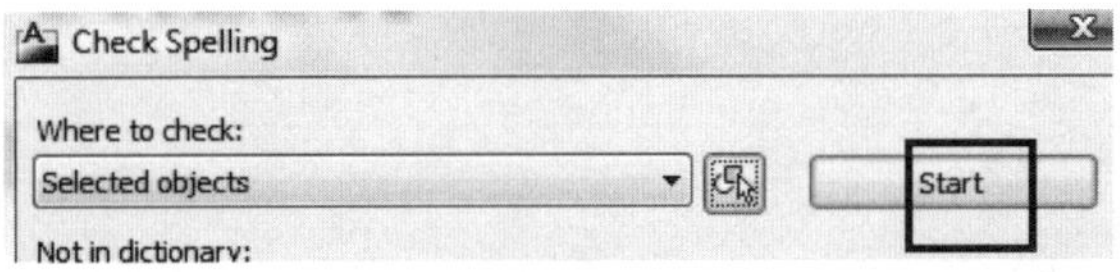

Press **Start**.

6. 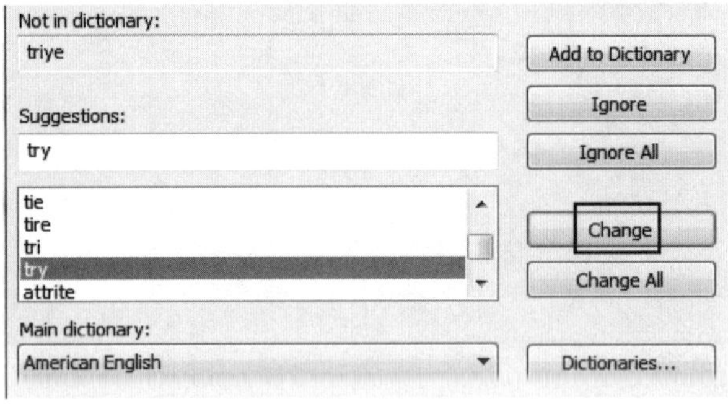

Locate the correct spelling under Suggestions and press **Change**.

7. The spell checker will advance to the next misspelled word. Change that one as well.

8. 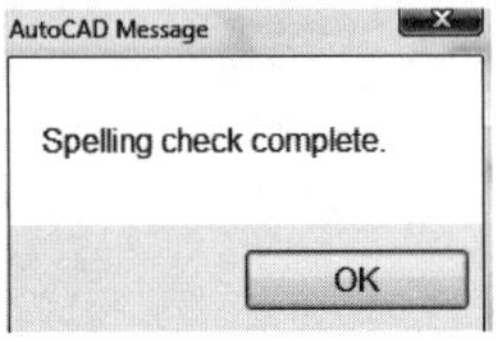

Press 'OK' when notified that Spell Check is complete to finish the command.

Close the Spell Check dialog.

Fields

Command Locator

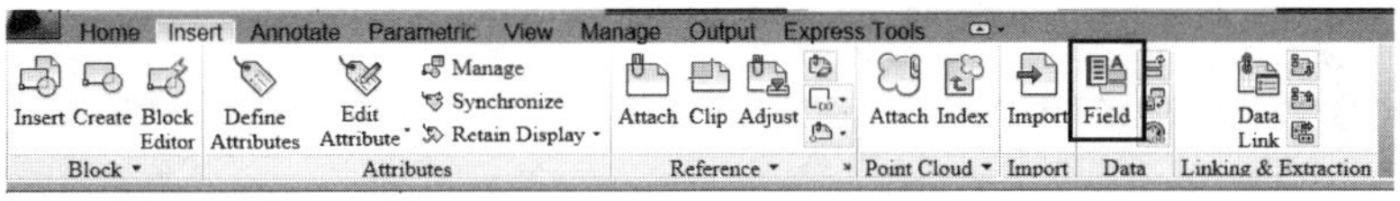

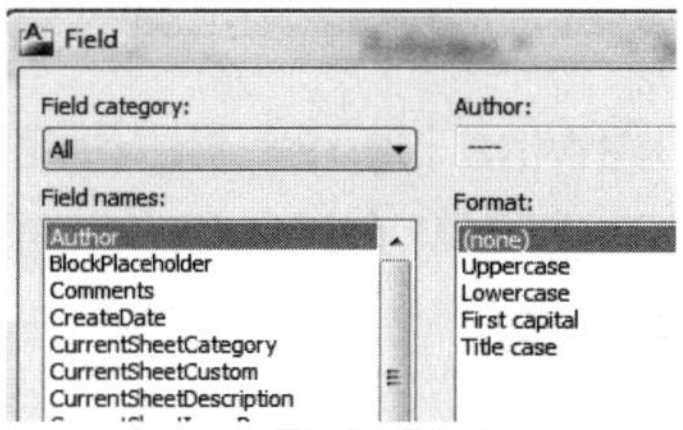

Insert Field Dialog

Pull Down Menu	**Insert→Field**
Command	**Field**
Alias	**Ctl+F**

Command Overview

Fields can be used in MTEXT or attribute definitions. You can use fields to display the area of a polygon or for title block information. Fields are also used in sheet sets. You can access the command by right clicking in the MTEXT window and selecting *Insert Field.*

There are several system variables that control how fields work. FIELDDISPLAY allows you to turn off the gray box under any defined fields. The gray box is not printed even when it is visible. FIELDEVAL sets how fields are updated, upon saving the drawing, plotting the drawing, or on Regen. FIELDUPDATE is used to update fields manually.

When you insert the field, there are two options available: Text Height and Justification.

General Procedures

Inserting a Field:

1. Go to Insert, Field.
2. Select the field data to use under the Field Category list.
3. Select the format (Upper Case/Lower Case/Sentence Case/Title Case) to be used for the field.
4. Press OK to close the dialog.
5. Select the insertion point for the field.

- The insertion point of the field is the upper left corner of the text.
- The Date field can only be updated using the UPDATEFIELD command.
- Spell check does not work on the values stored in fields.
- Fields are linked but not attached to objects. This means you can move the object and the field will not move with it. To have the field move with an assigned object, use **Group**.

Command Exercise

Exercise 11-12 – Adding Fields to Objects

Drawing Name: **fields2.dwg**
Estimated Time to Completion: 15 Minutes

Scope

Adding Fields to an object.

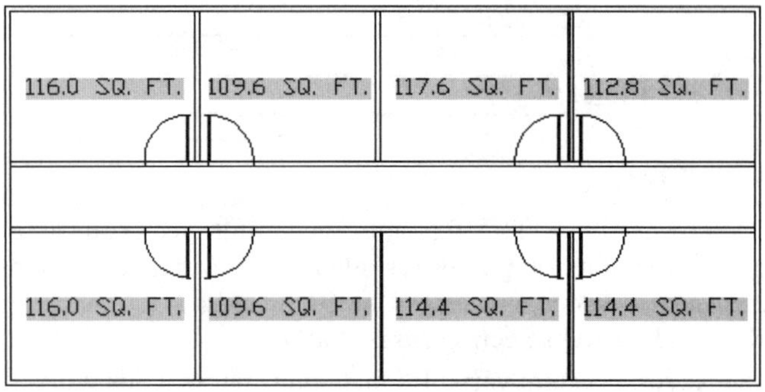

Figure 10 – Fields Exercise

Solution

1. 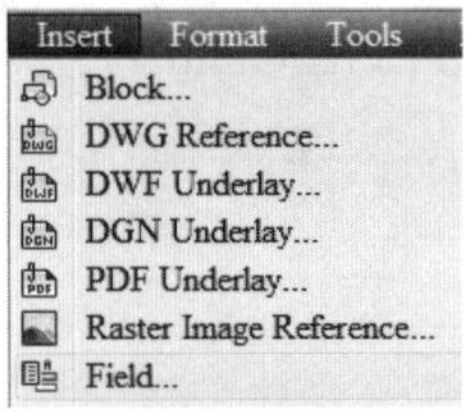

Invoke the **Insert→Field** command in the AutoCAD Classic workspace.

Or, use the Insert Ribbon and select the Field tool.

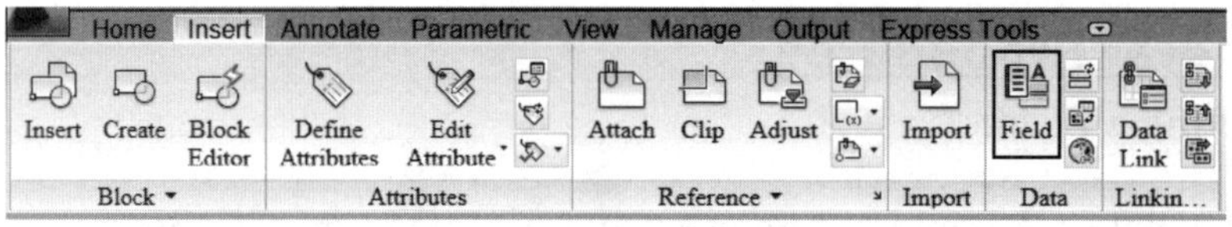

2. 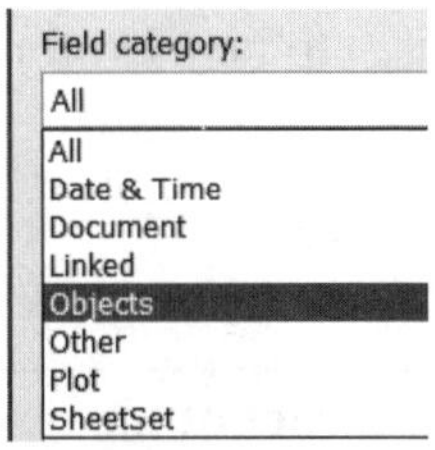

Under the Field Category, select **Objects**.

3. 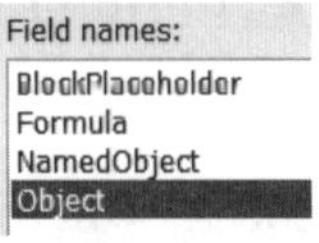

Highlight **Object** under Field names.

4. 

Select the **Select Object** tool.

5. 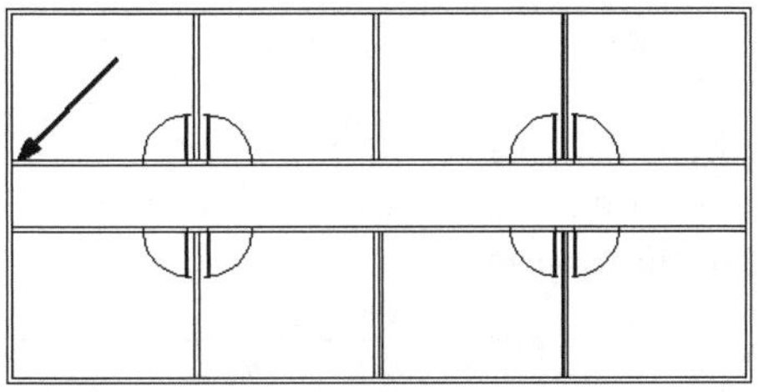

Select the first rectangle in the upper left corner.

> ***Tip:*** *Make sure you select the rectangle and not a line or the object properties will not display properly.*

6. 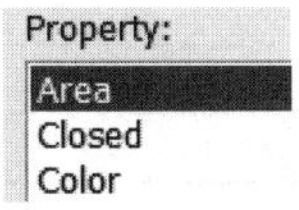

Highlight **Area** under Property.

7. 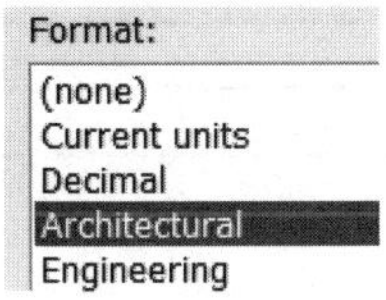

Select **Architectural** under Format.

8. 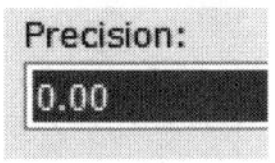

Set the Precision to two decimal places.

Press **OK**.

9. 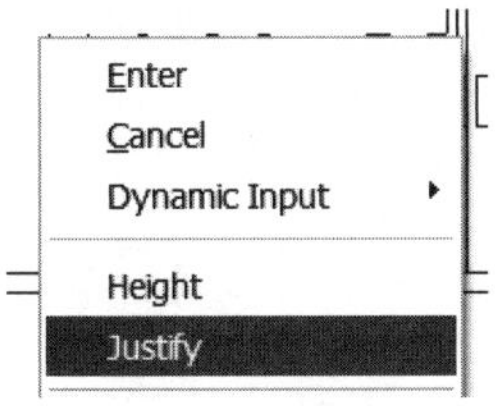

RMB and select **Justify**.

10. 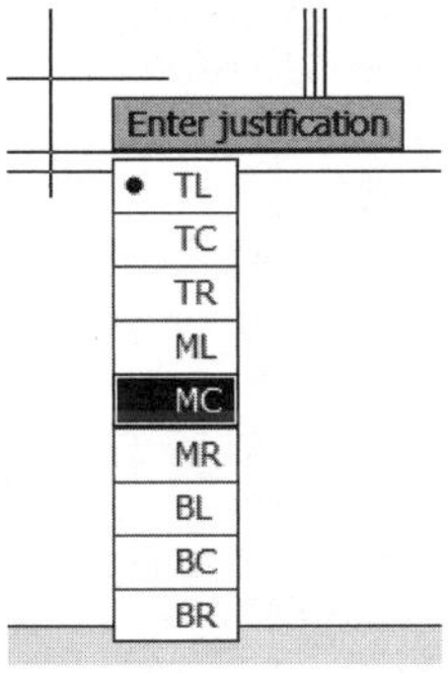

Select **MC** for Middle Center.

11. 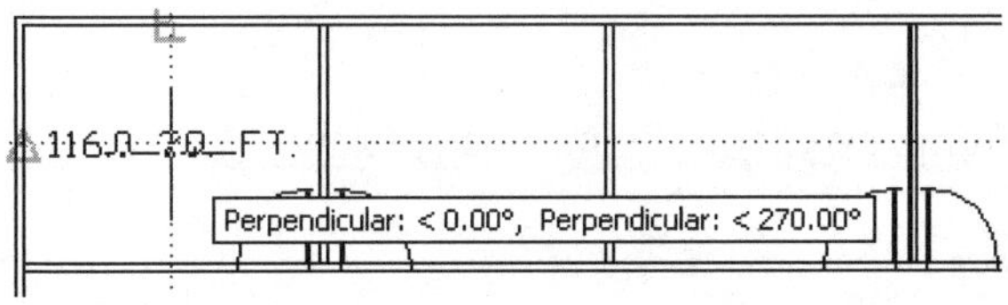

With Justification set to MC for Middle Center, use the Midpoint Object Snaps to place the field in the center of the room.

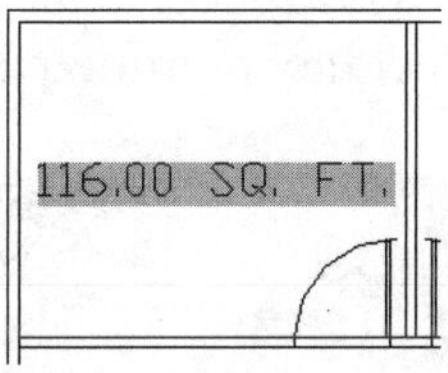

Extra: *Repeat for the other rooms in the layout.*

Tables

Tabulated Drawings: Many companies use tabulated drawings for their designs. A tabulated drawing is used when the basic design is the same, but the dimensions change depending on the part number. Tables can be used in these drawings.

Command Locator

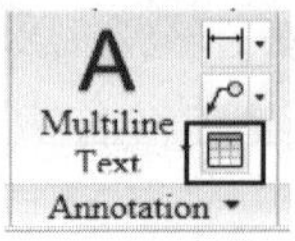

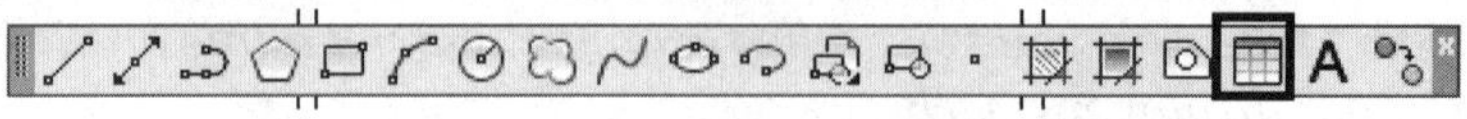

The Table Tool

Home Ribbon	**Annotation/Table**
Toolbar Menu	**Draw→Table**
Pull Down Menu	**Draw→Table**
Command	**table**
Alias	**tb**

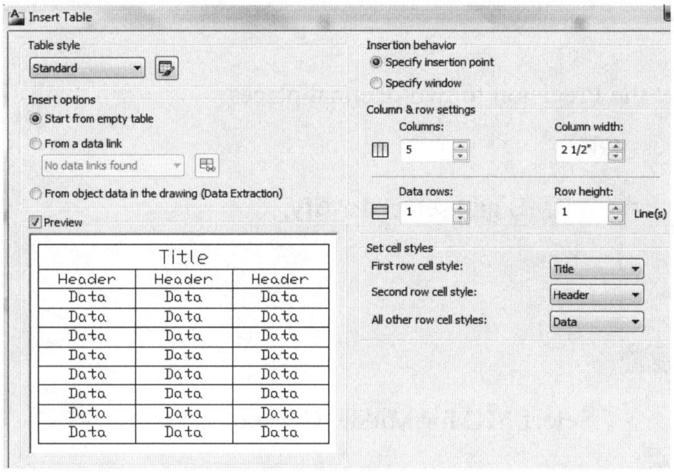

The Table Dialog

Command Overview

Tables can be defined with a specific number of columns and rows.
You can save table styles to be re-used in other drawings.

General Procedures

Inserting a Table:

1. Go to Draw, Table.
2. Select the number of columns, the column size, and the number of row.
3. Press OK to close the dialog.
4. Select the insertion point for the table.

Tips Tricks

- Tables can be exported to Excel or a text file.
- It is helpful to create text styles for the font styles to be applied to cells. Then you can simply select the cell(s) and assign the desired text style.
- Columns can be combined to create headers.
- Borders can be turned off and on to create more elaborate tables.
- Cells can be colored to provide shading.

Command Exercise

Exercise 11-13 – Adding a Table

Drawing Name: **table1.dwg**
Estimated Time to Completion: 15 Minutes

Scope

Adding a table to a drawing.

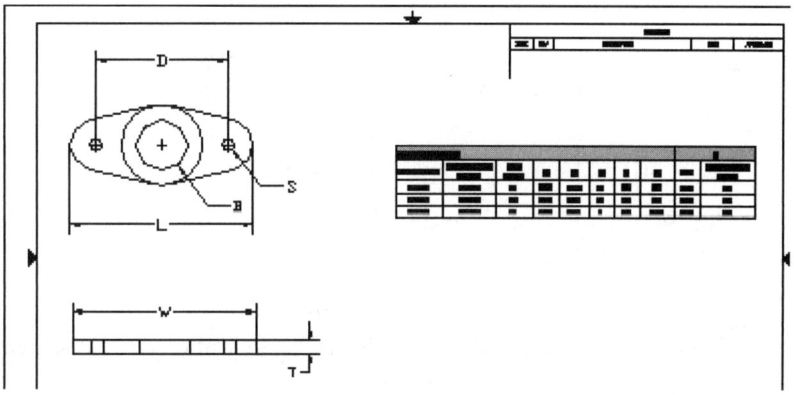

Figure 11 – Table Exercise

Solution

1. 

Activate the **Plan** layout by selecting it.

2.  Select the **Table** tool from the Drawing toolbar or from the Home ribbon.

3. 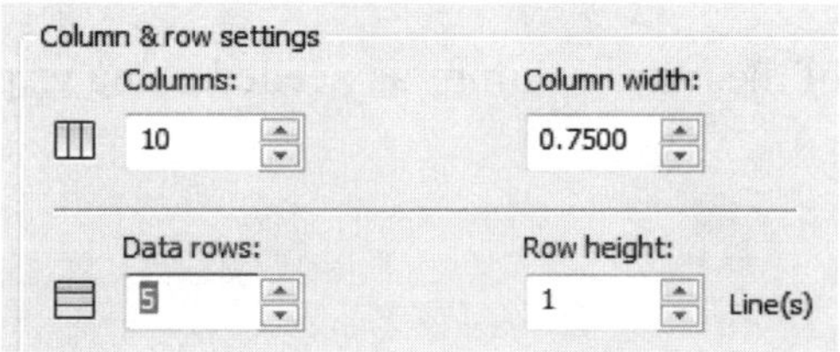

Set the Columns to **10**.
Set the Column width to **0.75**.

   Set the Data Rows to **5**.
   Set the Row Height to **1**.

   Press **OK**.

4. 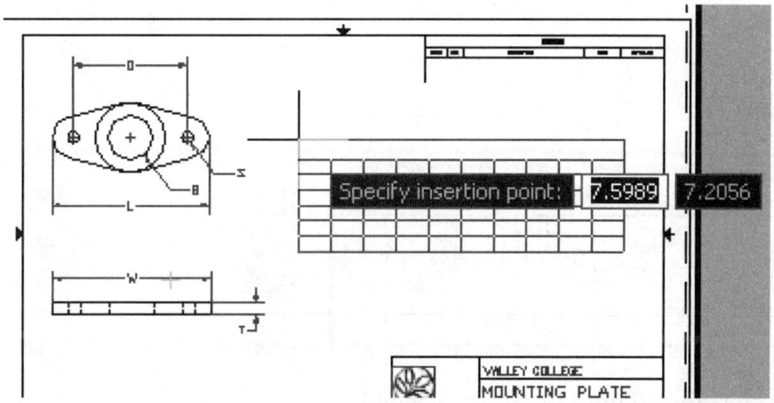

Place the table on the right side of the drawing.

5. 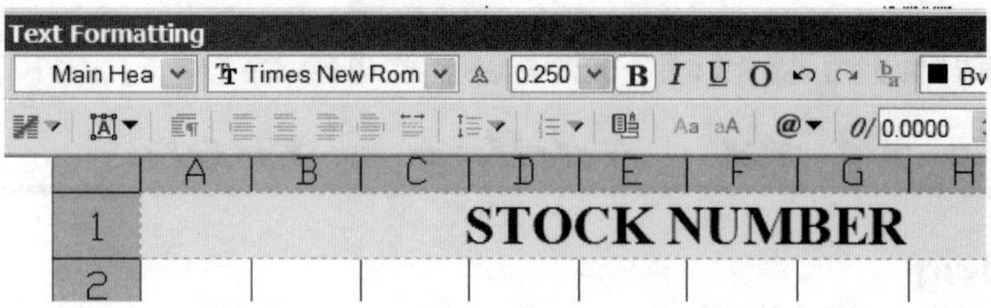

Enter **Stock Number** on the first row. Apply **Main Header** as the text style. Press **OK**.

6. 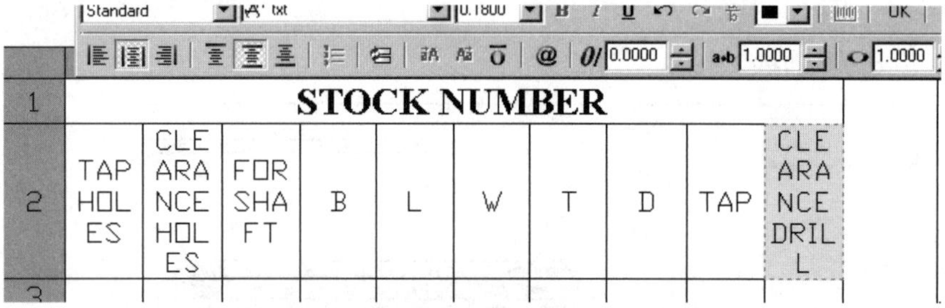

Fill in the cells for the second row. Use the <TAB> key to move to the next column. The cell is activated for data entry when it is shaded.

7. 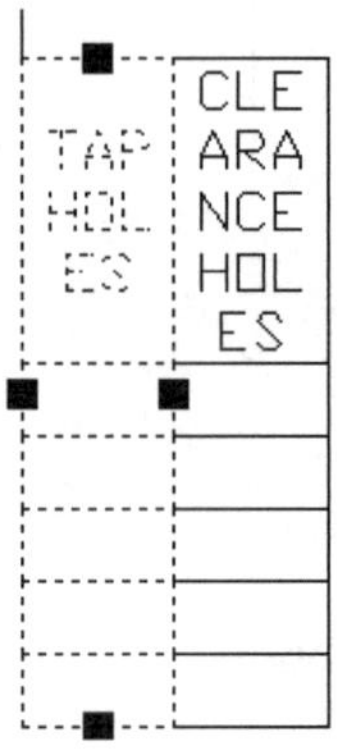

Use crossing to select the first column, rows 2 through 7.
You can also hold down the <SHIFT> key and select each cell.
Use grips to widen the column.

8. 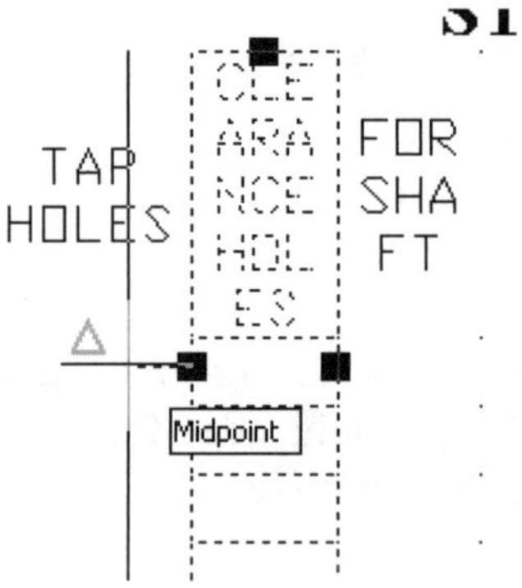

Adjust the width of the other columns as needed using grips.

9. 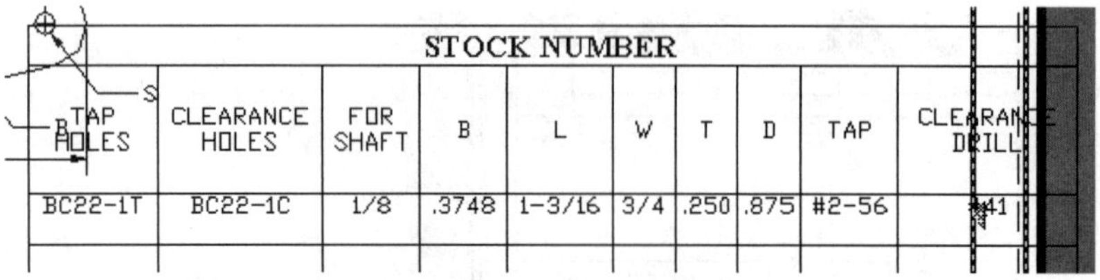

Fill in the third row. Adjust the column widths as needed.

10.

STOCK NUMBER									
TAP HOLES	CLEARANCE HOLES	FOR SHAFT	B	L	W	T	D	TAP	CLEARANCE DRILL
BC22-1T	BC22-1C	1/8	.3748	1-3/16	3/4	.250	.875	#2-56	#41
BC22-2T	BC22-2C	3/16	.4998	1-5/8	7/8	.312	1.25	#4-40	#31
BC22-3T	BC22-3C	1/4	.6248	1-3/4	1"	.312	1.375	#6-32	#26

Fill out the table as shown.

11. 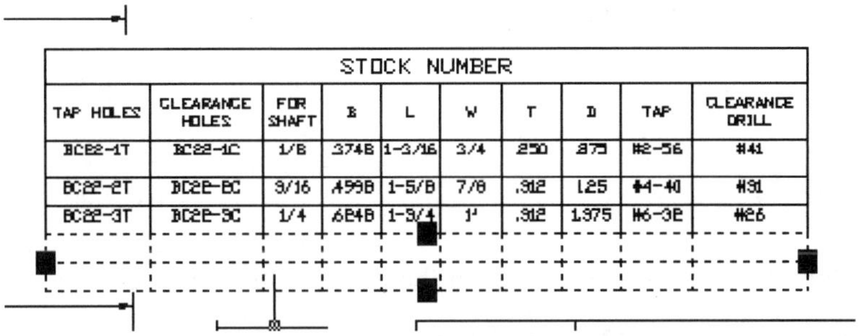

Hold down the <SHIFT> key and select the cells in the last two rows by picking each cell.

12. 

Select **Delete Rows** from the Table ribbon.

13. 

Select the top row.
Select **Unmerge Cells** from the Table ribbon.

14. 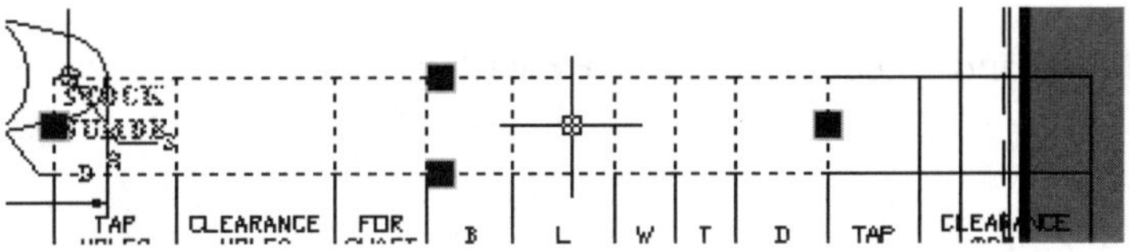

Select all the cells in the top row except for the last two column cells.

15. 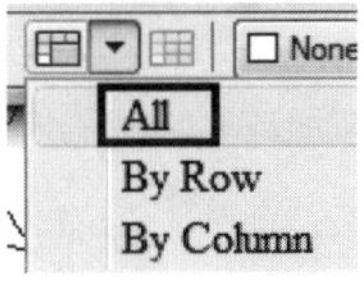

Select **Merge Cells→All** from the Table ribbon.

16. 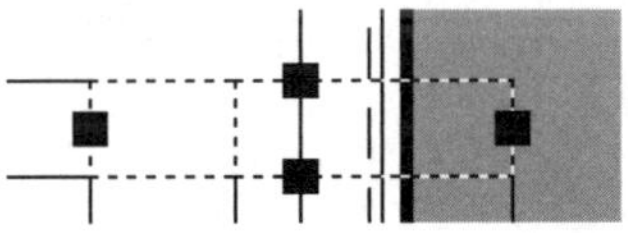

Select the last two cells in the top row.

17. 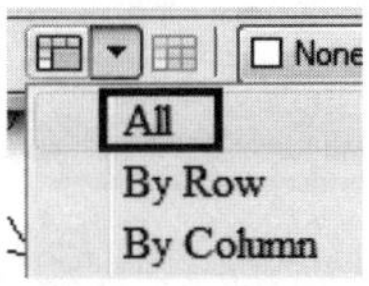

Select **Merge Cells→All** from the Table ribbon.

18. 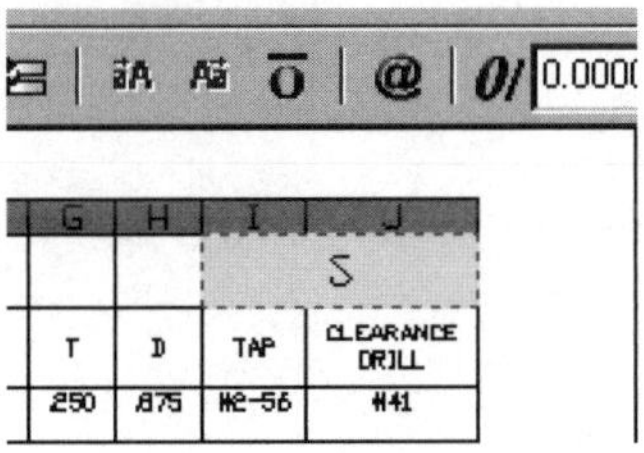

The columns are combined.

Enter **S** in the combined columns.

19. 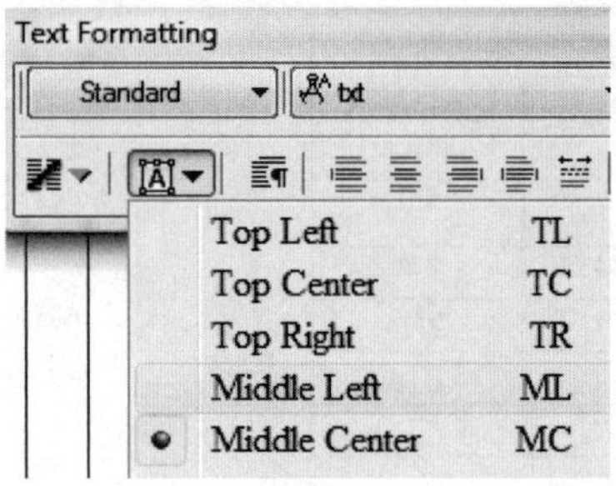

Set the first column, top row to **Middle Left Justified**.

To do this, highlight that cell, then select the Justification tool from the ribbon and select **Middle Left** from the drop-down.

20. Select the second first row column you merged on the top row, where you placed the 'S'.

21. 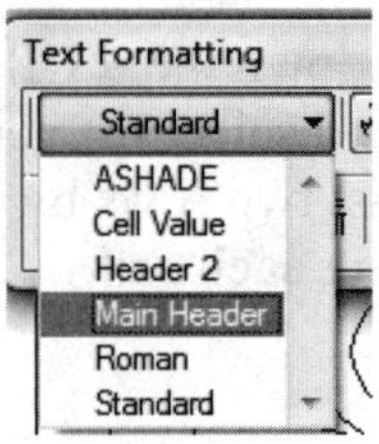

Set the Text style to **Main Header**.

22. 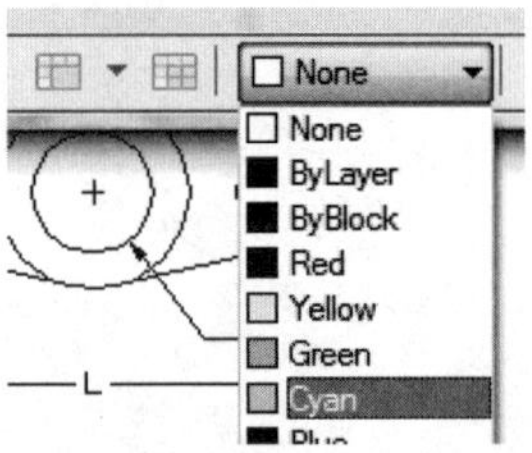

Exit Text edit mode and select the cell to enter Table edit mode.

Set the Background fill to **Cyan**.

23. 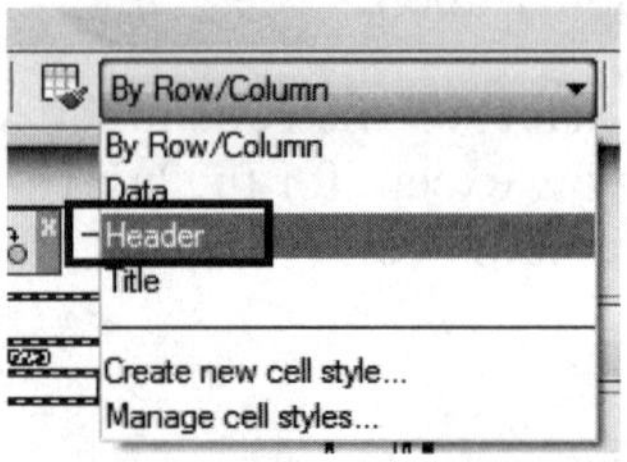

Select the columns in the second row.

RMB and select **Cell Style→ Header**.

24. 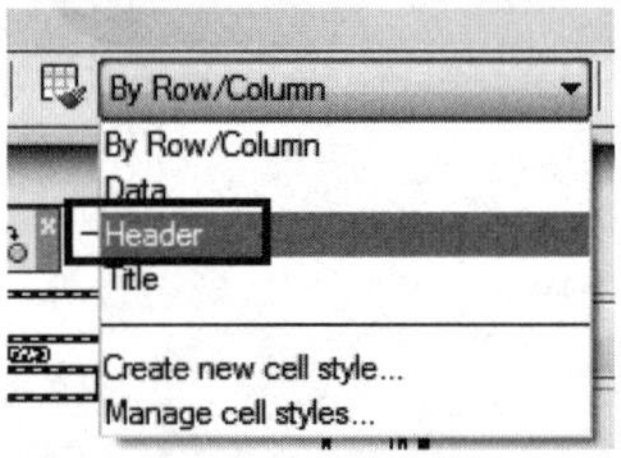

Set the Cell style to **Header2**.

25. 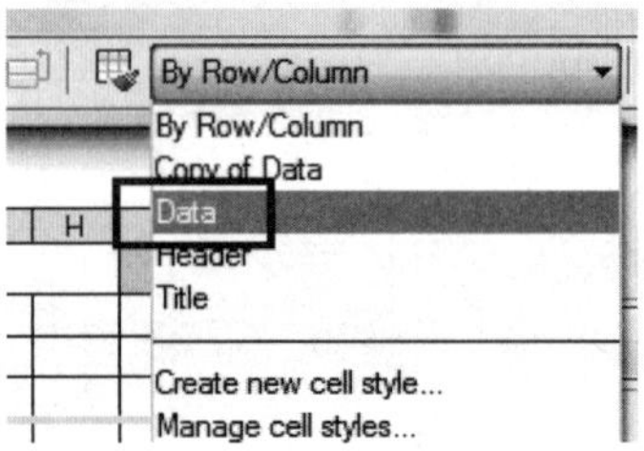

Set the Cell style to **Data**.

26.

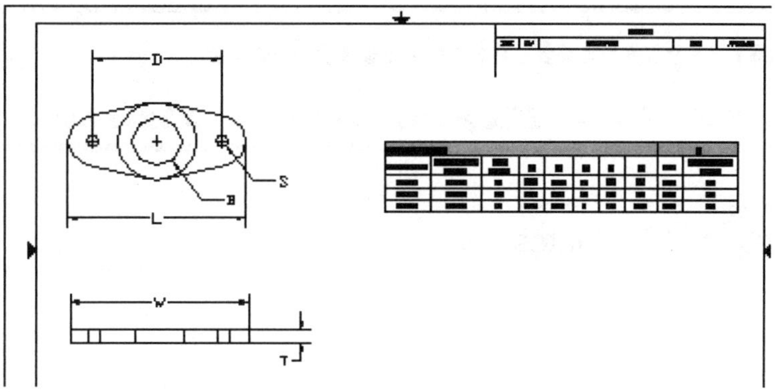

Adjust the location and size of the table so it fits onto the drawing properly.

Use the table below to assist you in creating your table.

STOCK NUMBER								S	
TAP HOLES	CLEARANCE HOLES	FOR SHAFT	B	L	W	T	D	TAP	CLEARANCE DRILL
BC22-1T	BC22-1C	1/8	0.3748	1-3/16	3/4	0.25	0.875	#2-56	#41
BC22-2T	BC22-2C	3/16	0.4998	1-5/8	7/8	0.312	1.25	#4-40	#31
BC22-3T	BC22-3C	1/4	0.6248	1-3/4	1"	0.312	1.375	#6-32	#26

Tip: *To change the colors used to indicate the cells and rows when a table is activated, select the table. Right click and select Table Indicator color. Select the desired color and press OK.*

Command Exercise

Exercise 11-14 – Exporting a Table

Drawing Name: **table2.dwg**
Estimated Time to Completion: 15 Minutes

Scope

Exporting a table to EXCEL.

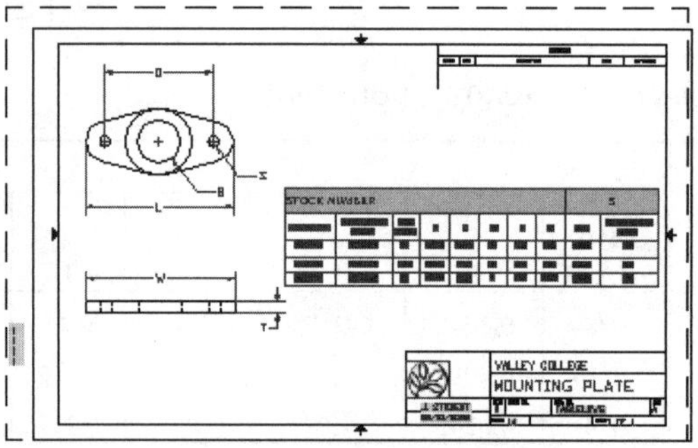

Figure 12 – Table Exercise

Solution

1.

Table Style
Size Columns Equally
Size Rows Equally
Remove All Property Overrides
Export...
Table Indicator Color...

Select the table in the drawing.

Right click and select **Export**.

2.

File name: Table1.csv
Files of type: Comma Delimited (*.csv)

Browse to the folder where you want to save the file.

Press **Save**.

3. Launch EXCEL.

File name:
Files of type: Text Files (*.prn; *.txt; *.csv)

Select **Open**.
Set the Files of type to Text Files.
Highlight the *table1.csv* file.
Press **Open**.

4.

Table1.csv

	A	B	C	D	E	F	G	H	I	J
1	STOCK NUMBER								S	
2	TAP HOLES	CLEARANCE HOLES	FOR SHAFT	B	L	W	T	D	TAP	CLEARANCE DRILL
3	BC22-1T	BC22-1C	1/8	0.3748	1-3/16	3/4	0.25	0.875	#2-56	#41
4	BC22-2T	BC22-2C	3/16	0.4998	1-5/8	7/8	0.312	1.25	#4-40	#31
5	BC22-3T	BC22-3C	1/4	0.6248	1-3/4	1"	0.312	1.375	#6-32	#26

You will have to format the columns to get the table to look proper.

> ***Tip:*** *You can only import text from a txt or rtf file. To import a Word file, save as txt or rtf.*

Command Exercise

Exercise 11-15 – Adding Blocks and Symbols to a Table

Drawing Name:**table3.dwg**
Estimated Time to Completion: 15 Minutes

Scope

Adding blocks and symbols to a table.

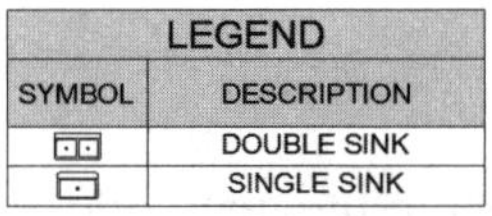

LEGEND	
SYMBOL	DESCRIPTION
	DOUBLE SINK
	SINGLE SINK

Figure 13 – Table Exercise

Solution

1. 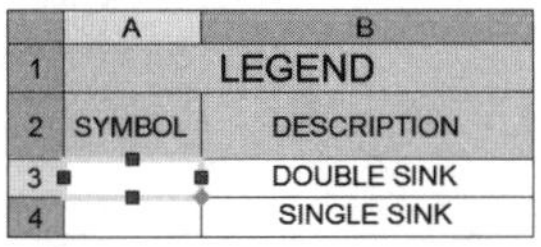

	A	B
1	LEGEND	
2	SYMBOL	DESCRIPTION
3		DOUBLE SINK
4		SINGLE SINK

Select the 3A cell.

2. 

Select the **Insert Block** tool from the Table toolbar.

3. 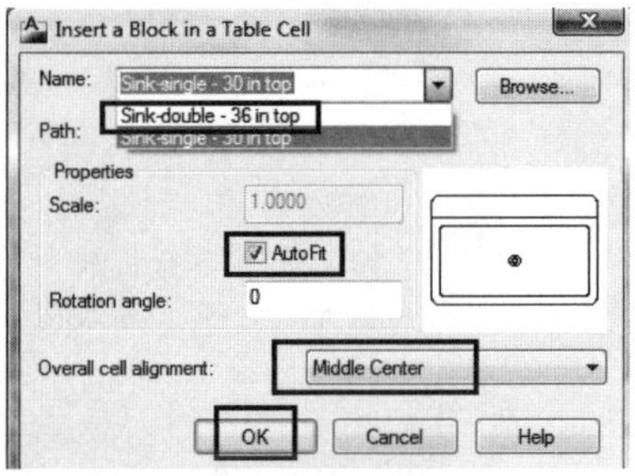

Select the **Sink-double-36 in top** from the drop-down.
These blocks are pre-loaded in the drawing. If you need to locate a block use the Browse button.
Enable **Autofit** to scale the block to the cell size.
Set the **Overall cell alignment** to **Middle Center**.
Press **OK**.

4. 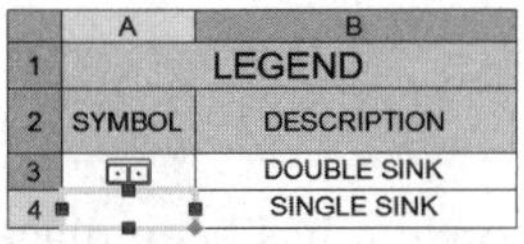

	A	B
1	LEGEND	
2	SYMBOL	DESCRIPTION
3		DOUBLE SINK
4		SINGLE SINK

Select the 4A cell.

5. 

Select the **Insert Block** tool from the Table toolbar.

6. 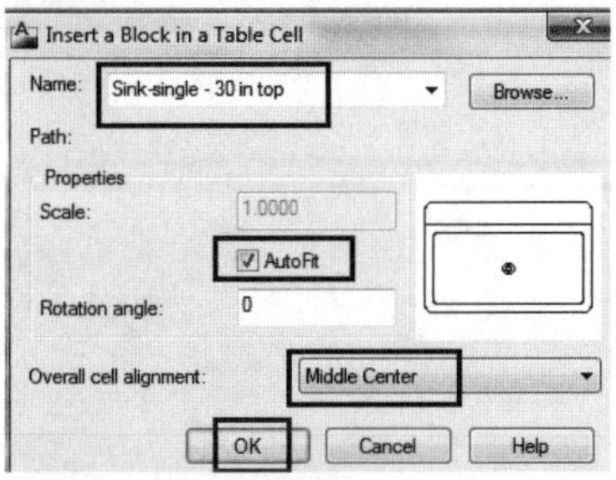

Select the **Sink-single-30 in top** from the drop-down.
These blocks are pre-loaded in the drawing. If you need to locate a block use the Browse button.
Enable **Autofit** to scale the block to the cell size.
Set the **Overall cell alignment** to **Middle Center**.
Press **OK**.

7. 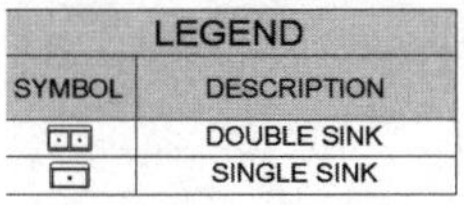

LEGEND	
SYMBOL	DESCRIPTION
	DOUBLE SINK
	SINGLE SINK

The legend is completed.

Review Questions:

1. To change the justification of text in the MTEXT dialog, select here.

2. To eliminate unused text styles in a drawing, use:
   - ❑ Erase
   - ❑ Purge
   - ❑ Delete
   - ❑ Eliminate

3. **T F** If a text height is specified in the text style, the user will not be prompted for the text height.

4. **T F** Spell check can be used on fields.

5. **T F** Fields can be applied to objects.

6. In order to import a text file into MTEXT, the file should be this format:
   - ❑ Txt or rtf
   - ❑ Doc or csv
   - ❑ Xls or csv
   - ❑ Txt or doc

7. Data exported from a table will be in this format:
   - ❑ Xls
   - ❑ Csv
   - ❑ Txt
   - ❑ Dwg

8. **T F** You can control the text style inside of tables.

9. **T F** You can not add or delete columns or rows from a table once it has been placed.

10. **T F** You can control the appearance of the MTEXT dialog.

Review Answers

1. To change the justification of text in the MTEXT dialog, select here.

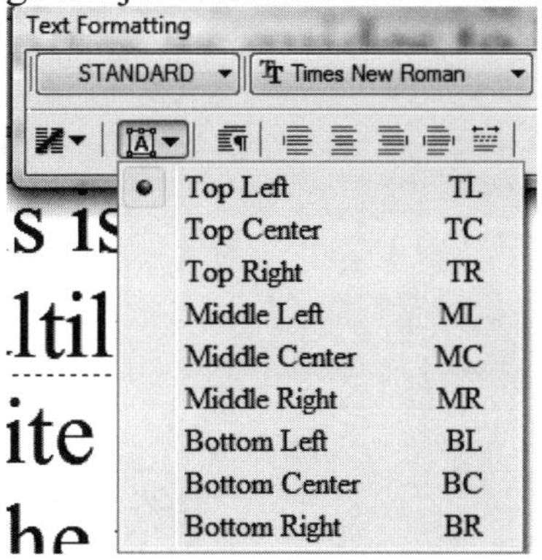

2. To eliminate unused text styles in a drawing, use:

   ❑ *Purge*

3. **T F** If a text height is specified in the text style, the user will not be prompted for the text height.

   True

4. **T F** Spell check can be used on fields.

   False

5. **T F** Fields can be applied to objects.

   True

6. In order to import a text file into MTEXT, the file should be this format:

   ❑ *Txt or rtf*

7. Data exported from a table will be in this format:

   ❑ *Csv*

8. **T F** You can control the text style inside of tables.

   True

9. **T F** You can not add or delete columns or rows from a table once it has been placed.

   False

10. **T F** You can control the appearance of the MTEXT dialog.

   True

NOTES:

Lesson 12.0 – Titleblocks and Templates

Estimated Class Time – 4 Hours

Objectives

Students will learn how to create Titleblocks and templates using drawing tools, fields, and attributes.

- **Templates**
  Templates are used as the starting point for a drawing and can store layers, linetypes, text styles and dimension styles.
- **Title Blocks**
  Titleblocks are used to track a drawing's name, part number, revision level, and other important information
- **Fields**
  Fields are linked to drawing properties
- **Attributes**
  Attributes store data and are easily edited.
- **The Define Attribute Command**

One of the options when you create a drawing is to use a template. Many companies set up and use templates to ensure their drafters comply with their internal standards. Templates are great because you only need to set up your layers, title blocks, and dimension styles once.

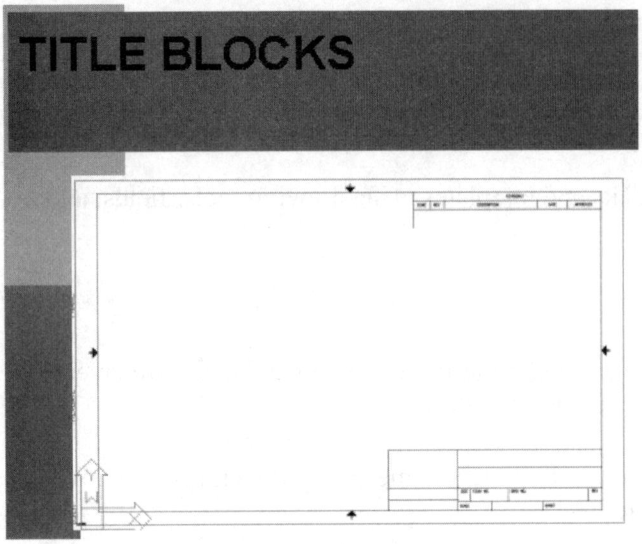

Standard Title Block

Technical drawings require a title block and a border.

You will notice that there are four arrows on the border, one on each side. The arrows are a leftover from the days when technical drawings were done on vellum. Drafters would create drawings using multiple sheets. Each sheet would act as a layer. The arrows were used to line up the views so that the overlays would match.

Most companies have a title block template that contains their company name and logo, as well as company address and contact information. As drafters, you need to know how to create and modify title blocks in case the company information changes and how to insert title blocks for use in your drawings.

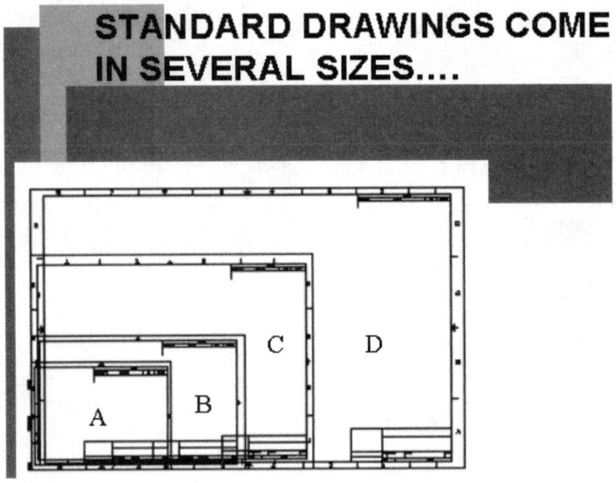

Each title block size is double the previous size...

A SIZE:	8-1/2 X 11
B SIZE:	11 X 17
C SIZE:	17 X 22
D SIZE:	22 X 34

In AutoCAD, all models and views are drawn 1:1. That way we can compare parts to make sure they fit together. In order to plot, we scale the title block and then scale the plot.

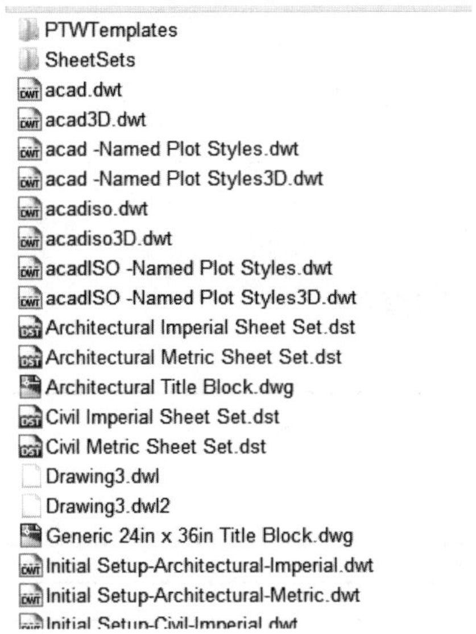

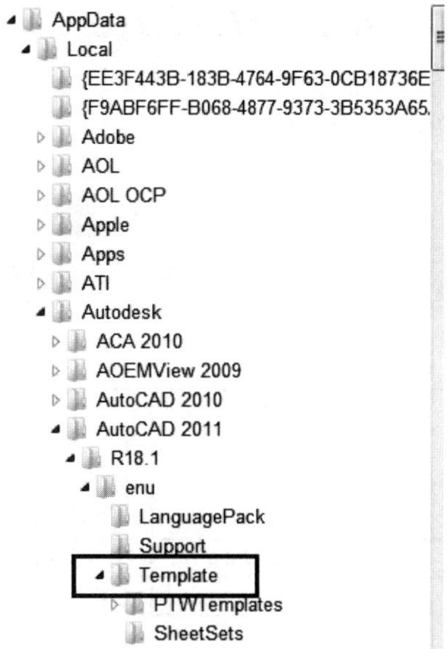

AutoCAD comes with standard title block templates. They are located in the Templates subdirectory under *Documents and Settings \<User Name> \Local Settings\Application Data\ Autodesk\ AutoCAD 2011\R18.1\enu \Template.*

If you are using VISTA, the templates are stored under *Users/<user name>/AppData/Local/ Autodesk/AutoCAD 2011/R18.1/enu/Template.*

Many companies will place their templates on the network so all users can access the same templates. In order to make this work properly, set the Options so that the templates folder is pointed to the correct path.

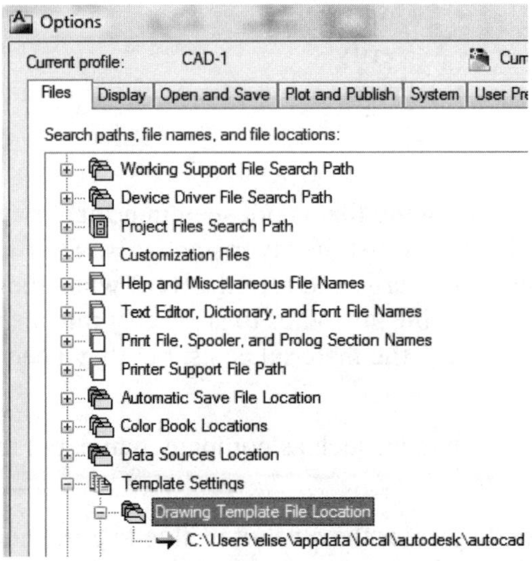

By adding attributes and fields to a title block, we can easily modify the text values and we can later learn how to export the attribute values to create a database for our parts drawings.

The Define Attribute Command

Command Locator

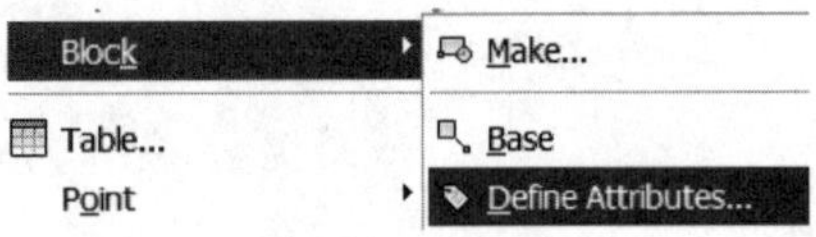

The Draw Menu

Insert Ribbon	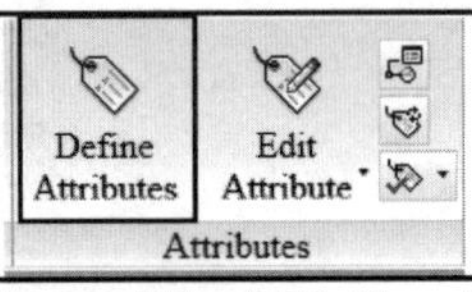
Pull Down Menu	**Draw/Block/Define Attributes**
Command	**ATTDEF**

> ***Tip:*** *To control the display of attributes use the command ATTDISP. Normal is normal/default viewing mode. ON allows you to see invisible and visible attributes. OFF makes all attributes invisible.*

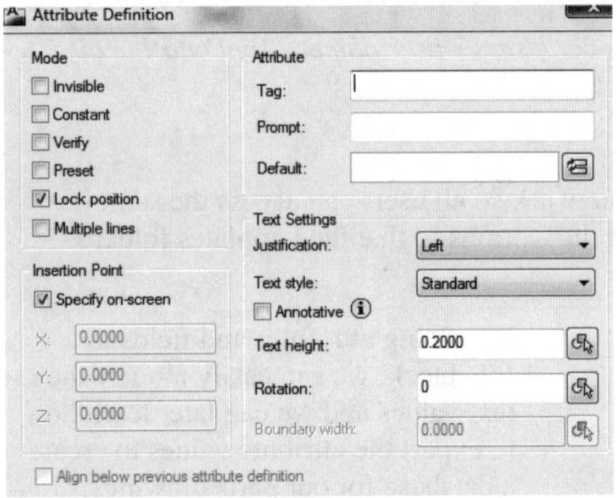

The Define Attribute dialog allows fields to be used as attributes. Field data is set up in the File Properties dialog. Once you enter the data in this dialog, the fields will automatically update in any corresponding locations.

There are four modes of Attribute definitions:

- Invisible
- Constant
- Verify
- Preset

Invisible attributes are used to store information in a drawing that is not seen in normal mode. Some companies will create a set of invisible attributes that list the layer standards. Drafters then turn the attribute display on so they can see the layer standards and turn them off when they are ready to plot their drawings. Other companies use invisible attributes to store cost information for parts. They don't want the customer to see how much the material costs, but they need the information to estimate project costs.

Constant attributes are used when the value does not change, such as company name, but the information is needed for extraction to a database.

Verify mode prompts the user with a Yes/No after they enter the attribute value to give them a chance to recheck their entry.

Preset sets the attribute to its default value when you insert a block containing a preset attribute.

Lock Position fixes the position of the attribute so it can not be moved.

Multiple lines allows you to create an attribute using the MTEXT editor. You can use the editor to determine the width of your paragraph.

Command Exercise

Exercise 12-1 – Adding Attributes

Drawing Name: **ANSI B.dwg**
Estimated Time to Completion: 70 Minutes

Scope

Add Attributes and fields to the title block.

Solution

1. 

Select the **Open** tool.

2. 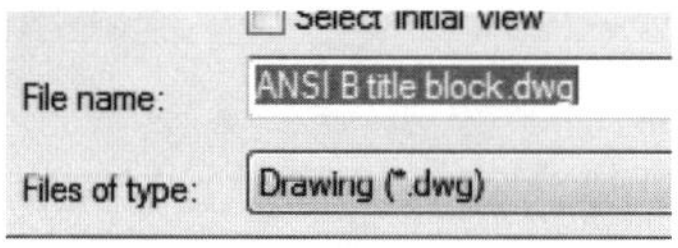

Locate the ANSI-*B title block.dwg* file.
This file is also available on the publisher's website if you have difficulty locating it on your system.

Press **Open**.

3. 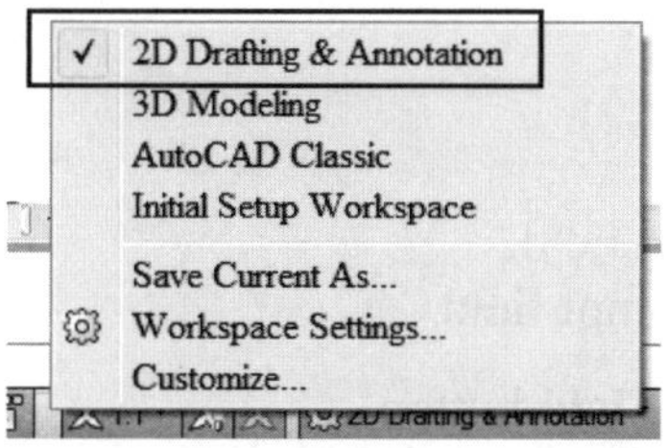

Verify that the active workspace is **2D Drafting & Annotation**.

4. 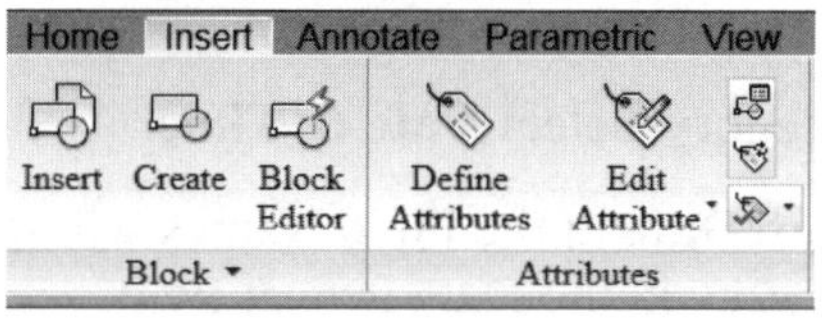

Activate the **Insert** tab on the ribbon.

5. 

Select the **Define Attributes** tool.

6. 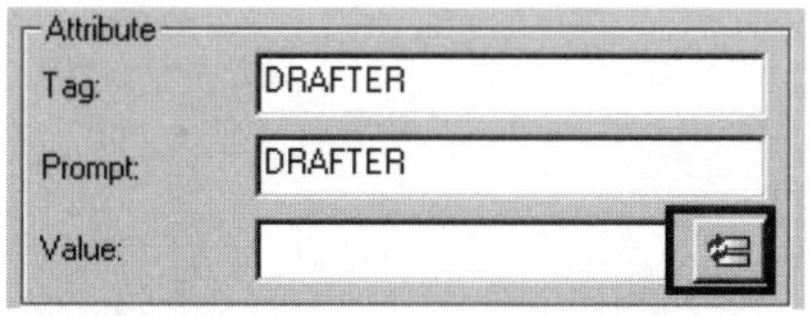

Enter **DRAFTER** in the Tag field.
Enter **DRAFTER** in the Prompt field.

Then select the **Insert Field** button.

7. 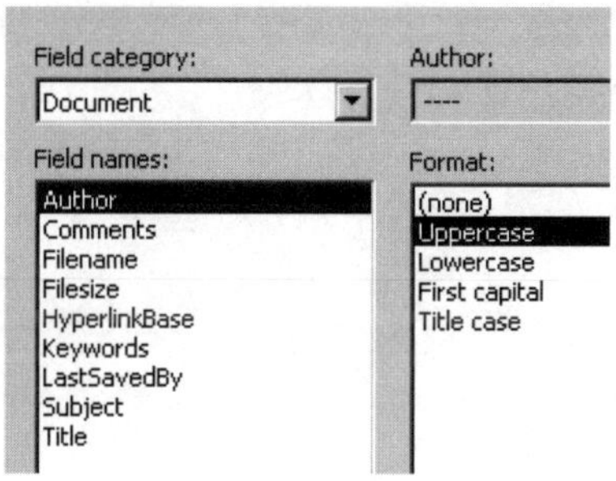

In the Field category, select **Document**.

Highlight **Author** in the Field Names window.
Highlight **Uppercase** in the Format window.

Press **OK**.

8. 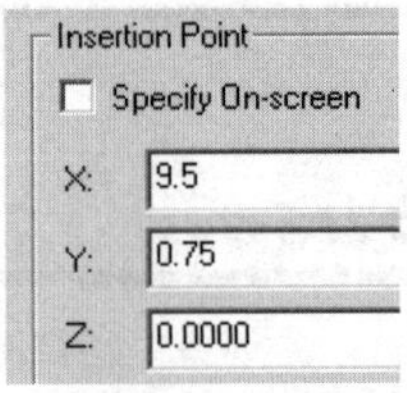

Under Insertion Point:

Set X to **9.5**.
Set Y to **0. 75**.
Set Z to **0**.

9. 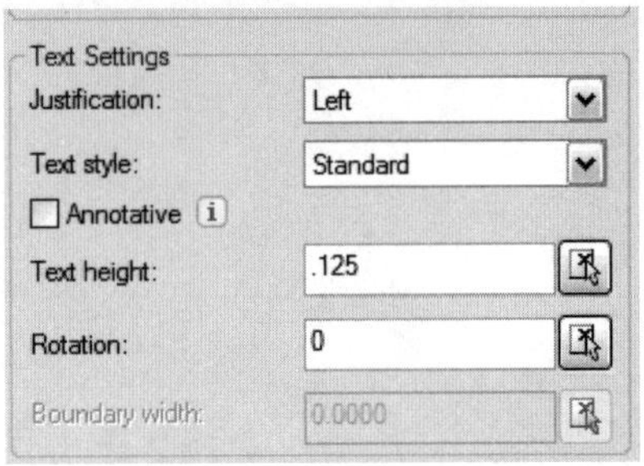

Under Text Options:

Set the Height to **.125**.

10. 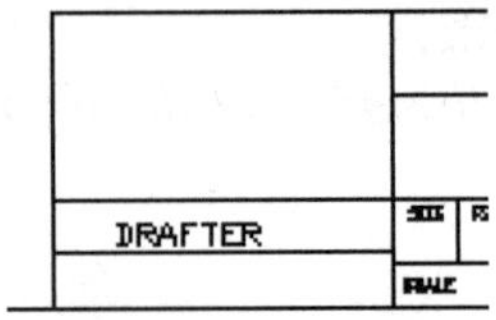

Press **OK**.

The field appears in the title block.

11. 

Select the **Define Attributes** tool.

12. 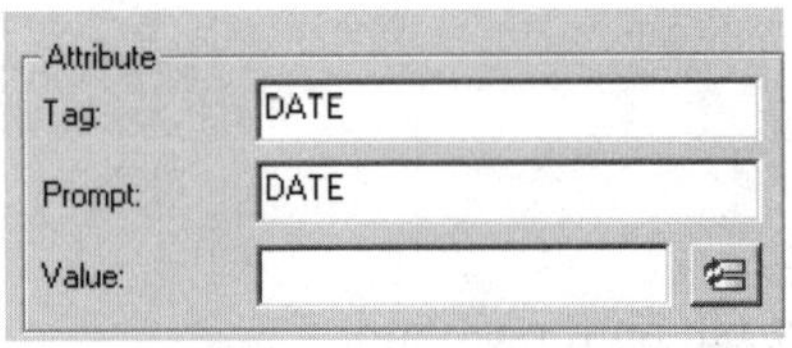

Enter **DATE** in the Tag field.
Enter **DATE** in the Prompt field.

Then select the **Insert Field** button.

13. 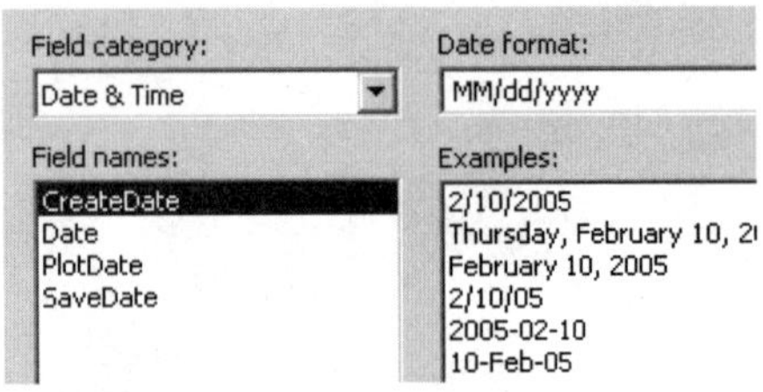

In the Field category, select **Date & Time**.

Highlight **CreateDate** in the Field Names window.
Type **MM/dd/yyyy** in the Date format field.

Press **OK**.

14. 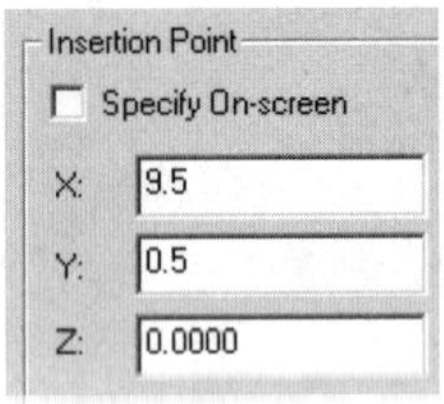

Under Insertion Point:

Set X to **9.5**.
Set Y to **0.5**.
Set Z to **0**.

15. 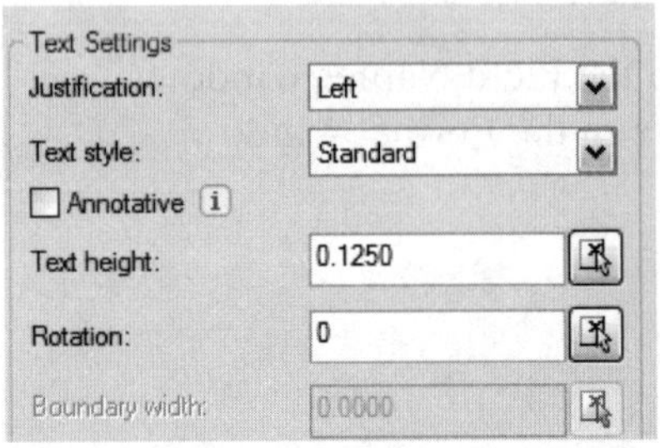

Under Text Options:

Set the Height to **.125**.

16.

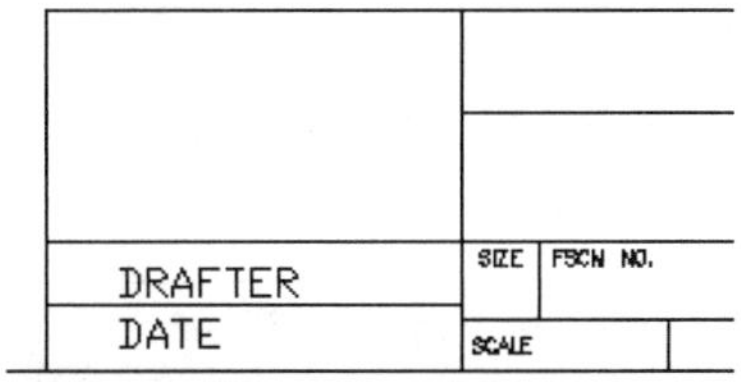

Press **OK**.

The field appears in the title block.

17.

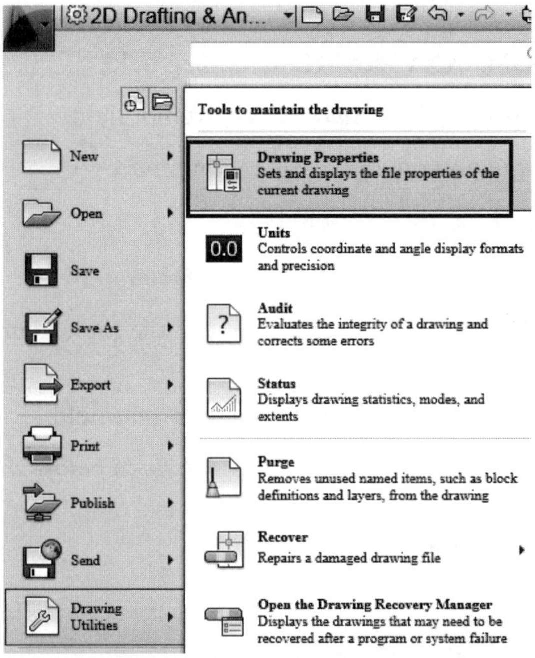

Go to **File→Drawing Utilities→Drawing Properties**.

18.

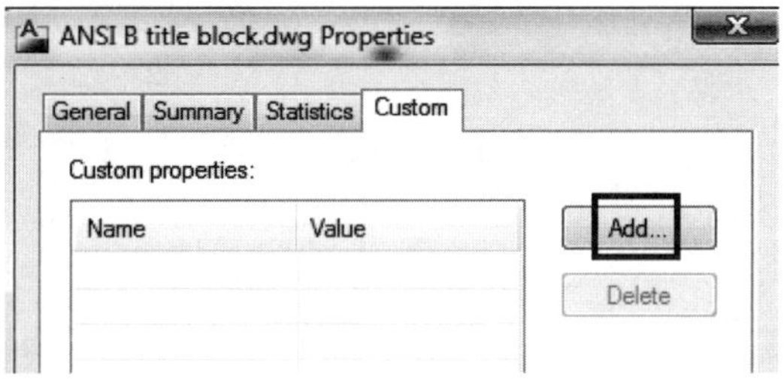

Select the **Custom** tab.

Press the **Add** button.

19.

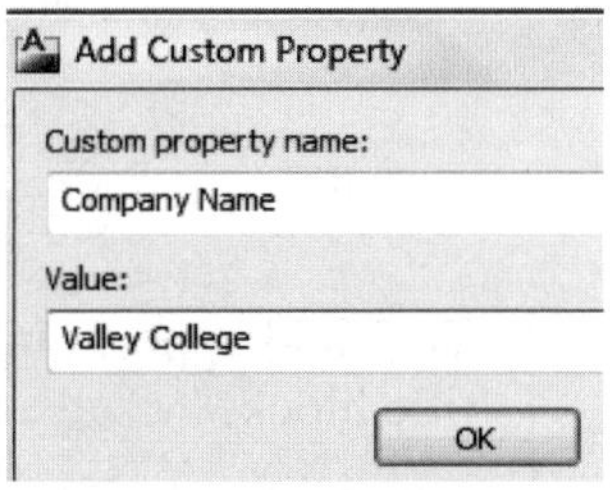

Type **Company Name** in the Custom property name field.

Type your school or company name in the Value field.

Press **OK**.

20.

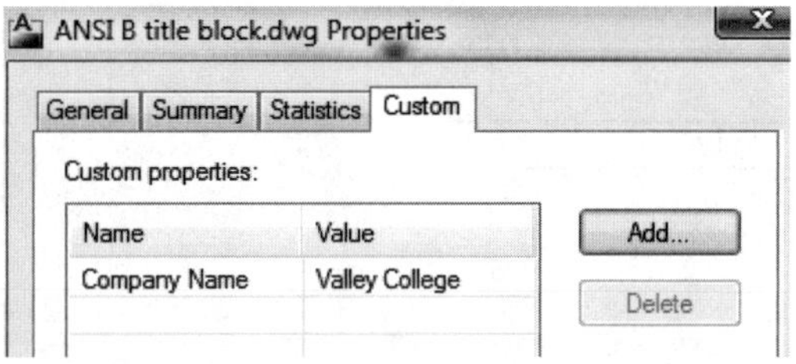

Press **OK**.

> ***Tip:*** *You could also add address, phone, and other data into this area if you want it included in the title block.*

21. 

Select the **Define Attributes** tool.

> ***Tip:*** *You can also right click and use Recent Input to access your most recent commands. Simply select the command you want to use from the list.*

22. 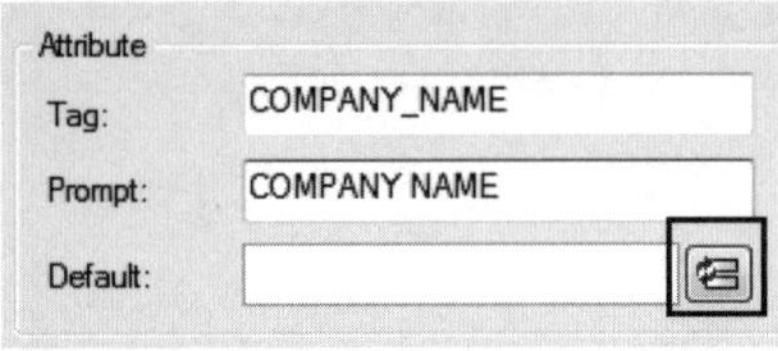

Enter **COMPANY_NAME** in the Tag field.

Enter **COMPANY NAME** in the Prompt field.

Note that the Tag field does not allow spaces.

Then select the **Insert Field** button.

23. 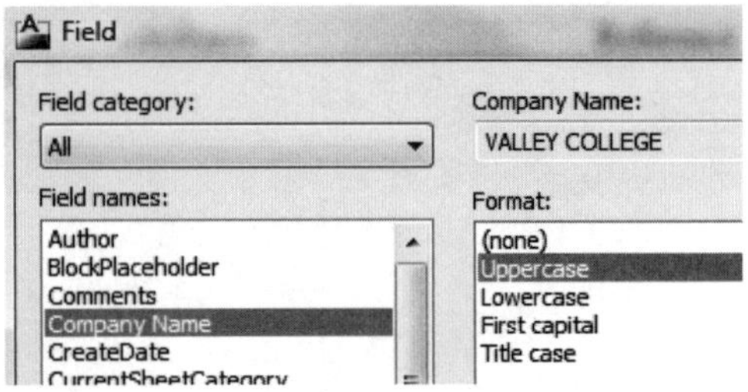

In the Field category, select **Document**.

Highlight **Company Name** in the Field Names window.

Highlight **Uppercase** in the format field.

Custom Properties must be defined before they are available as fields.

Press **OK**.

24. 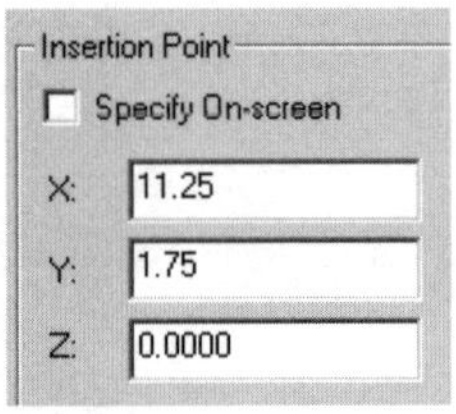

Under Insertion Point:

Set X to **11.25**.
Set Y to **1.75**.
Set Z to **0**.

25. 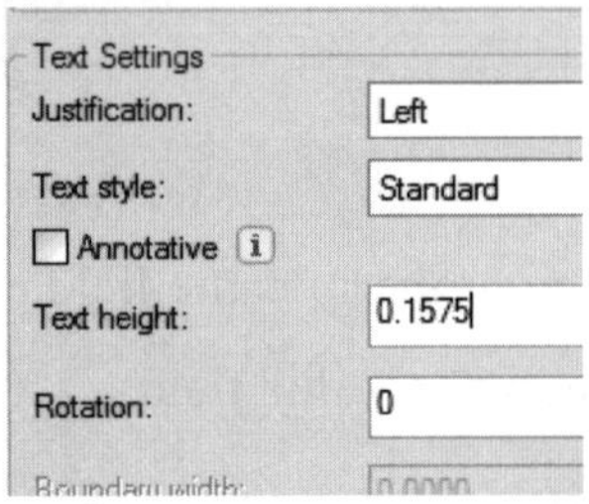

Under Text Options:

Set the Height to **.1575**.

Press **OK**.

26. 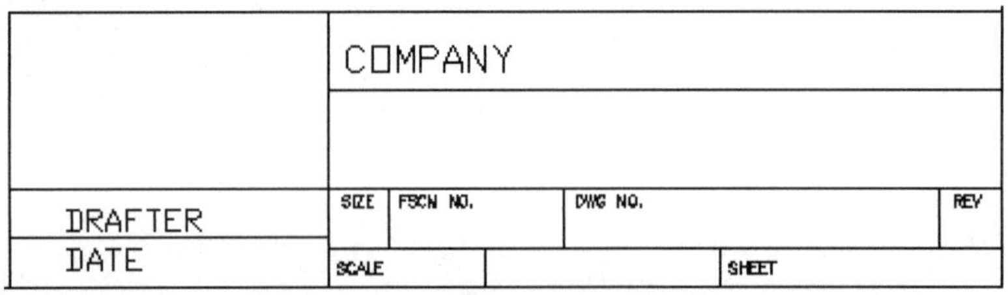

The field appears in the title block.

27. 

Select the **Define Attributes** tool.

28. 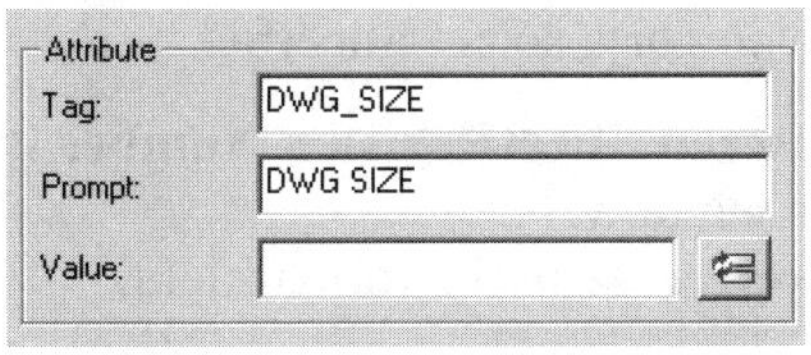

Enter **DWG_SIZE** in the Tag field.
Enter **DWG_SIZE** in the Prompt field.

Then select the **Insert Field** button.

29. 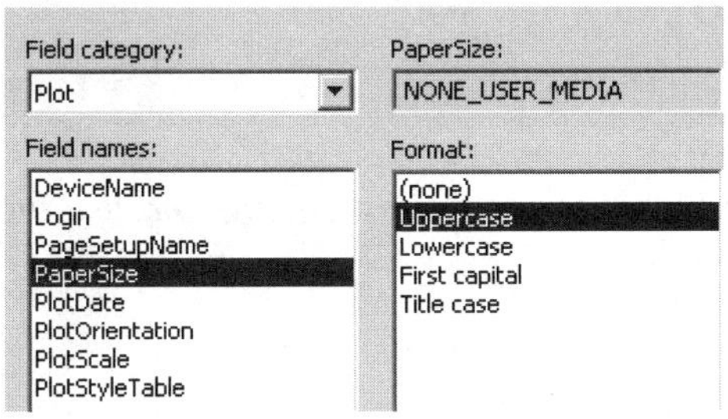

In the Field category, select **Plot**.

Highlight **PaperSize** in the Field Names window.

Highlight **Uppercase** in the format field.

Press **OK**.

By using a field for the papersize, the papersize will adjust based on the layout size used...you can change the papersize and the field will automatically update.

30. 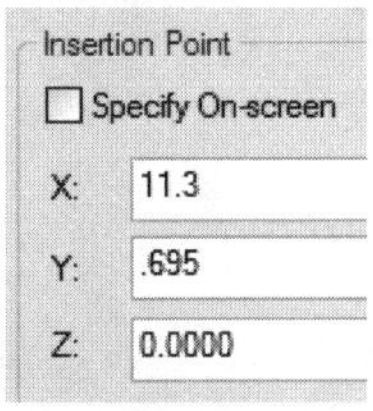

Under Insertion Point:

Set X to **11.3**.
Set Y to **0.695**.
Set Z to **0**.

31. 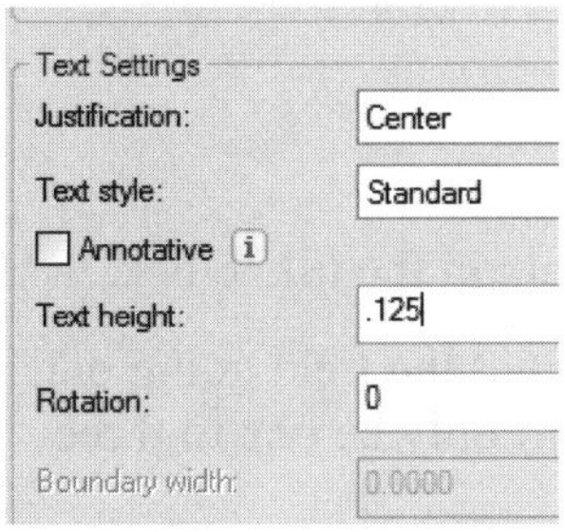

Under Text Options:

Set the Justification to **Center**.
Set the Height to **.125**.

32. 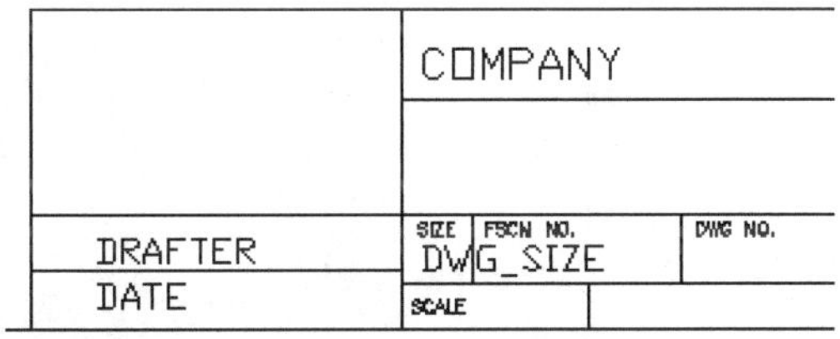

Press **OK**.

The field appears in the title block.

Don't worry about the field going outside the box as it will only be one character.

33. 

Select the **Define Attributes** tool.

34. 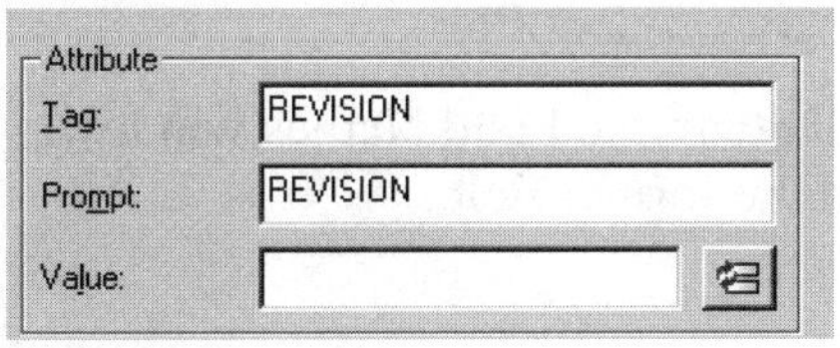

Enter **REVISION** in the Tag field.
Enter **REVISION** in the Prompt field.

Then select the **Insert Field** button.

35. 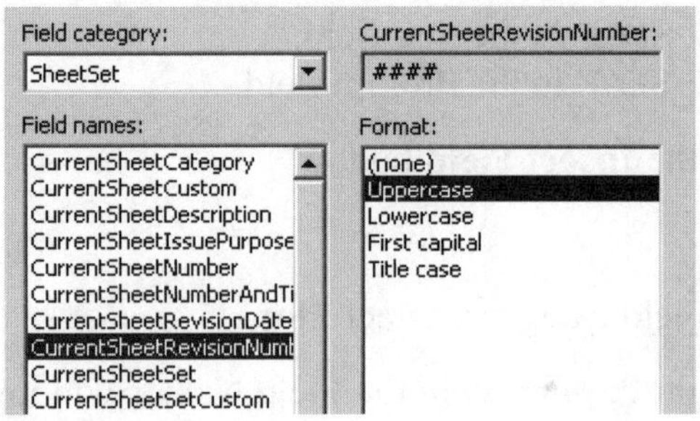

In the Field category, select **SheetSet**.

Highlight **CurrentSheetRevision Number** in the Field Names window.
Highlight **Uppercase** in the format field.

Press **OK**.

By using a field for the sheetset, you can have multiple layouts in a drawing and use the revision on that specific layout for the revision number.

36. 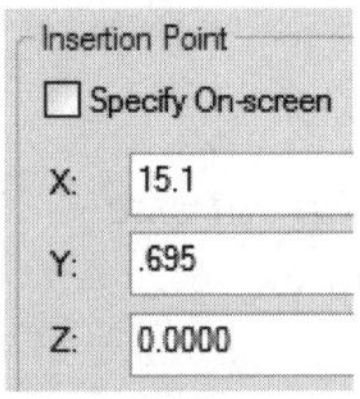

Under Insertion Point:

Set X to **15.1**.
Set Y to **0.695**.
Set Z to **0**.

37. 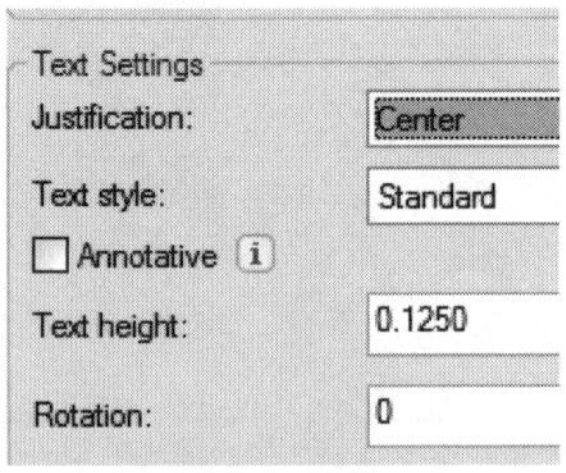

Under Text Options:

Set the Justification to **Center**.
Set the Height to **.125**.

38. 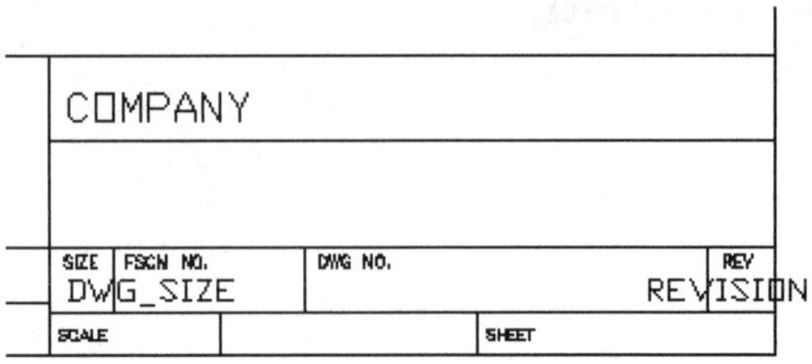

Press **OK**.

The field appears in the title block.

Don't worry about the field going outside the box as it will only be one to three characters.

39. 

Select the **Define Attributes** tool.

40. 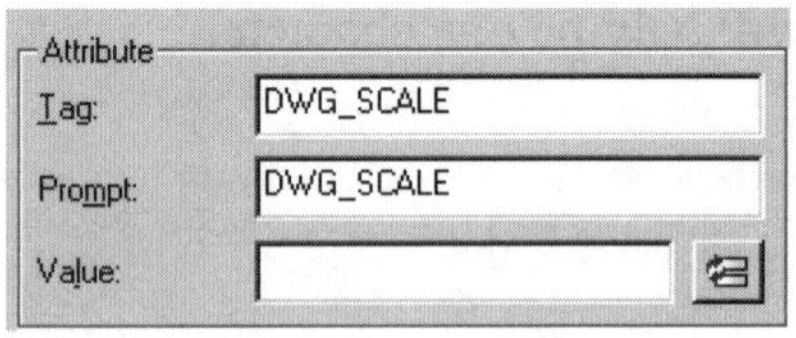

Enter **DWG_SCALE** in the Tag field.

Enter **DWG_SCALE** in the Prompt field.

Then select the **Insert Field** button.

41. 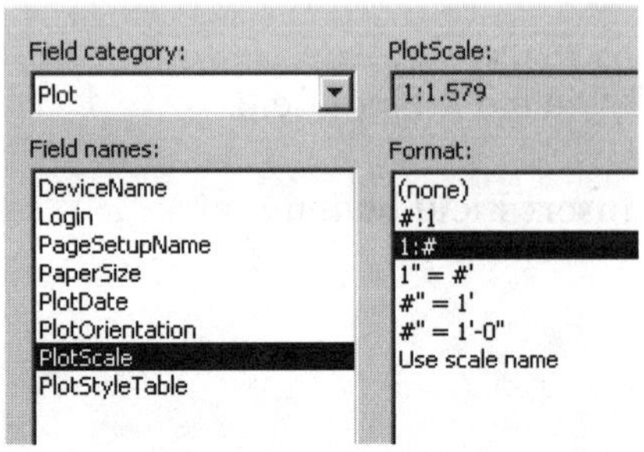

In the Field category, select **Plot**.

Highlight **PlotScale** in the Field Names window.
Highlight **1:#** in the format field.

Press **OK**.

By using a field for the plot scale, you can have multiple layouts in a drawing and use the plot scale on that specific layout.

42.

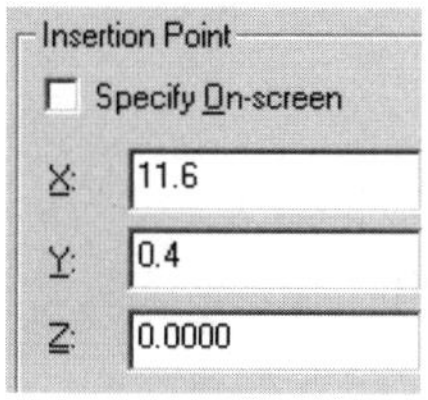

Under Insertion Point:

Set X to **11.6**.
Set Y to **0.40**.
Set Z to **0**.

43.

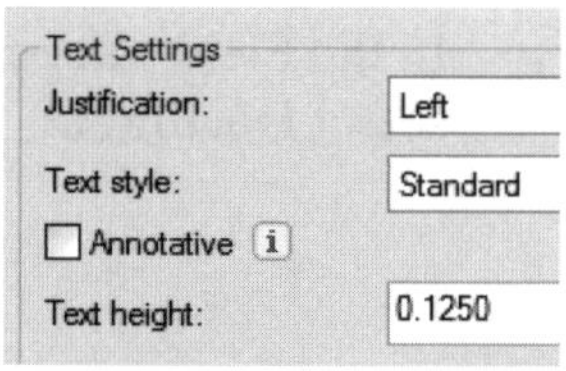

Under Text Options:

Set the Justification to **Left**.
Set the Height to **.125**.

44.

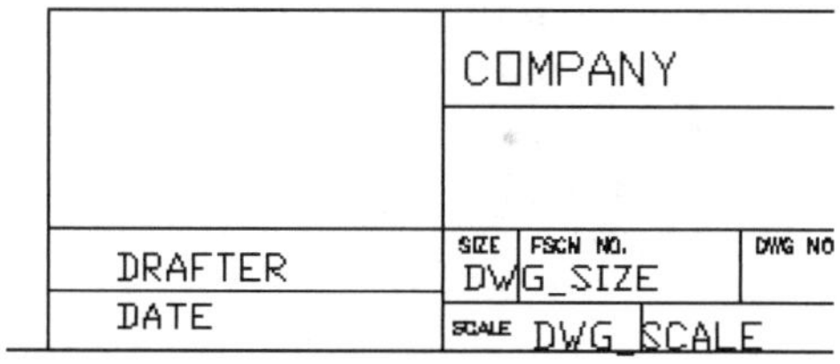

Press **OK**.

The field appears in the title block.

Don't worry about the field going outside the box as it will only be a few characters.

45.

Select the **Define Attributes** tool.

46.

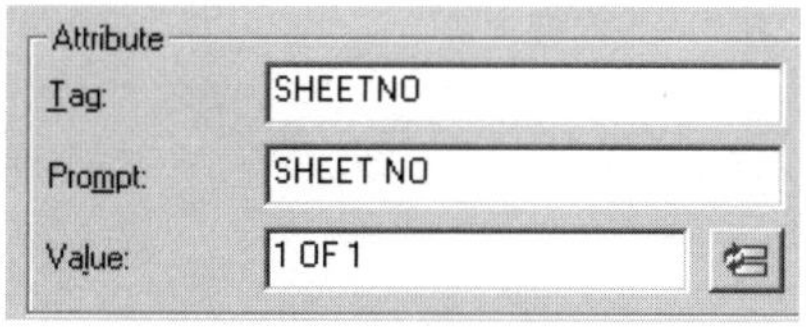

Enter **SHEETNO** in the Tag field.
Enter **SHEETNO** in the Prompt field.
Enter **1 OF 1** in the Value field.

47.

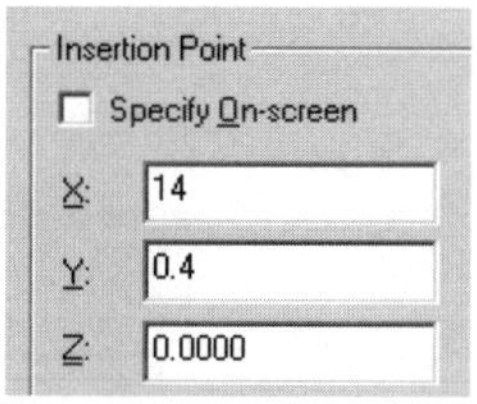

Under Insertion Point:

Set X to **14**.
Set Y to **0.40**.
Set Z to **0**.

48.

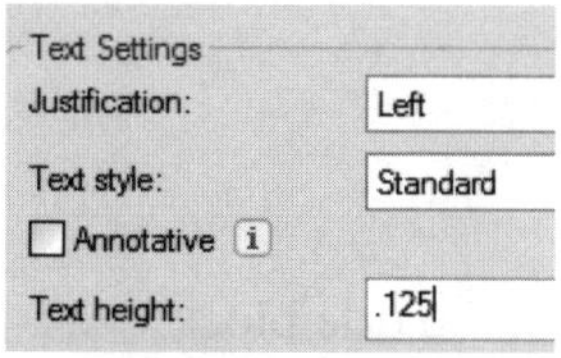

Under Text Options:

Set the Justification to **Left**.
Set the Height to **.125**.

49.

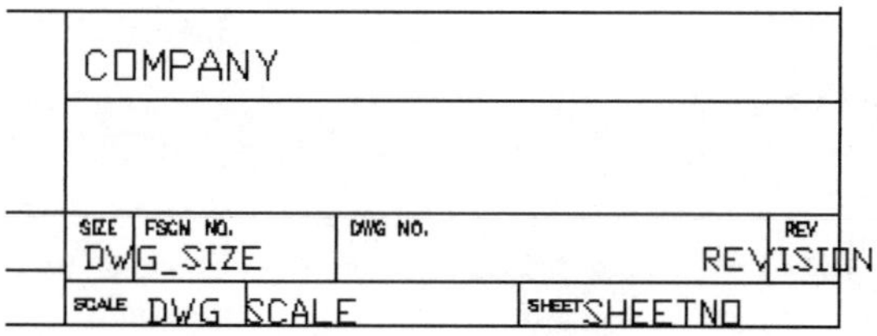

Press **OK**.

The field appears in the title block.

Don't worry about the field going outside the box as it will only be a few characters.

50. 

Select the **Define Attributes** tool.

51. 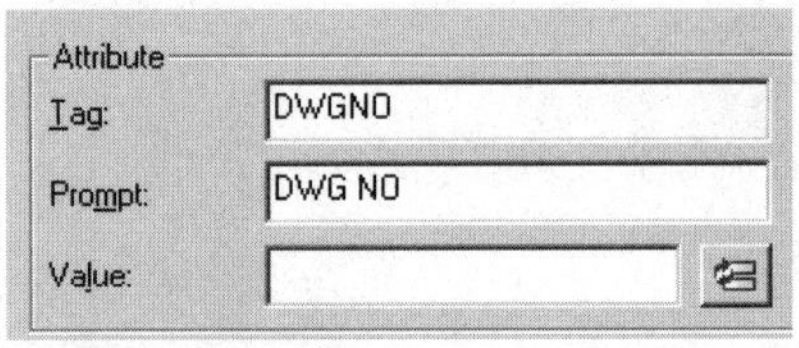

Enter **DWG_NO** in the Tag field.
Enter **DWG_NO** in the Prompt field.

Then select the **Insert Field** button.

52. 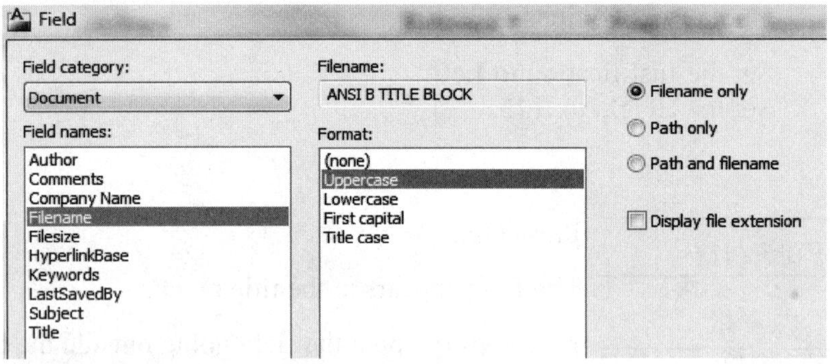

In the Field category, select **Document**.

Highlight **Filename** in the Field Names window.
Highlight **Uppercase** in the format field.
Enable **Filename only**.
Disable **Disable file extension.** *This removes the .dwg from the file name.*

Press **OK**.

53. 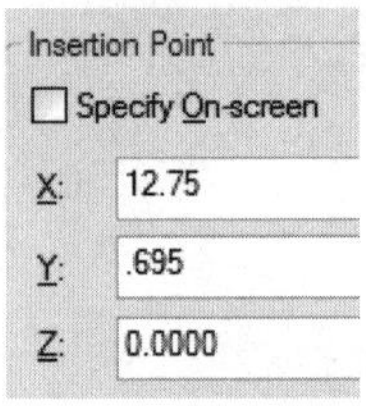

Under Insertion Point:

Set X to **12.75**.
Set Y to **0.695**.
Set Z to **0**.

54. 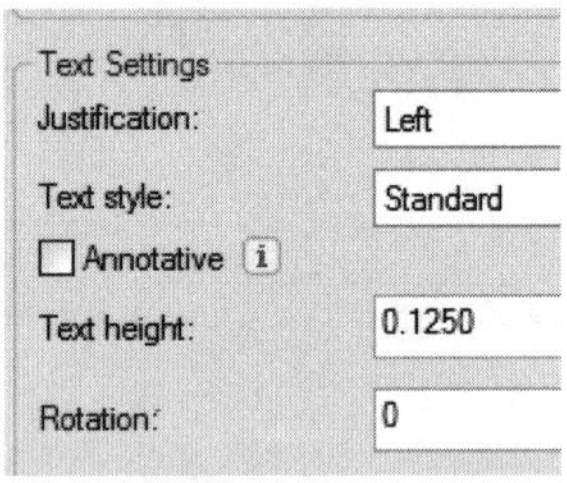

Under Text Options:

Set the Justification to **Left**.
Set the Height to **.125**.

55. 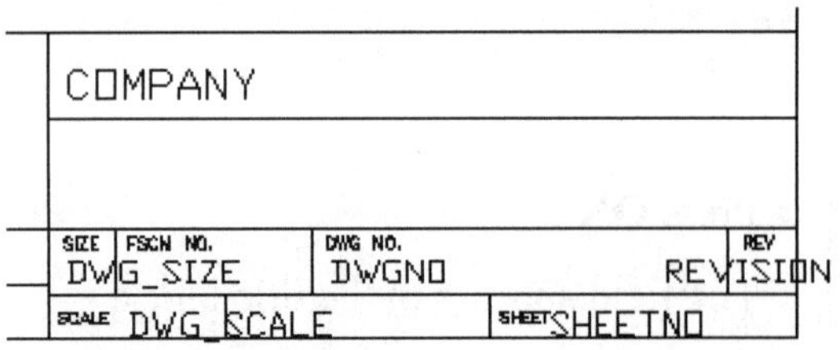

Press **OK**.

The field appears in the title block

56. 

Select the **Define Attributes** tool.

57.

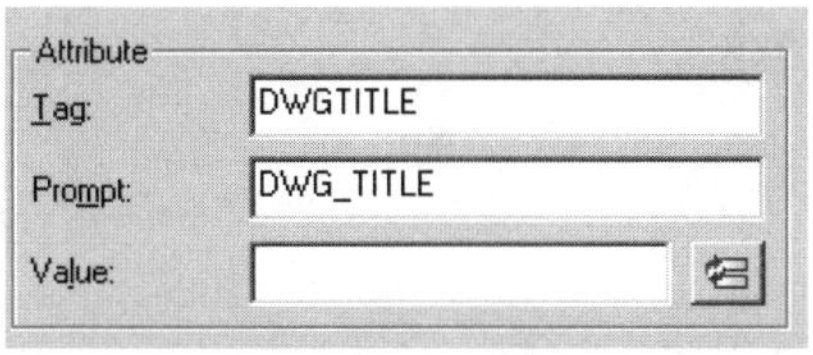

Enter **DWG_TITLE** in the Tag field.
Enter **DWG_TITLE** in the Prompt field.

Then select the **Insert Field** button.

58.

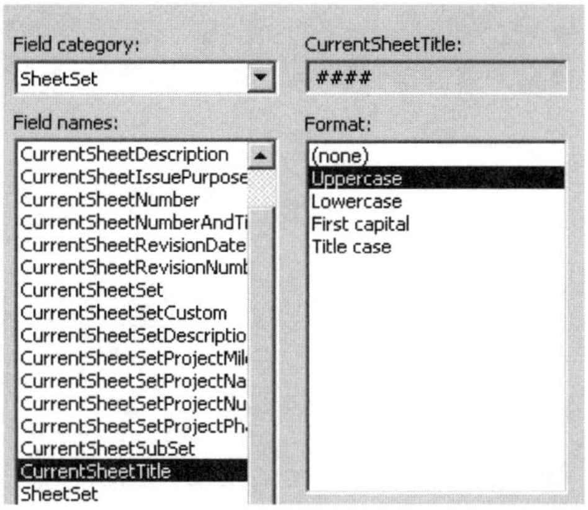

In the Field category, select **SheetSet**.

Highlight **CurrentSheetTitle** in the Field Names window.
Highlight **Uppercase** in the format field.

Press **OK**.

59.

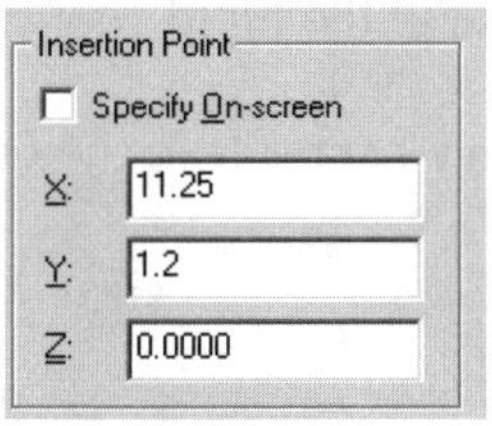

Under Insertion Point:

Set X to **11.25**.
Set Y to **1.2**.
Set Z to **0**.

60.

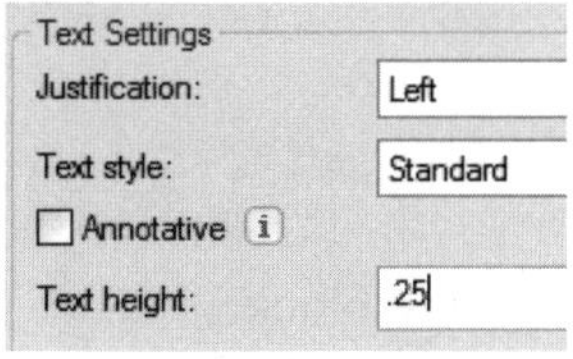

Under Text Options:

Set the Justification to **Left**.
Set the Height to **.25**.

> ***Tip:*** *The default insertion point is 0,0,0.*
>
> *If you forget to assign an insertion point, your attribute will be placed at 0,0,0. You can use the move tool to relocate the attribute into the title block.*

61.

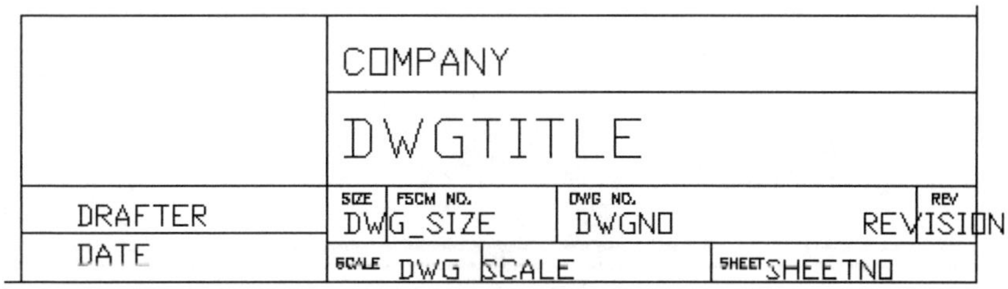

The title block should appear like as shown.

You'll notice that some of the attributes don't fit properly in the title block. This is OK. The values will fit just fine.

62. 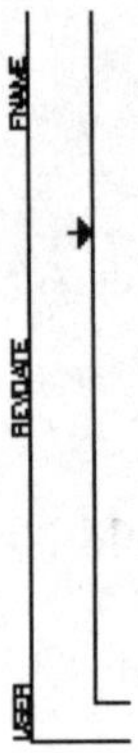

Erase the pre-defined attributes in the title block.

63. 

Select the **Field** tool from the Insert ribbon.

64. 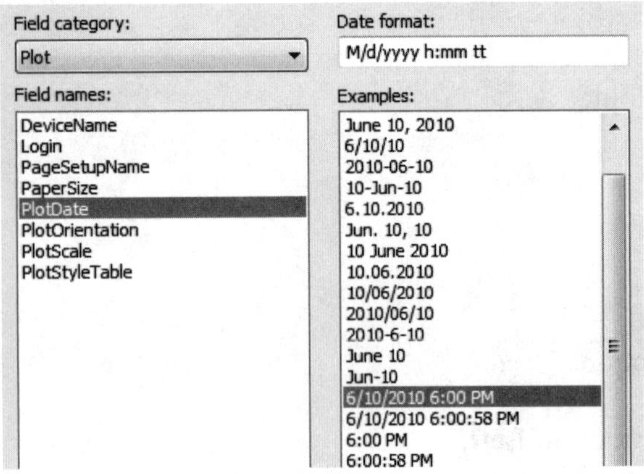

In the Field category, select **Plot**.

Highlight **PlotDate** in the Field Names window.
Highlight **M/dd/yyy h:mm tt** in the format field.

Press **OK**.

65. 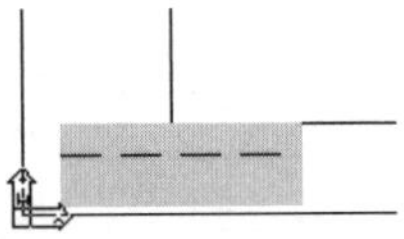

Place the field above the lower left corner of the title block.

66. 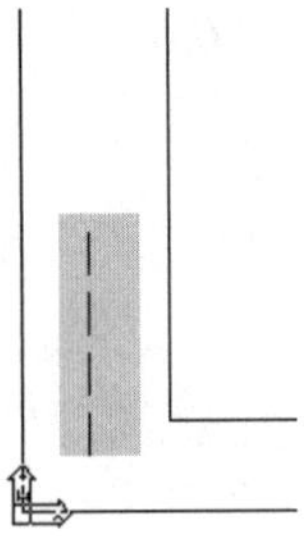

Rotate the field so that it is vertical.

This will act as a plot stamp for the sheet when it is plotted.

Adding a Logo

Many companies like to see their logo in the title block. AutoCAD allows you to insert graphics into drawings. Any gif, jpg, bmp, etc. can be inserted. For this lesson, we will use the logo for our college.

67. 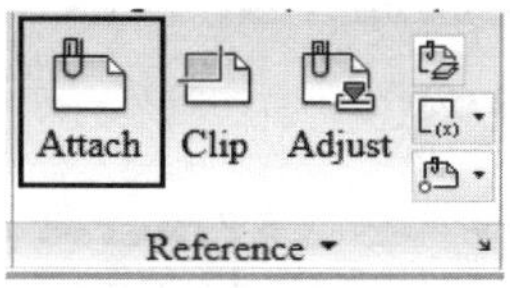

On the Insert ribbon, select **Reference→Attach.**

68. 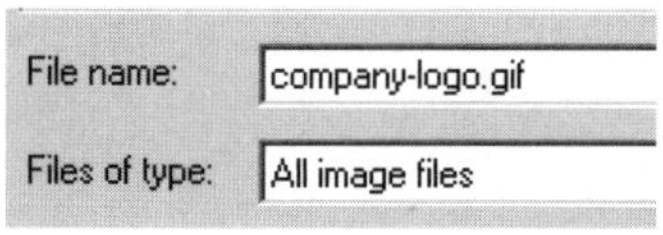

Use the **Browse** button to locate the image file.

Download the *company-logo.gif* file from the publisher.

69. 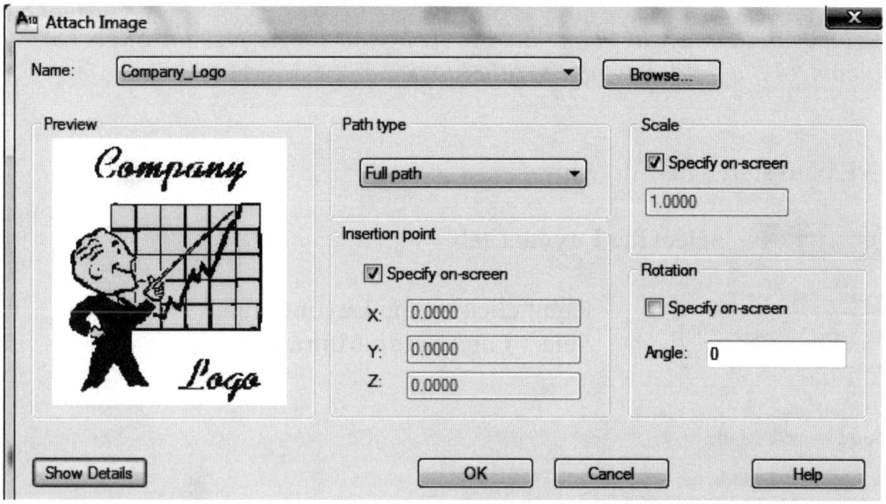

Press **OK**.

70. 

Locate the graphic as shown.
You can use the grips on the image to move and stretch the title block.

71. 

Save your file as *Custom-B.dwg.*

> ***Tip:*** *It is a good idea to save any custom blocks, toolbars, etc. in a separate directory away from AutoCAD. That way you can easily back up your custom work to use on another workstation and if you need to reinstall AutoCAD for any reason, you will not lose your work.*

Command Exercise

Exercise 12-2 – Inserting a Title Block

Drawing Name: **Custom B.dwg**
Estimated Time to Completion: 70 Minutes

Scope

Insert a title block onto a layout sheet. Set up the layout sheet. Use the Sheet Set Manager to control the field data on the title block.

Solution

1.  Start **QNEW** to start a new drawing.

2. 

Select the **Layout1** tab.

3. 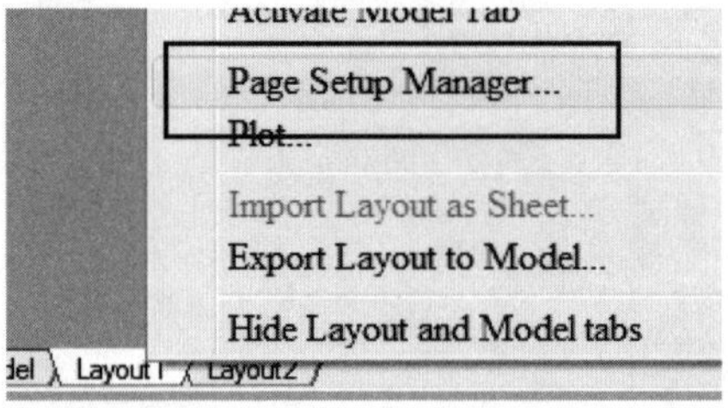

Right click on the **Layout1** tab.
Select **Page Setup Manager**.

4. 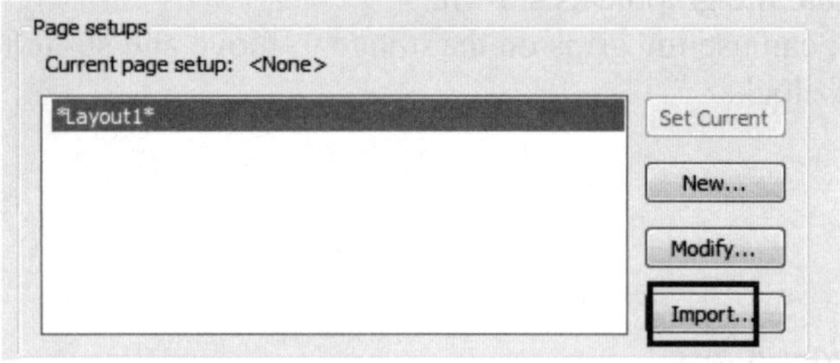

Select the **Import** button.

5. 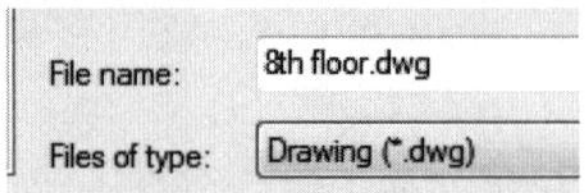

Locate the **8th floor** drawing in the exercise files.
Select **Open**.

6. 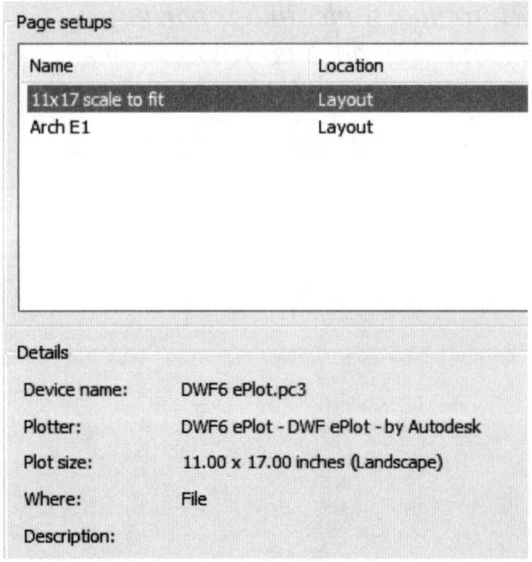

Highlight the **11 x 17 scale to fit** page set-up.

Note that the device name is set to DWF6. This is a virtual plotter.

Press **OK**.

7.

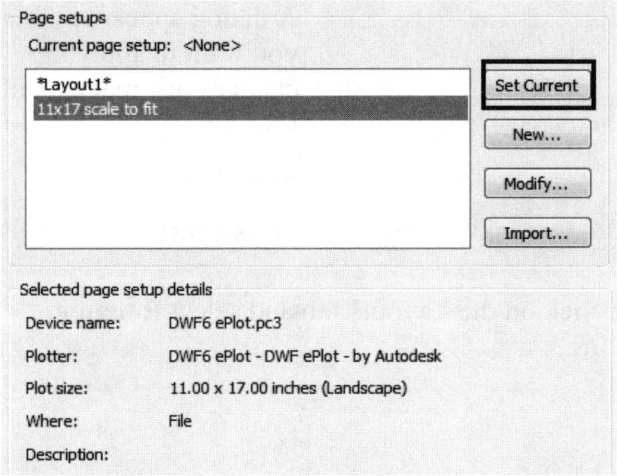

Highlight the new 11 x 17 page set-up.

Select **Set Current**.

Press **Modify**.

8.

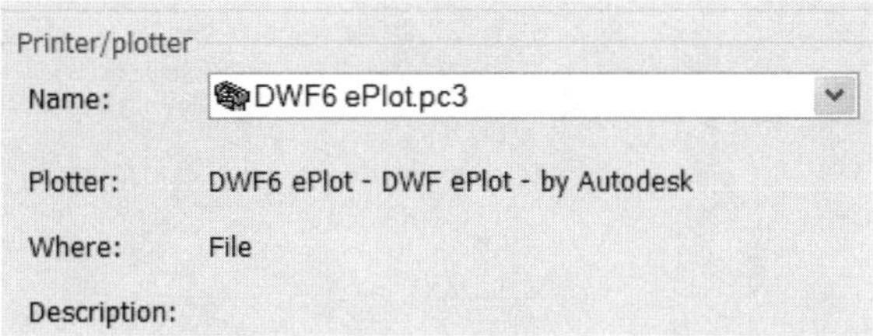

Note **DWF6 ePlot** is set as the plotter.

This driver creates a DWF file. A DWF file allows someone to view and plot an AutoCAD drawing file without having AutoCAD installed.

9.

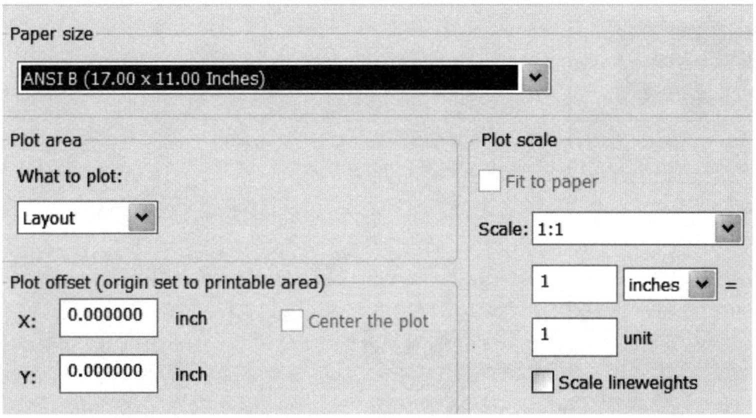

Select **ANSI B** as the paper size.

Set the Plot area to **Layout.**
Set the Plot scale to **1:1**.

10.

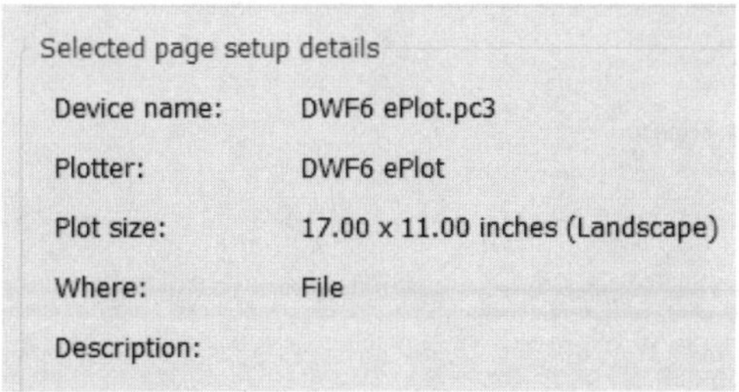

Confirm the page setup details.
Press **OK**.

11. 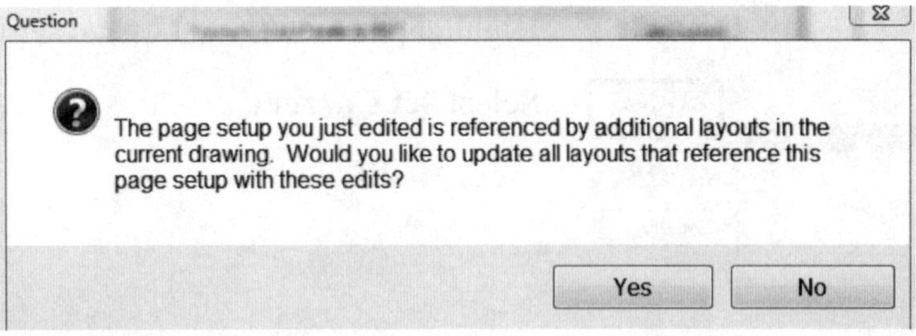

A dialog appears asking if you want to apply the changes just made to all layouts.

Press **Yes**.

Press **Close**.

12. 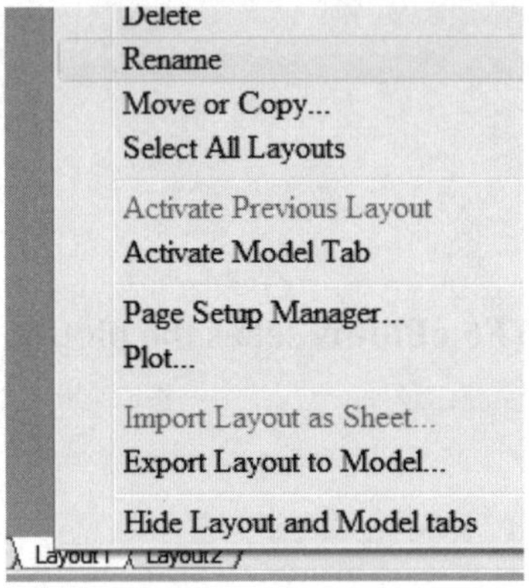

Right click on the Layout1 tab and select **Rename**.

13. 

Enter **Model Views** on the layout tab.

Inserting a Block:

Insert Menu	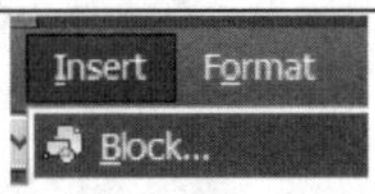
Draw toolbar	
Command line	Insert
Insert Ribbon	

14. 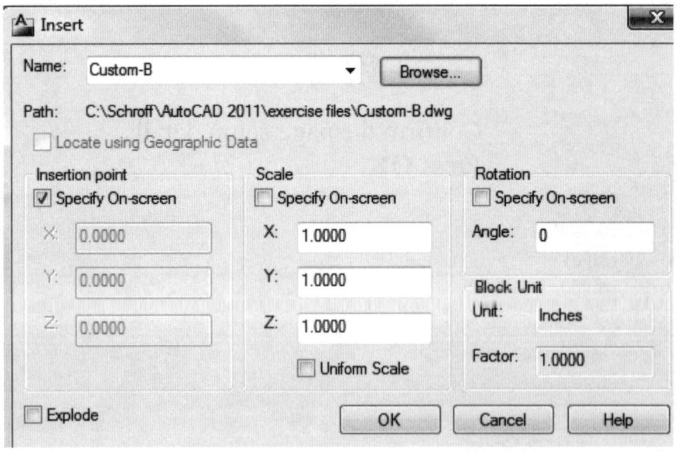

Select the **Insert Block** tool.
Locate your title block using the **Browse** button.
If you deselect the Specify On-Screen button under Insertion point, the title block will automatically insert at the origin (0,0,0).

15.

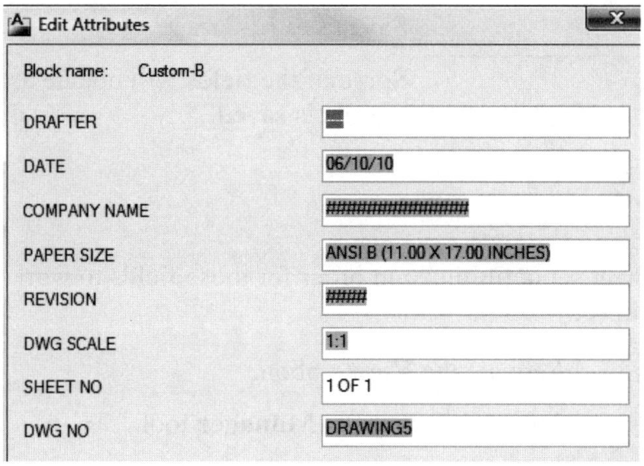

A dialog box will appear to prompt you for the attributes you defined.

Press **OK**.

> ***Tip:*** *If you were prompted on your command line for the attribute values instead of in a dialog box, then you need to reset your ATTDIA system variable. Type ATTDIA at the command line and enter '1'. This will enable the dialog box for attributes.*

16.

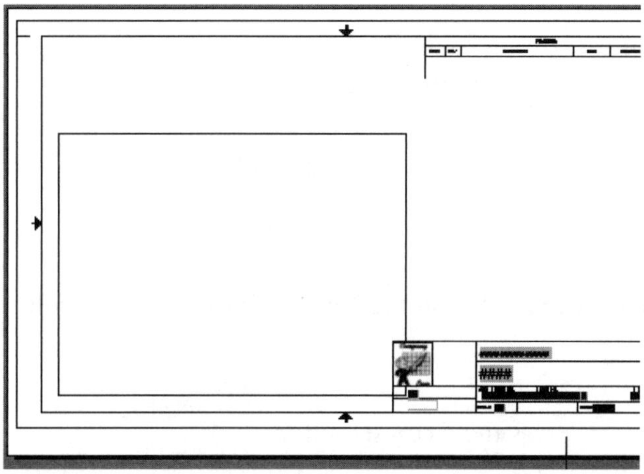

Your title block will appear in your drawing.

Notice that many of the fields are undefined.

17.

Go to **File→Drawing Utilities→Drawing Properties**.

18.

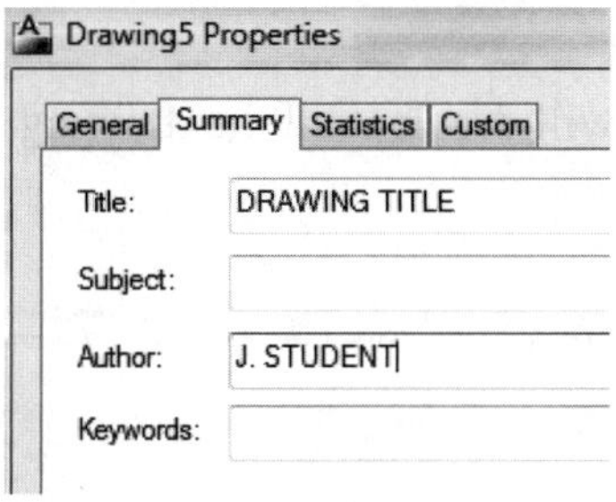

Select the **Summary** tab.

In the Title field, enter **DRAWING TITLE**.

In the Author field, enter your name.

Press **OK**.

19.

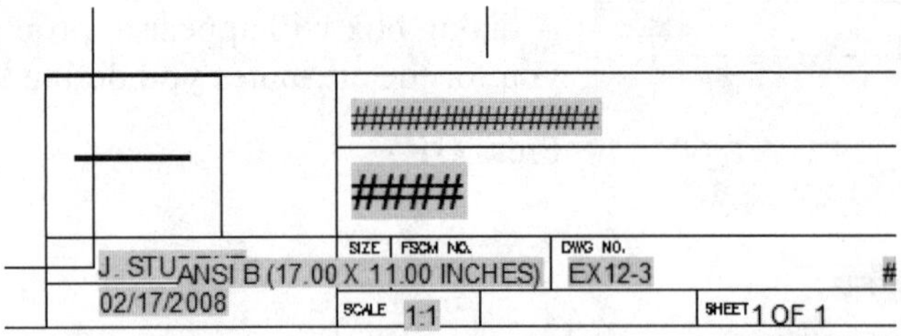

Save as *ex12-2.dwg*.

Some of the fields will update as soon the file is saved.

Many of the fields were linked to sheet set definitions; in order for those fields to work, the drawing has to be included in a sheet set.

20.

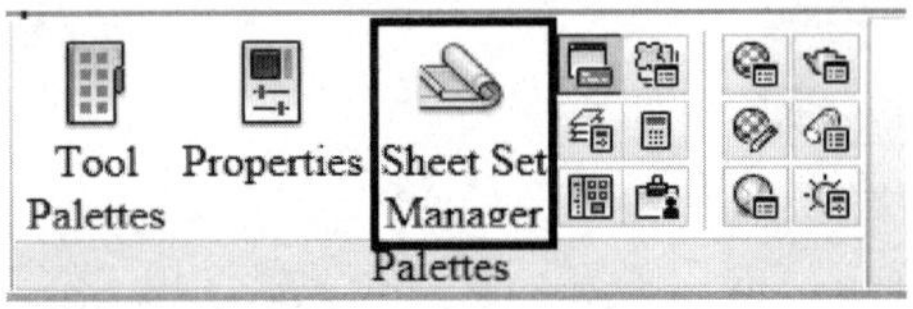

Activate the **View** ribbon.

Select the **Sheet Set Manager** tool.

21.

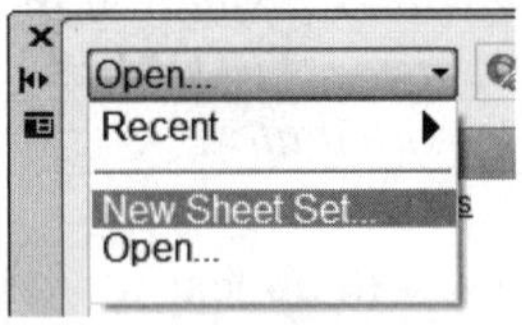

Go to **New Sheet Set**.

22.

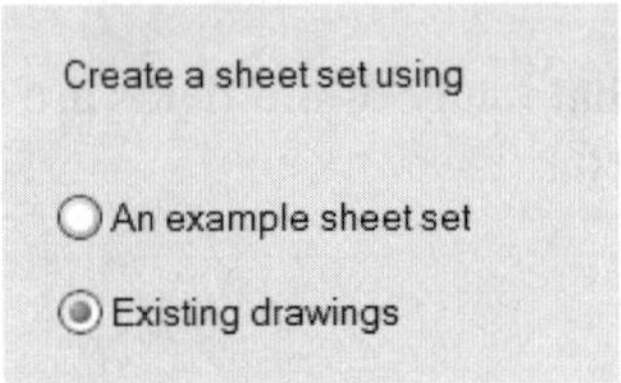

Enable **Existing drawings**.

Press **Next**.

23.

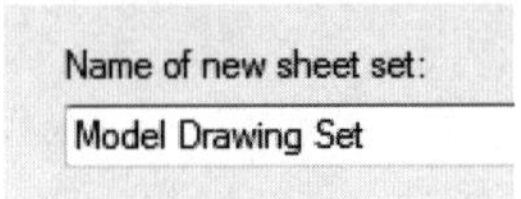

Enter **Model Drawing Set** in the Name of new sheet set field.

Press **Next**.

24.

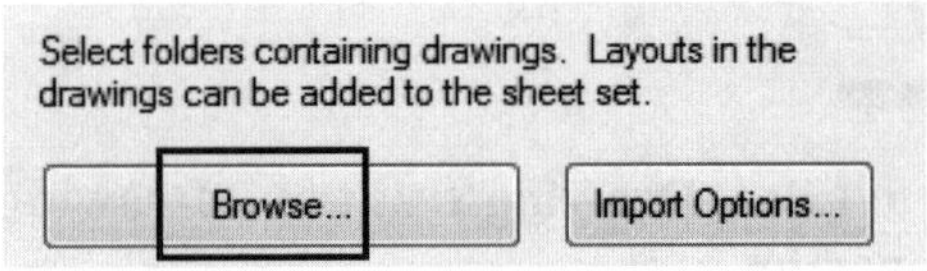

Press the **Browse** button.

25.

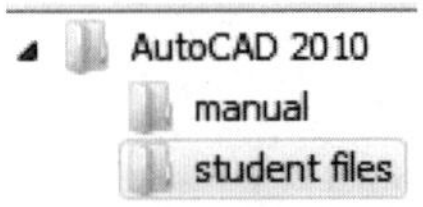

Locate the folder where you saved your file.

26.

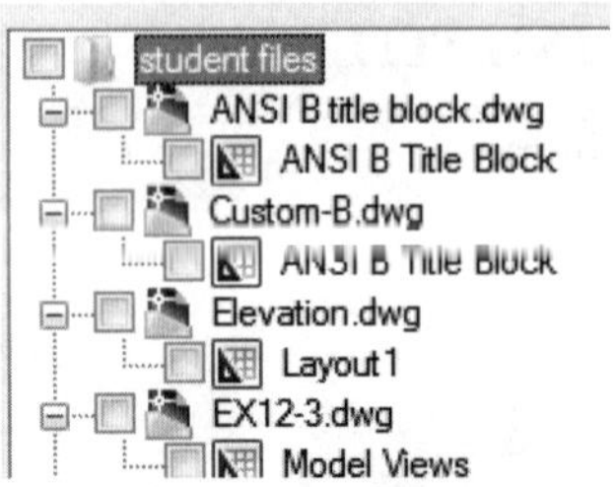

Uncheck the top folder. This will deselect all the drawing files in the folder.

27.

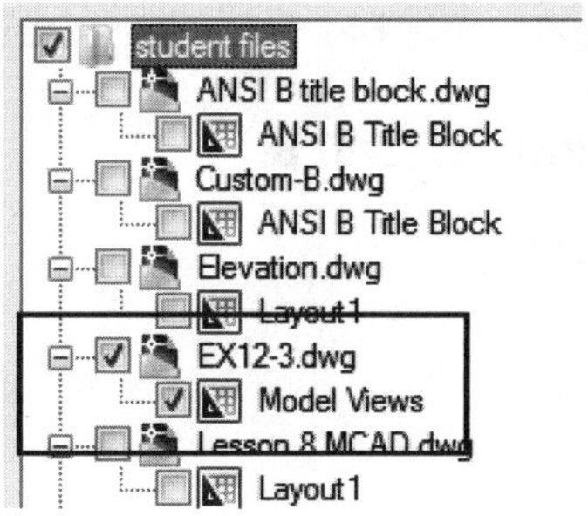

LMB on ***ex12-3.dwg***. This adds this file to the sheet set.

Press **Next**.

Press **Finish**.

28.

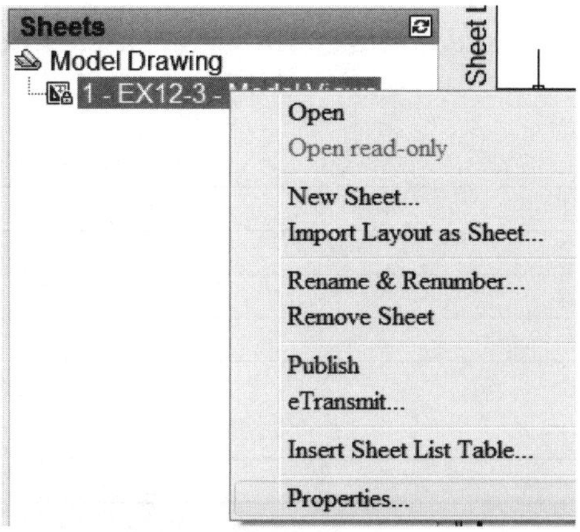

Highlight the Model Views sheet.

Right click and select **Properties**.

29.

Sheet	
Sheet title	Model Views
Sheet number	1
Description	MODEL LAYOUT
Include for publish	Yes
Expected layout	Model Views(C:\Schroff\AutoCAD 2009\student files\EX12-3.dwg)
Found layout	Model Views(C:\Schroff\AutoCAD 2009\student files\EX12-3.dwg)
Sheet set	Model Drawing
Revision number	A
Revision date	
Purpose	
Category	

Under Sheet title, enter **Model Views**.
Under Description, type **MODEL LAYOUT**.
Under Revision Number, enter **A**.

Close the dialog.

30.

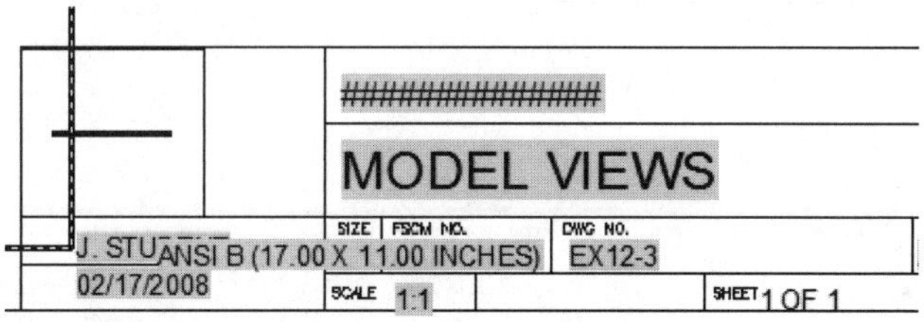

Type **REGEN** on the command line.

The Revision number now appears.

The Company data does not appear because that field was defined in the title block not in the current drawing.

31.

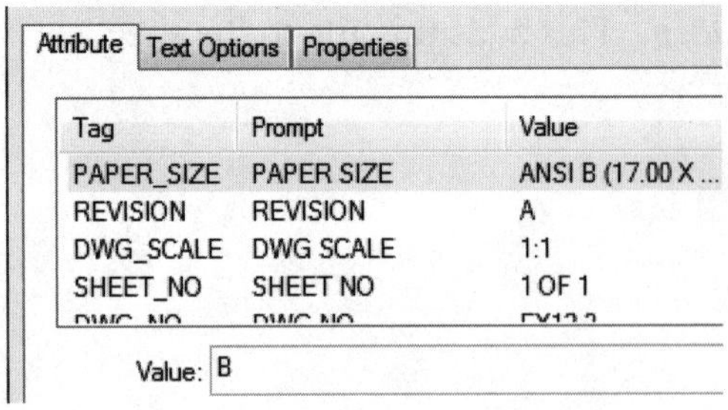

Double click on the title block and the Attribute Editor will appear.
Change the PAPER SIZE to **B**.

Save as *ex12-4.dwg*.

A good rule of thumb when plotting is that the plot scale is the inverse of the scale of the title block...

When plotting to an 81/2 x 11 size sheet of paper:

A size title block	1:1
B size title block	1:2
C size title block	1:4
D size title block	1:8

When plotting to an 11 x 17 size sheet of paper:

A size title block	1:2
B size title block	1:1
C size title block	1:2
D size title block	1:4

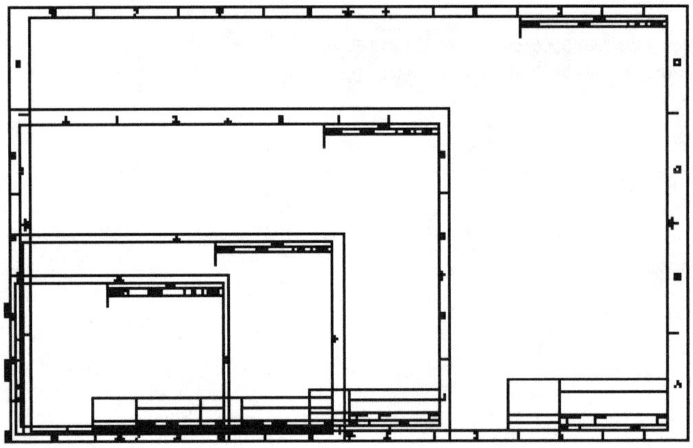

Command Exercise

Exercise 12-3 – Creating a Template

Drawing Name: **Custom B.dwg**
Estimated Time to Completion: 70 Minutes

Scope

Insert a title block onto a layout sheet. Set up the layout sheet. Use the Sheet Set Manager to control the field data on the title block.

Solution

1.  Start **QNEW** to start a new drawing.

2. 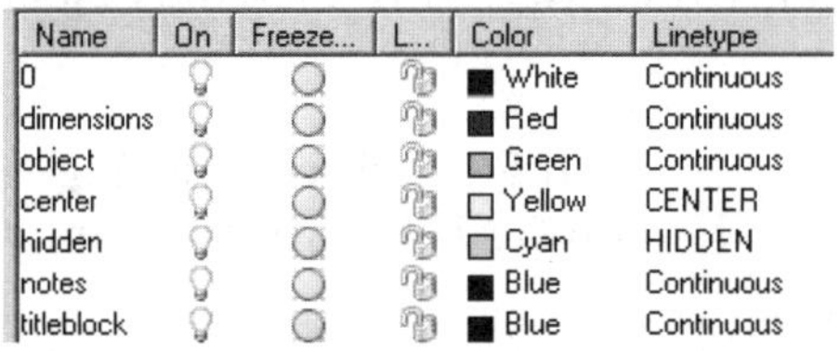 Set up your layers:

Name	On	Freeze...	L...	Color	Linetype
0				White	Continuous
dimensions				Red	Continuous
object				Green	Continuous
center				Yellow	CENTER
hidden				Cyan	HIDDEN
notes				Blue	Continuous
titleblock				Blue	Continuous

3. 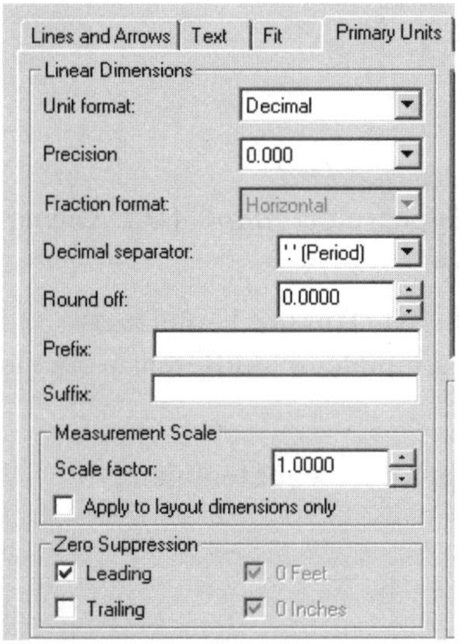

Set up your dimension style:

Set the Precision to **0.000**.
Suppress Leading Zeros.

Set the Fit to **Text**.

4. 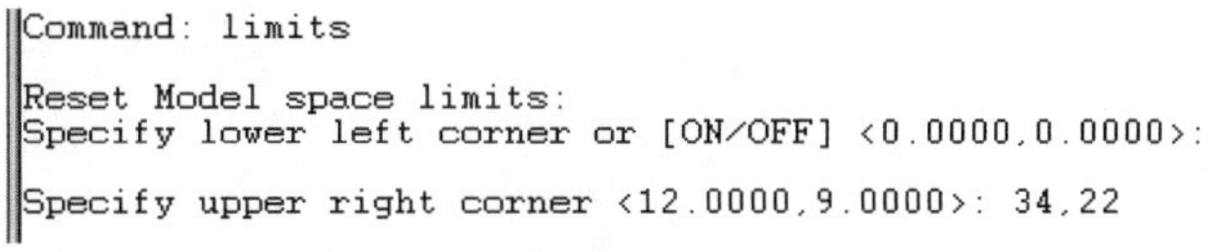

Set the limits.
Type **LIMITS** on the command line.

Set the lower left corner to the default.
Set the upper right corner to 34, 22.

Turn the UCSICON off.
Type **UCSICON** on the command line.
Type **OFF**.

5.  Select **Insert Block**.

6. 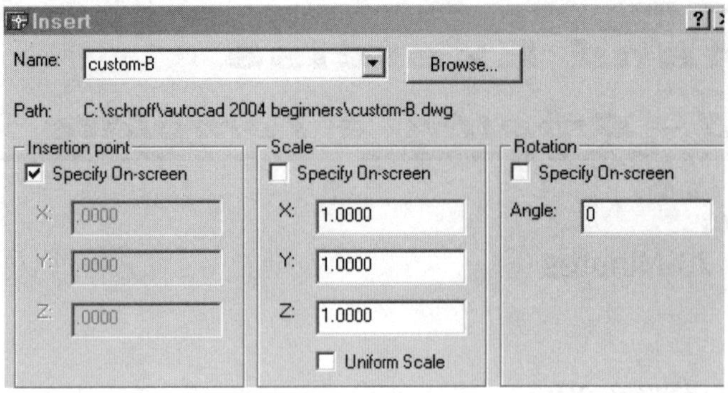

Locate the *custom-B* title block.
Enable **Specify On-Screen**.
Press **OK**.
Instead of selecting an insertion point, press **<ESC>**.

> ***Tip:*** *By pressing <ESC> you don't actually place the block. Instead you are storing it locally in the drawing, so you don't have to browse for it when you are ready to insert it.*

7. If you are planning on using layout sheets, you can insert the title block onto the first layout sheet instead of pressing <ESC>.

8. 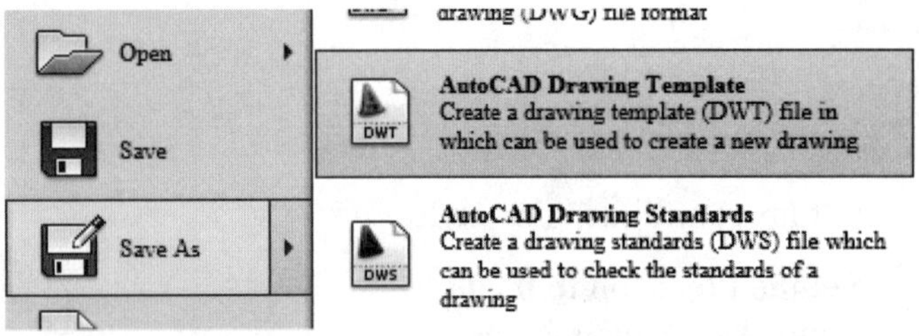

Go to **File→Save Drawing As→ AutoCAD Drawing Template**.

9. 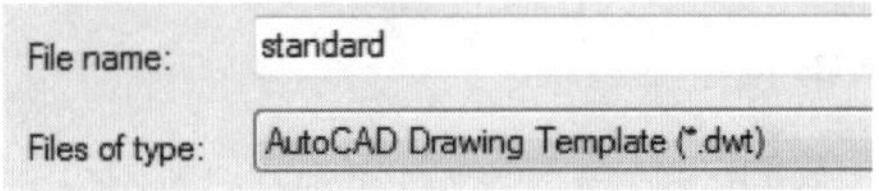

Call your template *standard.*
Under Files of Type, select *AutoCAD Drawing Template (*.dwt).*

Store your template in a directory away from AutoCAD – NOT in the Templates subdirectory. That way you can back up and copy your template to a different work station as needed.

10. 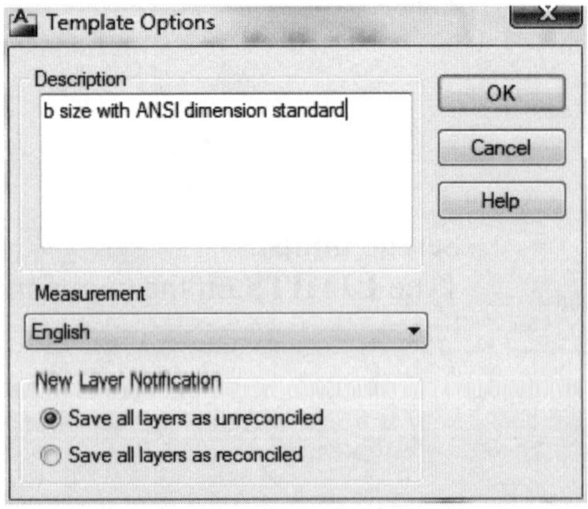

Enter a description for your template.

Press **OK**.

> ***Tip:*** *You can use the shortcut key Ctl+Shift+S to perform a File Save As.*

11. 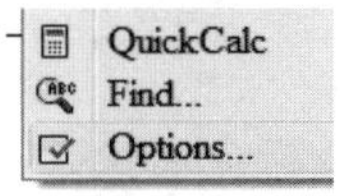

Right click in the window and select **Options**.

12. 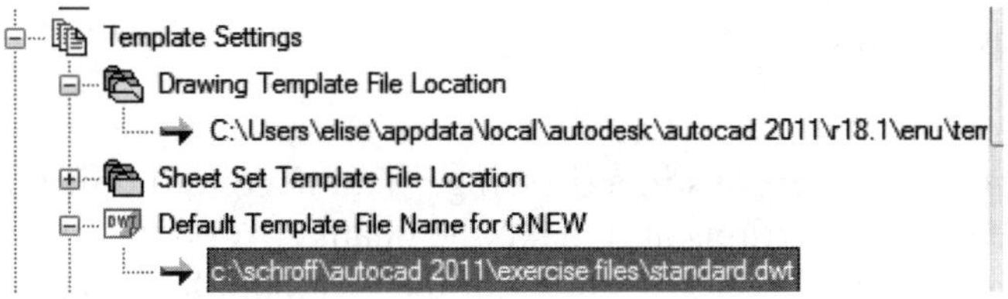

Select the File tab.
Under Drawing Template Settings, set the Default Template File Name for QNEW to use the standard.dwt file you just created.

Save and close the template file.

13. 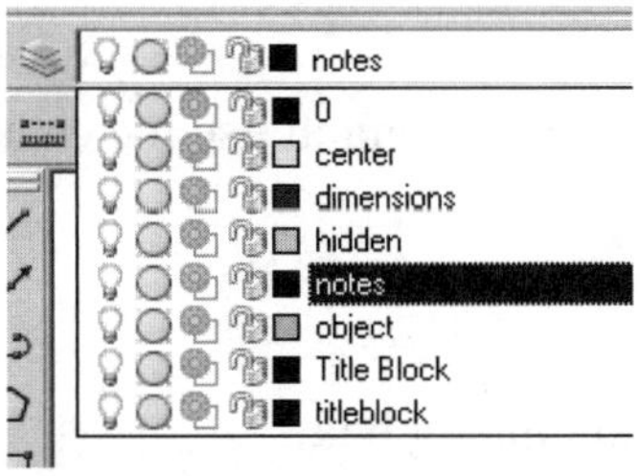

Start QNEW to start a new drawing.

Note your layers are already set up.

14.  Select the **Insert Block** tool.

15. 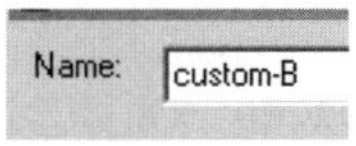

Press **Cancel**.

Note that your title block is already loaded and available to be placed.

Close without saving.

Review Questions

1. **T F** If you insert a titleblock into a drawing and then modify the external titleblock drawing, it will automatically update in the drawing(s) where it was inserted.

2. You have a local block with multiple insertions in a drawing. You need to modify the block. You explode one of the block insertions and make the change. You then use BMAKE and select the modified former block. You assign the original block name to the modified block. What happens to the other block insertions in the drawing?
   - ❑ They remain unchanged.
   - ❑ They are deleted.
   - ❑ They update to the new block definition.
   - ❑ They become unnamed blocks.

3. **T F** If you do not assign an insertion point to a block, it will by default use the center of the object selected.

4. An insertion point for a block can be defined by:
   - ❑ Entering an X, Y, and Z value in the Block Definition dialog box.
   - ❑ Entering an X, Y, and Z value in the Block Definition dialog box.
   - ❑ Enabling the Align Below Previous Attribute
   - ❑ All of the above

5. **T F** Blocks can have names up to 255 characters long and include spaces.

6. **T F** When defining a block, you can determine the units or if it will be Unitless. For example, if a block were defined with units of inches and then inserted into a drawing whose base units were millimeters, it would automatically scale by a factor of 25.4.

7. Attributes are created using the _________ command
   - ❑ ATTREQ
   - ❑ ATTDIA
   - ❑ ATTDISP
   - ❑ ATTDEF

8. You create a title block drawing with attribute definitions. Next you wblock it and try to insert it into a separate drawing. You then get this error message:
   - ❑ Block is Redefined
   - ❑ Block references itself
   - ❑ Memory overload
   - ❑ Fatal error – computer will now reformat your hard drive

Review Answers

1. **T F** If you insert a titleblock into a drawing and then modify the external titleblock drawing, it will automatically update in the drawing(s) where it was inserted.

   True

2. You have a local block with multiple insertions in a drawing. You need to modify the block. You explode one of the block insertions and make the change. You then use BMAKE and select the modified former block. You assign the original block name to the modified block. What happens to the other block insertions in the drawing?

   ❑ *They update to the new block definition.*

3. **T F** If you do not assign an insertion point to a block, it will by default use the center of the object selected.

   False

4. An insertion point for a block can be defined by:

   ❑ *All of the above*

5. **T F** Blocks can have names up to 255 characters long and include spaces.

   True

6. **T F** When defining a block, you can determine the units or if it will be Unitless. For example, if a block were defined with units of inches and then inserted into a drawing whose base units were millimeters, it would automatically scale by a factor of 25.4.

   True

7. Attributes are created using the _________ command

   ❑ *ATTDEF*

8. You create a title block drawing with attribute definitions. Next you wblock it and try to insert it into a separate drawing. You then get this error message:

   ❑ *Block references itself*

Notes:

Lesson 13.0 – Viewports and Layouts

Estimated Class Time – 2.5 Hours

Objectives

This section will cover how to create a drawing Layout from a Model and how to plot a drawing. The general idea is to create the drawing in the Model space window and plot the drawing from the paper space Layout window. Drawings may also be plotted in Model space. There are advantages and disadvantages to using the Model or Layout mode to plot a drawing.

Model Space is the environment in which you create your two–dimensional drawing, or your three–dimensional model. Paper Space (Layout) is the environment where you set up your drawing or model to plot. Although you can plot your drawing in Paper Space or in Model Space, there are certain advantages to setting up your drawing to plot in Paper Space. In Paper Space, you can create multiple views at multiple scales of the same model or drawing. You can also freeze layers in selected paper space view ports. There are a few tricks to working with Paper Space such as controlling line type scales and dimensioning.

Sheets Sets are used to plot multiple drawings. They are an easy way to organize drawing packages for plotting and editing.

Section Objectives:

- **Drawing Layout**
  Create a drawing layout from the drawing Model.
- **Drawing Layout Viewports**
  Insert a title block in the paper space Layout and create drawing views.
- **Adding Viewports**
- **Converting Existing Dimensions to Annotative**
- **Using Annotative Scales**
- **Controlling Viewport Properties**
- **Nonrectangular Viewports**
- **Using the Layout Wizard**
- **Controlling visibility of layers in viewports**
- **Plotting and Output**
- **Layout Settings**
- **Sheet Sets**
- **Sheet List Tables**

Option	Model	Layout
Drawing views	In model space, only one view of the drawing may be printed at a time.	In the Layout mode, or paper space, it is possible to plot multiple views of the same drawing. These views can show different parts of the drawing, and views can be zoomed at different scales.
Drawing Layers	In model space, layers are either visible or not since there is only one view port.	In the Layout mode, Layers can be frozen in one view port, but not in the other.
Plot Scale	In model space, the drawing must be plotted to scale. It is therefore important that the drawing limits and title block reflect the drawing scale. Text, Dimension Styles and LTSCALE (linetype scale) must also reflect the plot scale.	Drawings views placed in the Layout Mode must be zoomed to scale (X/XP). Dimensions, notes and the title block are placed in the Layout at a scale of 1. The drawing Layout is plotted at a scale of 1.
Drawing Revisions	In model space, the drawing must be revised in each instance the image is copied in the drawing (for instance if a detail was shown at a scale of 1:1 and 1:10).	In the drawing Layout, each view represents a single drawing. Therefore if a change is made to the drawing in Model space, the changes will automatically be reflected in the Layout view ports.

Drawing Layout

Command Locator

Toolbar Menu	**Layouts / New Layout** and **Layouts / Layout from Template**
Pull Down Menu	**Insert / Layout /** *(select option)*
Command	**Layout**
Dialog Box	**Page Setup Layout**

Command Overview

The first time the Layout tab is selected, the user will be presented with the Page Setup Layout dialog box. Plot settings for the drawing layout can be chosen here, or specified later by invoking the Plot command. If the default settings of the Page Setup Layer dialog box are accepted (press OK), the Layout will display a single view of the drawing. The dashed line in the drawing layout will represent the plot area of the paper.

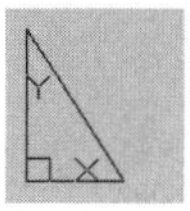

The icon in the lower left corner indicates that the user is viewing the drawing Layout or *paper space*. When the Zoom command is used in the PAPER space mode, the entire drawing layout is affected. When the Zoom command is used with the viewports in the MODEL space mode *(see next section)*, only the active viewport will be zoomed. The Title block should be inserted in the Layout PAPER space mode. The Title block should always be slightly smaller than the paper size, because the plot area will always be less than the paper size, as indicated by the dashed rectangle.

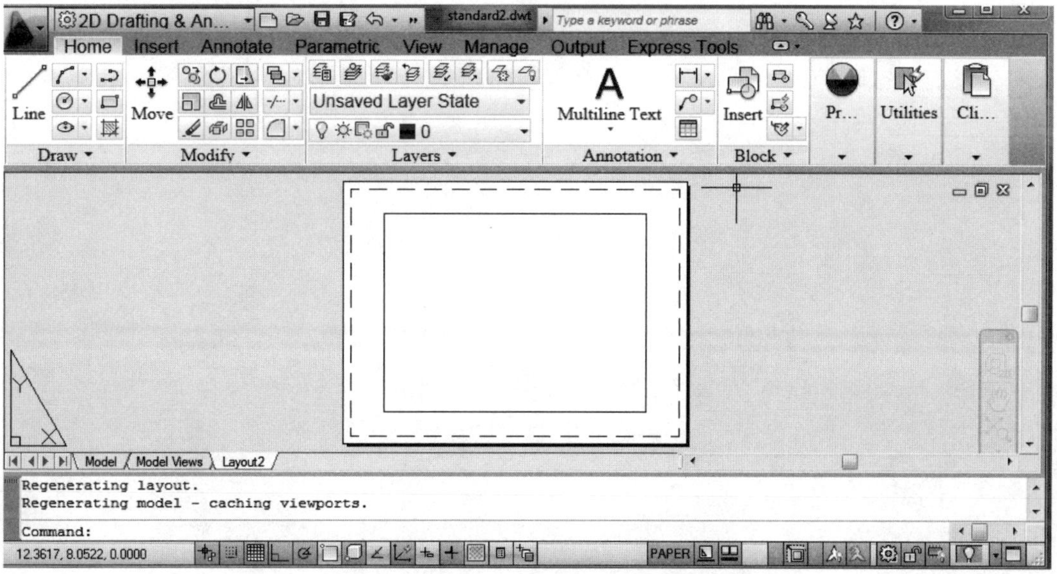

Drawing Layout, Paper Space

General Procedures

1. Create the drawing in Model space mode.
2. Select the Layout tab in the Drawing Window.
3. Select OK to accept the Page Setup Layout defaults.
4. Use the Block Insert command to insert a Title Block.

Tips & Tricks

- The Layout Page Setup can be changed by invoking the Plot command or the Page Setup command.
- Select the Model tab in the drawing window to return to Model space.
- The Title Block insertion point is typically 0,0. The scale factors should be 1 and the rotation angle should be 0.
- Place the viewport on a layer that is set not to plot and you will never have to worry about the viewport border being visible in your plots.
- Create as many layouts as needed to show all the views of the drawing necessary.
- You may name the layout using up to 255 characters, however, only the first 32 characters will show on the name tab.
- You can move your layouts so that they are in a desired order to make it easier to navigate through a drawing set.

Command Exercise

Exercise 13-1 – Creating a New Layout

Drawing Name: **nlayout1.dwg**
Estimated Time to Completion: 5 Minutes

Scope

Create a new layout in the drawing called 'Plan'.

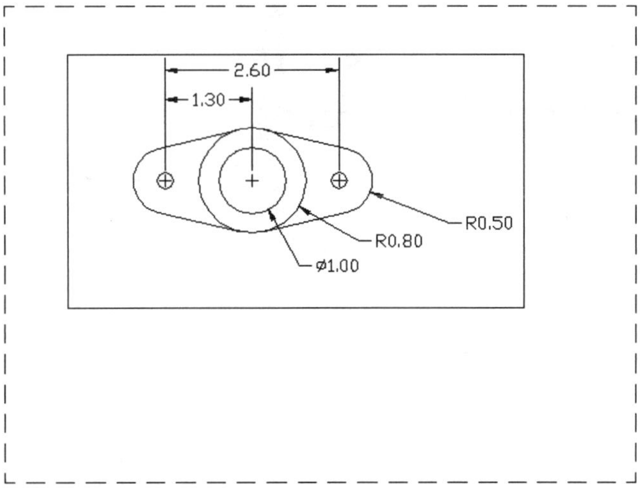

New Layout Exercise

Solution

1. 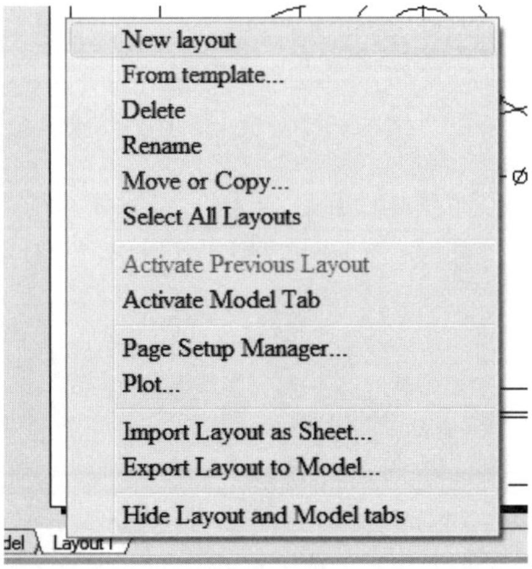

Right click on the Layout 1 tab and select **New layout**.

2. 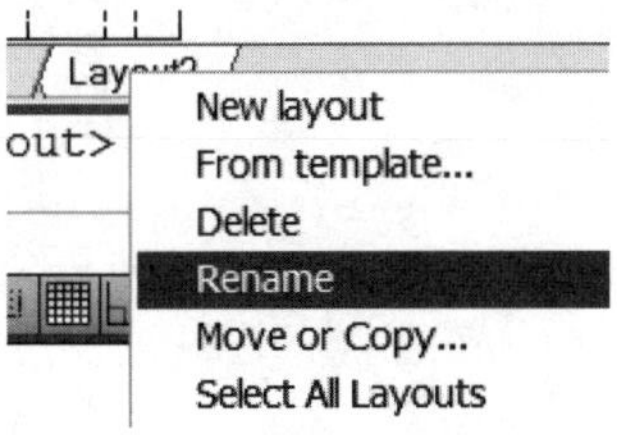

RMB on the new layout tab.

Select Rename.

Type **Plan** to change the layout name.

3. 

Click on the new **Plan** tab.

4. 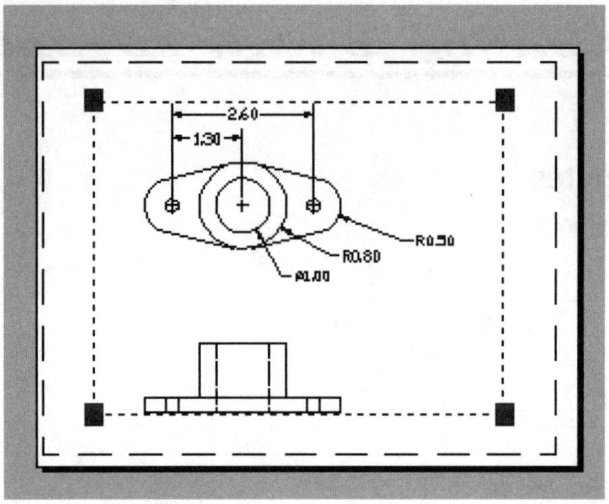

Click on the viewport border to activate its grips.

5. 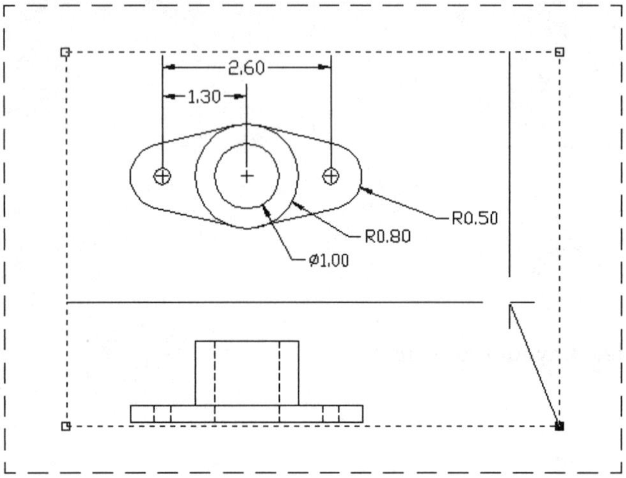

Specify stretch point or [Base point/ Copy/Undo/eXit]:
Stretch the border as shown in the following figure to show only the plan (top) view of the drawing.

Press <ESC> to release the grips.

Drawing Layout Viewports

Command Locator

View Ribbon	
Toolbar Menu	**Viewports**
Pull Down Menu	**View→Viewports** / *(select option)*
Command	**viewports**
Alias	**vports**
RMB Shortcut Menu	**Viewports** *(when New viewports is selected)*

Command Overview

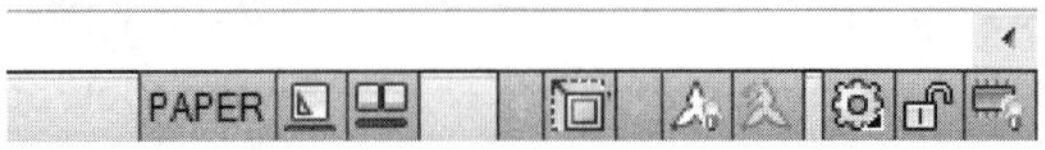

Unlike tiled viewports in the Model space drawing window, viewports in the Layout window can be rectangular or irregular polygon shapes. They can be moved, resized and copied using the grip options or the regular Modify commands, and they can be *clipped.* They can even overlap other viewports. For this reason, they are sometimes referred to as *floating* viewports. When the drawing is zoomed in the PAPER space mode, the entire Layout is zoomed.

When the Layout viewports are switched from the PAPER space mode to the MODEL space mode, from the Status Bar, only the active viewport will be zoomed. Select the viewport to zoom and Zoom All first. Repeat the zoom command by pressing <ENTER> or by typing Z. Type the scale factor, followed by XP (for *times paper space*). For example, 1xp would be a scale of 1:1, and 1/2xp would be a scale of 1:2. When all of the viewports have been properly zoomed, switch back to the PAPER space mode by selecting the word MODEL in the Status Bar.

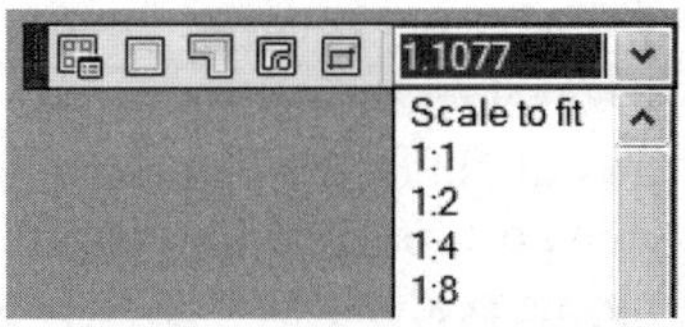

Applying a Viewport Scale

You may also use the Viewport Scale Control on the Viewports toolbar. This is a drop-down list of the available scales and is much easier to use than setting the zoom factor correctly. To use this, just select the border of the viewport to scale, then select the scale from the Viewport Scale Control.

The general rule is to create the drawing in the Model space window, and setup the drawing to plot from the Layout tab. Use either the PAPER or MODEL mode to adjust the viewport size and views. Then switch back to PAPER to plot the drawing.

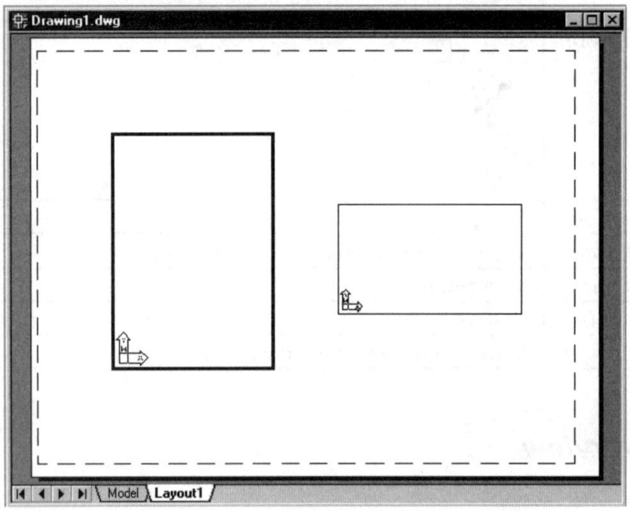

Drawing Layout, Floating Model Space Viewport

General Procedures

1. Create the drawing in Model space (the Model tab should be selected).
2. Select the Layout tab in the Drawing Window. Select OK to accept the Page Setup Layout defaults.
3. Use grips to re-size the viewport. Use the Viewports command options to create additional views.
4. Select PAPER in the Status Bar. This will switch the viewport mode to floating MODEL space. Select a viewport and Zoom the drawing view to scale.
5. Select MODEL in the Status Bar to switch the viewport mode back to PAPER space. Add notes, dimensions, etc. and plot the drawing.

- Make modifications to the drawing any time in the Model tab. Select Layout to switch back to the drawing Layout.
- Avoid placing one floating viewport inside another, as it may be difficult to select a floating model space viewport.
- After the drawing view is properly scaled in the floating MODEL space viewport, use the Pan command to adjust views without changing the scale.
- You can insert several drawings into model space using the INSERT or XREF command. Then create a layout for each drawing. Using this method, you can set up a master control drawing to allow you view a complete drawing package.

Command Exercise

Exercise 13-2 – Adding a Viewport

Drawing Name: **nlayout2.dwg**
Estimated Time to Completion: 15 Minutes

Scope

Create a new viewport. Add a scale to the scale list. Set the viewport scale. Lock the viewport display.

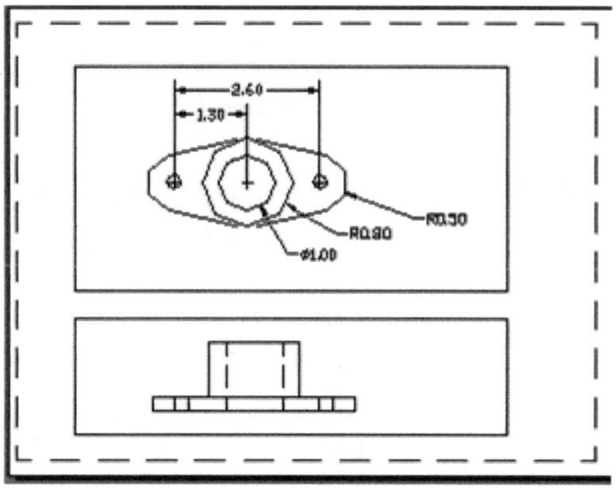

New Viewport Exercise

Solution

1. 

Select the Layout 1 tab.

   There should not be a viewport on it.
   You should see only a blank sheet of paper.
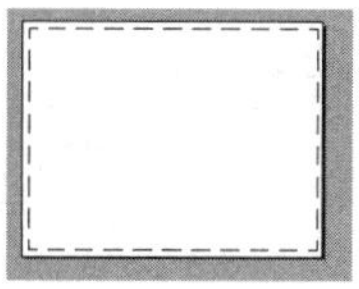

2. 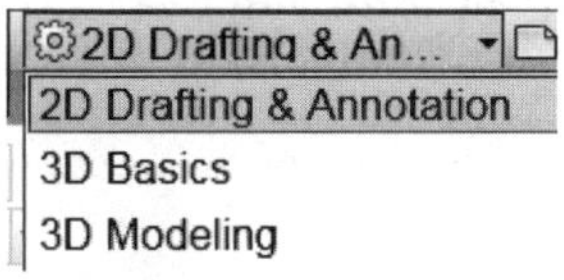

Set your workspace to **2D Drafting & Annotation**.

3. 
Verify that Quick Properties is **enabled**.

4. 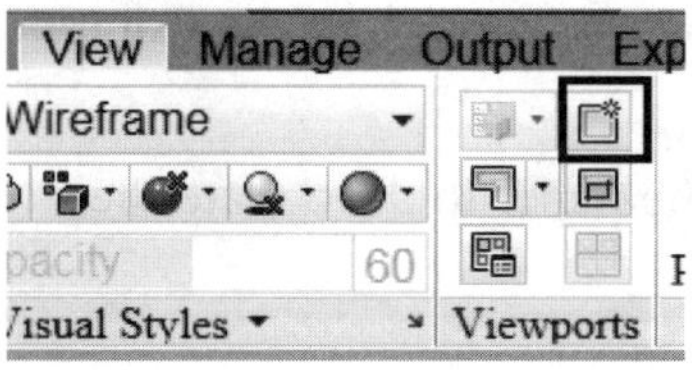

Select the **New** viewport tool on the View ribbon.

5. 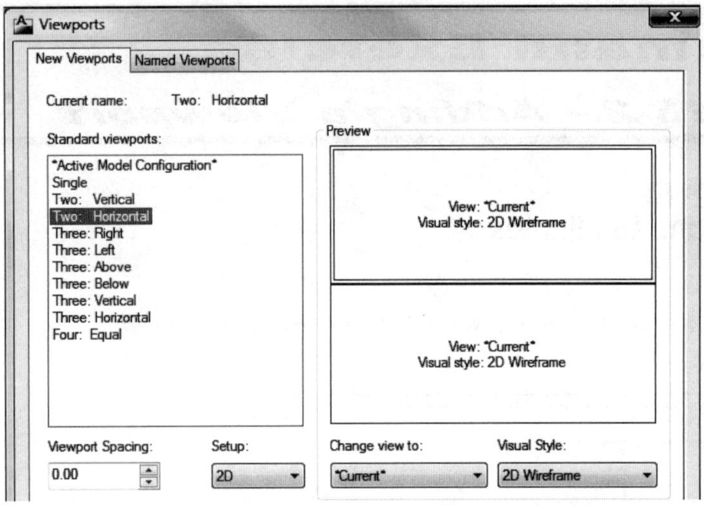

Select the **Two:Horizontal** option.

Press **OK**.

6. 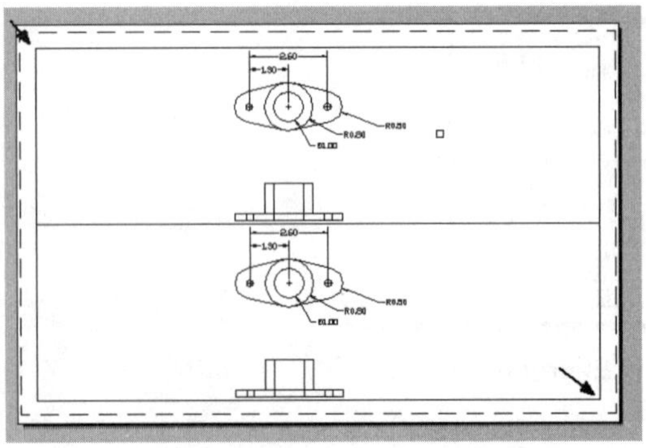

Select two points (similar to drawing a rectangle).

7. 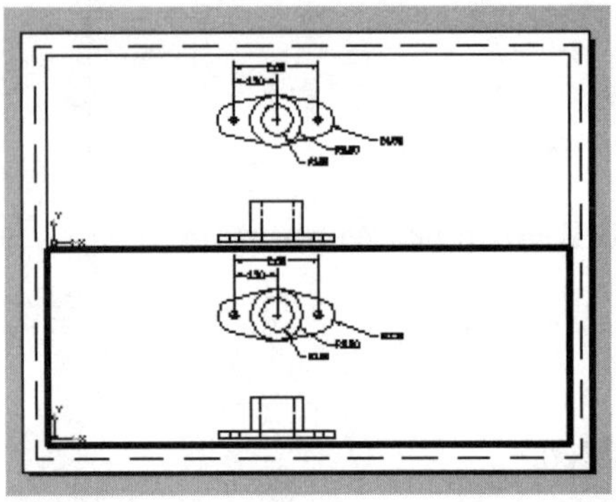

Double click LMB inside the lower viewport to activate MODEL space.

This will be indicated in two ways. The active viewport's border will appear bold and the word MODEL will be active in the Status Bar.

8. 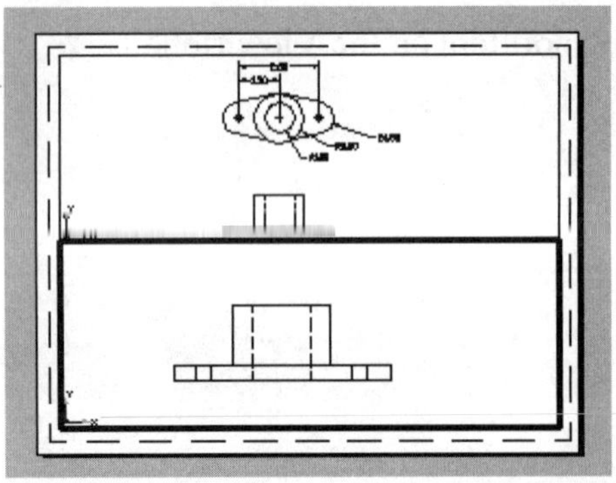

Use **Zoom Window** to zoom into the front view of the model.

Click outside of the paper to deactivate the viewport.

9. 

Select the viewport border so it highlights.

The scale of the viewport is displayed on the Status Bar.

10. 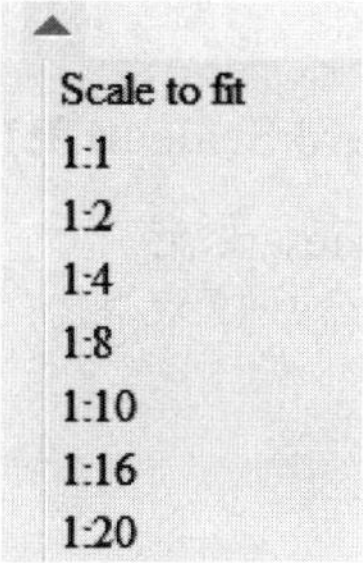

Left click on the viewport scale indicator.

A list of available scales is displayed.

We would like a 3:1 scale which is currently not available.

11. 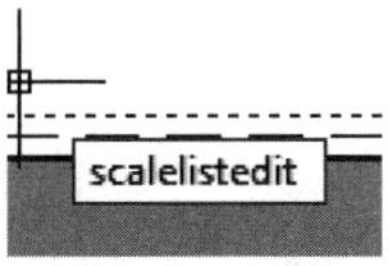

Type **SCALELISTEDIT**.

12. 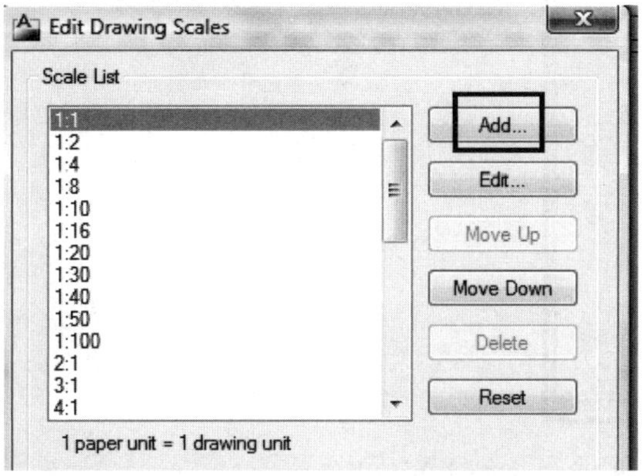

Select **Add**.

13. 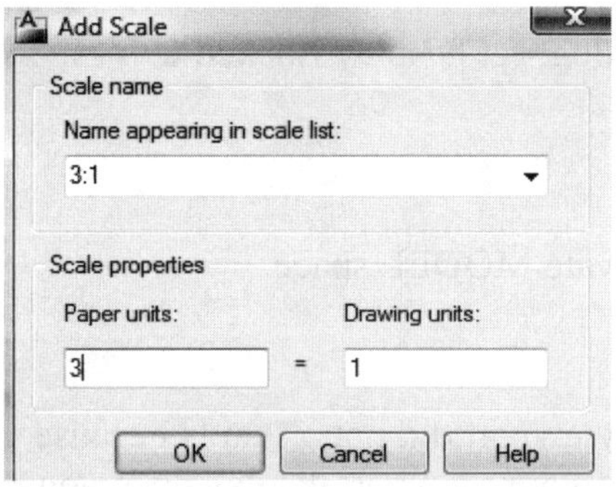

Type **3:1** in the first field.

Set the paper units to **3**.
Set the drawing units to **1**.

Press **OK**.

14. 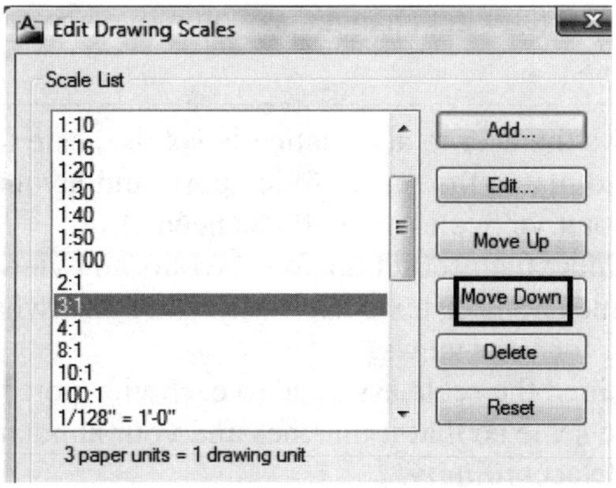

Use the **Move Down** button to position the 3:1 scale between the 2:1 and 4:1 scales.

Press **OK**.

15. 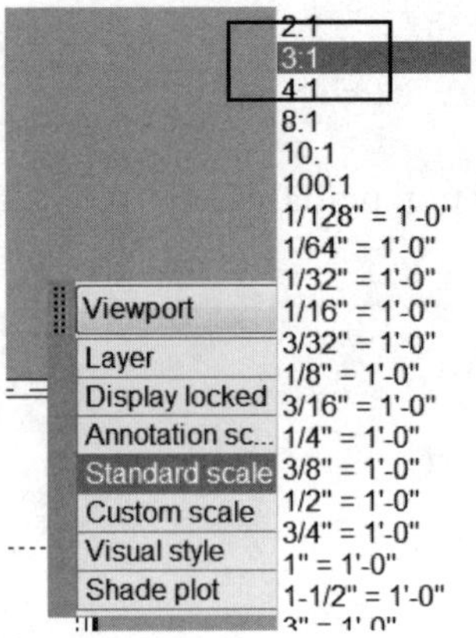

Select the bottom viewport so it highlights.

In the Quick Properties dialog, set the Standard Scale to **3:1**.

Click outside the sheet to deactivate for the viewport.
If clicking outside the sheet doesn't work, press <ESC>.

Repeat for the top viewport.

16. 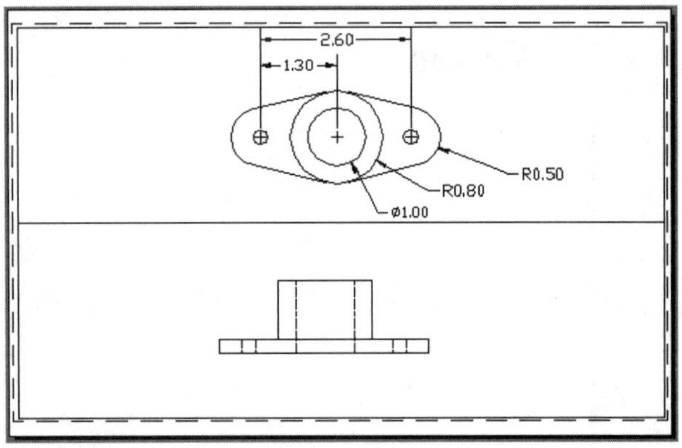

Line up the top and bottom views.

17. 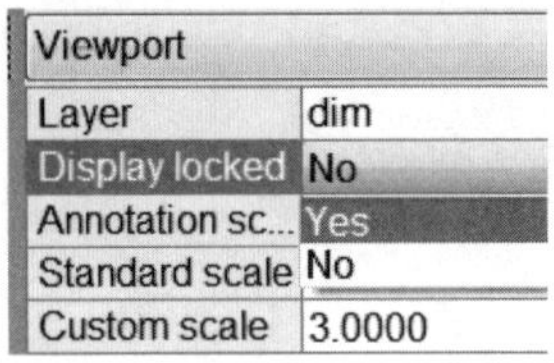

Select the viewport border so it highlights.

In the Quick Properties dialog, set Display Locked to **Yes**.

18. Double click LMB inside the lower viewport to activate MODEL space.

19. Select **Zoom Extents**.

20. Note that your display changed, but the view in the viewport did not. That is because you locked the viewport display. It is a good idea to lock your viewport display once you have set up your view to ensure that it does not accidentally get changed as you move about your drawing.

Tips & Tricks

- Annotative Scale allows the user to automatically set the scale for dimensions and notes to match the scale of viewports and layouts. You can reset the Annotative Scale on the fly as needed.
- If you elect to use this new feature, set up your layouts and viewports before you add any dimensions or text. That way you know what scale you will be using for your views.
- Once you have determined the scale assigned to each viewport, you can set your annotation scale so that it matches and your annotations will automatically scale accordingly.
- You can set the visibility of annotations so only those objects set to the active annotation scale are visible using the Annotation Visibility tool in the Status Bar tray.

Command Exercise

Exercise 13-3 – Converting Existing Dimensions to Annotative

Drawing Name: **nlayout3.dwg**
Estimated Time to Completion: 20 Minutes

Scope

Change existing dimensions to annotative, so that they can use Annotative Scale.

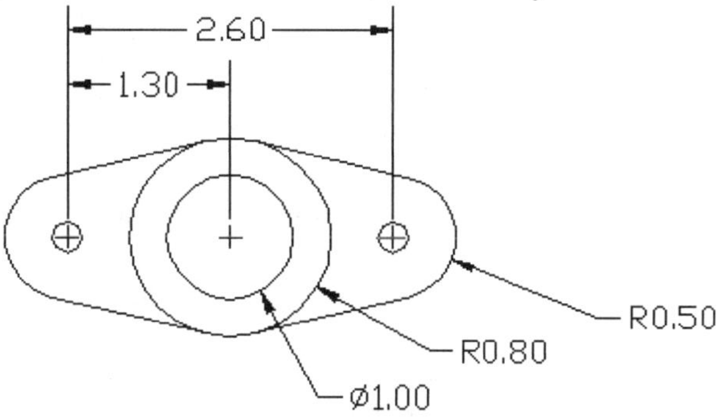

Converting Existing Dimensions to Annotative

Solution

1. 

Verify that the Model tab is active.

Verify that Quick Properties is **enabled**.

2. 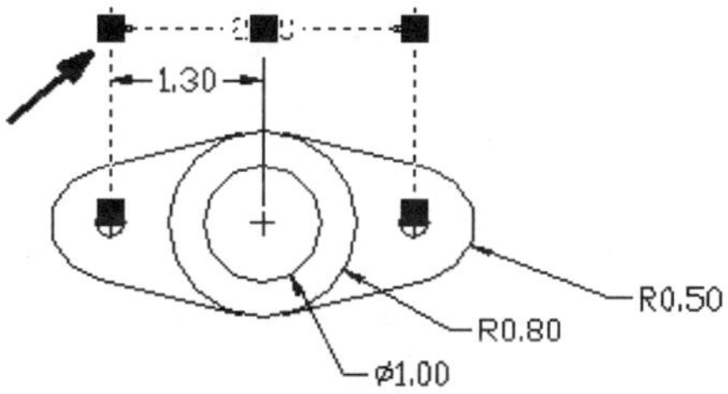

Select the 2.60 dimension so it is highlighted.

3. 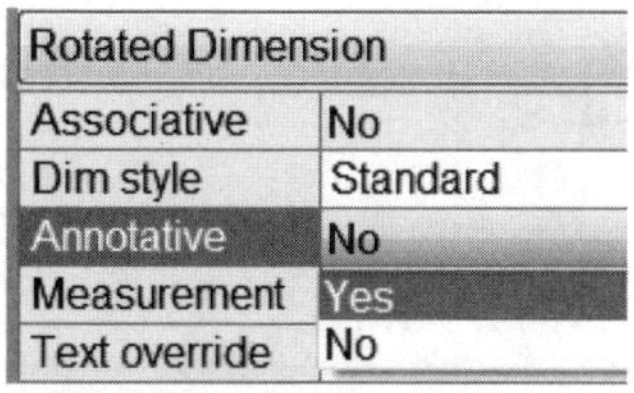

In the Quick Properties dialog:
Set Annotative to **Yes**.

4. 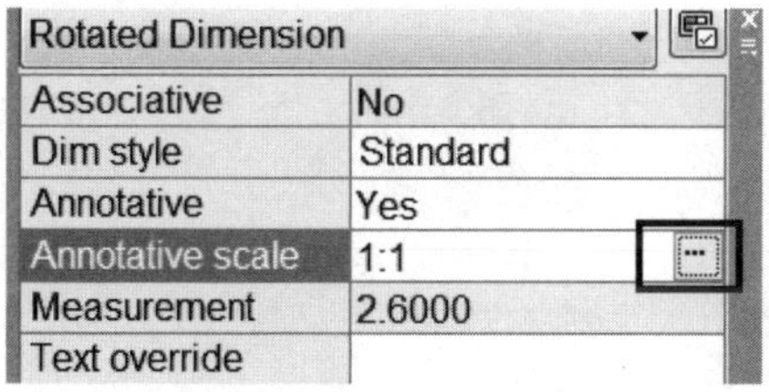

The Annotative scale field appears.

Select the **...** button.

5.

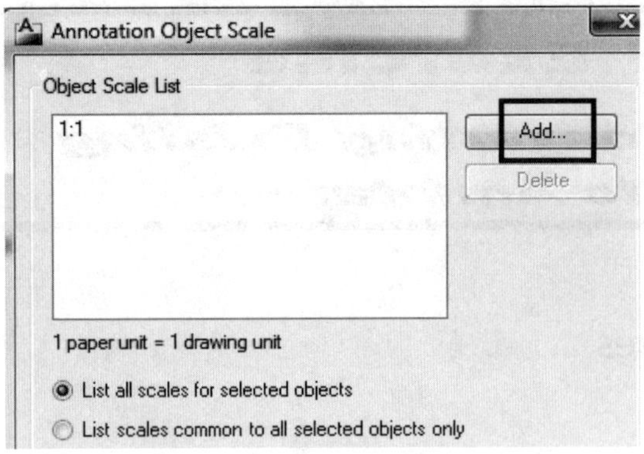

Select the **Add** button.

6.

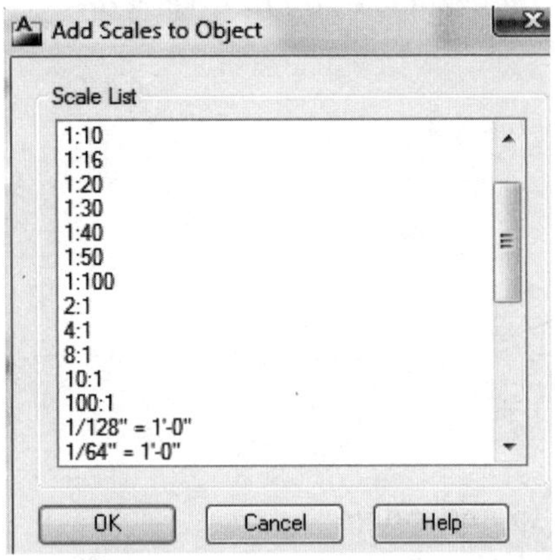

The 3:1 scale we created in the previous lesson does not exist in the list. This is because scales are associated with a drawing file and not with the application.

Press **Cancel** to exit the Annotation Object Scale dialog.
Press **<ESC>** to release the selected dimension.

7.

Type **scalelistedit** on the command line.

Tip: *If you press the <TAB> key after you type the first two letters, AutoCAD will fill in the rest.*

8.

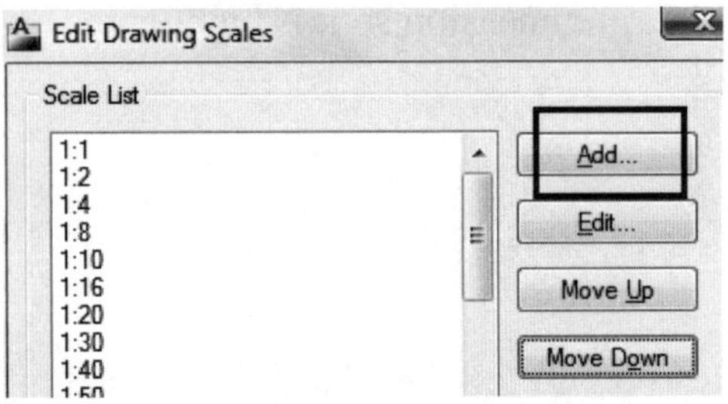

The list of available scales is shown.

Press the **Add** button.

9.

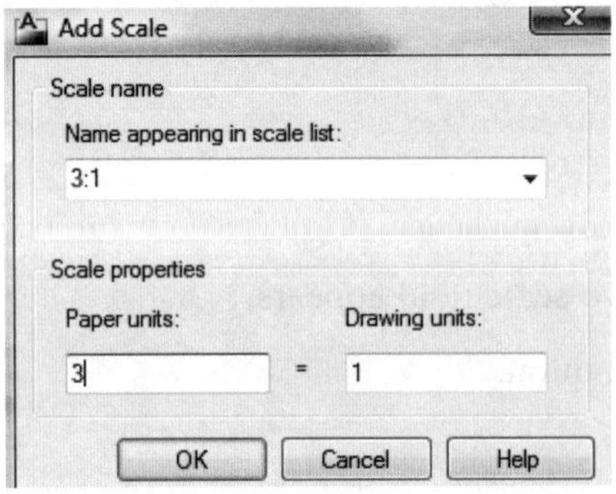

Type **3:1** in the first field.

Set the paper units to **3**.
Set the drawing units to **1**.

Press **OK**.

10. 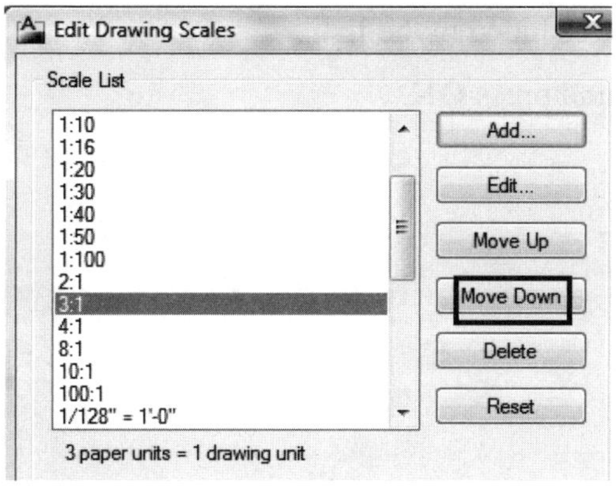

Use the **Move Down** button to position the 3:1 scale between the 2:1 and 4:1 scales.

Press **OK**.

9. 

Press **OK**.

10. 

Note when you mouse over the 2.60 dimension, a small icon now appears indicating that it is an annotative dimension.

11. 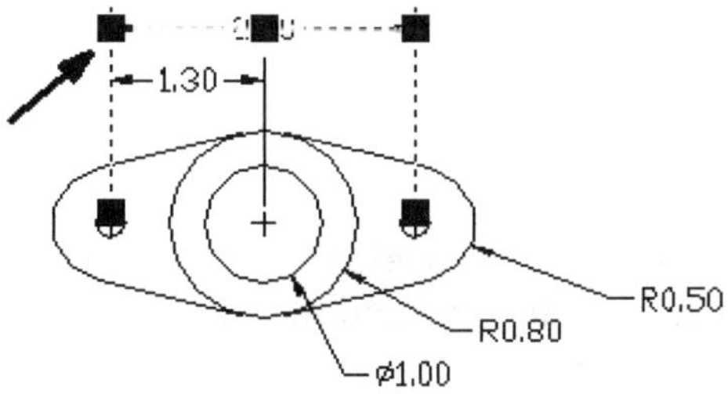

Select the 2.60 dimension so it is highlighted.

12. 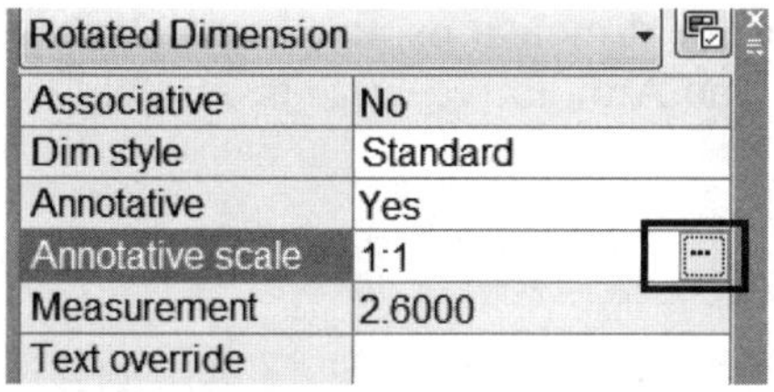

The Annotative scale field appears.

Select the **...** button.

13. 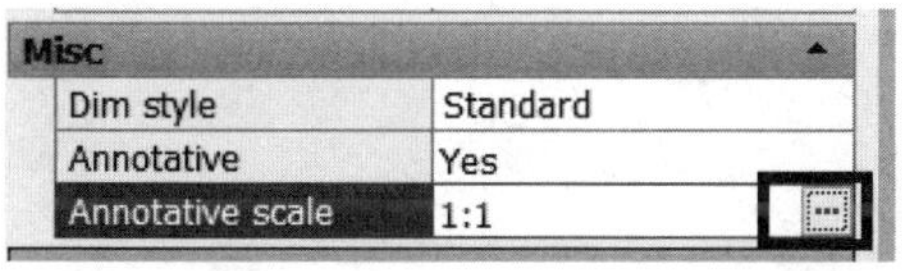

Select the **...** button in the Annotative scale field.

14. 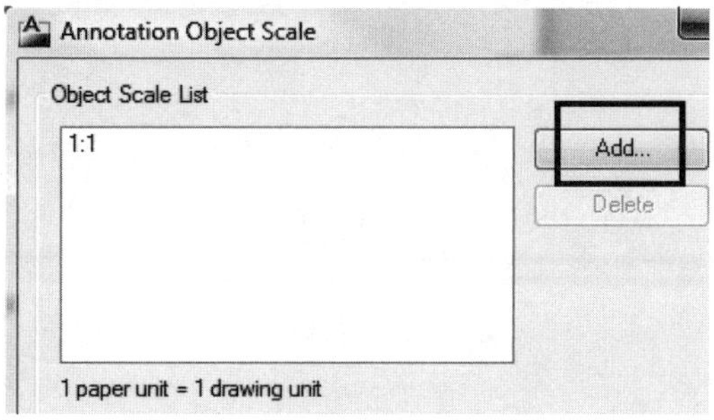

Select the **Add** button.

15. 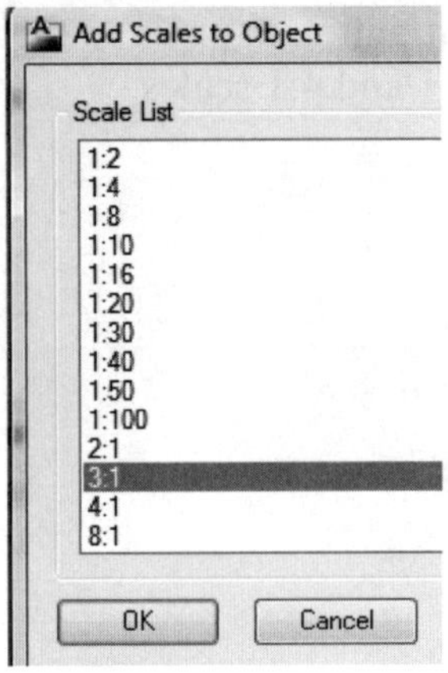

The **3:1** scale is now included in the list.

Highlight this scale and press **OK**.

16. 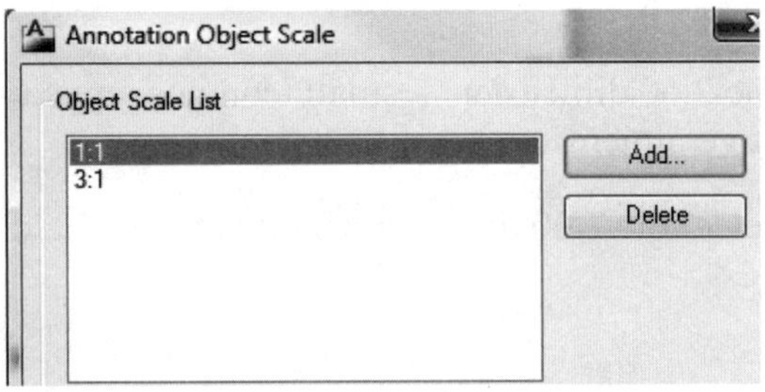

The 3:1 scale is now available for the dimension.

Press **OK**.

17. Set the remaining dimensions to Annotative and assign the 3:1 scale to them. You can select all the dimensions as a group and set them Annotative and add the 3:1 scale. *You do not have to select each one individually.*

18. 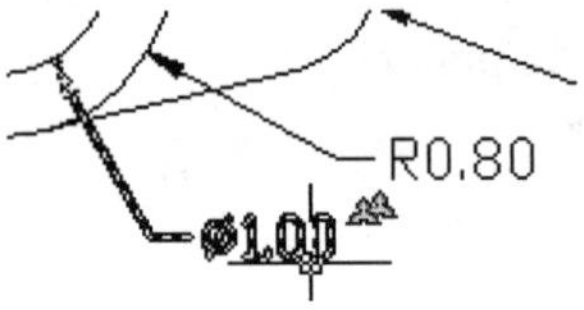

Note when you mouse over the dimensions, the Annotative icon now shows that more than one Annotative scale is available.

Command Exercise

Exercise 13-4 – Using Annotative Scales

Drawing Name: **nlayout4.dwg**
Estimated Time to Completion: 5 Minutes

Scope

Change the annotative scale used by a viewport.
Use the Quick View Layouts.

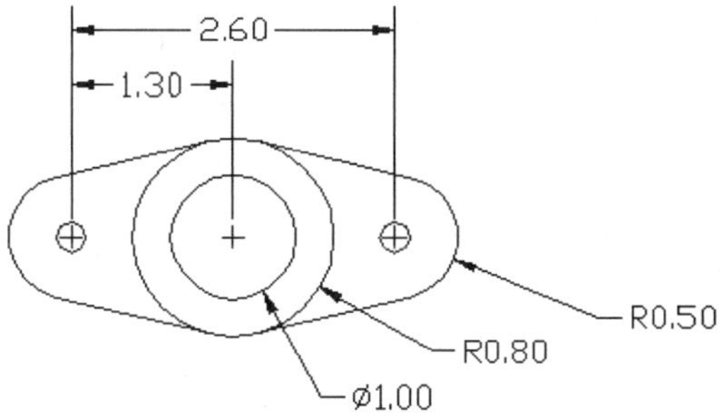

Changing the Annotative Scale for a Viewport

Solution

1. 

Verify that the **Plan** tab is active.

2. 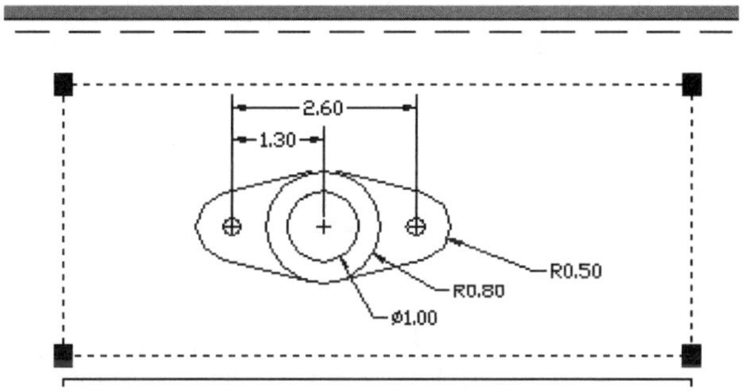

Select the top viewport so it is highlighted.

3. 

The Status Bar updates to show the VP Scale (viewport scale) and Annotation Scale.

4. 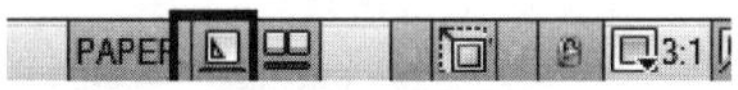

Select the **Quick View Layouts** icon.

5. There are four tools:

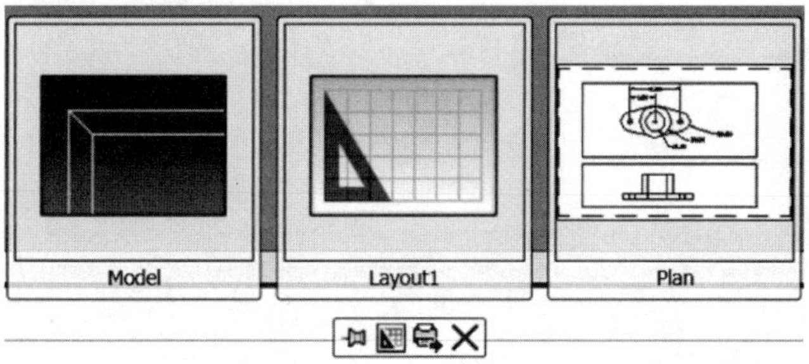

Pin – keeps the preview open

New Layout – adds a new layout tab

Publish –allows you to select and print layouts

Close – closes the Layout Preview.

6. 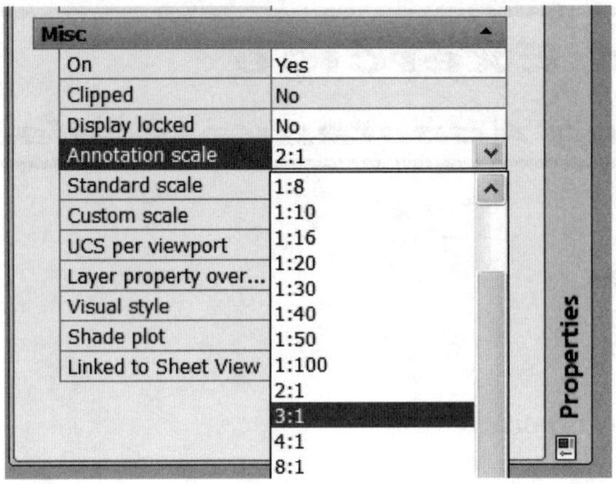

With the top viewport selected:

In the Quick Properties dialog:

Set Display Locked to **No**.

Left click on the down arrow next to the Annotation Scale and you will see the list of scales available.

Select **3:1**.

7. 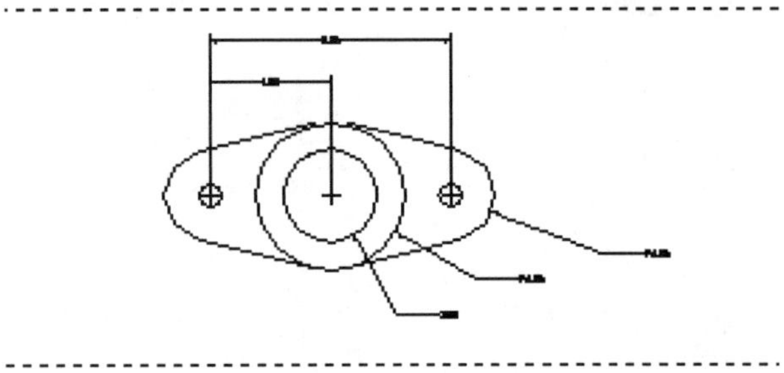

Note how the dimensions change size.

8. Select the Model tab.
Note that the actual size of the dimensions has not changed.

Command Exercise

Exercise 13-5 – Controlling Viewport Properties

Drawing Name: **paper2.dwg**
Estimated Time to Completion: 5 Minutes

Scope

Make the floating viewport window frame invisible. Use the Properties Command to set the viewport frame on the VP layer. Freeze the VP layer. Fill in the information in the title block.

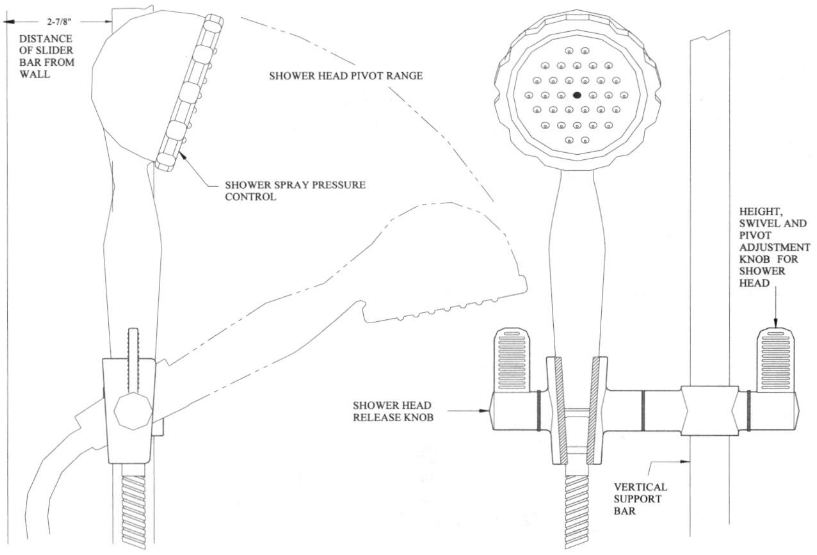

Drawing Layouts Exercise

Solution

1. 

Select the Layout1 tab at the bottom left corner of the drawing window.

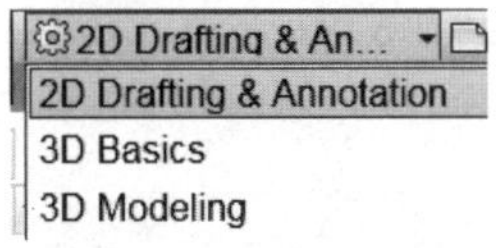

Set your workspace to **2D Drafting & Annotation**.

2. 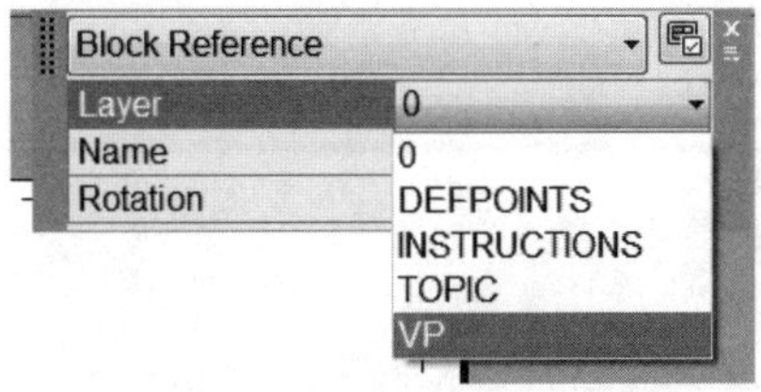

The drawing window will change to the Layout View.

Make sure Paper space is set at the Status line.

Select the border of the single viewport with the LMB and change the layer to **VP** in the Quick Properties dialog.

Notice that the single viewport window frame changes color. It is now on the VP layer. Deselect the viewport by clicking anywhere in the display window.

3. 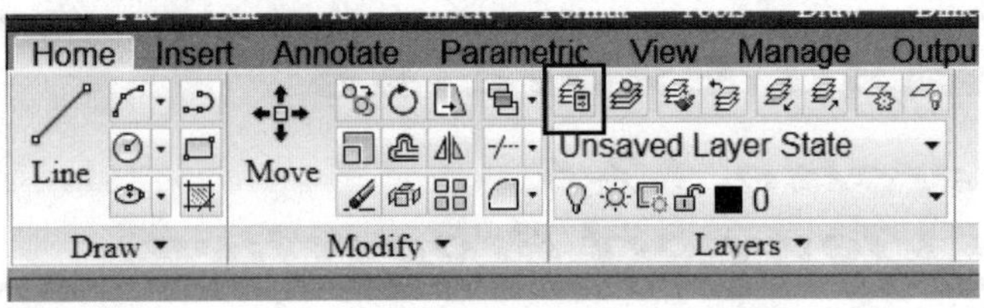

Activate the **Home** ribbon.

Select the **Layer Properties** tool.

4. 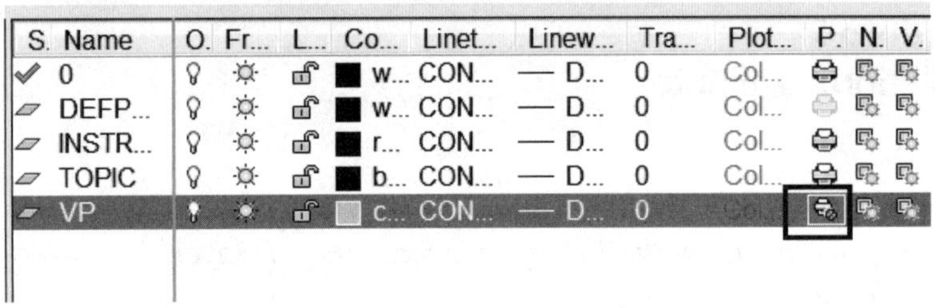

Set the VP layer to **No Plot**.

Close the Layer Properties Manager.

5. Activate the **Output** ribbon.

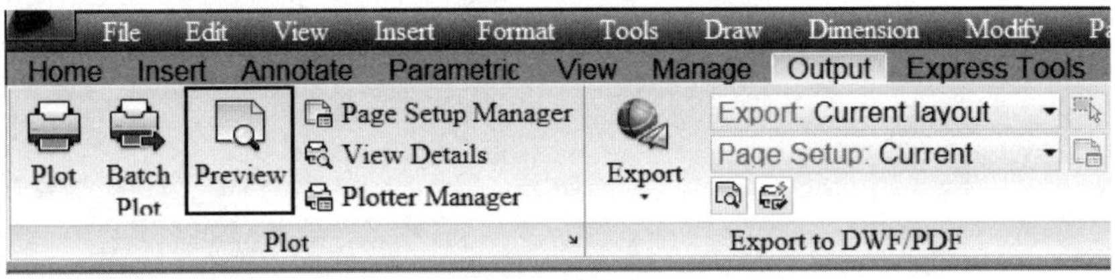

Select **Preview**.

The Plot preview shows that the Viewport border is not visible.

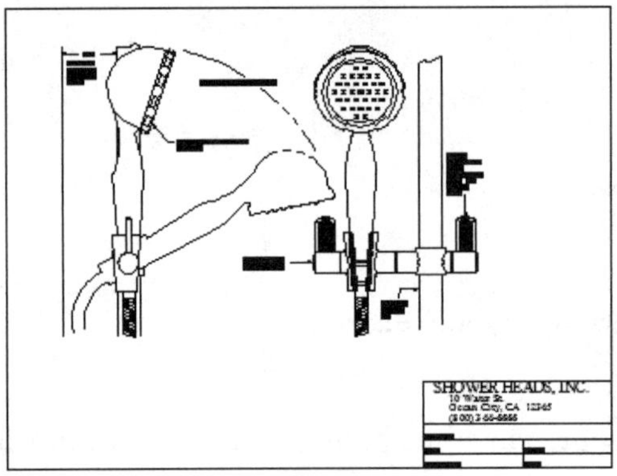

PAPER space must be on!
1.) With the properties command, select the paper space viewport.
2.) Change the layer to VP.
3.) Freeze the VP layer (model space freeze, not paper space).
4.) Zoom to the Title area and type your name and date where indicated.

6. 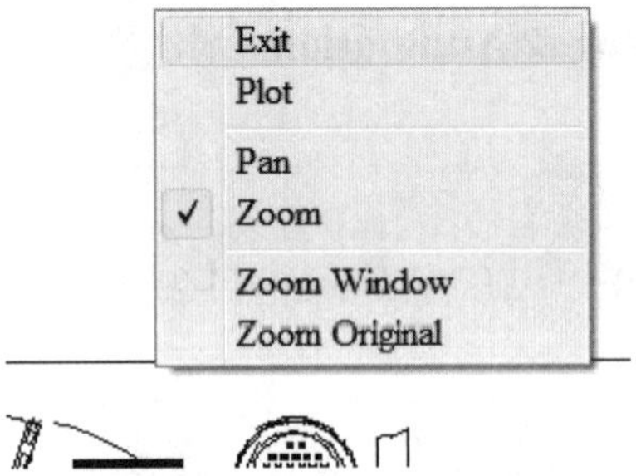

Right click and select **Exit** to exit the preview mode.

> ***Tip:*** *The white area in the layout indicates the actual piece of paper. This is controlled in the Page Setup dialog box. The dialog box can be activated from the <FILE<PAGE SETUP pull down menu.*

Command Exercise

Exercise 13-6 – Nonrectangular Viewport

Drawing Name: **nrview1.dwg**
Estimated Time to Completion: 10 Minutes

Scope

Create a viewport by drawing a hexagon. Then use the object option to create a viewport out of the star shape already in the drawing.

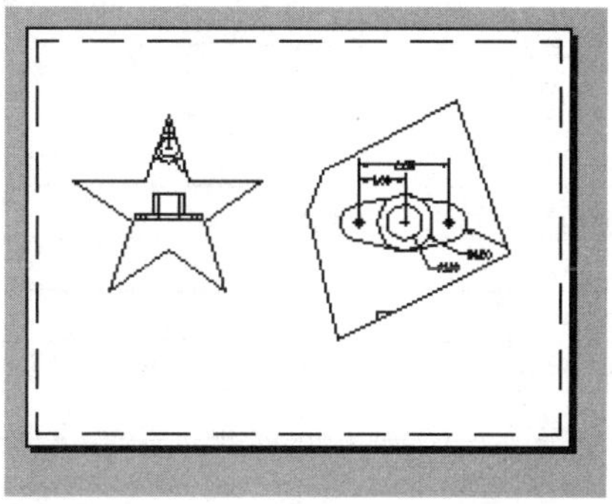

Nonrectangular Viewport Exercise

Solution

1. 

Select the Layout1 tab at the bottom left corner of the drawing window.

2. 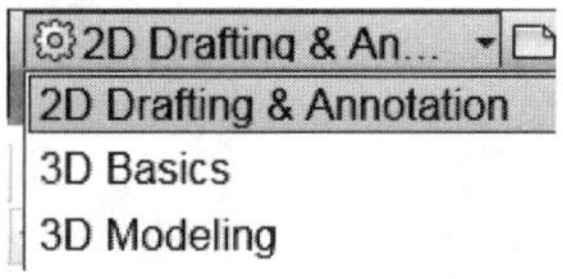

Set your workspace to **2D Drafting & Annotation**.

3. 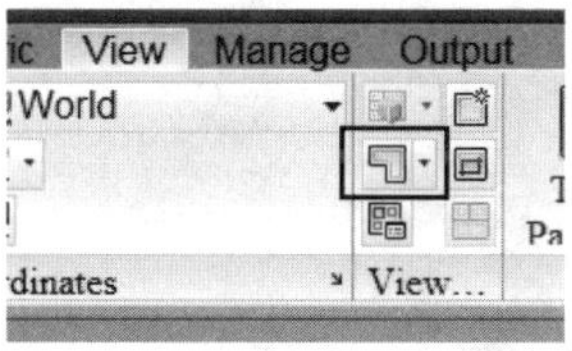

Invoke the Polygonal Viewport command, from the View ribbon, select **Create Polygonal.**

4. *Specify start point:*
Draw a closed hexagon shape, do not worry about it being a perfect hexagon.

5. 

Select the **Create from Object** tool on the View ribbon. This is located as a drop-down under the Create Polygonal tool.

6. *Select object to clip viewport:*
Select the star shape.

Extra: Activate each viewport and get the view to look proper.

Page Setup

Command Locator

Output Ribbon	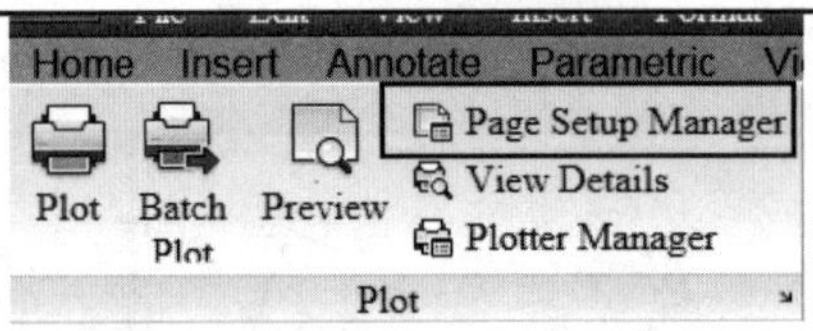
Toolbar Menu	**Layouts→Page Setup**
Pull Down Menu	**File→Page Setup…**
Command	**pagesetup**
RMB Shortcut Menu	**Right-click on the tab of the current layout/Page Setup…**
Dialog Box	**Page Setup**

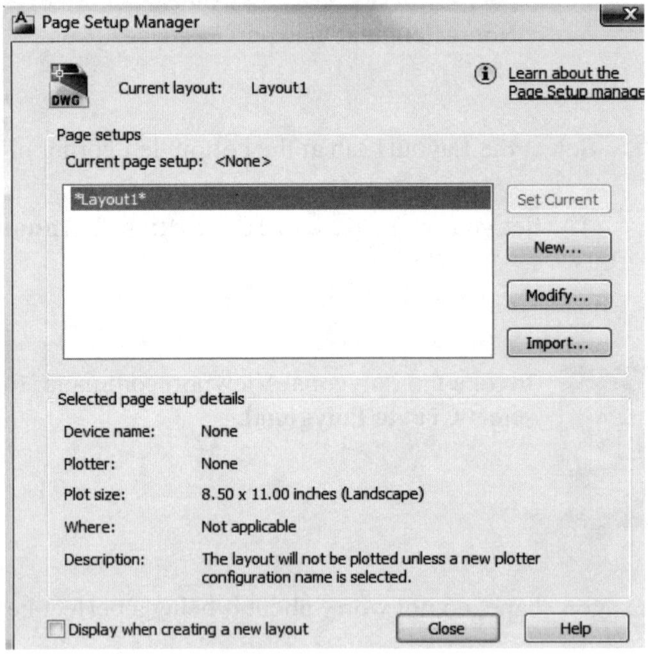

Page Setup Dialog Box

Command Overview

The Page Setup command is mixture of the old plot dialog box from earlier releases of AutoCAD and most windows print setup dialog boxes. In this dialog box, you can setup the layout and plotter settings for the current layout. This command is run automatically every time you select a layout tab that has not yet been set up. It is typically run whenever you create a new layout, unless this setting has been turned off by unchecking the 'Display when creating a new layout' checkbox at the bottom of the dialog box. The page setup is saved with its layout, so each layout in a drawing can have a different page setup.

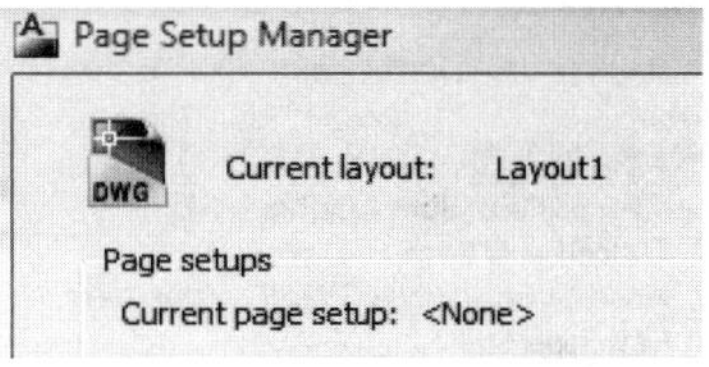

Top of Page Setup Dialog Box

You may edit the name of the layout in the Layout name field. The Page setup name is a drop-down list of available named page setups from which you can select a setup to apply to the current layout. If the setup you want is not in the available list, but is in a different drawing, or if you want to add a named setup, press the 'Add' button. This will open the User Defined Page Setups dialog box.

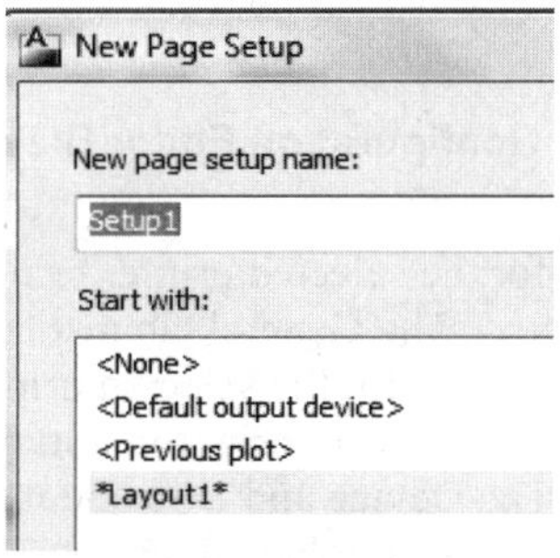

Page Setup Manager Dialog Box

To create a named page setup from the current settings, type in the name in the top field and press 'OK'. To rename an existing setup, click on the name of the setup to highlight it, press 'Rename' and type in a new name. To delete an existing setup, click on the name of the setup to highlight it and press 'Delete'. To import a setup from another file, press 'Import'. Select the file with the setup in the Select File dialog box and select the setup from the dialog box that opens.

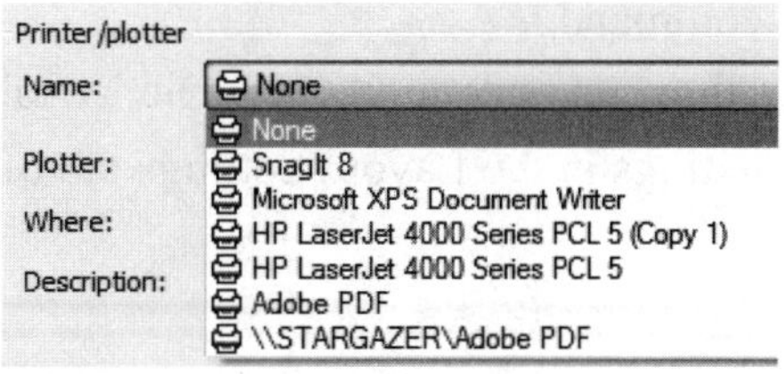

Plot Device Area of the Page Setup Dialog Box

The Plot Device tab of the dialog box allows you to select the plotter to use for the layout, its properties and a plot style table. There is a drop-down list of currently available printer/plotters. You must make sure to set up your printer/plotter in Windows before selecting it here. The 'Properties...' button opens the Plotter Configuration Editor dialog box.

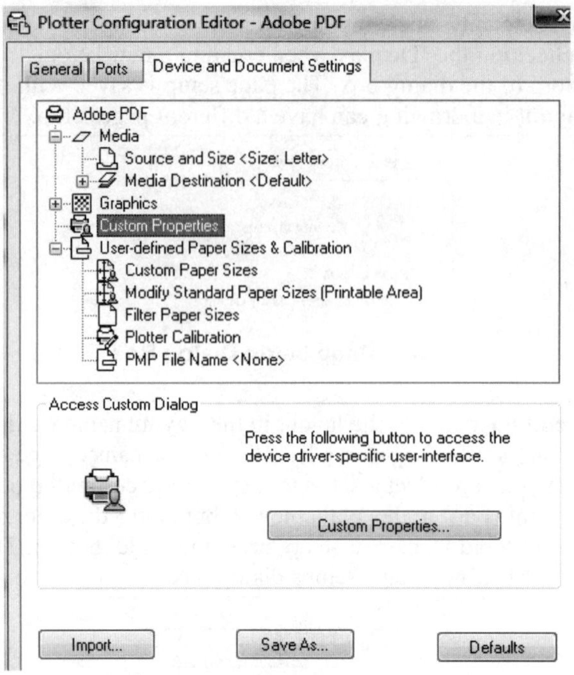

Plotter Configuration Editor Dialog Box

The Properties button for the selected printer brings up the Plotter Configuration dialog box. The General tab displays general information about the drivers for the selected printer/plotter. The Ports tab allows you to set which port to print to including the ability to print to a file or to a spool. The Device and Document Settings tab has many settings for the media to use, graphic quality, etc. Click on the setting to adjust and the bottom of the dialog box shows available settings to adjust.

Back in the Plot Device tab of the Page Setup dialog box, you may also select a plot style table to use for the layout. A plot style adjusts the color, lineweight, linetype, fill style, and other settings for plotted output. They are covered in more detail later in this section.

General Procedures

1. Invoke the Page Setup command.
2. Set the plotter configuration and style in the Plot Device tab of the dialog box.
3. Set the rest of the plot settings in the Layout Settings tab of the dialog box.
4. Press 'OK'.

Layout Wizard

Command Locator

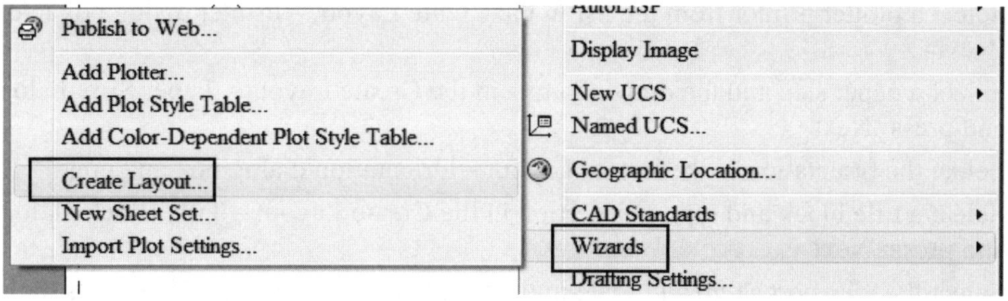

Pull Down Menu	**Tools→Wizards →Create Layout...**
Command	**layoutwizard**
Dialog Box	**Create Layout**

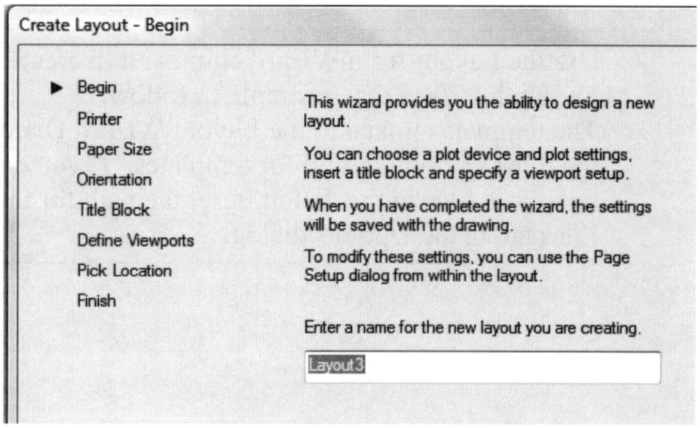

Layout Wizard Dialog Box

Command Overview

The Layout Wizard quickly steps through all of the settings to create a layout from the beginning. The wizard prompts you for the plotter to associate with the layout, the paper size to use, orientation of the paper, title block to insert and viewports to create. This is all done in a step by step dialog box. Once all of the prompts are responded to, the command creates the layout according to your settings.

General Procedures

1. From the Insert menu, select Create Layout from Wizard.
2. Type in the name of the new layout in the Create Layout – Begin dialog box and press 'Next>'.
3. Select a plotter/printer from the list in the Create Layout – Printer dialog box and press 'Next>'.
4. Select a paper size and the drawing units in the Create Layout – Paper Size dialog box and press 'Next>'.
5. Select the orientation in the Create Layout – Orientation dialog box and press 'Next>'.
6. Select a title block and type of insertion in the Create Layout – Title Block dialog box and press 'Next>'.
7. Select the viewport setup and scale in the Create Layout – Define Viewports dialog box and press 'Next>'.
8. Set the location of the viewport(s) in the Create Layout – Pick Location dialog box and press 'Next>'.
9. Press 'Finish'.

- Use the Layout from Wizard command to create a layout using a step by step interface that is simple to follow.
- The templates linked to the Layout Wizard Dialog are located using the Files Options setting for templates. If you do not see any templates files in the dialog, reset the path for the templates on the Files tab in the Options dialog.

Command Exercise

Exercise 13-7 – Layout Wizard

Drawing Name: **wlayout1.dwg**
Estimated Time to Completion: 10 Minutes

Scope

Create an A sized layout using the Layout from Wizard command.

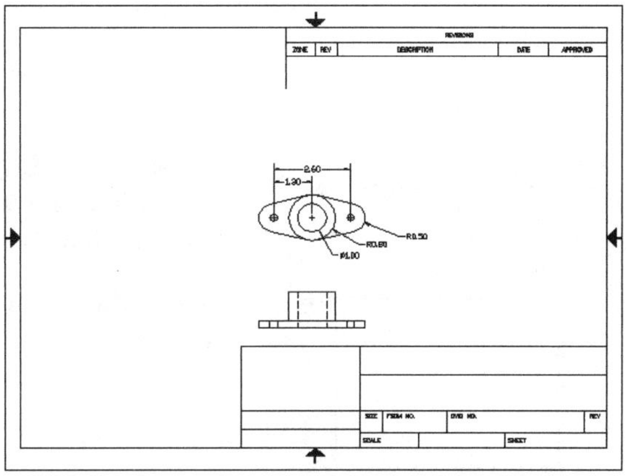

Layout Wizard Exercise

Solution

1. 

Set the Workspace to AutoCAD Classic.

2. 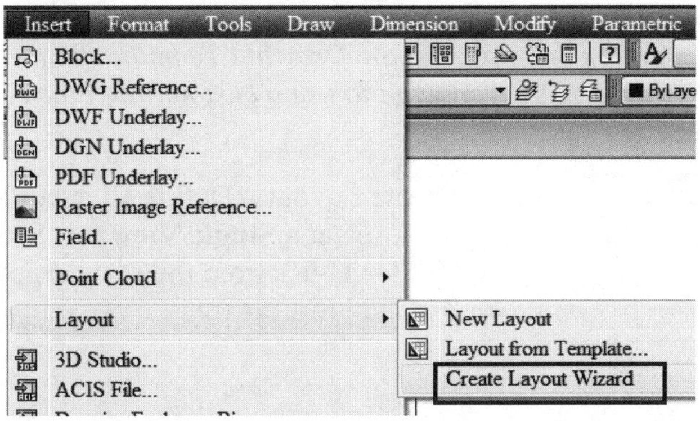

Invoke the **Layout Wizard** command by going to **Insert→Layout→Create Layout Wizard**.

3. 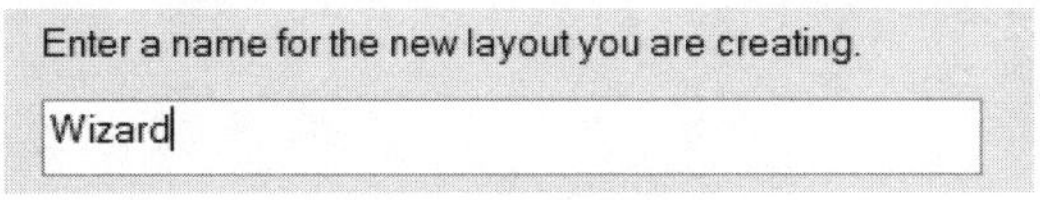

In the Create Layout – Begin dialog box, type in **Wizard** and press **Next**.

4. 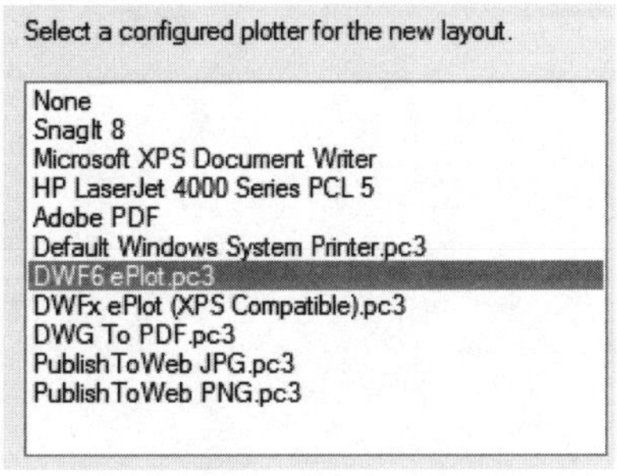

In the Create Layout – Printer dialog box, select **DWF6 ePlot.pc3** and press **Next>**.

5.

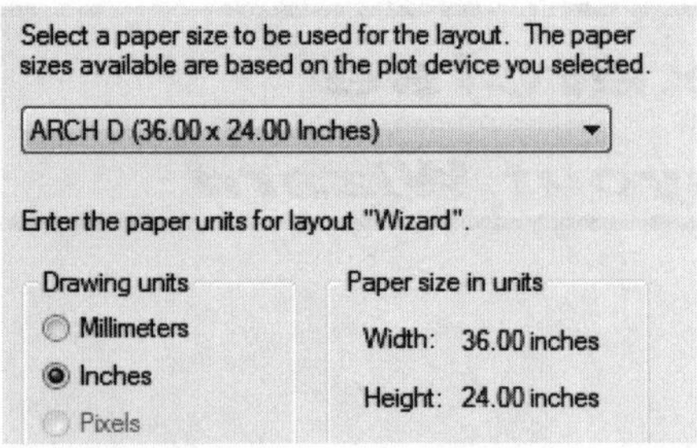

In the Create Layout – Paper Size dialog box, select **ARCH D (36.00 X 24.00 Inches)** from the drop–down list and Inches for units and press **Next>**.

6.

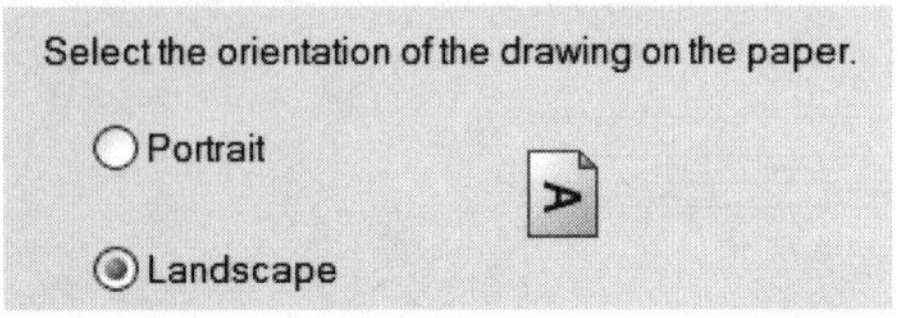

In the Create Layout – Orientation dialog box, select '**Landscape**' and press **Next>**.

7.

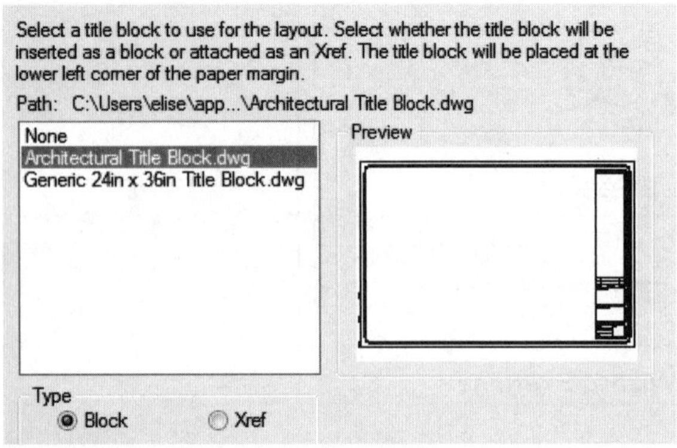

In the Create Layout – Title Block dialog box, select ***Architectural Title Block.dwg*** from the list.

Select **Block** for the type and press **Next>**.

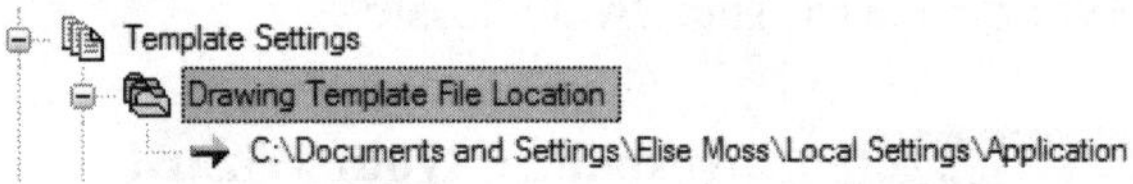

You will not see the list of title blocks unless you have set the Drawing Template path properly on the Files tab in the Option Dialog. If you want to use a custom title block set the path to the file in the Options Dialog.

8.

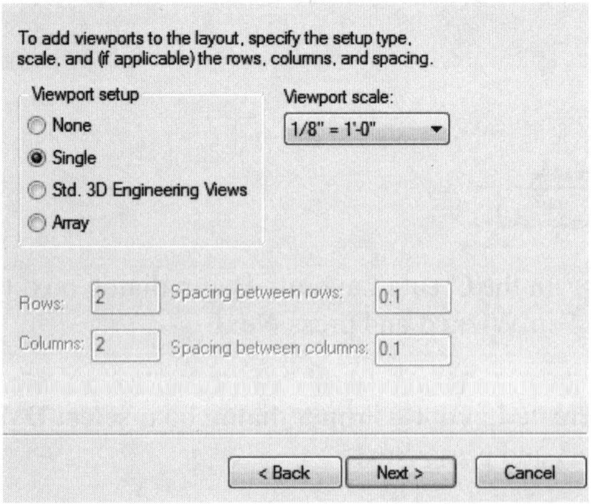

In the Create Layout – Define Viewports dialog box, select a **Single** Viewport Setup. Select **1/8″ = 1′-0″** from the scale drop–down list and press **Next>**.

9. 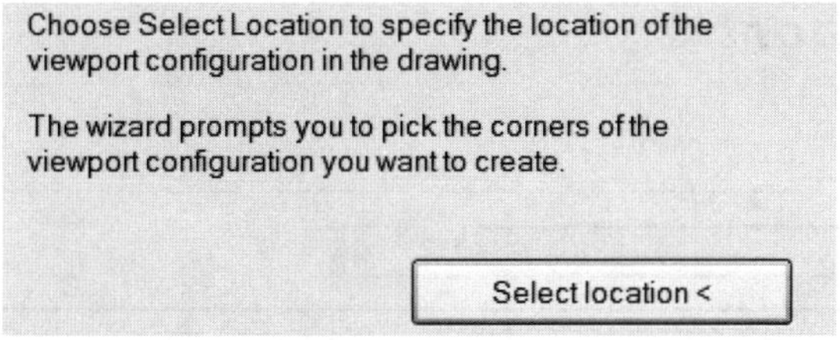

In the Create Layout – Pick Location dialog box, press **Select location <**.

10. *Specify first corner:*
Select a corner of the viewport to create just inside the title block.

11. *Specify opposite corner:*
Select the opposite corner of the viewport to create.

12. In the Create Layout
Finish dialog box, press **Finish**.

13. Double click in the viewport to activate.
Zoom Extents to see the model layout.

Controlling Layers per Viewport

Command Locator

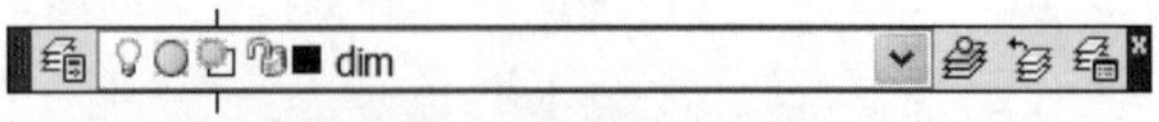

Home ribbon	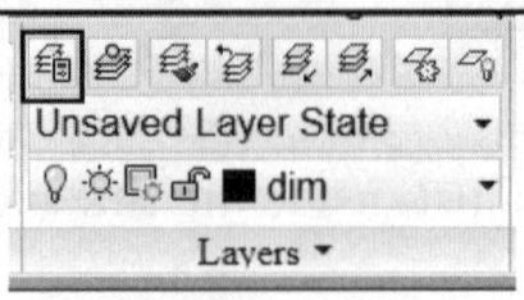
Toolbar Menu	**Object Properties**
Pull Down Menu	**Format →Layer…**
Command	**Layer**
Alias	**La**
Dialog Box	**Layer Properties Manager**

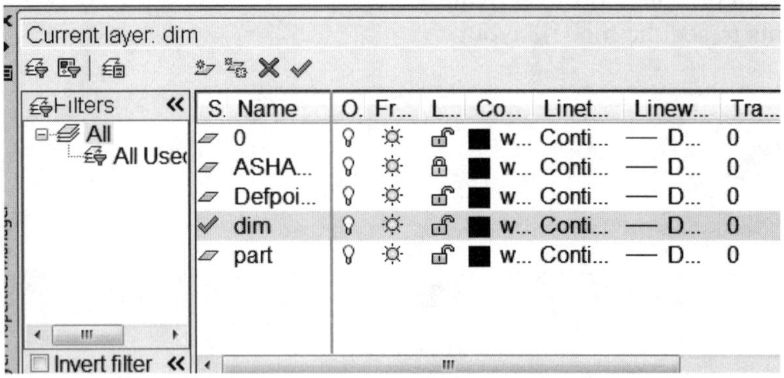

Layer Properties Manager Dialog Box

Command Overview

With TILE mode off, and MODEL Space on, layers can be frozen in selected viewports. Notice that the Layer Control Dialog now display two additional columns. 'Active VP Freeze' and 'New VP Freeze'

Options:

Active VP Freeze – This will freeze a selected layer in the active viewport.

New VP Freeze – This will freeze a selected layer in any new viewport created.

General Procedures

Freezing Layers in Active Viewport Only.

1. Select a floating model space viewport (TILE should be OFF, MODEL should be ON in the Status Bar).
2. Select from the Layers Dialog Box, the layer and select Active VP Freeze.
3. Select OK.

Freezing Layers in New Viewports Only:

1. Invoke the Layer command.
2. Select from the Layers Dialog Box, the layer and select New VP Freeze.
3. Select OK.

Command Exercise

Exercise 13-8 – Controlling Layers per Viewport

Drawing Name: **pslayer1.dwg**
Estimated Time to Completion: 5 Minutes

Scope

Switch to Paper Space and freeze (in paper space) the layers in the selected viewports, as indicated in the drawing. Freeze (in model space) the layers VP, which contain the paper space viewport borders, and Notes.

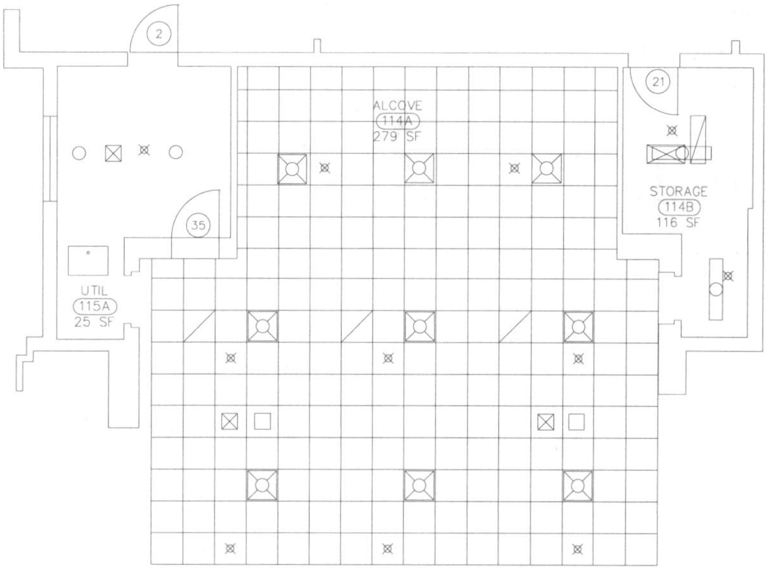

Paper Space Layers Exercise

Solution

1. Switch to Layout 1 by clicking on its tab at the bottom of the drawing window.

2. Activate the upper left viewport by double clicking within the viewport area.

3. 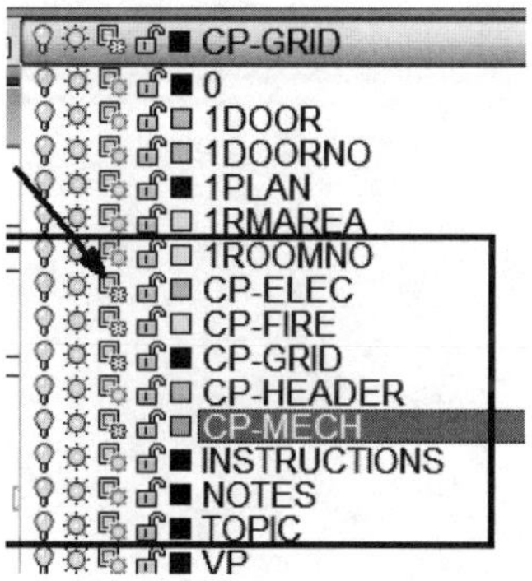

Select the Layers **CP–GRID**, **CP–FIRE**, **CP–ELEC**, and **CP–MECH** in the Layer drop-down and enabling the Freeze in Current Viewport option.

4.

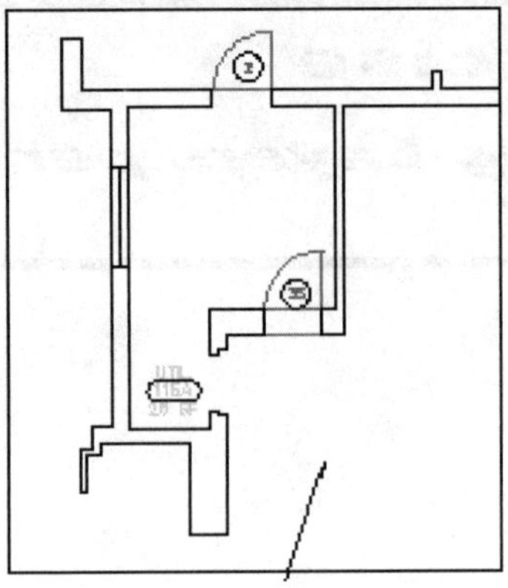

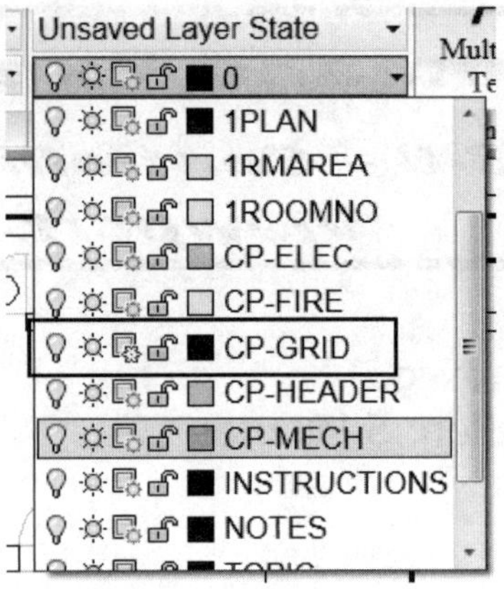

Activate the upper right viewport by clicking within its border. Using the Layer drop-down list freeze the layer CP–GRID in that view port.

5.

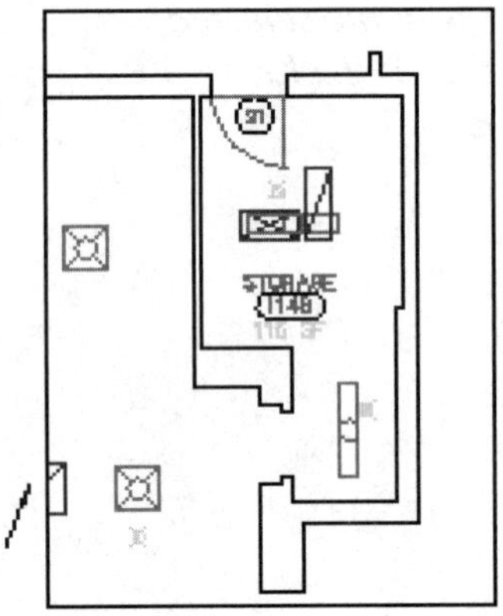

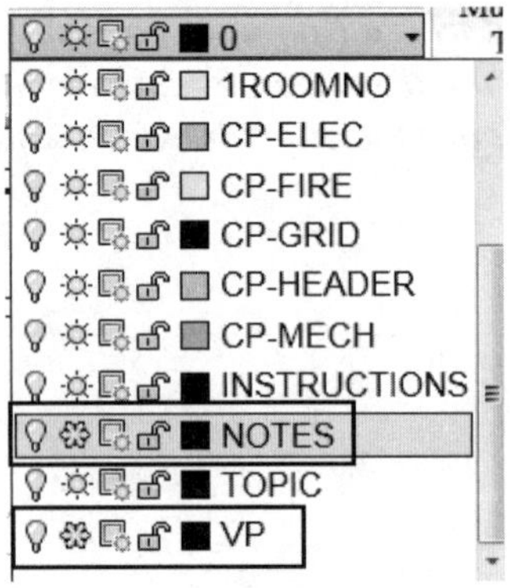

Freeze the layers named **VP** and **Notes** in all view ports by selecting the Layer Control drop down list, and choosing the **Freeze in ALL viewports** icon for both layers.

Plot Command

Command Locator

Output Ribbon	
Toolbar Menu	**Standard**
Pull Down Menu	**File →Plot**
Command	**Plot**
Alias	**Ctrl+P**
Dialog Box	**Plot**

Command Overview

Drawings may be plotted from the Model tab or the Layout tab. For 2-dimensional drawings, the user may opt to plot either way, though there are certain advantages to plotting from the Layout tab, such as including multiple views of the same drawing. For 3-dimensional drawing, it is necessary to use the Layout tab to print multiple views, such as a top, front and side view, of the 3-D Model on a single page. The Plot command will bring up the Page Setup dialog box. This dialog box includes the Plot Device tab and the Plot Settings tab. Basic options will be covered in this Tutorial. In addition to the plot command, is the Preview Plot command, which previews a plot according to the latest plot settings.

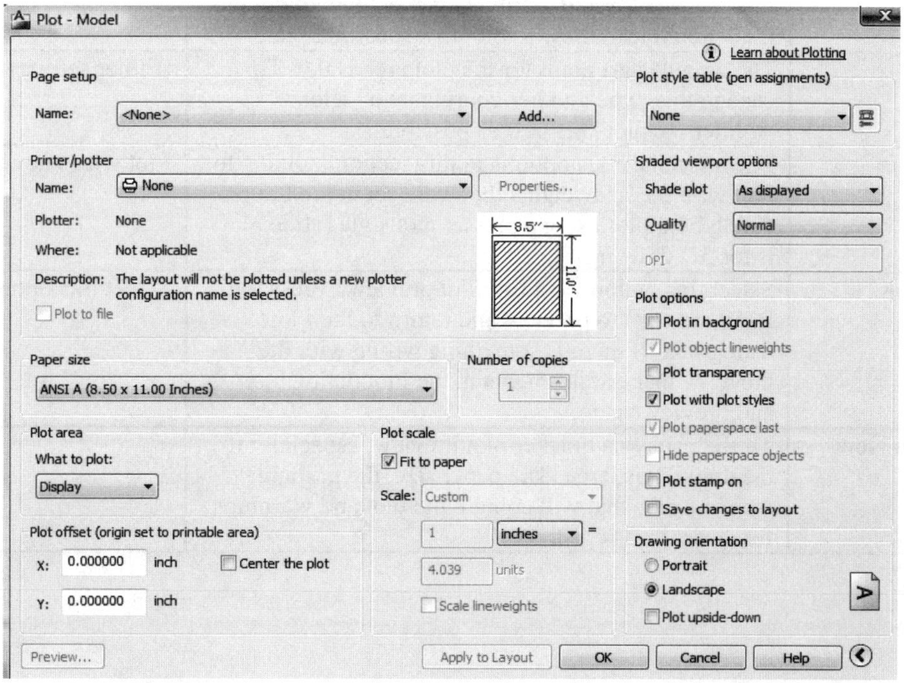

Plot Dialog Box

Plot Option	Overview	Typical Options to Choose
Plotter Configuration	Select a Plotting device from the drop down list, if the desired plotter does not appear at the top of this list. Select the Properties button to make changes to the Plotter Settings.	Use the default Plotter. Select a different plotter from the drop down list.
Plot Style Table (pen assignments)	This section allows the user to assign color numbers to pen numbers and set how objects are plotted.	Use the default setting (none)
What to Plot	Allows the user to plot all of the Layout tabs or only the Current tab. Multiple copies can be specified.	Current tab Selected tab All Layout tabs Any number of copies
Plot to File	This section allows the user to create a plot file (.plt) instead of an actual plot. Plot files contain the drawing information with all of the Plot command settings and can be plotted later.	None (leave blank)
Paper size and paper units	The available paper sizes will depend on the plotting device. The printable area will always be less than the paper size, because the rollers on the printer need to feed the paper through the machine. The printable area also depends on the printing device. Choose inches or mm, depending on the drawing units.	Select the paper size from the drop down list.
Drawing orientation	Choose Portrait, Landscape, or Plot upside-down. It is usually necessary to Preview the drawing first, to know which drawing orientation is correct.	Do a Full Preview first, then select Portrait or Landscape as required.
Plot area	The options in this area pertain to the part of the drawing that gets plotted: the drawing Limits, the drawing Extents, the current Display, or choose Window to make a window around the part of the drawing to plot.	Plot Limits *or* Select Window and make a window around the drawing area to plot.
Plot scale	This area controls the Plot scale. It is very easy at first to select "Scale to Fit", however, eventually the user should learn how to plot to a specified scale.	Select or type a Plot Scale
Plot offset	The default start point for the plot area is 0,0. To change this, type another coordinate or select "Center the plot" (as best as possible)	(Either setting)
Plot options	The miscellaneous options in this section include: to Plot with the lineweights that were set in the Layers dialog box, plot using a pre-set plot style (Hide plot is for 3D drawings.	Plot with lineweights
Full Preview	Select this button for a full Plot preview. Press the RMB (to exit) to preview and return to the Plot dialog box. If there is something wrong with the preview, make adjustments in the Plot dialog box, and Preview again.	Select this option
Partial Preview	This is usually a quicker plot preview, especially if the drawing is large. The paper size, the printable area, the area that will contain the plot and warnings for errors will be listed.	

General Procedures

Plot a drawing:

1. Invoke the Plot command.
2. Select the Plotter and Paper size.
3. Select the Plot area. Select or type the Plot scale.
4. Select "Full Preview". Right-click in the preview page and Exit to continue. Make any necessary adjustment to the Plot settings. Then press OK to plot.

Set up a Drawing to Plot the Layout tab:

1. Create the drawing in the Model tab.
2. Select the Layout tab in the Drawing Window. Select OK to accept the Page Setup Layout defaults.
3. Insert a Title Block where the insertion point is 0,0, the x and y scale factors are 0, and the rotation angle is 0.
4. Use grips to re-size the existing viewport, or use the Viewports command options to create additional viewports.
5. Select PAPER in the Status Bar. This will switch the viewport mode to floating MODEL space. Select a viewport and Zoom the drawing view to scale.
6. Select MODEL in the Status Bar to switch the viewport mode back to PAPER space. Add notes, dimensions, etc. and plot the drawing.

Set up a Drawing to Plot the Model tab:

1. Start a New drawing. Set the Drawing Units, the drawing Limits (according to the Drawing Limits / Scale Chart). Zoom All.
2. Insert a Title Block where the insertion point is 0,0, the x and y scale factors are equal to the Plot scale, and the rotation angle is 0
3. Create the drawing in designated drawing area, then plot the drawing.

Tips & Tricks

- When selecting Plot Extents, be careful that there is not any geometry that may have gotten thrown out into space by accident. This is one reason why it is good to periodically Zoom All, or Zoom Extents to erase errors such as this.
- To add a plotter, open the Plotter Manager from the File pull-down menu. Select, "Add a Plotter Wizard".
- Plot settings are saved on the computer and do not automatically go with the drawing. PC2 and PCP files save the plot settings. These are files separate from the drawing file. Plot settings can be saved and used with other drawings. The Batch Plot Utility command contains options that utilize PCP and PC2 files.

Plot Style Table Wizard

Command Locator

Pull Down Menu	**Tools / Wizards / Add Plot Style Table...**
Dialog Box	**Add Plot Style Table**

Plot Style Table Wizard

Command Overview

A Plot Style Table is a group of settings telling AutoCAD how to plot colors, dithering, gray scale, pen assignments, screening, linetype, lineweight, end styles, join styles, and fill styles. By changing the plot style, you can change the output of your drawing to get a different look for the same information. Plot styles can be set for objects, layers, layouts and viewports within layouts. There are two types of plot style tables, Color-Dependent and Named. **Color-Dependent** is similar to the old way of using AutoCAD where you assigned linetypes and lineweights based on an object's color. A color-dependent plot style table contains 255 plot styles and is saved with a CTB extension. A **Named** plot style table is independent of the object's color. You can assign any plot style to any object regardless of its color. This allows more freedom in selecting object color since it no longer controls how the object plots. Named plot style tables are saved with an STB extension.

The Plot Style Table Wizard allows you to easily create your own customized plot styles. When you run this command you have four options available, Start from scratch, Use an existing plot style table, Use My R14 Plotter Configuration, and Use a PCP or PC2 File.

Start from scratch will create a new plot style table that is not based on anything else. You will be prompted to select whether it is to be a Named or Color-Dependent table. You must supply a name for the new table. Then finally you are given the option of editing the default settings created in the new style.

Use an existing plot style table will create a new plot style table based on an existing one. You will be prompted to select the style table to base the new one on. You must supply a name for the new table. Then finally you are given the option of editing the settings created in the new style.

Use My R14 Plotter Configuration will create a new plot style table based on an existing Release 14 Configuration. You will be prompted to select whether it is to be a Named or Color-Dependent table. A Named table will have a plot style created for each unique pen definition in the configuration file. You will be prompted to select the configuration file to base the new style table on. You must supply a name for the new table. Then finally you are given the option of editing the settings created in the new style.

Use a PCP or PC2 File will create a new plot style based on a PCP or PC2 file from a previous release of AutoCAD. You will be prompted to select whether it is to be a Named or Color-Dependent table. A Named table will have a plot style created for each unique pen definition in the configuration file. You will be prompted to select the configuration file to base the new style table on. You must supply a name for the new table. Then finally you are given the option of editing the settings created in the new style.

General Procedures

1. Invoke the Add Plot Style Table Wizard command.
2. Follow the prompts in the dialog box and press 'Next>'.

Plot Style Table Editor

Command Locator

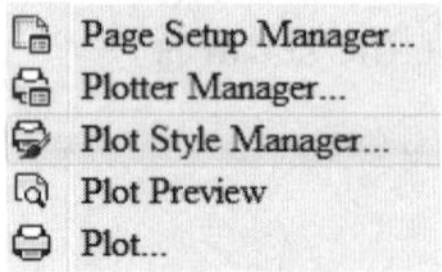

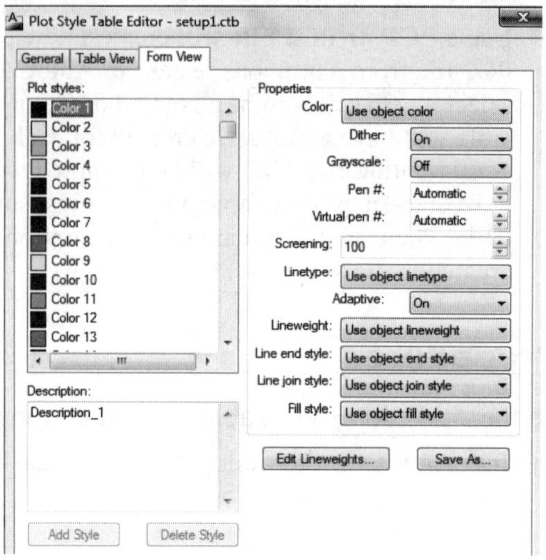

Plot Style Table Editor Dialog Box

Pull Down Menu	**File / Plot Style Manager...**
Command	**stylesmanager**
Dialog Box	**Plot Style Table Editor**

Command Overview

The Plot Style Table Editor allows you to edit the plot styles found in a plot style table. Color–dependent plot style tables must have 255 plot styles mapped to 255 colors so you cannot add or delete plot styles in this type of table. However, a named plot style table can have any number of plot styles and the editor will allow you to add and delete styles from this type of table.

The dialog box has three tabs. The first, General, gives general information about the table file. The second and third tabs contain the editable information about the plot styles in two formats, tabular and form. Select the tab of the format you prefer working with, both give the same information.

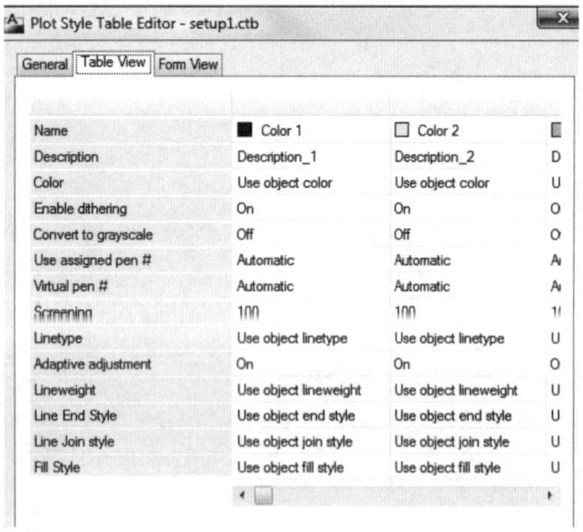

Plot Style Table Editor – Table View

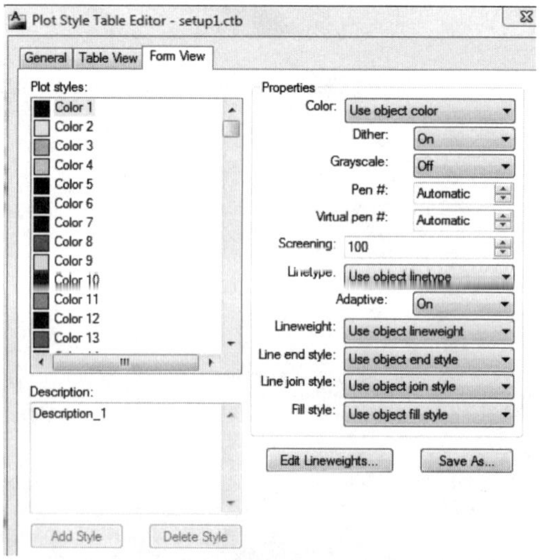

Plot Style Table Editor – Form View

Each plot style has a description and twelve properties.

Color sets the color the object will be plotted with regardless of the color the object was drawn with. The default setting is 'Use object color'.

Dither turns on or off dithering. This is the process of plotting lines as a series of dots in an attempt to create more colors in the plotted output.

Grayscale will convert the color of the object to grayscale.

Pen number sets the number of the pen to use for this style, available numbers are 1 – 32. If you have set the color to 'Use object color' or are using a color–dependent plot style table, you cannot change this setting from 'Automatic' which causes AutoCAD to use the pen with the closest color to that of the Color setting.

Virtual pen is used for non–pen plotters that are setup with virtual pens. Virtual pens can be programmed into many plotters to setup the pen's width, fill pattern, end style and color. If a virtual pen is selected, the other settings for the plot style will be ignored. If the plotter used is a pen plotter or does not have virtual pens setup, this setting is ignored.

Screening sets the intensity of the color to use as a percentage. Setting this to 0 will use no ink and therefore change the color to white, while 100 will set the color to full intensity.

Linetype allows you to set the linetype to use for the style. The default linetype is 'Use object linetype'.

Adaptive adjustment sets the linetype scale of the object to complete the linetype pattern without ending it in the middle. If your drawing looks correct, turn this off, if linetype scaling is not as important as making sure the linetypes show up correctly, turn this on.

Lineweight sets the lineweight of the objects. The default setting is 'Use object lineweight'.

Line end style sets the end style of your lines. The styles available are Butt, Square, Round and Diamond. The default setting is 'Use object end style'.

Line join style sets the style of the joints of lines. The styles available are Miter, Bevel, Round and Diamond. The default setting is 'Use object join style'.

Fill style sets the fill style for the objects. Styles available are Solid, Checkerboard, Crosshatch, Diamonds, Horizontal Bars, Slant Left, Slant Right, Square Dots and Vertical Bar. The default setting is 'Use object fill style'.

General Procedures

1. Invoke the Plot Style Manager command.
2. In the Plot Styles window, double click on the file to edit.
3. Set the desired settings in the dialog box.
4. Press 'Save & Close'.

Tips & Tricks

- Another way to get to the Plot Styles window is to double click on the Autodesk Plot Style Manager in the Windows Control Panel.

Section Exercise

Exercise 13-9 – Layout Setup

Drawing Name: **Section 13 aec.dwg**
Estimated Time to Completion: 10 Minutes

Scope

Select the Layout1 tab to create a new Page Setup. Select a Plotter and establish Layout Settings for plotting a D-size drawing. Then create Viewports, both rectangular and Non-rectangular.

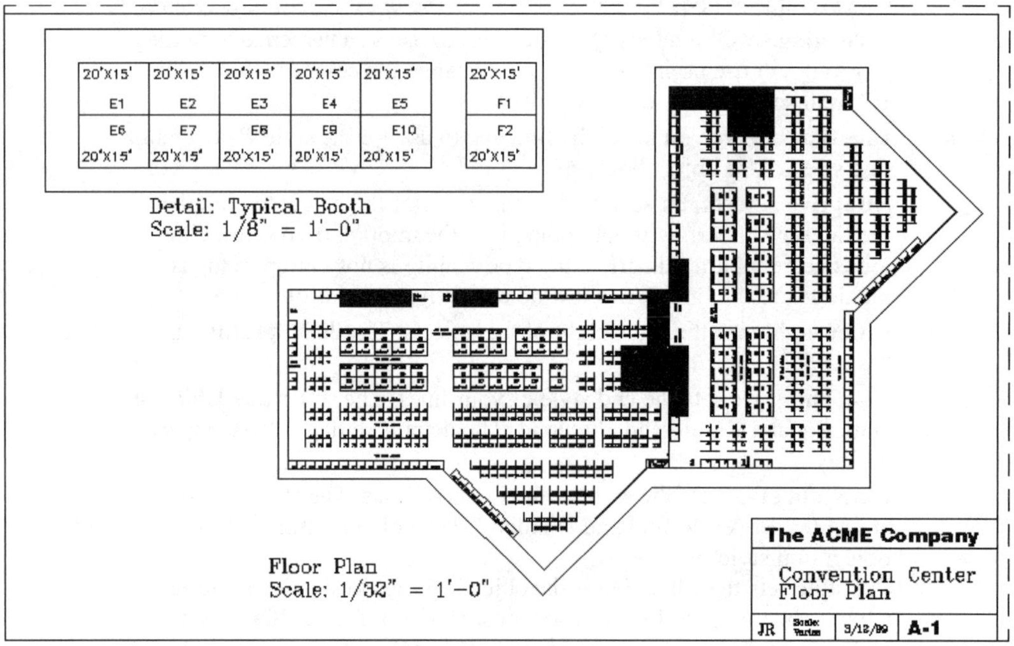

AEC Plotting and Output Exercise

Hints

1. Select the Layout1 tab and set the page settings.
2. Set the scale of the viewport created and then perform a polygonal clip on the existing viewport.
3. Create a rectangular viewport.
4. Insert the title block (there is a block in the drawing called Title).

> ***Extra:*** *Perform a Plot Preview to see what color the yellow entities will be when you plot.*

Sheet Sets

The Sheet Set Manager: Most users don't just create one drawing and send it off. Instead, they create documentation or drawing packages. These are mini-booklets of drawings that detail a mechanical assembly or building project. The problem many designers have is managing these documentation packages; making sure that the correct revision drawing is included in each package, that there are no missing drawings, etc.

The Sheet Set Manager allows you to manage your documentation package by creating a sheet set list, printing and publishing your sheets, add and delete sheets as needed. You can also create different versions of the same sheet set to send to different sub-contractors.

Command Locator

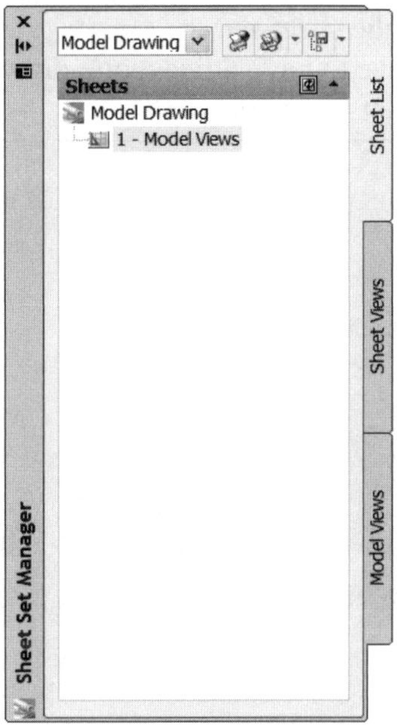

Sheet Set Manager

View ribbon	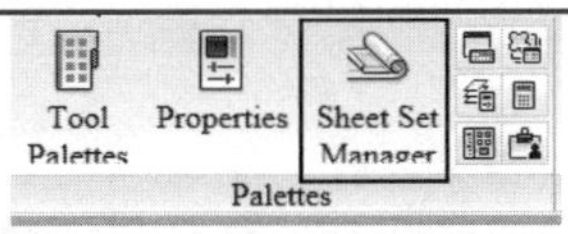
Pull Down Menu	**Tools/Sheet Set Manager**
Command	**Sheetset**
Alias	**SSM**
Keyboard Shortcut	**Ctl+4**

Command Overview

The Sheet Set Manager is used to print a documentation package. Users can add or delete sheets and create a sheet set list table.

General Procedures

1. Create drawings as usual. These are the resource drawings.
2. Create named views in model space. These are listed in the View List tab.
3. Invoke the Sheet Set Manager command.
4. Create the sheet set.
5. Assign a template to be used.
6. Create a table of contents for the entire sheet set.
7. Plot or publish the sheet set or a sub-set of the sheet set.

Tips & Tricks

- You can create different styles for your sheet set tables.
- You can use existing drawings to create your sheet sets or start with a new project.
- Once you have placed the sheet set table, you can update it if any of your sheets are modified.
- You can use the Sheet Set Manager to open and close drawings within the sheet set.
- You have to have at least one drawing open in order to launch the Sheet Set Manager.

Command Exercise

Exercise 13-10 –
Creating a New Sheet Set

Drawing Name: **8th floor.dwg**
Estimated Time to Completion: 15 Minutes

Scope

Create a new sheet set from an existing set of drawings.

Sheet Set Manager

Solution

Remember you have to have at least one drawing open in order to access the Sheet Set Manager.

1. Invoke the Sheet Set Manager.
   Type **SSM**.

2. 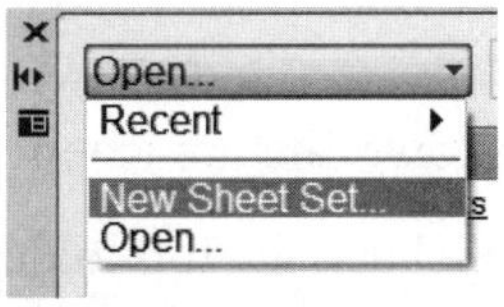

   Go to **New Sheet Set…**

3. 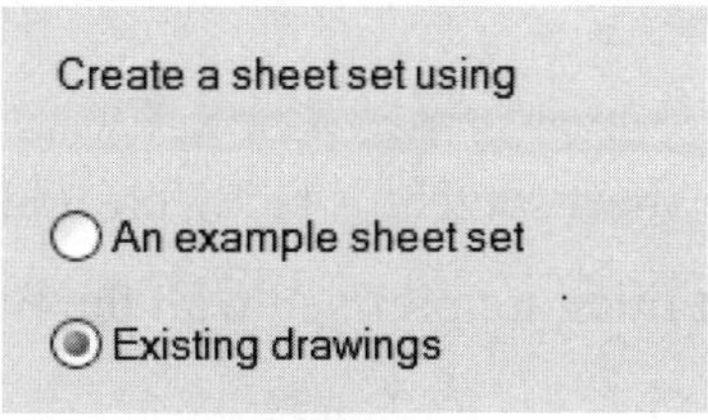

   Enable **Existing drawings**.
   Press **Next**.

4. 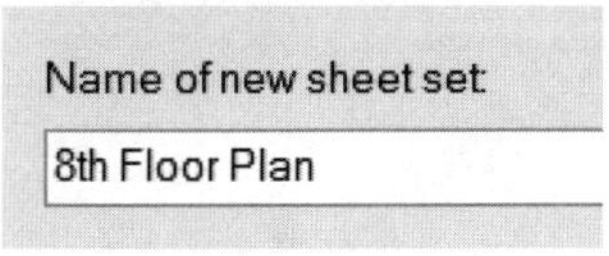

   Enter **8th floor plan** in the Name of new sheet set field.

5. 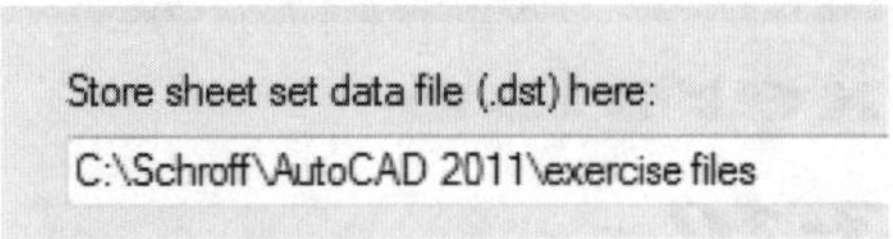

Browse to a location to store the sheet set data file. The data file keeps track of what drawings and views are included in each sheet set.

6. 

Press the **Sheet Set Properties** button.

7. 

Set the Sheet creation template to the *standard.dwt* file created earlier.

Press **OK**.

Press **Next**.

8. 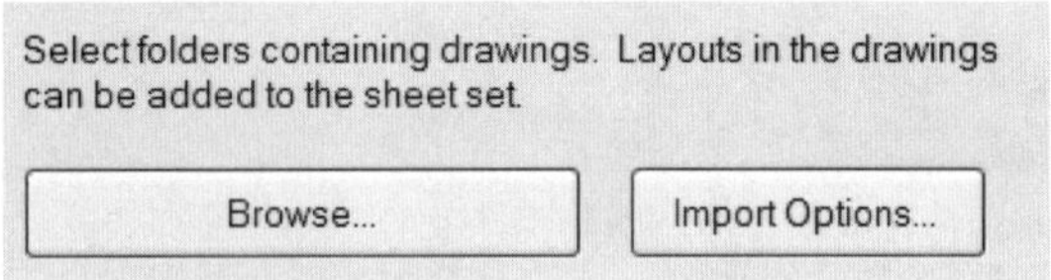

Select the **Browse** button.

9. 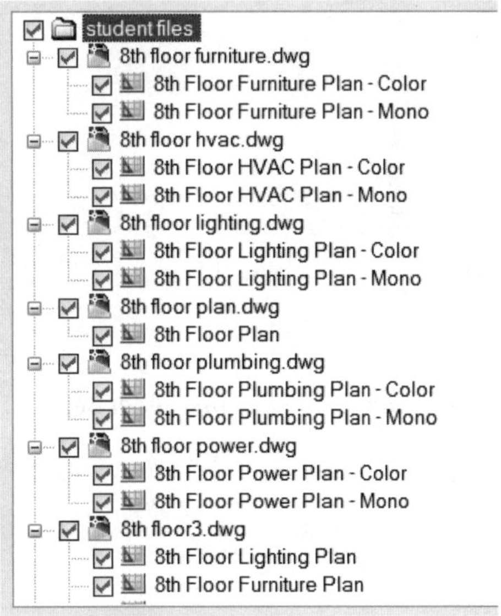

Locate the 8th floor drawings downloaded from the publisher's website.

10. 

Uncheck all the files except for the *8th floor3.dwg* file. Note that all the xrefs linked to the 8th floor3.dwg file are listed.

To clear all the selected files, simply uncheck the top folder. Then select only the *8th floor3.dwg* file.

Press **Next**.

11. 

You can preview the sheet set that is being created.

Notice how the sheet titles are prefixed with the file name.

Press **Back**.

12. 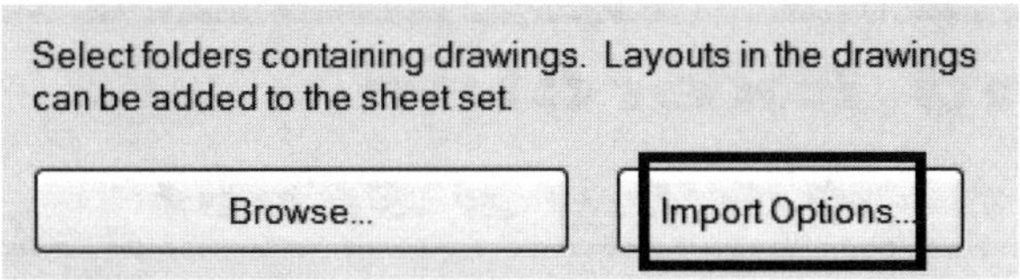

Press the **Import Options**.

13. 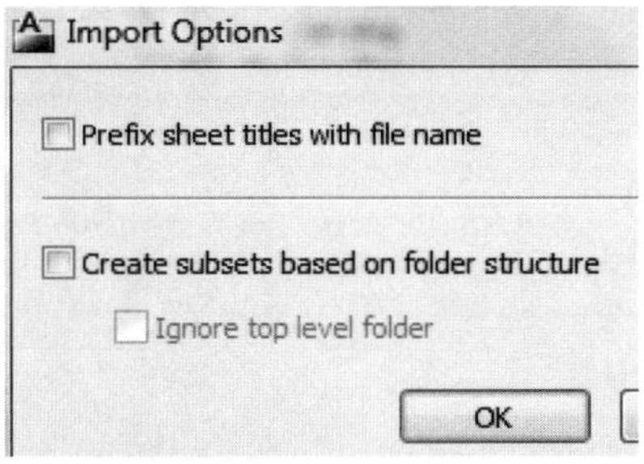

Disable the **Prefix sheet titles with file name** option.

Press **OK**.

Press **Next**.

14. 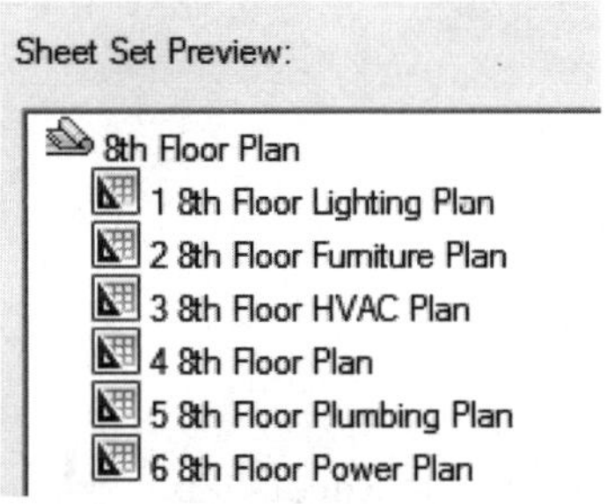

The preview now displays with the layout names only.

Press **Finish**.

15. 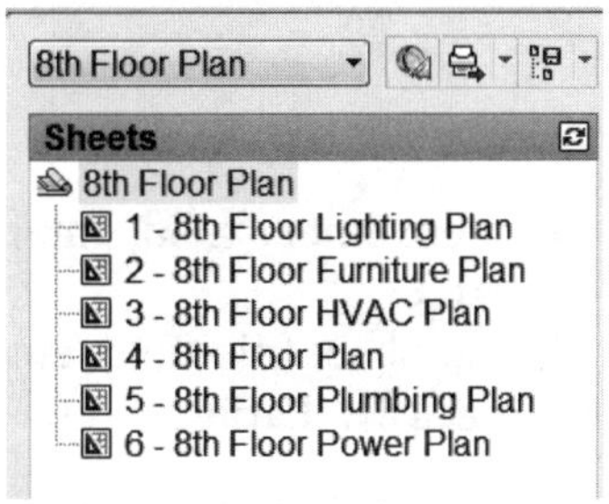

The sheets are listed in the Sheet Set Manager.

16. 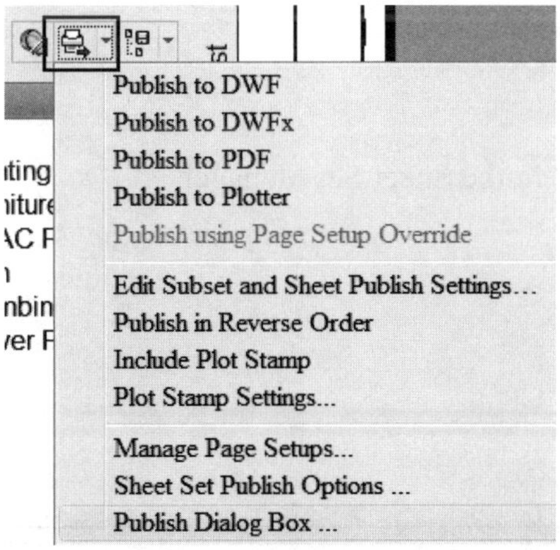

The Publish tool has a drop-down menu that allows the user to plot to DWF, PDF or plotter.

Command Exercise

Exercise 13-11 – Adding a Sheet

Drawing Name: **8th floor2.dwg**
Estimated Time to Completion: 5 Minutes

Scope

Adding a Sheet to the Sheet Set Manager.

Sheet Set Manager

Solution

1.

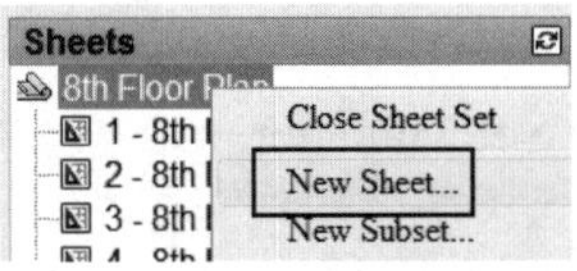

Highlight the **8th floor plan** header on the Sheets tab. RMB and select **New Sheet**.

2.

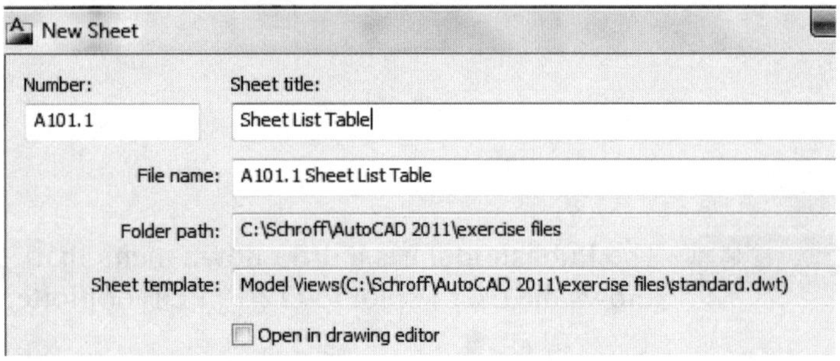

In the Number field, enter **A101.1**.
In the Sheet title field, enter **Sheet List Table**.

Press **OK**.

3.

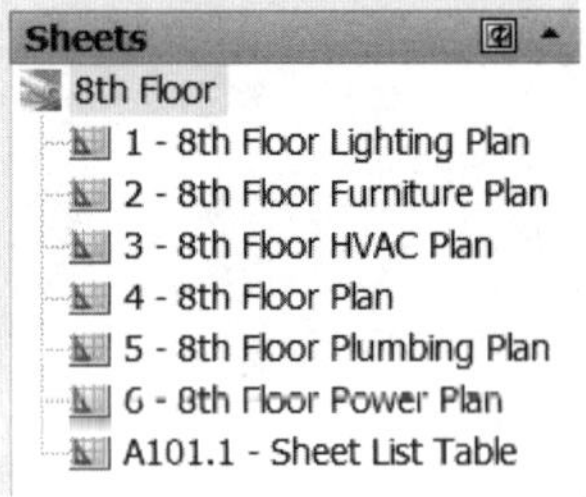

The new sheet is listed in the Sheet Set Manager.

Tips & Tricks

- To access shortcut menus needed for sheet list table operations, the Shortcut Menus in Drawing Area must be enabled in the Options dialog box, User Preferences tab.

Command Exercise

Exercise 13-12 – Creating a Sheet List Table

Drawing Name: **8th floor3.dwg**
Estimated Time to Completion: 15 Minutes

Scope

Creating a Sheet List Table.
Add the table to a sheet.
Modify the table.

Sheet List Table
Sheet List Table
8th floor - 8th Floor Furniture Plan
8th floor - 8th Floor HVAC Plan
8th floor - 8th Floor Lighting Plan
8th floor - 8th Floor Plan
8th floor - 8th Floor Plumbing Plan
8th floor - 8th Floor Power Plan

Sheet List Table

Solution

1.

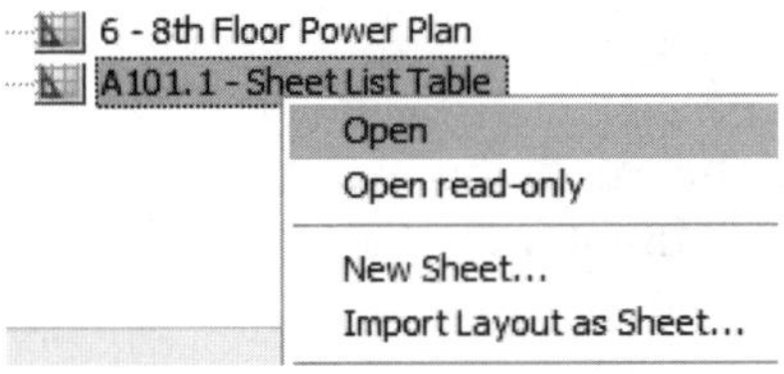

Launch the SSM if it is not already launched using Ctrl+4.

If the sheet set list is not visible, open the dst file created earlier.
Highlight the **A101.1 – Sheet List Table** drawing.

RMB and select **Open**.
The new layout sheet will open.

2.

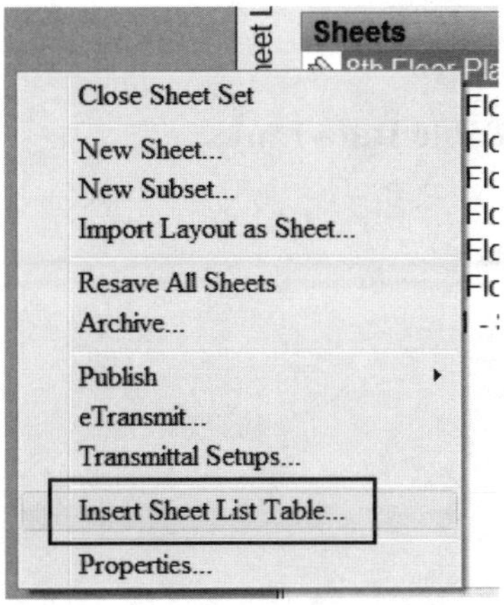

Highlight the 8th floor plan header.

RMB and select **Insert Sheet List Table**.

You must be in PaperSpace mode for this option to be available.

3.

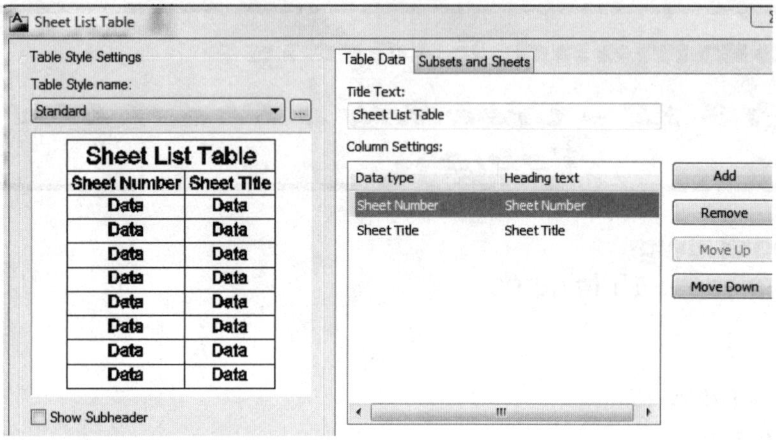

By default the sheet number, sheet title, and drawing title are displayed on the table.

If 'Show Subheader' is enabled, then the table will be organized by sub-categories.

4.

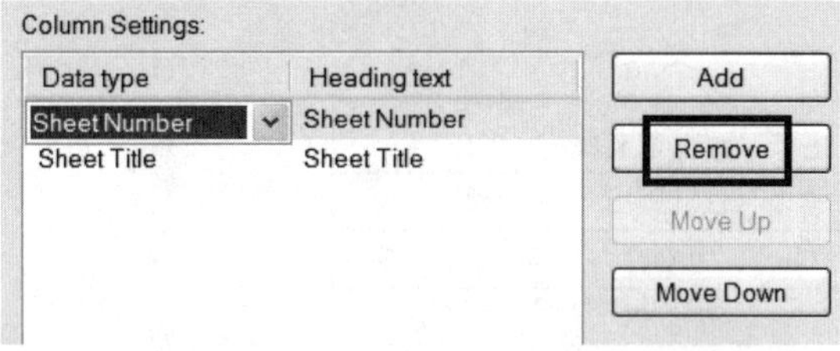

From the list, highlight Sheet Number and click **Remove** to remove it from the list.

Click **OK**.

5.

Place the table on the sheet.

6.

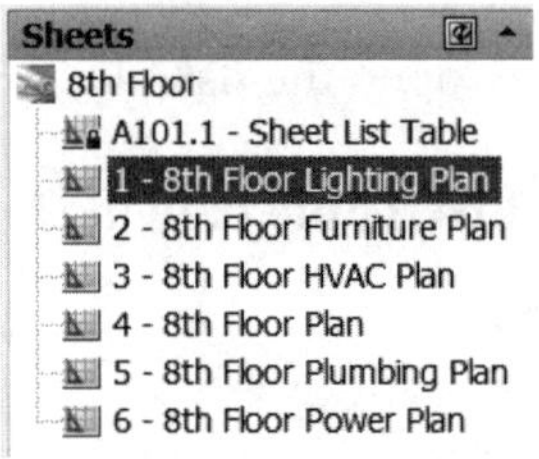

Move the Sheet List Table to the top of the list on the Sheet Set Manager by dragging and dropping it into place.

7.

Select the table so it highlights.

RMB and select **Update Table Data Links**.

8.

The table updates.

9. 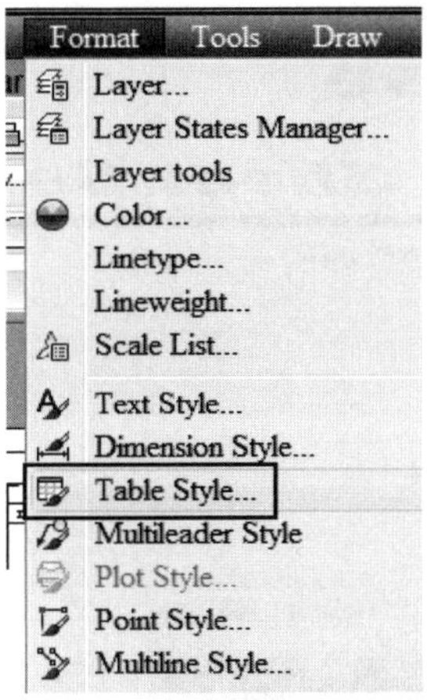

Go to **Format→Table Style**.

10. 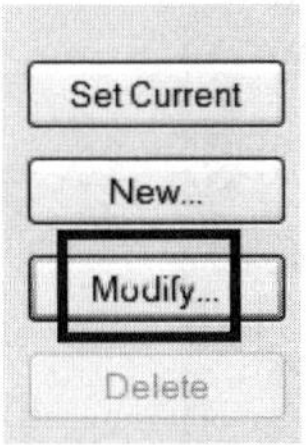

Press **Modify**.

11. 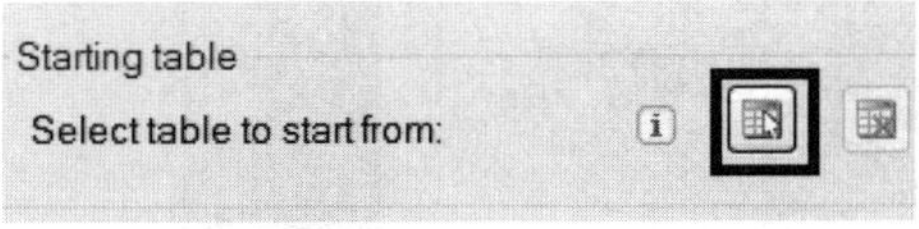

Select the table to start from button at the top of the dialog.

Then, select the Sheet List Table that is placed in the drawing.

12. 

Sheet List Table
Sheet Title
Sheet List Table
8th Floor Lighting Plan
8th Floor Furniture Plan
8th Floor HVAC Plan
8th Floor Plan
8th Floor Plumbing Plan
8th Floor Power Plan

A preview of the selected table will appear in the preview window.

13. 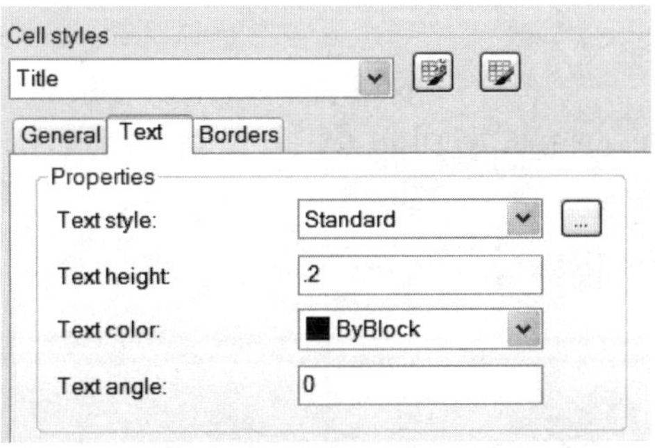

Select **Title** under Cell Styles.

Set the Text Style to **Standard**.
Set the Text height to **.20**.

Press **OK** to close the dialog.

14. 

Highlight the second row.
Two icons will appear when the row is selected.
The lock indicates the data is locked and cannot be modified.
The rings indicate that the data is linked to the Sheet Set Manager.

Command Exercise

Exercise 13-13 – Publishing a Sheet Set

Drawing Name: **sheetset5.dwg**
Estimated Time to Completion: 10 Minutes

Scope

Plot a sheet set to DWF.

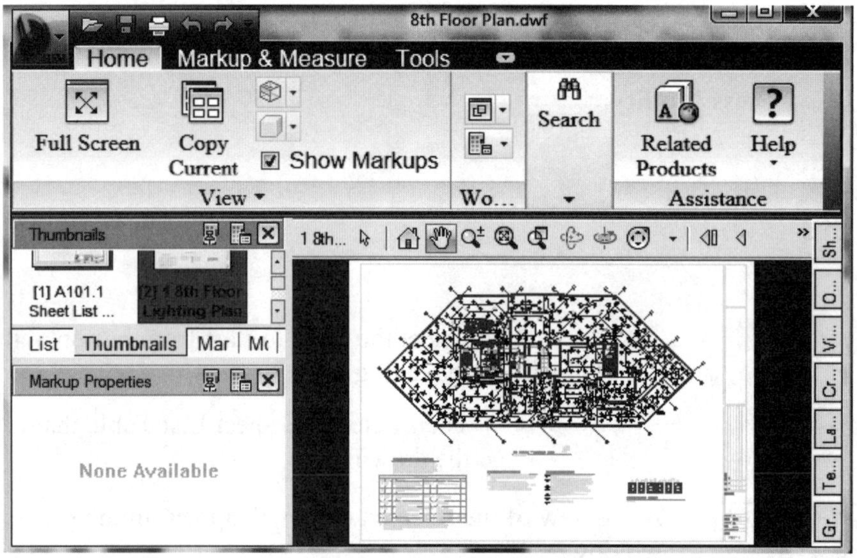

Publishing a DWF file

Solution

1. 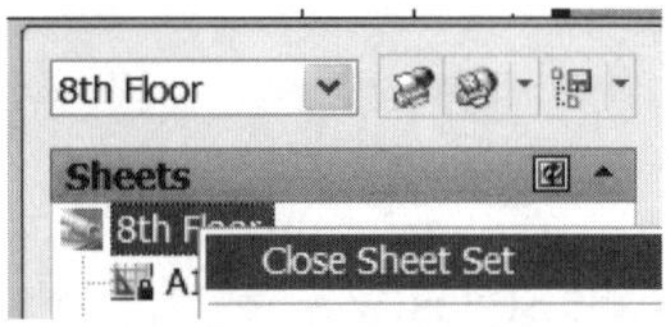

Highlight the **8th floor plan** header on the Sheets tab. RMB and select **Close Sheet Set**.

2. 

Go to **Recent…8th floor plan.dst** to re-open the sheet set.

3. 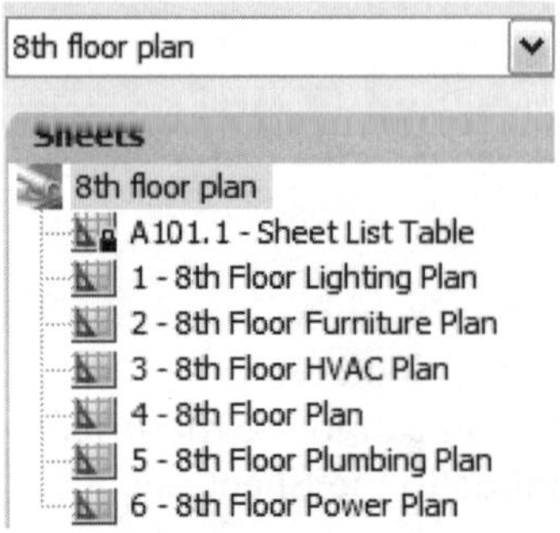

The sheet set is now listed.

4. 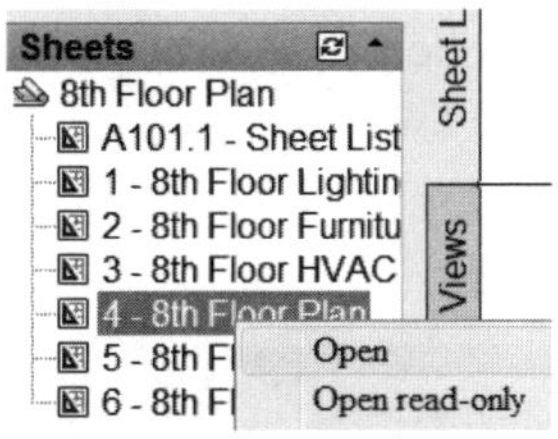

Highlight the 8th **Floor Plan** drawing (Item 4 on the list).

RMB and select **Open**.

5. 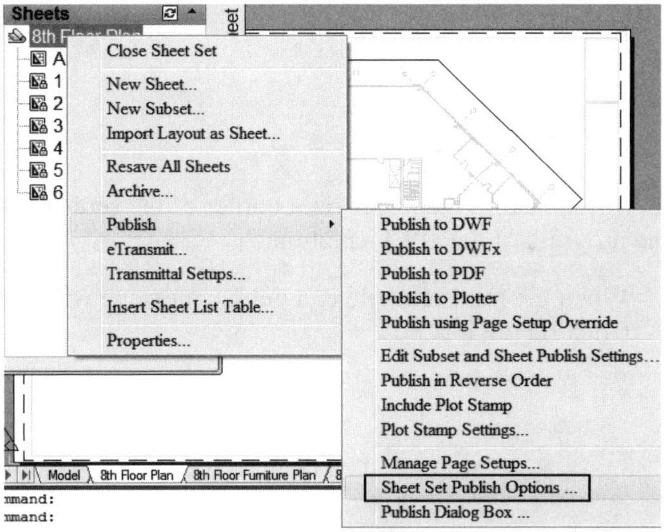

Highlight the sheet set header. RMB and select **Publish→Sheet Set Publish Options**.

6. 

Locate the folder where you wish to store the dwf file you will be creating.

7. 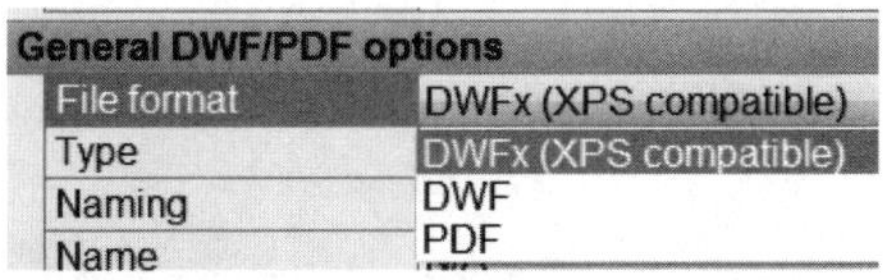

Under File format, select **DWF**.

Note that you can create a PDF document set, if desired. 2011 includes a free PDF writer.

8. 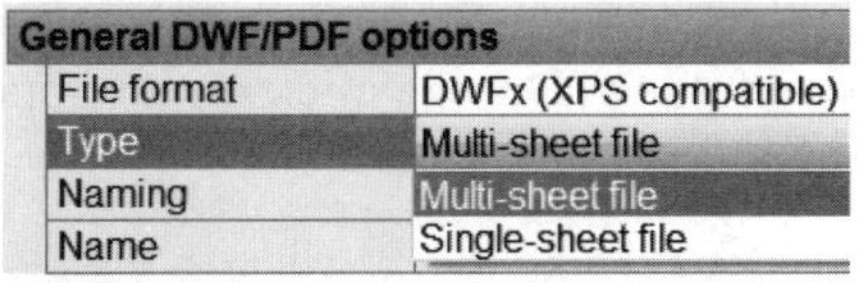

Enable **Multi-sheet file**.

9. 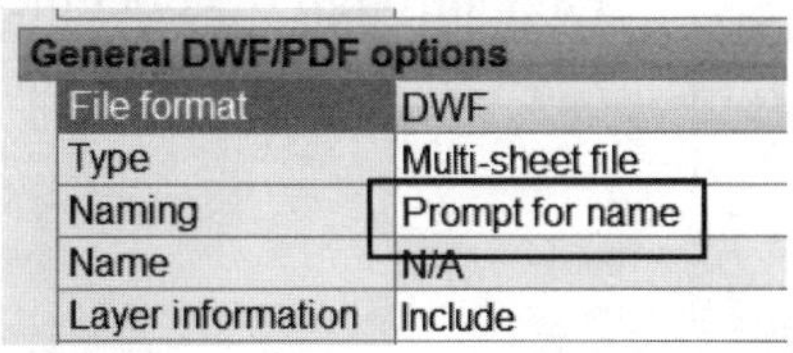

Enable **Prompt for name**.

Note that you can include the Layer information so users can turn layers on and off in the DWF viewer.

Press **OK**.

10. 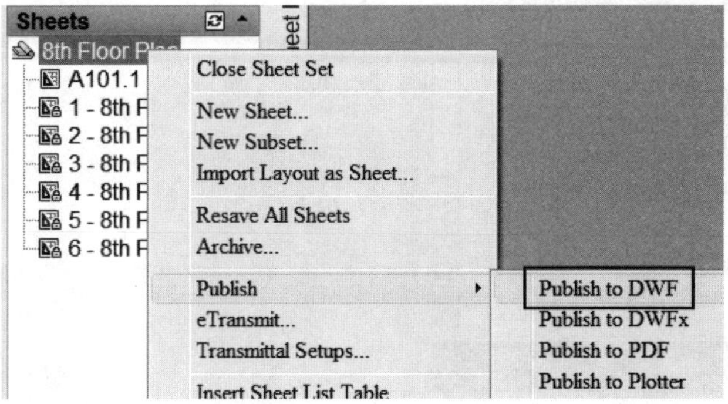

Highlight the sheet set header. RMB and select **Publish→Publish to DWF**.

11. 

The **Select DWF file** dialog will open to the folder specified.

Press **Select**.

12. 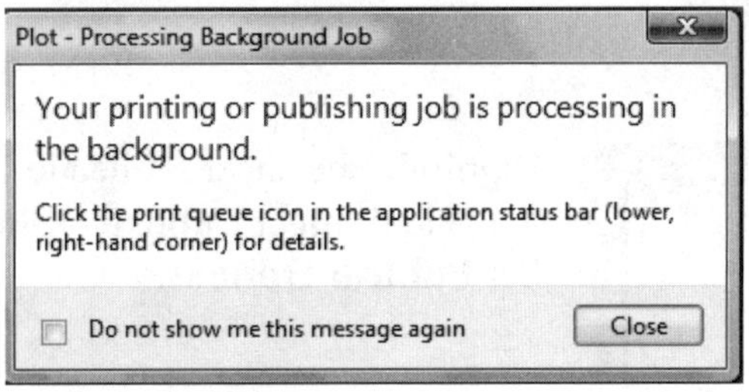

Press **Close**.

13. 

A plot icon will appear in the lower right corner of the screen, tracking the progress of the DWF creation.

14. 

When the job is complete, a bubble message will pop up. Click on the link.

15. 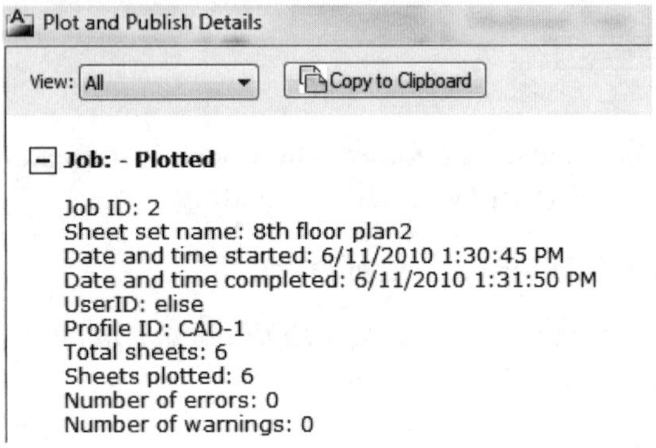

A log will be displayed detailing what was plotted.
Close the dialog.

16. 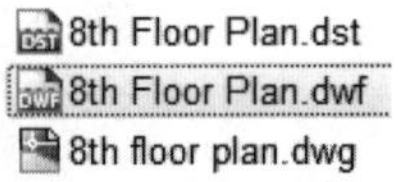

Locate the DWF file in the specified folder. Double click on it to open. This will launch Autodesk Design Review.

17. 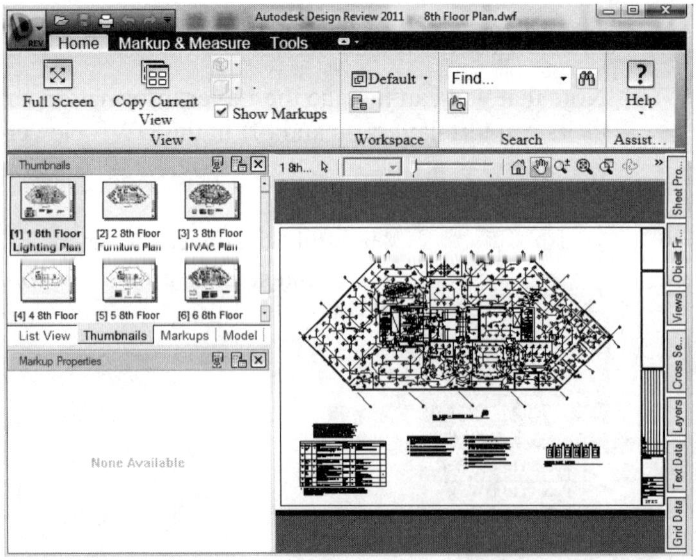

Page through the document to see how it looks.

Command Exercise

Exercise 13-14 – Export to PDF

Drawing Name: **pdf1.dwg**
Estimated Time to Completion: 10 Minutes

Scope

Export to PDF.

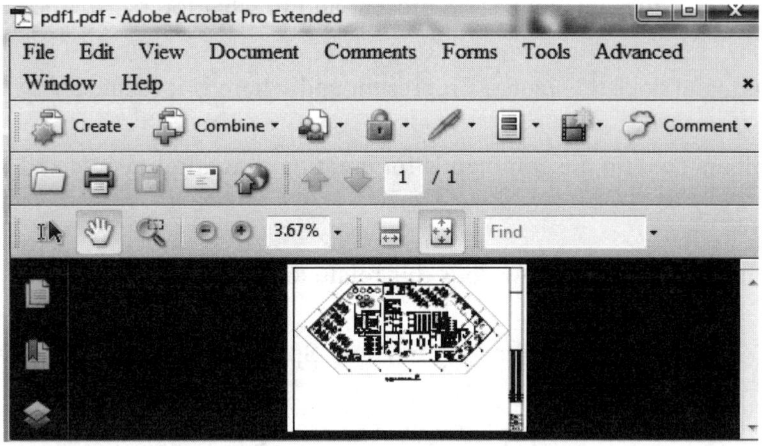

Publishing a DWF file

Solution

1. 

Set the Workspace to **2D Drafting & Annotation**.

2. 

Activate the **8th Floor Furniture Plan – Mono** layout tab.

3. 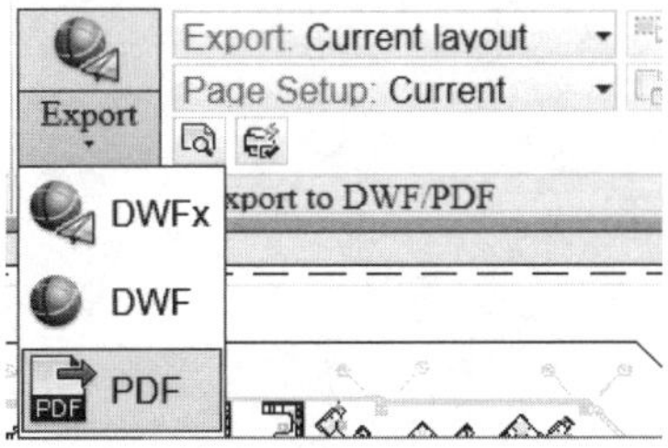

Set Export: **Current layout**.
Set Page Setup: **Current**.
Select **Export→PDF**.

4. 

Browse to the folder where you want to save the pdf file.

   Press **Save**.

5. 

A bubble will appear to alert you when the pdf is created.

6. Browse to the folder and open the pdf file to review.

Review Questions

1. What does this icon represent? 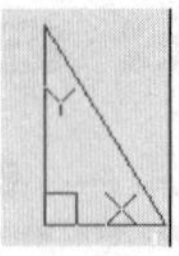

2. **T F** You should create your drawing in Model Space but you can plot your drawing from either the Layout tab (paper space) or the Model tab (model space).

3. From what pull-down menu can you access the Floating Viewports command?

4. What command does this icon  represent and in what toolbar is it located?

5. What command does this icon  represent and where is it located?

6. What toolbars contain the commands for creating drawing Layouts and Viewports?

7. What is the Plot Area and how does this relate to the paper size?

8. **T F** When you plot your drawing in Paper Space, your plot scale is 1=1.

9. What are some advantages to plotting your drawing in Paper Space?

10. What are the effects of the MODEL / PAPER Status Bar setting regarding Model Space and Layout?

    a. With the Model tab selected, what happens when you select the model button 

?

    b. With the Layout tab selected, the PAPER button switches to MODEL. What is the difference?

Review Answers

1. What does this icon represent? 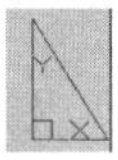

   PaperSpace

2. **T F** You should create your drawing in Model Space but you can plot your drawing from either the Layout tab (paper space) or the Model tab (model space).

   True

3. From what pull-down menu can you access the Floating Viewports command?

   View

4. What command does this icon  represent and in what toolbar is it located?

   Plot, Standard

5. What command does this icon  represent and where is it located?

   Plot Preview

6. What toolbars contain the commands for creating drawing Layouts and Viewports?

   Viewports

7. What is the Plot Area and how does this relate to the paper size?

   The Plot Area is the sheet size.

8. **T F** When you plot your drawing in Paper Space, your plot scale is 1=1.

   False…sometimes, but not always.

9. What are some advantages to plotting your drawing in Paper Space?

   You can be able to plan how your drawing will look when it is plotted.

10. What are the effects of the MODEL / PAPER Status Bar setting regarding Model Space and Layout.

    a. With the Model tab selected, what happens when you select the model button MODEL?

       You are in Model Space

    b. With the Layout tab selected, the PAPER button switches to MODEL? What is the difference?

       The Model Space is activated for a viewport or a viewport is made active.

About the Author

Elise Moss has worked for the past thirty years as a mechanical designer in Silicon Valley, primarily creating sheet metal designs. She has written articles for Autodesk's Toplines magazine, AUGI's PaperSpace, DigitalCAD.com and Tenlinks.com. She is President of Moss Designs, creating custom applications and designs for corporate clients. She has taught CAD classes at DeAnza College, Silicon Valley College, and for Autodesk resellers. She is currently teaching CAD at SFSU, in the College for Extended Learning campus and at Laney College in Oakland. Autodesk has named her as a Faculty of Distinction for the curriculum she has developed for Autodesk products. She holds a baccalaureate degree in Mechanical Engineering from San Jose State.

She is married with three sons. Her older son, Benjamin, is an electrical engineer. Her middle son, Daniel, works with AutoCAD Architecture in the construction industry. His designs have been featured in architectural journals. Her youngest son, Isaiah, is starting high school, but shows signs of being a budding engineer. Her husband, Ari, has a distinguished career in software development.

Elise is a third generation engineer. Her father, Robert Moss, was a metallurgical engineer in the aerospace industry. Her grandfather, Solomon Kupperman, was a civil engineer for the City of Chicago.

She can be contacted via email at elise_moss@mossdesigns.com.

More information about the author and her work can be found on her website at www.mossdesigns.com.

<u>Other books by Elise Moss</u>

AutoCAD Architecture 2011 Fundamentals
Autodesk Revit Architecture 2011 Basics

NOTES:

NOTES: